NORTHAMPTONSHIRE ARCHAEOLOGY, 35
2008

Contents

The Publication of Northamptonshire Archaeology Andy Chapman	1
Dennis Jackson – 80 not out Andy Chapman	5
A Collared Urn burial from Upton, Northampton Anne Foard-Colby	15
Excavation of a Romano-British Enclosure Complex at Burton Wold Farm, Burton Latimer Matt Edgeworth	27
Excavation of the Roman Villa and Mosaic at Rowler Manor, Croughton Michael Dawson	45
Archaeological recording of a Roman Villa at Brigstock Road, Stanion, 2002 Martin Tingle	95
Bury Mount: A Norman Motte and Bailey Castle at Towcester Jim Brown and Iain Soden	137
A riverside timber revetment at 130 Bridge Street, Peterborough Ian Meadows	163
Archaeological excavation at the corner of Kingswell Street and Woolmonger Street, Northampton Jim Brown	173
A medieval potters' tenement at Corby Road, Stanion Pat Chapman, Paul Blinkhorn and Andy Chapman	215
The Tin Tabernacle, Havelock Street, Desborough Joe Prentice	271
A prefabricated building at the Primary School, Cranford Antony Walsh	277

Notes **287**

An eleventh-century copper alloy stirrup-strap from Overstone, Northamptonshire 287
Steven Ashby

Northamptonshire Portable Antiquities Scheme 2007 Steven Ashby 288

Some recent archaeological publications Andy Chapman 291

Northamptonshire Archaeology Reports online Andy Chapman 293

Archaeology in Northamptonshire, 2007 **295**
Compiled by Pat Chapman (Northamptonshire Archaeology),
with additional contributions from Richard Ivens

(CD in back pocket; pdf files)

The Journal of Northamptonshire Archaeological Society,
Northamptonshire Archaeology: **Volume 9, 1974 to Volume 19, 1984**
(including microfiche sections)

Contents and Place-name Index to *Northamptonshire Archaeology*, **Volume 1, 1966 to Volume 34, 2006**
Andy Chapman

Stanion pottery: photographic archive

The publication of Northamptonshire Archaeology

by

ANDY CHAPMAN

WHATEVER HAPPENED TO 2007?

Observant readers will have noticed that we have gone from volume 34, 2006 to volume 35, 2008, with 2007 banished from existence. There is a good reason for this. While we have managed to produce six consecutive journals annually from the 2000-01 issue to 2006, from the mid-1980s to the beginning of the 2000s several journals appeared as biennial issues, dated to two-year spans. The years also slipped one behind in this period, so that last year we published at the end of 2007, with distribution continuing into early 2008, the journal for 2006. This has not caused our ordinary members any evident concern, but over the years it has confused some of our institutional members, and each year we receive a few letters from institutional libraries enquiring as to why they have still not received the previous year's journal. (No doubt next year we will receive similar letters asking, "Where is the journal for 2007?".)

It has also meant that for bibliographic referencing the publication year as indicated by the date on the volume, has been a year behind the actual date of publication. Whilst unlikely, given how long it usually takes most of us to get our reports written, under the old formula it would have been possible to carry out some fieldwork in the early months of, say, 2007, to write a quick report and get it in the journal for 2006, which really would make the author prompt with his publication! Regrettably, the possibility of having a publication date in advance of the fieldwork date is now lost.

We could have double-dated this issue to 2007-08, but my personal feeling is that this looks ugly in bibliographies (can those people not make their minds up which year they are publishing in?), and it might be taken to imply that we were again producing a biennial issue. We have therefore chosen the simple option of jumping a year so that the journal appearing at the end of 2008 to early 2009 will be the journal for 2008, which seems most logical.

THE CHANGE OF FORMAT

Of course, we have changed rather more than just the publication year, the whole format of the journal has been revamped with the move to A4 and digital printing, to bring in lots of colour, and a change of font for the headings to give the presentation of the text a new look as well.

As this editorial is being written I can only hope that the published journal lives up to my own expectations, and I hope that at least a majority of our readers enjoy the introduction of both colour illustrations and photographs.

This volume does of course show the submitted material in transition, with some articles prepared for traditional printing and others prepared for full colour throughout, while others are somewhere between.

As discussed in the editorial last year, this volume also includes some extreme contrasts of style from lengthy traditional reports accompanied by lengthy specialist reports and much tabulated data, while others present briefer syntheses of the results and direct the interested reader to the archive reports, while others have replaced the finds drawings with colour photographs.

PRODUCTION COSTS

In looking at the need for change in the style and format of the journal one aspect considered was the cost of publication. To do this I have tracked back through the annual accounts to look at the costs of production and printing over the years, for which I have found figures back to 1983 (Table 1). (If anyone can provide details of the costs of earlier issues I would be pleased to hear from them.) As the cost per page is the most accurate measure of changing costs (Table 2), the total costs have been set against the length of the journals (Table 3) to establish this.

As can be seen, the total cost of producing the journal by traditional typesetting and offset litho production rose steadily through the 1980s, no doubt reflecting steadily rising costs in a period of high inflation. A peak was reached in 1989, volume 22, when the society spent £10,770 on printing the journal at a cost of nearly £60 per page. Fortunately for the society's bank account, £7,087 of that was covered by publication grants from the Historic Buildings and Monuments Commission for England (HBMCE), now English Heritage, who in those days funded much of the "Rescue" archaeology in advance of development works.

From the peak of 1989 there was an equally dramatic fall in production costs through to the mid-1990s, which I assume is due to the introduction of digital typesetting leading to a substantial saving compared to traditional typesetting costs. A reduction in the use of microfiche in the early 1990s, and coming to an end in 1995, would also have given some savings.

The overall costs show a slow rise through the later 1990s, but this was a result of a general increase in the length of the volumes at this time, reaching an all-time high of 240 pages in 2001, volume 29 (Table 3). As can be seen from the cost per page, costs have actually remained pretty static from the mid-1990s to the present day, a period of very low inflation, oscillating between £25 and £30 per page, about the same as in the early 1980s.

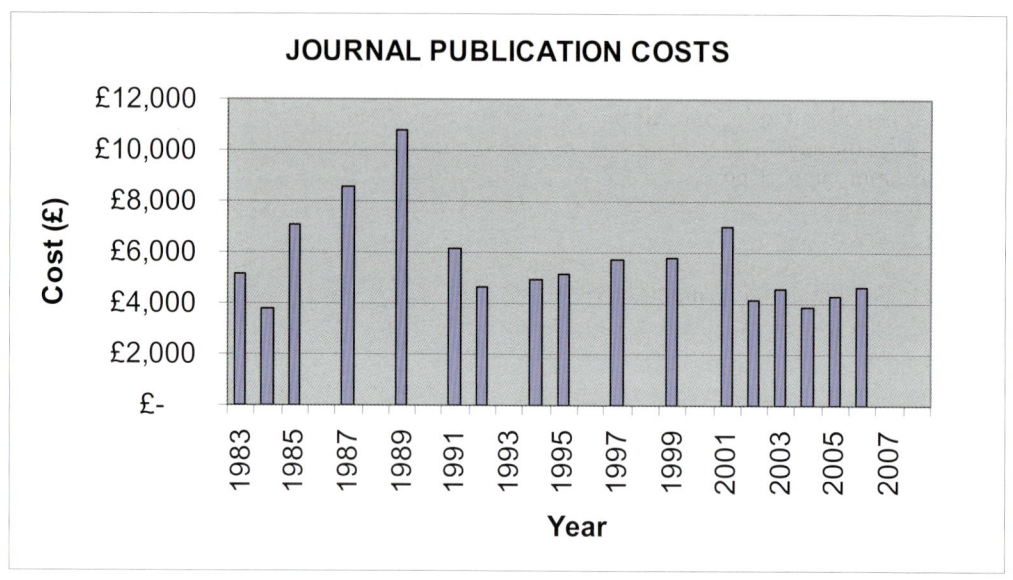

Table 1: Journal publication costs 1983-2006

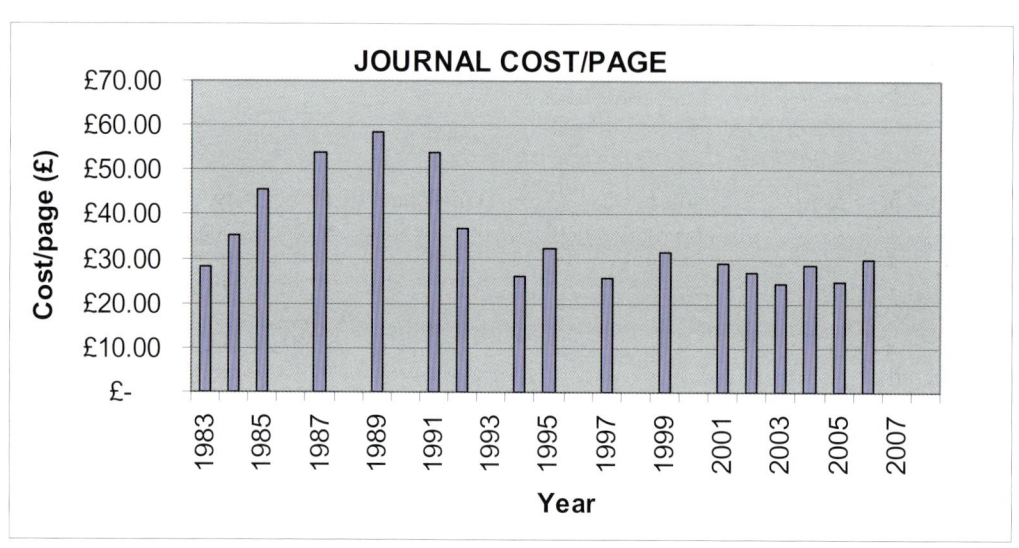

Table 2: The journal cost/page 1983-2006

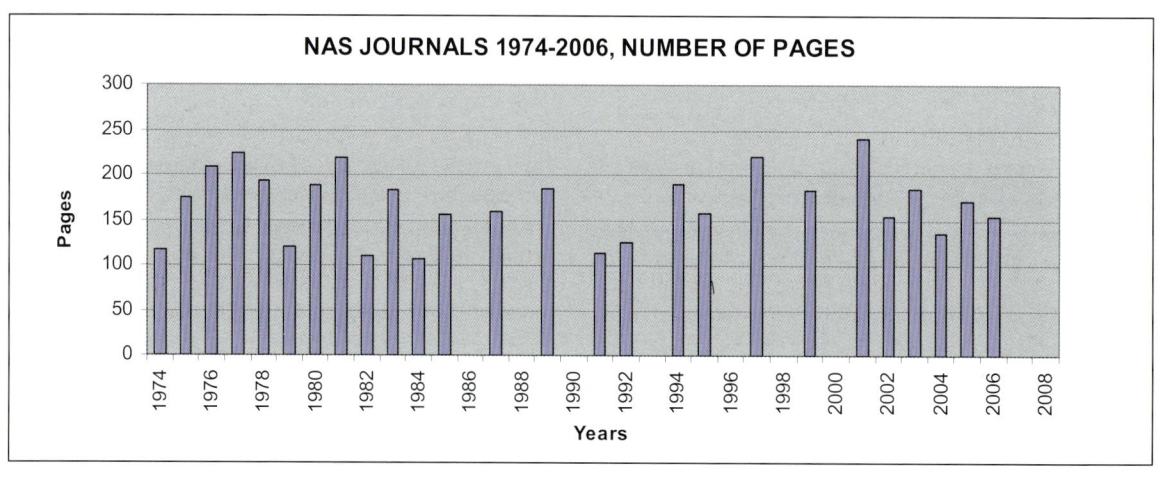

Table 3: Variations in the length of the journal 1983-2006

It should also be noted that from the early 1990s onward the funding of the journal has changed dramatically. Up to 1990 the HBMCE provided publication grants for much of the work reported in the journal carried out as "Rescue" projects. With the advent of developer funding, the majority of the grant support now comes from the archaeological contractors as part of the costs charged to their clients, the developers themselves.

This analysis of past costs will allow us to look at the cost of the change to A4 and digital printing to see how it compares in terms of value for money in comparison to past journals. The aim is to bring in the colour content by using digital printing but without this significantly increasing our costs.

A few more statistics to finish with:

From 1983 to 2006 the society spent £96,000 pounds on the publication of the journal, at an average cost of £5650 per journal. From 1974 to 2006 we published some 2800 pages of text and illustrations, an average of 176 pages per journal, with around 153 main articles and 120 notes; 273 separate pieces of work. Of course, these totals do not include the hundreds of pages of microfiche text published between 1979 and 1995 and the numerous pieces of work that have appeared in the annual notes, which have not been counted!

THE DIGITAL JOURNAL

The digitising of all past copies of the journal has cost the society just under £1,000. In addition, we have paid a £500 grant to the Council for British Archaeology (CBA) to be a partner in their online Archaeology Library of county and national journals (ArchLib). Under this scheme individual articles can be tracked down and viewed or copied either for free or on payment of a fee. In particular, the site has a search capacity so that researchers can gather relevant material by period or specific themes or geographical areas, and so on. Go to the CBA website (www.britarch.co.uk) and follow the links to Online Publications and ArchLib.

Hopefully more counties and national journals will join this scheme so that it will become a major tool for archaeological research, with Northamptonshire taking its place as part of national and international research. At the moment we have some 50 institutional members in Britain and abroad, but this means that a majority of archaeological departments in Britain do not take the journal and are therefore less likely to include Northamptonshire material in their research.

We will be making articles from all earlier copies of the journal freely available, on the basis that one of our main purposes is the dissemination of information and the promotion of archaeology in Northamptonshire. However, there will be a small charge per article for material published within the past five years, and the latest online journal will always be a year behind. These safeguards are to encourage everyone to maintain their membership and support of NAS, so that we can go on publishing the journal.

In addition, we continue making digital copies of the journal directly available to our members. Last year's journal included a CD containing the eight bulletins of the Northamptonshire Federation of Archaeological Societies. This year we extend the sequence by providing a CD containing volumes 9-19 of the journal, covering the years 1974-1984, the final year in which Tony Brown was editor. Next year there will be a further 10 or so journals to take the sequence to the early 2000s.

THE JOURNAL INDEX

To help readers of both the paper and digital copies find the material they are looking for, we are also publishing a full contents index and a place-name index to Volumes 1-34. This has been added to the CD and will also be available on the society website. The pdf has been formatted to print as back-to-back pages.

If there is anyone who wishes to have a paper copy who does not have access to a computer so they can print their own, please get in touch and we will arrange to provide a copy.

JOHN WILLIAMS

On behalf of the society, we pass our congratulations to Dr John Williams, who has recently retired from the position of Head of Heritage Conservation, Kent County Council, for the award of an MBE in the Queen's Birthday Honours.

John was head of the Northampton Development Corporation (NDC) Archaeological Unit from the early 1970s through to its demise in the mid-1980s. He was responsible for the excavation, and prompt publication, of a series of excavations around St Peter's church, Northampton that led to the discovery of the Saxon "Palaces" site, now generally considered to have been a timber, and later stone, hall at the centre of a middle Saxon minster complex that included the churches of St Peter and St Gregory.

John was also one of those involved in establishing *Northamptonshire Archaeology* as the county journal, and supported its publication by the contribution of numerous grant-funded articles accounting for the smaller projects carried out by the NDC.

He was also involved in setting up a county archive under the management of Northampton Borough Council through the Central Museum and Art Gallery. Alas, while *Northamptonshire Archaeology* survives, the Borough withdrew from its role as the county archive curator some years ago, a decision that has left so much of our excavated heritage homeless and inaccessible.

ANDY CHAPMAN

Dennis Jackson – 80 not out

by

ANDY CHAPMAN

INTRODUCTION

In Volume 1 of the *Bulletin of the Northamptonshire Federation of Archaeological Societies*, published December 1966, the very first page of fieldwork summaries contains an account of 'An Iron Age and Saxon site ... exposed by road improvements and excavated and recorded between July and December 1965' at Upton, Northampton.

This was a rescue excavation (but before the word rescue had been coined), which was partly funded by the then Ministry of Public Buildings and Works. The success of this project encouraged Dennis Jackson to take up field archaeology as a full-time profession, and much of Dennis's work as a freelance excavator over the following decades was also funded by the Ministry and its successors, the Department of the Environment (DoE) and English Heritage, although by his retirement archaeology had entered the age of developer-funded projects.

The opening two articles in the very first volume of the journal itself, Volume 9, 1974, were further sites excavated by Dennis: 'Bronze Age Burials at Weldon', describing rescue excavation in advance of ironstone quarrying near Weldon in 1970, and 'Two new pit alignments ... from Northamptonshire' describing the excavations of a pit alignment at Briar Hill, Northampton in 1969 in advance of new housing and a pit alignment at Gretton in 1972 prior to ironstone quarrying. Similar contributions were to continue journal after journal, with a decline only in recent years, although there are still a few Iron Age pottery reports awaiting publication in future issues, as well as an account of some recent trenches excavated at Hunsbury Hill, with Martin Tingle. A bibliography of Dennis's many publications in *Northamptonshire Archaeology* and a range of national journals, up to that date, appeared in volume 28, 1998-99.

Dennis's contributions to the journal by far outnumber those of any other contributor, and it is therefore appropriate that this opening volume of the journal in its new A4 format with digital (colour) printing should begin with a brief retrospective of the career of this most prolific Northamptonshire archaeologist, and one whose work on Iron Age settlement and Iron Age and Roman ironworking will stand as the bedrock for all future studies.

On the occasion of Dennis's 80th birthday in 2008, there was a small gathering of just some of the many archaeologists and society members that Dennis has worked with over the years – Roy and Diana Friendship-Taylor, Burl Bellamy, Robert Moore, Brian Giggins, John Small, David Hall, Steve Parry, Ian Barrie, and Andy and Pat Chapman. Dennis had made a small selection of slides providing a glimpse of his career, and these were passed around before dinner. Those slides are compiled here as a pictorial autobiography of just some of the highlights from the career of Dennis Jackson, the archaeologist of Iron Age Northamptonshire, and much more besides.

ROAD WIDENING AT UPTON, NORTHAMPTON, 1965

In 1965, as part of the recently formed Upper Nene Archaeological Society (UNAS), Dennis directed the excavation of Iron Age settlement and Saxon occupation at Upton, Northampton during road improvements to the Weedon Road, the creation of the dual carriageway that

Fig 1 Excavation during widening of the Weedon Road at Upton in 1965

we drive along today. The photograph includes other local archaeologists, Robert Moore (centre) and Richard (Dick) Hollowell (with camera, right). The results were published as: Jackson, D, Harding, D W, and Myers, J N L, 1969 The Iron Age and Anglo-Saxon site at Upton, Northants, *Antiquaries Journal*, **49:2**, 202-221.

TWYWELL IRON AGE SETTLEMENT

During late 1966 and throughout 1967 Dennis excavated an area of Iron Age settlement within an ironstone quarry near Twywell (Jackson, D A, 1975, An Iron Age site at Twywell, Northamptonshire, *Northamptonshire Archaeology*, **10**, 31-93). The work began with the help of the Upper Nene Archaeological Society and pupils from Kettering Grammar School, including Brian Dix, and was later supported by the Ministry of Works. An enclosure and several adjacent roundhouses were excavated, along with numerous pits. The photograph (Fig 2) shows the young Brian Dix posing next to a group of excavated pits, with the one in the foreground containing a pig burial.

ALDWINCLE NEOLITHIC MORTUARY ENCLOSURE

The extraction of gravel at Aldwincle quarry ran from 1967 to 1971 and Dennis directed the rescue excavation of various sites spanning the Neolithic, Bronze Age, Iron Age, Roman and Saxon periods.

The presence of a number of these sites had been known from aerial photographic evidence, but the Neolithic mortuary enclosure was only revealed in 1968 during the removal of overburden prior to gravel extraction (Jackson, D A, 1976, The excavation of Neolithic and Bronze Age Sites at Aldwincle, Northants, 1967-71, *Northamptonshire Archaeology*, **11**, 12-70). When recognised, the over-burden had been removed across the south-western half of the monument, leaving only the features cut into the gravel, while to the north-east there was surviving stratigraphy. The photograph below vividly depicts the situation (Fig 3). An *in situ* crouched inhumation burial and an adjacent deposit of disarticulated bones from a second individual lie poised on the edge of the stripped area (to the left), when one more pass of overburden removal would have taken them out. The ranging pole in the foreground stands in one posthole of the mortuary structure, and had contained a D-shaped upright, with the opposing post set to the right of the two burials to form the other end of the mortuary house containing them. Nearby round barrows included two coffined Beaker burials.

Fig 2 Excavated pits at Twywell Iron Age settlement

Fig 3 The inhumation burials at the heart of the Neolithic mortuary enclosure at Aldwincle

EARLS BARTON BRONZE AGE BARROW

In the winter months of early 1969 Dennis directed the rescue excavation of an upstanding barrow mound, which had been identified by Dick Hollowell, in advance of its destruction by gravel quarrying (Jackson, D A, 1984, The Excavation of a Bronze Age Barrow at Earls Barton, Northants, *Northamptonshire Archaeology*, **19**, 3-30).

This was the first site in the country to provide a radiocarbon date associated with a Wessex Culture bronze dagger, which caused some controversy at the time as the date was unacceptably late. However, with the recognition that radiocarbon years did not equal calendar years, and the consequent need to recalibrate dates, the Earls Barton date became more acceptable.

Despite the excavation being carried out in January, initially the weather was reasonable as sections were excavated by hand to give a complete cross section of the mound (Fig 4). Subsequently work had to be abandoned for a while (Fig 5). The technique of cutting multiple sections into barrow mounds had been pioneered by T C M Brewster in Yorkshire.

Fig 4 The excavated barrow ditch at Earls Barton, 1969 (the team included young local archaeologist John Small (centre)

Fig 5 The excavated barrow mound at Earls Barton during January 1969, with gravel pit plant and equipment in the background

ALDWINCLE ROMAN BRIDGE

Meanwhile, back at Aldwincle quarry there was another fortuitous survival, when the timbers of a Roman bridge were exposed in the section at the quarry edge (Jackson, D, and Ambrose, T, 1976 A Roman Timber Bridge at Aldwincle, Northants, *Britannia*, **7**, 39-72).

Fig 6 Aldwincle; the timbers of a Roman bridge exposed in section at the quarry edge (with Dick Hollowell looking on)

Fig 7 An exceptionally deep enclosure ditch at Weekley Iron Age settlement (with Brian Dix standing in the bottom)

WEEKLEY LATE IRON AGE AND ROMAN SETTLEMENT

Rescue excavations were carried out in 1970-71, with further work in 1975-78, in advance of ironstone quarrying near Weekley (Jackson, D, and Dix, B, 1986-87 Late Iron Age and Roman settlement at Weekley, Northants, *Northamptonshire Archaeology*, **21**, 41-94). A series of ditched enclosures spanned the late Iron Age into the Roman period, as precursors to a nearby villa. The site produced a large collection of La Tene style, curvilinear decorated globular bowls, with imported vessels indicating the high status of the site from an early date. Enclosure C had an elaborate entrance gateway and the ditch averaged 3.0m deep (Fig 7).

The late Iron Age enclosures had continued in use into the Roman period. The remains of 14 small pottery kilns were scattered across the area, and a lime kiln (Fig 8), dated to the mid-2nd century, may have served in the preparation of mortar for use in the nearby villa (Jackson, D A, Biek, L, and Dix, B F, 1973 A Roman lime kiln at Weekley, Northants, *Britannia*, **4**, 128-40).

Fig 8 A Roman lime kiln at Weekley, showing the stepped stone-lining of the circular kiln with the rectangular stoke pit beyond

Fig 9 The Roman column base from Ringstead, weighing 128.5kg, perhaps part of a Jupiter column

ROMAN BUILDINGS AT RINGSTEAD

In 1971, a drainage trench excavated prior to gravel extraction revealed part of a previously unknown Roman building, and the threatened area was excavated during the late autumn to early winter of 1971-2 (Jackson, D A, 1980 Roman buildings at Ringstead, Northants, *Northamptonshire Archaeology*, **15**, 12-34). In 1975 a large decorated limestone drum from a Roman column was found in this area during gravel extraction, which Dennis counts as his largest small find (Fig 9)!

BRIGSTOCK IRON AGE ENCLOSURE

While our Iron Age settlements have typically been ploughed flat over the centuries, an earthwork enclosure at Brigstock had lain within the confines of Brigstock Great Park during the medieval period and had escaped this fate until modern times. According to local farm workers, the bank had previously stood to a considerable height but had been ploughed twice in the last war and several times in the 1950s. After this it had reverted to pasture until the late 1970s, when the farmer turned it back to the plough and was intending to gradually level out the earthworks because of the problems they caused to modern harvesting machinery.

In the autumn of 1979 Dennis excavated the eastern side of the enclosure, where the entrance stood, working on behalf of the Department of the Environment (DoE) and Northamptonshire County Council, to establish the state of preservation and the effects of ploughing (Fig 10). The remainder of the interior was excavated in 1979 (Jackson, D, 1983 The excavation of an Iron Age site at Brigstock, Northants, 1979-81, *Northamptonshire Archaeology*, **18**, 17-42).

The site comprised a single roundhouse set towards the southern side of a ditched enclosure, with an internal clay bank up to 4m wide but then no more than 300mm high. On the eastern side a stone path, of cobbles and limestone, ran through the opening in the bank and up to door of the roundhouse. Much of the shallow slot defining the house wall survived. Within the house there was the remnant of a laid floor of chalk grits inside the doorway, and a spread of limestone inside the wall around the northern half of the building may have been the base of a broad stone bench.

This site has given us a glimpse of what we have lost on our ploughed settlement sites.

Fig 10 Brigstock Iron Age enclosure with its upstanding bank and paved pathway leading to the door of the roundhouse

ROMAN IRONSMELTING FURNACES AT LAXTON

In 1985, during road improvements on the A43 at Laxton Lodge, the contractor's groundworks uncovered a major Roman ironworking site as well as occupation evidence and a cemetery. The hastily arranged rescue excavation uncovered a row of exceptionally large ironworking furnaces, with chambers 1.35m in diameter, and an adjacent small valley had been filled with slag and furnace debris (Jackson, D, and Tylecote, R, 1988 Two new Romano-British ironworking sites in Northamptonshire – A new type of furnace, *Britannia*, **19**, 275-298).

Fig 11 The rescue excavation of Roman smelting furnaces at Laxton in advance of road building

Fig 12 An unusual burial posture in the Anglo-Saxon cemetery at Wakerley

WAKERLEY ANGLO-SAXON CEMETERY

To finish, we return to the ironstone quarries and the excavation of an Anglo-Saxon cemetery, between 1968 and 1969, in advance of open-cast ironworking to the south-west of Wakerley. A total of 85 burials were recorded. This included a group of 6th to early 7th-century burials furnished with a range of grave goods, and a separate group of 7th-century graves. The first half of the work was carried out during the winter on the bleak hillside exposed to the worst of the weather, while the work was completed in the summer months (Adams, B, and Jackson, D, 1988-9 The Anglo-Saxon cemetery at Wakerley, Northamptonshire: Excavations by Mr D Jackson, 1968-69, *Northamptonshire Archaeology*, **22**, 69-183).

DENNIS JACKSON

Dennis retired from full-time fieldwork in 1999, when he became, and remains, a vice-president of the society, only rarely missing a committee meeting. His involvement

Fig 13 Dennis on a watching brief on the M40 near Banbury, one of his last fieldwork projects

Fig 14 Aerial view of Hunsbury Hill, Northampton, which in the 1970s became surrounded by housing estates and now suffers from neglect and vandalism (Northamptonshire County Council)

and interest in the archaeology of the county continues, particularly with his recent efforts to promote an interest in the preservation, presentation and research of the neglected site of Northampton's own Iron Age hillfort at Hunsbury Hill (Fig 14). However, Dennis does now also have time to devote to other interests including bird watching and the fortunes of his near neighbours, Northamptonshire County Cricket Club, and we all hope that Dennis will remain 80 not out for many years to come.

A Bronze Age Cremation Burial from Upton, Northampton

by

ANNE FOARD-COLBY

with contributions by
Andy Chapman, Pat Chapman, Rowena Gale and Sarah Inskipp

SUMMARY

Between September and November 2007, an archaeological watching brief was carried out by Northamptonshire Archaeology during flood attenuation works on the north side of the River Nene, between Kislingbury and Upton, Northampton. The topsoil was stripped in three separate areas. In one area a small pit contained the cremated bones of an adult within an inverted Collared Urn. This burial has been radiocarbon dated to the early 2nd millennium BC, the early Bronze Age. A number of postholes lay nearby, one of which cut the cremation pit and may have contained a grave marker. However, there is no indication that this burial lay close to a round barrow or any other funerary deposits, so it appears to have been an isolated burial. A series of undated shallow, parallel gullies and postholes, possibly part of a water-meadow management system, and a post-medieval or modern boundary ditch were recorded in the other watching brief areas.

INTRODUCTION

Between September and November 2007, Northamptonshire Archaeology maintained an archaeological watching brief during groundworks for the Upton Flood Attenuation Scheme (Phase 2), Northampton (NGR SP 703 599 to SP 719 593, Fig 1). The Collared Urn burial lay at SP 7065 5987.

The work was commissioned by Birse Civils and was undertaken in order to meet the archaeological conditions, requested by Northampton Borough Council's Archaeological Advisor, which had been attached to the planning consent for the flood alleviation works. The purpose of the archaeological investigation was to mitigate against the impact of groundworks on archaeological remains in three areas, comprising two spurs for the construction of banks and an area of floodplain lowering.

The fieldwork was carried out in accordance with a specification written by Northamptonshire Archaeology (NA 2007) based on the specification produced by Halcrow (2007), who were advised by the former Archaeological Planning Officer for Northamptonshire County Council Historic Environment Team (NCCHET).

ACKNOWLEDGEMENTS

The project was sponsored by English Partnerships, and was managed by James Goad for the Halcrow Group Ltd, as archaeological consultants, and by Anthony Maull and Simon Carlyle for Northamptonshire Archaeology. The fieldwork was carried out by Anne Foard-Colby, Mark Patenall and Yvonne Wolframm-Murray. The illustrations are by Carol Simmonds and Andy Chapman. This published report focuses on the Collared Urn cremation burial, but further details of the other features and finds recorded can be found within the client report (Foard-Colby 2008).

TOPOGRAPHY AND GEOLOGY

The watching brief area was situated to the north of the River Nene, between the village of Kislingbury to the west and Upton, Northampton to the east (Fig 1). The ground rises from 60m aOD on the floodplain to 72mOD on the lower slopes to the north of the river. The land comprised water meadow and pasture for grazing sheep and cattle.

The British Geological Survey has mapped the area as a mixture of alluvium and glacial boulder clay, sand and gravel, overlying Middle Lias clay, mudstone and ironstone (BGS 1980). The soils belong to the Fladbury 2 soil association, comprising stoneless clayey soils, variably affected by groundwater (SSEW 1983).

ARCHAEOLOGICAL AND HISTORICAL BACKGROUND

A search of the Historic Environment Record (HER) shows that the area of the flood attenuation works lies within a landscape containing archaeological remains ranging in date from the prehistoric to the post-medieval periods. The Neolithic Causewayed Enclosure of Briar Hill lay 2.5km to the south-east on the southern slope of the river valley (Fig 1), and was excavated in the mid-1970s (Bamford 1985). A small cremation cemetery, dated to the middle Bronze Age lay within the Causewayed Enclosure at Briar Hill (Bamford 1985), and another small cremation cemetery of possible middle Bronze Age date has recently been excavated at Pineham Barn, also south of the river (Fig 2, Brown 2007).

Possible prehistoric ditches were investigated between 1991 and 1992 by Northamptonshire Archaeology (Fig

Fig 1 Site location

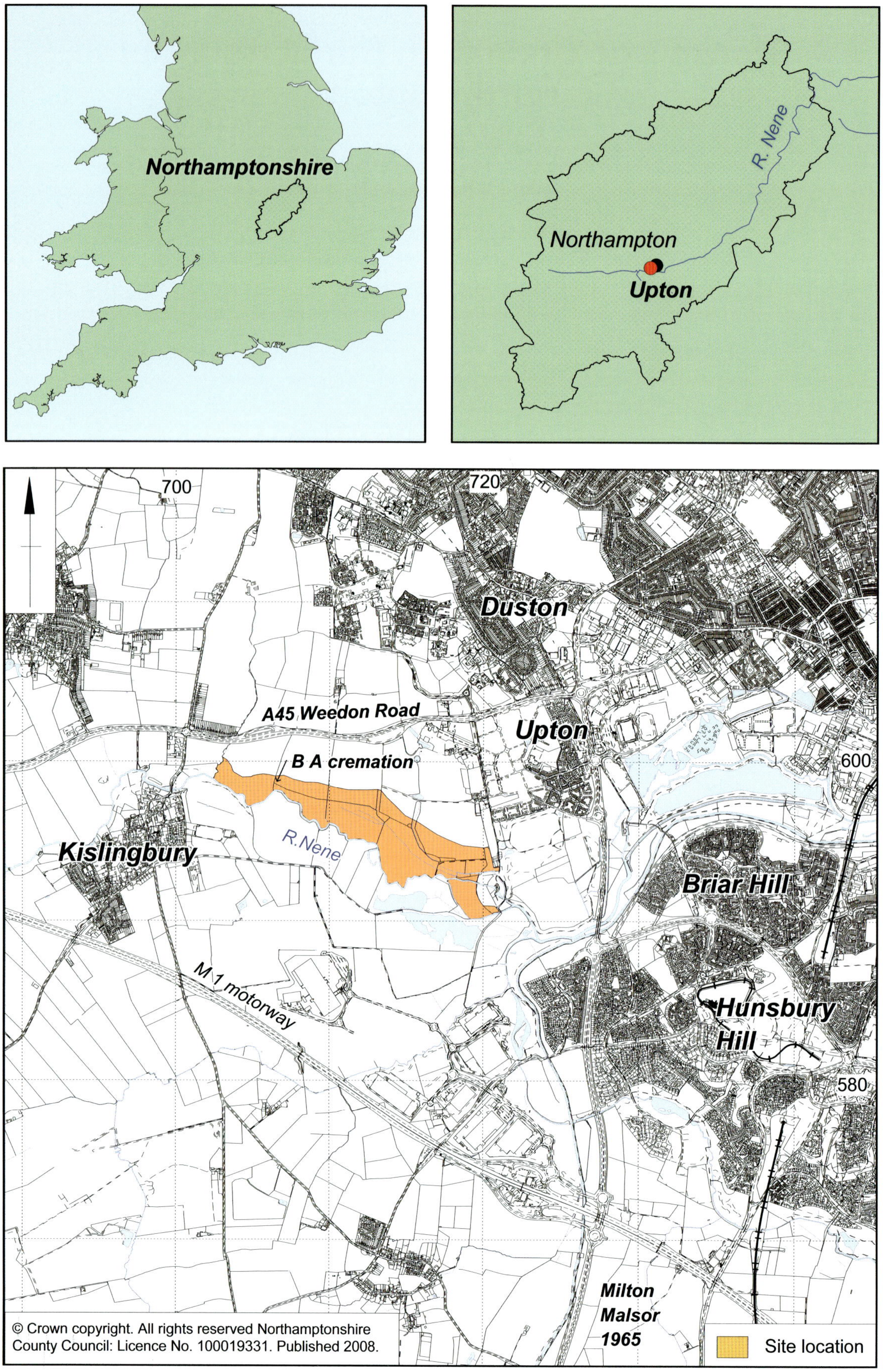

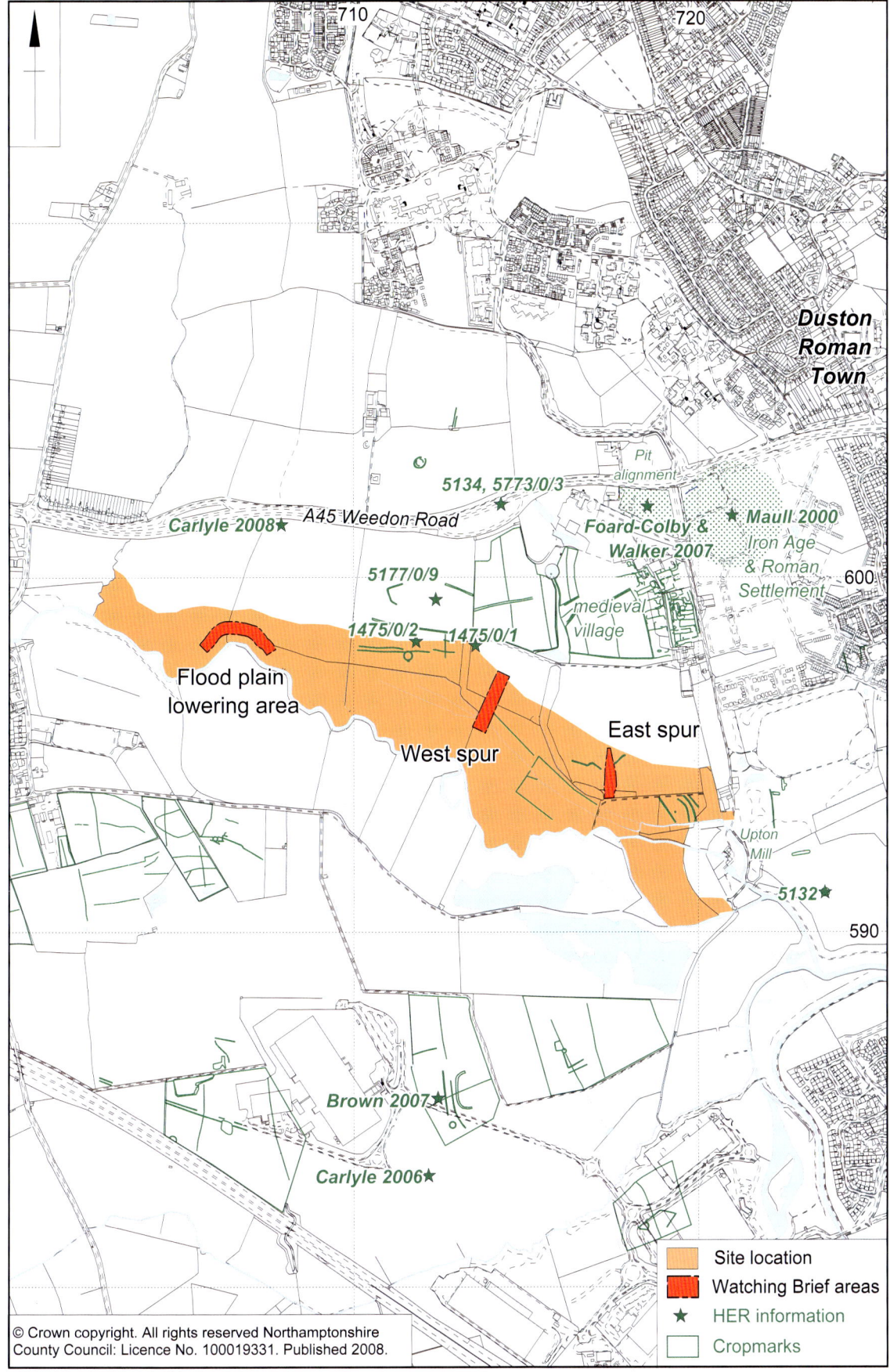

Fig 2 Historic Environment Record (HER) sites

2; NSMR 1475/0/1-2; Jackson 1993a; 1993b, 74-75).

Hunsbury Hillfort, a major Iron Age tribal centre overlooked the valley from the ridge to the south-east (Fig 1). To the north of the watching brief area, Iron Age pits and ditches were excavated during the widening of the A45 in 1965 (NSMR 5134; Jackson *et al* 1969), and to the north-east an Iron Age pit alignment was excavated at Upton, east of Quinton House School (Maull 2000, Foard-Colby and Butler 2006). A further pit alignment lying to the north of the watching brief area has been identified and examined prior to the construction of the Cross Valley Link Road (Fig 2, Carlyle 2008).

To the north-east, Late Iron Age and Roman settlement was excavated prior to residential development at Upton, and has been shown to continue westward into the grounds of Quinton House School (Maull 2000, Foard-Colby and Butler 2006, Foard-Colby and Walker 2007). These sites lie at the south-western margin of Duston Roman town.

To the south of the river, extensive Iron Age and Roman settlement has recently been excavated at Pineham Barn (Fig 2; Carlyle 2006 and Brown 2007; and NSMR 5088/0/1 and 5092/0/6; JSAC 1999; 2000; Buteux & Jones 2000; Morris 2000; Pears 2005), with further Iron Age and Roman settlement to the south-east at the Swan valley area (Holmes and Chapman 2005).

A Saxon *Grubenhaus* was excavated during widening of the A45 in 1965 (SMR 5773/0/3; Jackson *et al* 1969, 213) and possible Saxon or early medieval ditches were identified from aerial photographs (SMR 5177/0/9).

OBJECTIVES

The objectives of the watching brief were to provide monitoring of selected areas of groundworks where there were known archaeological features in the vicinity, or where there was deemed to be areas of archaeological or palaeoenvironmental/geoarchaeological potential. If possible, environmental samples would be collected from peaty deposits exposed within the river re-alignment works, which could be used as the basis for an environmental assessment of the historic landscape in

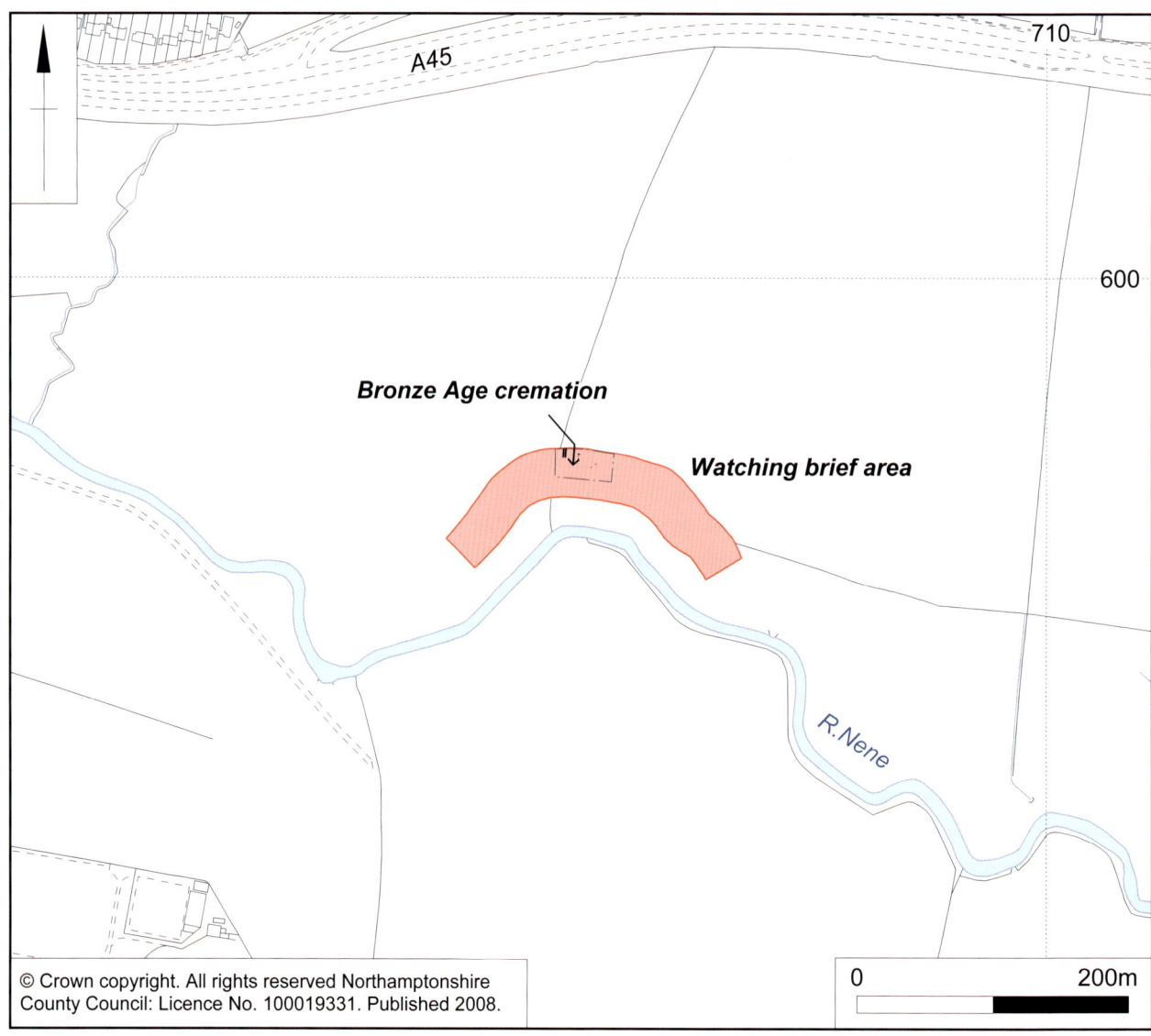

Fig 3 Location of western area (flood plain lowering area)

this part of the River Nene valley. No such deposits were encountered.

FIELDWORK METHODOLOGY

Topsoil stripping was undertaken by mechanical excavator under archaeological supervision. All potential archaeological features were examined by hand excavation. The location of the stripped areas was related to the Ordnance Survey National Grid. Contexts were recorded on *pro-forma* sheets with a unique context number being allocated to each distinct deposit. Plans and sections were drawn at the appropriate scale. A photographic record comprising both 35mm black and white negatives, with associated contact prints, and colour transparencies was maintained, with additional digital photographs. The site code is UFA 07.

All works were carried out in accordance with the Institute of Field Archaeologists *Code of Conduct* (IFA 1995, revised 2006) and *Standards and guidance for archaeological watching briefs* (IFA 1994, revised 2001), and complied with the *Policy and Guidance for Archaeological Fieldwork Projects in Northamptonshire* (NCCHET 1995). All procedures complied with the Northamptonshire County Council Health and Safety provisions.

THE WATCHING BRIEF

WESTERN AREA (AREA OF FLOODPLAIN LOWERING)

The area of floodplain lowering was at the western end of the watching brief area (Figs 2 & 3). Here excavation revealed a sequence of alluvial deposits, into the surface of which was cut a number of archaeological features, including a Bronze Age cremation burial.

At 1.2m below the stripped surface there was dark blue-grey silty clay with gravel inclusions, succeeded by a layer, 0.6m thick, of light yellow-brown silty clay. A layer of light to mid grey and yellow-brown silty clay, of a similar thickness, slightly overlay or abutted this layer. Together, they may be terraces associated with the nearby River Nene. Sealing these deposits was mid orange-brown alluvium with river gravel inclusions.

Close to the northern edge of this area there was a cremation burial within an inverted Collared Urn of early Bronze Age date (Fig 4). The urn had been intact but the base was damaged during stripping of the topsoil (Fig 5). It lay within a pit [306] with an adjacent pit/posthole [316] that may have held a marker-post (Figs 6-8). The burial deposit is described in detail below.

To the south-west of the cremation was a shallow posthole [309], 0.29m in diameter and 0.12m deep, and

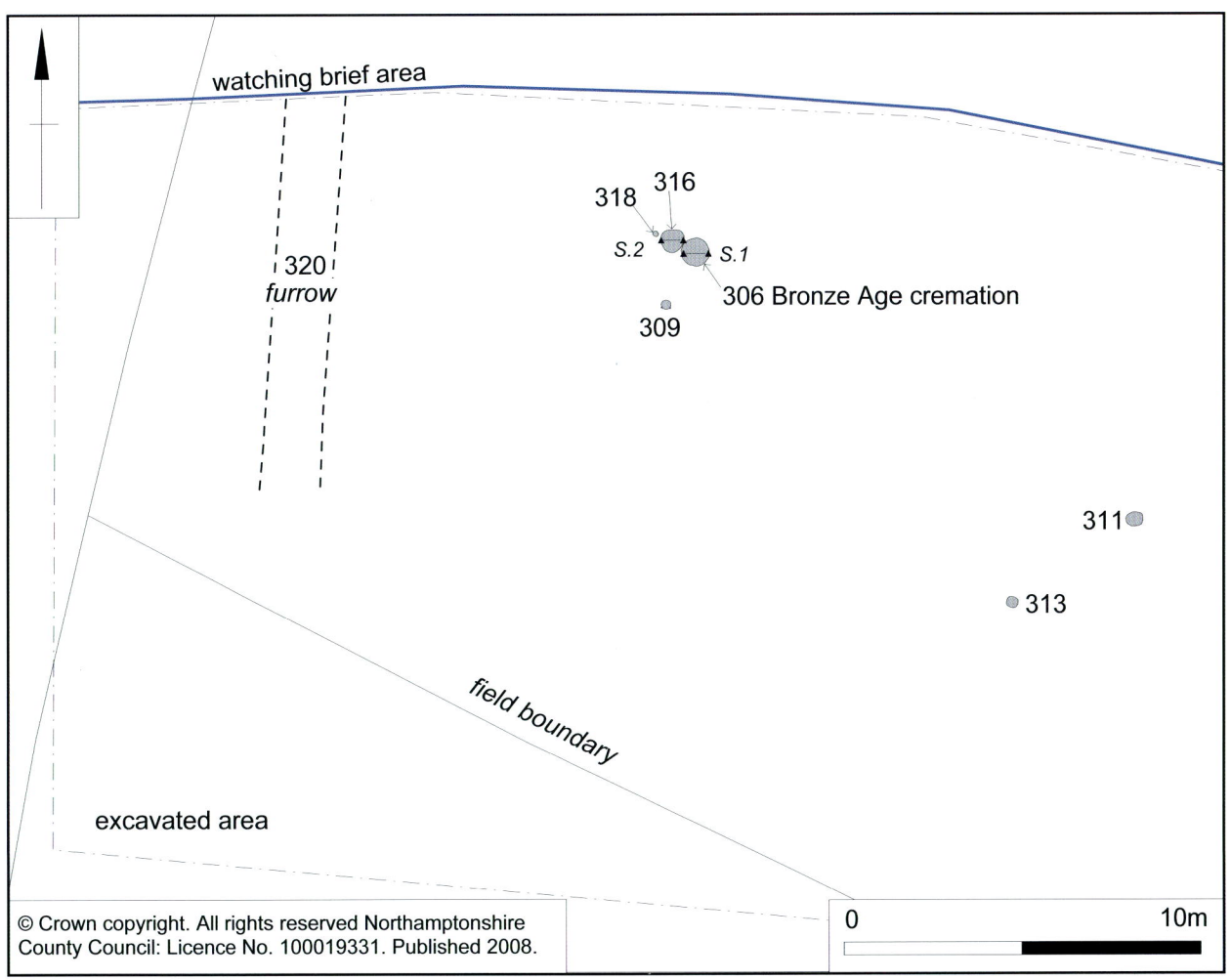

Fig 4 Flood plain lowering area, plan of features

Fig 5 Base of urn exposed and damaged in machine stripping

Fig 6 The inverted urn exposed for lifting

immediately to the north-west of posthole [316] was a shallow stakehole [318] (Fig 4). Both features were filled with mid grey-brown silty clay loam with gravel and charcoal flecks.

Two further shallow postholes lay to the south-east. Postholes [311] and [313] were 0.29m and 0.43m in diameter and 0.07m to 0.09m deep, and filled with mid grey-brown silty clay loam with occasional river gravels. The fill of posthole [311] contained two pieces of worked flint.

Approximately 8m to the west of the cremation there was a shallow, linear feature [320], probably a furrow, aligned north to south, 1.5m wide by 0.08m deep. Its fill of light brown silty clay contained sherds of abraded medieval pottery dated to the 13th to 14th centuries.

All of the features were sealed by topsoil (301), which ranged from 0.3m to 0.4m thick.

WEST SPUR

The remains of a north-west to south-east aligned boundary ditch was visible in the fields to the east and west of the watching brief area (Fig 2). It was parallel to field boundaries to the north and south. Within the stripped area, the ditch, which was cut into alluvium, was 1.4m wide and was filled with dark grey brown silty clay loam with gravel inclusions. It was overlain by topsoil. No dating evidence was recovered, but it is probably post-medieval or modern in date.

EAST SPUR

In this area there were two ditches (Fig 2). One contained eleven pieces of residual worked flint, the other contained abraded fragments of brick, tile and a piece of fuel ash slag. In addition, there was a series of short, roughly parallel, undated shallow gullies and a scatter of shallow pits and postholes, all cut into the alluvium. The topsoil was 0.25m to 0.40m thick.

THE BRONZE AGE CREMATION BURIAL

A cremation burial within a Collared Urn (304) was recovered from a pit [306] (Figs 4-6). The pit was steep-sided, 0.69m in diameter and 0.34m deep (Fig 7, Section 1). Although the fill (305) was fairly homogeneous, there appears to have been two phases of soil deposition as the urn was apparently placed upon a primary fill, 0.06m thick. The pit was backfilled around the urn with red-brown sandy-silt, with gravel inclusions (305), which contained no pyre debris. The contents of the urn are described in detail below.

The north-west edge of the pit was cut by a pit/posthole [316], 0.55m in diameter and 0.28m deep (Fig 7, Section 2 & Fig 8). It was steep-sided with a deeper hole in the base. It is possible that this was a post-pit that had held a grave marker post.

THE BRONZE AGE URN
Andy Chapman

The Collared Urn (Figs 9-11) stands *c* 250mm high, with a flat base, 105mm in diameter, and a rim diameter of 215mm. The fabric contains no evident mineral inclusions and is black throughout, apart from the outer skin, 1-2mm thick, which is red brown. The colour differentiation indicates that the pot had stood rim down in a bonfire, so that only the outer surface was oxidised. The base is 16-18mm thick, while the body is consistently 10mm thick, but slightly thicker at the carination and at the base of the collar, at 15mm thick. There is an oblique coil join just above the carination, which had been a major point of fracture. The rim is rounded and undecorated.

This is a tripartite vessel, with a shallow collar, 43mm thick, above a concave neck, 65mm deep, with a marked carination at the base of the neck. The collar and the neck are decorated with a herringbone motif, executed in incised lines. There are six lines on the neck while on the collar there are abrupt changes from five to four lines (Fig 12). In some places adjacent lines meet at an apex or overlap slightly, while in other places there is a gap between the adjacent lines.

The narrow collar and the presence of decoration below the collar, places this urn in Longworth's Primary Series and in Burgess's Early style (Gibson & Woods 1997, 126-131).

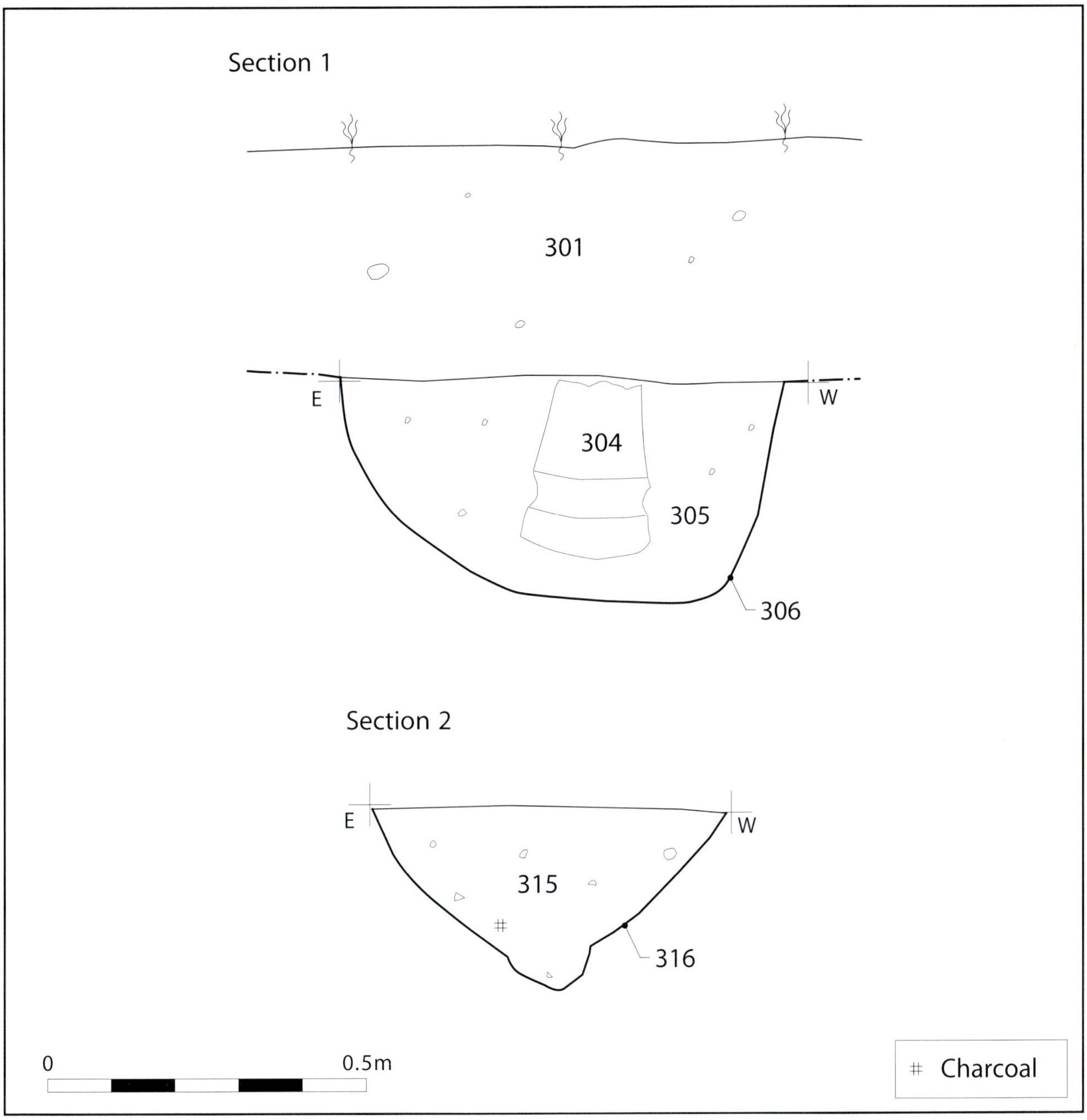

Fig 7 Pit 306 containing inverted Collared Urn (304), and posthole 316

Fig 8 Pit 306 and adjacent posthole 316, looking south

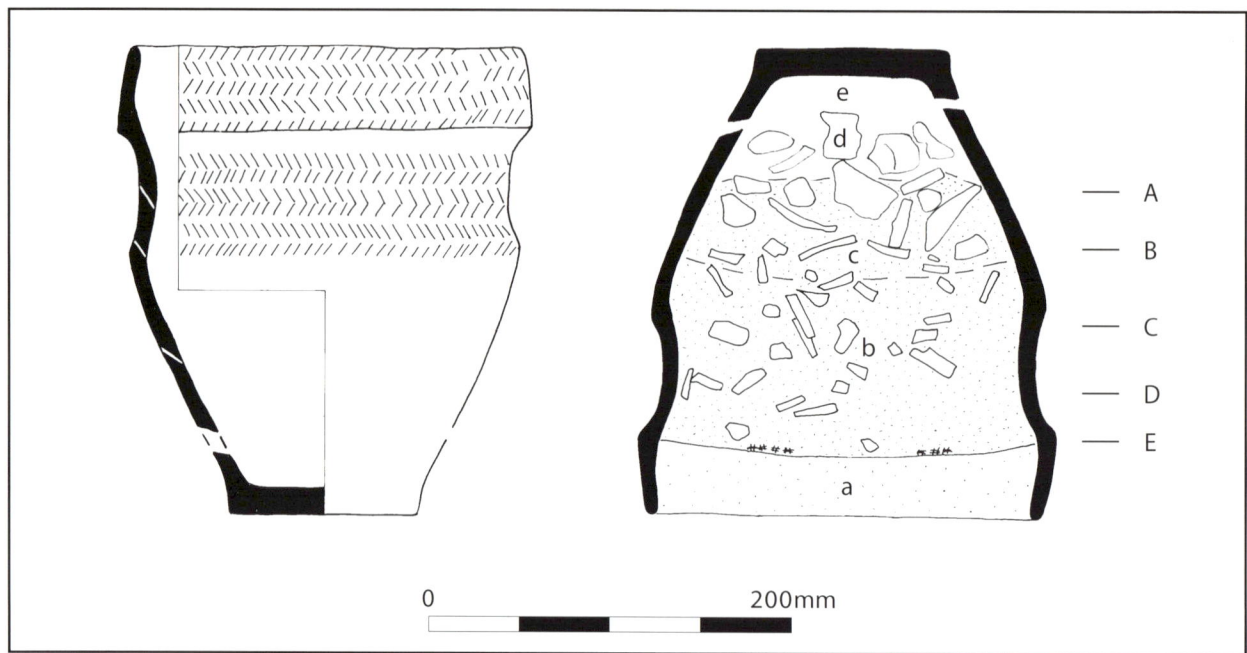

Fig 9 The Collared Urn 304 and section showing contents of urn

Fig 10 The Collared Urn, after initial cleaning and before excavation of its contents

Fig 11 The Collared Urn after excavation and dismantling

Fig 12 The Collared Urn, showing the change from four to five rows of herringbone decoration on the collar

THE CONTENTS OF THE COLLARED URN/THE CREMATION DEPOSIT
Andy Chapman and Pat Chapman

METHODOLOGY

The base of the inverted urn had been removed by the excavating machine when the urn was uncovered. However, the urn was evidently already fractured at the base before this. This fracture had permitted water to trickle in, and loose bone within the void at the base of the pot had become coated with a thin layer of silt. The extent to which the soil content, or a proportion of it, may have come into the pot following deposition is uncertain.

Following cleaning of the exterior of the pot, the outside was treated with a weak solution of PVA to provide some strength to the fabric. One side of the vessel was in particularly poor condition, with an old oblique fracture along a coil join near the carination, so that the lower body had slipped down and slightly overlapped with the upper body. In addition, there were numerous other fractures throughout the vessel, which had essentially been held together by the soil adhering to its surfaces. The more damaged side of the vessel was removed to provide both a section of the contents (Figs 9 & 13) and access to the interior for the excavation of the contents (as it was not possible to turn the urn upright given the damage to the base and the presence of a void). The bone and soil deposit was taken down in a series of five spits, each *c* 30mm thick, over a total depth of 180mm (Fig 9, A-E). The uppermost spit comprised loose bone (Fig 14), while the others were all in a matrix of sandy loam. At each level the exposed surface was drawn and photographed (Fig 15, level A). The matrix was retained for wet sieving, which produced nothing of significance. Once the contents of the urn had been removed, the remainder of the urn was in such a fragile condition, with multiple fractures, that it was not possible to keep it together (Fig 11).

THE CONTENTS OF THE URN

The void in the base of the pot was up to *c* 30mm deep and extended down parts of the sides for up to 60mm (Fig 9, e). At the base of the pot, the first material to be deposited in the urn, there were loose large bone fragments often up to 60mm across (Figs 9, d and Fig 14). There was a mixture of body parts, including fragments of skull, long bone and a number of recognisable fragments of the drums and the detached processes and spine of vertebra. Below this there were similarly large bone fragments, with the same broad mix of body parts, in a matrix of clean brown sandy loam (Figs 9, c and Fig 15). At a depth of 120mm from the top of the bone deposit (60mm above the base of the deposit), there was a gradual change to smaller bone fragments, of up to 30mm, closely packed in a firm deposit of brown sandy loam (Fig 9, b). The

Fig 13 The cremated bone deposit in section

Fig 14 The loose bone in the base of the urn

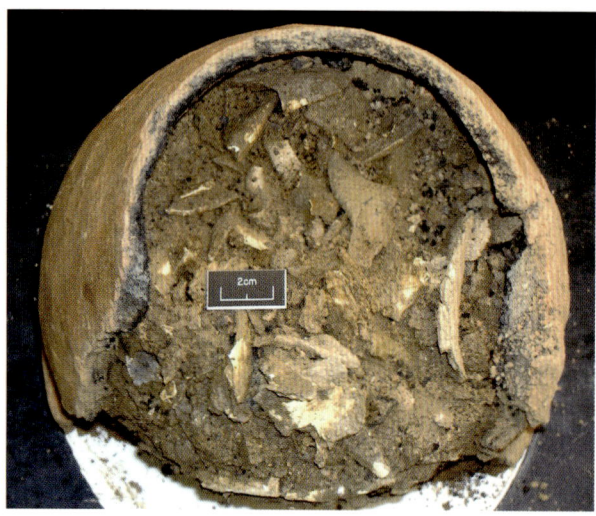

Fig 15 The bone deposit in plan, level A

bottom 20mm of the deposit was very densely packed in a compact matrix of brown sand, which also contained sparse small flecks of charcoal. This still contained some pieces of bone of up to 30mm, but the proportion of small fragments was higher. The lower half of the deposit still contained a mix of body parts.

It was notable throughout that, apart from very sparse and small charcoal flecks, the matrix was of clean sand, which had evidently not come from the pyre. There were no stone inclusions, even down to the smallest pebble.

The base of the bone deposit lay 35mm above the rim of the urn, with a slight hollow in the top of the underlying deposit (Fig 9, a). At the interface between the cremated bone and the underlying sand there were a few fragments of oak charcoal, measuring 40-60mm long, which suggests that a few lumps of carbonised wood had been deliberately placed on top of the bone deposit before the urn was inverted for deposition. It is this charcoal that has given a radiocarbon date in the early 2nd millennium BC (see below). In addition, there was a single piece of natural flint.

The top 30-40mm of the urn was filled with clean light brown sand, containing fine gravel, closely similar to the light brown sand adhering to the outer surface of the pot.

Given the presence of a void at the base of the urn, it seems unlikely that the pot had been "topped-up" with sand prior to being inverted and deposited, as this would have prevented the contents from settling to form a void. It seems more likely that some organic filler or cover had been used to prevent the contents from falling out on inversion. It is suggested that the decay of some organic filler had allowed the formation of a void at the base of the inverted pot. The pot may also have sunk into the underlying sand by up to 40mm.

THE HUMAN BONE
Sarah Inskip

(The full report is included in the client report and will be available from the Northamptonshire HER, online through ADS and in archive.)

The bone deposit weighed 2.3 kg. This is average for a complete, adult modern cremation. The total weight and virtual complete representation of skeletal elements suggest that the very complete remains from a single entire individual had been collected and placed in the urn. Every long bone is represented and furthermore, the small bones of the hand and foot were recovered, including three sesamoid bones and many distal phalanges. All the major bones of the skull are present as well as a large number of each of the four types of vertebrae. The deposit was checked for the presence of more than one individual but no repeated, sided fragments were found.

The colour of the bone, 90% of which is cream/white, indicates a pyre temperature above 600° C. There were few fragments of black and grey bone. There were no significant colour differences between the groups and uniformity in bone fragment colour suggests that the high temperature of the pyre was consistent around the body. There was a large variation in bone fragment size; the largest was a tibia fragment measuring 62mm x 40mm, while the smallest fragments were less than 1mm. The majority of the bone (82%) was in the 10mm and 5mm sieve fractions.

The osteological evidence suggests that this person was adult and the auricular surface indicates that they were a middle adult onwards (at least 25 years old). This is further reinforced by the presence of age related pathology, as there are changes in the spine that are consistent with osteoarthritis, which would also suggest an older adult, although such changes can also be activity related. Unfortunately, it was not possible to determine the sex of the individual.

THE CHARCOAL
Rowena Gale

A sample of charcoal recovered from the Collared Urn at the interface between the bone deposit and the underlying sand, was identified to genus level prior to radiocarbon dating.

The charcoal was extremely friable and also infiltrated with sediments, which made it rather difficult to examine. The sample was prepared using standard methods (Gale and Cutler 2000). Anatomical structures were examined using incident light on a Nikon Labophot-2 compound microscope at magnifications up to x400 and matched to prepared reference slides of modern wood; where possible, the maturity of the wood was assessed (i.e. heartwood/ sapwood). The samples were identified as:

Context (303)   1 x oak (*Quercus* sp.) sapwood, <1g
                26 x oak (*Quercus* sp.) heartwood

RADIOCARBON DETERMINATION

A sample of oak sapwood charcoal from the fill (303) of the Collared Urn was submitted for radiocarbon determination (Table 1 - see p. 25).

WORKED FLINT
Andy Chapman

Eighteen pieces of flint were recovered during the

Table 1: Radiocarbon determination of the charcoal from cremation pit [306]

Lab no. and sample no.	Origin of sample	Sample details	13C/12C ratio	Conventional radiocarbon age BP	Cal BC 68% 95%
Beta-238910 UFA07/303	Fill 303 of urn	Oak (*Quercus* sp.) charcoal	-24.0 0/00	3560 +/-40	1940-1870 1980-1750

Radiocarbon dating laboratory: Beta Analytic, University of Florida, Miami, USA
Method of analysis: AMS - standard
Calibration: Reimer *et al* 2004; OxCal v3.10; Bronk Ramsey; curb r:5 sd:12 prob usp (chron)

fieldwork. Four pieces came from the subsoil and eleven from the fill of the ditch on the eastern spur, and two pieces are from context (310), posthole [311] from the floodplain lowering area, near the cremation burial.

In addition, there is a single piece that had been placed within the Collared Urn on top of the cremated bone (303). This was a piece of natural flint, 45mm long by 36mm wide and 15mm thick, from a patinated and rolled pebble that had probably fractured along a natural plan of weakness.

The raw material is either grey, or occasionally brown, vitreous flint with a brown to light brown cortex or a grey granular opaque flint with a light brown to white cortex. Most pieces are between 20-30mm long, often with some cortex surviving, indicating that most come from quite small pebbles, as can be found within the local gravels.

The group includes 13 flakes, two blades and two cores. The flakes are typically short and squat, and only a couple show clear edge damage, perhaps from utilisation. There are two blades, one of which shows both edge damage and some retouch.

The two cores are both crudely worked pebble cores, 50mm and 52mm in diameter. One has a single platform while the other is discoidal, with small flakes removed around the circumference. Both cores are in grey opaque flint, with white cortex.

This small group of flint contains too few diagnostic features to enable any general characterisation, although all would be broadly appropriate to Neolithic to early Bronze Age assemblages utilising poor-quality flint obtained as pebbles or small cobbles from the local gravels.

DISCUSSION
Anne Foard-Colby and Andy Chapman

In the early second millennium BC, the early Bronze Age, a Collared Urn containing the cremated remains of a single mature adult, was inverted and buried in a small pit, close to the banks of the River Nene. This cremation deposit is unusual in that it contains virtually the entire individual, with all the major bones present along with the small hand and foot bones. This indicates that great care had been taken in recovering this material from the pyre. The lack of charcoal and burnt soils also indicates that care had been taken to exclude other pyre debris, perhaps through a combination of careful selection from the pyre and subsequent cleaning, possibly washing, of the bone. The distribution of the material within the urn indicates that the larger bone fragments had been placed in the bottom and then progressively smaller bones were added above this. The bone was probably deposited within a matrix of clean sand, as it seems unlikely that this had all accumulated as a result of silts infiltrating through fine cracks in the urn, although this had certainly been occurring. Once all the bone had been deposited in the urn, a few token fragments of charcoal, presumably taken directly from the pyre, which had been fuelled with oak timbers, had been placed on top of the bone, along with a square piece of natural flint. The urn was then inverted and placed in its pit for burial.

Immediately adjacent to the burial pit there was a second pit, which may have held a timber post as a grave marker. However, there was no evidence for a surrounding ditch to indicate that this burial had lain beneath a round barrow, or for the presence of a nearby barrow. Four small, shallow postholes lay close by, but the lack of dating evidence precludes establishing an association with the grave. This would therefore appear to be an isolated cremation burial with no relation to a round barrow or other funerary deposits.

There are only a few known funerary sites of Bronze Age date in the immediate vicinity. A supposed round barrow, the Upton Barrow (Scheduled Ancient Monument 13674; NSMR 5132/0/3), lies approximately 285m south-east of Upton Mill, but investigation in the early 1990s was inconclusive in establishing a date, and it was suggested that the monument probably post-dated the Roman period (Jackson 1993a, 8-9; 1993b, 72-73). A cremation deposit within a Collared Urn was discovered in a sand pit at Milton Malsor in 1965 (RCHME 1982, 102), but the context of the burial is unknown (Fig 1, Milton Malsor 1965). It would have lain quite close to a tributary stream running into Wootton Brook, itself a tributary of the River Nene. In Northampton, a small Collared Urn was found at St. Peter's Street, and is believed to have been an accessory vessel, perhaps associated with a nearby round barrow (Humble, in Williams *et al*, 1985, 46).

Of a slightly later date, at Pineham Barn, to the south of the River Nene, a small cremation cemetery contained the remains of seven individuals, one of which was contained within a vessel probably of middle Bronze Age date (Brown 2007). A nearby cluster of pits produced early Bronze Age pottery and a nearby ring ditch is interpreted as a possible barrow, although this is undated.

Within the broader landscape, the site lies 2.5km to the west of the Neolithic Causewayed Enclosure at Briar Hill, which was a major focus for ritual and funerary activity in this stretch of the Nene valley from the Neolithic to

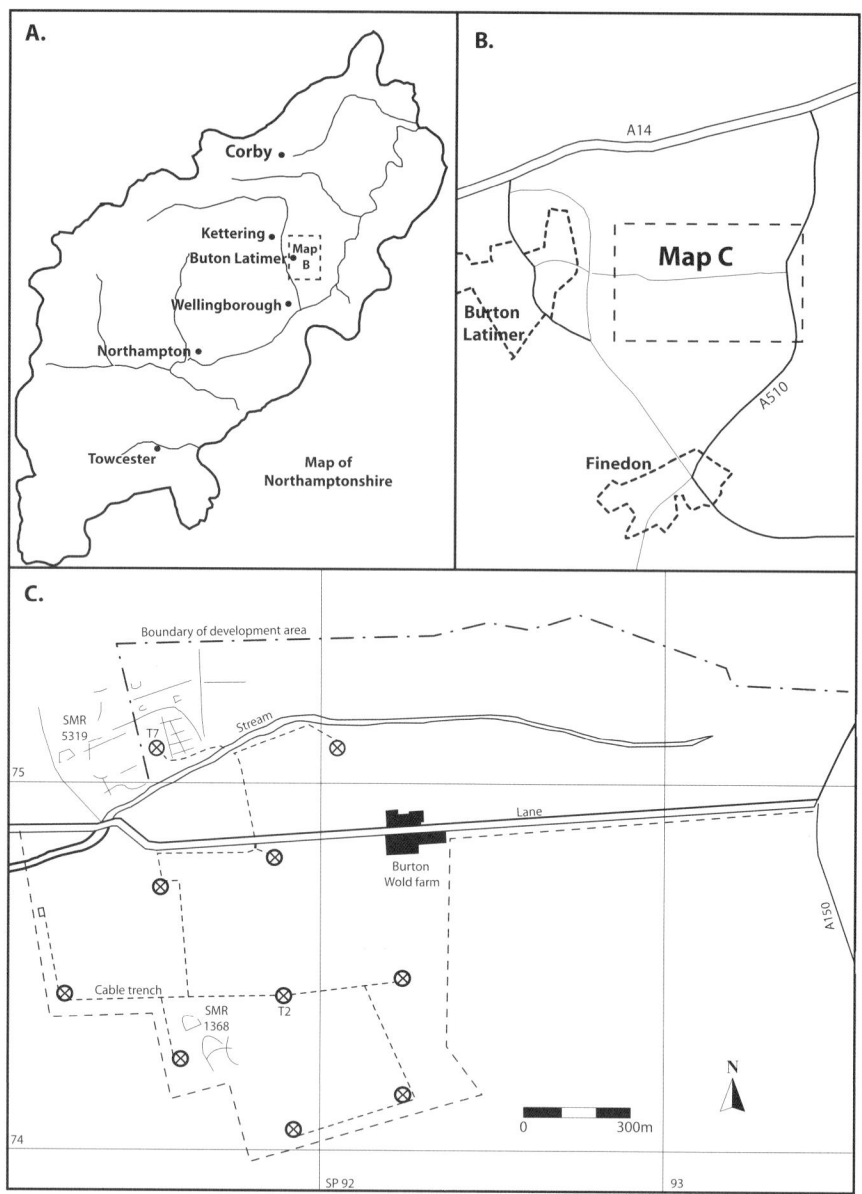

Fig 2 Location maps

the landscape rather than set out in a linear row. Figure 2 shows the boundaries of the development area and the position of turbines within it, together with the cable trenches between turbines and already existing landscape features such as the small stream. Also depicted are the cropmarks of archaeological sites known from aerial photography and recorded in the SMR: these will be described in more detail below.

The general topography of the area is characterised by large and fairly flat arable fields with an average height of 80m above sea level. The land rises slightly towards the north and east, with a small stream running in an east to west direction to the north of the Burton Wold Farm road. Soil consists of shallow boulder clay on an underlying Blisworth limestone (British Geological Survey 2003). In the area of T7, however, the boulder clay seems to be largely absent. The presence of more easily drained sandy clays here and the proximity just to the south of the stream mentioned above, as well as the slight protection offered by the rise in land towards the north, were probably major factors in the location of the complex of enclosures and associated settlement in the late Iron Age and early Roman period.

The earliest surviving map of the area is an Enclosure Award map of 1803/4 (NRO 2799). This shows the layout of fields at the time of enclosure. Most of the field boundaries depicted are subdivisions of what were formerly much larger open fields, such as South Fields and Wolds on the southern side of the farm road. No structures of any kind within the area of the wind farm are marked on the map.

AERIAL PHOTOGRAPHY

There are two areas where cropmarks of significant pre-modern archaeological activity have been discerned on aerial photographs (apart from medieval ridge-and-furrow, traces of which were identified in the central part

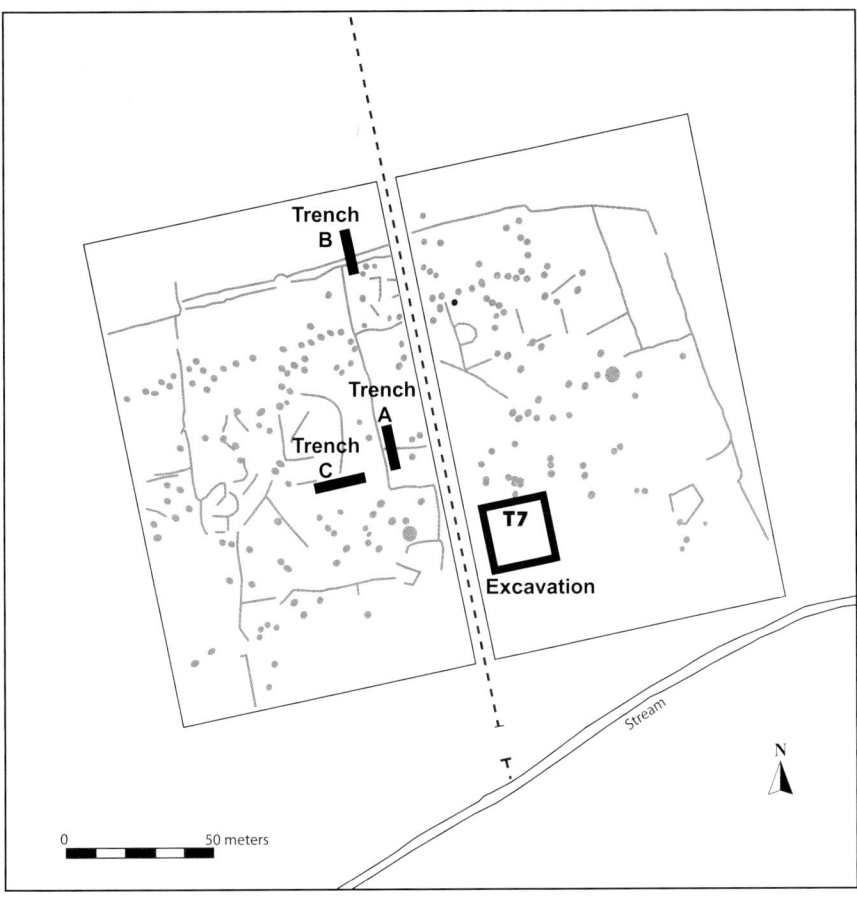

Fig 3 Results of magnetometer survey, and trench locations

of the site). Firstly, in the southern part of the Development Area, a small group of rectilinear and curvilinear enclosures was recorded as SMR 1368 (NGR SP 917 743). Secondly, in the northern part of the Development Area, a large rectilinear enclosure measuring about 200m x 120m with some smaller rectilinear and polygonal enclosures and outlying field boundaries is recorded as SMR 5319 (NGR SP 916753). Both are shown on Figure 2. While SMR 1368 was not due to be directly affected by the construction of wind turbines, the proposed location of T7 was inside the area of cropmarks known as SMR 5319. As it would be directly impacted upon by groundworks, the cropmark complex was investigated further by means of geophysical survey and trial trench evaluation.

GEOPHYSICAL SURVEY

The geophysical survey was undertaken by Northamptonshire Archaeology in two 1.6ha blocks, either side of a hedge running roughly north-south, using a fluxgate magnetic gradiometer (Butler 2003). The total area covered corresponded to the area of known cropmarks recorded as SMR 5319. The results of the survey, in the form of linear and discrete anomalies detected, are shown in Figure 3. Positions of subsequent excavation trenches are also shown, as it is useful to place the results of these within a representation of the enclosure complex as a whole.

Large numbers of positive magnetic anomalies representing linear, curvilinear and discrete archaeological features were detected. Two distinct phases of archaeological activity could be discerned. The latest phase was represented by the parallel linear features running in a north-north-west to south-south-east direction across the whole of the surveyed area, spaced on average about 8m apart. These were the remains of a medieval ridge-and-furrow field system, and have not been marked on Figure 3. The fact that they all run in the same direction indicates that this whole area was part of a single large open field prior to parliamentary enclosure.

The pre-medieval phase is represented by linear, rectilinear and curvilinear features detected within a rectilinear area bounded to the north and east by a straight linear ditch, slightly curving at the corner. This corresponds to the large enclosure visible on aerial photos. The ditch measures approximately 160m from west to east and 90m from north to south, perhaps with further extensions taking it beyond the edges of the survey area. A 55m long stretch of ditch defines part of the southern side of this large enclosure, inside of which there are numerous subdivisions and smaller enclosures, mostly with sides aligned towards the cardinal points. In some cases there appear to be entrances or gaps in the ditches of small rectilinear or polygonal enclosures within the larger complex. Also visible are many discrete anomalies - probably pits - some of which form alignments or linear patterns. These could be ritual in character or of a more practical function. In particular there is an alignment of up to thirty pits in the north-west part of the surveyed area, running parallel to the outer enclosure ditch but crossing some of the internal subdivisions – indicating that this pre-medieval phase of activity is itself comprised of multiple phases. Industrial activity may be suggested by several intense discrete anomalies which could be thermoremnant and might possibly be the remains of kilns or ovens (Butler 2003).

It is interesting to note that the geophysical survey results for land on the western side of the modern field boundary are much clearer than those on the eastern side. There could be several reasons for this, perhaps the most significant of which is that, as excavation showed, depth of overburden seems to be greater on the eastern side. Slightly different geological conditions were also encountered on either side of the boundary. To the west, archaeological features in evaluation trenches A and B were cut into limestone bedrock, which outcrops at between 0.30m and 0.60m below the modern ground surface. To the east, features in T7 were cut into sandy clay soils at a depth of between 0.50 and 1.00m, indicating that the bedrock must have dipped or shelved down, creating different conditions both for agriculture (enabling deeper ploughing) and for the magnetic survey itself.

RESULTS OF EXCAVATION

METHODOLOGY

Excavation of archaeological features took place in four stages. The first (evaluation) stage involved the excavation in 2003 of three trial trenches – 20m, 15m and 15m in length and 1.7m wide – on the complex of cropmarks recorded as SMR 5319 which has already been described. Information from the geophysical survey was used to locate the trenches, in order to target the investigation on the outer enclosure ditch as well as internal boundary ditches and pits. Upper levels were removed by mechanical excavator. Archaeological levels were then cleaned, photographed, investigated further through hand excavation, and recorded using Cambrian Archaeological Projects Ltd recording systems. The aim was to assess the survival, quality, condition, date and significance of archaeological features and deposits which might be impacted upon by the construction of Turbine 7.

Rationales and guidelines for the next stages were set out in the *Brief for a Recording Action* (Flitcroft 2004). The second stage, undertaken by Cambrian in the summer of 2005, consisted of monitoring of the construction of access roads and archaeological supervision of a 25 x 25m trench for each of the ten turbine sites. The aim was to ensure that any archaeological deposits present would be investigated and recorded prior to the construction of the circular turbine base foundations, each of which were to be 17m in diameter. Upper layers were removed by mechanical excavator, either to the level of the uppermost surviving archaeological horizons, or to the upper surface of the natural geological layers – in most cases boulder clay. Eight of the turbine sites were shown to be archaeologically blank. However, two parallel linear features were identified on the site of Turbine 2. As expected, large numbers of archaeological features of various kinds were observed on the site of Turbine 7, situated as it is near the centre of a known cropmark complex. These two areas (henceforth called T2 and T7) were earmarked for further investigation through hand excavation.

The third stage of excavation was undertaken by Cambrian over a period of four weeks in the autumn of 2005. Archaeological surfaces in T2 and T7 that had been revealed during the watching brief were cleaned and features excavated by hand, following the guidelines set down in the Brief (Flitcroft 2004) which stated that at least 10% of fills of linear features and 50% of pit fills should be sampled by means of excavation. Particular attention was focused in understanding stratigraphy at the intersections of features. The general aim was to identify, investigate through excavation, and make an appropriate record of archaeological remains about to be destroyed by the development. Specific aims were to establish: 1) the chronological development of settlement occupation and activity; 2) its economic basis; 3) the nature of social organisation within the settlement; and 4) the dates of abandonment or change in landscape use.

A fourth (watching brief) stage followed on from the excavation of T2 and T7. Digging of cable trenches between turbine sites and associated groundworks for the construction of a small electricity substation were monitored by an archaeologist.

All cuts, fills and layers were allotted context numbers during on-site recording. In post-excavation analysis, contexts were combined into a structural hierarchy of sub-groups, groups, landscapes and phases. For the purposes of this paper, group numbers (eg G1) have been assigned to single features such as ditches or pits which might have been investigated and recorded in terms of multiple excavated segments and recorded contexts. Landscape numbers (eg L1) have been assigned to landscape features that consisted of more than one feature, such as the droveway which is formed by parallel ditches in T2. Evidence is divided into two broad phases, corresponding to the three principal periods of activity of which traces are found: 1.Late Iron Age to Early Roman; 2. Medieval; and 3. Modern.

EVALUATION TRENCHES

The three trenches were all located in the western half of the complex of enclosures (Fig 3). Evidence from each trench is described separately below (Fig 4).

TRENCH A

Phase 1: Late Iron Age to Romano-British
Pit G1 had a semi-circular cut that continued into the eastern section of the trench, measuring 1.7m in width from north to south and with a depth of 0.40m. It had a vertical northern edge and a gently sloping southern edge. It may be part of a large circular pit. The fill was compact orange-brown silty clay. It contained pottery of the 1st-2nd century AD.

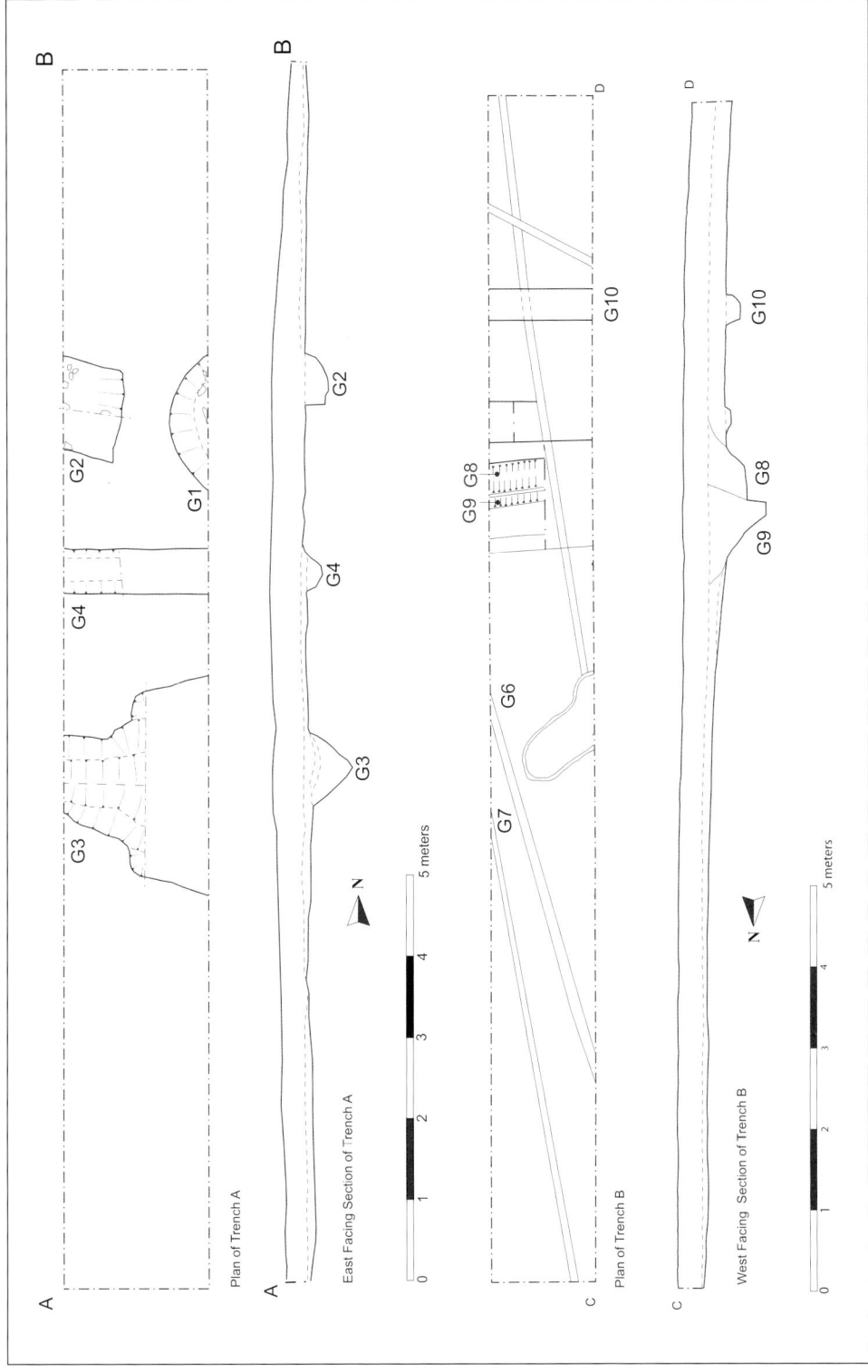

Fig 4 Evaluation trenches, plans and sections

Pit G2 was a sub-rectangular shape, extending into the western section of the trench. It measured 1.00m in width from north to south and was 0.40m deep with irregular edges and base. It was filled by a compact orange-brown silty clay. Like the fill of Pit G1, it contained 1st-2nd century pottery.

Pit G3 was a large and irregularly shaped but symmetrical feature extending into the sections on either side. It measured 2.5m in width on the eastern side, narrowing to 1.2 m wide on the western side, with a maximum depth of 0.60m. Its gently sloping sides at the top changed sharply into a steep V-shaped cut at the base. Interpreted as a pit, there is a possibility that this feature could be a boundary ditch running east-west. The lower fill was greyish-brown clay. The upper fill contained a deposit of ash and cinder.

Ditch G4 was a linear cut feature oriented east-west across the trench, extending into and beyond both sections. It was 0.55m wide and 0.30m deep, with sloping sides and a fairly flat base. The fill was a compact orange brown silty clay, within which pottery sherds of the 1st-2nd century AD were found. This feature is interpreted as an internal boundary gully or ditch within the larger enclosure complex.

TRENCH B

Phase 1: Late Iron Age to Romano-British

Ditch L1 ran from east to west and consists of ditch G8 and the recut G9. Ditch G8 has a gently sloping southern edge and a flat base. It was 0.60m deep, filled by a compact dark brown silty clay which contained 1st-2nd century pottery. This was cut by the ditch G9, which represents a recut of the same linear feature. This had a steep near-vertical southern edge and a more gently sloping northern edge, with a flat base 0.20m wide. The maximum depth of the feature was 1.10m. Its fill was similar to that of G8 except less stoney. The sherds of shell-tempered ware it contained cannot be precisely dated. This recut ditch was the main boundary ditch in the northern part of the enclosure complex, and in fact defined its northern limits. It can be correlated with the northern boundary ditch clearly visible on the geophysical survey and aerial photos. As a major boundary, it is likely to have had a bank and/or hedge associated with it, though no evidence of this survives in the ground.

Ditch G10 was a smaller linear feature running parallel with and about 2.00m south of the main boundary ditch L1. It measured 0.50m in width and 0.20m in depth, with gently sloping sides and a flat base. Its fill was a compact dark brown silty clay. It may well have been associated with the main boundary ditch L1, perhaps forming part of the same boundary (one possibility, for example, is that it delineates the southern edge of an internal bank, of which no other trace survives). Or it may represent an earlier and smaller version of the northern boundary.

Phase 2: Medieval

Three plough scars G5, G6 and G7, approximately 0.15m wide and up to 0.08m deep, ran across the trench from north-north-west to south-south-east. These were filled with a dark brown silty clay. Their orientation is the same as the linear features, interpreted as furrows, which showed up on the geophysical survey. Cutting the earlier linear features of Romano-British date, they are thought to be of medieval date.

TRENCH C

No features were encountered in this trench.

TURBINE SITE 7: EXCAVATION

Topsoil and subsoil layers were removed by machine to a total depth of between 0.60m and 1.00m, over an area of about 23 x 23m, revealing a natural surface of firm mid orange-brown sandy clays and silty clays, with small areas of limestone outcrop. Many archaeological features were cut into these natural layers, their darker fills showing up clearly against the lighter background. The position of T7 in relation to features picked up on geophysical survey is shown on Figure 2.

A general plan of T7 is shown in Figure 5.

Phase 1: Late Iron Age to Romano-British

Main enclosure ditches

The principal landscape features encountered were the north-south ditch L3 and the east-west ditch L4. These are regarded as main enclosure ditches which were part of the overall internal pattern of rectangular enclosures within the complex as a whole. The ditches were found to have been re-cut several times, indicating that the use of these internal boundaries persisted for some length of time.

Main north-south enclosure ditch L3

This composite feature – actually comprised of an accumulation of cuts and recuts – extended the whole length of the trench from north to south, measuring up to 4m in width. Two segments were excavated across it and a further box segment located on its intersection with L4. There was much variation between the three sections. Patterns of recutting encountered are best illustrated by means of the section drawings in Figure 6.

In all cases the main part of the composite feature was formed by the latest recut G17. This ditch cut was 2m wide and between 0.45 and 0.90 deep. The profile varied from a fairly steep-sided V-shape in the north to a shallower concave shape in the south. In the former, a sequence of four fills ranged from mid orange-brown silty clays near the base of the ditch to much darker and more charcoal laden grey-brown silty clay, lightly specked with small fragments of limestone near the top.

G18 was a steep sided gully or trench cut by G17 on its eastern side. It extended for at least 5m, was up to 0.4m wide and 0.55m deep. This could have marked the north-south internal boundary before the later ditch was dug. The fill was a grey-brown silty clay.

G19, G20 and G21 were all earlier cuts of the ditch, truncated by the later recut G17. These are best seen in the section across the southern part of L3.

All these features are taken to be part of a single composite landscape feature which retained its integrity as an internal boundary throughout numerous episodes of recutting. Traces of a possible bank on the eastern side of L3 were recorded in the northern south-facing side of the excavation trench.

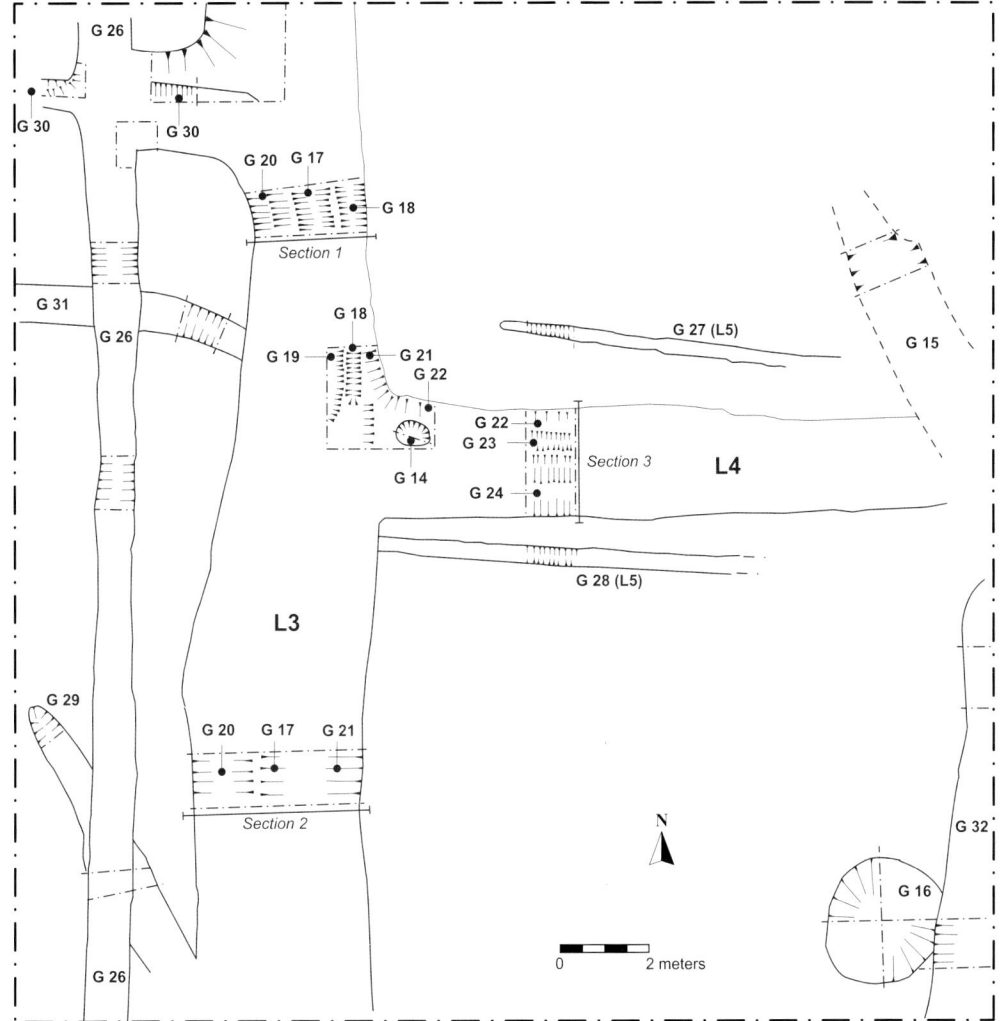

Fig 5 General plan, T7

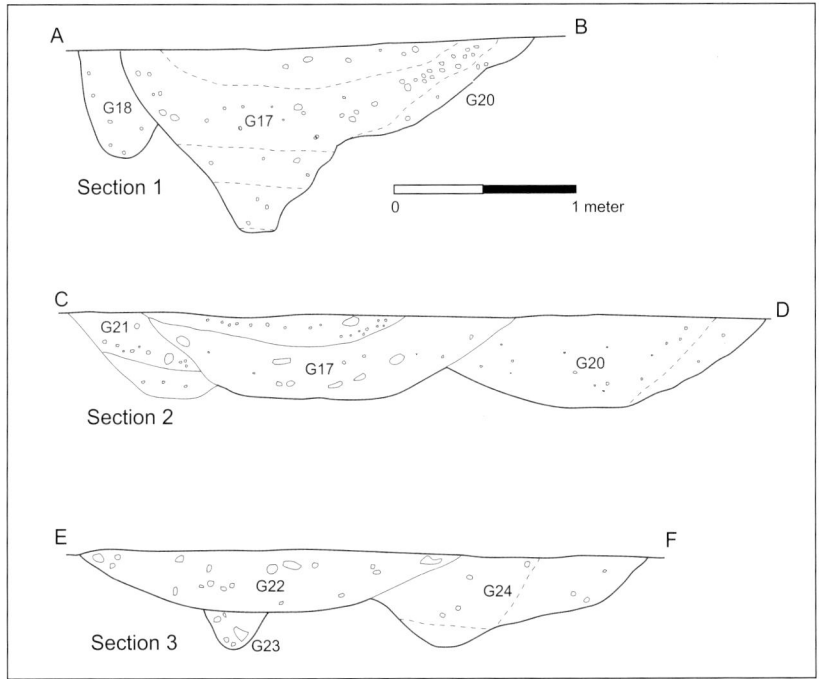

Fig 6 Enclosure ditch sections, T7

Relationship between L3 and L4

The box segment excavated to explore the intersection with L3 revealed a complex relationship of intermeshing stratigraphy, from which it can be inferred that neither L4 nor L3 is earlier or later than the other. Rather it can be said that both co-existed as part of the same system of internal division, and both were presumably recut as and when required, probably at the same times. No attempt is made here, then, to unpick the very complex sequence of deposits at the junction.

Main east-west enclosure ditch L4

Again it should be noted that this is a composite feature, comprised of a later recut and at least two earlier cuts, either of which could be the original. It extended from its junction with L3 right up to the eastern side of the excavation trench and beyond. Its width was up to 2.8m. Apart from the box segment, a further segment was excavated across L4 further to the east.

The main part of L4 consisted of the latest recut G22. This was up to 2m wide and 0.32m deep, with a fill of dark orange brown silty clay. G25 was a posthole cutting the base of this feature and thought to have been dug while the ditch was open and before it silted up. It measured 0.7 x 0.6m and was 0.2m deep, with a fill of mid orange brown clay, slightly lighter than that of the ditch fill above.

An earlier gully G23, running east to west, cut by the base of G22. This was 0.53m wide and 0.23m deep, with quite steep sides and a stony fill of mid grey-brown silty clay.

G24 was the earliest and original cut of ditch L4, surviving on the southern side in truncated form to a depth of up to 0.5m. Its fills of dark grey-brown to orange-brown silty clay contained some flecks of charcoal and small stones.

Smaller ditches

East-west gullies L5. This pair of parallel gullies, G27 and G28 ran either side of, and parallel to, the main east-west ditch L4. They may have been associated with that larger feature, or were perhaps precursors or successors to it – marking the same internal enclosure boundary. Unfortunately, there is no stratigraphic evidence to prove the point either way. Each gully was about 0.4m wide and 0.2m deep, with concave or flattish base, filled by mid orange brown silty clay.

North-south ditch G26. A very straight ditch, up to 1.2m in width and 0.3m deep, that ran parallel and to the west of the main N-S ditch L3. It was filled by a mid greyish brown silty clay with frequent small roundish stones. Sides partly destroyed by a later field drain that followed roughly the same course.

South south east – north north west ditch G29. Unusual for being off the general alignment of most other ditches, and may therefore represent a different, earlier, phase. Cut by G26. It was up to 1m wide and only 0.12m deep, with a mid orange-brown silty clay fill.

East-west ditch G30. This ditch ran off from the main north-south ditch L3 on its western side, and might effectively consist of one of the recuts of that ditch turning a corner – perhaps indicating increased subdivision of the site over time. Its stratigraphic relation with G26 could not be ascertained for sure, though it is thought to be earlier. It was a steep-sided ditch, up to 1.6m wide, narrowing to 0.7m wide towards the west, and was filled by mid - light orange brown sandy clays.

East-west ditch G31. A slightly curving ditch with concave sides that was cut by both L3 and G26. It was 0.75m wide and 0.3m deep, and its fill was a grey-brown silty clay.

North-south ditch G32. Situated on the east side of T7, this ditch cuts and is therefore stratigraphically later than pit G16. As far as is possible to tell, it seems to turn to the east at its northern end on the very edge of the trench. At least 2m wide and 0.6m deep, its full width was obscured by the trench side. Its fill was an orange-brown silty clay.

Pit

Pit G16 measured 3.00 x 2.60m in plan, and was 1.25m deep. It was excavated in two quadrants, though full excavation of the north-western quadrant was impeded by the presence of a large slab of stone extending into the section. The sides were quite steep and partially stepped on the south-eastern side. The bottom of the pit was fairly flat. Fills of the pit can be divided into three subgroups, which represent the different mini-phases of (a) **erosion** of lower sides while the feature was in use, probably as a water-pit; these were mainly interface layers that consisted of a mix of the organic 'peaty' deposits described below with natural clays originating from the sides, (b) **silting up** of the lower half of the feature after it had gone out of use; these heavily waterlogged layers were dark greyish-black silty clays with a 'peaty' consistency and a high organic content of woody fibrous material, obviously with potential for environmental analysis, and (c) **backfilling** of the top half of the feature; these layers were mainly dark brown or orange-brown compact or plastic sandy clays, including tipped layers containing quantities of large limestone slabs, which may have originated from a nearby building, wall or other structure (see Figure 7).

The lower 0.50m of fills were largely waterlogged; indeed the top of the layers of phase (a) represents approximately the current level of the water table. If the pit was originally dug as a water-pit, then it is reasonable to assume that the level of the water table then was more or less the same as it is now. While the lower fills may have accumulated through natural silting after abandonment of the water-pit, as suggested above, it was thought possible that the disused water-pit was re-used as a cess-pit, and this might account at least partially for the build-up of these organic layers. However, analysis of soil samples showed low levels of edible food remains such as fruit pips, discounting this theory.

Column samples were taken from all fills for pollen analysis and bulk samples were taken from the waterlogged layers for flotation, in search of charcoal, charred seeds or grain. Results are presented later in the section on environmental evidence.

It is now considered in the light of that evidence that

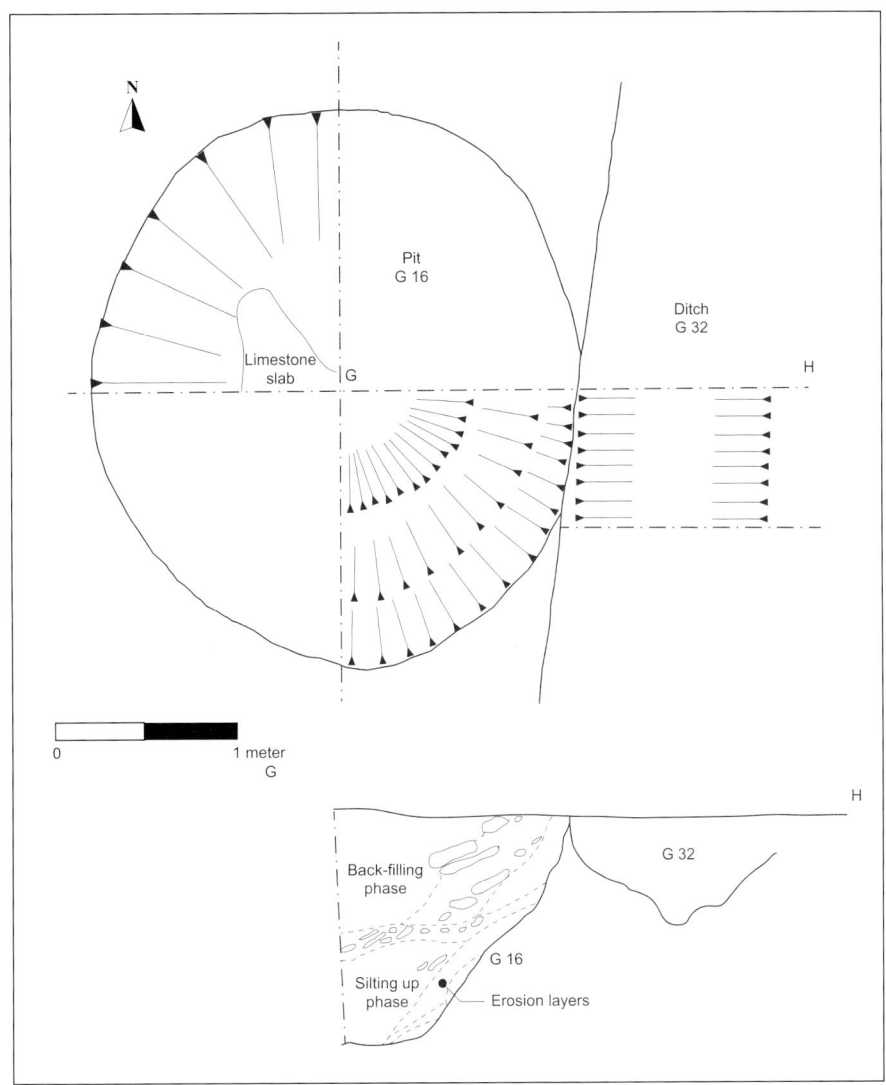

Fig 7 Plan and section of pit G16, T7

the pit was deliberately backfilled with material from elsewhere on site, including construction debris. The stratigraphy of the pit fills indicates several episodes of backfilling, though it is likely that these took place over a fairly short period of time. The considerable quantities of pottery sherds found date the backfilling events to the 3rd-4th centuries AD.

One of the finds from the backfilling of the pit was the shaped fragment of a top stone from a small puddingstone quern (small find 4). This is probably a domestic item rather than an artefact for the large scale processing of grain. Along with the numerous pottery sherds, it indicates that domestic activity was taking place nearby, even if no evidence for structures was found in T7. The existence of the water-pit itself suggests occupation nearby, since its function was probably to provide water for a dwelling or group of dwellings.

Figure 8 shows recording of the pit in progress.

Posthole

There were practically no surviving postholes, despite intensive efforts made to find traces of such features in areas of natural sands and gravels between the enclosure ditches. The only posthole was in fact found on the base of the east-west enclosure ditch L6.

Posthole G14 was oval in shape and measured 0.70 x 0.60m. It was steep-sided with a concave base, filled with a compact mid orange-brown sandy clay. This feature was cut into the base of the ditch while the ditch was open and before it silted up.

The absence of posthole structures generally within T7 indicates that settlement and domestic activity was for the most part located elsewhere (though close by) within the wider complex of enclosures.

External Surface

Linear gravel surface G15, interpreted as a possible path, extended in a north west to south east direction for a distance of about 8.00m. It was up to 1.20m wide and 0.5 m deep, and consisted of frequent small-medium stones in

Fig 8 Recording of south east quadrant of pit G16 in progress

a loose greyish-brown clay matrix. Further traces of this feature were picked up further to the north-west, though its precise outline was difficult to establish. Overlying one of the pair of parallel gullies L5 as well as the main east to west running enclosure ditch L4, this was one of the latest features of Phase 1. As such its use cannot be associated with that of other features, which are earlier in date and mostly of different orientation. Amongst the inclusions was a small, shaped stone artefact, possibly an ornamental whetstone (small find 1), which is discussed in more detail later. It seems likely that the path may have led to or from a dwelling just outside of T7, perhaps on slightly higher ground to the north.

TURBINE SITE 2: EXCAVATION

Topsoil and subsoil were removed by machine to a total depth of about 0.35-0.50m over an area of approximately 25m square revealing the surface of natural boulder clay of glacial origin (Figs 2 & 9). This natural layer was a firm light yellowish brown with occasional small chalk particles, fairly typical of the boulder clay across most of the wind farm development area as a whole. Cutting into the clay were two straight parallel linear features which together defined the shape of droveway L1. Several possible postholes were investigated but only one proved to be real. A 1m wide modern ditch (on the line of the hedgerow that had been uprooted from beside the road) ran from east to west along the southern edge of the trench.

Droveway

The possible droveway L2 consisted of two ditches G11 and G12, both of which were aligned north-north-east to south-south-west and were of similar shape and dimensions. The distance between the ditches at any given point was about 7m.

Ditch G11 was 17m long, continuing beyond the northern trench edge and coming to a butt-end in the southern half of the trench. It forms the western side of the droveway. Three segments, each 1m in length, were excavated through the ditch. These proved to be between 0.70 and 0.80m wide, and between 0.20 and 0.30m deep. The profile of the ditch changed along its length. While flat-bottomed and fairly steep-sided at either end, it was more of a concave shape in the middle segment. In all three segments there was a fill of hard, light greyish-brown silty clay – similar to but slightly darker than the surrounding natural, with some patches of orange oxide staining and containing occasional small to medium stones. There were no pottery or other finds.

Ditch G12 was uncovered to a length of 13m. It forms the eastern side of the droveway. Like ditch G11, it clearly continued on beyond the northern trench edge, while coming to a butt-end in the middle of the trench. Four segments of various lengths were excavated, showing the ditch to be between 0.60 and 0.90m wide, and between 0.15 and 0.20m deep. The profile of the ditch was concave, although in one segment the inner side was very steep relative to a much shallower outer side. The fill was a hard mid greyish-brown silty clay, with occasional small stones. As in the fill of G11, there were no finds.

Posthole

Only one posthole was discovered, despite extensive cleaning of surfaces and investigation of other possible candidates for postholes or pits that turned out to be natural features.

Posthole G13 was situated just to the east of droveway ditch G12. It was an irregular circular shape, 0.26m in diameter and 0.10m deep with an uneven base. The fill was a firm dark greyish-brown/black clay with occasional small stone inclusions. Again, there were no dateable finds.

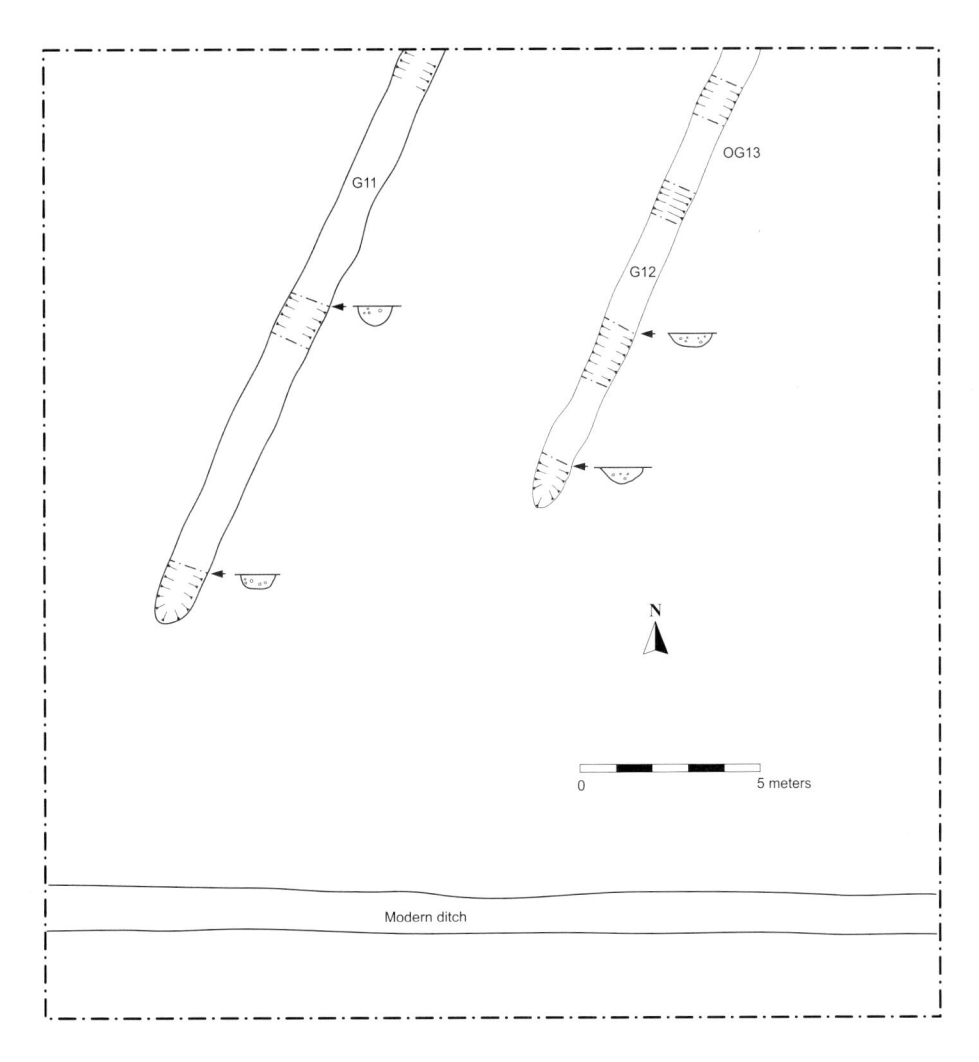

Fig 9 General plan and sections, T2

THE POTTERY
Peter Webster

INTRODUCTION

The Burton Latimer pottery consists mainly of small and medium sized sherds with relatively few rims. As an assemblage, it appears to be more local in origin and more kitchen-oriented than one would expect, for instance, from an urban or upper class rural site. In general, contexts seem to be mixed in date. The overall chronological spread is probably later 1st or 2nd century to earlier 4th century but the number of truly diagnostic pieces is low making the dating of individual features problematic.

All pottery from the site has been examined and listed in an archive. The collection is too small for much in the way of meaningful quantification. There are too few rims and bases to make the calculation of EVES a viable statistical tool. Quantification by weight was considered but this would have given undue prominence to the heavier grog-tempered fabrics (for instance) at the expense of others. The most practical way to represent the proportion of each fabric within the whole assemblage was by sherd count supplemented, where possible, by the isolation of specific vessels. A summary list arranged by context, fabric and sherd numbers will be placed in the archive.

CHRONOLOGY

The great majority of the pottery is from local sources and, as so often in such cases, this makes dating problematic. In our case, this is compounded by the fact that both the wide mouthed jars in sandy fabric and the 'lid-seated' jars in shell and grog tempered fabrics do not show the sort of development which encourages firm typologies. The latter may be confidently placed in the 1st and 2nd centuries and may well have survived into the 3rd century, but it is not clear if the Burton Latimer site extended over the whole of this period. There are a few pieces which seem more likely to be 1st or early 2nd century rather than later (from G2, G8, G16c, G17, G24, and G31). However, the absence of south Gaulish samian (even in an assemblage so lacking in samian) might suggest that extensive 1st century occupation is unlikely and a late 1st to early 2nd century start on our site is preferred. There seems no reason why this occupation should not have extended across the 3rd century and there are certainly a few pieces of late colour coated ware (from G17, G36, G37, and possibly G31) which are likely to be 4th century. However, the absence of the later shell-tempered jar forms (eg Tyers 1996, fig 242, 2-4) suggests that occupation probably did not extend long into the 4th century.

POTTERY SOURCES

The collection as a whole can be summarised by source as follows:

FINEWARES

Samian
Extremely scarce, only 6 sherds, just under 1% of all sherds found. Only five contexts yielded even small sherds:

Form 31 Central Gaulish; from G17.
Form 33 Central Gaulish; from G1 and a probable example from unstratified contexts.

There are also small scraps of Central Gaulish samian from G8 and unstratified contexts.

It is noticeable that all the samian is from Central Gaul and from common plain forms (2 cups, one bowl). As a collection they fall within the period cAD 120-200. The form 31 is certainly and the form 33 is probably Antonine, giving a distinctly mid-late 2nd century bias to the collection.

Other fineware
With the exception of one colour coated sherd (from G16c) which may be from Hadham, all fineware is in the white fabric with colour coat characteristic of the Nene Valley. Again the numbers are low, 16 sherds or 2.5% of all sherds found:

G16c	Small sherd of indented beaker, 3rd-4th century
G16c	Beaker base (probably from a vessel such as Howe, Perrin & Mackreth 1980, no.27 (3rd century) although the later no. 55 is also possible)
G17	Basal section of a large beaker (Howe *et al* 1980, no. 27), early 3rd century
G17	Bowl (Perrin 1999, fig. 63, 239), first half of 4th century
G17	Dish (Howe *et al* 1980, no.57), 4th century
G18	Fragment from a fairly large vessel
G24	Probable beaker fragment
G31	Bowl base, probably 4th century
	Small barbotine decorated sherd (probably later 2nd or 3rd century)
G36	Fragment of rouletted beaker (possibly as Howe *et al* 1980, nos.32-4, but more probably nos. 55-7), probably 4th century
G37	Dish (Howe *et al* 1980, no.87), 4th century; also a fragment possible once colour coated
Unstrat.	Dish base, probably 4th century

The list seems small considering the likely chronological spread of the site and its proximity to the Nene Valley.

It is also noticeable that forms represented have a preponderance of the coarser later forms. Small barbotine decorated beakers are, for instance, almost totally absent (just one small scrap from G31). The comparatively impoverished nature of the ceramic assemblage is clear.

In addition there are a number of sherds of white ware from the same source as the above:

G1	Jar
G4	Probable wide mouthed jar
G17	Jar fragment
G24	Six sherds
G30	One sherd
G36	Jar sherd

COARSEWARES

The great majority of the pottery from the site (over 84% of all sherds) falls into three broad categories, local shell-tempered, local grog tempered and local grey sandy wares:

Local Shell Tempered Ware
The fabric was present in most contexts and formed almost 26% of all sherds found. It falls within a general South Midlands tradition of shell-tempered pottery and a local source is implied. All or most fragments come from jars. It is noticeable that the late hook-rim jars are absent. The most common rim form present is a solid almost wedge-like rim with internal depression or groove as if for a lid. The total absence of these putative lids is however, noticeable implying some other use for this feature (see below). These rims appear to have an origin in the pre-Roman period and are found in quantity in the 1st and 2nd centuries (see for instance, Woods 1970, fig 34, 244-7 and Marney 1989, fig 21, 1-10). Similar rims appear elsewhere into the 3rd century (see Segontium, Period 7, Casey & Davies 1993, fig 17.11, 329, fig 17.13, 381; also Leicester, Kenyon 1948, fig 30, 18) and it is likely that the shell-tempered ware at Burton runs through into this period also. Sooting, especially externally, suggest use in cooking.

Local Sandy Wares
The fabric is most commonly reduced grey in colour, with a fine sand content and slightly darker core and surface. However, both darker and oxidised versions also appear along with a number altered by later burning. It formed the most common of all fabric found (making up almost 40% of all sherds). The tradition appears to be that found throughout the Nene Valley (cf Perrin 1999, 78 for instance; also discussion in Marney 1989, 70-87). The most common vessels are wide mouthed jars with tall often near upright necks (see for instance the many fragments of such a vessel from contexts G30 and G32). Most would seem to be 2nd and 3rd century, but the form does not seem to change sufficiently across time to give confidence in any detailed typology.

Grog-tempered Wares
This fabric clearly formed a staple for kitchen use and made up over 18% of all sherds found. The fabric tends to be oxidised with lumps of fired clay and a smoothed but pimply surface. Many examples are burnt suggesting

use on or near a fire. The tradition is a local one (see Marney 1989, 64-9 & 87-94). The most common rim form closely resembles that of the shell tempered jars and one suspects a common local tradition (and use, see below). There are also a number of jars with chunky everted rims. As with the shell-tempered vessels, a 1st to 3rd century date seems probable for most examples.

OTHER ROMAN FABRICS AND VESSELS
Mortaria
Only two mortarium fragments were noted, a Nene Valley mortarium from G16c and a flange of unknown source from an unstratified context. The dearth of these vessels so close to a source of mortarium manufacture is notable.

There were also a small number of sherds (about 10% of the whole) not certainly from the sources listed above, although a local origin cannot be ruled out for most.

POST-ROMAN POTTERY

The site was almost totally devoid of pottery which could certainly be ascribed a post-Roman date. The only exception were a few pieces of glazed earthenware from unstratified levels and from G8.

ECONOMIC AND SOCIAL IMPLICATIONS

The collection appears to be almost entirely kitchen oriented. The low percentage of finewares (3.5% of sherds) is noticeable. Samian is barely represented (a mere 6 sherds or 1% of the whole). Despite the proximity of the kilns, Nene Valley colour coated ware is only marginally more popular (16 sherds or 2.5%). Even among the latter, the majority are the late coarser kitchen wares rather than the earlier more delicate beakers. The enormous preponderance of shell-tempered, grog-tempered and local sandy wares (86% of all sherds) are almost all in forms which one might expect to be found in the kitchen. All, therefore, points to a way of life which was concentrated on the practicalities of living, rather than in its refinements. This may not be subsistence level farming, but it does not appear to be a great deal above that.

One other aspect of the collection calls for note. The great majority of the vessels recovered are jars. Among those jars, the so-called 'lid-seated' jar has already been noted as has the absence of lids. There seems little doubt that these vessels saw use on a fire as many show signs of sooting and burning, especially externally. They appear to be indicative of a particular form of cuisine concentrated on the cooking pot, rather than the dish and casserole. If so, then it may be that the 'lid-seating' supported not a lid, but other types of vessel. It would, for instance be possible to use the 'lid-seating' to support shallow wicker or similar vessels placed over the jar in cooking, after the manner of a steamer. It is a supposition impossible to prove from the Burton Latimer evidence, but perhaps one worth investigation on a more regional basis.

COPPER ALLOY BROOCH
Janet Webster

A simple one-piece brooch of the so-called Nauheim derivative type (see Webster, in Manning, Price & Webster 1995, 64-5 and references therein). The undecorated bow is of rod-like form with a roughly square cross-section and a single flattish curve in profile (Fig 10). Behind the head, where the rod of the bow is coiled back to form the spring, the metal has been flattened to produce coils of a broader rectangular cross-section, but with a more slender pin emerging from the rear. The bow tapers to a knife-edged foot with a simple trapeziform catchplate.

Although Hull was of the opinion that the Nauheim derivative in Britain was essentially a pre-Flavian form (Hull 1967, 28, footnote 49; Simpson 1979, 338), recent assessment of the dating evidence for this varied class of brooches has suggested that the rod-bow form survived in currency somewhat longer than the flat-bowed types (Bayley & Butcher 2004, 147), into the last quarter of the first century.

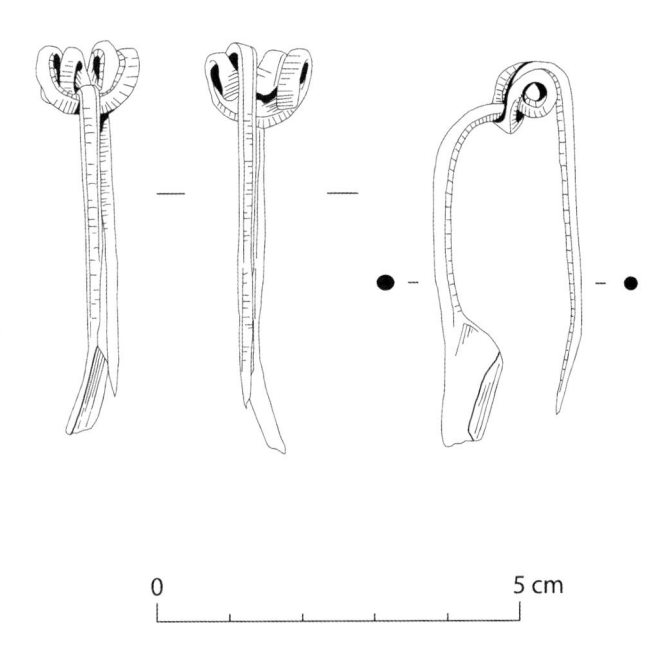

Fig 10 Copper alloy brooch (Scale 50mm)

STONE ARTEFACTS
Kevin Blockley

Quern (not illustrated). This is the top stone from a small quern 180mm in diameter, made from a conglomerate sandstone or 'puddingstone'. The central hole is evident, around 10mm in diameter. The thickness of the quern varies from 80mm in the centre to 55mm at the edge, although the original thickness of the quern has been lost since the underside is broken. The top surface and edge of the stone are smoothly worked.
Small find 4, from G16c.

Whetstone (not illustrated). This object is made from iron-rich fine-grained sandstone. It measures 12mm by 10mm in cross section, but its original length has been lost since both ends are broken. Three of the faces are smooth and one face has a slight depression which is very smooth. Probably used for sharpening a small iron blade. The surviving length is 31mm.
Small find 1, from G15.

THE ANIMAL BONE
Kevin Blockley

A total of 264 fragments of animal bone were recovered from the evaluation trenching (7 fragments) and larger scale excavation (259 fragments). The assemblage was well preserved but very fragmentary and not a large enough collection for metrical analysis to have been undertaken.

Present in the collection were sheep and cattle bones. One mandible from an adult dog was found in the same context as a bone from a rat.

SHEEP

Mainly fragments from mandible and teeth and leg bones. The bones represent a minimum of one lamb and one adult sheep. One fragment of mandible showed evidence of gnawing from a canine. No butchering marks were evident. It is thought that these bones were from casualties around the farm rather than the result of butchery and meals.

CATTLE

The bones are mainly from mandibles, teeth, lower legs, vertebrae and ribs. The bones represent a minimum of one calf and one adult cow. The only butchering mark is on a fragment of rib. This is evidence of butchered and prepared food, but in this context perhaps a discarded bone which has been moved from the site of occupation by a canine, the remaining fragments are thought to have been casualties around the farm rather than the results of butchery and meals. A single horn core indicates that polling of the cows was not undertaken.

DOG

Two mandibles from an adult dog were recovered. These are from one medium sized dog perhaps the size of a modern sheep dog.

RAT

A single rib bone from a rat attests the presence of this rodent on the site.

THE ENVIRONMENTAL EVIDENCE
Gemma Swindle, Barbara Silva, Nick Branch and Chris Green
(Department of Geography Royal Holloway University of London)

Assessment of one bulk sample and two sequences of monolith samples from contexts within the north-south ditch G17 and the fills of large pit G16 aimed to provide:

A record of the sedimentary sequence in order to establish the function of the archaeological features

A record of the concentration and preservation of archaeobotanical remains

An evaluation of the potential of the archaeobotanical remains for reconstructing the economy and diet of the Roman inhabitants, and the local environment.

POLLEN ASSESSMENT

Five sub-samples were extracted from monolith samples from ditch G17, and 11 sub-samples extracted from monolith samples from Pit G16 for assessment of the pollen content. For a detailed account of methodology and results refer to the archive report.

Fills of Ditch G17

The assessment indicates that pollen grains and spores are poorly preserved and in low concentration. Those grains identified are highly resistant to chemical or biological degradation due to their higher sporopollenin content, and tend to be preferentially preserved. Therefore, the results are inconclusive and no information can be ascertained on the nature of the local environment.

Fills of Pit G16

The assessment of Pit G16 indicates that pollen grains and spores are preserved better than in Ditch G17, although overall the concentration and preservation are below acceptable levels. Nevertheless, those pollen grains and spores recorded indicate the presence of grassland (Poaceae), waste ground (eg thistle and ribwort plantain), open dryland woodland (eg oak, ash and birch), and wet ground (sedges and alder).

PLANT MACROFOSSIL ASSESSMENT

A one-litre sub-sample was taken from from the basal fill of Pit G16. The sample was wet-sieved and the wet residues scanned using a low power zoom-stereo microscope. Identifications were made with reference to the modern seed collection at Royal Holloway University, London.

The 1-litre sub-sample processed for this assessment contained very occasional charcoal and charred seeds that are poorly preserved and unidentifiable. The sample also contained a frequent number of waterlogged seeds, which were provisionally identified as *Rubus fruticosus* (blackberry), *Juncus sp* (rush), *Chenopodium album* (fat hen), *Alnus glutinosa* (alder), *Rumex sp* (docks and sorrels), Apiaceae (carrot family) and Caryophyllaceae (campion family). This assemblage of plant remains indicates the presence of wet ground and possibly shallow open water fringed by alder and rushes, shrubland with blackberry bushes, and waste ground / grassland with short and tall herbs. The absence of a range of taxa representing edible food eg fruit, suggests that the feature is unlikely to have been a cesspit, but instead may have been utilised as a waterhole. The low concentration of charcoal and charred seeds suggests that these were probably deposited accidentally in the pit, perhaps by wind or water.

DISCUSSION

This discussion refers mainly to the interpretation of the enclosure complex initially known from aerial photography and classified as SMR 5319, later subject to evaluation by trial trenching and geophysical survey, then to excavation of a small area within it on the site of Turbine 7. Evidence from other turbine sites, and from the watching brief of groundworks within the development area as a whole, will be used to shed light on the landscape context within which the enclosure complex was situated.

The excavation of T7 took place within an area of the enclosure complex that was relatively free of features picked up by geophysical survey. Even so, a considerable number of features - especially ditches - was uncovered. This indicates that the site as a whole has much more interior structure to it than the aerial photograph or geophysical evidence might suggest. Although not picked up on the survey, the main north-south and east-west ditches encountered fit within the general orientation of the enclosure complex as a whole; these can be taken to be internal boundaries. The large pit in the south-east corner of T7 can perhaps be taken to be fairly representative – in the sense of providing a good idea of size, shape and environmental potential - of the many other pits whose location is indicated on the survey.

The best indicator for the date of the enclosure complex is the pottery, which has an overall chronological spread from the later 1st or 2nd century to the earlier 4th century. This suggests the complex was in use for a period of approximately 200-300 years. Although its origins may lie in the very late Iron Age, the site is primarily of Romano-British date and character. Heavy recutting of ditches indicates a continuity of form, with the same internal boundaries being re-formed and re-used again and again. Even when new ditches are cut, they tend to respect the general alignment of the older ones. All of this seems to suggest a settled way of life of the farming community that lived and worked here, and this is reflected by the internal coherence of the enclosure complex throughout its period of its use.

What was the primary function of the enclosure complex? That settlement did take place is indicated by considerable quantities of domestic pottery found in ditch and pit fills, with the large pit itself probably serving as a water-pit for the community that lived nearby. On the other hand, the lack of postholes or other evidence of buildings within the excavation trench, where conditions were excellent for showing up such evidence if it had existed, shows that parts of the site were not inhabited as such. Areas of settlement were probably localised in particular areas and not spread out uniformly over the complex as a whole. A significant possibility is that the east-west pit alignment identified in the geophysical survey might have formed an internal boundary between a settlement area on higher ground to the north and animal enclosures to the south.

This also gives support to the idea that the primary function of the enclosure complex was more to do with the activity of farming itself. The interpretation of enclosures as animal pens was initially put forward in the evaluation report and this is not refuted by the results of excavation from T7. Indeed it may explain the absence of traces of domestic structures. Banks and possibly hedges associated with ditches could have played a major role in facilitating the control of animals through providing barriers to the movement of stock. These would have had considerable durability through time, with each recutting of a ditch serving to replenish the already existing bank.

It is possible that animals were overwintered here on the dryer, better drained and more sheltered ground next to the stream, while being led out to graze more widely in summer months. Unfortunately, the assemblage of faunal remains – with a fairly typical ratio of cattle and sheep bones - is not particularly large and it is difficult to extrapolate much information from such a small sample.

There was little evidence of arable farming. The quern found in a pit is probably the kind of artefact that would be found in any Romano-British household. Not too much interpretation should be placed upon the negative evidence of the general absence of grain in pit and ditch fills, but this could be taken as being indicative of an economy based largely on other resources. The Boulder Clay in the vicinity may have been much more suitable for animal grazing than for arable farming.

Evidence of a droveway in T2, hints at the kind of system of communications within which the enclosure complex may have been embedded. Although the nearest known Roman road is some distance away, it is likely that small enclosures or enclosure complexes were linked together by a system of droveways, which provided routes for controlled animal movement across the landscape. This was certainly a characteristic of late Iron Age landscapes in upland boulder clay areas of the midland region – as for example at the recently excavated site on the Stoke Hammond Bypass in Buckinghamshire (Edgeworth 2006). It is probable that these patterns of communication, and agricultural practices associated with them, carried through into the Romano-British period.

The identification of the two parallel ditches in T2 as a droveway is of course a provisional interpretation, based mainly on comparison with similar features on other Iron Age and Romano-British sites. In this case there is no dating evidence, however, and the continuation of the feature does not show up on any aerial photographs. While it appears that the ditches both stop before they reach the southern edge of the trench, it is possible that they continue on in segmented form, or perhaps as shallower ditches which have since been ploughed out. The droveway – if that is what it was - was probably associated with banks and hedges, traces of which no longer survive. Absence of pottery in the fills, relative to the large amounts of pottery found in T7, indicates that the droveway passed through a tract of land which was not settled at this point, though it no doubt linked farmsteads or pockets of small scale settlement that were dispersed across the landscape.

Jeremy Taylor noted the association of droveway and rectilinear enclosures in his assessment of the Roman archaeological resource in the East Midlands region as a whole. Together with the simple farmsteads or small enclosed settlements like Wootton Hill (Jackson 1988-89) and Wollaston (Meadows 1996), he noted groups of individual rectilinear enclosures and enclosure complexes alongside long distance and local tracks and droveways" (Taylor 2001-2, 10). He associates these larger enclosure complexes with a restructuring of rural settlement which occurred from the Late Iron Age to the 2nd century AD, but only with regard to the "extensive and highly structured agricultural landscape of the river valleys" (*ibid*, 10-11). What the evidence at Burton Wold suggests is that such networks of enclosure complexes, linked by droveways, might have extended up onto the clay uplands too.

Most of the known Iron Age and Romano-British rural settlement sites in Northamptonshire are situated in lowland situations, often on the river gravels and away from the clay uplands. Until recently, it was assumed that the greater proportion of the Boulder Clay zone of the midland region was devoid of settlement at that time. The unquestioned belief until recently was that these areas were largely covered with woodland.

For a refutation of this, see Foster's study of extensive occupation on Boulder Clay and Oxford Clay during the Iron Age and Roman periods in the Brigstock area (Foster 1988). At Mawsley New Village, Cransley Lodge, Kettering both enclosed and unenclosed structures dated to the middle Iron Age were found on the heavy boulder clay (Hull and Preston 2002). These suggest that exploitation of such supposedly marginal landscapes may have been well established before the Romano-British period.

Exploitation of the Boulder Clay zone, of course, does not necessarily imply an arable landscape any more than it does a wooded one. If sites like the enclosure complex at Burton Wold were primarily supported by a pastoral economy, this implies a fairly open grassed landscape, perhaps shaped and divided up more by droveways than by a patchwork of arable fields.

Admittedly only a small part of the enclosure complex at Burton Wold has been investigated by excavation and many questions about the site as a whole remain. Why were there so many pits? What was the function of the pit alignments? Where was domestic settlement located within the complex? Even so, the site is special in that it provides a concrete example of settlement and exploitation of the Boulder Clay zone during the Romano-British period. It points, perhaps, to the possible existence of many more such sites – not previously suspected because not situated on valley floors where most known sites are located, and perhaps not with such high visibility on aerial photos or geophysical survey due to the soil conditions. A very interesting facet of the excavations here was how features on the limestone outcrop (eg enclosure ditches in T7) showed up extremely well on aerial photos, whereas features on the Boulder Clay itself (eg droveway ditches in T2) did not show up at all. Further illustration of this was provided by the geophysical survey of the enclosure complex itself. Features showed up much more clearly on the western side of the modern field boundary (where the limestone bedrock outcrops quite close to the surface) than on the eastern side (where the bedrock shelves down beneath sandy clays).

All this goes to show that sites and features in the Boulder Clay zone which are not conveniently located on limestone outcrops may be getting missed by archaeologists because their presence is masked by the drift geology on which they are situated.

ACKNOWLEDGEMENTS

This report is a compilation of the work of many individuals and organizations. For Cambrian Archaeological Projects Ltd, Richard Jones wrote the desk-based assessment, Phil Evans carried out the archaeological evaluation, while Kevin Blockley carried out parts of the watching brief and managed the project as a whole. Darren Baker, Paula Howell, Daniel Jones, Hywel Keen and Kevin Moore worked on the excavation of T2 and T7. Cambrian would like to thank Myk Flitcroft, formerly of the Historic Environment Team at Northamptonshire County Council, Alison Smith of the HER office, Mark Osborn and Eddie Whittle of Breheny Civil Engineers, and the staff of Enercon for their assistance. We are grateful to Enercon for the funding of the archaeological work.

BIBLIOGRAPHY

Bayley, J, & Butcher, S, 2004 *Roman Brooches in Britain. A Technological and Typological Study based on the Richborough Collection*, Report of the Research Committee of the Society of Antiquaries of London, **68**

British Geological Survey 2003 digital geology sheet, EW186

Butler, A, 2003 *Geophysical Survey at Burton Wold Farm, Kettering, Northamptonshire*, Northamptonshire Archaeology report

Casey, P J, and Davies, J L, 1993 *Excavations at Segontioum (Caernarfon) Roman Fort, 1975-1979*, Council for British Archaeology, Research Report, **90**, London.

Edgeworth, M, 2006 Changing Landscapes: Archaeological Investigation of an Iron Age Enclosure on the Stoke Hammond Bypass, *Records of Buckinghamshire*, **46**, 119-148

Evans, P, 2003 *Interim Report on an Archaeological Field Evaluation at Burton Wold Farm, Kettering, Northamptonshire*, Cambrian Archaeological Projects report, **254**

Foster, P J, 1988 *Changes in the Landscape: An Archaeological Study of the Clay Uplands in the Brigstock Area of Northamptonshire*, BA Dissertation, University of Sheffield

Flitcroft, M, 2004, *Wind Farm at Burton Wold Farm, Thrapston Road, Burton Latimer: Brief for a Recording Action*, Northamptonshire County Council, Historic Environment Team report

Howe, M D, Perrin, J R, & Mackreth, D F, 1980 *Roman pottery from the Nene Valley: a Guide*, Peterborough City Museum, Occasional Paper, **2**

Hull, M R, 1967 The Nor'nour Brooches, in D Dudley, Excavations on Nor'nour in the Isles of Scilly, 1962, *Archaeological Journal*, **124**, 1-64

Hull, G, and Preston, S, 2002 Middle Iron Age Occupation at Mausley New Village, Cransley Lodge, Kettering, Northamptonshire, *Northamptonshire Archaeology*, **30**, 1-20

Jackson, D A, 1988-89 An Iron Age Enclosure at Wootton Hill Farm, Northampton, *Northamptonshire Archaeology*, **22**, 3-21

Jones, R S, 2003 *Burton Latimer, Kettering: Archaeological Desk-based Assessment*, Cambrian Archaeological Projects report, **245**

Kenyon, K M, 1948 *Excavations at the Jewry Wall Site, Leicester*, Report of the Research Committee of the Society of Antiquaries of London, **15**

Kidd, A, 2001-2 *An Archaeological Resource Assessment of the Later Bronze and Iron Ages (the First Millenium BC) in Northamptonshire*, East Midland Archaeological Research Framework Available: http://www.le.ac.uk/archaeology/research/projects/eastmidsfw/ (accessed 10/11/05).

Manning, W H, Price, J, & Webster, J, 1995 *Report on the Excavations at Usk 1965-1976. The Roman Small finds*, University of Wales Press

Marney, P T, 1989 *Roman and Belgic pottery from excavations in Milton Keynes, 1972-82,* Buckinghamshire Archaeological Society Monograph Series, **2**

Meadows, I, 1996 Wollaston, in *Current Archaeology*, **150**, 212-15

Taylor, J, 2001-2a *An Archaeological Resource Assessment of Roman Northamptonshire*, East Midland Archaeological Research Framework
Available: http://www.le.ac.uk/archaeology/research/projects/eastmidsfw/ (Accessed 10/11/05)

Taylor, J, 2001-2b *An Archaeological Resource Assessment and Research Agenda for the Roman Period in the East Midlands*, East Midland Archaeological Research Framework
Available: http://www.le.ac.uk/archaeology/research/projects/eastmidsfw/ (Accessed 10/11/05)

Taylor, J, & Flitcroft, M, 2004 The Roman Period, in M Tingle (ed), *The Archaeology of Northamptonshire*, Northamptonshire Archaeological Society

Tyers, P, 1996 *Roman Pottery in Britain*, London

Woods, P J, 1970 *Brixworth Excavations 1. The Romano-British Villa, 1965-70. Part 1 – The Roman coarse pottery and decorated samian ware*, Journal of the Northampton Museums and Art Gallery, **8**, 1-102

Excavation of the Roman Villa and Mosaic at Rowler Manor, Croughton, Northamptonshire

by

MICHAEL DAWSON

with contributions by

Simon Carlyle, Andy Chapman, Hillary Cool, Peter Guest, Tora Hylton, Natasha Hutcheson, Ian Meadows, Phil Mills, David S Neal, Andrew Payne, Rob Scaife, Robin P Symonds and Ros Tyrrell

SUMMARY

Investigation of the Roman villa site at Croughton began in 1991 when evidence of settlement was unearthed during the construction of a gas pipeline. Subsequently the location of a villa was revealed by the presence of tesserae found during fieldwalking and metal detecting. Excavation exposed a mosaic pavement portraying Bellerophon slaying the Chimaera. Assessment and evaluation by English Heritage led to scheduling in 1995. A change of ownership raised the possibility of displaying the mosaic in situ beneath a cover building. This required Scheduled Monument consent which was granted, but a further change in ownership resulted in the re-burial of the mosaic and its continued preservation in situ. This report presents the results of investigations at the site since 1991; it includes a full account of the mosaic pavement and excavations as well as episodes of trial trenching, geophysical survey and fieldwalking.

INTRODUCTION

The Roman settlement at Rowler Manor Estate was first recorded in 1991 during the construction of a gas pipeline which ran through an area of Roman period archaeology (Figs 1 and 2). Subject to a watching brief, quantities of Roman pottery and two small coin hoards were recovered. Later investigation to the south of this line led to the excavation of a 4th-century AD mosaic floor and a small area of structural stonework. The mosaic showed the Greek hero Bellerophon slaying the mythical beast Chimaera, set within a frame of geometric design, located within a stone building, or 'villa'.

Subsequent assessment and evaluation established that the site at Rowler Manor Estate probably comprised a stone-built house. Aerial photographs show cropmark enclosures extending over a 5ha site, including part of a now dry streambed to the east of the main house, suggesting the 'villa' was part of a complex of buildings at the centre of a country estate.

A single La Tène II spearhead hinted at activity on the site in the 2nd century BC whilst the ceramic assemblage from fieldwalking and evaluation trenching suggests the most intense period of occupation of the villa was from the 2nd to the 4th centuries AD. The mosaic dates to the mid-4th century. Beads dating to the 5th to 6th centuries found on the mosaic and burning on its surface, as well as Anglo-Saxon period ceramics in the vicinity, hint at occupation continuing in the 6th century some time after the end of the Roman province.

The site is located in farmland that is presently part arable land, part wooded. It occupies a southward facing slope at the head of a shallow valley which, although culverted and dry today, was once an open stream course. The site is presently a Scheduled Ancient Monument: *Roman Settlement 600m north east of Rowler (Nat Monument no 22703; NSMR 5717)*. It was scheduled in 1995.

In 1998 Rowler Manor Estate was sold and during the restoration some inadvertent damage was done to the Scheduled Area. The damage assessment by English Heritage (Wilmott 2001) re-opened the debate about the future of the mosaic and with the new owner's enthusiasm and interest in the pavement and its context, a plan to put the mosaic on limited display beneath a protective cover building was developed (Dawson 2003). This report draws together the archaeological evidence gathered at Rowler from the first discovery of the site in 1991. It presents the excavated evidence in the context of the wider landscape and includes the specialists' reports on significant artefacts as well as the Bellerophon mosaic.

GEOLOGY AND TOPOGRAPHY

Historically the site is located within the parish of Croughton and Newbottle in Sutton hundred, a medieval sub-division of Northamptonshire. The site is located some distance to the north of the village of Croughton. The village, originally *Criweltone* (AD 1086 DB), which means a settlement, *tun*, at a fork in the river (Ekwall 1980, 133), was founded by the late Saxon period. Rowler probably means rough, OE *rūh*, in the sense of uncultivated clearing in the woods, OE *leah*.

The solid geology of the area comprises Blisworth Limestone of the Great Oolite Series, with underlying strata of Northamptonshire sands. The site is situated on level ground at approximately 143m OD above a shallow valley of a tributary stream of the River Cherwell. The soils are calcareous loams of the Aberford Association traditionally associated with stock rearing and occasionally winter cereals (Soil Survey of England and Wales 1983, Sheet 4).

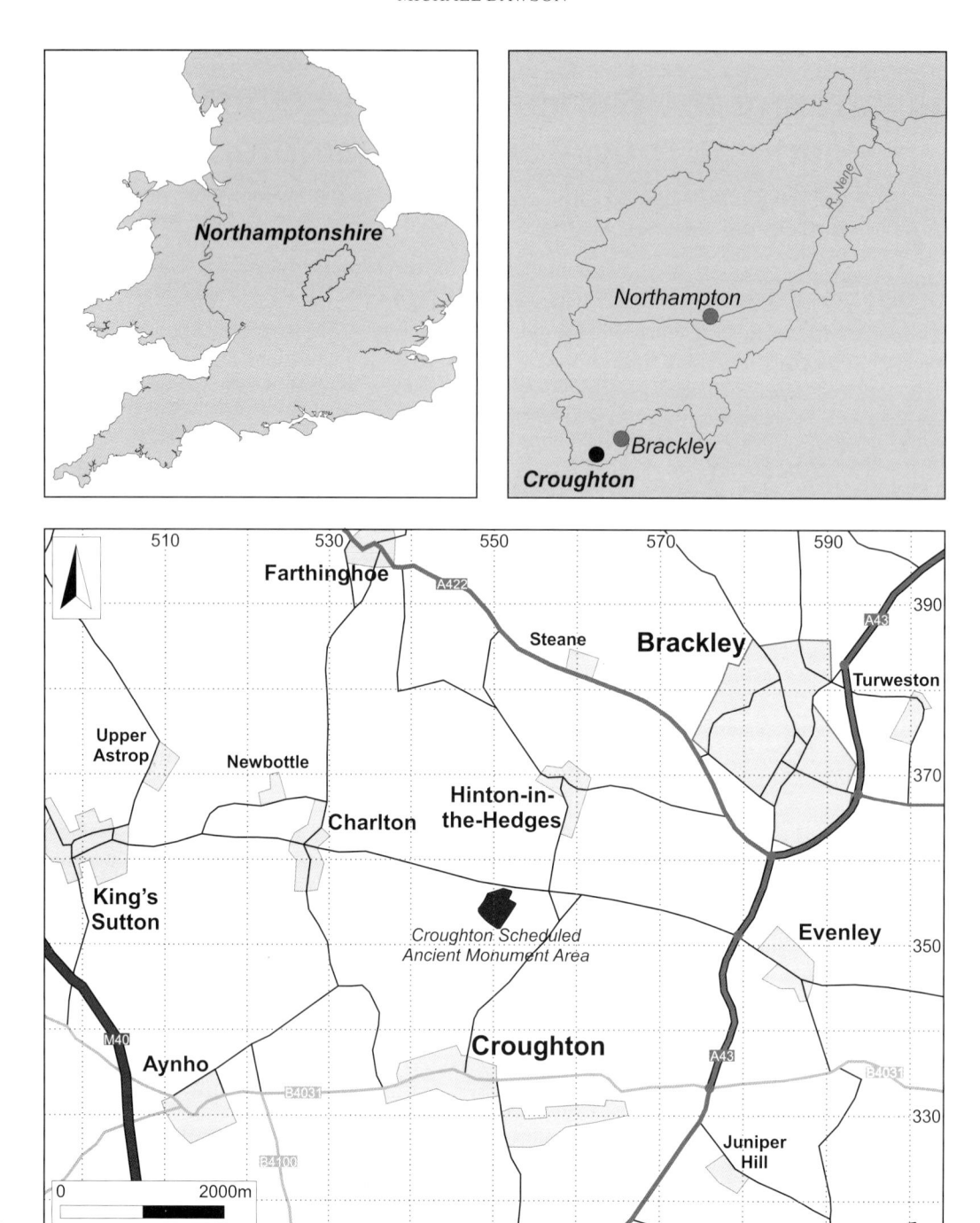

Fig 1 Location plan showing the position of the Scheduled Ancient Monument on the Rowler Manor estate at Croughton

THE ARCHAEOLOGICAL INVESTIGATIONS

In early July 1991 during construction of a gas pipeline to Brackley, Northamptonshire, metal detectorists discovered coins, a belt buckle and a brooch. A subsequent watching brief by Northamptonshire Archaeology recorded the remains of stone walls, a surface or roadway close to the bridleway south of Charlton Road. The watching brief also recovered tile, pottery and a small coin (RN 5535/004) (Table 1 see p. 48).

In October 1991, the presence of tesserae in field OS 0557 (Ordnance Survey Land parcel number) alerted two local amateur archaeologists and metal detector users to the possibility of a mosaic in the area. With the permission of the owners, Mr and Mrs Bryan Harris, a small excavation was mounted and several square metres of decorative mosaic pavement were revealed (*Independent*, 17th Oct 1991). The mosaic was subsequently re-buried on the advice of English Heritage.

In October 1992 and January 1993 the Ancient Monuments Laboratory carried out an extensive geophysical survey to establish the limits to the site and to determine the form of any buildings (David and Payne 1993). In July 1993 English Heritage re-excavated the mosaic 'to

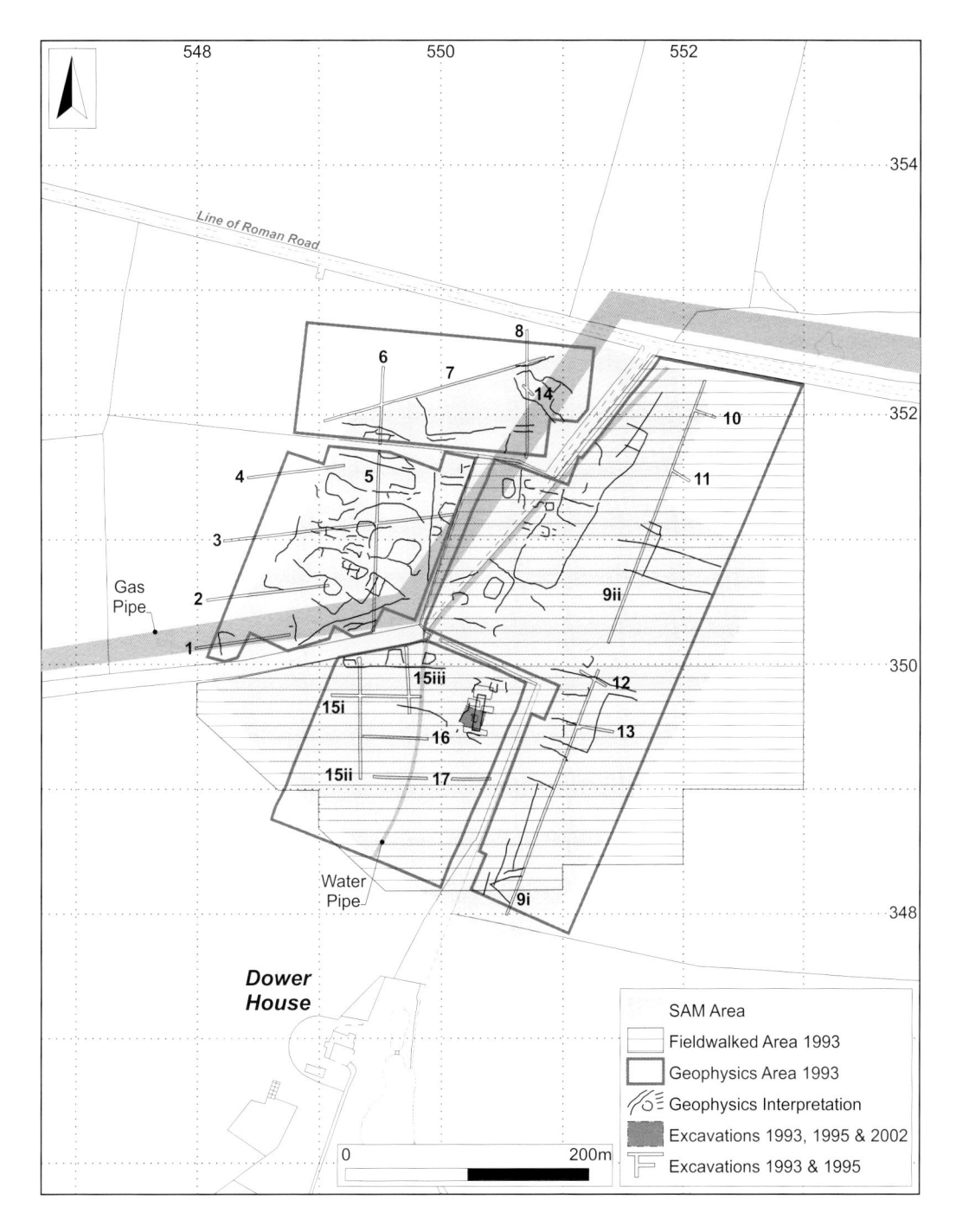

Fig 2 Archaeological interventions plan: geophysics (EH), trial trenches (EH), field artefact collection (NA), excavation trenches (EH) and damage assessment (EH)

assess the...condition of the mosaic and to backfill the area of disturbance with more suitable material' (Blore 1993). The original excavation had been backfilled with sand and the mosaic covered by a steel mesh to deter metal detectorists. David Neal was one of the first people to inspect the Bellerophon mosaic (Mosaic 1) in 1991 and when the pavement was re-exposed in 1993 made a painting of it based on photographs.

In November 1993 Northamptonshire Archaeology carried out field artefact collection on several fields and a contour survey in September 1994 (Shaw and Auduoy1993, NA 1995).

Building on the results of the early interventions and assessments the site was scheduled by the Secretary of State in July 1995. In order to characterise the site further English Heritage undertook a final season of evaluation in the summer of 1995. Seventeen trial trenches were excavated, largely in the western half of the Scheduled Area, with several more trenches opened to test the extent of the 'villa' building and re-examine the condition of the

Table 1: Datasets from investigations at Rowler Manor Farm

Episode	Site Codes	Contexts used in this Report	Archive Location	Reports
Watching Brief 1991	WB 91	-	Northamptonshire SMR	Watching Brief Sheets
Mosaic Excavation 1991	CRV 91	-	Northampton Museum	
Geophysical Survey 1993	AML 15/93	-	EH	AML 15/93
NA Field Artefact Collection 1993	Fields 4148, 0557, part 7100, part 7158	-	Northamptonshire Archaeology and Rowler Manor Estate	NA 1995
EH 1993 Excavation of mosaic trenches A-E	CAS 492		Rowler Manor Estate	Blore 1996
EH 1995 17 trial trenches	CAS 492	1001-1106	Rowler Manor Estate	Blore 1996
EH Damage Ass of Water Main	CAS 662 0-82	6201-6282	Rowler Manor Estate	Wilmott 2001
NA excavation 2002	RMF 02 0-84	0-84	Rowler Manor Estate	Carlyle 2002

mosaic and to record it fully (Blore 1996). Re-exposure provided an opportunity to make a measured drawing of the mosaic and create a new painting, since slightly more of the pavement had been exposed.

In mid-2001 excavation of a new water pipe trench by contractors across the Scheduled Area led to a campaign of evaluation by English Heritage (Wilmott 2001) when the pipe-trench was partially re-excavated and examined.

In 2002, subject to Scheduled Monument Consent, excavation was carried out by Northamptonshire Archaeology and managed by CgMs Consulting in order to assess the potential to display the Bellerophon mosaic and to set the mosaic in context. With the full exposure of the mosaic in 2002 the 1995 survey and painting were updated, whilst a photographic survey was undertaken by David Andrews of English Heritage (Andrews et al 2005).

STRUCTURAL EVIDENCE

INTRODUCTION

The evidence for the Roman settlement at Croughton comes from several sources, a watching brief, aerial photography, field artefact collection, sample trial trenching, several stages of geophysical survey and excavation.

Gathered over the past 12 years, no significant attempt has been made to characterize the site except in its broadest terms and today the site is referred to in the scheduling description as 'Croughton Roman settlement' and is generally known as a Roman villa.

The contextual data recovered from the site suggests that the villa is at the core of a larger estate centre. Contexts are referred to conventionally as [cut] and (fill). Because of duplicated context numbers a context concordance was drawn up for the publication and remains with the archive (Table 1).

THE PERIPHERY
A Payne and M Dawson

The evidence of activity at Croughton extends over an area of some 6ha. Geophysical survey has revealed a concentration of enclosures on the higher ground to the north with several rectangular areas, probably fields, enclosed by ditches along both banks of a spring fed stream, Rowler Brook, which runs along the eastern side of the site. The stone building, characterised as the villa, occupies a locally prominent position on the southern periphery of the site. It overlooks the brook and is opposite a series of intercutting enclosures.

The stone building, which appears to form the focus of activity in the 3rd and 4th centuries AD at Croughton, was part excavated whilst the structures and enclosures around the periphery have only been assessed for the purposes of scheduling. Consequently the following comprises only a preliminary description based on the results of the evaluation (Fig 2).

The villa building lies to the south-east of the main complex of cropmarks and enclosures, features which primarily consist of ditches defined by geophysical survey as positive anomalies in the magnetic coverage. Several linear positive anomalies (Fig 3, 2 - 4) appear to indicate a series of long straight ditches perhaps defining a system of larger angular enclosures and linear boundaries sub-divided by roadways. Within the areas bounded by the longer linear features, the magnetometer has mapped a very dense complex of anomalous activity including intercut ditches and gullies defining small square and sub-rectangular enclosures (Fig 3, 5-7), larger ditched enclosures (Fig 3, 8-10), hut emplacements (Fig 3, 11-12), clusters of pits (Fig 3, 13) and probably some industrial activity. The density and superimposition of many of the anomalies in these areas suggests several phases of modification of the settlement indicative of prolonged activity. Peaks in topsoil magnetic susceptibility occur in a zone associated with the partially excavated Roman building, the villa, and extending some 50m to the north of it. Further localised peaks in topsoil magnetic susceptibility suggest the presence of high temperature industrial activity within one of the enclosures some 200m north of the villa (Fig 3, 14). The earliest activity seems to have occurred on the northern periphery where a polygonal enclosure was identified by

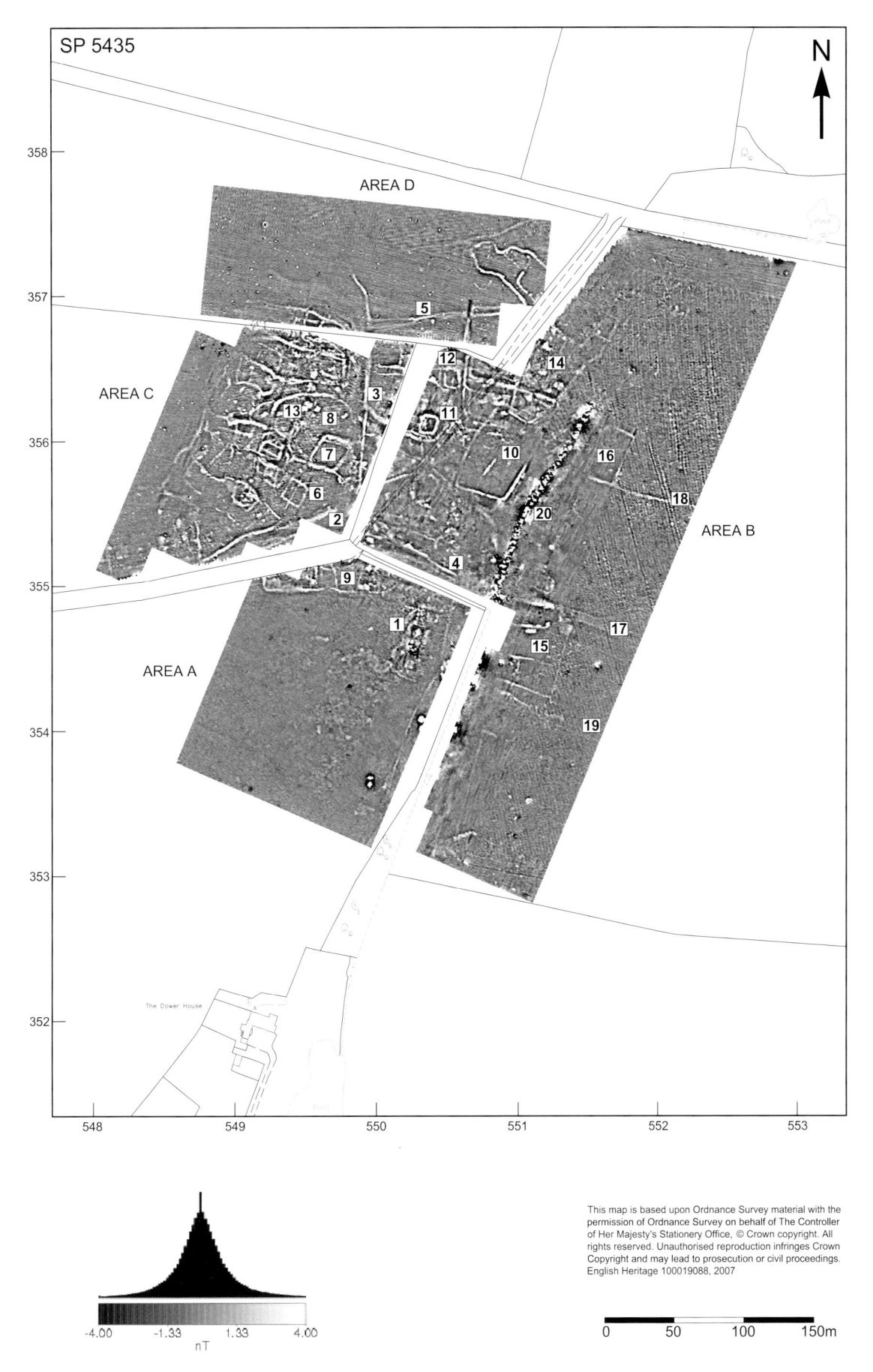

EXCAVATION OF THE ROMAN VILLA AND MOSAIC AT ROWLER MANOR, CROUGHTON, NORTHAMPTONSHIRE

Fig 3 Geophysical survey showing areas of significance

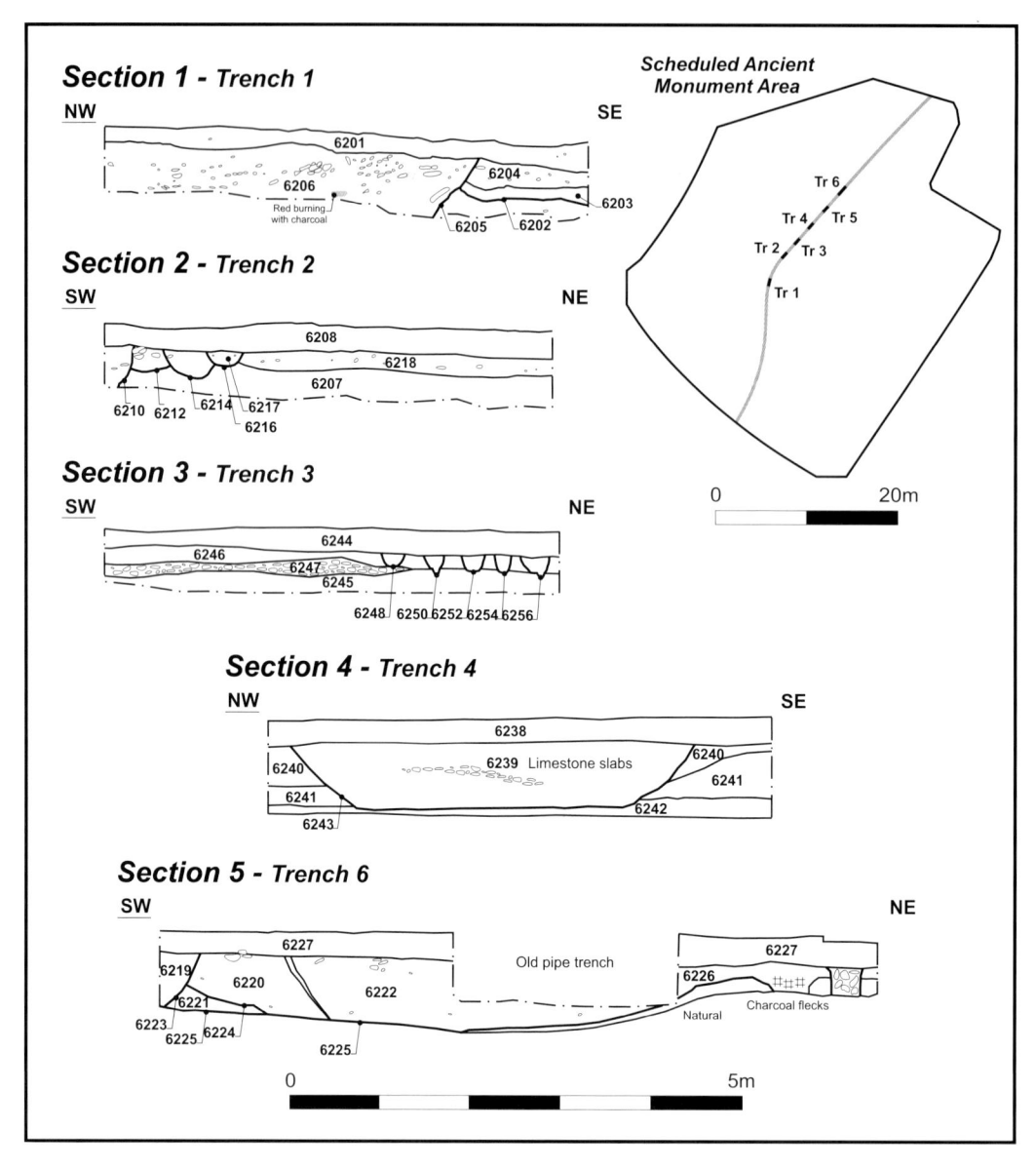

Fig 4 Damage assessment: the water pipe sections (Wilmott 2000)

the geophysics and partially sampled in trenches 7, 8 and 14. Trench 8 (1010) and trench 7 (1009) in fact revealed several ditches and cobbled areas whilst trench 14 (1016) seemed to pick up the line of the enclosure ditch from trench 7. Ceramic dating, however, from (1010) spanned the period AD 170-400 although a La Tène II spearhead characteristic of the period 300-100 BC was recovered from the primary fill of a ditch (1010) (Fig 12.1). The northern area also produced 1st-century coins from a small hoard during the watching brief amongst contexts which suggested later settlement activity.

On the western side of the complex the evidence is of settlement typified by post-built structures, metalled limestone surfaces and trackways amongst ditched enclosures. Animal bone, pottery, fragments of tile and some fired clay fragments suggest a predominantly agricultural settlement. The ceramics produced from this area suggest a later period of activity with a date range of AD 270-400 from contexts (1003), (1004), (1005), (1006), (1008), (1009) in trench 10 (Fig 2). On the eastern margin of this concentration along the upper slope of Rowler Brook investigative trenching (Wilmott 2001) hinted at a shifting pattern of settlement with buried soil horizons (6218), (6246), (6222) (Fig 4) around several post-built buildings producing ceramic dates of AD 170-400.

A series of positive linear magnetic anomalies (Fig 3, 15-16) on the eastern side of the former stream course indicate a pattern of rectilinear enclosures following the course of the stream from north to south. Magnetic activity is more limited within these enclosures compared to those west of the stream, suggesting they probably represent fields and paddocks. Settlement activity appears to fall off considerably in the direction of the higher ground to the east of this linear system of enclosures. A sparser number of weaker linear anomalies here may indicate a trackway running into the settlement from the higher ground to the east (17) (Fig 3) and further field boundaries associated with the Roman settlement (Fig 3, 18-19). Activity does not seem to have spread significantly to the eastern bank of Rowler Brook until the 3rd and 4th centuries. In the northern end of trench 9 (ii) a T-shaped stone-built corn dryer (1011) was dated by ceramics to AD 300-400 and in the southern sector a single refuse pit (1011/1014) and a ditch produced slightly earlier dates AD 270-400. The evidence in this area may represent stock enclosures.

THE ROMAN VILLA
S Carlyle

Located on the upper slopes of the small valley above the Rowler Brook, but firmly on the southern edge of the main concentration of activity at Rowler, lie the remains of a substantial stone built Roman period building. The outline of the building, which included at least two mosaic pavements, was indistinct in the geophysical survey, but appears to consist of a rectangular structure with dimensions of approximately 8m x 30m, aligned nearly north-south (Fig 5). The wall foundations are marked by negative magnetic anomalies. The mosaic seems to be in the centre of this rectangle. Immediately surrounding the rectangle, and further to the south-west, disturbance was apparent but with no coherent pattern. Trenching to the west of the building confirmed the absence of any significant activity close to the building, but demonstrated that the building comprised at least five rooms, possibly a row type house

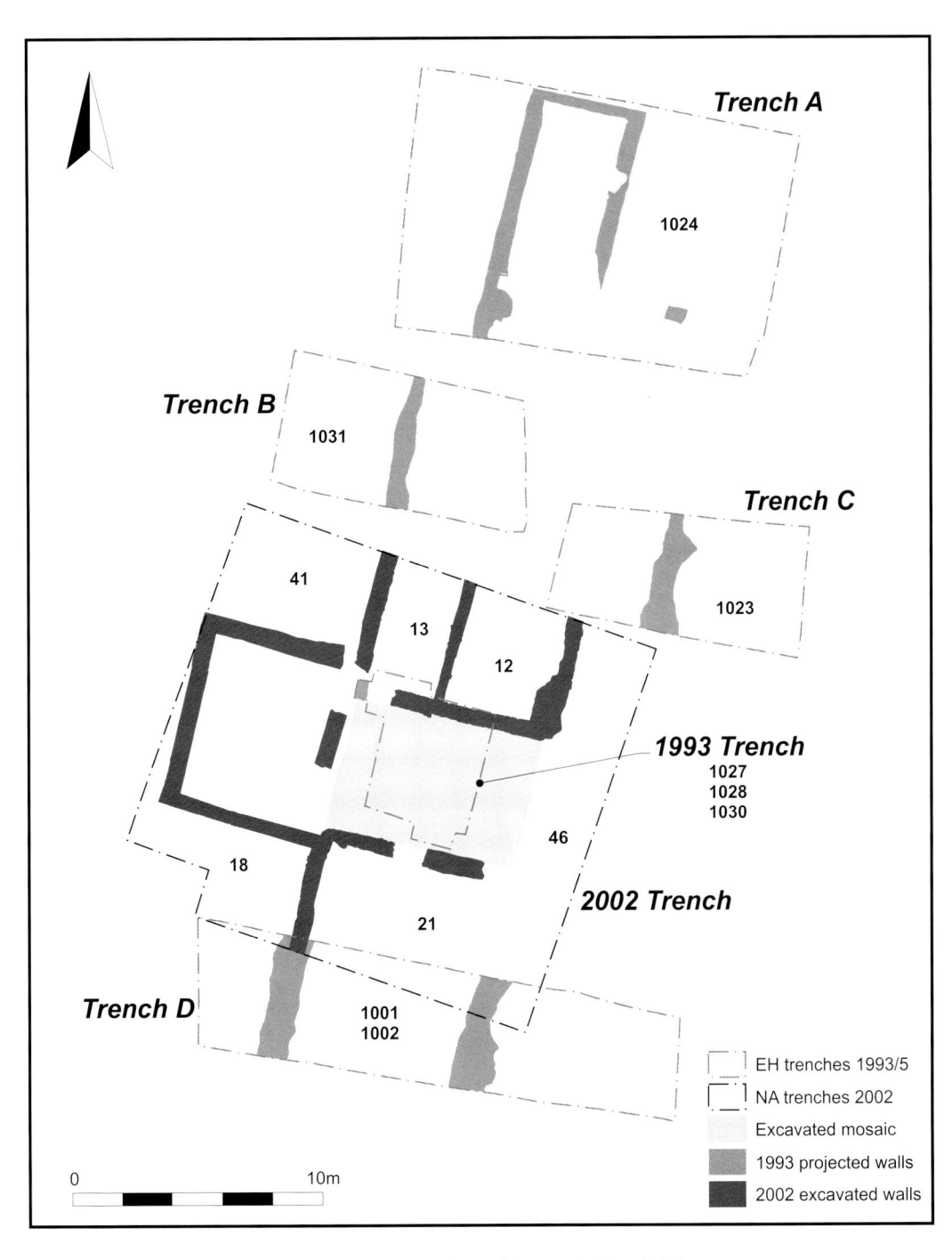

Fig 5 Excavation of the villa core (EH and NA)

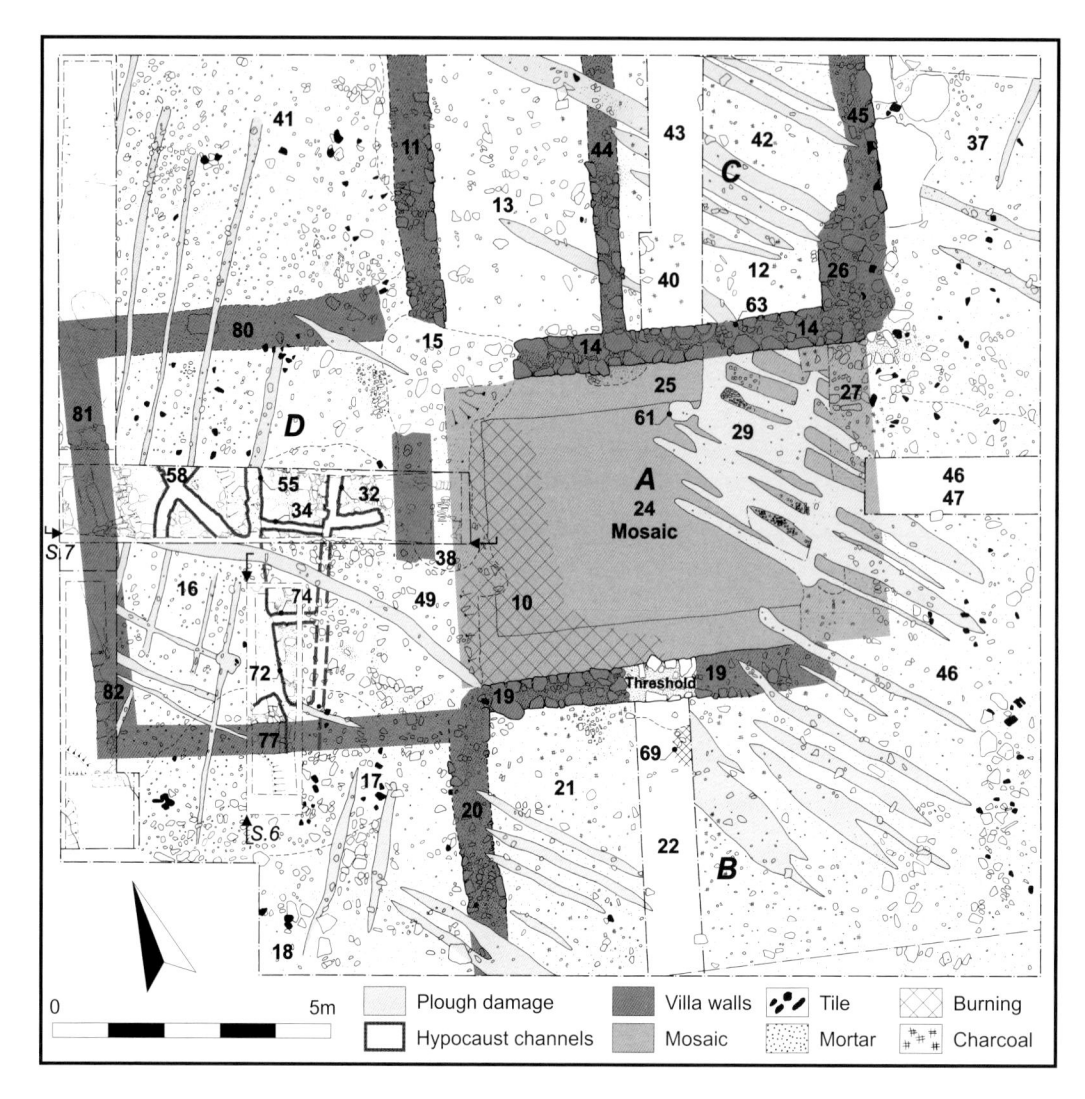

Fig 6 Details of the 2002 excavation

(Smith 1997, 46-64) and probably a villa. The remains of four rooms, designated A to D, were investigated in 2002, three arranged on a north to south axis, and a fourth, which contained a hypocaust and the fragmentary remains of a second mosaic, situated to the west (Fig 6).

The villa was built on prominent ground above the small stream to the east in an area of modern day pasture. The site was covered by demolition material from the building with a robbing horizon (37) to the north containing fragments of limestone, *tegulae*, plaster, charcoal and iron nails. It was some 0.10m thick and included pottery dating to the late 3rd and 4th centuries AD. To the east robbing spoil (46) overlay a brown sand (47), approximately 0.08m thick, over limestone bedrock. In the north-west pottery recovered from the demolition material dated to the 4th century AD with two coins of Tetricus I (AD 270-273). To the south (17) extending beyond the limits of excavation, a mid greyish-brown sand (18) with limestone slabs, ceramic tile fragments, charcoal flecks, tufa pieces and fragments of flue tile yielded a bronze coin dating to the first half of the 4th century AD (Fig 6).

In the centre of the excavation, Room A contained a mosaic pavement depicting the Greek hero Bellerophon (Fig 7). The mosaic, which was set in a shallow bedding layer of *opus signinum*, on a sub-base of compacted light yellowish orange sand (25) occupied the entire room, 6.5m from east to west, 5.1m from north to south. A single sherd of pottery dated only to the Roman period was recovered from beneath the mosaic.

Lying over the mosaic pavement was a coarse horizon of demolition material (9) (23) (not illustrated) of sandy silts, angular limestone fragments some burnt red, fragments of *tegulae*, plaster, charcoal, pieces of daub, iron nails, melted glass and loose tesserae (not illus). Along the western edge of the mosaic the deposit (9) was up to 0.22m thick, while along the eastern side the deposit (23) was heavily disturbed by ploughing, and only 0.14m deep. In the south-west corner of the pavement the demolition deposit (9) overlay dark grey, almost black sandy silt (10) with a very high charcoal content. This layer contained occasional angular limestone pebbles some burnt, flecks and lumps of plaster, decorative glass beads, loose tesserae and fragments of copper alloy objects. Pottery recovered from these deposits generally dates to the late 3rd and 4th centuries AD. Two glass

Fig 7 The re-exposure of the Bellerophon mosaic in 2002

beads, found on the mosaic pavement, date to the 5th and 6th centuries AD (Fig 14). On the eastern side of the mosaic a similar horizon (29) sealed the mosaic surface.

The remains of the north and south walls [14] and [19] were approximately 0.7m wide, survived to two courses and comprised angular limestone ashlars, bonded with light yellowish-white mortar. With the exception of a small section at its northern end, the east wall was entirely ploughed away, and the west wall had been completely robbed out (see Room D below). The remaining length of the east wall [27] was also heavily disturbed by ploughing.

Close to the northern edge of Room A and cutting through the mosaic were two postholes [61] and [63]. Neither feature was excavated (Fig 6).

To the south Room B lay partly beyond the limits of the excavation. The west wall [20] 0.7m wide was a single surviving course of angular limestone, bonded with light yellowish-white mortar. In places it was largely ploughed away but was still visible as a band of mortar. In the centre of the north wall [19], the worn edges of several stones suggest a threshold between rooms A and B (Fig 6).

The ploughed-out remnants of the east wall survived sufficiently to suggest its position, giving the room an approximate width of 6.5m. The south wall of the room lay beyond the excavation and it is likely that the room was sub-divided by at least one internal wall. Within, Room B was covered by a shallow demolition layer (21), 0.06m thick. This had been heavily scarred by ploughing but it had protected a possible floor surface (22) of compacted light yellowish-white mortar. The floor also contained angular limestone pebbles and small cobbles, some burnt, embedded in its surface, and reddish pink patches of burning. At the north end at the base of wall [19], was a surviving fragment of plaster that had probably fallen from the wall; this was left *in situ*. At the south end a posthole [69] *c* 0.28m in diameter, cutting through the floor surface, was also left *in situ*.

Room C to the north was sub-divided into two by a slim partition wall [44]. The west wall [11] was 0.7m wide, its northern end damaged by ploughing. It appeared to have been modified, with two phases of construction. The original east wall [26], of which only a single course survived was also constructed of angular limestone slabs and cobbles, bonded with mortar. It was built on the same line and was of a similar width (0.7m) to the east wall of Room A [27], which originally extended along the east side of room C where it was evident only from the hollow left by stone robbing. Above and slightly offset to the east was a wall of angular limestone, surviving only one course high [45], probably a rebuilding of the original. At its southern end there were the remnants of a tile course, formed from *tegulae*. The sub-dividing wall [44], abutted wall [14], suggesting a later adaptation, its north end ploughed away, originally no doubt continuing beyond the limits of the excavation. Traces of wall plaster still survived *in situ* on its eastern face but were not excavated. In the western part of the room the demolition deposit was not excavated, but comprised light yellowish brown silty sand (13), largely mortar, with angular limestone, some burnt, occasional charcoal flecks and tile fragments both ceramic and Collyweston type. In the area to the east the demolition deposits (12)

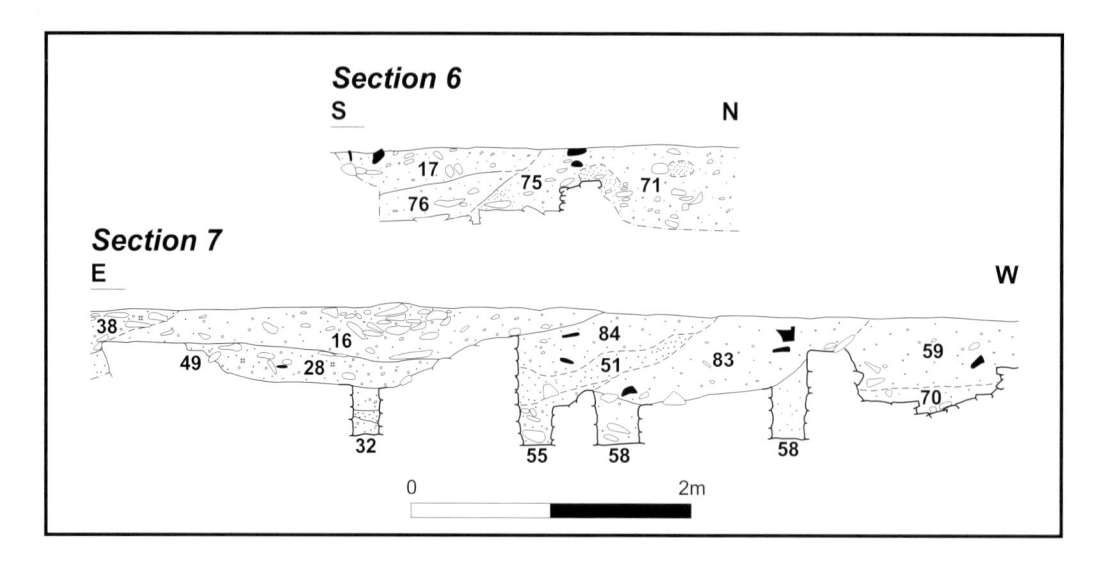

Fig 8 Sections from the 2002 excavations

and (42) were identical to (13) but amongst this deposit were 14 coins dating to the mid to late 4th century (*Guest below*). Underlying the demolition deposits was a mid-grey-brown sand (40) which may represent a buried soil horizon, possibly the remnants of the original soil cover on the site prior to the construction of the villa. This deposit was not excavated. A similar deposit (48) was noted beneath the sand sub-base of the mosaic in Room A (Fig 6).

Excavation west of room A revealed the remains of a fourth room, D, where a hypocaust was sealed by demolition material. Partially excavated (Figs 6 and 8), the hypocaust contained the fragments of a second mosaic, superior in quality to that of the surviving Bellerophon mosaic. The room was approximately 5.1m from east to west and 6.5m from north to south, identical to Room A, the long axis of the room aligned north to south. The east wall, separating rooms A and D, had been partially robbed, together with the mosaic and parts of the hypocaust. The surviving footing for the east wall, a linear mass of mortar limestone slabs and cobbles [49], was c1.0m wide and 0.6m deep, set in a foundation trench. The wall footing was integral with the mass of mortar and stone forming the hypocaust (see below), indicating that Rooms A and D were probably contemporary. A small area of pitched stone, in the demolition material lying on top of the foundation may be the remains of a threshold between the two rooms. The north wall of the room had been entirely robbed, its position revealed by a linear trench [80] separating the demolition deposits within the room from the relatively sterile layer (41) to the north. The robber-trench was between 0.6m and 0.7m wide, 0.42m deep and contained three fills, two of which contained significant quantities of plaster and mortar. Two short stretches of the west wall survive, limestone, [81] and [82], bonded with light yellowish white mortar, approximately 0.7m wide in places up to three courses high (Fig 6).

The south wall [77], also limestone, included the remains of a stokehole for the hypocaust. Constructed from angular limestone, it was faced with alternating limestone slabs and floor tiles defining an opening in the wall to one of the main hypocaust vents. Four courses survived, forming the western side of an archway over the stokehole. Radiating out from the stokehole was an irregular pattern of hypocaust vents, formed from angular limestone slabs and ashlars, set in mortar. The vents, which were typically c 0.25m wide, were up to 0.35m deep, with vertical sides. They contained tesserae and broken fragments from the second mosaic which had once formed the floor of Room D.

The internal area of Room D contained a complex series of demolition layers overlying and infilling the remains of the hypocaust. These deposits, c 0.6m thick, appear to have been cast up in the direction of the west wall, probably when the mosaic was broken up to gain access to the stone in the upper courses of the hypocaust. This perhaps preceded the final robbing of stone from the walls, which may have been deliberately toppled as many of the stones near the surface of the demolition deposits were pitched to the north and north-west. The demolition deposits typically comprised mid-brown sand, limestone, plaster, occasionally charcoal, tesserae and fragments of *tegulae* and flue tile. Some of the deposits (51) may derive from the sub-base of the mosaic in this room (Fig 7). Pottery recovered from these deposits generally dates to the late 3rd and 4th centuries AD, (*Symonds below*) and there are sherds of cylinder blown window glass typically date to the 4th century AD (*Cool below*).

THE ROMAN MOSAIC PAVEMENTS
D S Neal

INTRODUCTION

During fieldwalking and the excavation of the villa building at Croughton the remains of two mosaic pavements were revealed. The first and best preserved, Mosaic 1, comprised a figured pavement of Bellerophon found almost intact in Room A (Figs 7, 9 & 11) and the second, Mosaic 2, found in pieces filling the hypocaust channels in Room D (Fig 10). The loose tesserae associated with Mosaic 1 are not discussed here as they duplicate the evidence on the surviving floor. However, covering the surfaces of the north parts of the *in situ* mosaic, and some of the loose fragments associated with Mosaic 2, is pink tile mortar the presence of which may have a bearing on the demise of the villa.

THE BELLEROPHON MOSAIC (MOSAIC 1)

Dimensions: room 6.50m by 5.10m; Panel A 3.60m square, Panels B and C 3.60m by 1.05m. Tesserae: grey, red, white, buff, yellow ochre and dark wine red, 15mm. Border: red and buff, 35mm-50mm (Figs 9 & 11).

The full excavation of the Bellerophon mosaic in 2002 necessitates the amendment of the initial description and illustration in Neal and Cosh 2002 (Mosaic 86.1). The

Fig 9 The Bellerophon mosaic (Mosaic 1), painted by David Neal

Fig 10 Fragments of the second mosaic (Mosaic 2), painted by David Neal

Fig 11 English Heritage orthophotograph of the Bellerophon mosaic

scheme of the mosaic comprises three panels, a central square (Panel A) flanked on the east and west sides by long rectangles (Panels B and C respectively).

PANEL A

A square panel worked in simple guilloche outlined grey with red and two white strands, with oblique bands of simple guilloche across its corners to create an octagon. Within and tangent to the sides of the octagon is a pair of interlaced squares in simple guilloche, one in the same colours as before and the other with buff and two white strands. The draughtsmanship is so poor that the intended circle of right-angled Z-pattern in the octagon, formed by the interlaced squares, only features around two thirds of the surround. Likewise, a grey octagonal line between the right-angled Z pattern and the interlaced squares stops short. In triangular interspaces created by the interlaced squares are red triangles outlined grey, and in lozenge-shaped interspaces between the interlaced squares and the octagonal panel are lozenges outlined with grey dentilled bands and containing smaller lozenges in grey and red with white centres. Three triangular panels at the corners of the panel survive and all contain a red heart-shaped leaf with curving stems. Unusually, the clefts of the leaves are looped around a single white tessera and the red tips are partly white.

The central circle contains a scene of Bellerophon, viewed from the south, riding the winged horse Pegasus and slaying the three-headed monster, the Chimaera, all worked in a linear style. Bellerophon is shown looking behind him and holding a spear in his outstretched right hand. His face is white and he has deep red hair. He wears a white tunic and breeches, and across his chest and over his right shoulder is a red cloak, possibly fixed by a rounded grey brooch or clasp on his right shoulder. His shoes and waistband are red and his cuff grey, and on his knee is a grey circular ornament (*orbicula*). Pegasus is outlined in grey and shaded white with the exception of his ears, which are red; his hind legs stretch out behind him and although the front legs are damaged they also appear to have been outstretched originally and in a 'flying' pose. He has a thin tail and a finely drawn mane accentuated by a line of buff, which runs down the back of the neck and also under his head and around his chest. His wing, in alternating grey, buff and white lines, passes in front of Bellerophon and its top edge is confused with, and parallel to, the spear. Pegasus' bridle is red, as is the saddle-cloth which can be seen in the form of an outline below and above Bellerophon's leg. The Chimaera is predominantly in yellow ochre but its legs are white, as is its feline head, which faces upwards and displays a row of grey triangular teeth and an arrow-shaped tongue spitting fire at the tip of the spear which threatens to pierce its mouth. The front of the beast has a series of parallel grey, right-angled lines, which are intended to represent the mane. From the back of the Chimaera is the head of a goat, with a round eye and a grey collar, so badly drawn that it resembles a duck. Its mouth is wide open, displaying a red tongue, and faces the feline; three red lines indicate that it breaths fire. The tail is turned across the back of the animal and, conventionally, bears the head of a serpent, here with a tiny grey eye and a red tongue. The male genitalia of the beast are shown in grey. In front of the Chimaera are nine single grey tesserae on a field of white and believed by Beeson to be an attempt to represent water as a reference to Pegasus's spring-making qualities (Beeson 1996, 20-1). To the right and left of Bellerophon's head are four red crosses, perhaps intended to represent stars in the sky and an allusion to the apotheosis of Pegasus as he rose into the heavens (Beeson 1996, 21).

PANELS B AND C

Except for its south end, much of Panel B has been destroyed by ploughing. What survives is virtually identical to Panel C to the west and will not be described further. Panel C is bordered by a band of three-strand guilloche, outlined grey and with red and white (x2) strands (in places the double white strands are conventionally shaded red, white and yellow ochre). The panel surrounds a broad strip of straight-tongued double guilloche in the same shades as the three-strand guilloche and with similar inconsistencies in the colouring.

WORKMANSHIP

Although the figured panel has been drawn in a lively linear style the geometry and workmanship elsewhere is decidedly poor. The mosaicist has misaligned the radial point of the central panel in relationship to the pair of surrounding interlaced squares resulting in the circular right angled Z-pattern border 'around' Bellerophon being absent on the east side. The style of the guilloche is decidedly unusual; in places, particularly the surround of Panel A, the outer edges of the guilloche are drawn as single or double fillets with little or no attempt to link the grey outline of the braids to the fillets and, in places, white tesserae are set between them as if the mosaicist was trying to create the impression of the braids being on a white background. The guilloche on the western side of Panel C is more crudely drawn as if by a separate hand; the grey outlines to the braids do not curve, as is conventional, but are treated as a series of straight lines.

DISCUSSION

There are three other examples of Romano-British mosaic with scenes of Bellerophon killing the Chimaera; they include the mosaics from Lullingstone, Kent, and Frampton and Hinton St Mary, Dorset. In the case of the examples from Frampton and Hinton St Mary, mosaics almost certainly constructed by the same mosaicist, the scene is associated with Christian iconography, with the Chi-Rho represented and at Hinton St Mary with the symbol superimposed by a male figure believed to represent Christ (Toynbee 1964). There is no Christian iconography overtly displayed on the Lullingstone mosaic but Henig has interpreted the couplet as possibly concealing a reference to Jesus (Henig 1997, 5). The painted wall plaster recovered from the cellar is indisputably Christian with human figures in the *Orans* attitude of prayer and with Chi-Rho monograms. The Lullingstone plaster came from a house church and it is quite possible that one of the functions of the rooms both at Frampton and Hinton St Mary was the same and a place where guests with the same beliefs could be entertained and perhaps worship. Even though there is no direct evidence for Christian association on the mosaic, or wall plaster, from Croughton, the very fact that the other mosaics in Britain depicting Bellerophon killing the Chimaera have Christian associations, strongly implies that the Croughton mosaic could also have paved a house church. Placing the mosaic within the genre of mosaic workshops is problematic because of its inept layout and workmanship. However, the method of laying the guilloche recalls the workmanship on the mosaic from Thenford and it should also be noted that the use of Pennant stone tesserae for the hair (a material not indigenous to the area and only used sparingly, therefore) also occurs in the hair of Venus at Thenford. Figured mosaics are rare in Northamptonshire, only occurring to the west of the county. The mosaic from Whittlebury is the only other example. For this reason the mosaics have been assigned to the Northamptonshire Figured Group (Neal and Cosh 2002, 29) and attributed to the late 4th century.

FIGURED MOSAIC (MOSAIC 2)

Dimensions: room 5.10m by 6.50, panel: not known. Tesserae: grey, red, white, off-white, buff, yellow ochre, very pale blue-grey and dark wine red, 15mm (Fig 10).

It is not possible to provide clues as to the scheme of this mosaic found in pieces in the hypocaust channels of Room D, although a fragment from context (53) might be part of a lozenge and, therefore, part of a lozenge-based design. However, from the numerous fragments in context (29) it is possible to say with certainty that the mosaic was figured. Two fragments (Fig 10), which almost certainly joined originally, show two grey fillets separating an area of red. This looks as if it might be an arm or leg. It is not part of a conventional motif. Another fragment from the same context has a series of sinuous grey and white lines (Fig 10) against a pale yellowish-grey background. Possibly the sinuous lines represent hair. However, on neither fragment is there sufficient evidence to determine whether the figure is human or animal.

The materials of the tesserae used in Mosaic 2 differ from those in Mosaic 1 in that there is a wider palette of colour. The general background tesserae are off-white rather than white and on the fragment from context (53) the fillets forming the supposed lozenges are of a blue-grey oolitic limestone similar to Raunds or Stanwick 'marble', a material not noted on the Bellerophon mosaic. There is also a greater use of Pennant sandstone. On the Bellerophon mosaic, Pennant sandstone only occurs in Bellerophon's hair but at least five fragments from Mosaic 2 include this material. A chevron-shaped design on a fragment from context (71) (Fig 10) could be from a variant of round-tongued guilloche but this is uncertain. It is shaded grey and deep red/brown Pennant sandstone.

WORKMANSHIP

The evidence suggests that the workmanship of Mosaic 2 is superior to Mosaic 1. The tesserae are more closely set, and tesserae as small as 5mm are occasionally used for detail. The fact that the background tesserae are off-white, rather than white, suggests the work to be by a different hand but whether any appreciable time separate their construction is unlikely.

A characteristic of both Mosaic 1 and the fragments of Mosaic 2 from (29) is that the surfaces of the tesserae of the actual mosaic (and not just the coarse border tesserae) are covered, in places, with a fine red tile mortar (*opus signinum*) possibly used to grout the mosaics. On one fragment this is 8mm thick. It could be argued, therefore, that the mosaics were never finished (in antiquity grouting mosaics usually took place after the painted wall plaster had been applied which explains why quarter-round moulding, for example, seals both walls and floors). To account for this phenomena two scenarios are possible: an event, such as the fire known to have destroyed the building, happened during building work and mosaic construction or, alternatively, the fire took place during restoration of the building following a period of occupation. The writer knows of no parallel for a mosaic being covered in such material although the mosaic (panel only) from the church at Silchester was sealed with opus signinum to create a new surface.

PREHISTORIC ARTEFACTS

FLINT
Andy Chapman

A total of three pieces of flint were recovered during the excavation of 2002, and a further six came from the excavation in 1995. All nine pieces have opaque heavily patinated surfaces, either creamy white to light grey or a mottled blue-grey colour.

The group comprises seven flakes (one burnt), one irregular shattered piece and one natural, gravel pebble. There are few diagnostic features, although the presence of large and irregular flakes would suggest that they come from an industry no earlier than the later Neolithic, and they could represent a later casual usage of flint.

WEAPONS
Natasha Hutcheson

La Tène II spearhead
This spearhead was found on the outskirts of the Roman settlement at Croughton, from context (1010), the primary fill of a ditch-like feature (Fig 2 Trench 8).

ILLUSTRATED FIND (Fig 12)

1   Spearhead, Iron Age, La Tène II (*c* 300BC – 100BC) The spearhead is made of iron and is complete. The socket, which is closed, is 75mm in length. The blade, which has a raised central midrib, is 195mm long. There is some suggestion of a hole in the socket, presumably for a rivet to pass through and aid the attachment of a wooden shaft. (sf86)

The most distinctive attribute of this spearhead is the shape of the blade. Rather than leaf-shaped, it is sinusoidal

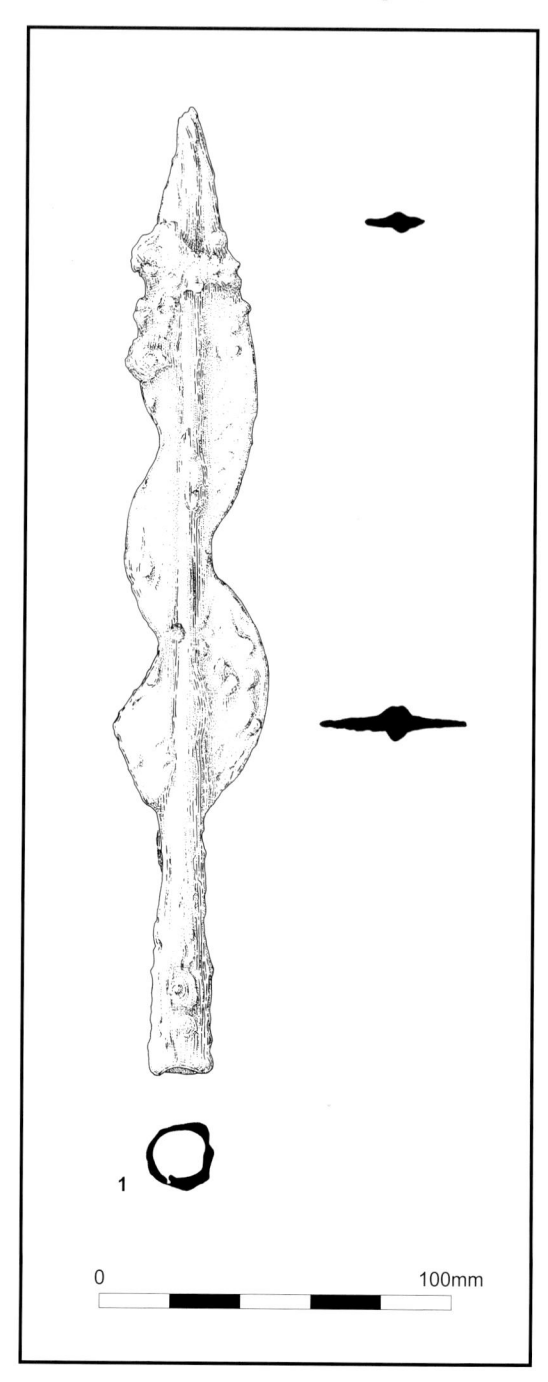

Fig 12 Other finds: The Iron Age spearhead

or curvilinear in form. In order to achieve this shape it seems likely, given that the midrib is straight, that the spearhead was initially smithed into a leaf shape. This was then cut whilst hot into its current sinusoidal form. It is impossible to tell whether this was all undertaken as one task, ie we do not know whether the maker of the spearhead intended to create this shape, or whether the spearhead was reheated and altered at a later stage.

Other Iron Age spearheads are known from Britain, the two largest collections being those from Hunsbury hillfort, also in Northamptonshire (Fell 1936) and those in the Durden collection from Hod Hill in Dorset (Brailsford 1962). The examples from Hunsbury, which are likely to be of Iron Age date, have been categorised into three main types; 'the small javelin head, the long narrow spear-head with slight mid-rib, and the broad leaf-shaped form with distinct mid-rib' (Fell 1936, 66). The example from Croughton does not fit closely in any one of these categories, but if the blade were straight sided it would fall across two of Fell's types. In particular, it can be seen that the Croughton example displays the narrowness of a 'long narrow spear-head' with the broad, blade-base more reminiscent of the 'broad leaf-shape' type.

Given the possible Roman component of the assemblage from Hod Hill, it is not known how many of the examples from this site are Iron Age and therefore close in date to the Croughton example. Manning suggests that the 'majority of the objects from the Durden collection are certainly Roman' (Manning 1976, 18), although recent metallurgical analysis of Iron Age and Roman iron implements demonstrates that such suggestions cannot be confirmed on a morphological basis alone (Hutcheson 1997). However, whether Iron Age or Roman, none of the Durden collection spearheads closely resemble the Croughton example. In addition, this example is not closely paralleled at Danebury (Sellwood 1984; Cunliffe and Poole 1991) or Maiden Castle (Wheeler 1943). It appears at present to be unique to this country. Sinusoidal-shaped spearheads are known from the continent with eleven examples recovered from the site at La Tène in Switzerland (Vouga 1923). The spearheads from the site of La Tène vary in size between 350mm and 450mm and are rather larger than the Croughton example. Given that this spearhead appears to be unique in this country, it is possible that it is an import. If not an import, it is likely that the smith who made it, or the person who 'commissioned' it had seen and was emulating these continental forms.

How this spear was used is unclear, it might have been an implement of war or used for hunting. Given the decorative shape, it could be that it was used more specifically for its visual attributes, perhaps as a 'banner' or 'standard'. With regard to its deposition, it is possible that this spearhead, which is undamaged, was purposefully deposited into the ditch from which it was recovered. The practice of deliberately depositing material, including iron objects such as currency bars into pits, ditches or watery locations is a practice that is well documented for the Iron Age (Hingley 1990; Hill 1995).

ROMAN AND EARLY MEDIEVAL ARTEFACTS

Archaeological fieldwork between 1991 and 2002 produced a range of finds from the Roman and early medieval periods. The majority of finds are Roman and were recovered from topsoil and demolition deposits during excavation and trial trenching although several coins and a buckle fragment came from the watching brief in 1991. The largest group of finds is coins with 22 further small finds, excluding nails, that may be dated stylistically to the Roman period. Many of the nails and undiagnostic fragments were difficult to identify and date with any degree of certainty and have been excluded from this report.

Despite the limitations this small assemblage provides an insight into aspects of life at the settlement and includes items for personal use and recreation, as well as structural fittings and a small number of tools. Most of the finds appear to date to the late 3rd - 4th centuries mirroring the date of the pottery. Most importantly a glass bead dating to the 6th century AD and probably part of a necklace suggests continuing occupation of the villa site into the early medieval period.

All of the individually recorded finds have been entered on to an Access database. A basic catalogue has been compiled, comprising material type and object identifications, together with stratigraphic information. Each object has been described and measured and a descriptive catalogue is retained in archive.

THE ROMAN COINS
P Guest

One-hundred-and-three Roman coins were recovered from the settlement at Croughton between 1991 and 2002. Messrs Shelley and Heritage discovered 44 Roman coins (and a modern halfpenny) while metal-detecting in July 1991, and a further two coins came to light during the watching brief and excavation of the mosaic later that year. Twenty more coins were recovered from the evaluation trenches excavated in 1995, while the 2002 re-excavation of the mosaic produced a further group of 37 Roman coins. Of the 46 coins discovered in 1991, six *sestertii* were found together as a small hoard and these are, therefore, considered separately from the 97 excavated and detected site-finds. The catalogue of excavated coins is presented in Table 3; the metal-detected coins are listed in Table 4, while Table 5 records the coin hoard. A summary of the excavated and metal-detected groups of coins is presented in Table 6.

Of the 97 coins classed as site-finds, 80 could be identified to an emperor's reign or period of issue. Table 2 clearly shows that the majority of these coins were produced between the late 3rd and late 4th centuries, with a particular concentration of coins from the middle decades of the 4th century (AD 330-378). The assemblage contained a single silver coin (a clipped *siliqua* of Valens found in 2002 – sf 27), while the remaining coins were all bronze or silvered bronze denominations. The remaining 17 coins could only be described in more vague terms - 'late 3rd to 4th centuries'.

Only two coins from the excavations and metal-detector

surveys predated the mid-3rd century (both recovered by detector); a *sestertius* of Hadrian (1991, no. 27) and an *as* of Marcus Aurelius as Caesar (1991, no. 13). The main concentration of coins, however, extends from the late 3rd to the end of the 4th centuries. The late 3rd century (Issue Periods XIII and XIV) is represented by 15 coins, including five barbarous radiates and a *quinarius* of Allectus (2002, sf 22), while 63 coins were struck during the 4th century (Issue Periods XV to XXI). Issues of the 330s and 350s were particularly common, especially the FEL TEMP REPARATIO types and their imitations, although significant quantities of Valentinianic and Theodosian coins from the later 4th century were also recovered during excavation and by detector.

Although the coins indicate that the main period of coin loss occurred during the later Roman period, this does not mean that the settlement was unoccupied before this time or that coins did not circulate during the 1st or 2nd centuries. Coinage of the early Roman period in Britain consists of high value silver *denarii* or large bronze denominations (such as the *sestertius*, *dupondius* or *as*), which will have been more zealously and easily recovered if lost than the smaller, lower value, coinage of the later 3rd and 4th centuries. However, the preponderance of later Roman coins is significant, particularly for the dating of the Bellerophon mosaic. Unfortunately, only one coin recovered in 2002 was found in a context that might date the construction and/ or use of the mosaic; a small bronze of Arcadius struck 388-402 (sf 37) which was found in the hypocaust flue (33), although it could have been lost once the hypocaust went out of use. The deposits excavated in 2002 were associated primarily with demolition activity and as a result the coin assemblage provides relatively reliable dating for the disuse and collapse of the building containing the mosaic. Altogether, 23 coins were recovered from demolition deposits, while 14 coins were found within context (12) a layer consisting of decayed mortar found in room C to the north of the mosaic. These coins generally span the period from the 330s to the 370s, suggesting that the building was disused and neglected certainly by the end of the 4th century, or possibly as late as the 5th century.

Interestingly, the coins detected in 1991 show a similar chronological distribution to those recovered from the excavations in 1995 and 2002, as if the building housing the mosaic shared the same history as the wider settlement. Therefore, by combining together all of the coins found at Croughton we should have a representative assemblage from the settlement as a whole, which can then be compared to other groups of site-finds from Roman Britain. The first stage of this analysis involves setting the Croughton coins against the background of coin-supply to Britain in order to see when and how they deviate from the notionally average Romano-British site (Reece 1995). Firstly, the coins must be converted into 'coins per thousand' values (Table 6) which are then added cumulatively. These are deducted from the Romano-British mean (an average of the coins from 140 sites) to produce a sequence of values that shows when and to what extent the Croughton coins deviate from this mean. Table 2 plots the same data as a chart (the x-axis representing the Romano-British background), which shows the concentration of late Roman coins recovered from the settlement. The Croughton coins are always below the x-axis because the site produced significantly fewer early coins (and therefore significantly more later 3rd and 4th-century coins), than the hypothetical average Romano-British site.

When the Croughton coins are compared to other assemblages it is apparent that this pattern of coin-loss identified from Croughton is very similar to the assemblages recovered from the excavations at Nettleton Scrubb, Lamyatt Beacon, Uley, Lullingstone and Gatcombe (Reece 1995, 197-203 & fig. 27). In fact, the settlement at Croughton exhibits the Valentinianic and Theodosian peak of coin-loss characteristic of settlements that were important religious *foci* during the last decades of the Roman period in Britain. Therefore, Croughton finds itself grouped together with the temples at Lamyatt, Nettleton, Uley and the 'villas' at Lullingstone and Gatcombe. Lullingstone was clearly an important pagan (with a Bellerophon mosaic) and later Christian place of religious worship, while at Gatcombe the excavations concentrated on the periphery of a settlement enclosure in which the supposed villa had been destroyed during the construction of a railway cutting in the 19th century (Meates 1979; Branigan 1977). From this comparative analysis, admittedly of the coins alone, it seems reasonable to conclude that the settlement at Croughton was a site of some religious significance during the later Roman period (from about 350 until some time in the 5th century), perhaps with the Bellerophon mosaic at its centre.

The Croughton site produces only limited evidence for coin use before the end of the 3rd century, although interestingly that evidence includes a small hoard of 2nd-century *sestertii* (Table 5). The hoard was found by metal detector in 1991 and the constituent coins had become stuck together into a column after having been kept in a narrow (probably textile) bag (Curteis 2003). The earliest coin is a *sestertius* of Trajan struck in 101-02, while the *terminus post quem* for the hoard is provided by the coin struck for Lucilla between 161-69. In the preliminary report Mark Curteis pointed out that the *sestertius* of Antoninus Pius was not attached to the rest of the coins. However, this coin shared the same level of wear as those in the column and as there are so few pre-3rd-century coins from Croughton it seems likely that the Antoninus *sestertius* was originally part of the hoard. Although 2nd-century *sestertii* are found in a number of 3rd-century hoards (up to the 260s), generally these are much larger than 2nd-century hoards and, therefore, it is likely that the Croughton hoard was deposited at some time between 161 and 200.

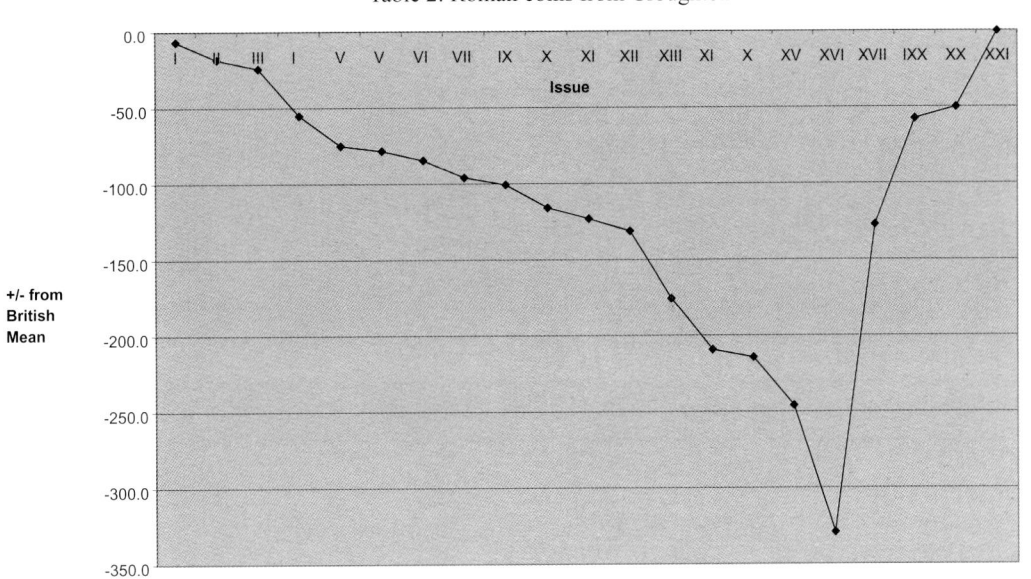

Table 2: Roman coins from Croughton

Table 3: Catalogue of excavated coins from Croughton, arranged by year (1995 & 2002) and context

Year	Small find (Context)	Denom	Date	Obverse	Reverse	Mint mark	Reference & Remarks
2002	1 (1)	AE3	353-60	CONSTANTIUS II	FEL TEMP REPARATIO - falling horseman	//CPLG Lyons	CK: 253, 256
2002	22 (1)	quinarius	293-96	ALLECTUS	VIRTVS AVG - galley	//QL	RIC: 55
2002	4 (2)	AE3 copy	350s?	DN Constantinus Aug	2 victories facing, holding shield on column	//[.....]	
2002	44 (9)	AE4 minim	4th c?	illegible	illegible	//[.....]	6mm diam.
2002	11 (12)	AE3	330-35	CONSTANTINOPOLIS	Victory on prow	//TR●P Trier	HK: 66
2002	13 (12)	AE4 copy	353-64	as House of Constantine	as Fel Temp Reparatio - falling horseman	//[..]N	9mm diam
2002	14 (12)	AE4 minim	4th c?	illegible	illegible	//[.....]	6mm diam
2002	15 (12)	AE3	330-35	CONSTANTINOPOLIS	Victory on prow	//cres.PLG Lyons	HK: 196
2002	16 (12)	AE4 minim	4th c?	illegible	illegible	//[.....]	4mm diam
2002	23 (12)	AE4 copy	353-64	as House of Constantine	as Fel Temp Reparatio - falling horseman	//[.....]	10mm diam
2002	29 (12)	AE3	4th c	diademed bust	illegible	//[.....]	
2002	30 (12)	AE3	353-60	CONSTANTIUS II	FEL TEMP REPARATIO - falling horseman	//[.....]	
2002	35a (12)	AE4	4th c	illegible	illegible	//[.....]	8mm diam
2002	35b (12)	AE4 copy	353-64	as House of Constantine	as Fel Temp Reparatio - falling horseman	//[.....]	8mm diam
2002	35c (12)	AE4 copy	353-64	as House of Constantine	as Fel Temp Reparatio - falling horseman	//[.....]	7mm diam
2002	35d (12)	AE4 copy	4th c	diademed bust	illegible	//[.....]	6mm diam.
2002	35e (12)	AE4 minim	4th c	illegible	illegible	//[.....]	6mm diam broken half
2002	35f (12)	AE4 minim	4th c	illegible	illegible	//[.....]	4mm diam

Table 3 (cont.): Catalogue of excavated coins from Croughton, arranged by year (1995 & 2002) and context

Year	Small find (Context)	Denom	Date	Obverse	Reverse	Mint mark	Reference & Remarks
2002	27 (16)	siliqua	374-77	VALENS	VRBS ROMA - seated	//TRPS• Trier	RIC: 27b/45a clipped close to bust
2002	18 (18)	AE3	330-37	VRBS ROMA	Wolf & twins	//PLG Lyons	HK: 184, 224
2002	32 (28)	Follies	294-307	MAXIMINUS	GENIO POPVLI ROMANI	//Q[..]	8.9 gm.
2002	37 (33)	AE4	388-402	ARCADIUS	VICTORIA AVGGG	//[.....]	
2002	39 (37)	AE4 copy	353-64	as House of Constantine	as Fel Temp Reparatio - falling horseman	//[.....]	10mm diam
2002	46 (38)	AE3	353-60	CONSTANTIUS II	FEL TEMP REPARATIO - falling horseman	//C[PLG] Lyons	CK: 253, 256
2002	41 (40)	AE3 copy	330-48	as Constantinopolis	as Victory on prow	//[.....]	
2002	34 (41)	AE3	367-78	VALENS	SECVRITAS REIPVBLICAE	//SM♥RP Rome	CK: 725, 730
2002	42 (41)	AE3	367-75	VALENTINIAN I	SECVRITAS REIPVBLICAE	•/-//[PC]ON Arles	CK: 501
2002	47 (41)	radiate	270-74	TETRICUS I	illegible		
2002	49 (41)	radiate	270-74	TETRICUS I	LAETITIA [AVGG]	Mint II	
2002	28 (42)	AE3	335-37	CONSTANTINE I	GLORIA EXERCITVS (1 std)	Constantinople	HK: 1025
2002	40 (42)	AE3	348-50	CONSTANTIUS II	FEL TEMP REPARATIO - galley (2)	//TRP Trier	CK: 42
2002	24 u/s	AE4	late 3rd-4th c	illegible	illegible	//[.....]	9mm diam
2002	25 u/s	AE4	late 3rd-4th c	illegible	illegible	//[.....]	11mm diam
2002	26 u/s	AE4	388-402	House of Theodosius	[VICTORIA AVGGG]	//[.....]	
2002	48 u/s	AE3	330-35	CONSTANTINOPOLIS	Victory on prow	//[.....]	
2002	53 u/s	AE4	378-83	VALENTINIAN II	VOT / V / MVLT / X	//[.....]	
2002	56 u/s	AE4	4th c.	diademed bust	illegible	//[.....]	
1995	128 (1007)	AE2	348-50	CONSTANTIUS II	FEL TEMP REPARATIO - hut	//TRP Trier	CK: 28
1995	105 (1024)	AE3	364-78	House of Valentinian	SECVRITAS REIPVBLICAE	//[.....]	
1995	106 (1024)	barb. radiate	270-96	stylised radiate bust	stylised stdg figure?		6mm diam
1995	107 (1024)	AE4	388-402	House of Theodosius	VICTORIA AVGG[G]	//[.....]	
1995	108 (1024)	AE3	330-40	CONSTANTINOPOLIS	victory on prow	//TRP• Trier	HK: 59
1995	127 (1024)	AE4	mid-late 4thc	illegible	illegible	//[.....]	
1995	128 (1024)	radiate	273-74	TETRICUS II	PRINC IVVENT		reverse very worn
1995	129 (1024)	AE3	335-40	House of Constantine	GLORIA EXERCITVS (1 std)	//[.....]	
1995	130 (1024)	AE3	337-40	CONSTANS	GLORIA EXERCITVS (1 std)	M//[.....] Trier	HK: 133
1995	131 (1024)	AE3 copy	353-64	as House of Constantine	as Fel Temp Reparatio (falling horseman)	//[.....]	15mm diam
1995	132 (1024)	AE4 copy	4th c.?	stylised (diademed) bust	abstract curved lines & dots	//[.....]	8mm diam

Table 3 (cont.): Catalogue of excavated coins from Croughton, arranged by year (1995 & 2002) and context

Year	Small find (Context)	Denom	Date	Obverse	Reverse	Mint mark	Reference & Remarks
1995	133 (1024)	AE4	388-92	VALENTINIAN II	VICTORIA AVGGG	//[PC]ON Arles	CK: 564
1995	134 (1024)	AE2	351-53	DECENTIUS	VICTORIA DD NN AVG ET CAE[S]	//[.....]	
1995	135 (1024)	AE3/4	388-402	House of Theodosius	SALVS REIPVBLICAE	//[.....]	
1995	184	AE4 copy	353-64	as House of Constantine	as Fel Telp Reparatio (falling horseman)	//[.....]	8mm diam
1995	187 (1024)	AE4 copy	353-64	as House of Constantine	as Fel Telp Reparatio (falling horseman)	//[.....]	9mm diam
1995	188 (1024)	AE4 copy	late 3rd-4th c.	illegible	illegible	//[.....]	6mm diam
1995	189 (1024)	AE3	364-78	House of Valentinian	SECVRITAS REIPVBLICAE	//[.....]	
1995	103 (1027)	AE4	388-402	ARCADIUS	VICTORIA AVGG[G]	//[.....]	
1995	104 (1027)	AE3	364-78	VALENS	SECVRITAS REIPVBLICAE	//[.....]	

Table 4: Catalogue of the metal-detected coins from Croughton

Coin no./ Context	Denom	Date	Obverse	Reverse	Mint mark/ mint	Reference & Remarks
1 u/s	AE4	388-402	House of Theodosius	[SALVS REIPVBLICAE]	//[.....]	recovered during mosaic excavation?
2 near N wall	Radiate	268-70	VICTORINUS	PIETAS AVG		recovered during watching brief?
3	barb. radiate	270-96	illegible	illegible		10mm diam.
4	Radiate	286-93	CARAUSIUS	[PAX AVG]	//[.....]	
5	AE3	353-60	CONSTANTIUS II	FEL TEMP REPARATIO - falling horseman	//[.....]	
6	AE3	353-60	CONSTANTIUS II	FEL TEMP REPARATIO - falling horseman	//[.....]	
7	AE4	347-48	CONSTANS	VICTORIAE DD AVGGQ NN	//? Trier	RIC VIII: Tr 199
8	AE3	364-75	VALENTINIAN I	GLORIA ROMANORVM	//[.....]	
9	AE3	364-78	VALENS	SECVRITAS REIPVBLICAE	//[.....]	
10	AE3	364-78	House of Valentinian	GLORIA ROMANORVM	//[.....]	
11	AE3	364-78	House of Valentinian	illegible	//[.....]	
12	AE?	Late 3rd-4th	illegible	illegible	//[.....]	
13	As	140-44	MARCUS AURELIUS Caesar	[IVVEN]TA[S] - SC	Rome	RIC: (Pius) 1238
14	Radiate	268-70	VICTORINUS	PAX AVG		
15	Radiate	270-74	TETRICUS I	illegible		
16	Radiate	270-74	TETRICUS I	[SPES]		
17	Radiate	259-74	illegible	illegible		
18	barb. radiate	270-96	illegible	illegible		8mm diam.
19	barb. radiate	270-96	illegible	illegible		7mm diam.

Table 4 (cont.): Catalogue of the metal-detected coins from Croughton

Coin no./ Context	Denom	Date	Obverse	Reverse	Mint mark/ mint	Reference & Remarks
20	AE	318-19	CONSTANTINE I	VICTORIAE LAETAE PRINC PERP	//[.....]	
21	AE	337-40	HELENA	PAX PVBLICA	//[.....]	
22	AE	353-55	CONSTANTIUS II	FEL TEMP REPARATIO - falling horseman	//? Trier	RIC VIII: Tr 350
23	AE3	353-60	'CONSTANTIUS II'	FEL TEMP REPARATIO - falling horseman	//[.....]	
24	AE3	353-60	'CONSTANTIUS II'	FEL TEMP REPARATIO - falling horseman	//[.....]	
25	AE3	353-60	'CONSTANTIUS II'	FEL TEMP REPARATIO - falling horseman	//[.....]	
26	AE3	353-60	'CONSTANTIUS II'	FEL TEMP REPARATIO - falling horseman	//[.....]	
27	AE3	347-48	House of Constantine	VICTORIAE DD AVGGQ NN	//[.....]	
28	AE3	350-53	MAGNENTIUS	VICTORIAE DD NN AVG ET CAES	//[.....]	
29	AE3	367-75	VALENTINIAN I	GLORIA ROMANORVM	//?	CK: 525
30	AE3	364-78	VALENS	GLORIA ROMANORVM	OF/I//[.....]	
31	AE3	364-78	House of Valentinian	SECVRITAS REIPVBLICAE	//[.....]	
32	AE3	364-78	House of Valentinian	illegible	//[.....]	
33	AE4	388-402	House of Theodosius	VICTORIA AVGGG	//LVGP Lyons	
34	AE	4th C.	illegible	illegible	//[.....]	
35	sestertius	119-22	HADRIAN	figure seated left		
36	barb. radiate	270-96	illegible	illegible		10mm diam.
37	AE	347-48	House of Constantine	VICTORIAE DD AVGGQ NN	//[.....]	
38	AE	350-53	MAGNENTIUS	SALVS DD NN AVG ET CAES	//[.....]	overstrike on coin of Constantius II
39	AE3	364-78	House of Valentinian	GLORIA ROMANORVM	//[.....]	
40	AE	Roman	illegible	illegible		

(Note: Coins 1 and 2 identified by the author, information on the remaining coins from Curteis 2003)

Table 5: Catalogue of the Croughton coin hoard (Curteis 2003)

Coin no.	Denom	Date	Obverse	Reverse	Mint	Reference & remarks
1	sestertius	101-02	TRAJAN	[TR POT COS IIII PP - SC]	Rome	RIC: 426 very worn
2	sestertius	103-17	TRAJAN	illegible	-	very worn
3	sestertius	117-38	HADRIAN	illegible	-	very worn
4	sestertius	154-56	ANTONINUS PIUS	[FIDES EXERC COS IIII - SC]	Rome	very worn
5	sestertius	161	MARCUS AURELIUS	[PROV DEOR TRP XV COS III - SC]	Rome	RIC: 812 very worn
6	sestertius	164-69	LUCILLA	[VENVS - SC]	Rome	RIC: 1772 very worn

Table 6: Roman coins from Croughton

Date	Issue Period	2002 No. of coins	1995 No. of coins	1991 No. of coins	CROUGHTON No. of coins	‰ of coins
to AD 41	I	-	-	-	-	0
41-54	II	-	-	-	-	0
54-68	III	-	-	-	-	0
69-96	IV	-	-	-	-	0
96-117	V	-	-	-	-	0
117-138	VI	-	-	1	1	12.5
138-161	VII	-	-	1	1	12.5
161-180	VIII	-	-	-	-	0
180-192	IX	-	-	-	-	0
193-222	X	-	-	-	-	0
222-238	XI	-	-	-	-	0
238-260	XII	-	-	-	-	0
260-275	XIII	2	1	5	8	100.0
275-296	XIV	1	1	5	7	87.5
296-317	XV	1	-	-	1	12.5
317-330	XVI	-	-	1	1	12.5
330-348	XVII	6	3	4	13	162.5
348-364	XVIII	10	5	9	24	300.0
364-378	XIX	3	3	9	15	187.5
378-388	XX	1	-	-	1	12.5
388-402	XXI	2	4	2	8	100.0
	Sub-total	26	17	37	80	1000
Æ - late 3rd-4th c.		2	1	1	4	
Æ - 4th c.		9	2	1	12	
Æ - 'Roman'				1	1	
Total		37	20	40	97	

PERSONAL POSSESSIONS
Tora Hylton

This category comprises small portable items which would have formed part of a persons clothing (costume fittings), either worn as jewellery, or held by an individual for personal use, such as toilet equipment and objects for recreational use.

COSTUME FITTINGS

Buckles

Part of a cast copper alloy belt buckle was recovered during a metal detector survey in 1991 at Croughton (Northampton Borough Museum and Art Gallery – Acc. No 1991.132). The buckle, now missing, has not been viewed, therefore, this brief description has been compiled using a sketch illustration supplied by Northamptonshire Archaeology.

ILLUSTRATED FINDS (Fig 13)

2   **Zoomorphic buckle,** small and crudely manufactured fragment probably part of a well known type representing two confronting dolphins with open jaws, holding a pellet. The eye of the dolphin is represented by a ring-and-dot motif, the open jaws by opposing chevrons and the crest is defined by shallow grooves. Stylised dolphins were a common motif during the Roman period and although they have complex levels of symbolism, their use was often for purely decorative purposes (Johns 1998, 2000).

It is impossible to ascertain whether the buckle originally formed part of a Hawkes and Dunning Type IA or IIA buckle (1961, 21), since the diagnostic section of this buckle is now missing. Type IA buckles are cast in one piece, with a closed 'D-shaped' loop with integral hinge bar (ibid 41). Type IIA buckles are composite, they are cast in individual sections, comprising an open-loop, tongue and plate, held together by a bolt (ibid 50, 51). Both types have been recovered in considerable numbers across the country and evidence tends to suggest that they date from the late 4th – 5th centuries (ibid 26).

JEWELLERY

Objects for personal adornment are represented by two brooches, a finger ring and fragments from seven armlets.

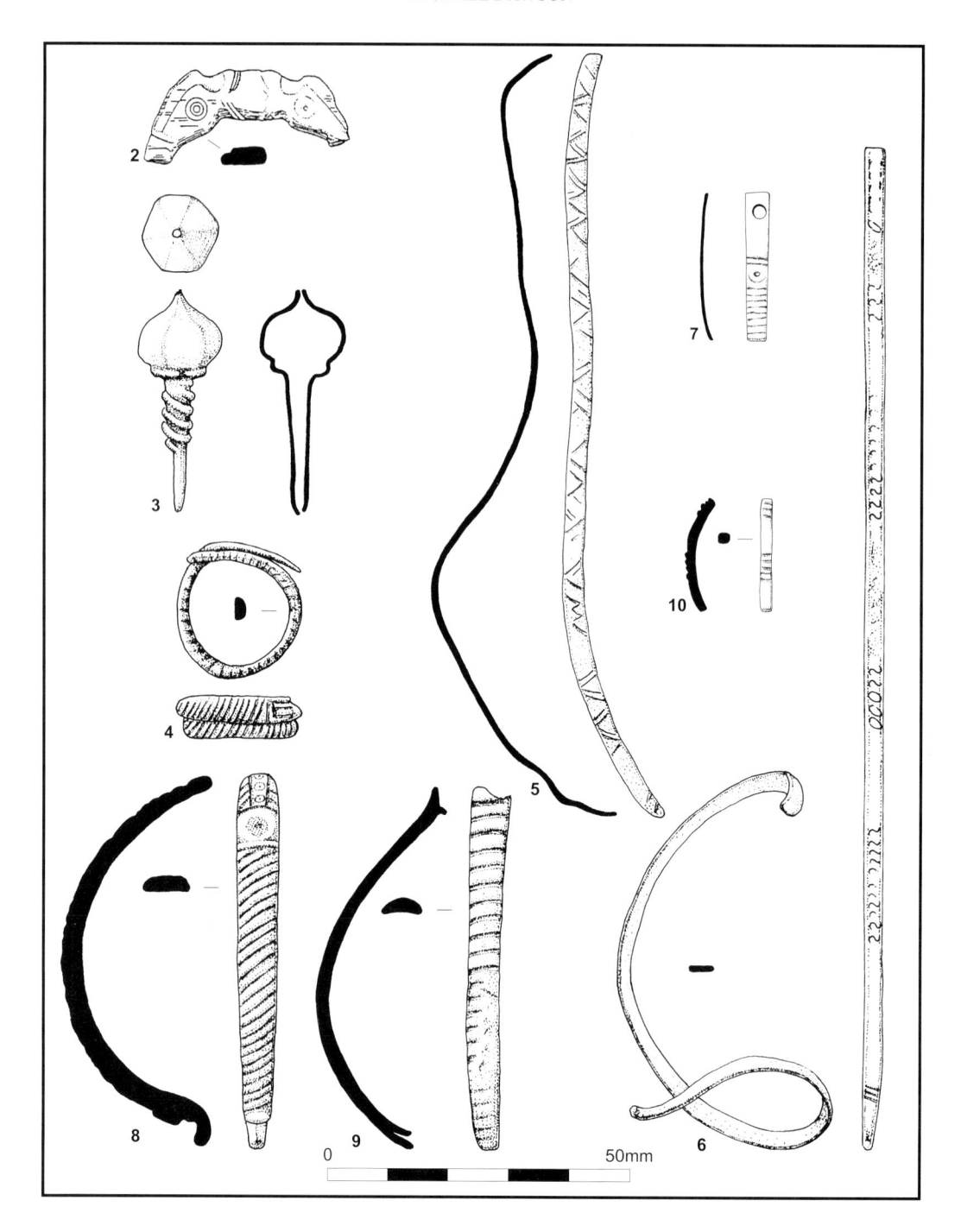

Fig 13 Other finds: 2, zoomorphic buckle; 3, crossbow brooch; 4, finger ring; 5, armlet; 6, armlet; 7, armlet; 8, armlet; 9, armlet; 10, armlet

Brooches
D Mackreth

ILLUSTRATED FINDS (Fig 13)

3 **Crossbow brooch**, the left hand terminal and screw from a Crossbow brooch. The knob is made of sheet and is in the form of a hexagon with an onion-shaped profile with a piece of wire wound round its base as a moulding. The shank on which it is built has a tapering screw of four and half turns and ends in a plain pin with appointed end. The pin would have engaged in the loop at the head of a brooch pin which was secured in a sleeve or tube behind the lower bow. The minimum spread of the head of the Crossbow brooch would have been 60mm. sf150, (1024)

The brooch terminal is similar to Keller's Type 5 (Keller 1971), although dated by Keller (ibid, Abb.12) to AD 370-400, no coin from the South Bavarian graves was later than 380. The brooches are made from sheet metal. The bow and foot tend to be the same width, and at best the two are of equal length. The knobs are definitely wider than they are long. Gilding is frequent, if not actually obligatory, and the incised decoration can be very elaborate.

These brooches were made to look massy yet be light. This says more about the fabrics with which they were worn than anything else. These brooches were not made for ordinary people and were designed to be a recognizable badge of rank or office, the two hardly being separate out in the remote Provinces. Their distribution includes Kent, Huntingdonshire, Sussex, Gloucestershire, Herefordshire, Suffolk, Norfolk, Cambridgeshire and Shropshire.

If these brooches represent the presence of high officials, then they were to be found more commonly along the Severn Valley and in East Anglia than elsewhere. Those from Gloucestershire are either from Lydney or Cirencester. The former close to a naval headquarters and the latter a provincial capital.

The terminal from Rowler also bears a close resemblance to Keller's Type 6, dated AD 400-*c* 450 (ibid 53). The chief feature of this type is the free-standing border consisting of conjoined open-work Cs along each side of the foot. There is, however, one technical innovation which belongs here alone: a pin secured by another. In most instances this extra pin is provided by one of the knobs on the head being screwed into position, the end of the knob having a pin which passes through the hole in the real brooch pin once occupied by the axis bar. This was means of making sure that the brooch could not just fall off or be pulled off without considerable force. The pin is frequently housed in a tube running along the back of the foot. It is not necessary that every brooch has both the screwed terminal and the open-work decoration, but one or the other must be present.

These brooches occur in two sizes: those like Type 5, and those which have much longer feet. The latter have very narrow faces down the front of the bow, in the case of the brooch from Icklingham, 10528 (Keller 1971), actually creased to form an arris. The foot as a consequence also has a very narrow central face. In primitive terms, Keller's Type 6 should always be recognizable by its foot or, failing that, by the narrow front face of the bow in proportion to the depth of the bow which, in any case, is narrower than the foot.

There may be a chronological difference between the short and squat Type 5-derived examples and the elongated Type 6, but dating is virtually non-existent. The Diptych of Stilicho provides a convenient reference point for Type 6, and one may note the giant gold Crossbows somewhat crudely shown on the entourage attending Justinian in San Vitale, Ravenna, which, incidentally all show the brooches being worn with what we normally call the 'foot' sticking up in the air.

Finger rings
Tora Hylton

A single penannular finger ring was recovered from the topsoil overlying Trench B (1022).

ILLUSTRATED FINDS (Fig 13)

4   **Finger ring**, copper alloy. Incomplete, one terminal missing, crudely coiled fingering with D-shaped cross-section. One end is rounded with two short lateral grooves, representing a serpent's head, the other end is missing. Int. Diameter: 167mm, Height: 4mm, Th: 1.5mm. sf71

The finger ring is crudely manufactured from a reused bracelet fragment decorated with oblique, incised grooves. The one surviving terminal of the original bracelet comprises a rounded end with two short lateral grooves and probably represents a stylised devolved serpent's head. Such representations on items of jewellery are common during the Roman period and represent health and healing, rebirth and the spirits of the departed (Johns 1998, 7). For a discussion on bracelets and rings in the form of snakes see Johns 1996 (334). Signs of extreme wear are visible on the back of the ring, but not on the front, suggesting that the ring was in use for a long period of time. Finger rings manufactured from reused bracelet fragments are not uncommon and similar examples are known from Colchester (Crummy 1983, fig 50, 1758) and Verulamium (Waugh and Goodburn 1972, fig 32, 28).

Armlets
Fragments from seven individual armlets were recovered, six of copper alloy and one of shale. All the copper alloy examples were recovered from topsoil deposits, five from Trench A and one from Trench 5. Three small fragments from a shale armlet were recovered from demolition deposits overlying the Bellerophon mosaic, Room A.

ILLUSTRATED FINDS (Fig 13)

5   **Armlet**, copper alloy. Ribbon strip type, almost complete but damaged, one terminal missing and the other is rounded. Exterior surface decorated with a crudely executed pattern of pairs of incised oblique grooves in opposing directions, forming a V-shaped motif. Patina flaking. Length: *c* 145mm Height: 3.5mm Th: 0.5mm. sf 149, (1024), trench A, topsoil

6   **Armlet**, copper alloy. Ribbon strip type, almost complete, one terminal missing. Parallel sides with flat cross-section, tapering towards a hooked terminal (hook and eye clasp). The exterior surface is decorated with a panel of stamped reversed S-shaped motifs within marginal grooves. Three transverse grooves separate the hook with the decorated section. Length (incomplete): 130mm Height: 3mm Th: 1mm. sf 125, (1007), trench 5, topsoil

7   **Armlet**, copper alloy. Ribbon strip type, terminal fragment only. Terminal perforated (hook and eye clasp). Decorated with incised transverse grooves and ring and dot. Length (incomplete): 13mm Height: 4mm Th: 1mm. sf 151, (1024), trench A, topsoil

8   **Armlet**, copper alloy. Incomplete, D-shaped cross-section with hooked terminal. Decorated with multiple motifs, comprising oblique transverse mouldings close to the hook, a plain recessed band and then a centrally placed line of 6 ring-and-dots flanked by pairs of lateral grooves, the outer groove is cut by short equidistant oblique incisions. Diameter: *c* 60mm Height: 7mm Th: 3mm. sf 147, (1024), trench A, topsoil

9 **Armlet**, copper alloy. Incomplete, fragment only. D-shaped cross-section, decorated with transverse grooves. The grooves have been subjected to extreme wear in places, their presence only visible on the extreme outer edge. Height: 6mm. sf 148, (1024), trench A, topsoil

10 **Armlet**, copper alloy. Incomplete, fragment only. Circular cross-section, outer edge 'castellated' with panels of four ?hand-cut transverses grooves. Good patina, Height: 2mm Th: 2mm. sf 186, (1024), trench A, topsoil

The copper alloy armlet fragments are from forms commonly found on Roman settlement sites. Three forms are represented:

> armlets with a flat rectangular cross-section 'ribbon-strip types'(3 examples)
> armlets with a D-shaped cross-section (2 examples)
> armlets with a circular cross-section (1 example)

Four of the armlet fragments still retain one of the original terminals, providing evidence for the type of fastening; three armlets have hook-and-eye fastenings (Fig 13. 6, 7, 8), and one has a rounded terminal, indicating that it is penannular (Fig 13.5). All the armlets are decorated with hand-tooled decoration, comprising either incised grooves or stamped motifs, and in some cases both techniques are used. The range represents stylistic features generally observed on armlets that date to the late 3rd and 4th centuries, and can be likened to those recovered from the cemetery at Lankhills (Clarke 1979) and Colchester (Crummy 1983).

The ribbon-strip type armlets are decorated with incised or stamped ornament. One or both decorative techniques have been applied as surface decoration. One armlet is decorated with incised double chevrons (Fig 13.5) and is not dissimilar to the motif on the inner face of a finger ring manufactured from an armlet found in Colchester (Crummy 1983, fig 50, 1774). The other two armlets are ornamented with both incised and stamped motifs. One has a panel of reversed S-shaped motifs, sandwiched between incised marginal grooves (Fig 13.6), similar to an example from Colchester (Crummy 1983, fig 43, 1700). The other is furnished with a single stamped ring-and-dot motif, flanked by transverse grooves (Fig 13.7), and it parallels a 4th-century example from Richborough (Henderson 1949, plate XLIX, 9). Two armlets have D-shaped cross-sections. One is elaborately decorated with distinct panels of decoration (Fig 13.8), similar to examples from Poundbury, Dorset (Cool 1993, fig 66, 19) and Shakenoak (Brodribb *et al*, 1973, fig 54, 194). Armlets of this type are usually referred to as 'multiple unit' armlets; they are decorated with a symmetrical pattern of five or more panels. Where they have been recovered from datable contexts, they are generally 4th century in date or later (Clarke 1979, 307) but Cool suggests that there are some indications that the type developed in the late 3rd century (Cool 1993, 89). The other armlet is faintly decorated with equidistant transverse grooves (Fig 13.9), similar to segmented forms recovered from the Caerleon Canabae (Lloyd-Morgan 2000, fig 80, 59) and a 4th-century penannular bracelet from Colchester (Crummy 1983, fig 44, 1683). The remaining armlet fragment appears to have been manufactured from a circular-sectioned rod fragment (wire), the outer face of the piece is 'crenellated' with alternate panels of plain and raised,?hand-cut, transverse incisions (Fig 13.10). Similar examples have been recorded at Colchester (Crummy 1983, fig 46, 1721) and Shakenoak (Brodribb *et al* 1973, fig 54, 192) and at Bancroft Villa, Milton Keynes (Hylton and Zeepvat 1994, fig 144,71), the latter recovered from a late 3rd to mid 4th century deposit.

Three small abraded fragments of shale were recovered from demolition deposits overlying the Bellerophon mosaic (10). Although they do not appear to join together, the curvature of one of the pieces suggests that it may have been part of an **armlet** (not illus).

Beads
H E M Cool

Four glass beads and a fragment that may be a much decayed fifth bead were found during the 2002 excavations in the deposit above the floor (10).

ILLUSTRATED FINDS (Fig 14)

14 **Annular bead**, Asymmetric. Body appearing black with opaque red marvered zig-zag around the outside face. Diameter 15mm, perforation diameter 7mm, maximum thickness 7mm. sf 8.1 (10)

15 **Annular bead**, Body appearing black with marvered zig-zag trail around the outside face; trail mostly missing but appears likely to have opaque white or yellow. Diameter 12mm, perforation diameter 5.5mm, maximum thickness 5.5mm. sf 8.2 (10)

16 **Annular bead**, Asymmetrical. Light yellow/brown. Diameter 13 x 12mm, perforation diameter 5mm, thickness 5.5mm. sf 8.3 (10)

17 **Annular bead**, Translucent deep blue. Diameter 10.5mm, perforation diameter 4mm, thickness 4.5mm. sf 8.4 (10)

   Annular bead, fragment. Probably highly decayed glass. Diameter 15mm. sf 8 (10) (not illus)

All the beads are annular forms. The two monochrome examples (Fig 14. 16, 17; sf 8.3 and sf 8.4) cannot be closely dated as they are a simple long-lived form. The polychrome beads though are a distinctive Saxon form in use during the 5th and 6th centuries. Sf 8.1 (Fig 14. 14) has a red trail marvered into glass that appears black, whilst on the other 'black' bead the trail has much decayed but appears to have been a yellowish colour. Both belong to Guido's Schedule D type vi (Guido 1999, 178-80). Beads such as sf 8.3 and sf 8.4 were in use contemporaneously so the group as a whole may be taken as indicative of occupation in the 5th to 6th centuries.

Toiletry equipment
Tora Hylton

One almost complete double-sided composite bone comb was recovered from topsoil deposits overlying Trench A.

ILLUSTRATED FINDS (Fig 14)

11 **Double-sided composite comb**, Bone. Incomplete, comprises 1 end segment, 1 tooth segment, 2 connecting plates and a small number of loose

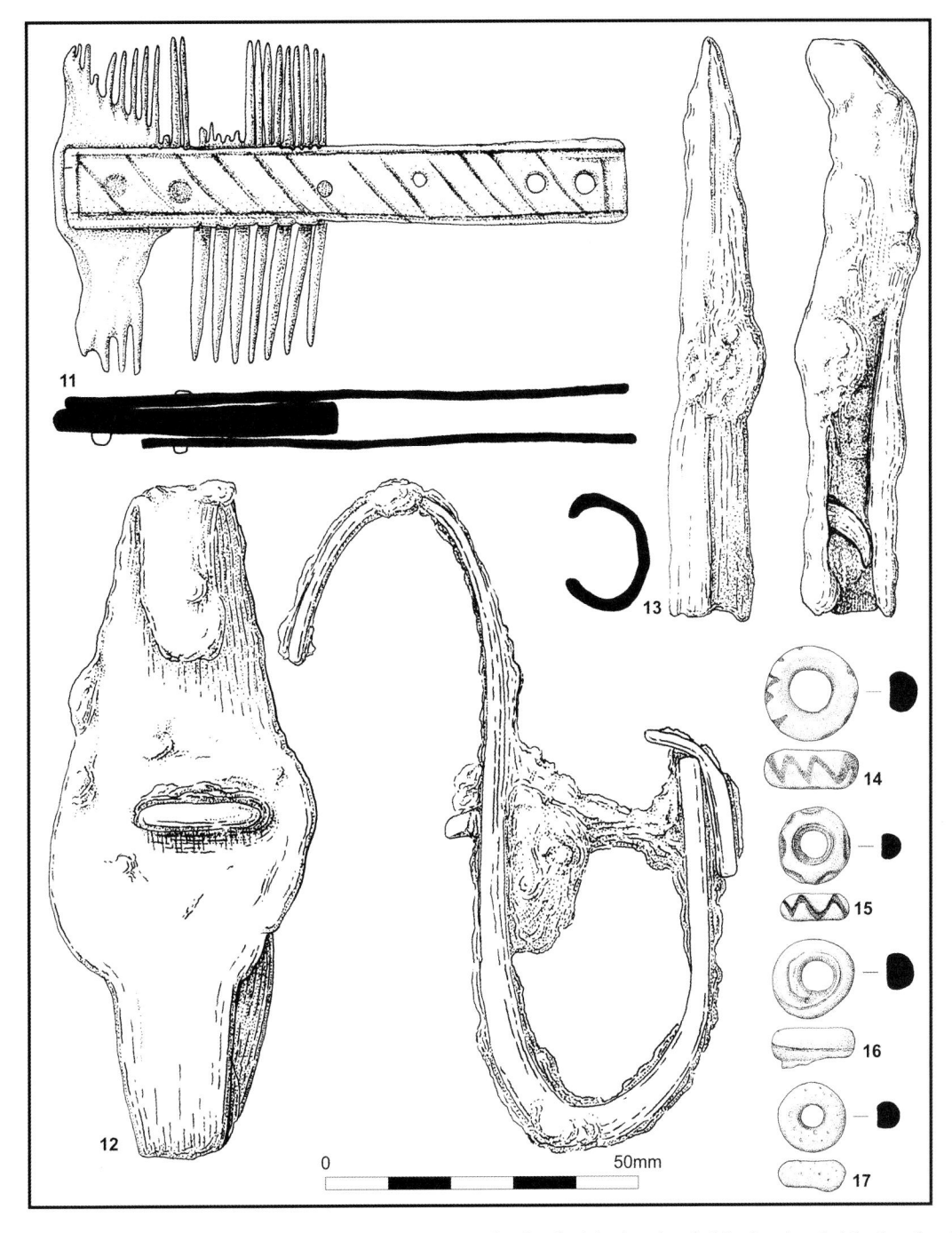

Fig 14 Other finds: 11, comb; 12, drop hinge; 13, pruning hook; 14, glass bead; 15, glass bead; 16, glass bead; 17, glass bead

teeth (originally there would have been 2 end segments and 2 teeth segments). The vertical edge of the surviving end segment has a concave curve either side of the connecting plate and the teeth are graduated. There are two sizes of teeth, fine (8 per centimetre) and coarse (4 per centimetre) on either side of the comb, they appear to be slightly worn and measure 18-19mm in length. The end segment and teeth segment is supported by two connecting-plates secured by six iron rivets (three extant) that pass through the end/tooth segments. The connecting-plates are ornamented with irregularly spaced oblique incisions within an incised marginal groove. The outside longitudinal edges of the connecting-plates are furnished with tiny equidistant notches, spaced according to the size of the teeth. These were most probably created during the cutting of the teeth. Length: 90mm Width: 48mm Depth: 8mm. sf 152, (1024), trench A, topsoil

The comb is fairly well preserved, though the side that had been facing down and in contact with the soil is slightly pitted. Combs were popular in the late Roman period (Galloway 1979, 247) and stylistically this comb displays similarities to late 4th-century examples. Stylistically, features observed on combs of this date are similar to those seen on continental examples (Galloway 1993, 108) and include being rectangular in shape with flat connecting-plates and profiled end segments. The main feature that differentiates them from the continental combs is, that like the example from Croughton, they are less elaborate and more simply decorated. Galloway has postulated that this suggests that the combs may have been manufactured locally, but they still retain the general characteristics of the continental combs (1979, 108). Stylistically the Croughton example displays similarities to late 4th-century examples from the cemeteries at Poundbury, Dorset (Farwell and Molleson 1993) and Lankhills, Hampshire (Clarke 1979). The profile of the end segment may be paralleled by examples from Poundbury (Galloway 1993, fig 78, 3), Lankhills (Galloway 1979, fig 31, 64) and Thorplands, Northampton (Oakley 1977, fig 19, 279), the latter was recovered from a late 1st to 3rd-century deposit.

The connecting-plates are crudely decorated with a linear ornament; the marginally placed horizontal and vertical incised grooves may be paralleled by a comb from Lankhills (Galloway 1979, fig 31, 64) and Poundbury (fig 78, 1). It is, however, possible that such a decorative technique may be a crude representation of the stepped bevelling seen on combs of a similar date (Galloway 1979, fig 78, 2).

RECREATION

A single ceramic roundel was recovered from the topsoil during trial trenching in 1995.

> Ceramic **roundel**, manufactured from the complete base of a Nene Valley Colour Coat beaker (grey coat), a fabric which dates to the mid 3rd and 4th centuries. The roundel measures 39mm in diameter and the broken edges appear to have been grounded down to form a flat edge. Similar examples are known from Colchester (Crummy 1983, fig 98, 2449). Trench 9 (1011)

Ceramic roundels are often recovered from Roman sites and they may have had any number of uses, including, reckoning counters or gaming pieces. (For a full discussion on their possible uses, see Crummy 1983 (93)).

BUILDING EQUIPMENT

There are a small number of objects which may have formed part of or been attached to, the villa building. Apart from a drop-hinge recovered from demolition deposits (16), the objects were recovered from topsoil.

ILLUSTRATED FINDS (Fig 14)

12 **Drop-hinge** for supporting a door or shutter. It has been manufactured from a single piece of sheet metal folded over to form a U-shaped hanging eye. Although incomplete, one terminal missing, it comprises a short arm, a longer 'shaped' arm (incomplete) and the hinge would have been secured by a nail (extant) which passes through both arms. Similar examples are known from Lakenheath (Manning 1985, plate 58, R9). Recovered from demolition deposits lying to the west of Room A (16)

Not illustrated

Fragments from two **split-spiked loops** for attaching rings and fittings. One has an out-turned spike and the distance between the loop and the clenched spike suggests that whatever the split-spiked loop had been passed through, measured c 8mm thick. Trench 12 (1014) and trench A (1024). For similar examples see Manning 1985 (plate 61, R49-50).

A **joiners-dog** would have been used for joining timbers. Topsoil overlying trench 2 (1002). (Manning 1985, 131).

Lastly, a perforated **leaf-shaped terminal** is either part of a decorative binding strip or a terminal from a box fitting, comparable to an example from Fishbourne (Cunliffe 1971, fig 62, 61). Topsoil overlying trench 5.

Nails

A total of 199 nails were recovered, including four hobnails which presumably derive from footwear. Stratified nails (54) were recovered from demolition deposits overlying Rooms A (90), (10), (23), C (12), (13), (42) and D (16), (28), (38), (59) and just outside the east wall (46). The remainder (145) derived from topsoil deposits overlying the footprint of the villa and a series of trenches excavated to the north-west of the building (Fig 2) (trenches 1, 2, 3 and 5) and are therefore unstratified.

Of the total number 13% (26 nails) are of indeterminate form, with their heads missing etc, the remainder have been classified according to Mannings Type series (1985, 134ff). The majority of the identifiable nail types are Mannings Type 1B (62%), which range in recorded length from 44-100mm. The majority clustered between 40-55mm and were presumably used for furniture or light structural fixings. Other types represented include, large structural nails, possibly for securing major timbers (Type 1A, 3%), nails with T-shaped heads (Type 3, 9%), nails with 'L' shaped heads (Type 4, 5%), nails lacking a distinct head (Type 5, 1%), nails for upholstery (Types 7, 2% and 9, 1%) and hob nails (Type 10, 1%).

TOOLS

Tools are represented by a pruning hook and a fragment of a spindle whorl (not illus), both were recovered from topsoil deposits.

ILLUSTRATED FINDS (Fig 14)

13 **Pruning hook**, iron. Complete. Short curving blade, oval-sectioned open socket. Cutting edge proceeds directly from the top of the socket. Length: 88mm Blade – Width: 14mm Socket – Diameter: 1.6mm sf 257, context 1, topsoil, unstratified

The presence of an iron pruning hook/small hook attests to some form of agricultural/horticultural activity during the lifetime of the settlement. The pruning hook is small and displays similarities to Rees Type 1a, the most common type (Rees 1979, 461). It has a short gently curving blade with open socket, rather like an example from Pitney, Somerset (ibid, fig 195c). Although prune/small hooks may have been used for agricultural/horticultural purposes, the small size of this example, suggests that its function may well have been more general purpose.

A fragment of a burnt/charred **spindle whorl** (not illus) was recovered from trench E, its presence possibly attesting to textile manufacture, or certainly spinning. Although incomplete, diagnostic features suggest that originally the whorl may have been plano-convex. The centrally placed perforation is waisted, indicating that it had been drilled from both sides.

Lead

Fourteen pieces of lead were recovered, seven from Roman contexts, four from topsoil over lying trenches 1, A and C, and three unstratified. Lead from Roman deposits were located mainly within demolition deposits overlying Room C1 (13), Room D (17, 35) and Room B (21). In addition, one fragment of lead waste was recovered from the hypocaust (72) and 2 from subsoil (2) (Fig 6).

There are no complete objects and the entire assemblage comprises undiagnostic fragments, represented mainly by cut sheeting and fused lumps. Fragments of sheeting measure up to 100 x 70mm and up to 7mm thick. Two fragments still retain perforations, indicating that they may have originally been used as flashing on the building. One piece measuring 100 x 70mm was recovered from demolition deposits overlying Room C1 (13) and the other measuring 8 x 8mm, with two square perforations is unstratified. The assemblage also includes a small number of molten fragments suggesting that after the building had been abandoned, lead was removed and possibly melted down for reuse elsewhere.

BUILDING MATERIALS

Window glass
H E M Cool

All of the window glass is of the cylinder blown variety, typical of the 4th century. Although it is thin, averaging 2mm in thickness, this would not have been the sort of glass you could see through because it is translucent rather than transparent. Light would have come through but it would have been tinted green. The greatest concentrations, judged by areas recovered, came from trench A and the hypocaust (Figs 5 & 6).

Painted Wall Plaster
Ros Tyrrell

This report concerns 479 fragments of painted plaster, weighing 12.186kg from the 1993 and 2002 excavations, and 1.778kg from the 1991 salvage work. A further 27.559kg of 'undecorated or plaster backing' pieces were discarded on site. No comment can be made as to the fabric or type of this material, or whether the

Table 7: Window glass

Context	Colour	Area cm^2
0	Light green bubbly	11
0	Light green bubbly	14
1	blue/green bubbly	3
1	Light green bubbly	0
57	Light green bubbly	5
70	Light green bubbly	34
70	Light green bubbly	17
75	blue/green bubbly	9
75	Light green bubbly	38
75	Light green bubbly	35
1002	Light green bubbly	3.5
1002	yellow green bubbly	2.5
1023	Light green bubbly	3.5
1024	Blue/green	7
1024	blue/green bubbly	2.5
1024	Light green bubbly	9
1024	Light green bubbly	12
1024	Light green bubbly	6
1024	Light green bubbly	8
1024	Light green bubbly	12
1024	Light green bubbly	12
1026	Light green bubbly	11

back retained any impressions of the wall or ceiling on which it had been mounted. No measurement of the size of the fragments has been made but visual assessment suggests that most of the fragments are small. In fact, few fragments are as large as those found in 1991 (75 x 80mm). This is probably partly due to plough damage as well as the demolition of the building and later robbing.

The largest amounts of plaster were found in Rooms A, 6.895kg, and D, 5.250 kg, which were the rooms with evidence of having been floored with mosaics. These relative quantities, however, were increased by the sampling strategies used on the site. Fragments of material lay in Room B and traces of plaster *in situ* were seen in Room C, but were not excavated or described. It is presumed that there were no colours visible.

The fabric of the wall plaster is made up of a yellow sandy matrix with rounded chalk and ironstone inclusions. The thicker pieces have a darker yellow version of this material with larger inclusions as the base coat on which the finer 10–15mm plaster is laid to take the paint. Of the plaster kept for the archive, 44% was burnt to a dark orange-red. The discolouration of these pieces in some cases started on the painted surface but did not penetrate to the backing and on others the opposite had happened.

Two impressions of box flue tile combing were noted on the back of plaster from Room D. Many other fragments had the imprint of the stone walls of the building preserved, but the generally small size of the fragments does not favour the preservation of this type of detail. There were also two pieces of white painted, round edged door or window mouldings from Room A.

Onto these fabrics a number of colours have been applied. Pink, red, yellow, light blue, white and black were used. These are probably not exotic or expensive pigments and are singly applied, with no undercoats, used to improve the tones of colours. There is no evidence for replastering or repainting. Lines, borders and possibly some mock marbling seem to be the designs represented by the fragments. There are no pieces that displayed evidence of any figured scenes. Colour combinations of a white line on red, yellow and white divided by a black line, a red line on yellow, are probably panel divisions. The predominance of white and black fragments suggests that these may have been background colours. Fragments found in 1991 suggested *c* 50mm wide pink band and *c* 45mm red band divided by a white 5mm line. The red is bordered on the other side by an area of black and white mock marbling. The colours on the burnt fragments are more difficult to describe, but it is mostly possible to see lines and indications of the colours, if not the actual shade. The plaster is well finished, although there are no signs of the polished surfaces of the highest quality wall paintings.

Due to plough disturbance and the small size of the assemblage it is not possible to make any assumptions as to the décor of each room. Thus the possible designs of the room with the Bellerophon mosaic remain enigmatic.

Stonework
Ian Meadows

A total of 40 pieces of stone were retained, seven as small finds, from the evaluation of 1995. Most was unworked.

sf 70 A small fragment of a limestone peg tile, the peg hole is 5mm diameter. This piece is a maximum of 95 x 85mm and 16mm thick and is of a Jurassic shelly limestone. The piece may have part of two original edges suggesting an original lozenge shape for the tile. It comes from an unknown context, it is itself undateable, and stone roof slates are common in this area throughout the last two millennia.

sf 100 Two non-joining fragments of Jurassic oolitic limestone from a curved, possibly circular, object with an original potential diameter of at least 1.5m. The piece thickens towards the edge where it has a slightly raised lip on one face with an incised line at the base of this lip. At one point on the edge there is evidence for knife sharpening. This piece was tentatively identified by the excavator as a stone basin, however, if this was the case it would only be a few millimetres deep, which would appear to militate against such an interpretation, elsewhere such stone basins are generally over 40mm deep. Perhaps a more likely function is as a limestone tabletop. Stone tabletops have been recovered from several sites and they come in rectangular and bowed form (Solley 1979). The date placed on such elements is generally 3rd or 4th century with provenances either urban or villa. On continental sites where similar finds occur a possible role in religious practice has been suggested.

sf 118 A large fragment of fine-grained fissile Jurassic limestone with many shell fragments. The piece measures 210 x 130mm and is up to 30mm thick. The piece shows no signs of working although a small part of the surface is smoothly worn, but this could be a natural feature as well as the possible result of usage wear. The piece is perhaps part of a stone floor slab.

sf 119 A fragment of the lower stone from a probably Derbyshire gritstone rotary quern with an original diameter of at least 240mm, unfortunately none of the original edge survived. The piece is 220 x 170mm and 70mm thick. The upper, grinding, surface is worn to a smooth polish. The round perforation had been drilled from both sides, and is a maximum of 25mm diameter at the grinding surface, narrowing to about 10mm before flaring to the underside surface (50mm). This piece could date to either the later Iron Age or Roman period but is itself not closely dateable.

Most of the stone are natural unworked fragments. These are catalogued in the archive.

VESSEL GLASS
H E M Cool

The earliest vessel glass comprises a few fragments of blue/green glass. All those that can be identified as to form come from the range of square bottles in common use from the later 1st century, throughout the 2nd and into the 3rd century. These utilitarian vessels are common on rural sites.

The majority of the vessel glass fragments, however, come from 4th-century drinking vessels. Where the forms can be closely dated, they belong to the second half of the century and into the 5th century. Again, it is not unusual to have an assemblage like this on a late villa site. By the 4th century glass was overwhelmingly used for drinking vessels.

INDUSTRIAL PROCESSES
A Chapman

Two contexts, (1007) and (1024), produced very small quantities (230g and 90g) of undiagnostic ironworking slag. This small quantity indicates the occurrence of iron smithing nearby.

THE ROMAN POTTERY
R P Symonds

INTRODUCTION

(This is an abbreviated report on the pottery. A full copy is held with the archive.)

Roman pottery was recovered from Croughton during field artifact collection in 1993 (Shaw and Audouy 1993), trial trenching in 1993 and 1995 (Blore 1996), from damage assessment in 2001 (Wilmott 2001) and during excavation of the mosaic in 2002 (Carlyle 2002). The assemblages from the fieldwalking in 1993 and trial trenching in 1993/5 both came from topsoil as no excavation was undertaken during the trenching, whilst the damage assessment and 2002 excavation produced a small quantity of stratified material.

The pottery has been reported on by Robin Symonds using methodology developed by the Museum of London. The forms were recorded following the MoLSS/MoLAS system, which in turn is based on the system devised

Table 8: List of fabrics present

Fabric	Description	Edate	Ldate
NVCC	Nene Valley colour-coated ware	150	400
OXRC	Oxfordshire red/brown colour-coated ware	270	400
OXWC	Oxfordshire white colour-coated ware	240	400
BB1	black-burnished ware 1	120	400
FINE	unsourced fine wares	50	400
AHFA	Alice Holt/Farnham ware	250	400
SAND	unsourced sand-tempered wares	50	400
VRG	Verulamium region grey wares	50	200
CALC	late Roman 'calcite-tempered' ware	300	400
COAR	unsourced coarse wares	40	400
GROG	unsourced grog-tempered wares	40	400
PKG	pink-grogged ware	50	400
OXID	unsourced oxidised wares	50	400
OXIDF	unsourced fine oxidised fabric	50	400
OXWW	Oxfordshire white ware	180	400
VRW	Verulamium region white ware	50	160
CC	unsourced colour-coated wares	50	400

by Marsh and Tyers (1978), more recently updated (Symonds (ed) 1999); for details of the use of rows see Symonds and Rauxloh (2003).

FIELDWALKING 1993

The area of fieldwalking is outlined on Figure 2 and details of the stints and collection points form part of the site archive. A total of 1845 sherds weighing 8374 grammes were recorded from 109 stints. The assemblage consisted almost entirely of small, badly abraded and difficult-to-identify sherds, with an average weight of 4.5 grammes. The assemblage can be broadly dated to the late Roman period (AD 200-400), with just four sherds likely to be residual by AD 200 (see Table 9 p. 74).

The Ceramics Fabrics

The most common fabric in the assemblage is pink grog-tempered ware (PKG), with 31.7% by rows, 33.2% by sherd-count and 43.5% by weight (Table 10) with five or six common fabrics. (For the nature and characteristics of PKG see Woodfield 1983, 78-9, Booth and Green 1989, Marney 1989, 64-7, Tomber 1989, 67-9, and in Booth *et al* 2001, 328-31).

Unsourced oxidised wares are the second most common fabric by rows and sherd-count, but not by weight, with both unsourced grog-tempered wares and unsourced sand-tempered wares more common by weight. Although Oxford red-brown colour-coated wares are the fifth most common fabric type (118 sherds), it may be that some unsourced oxidised wares and fine oxidised wares were not recognised as Oxford products because of surface abrasion and the small size of many sherds. In the same way other fabrics likely to have been under-identified are Oxford white ware (OXWW) and Oxford white colour-coated ware (OXWC), as well as late Roman calcite-gritted ware, for which identification is usually helped by some horizontal rilling on the exterior of jar forms, often absent from badly abraded small sherds. Although pink grog-tempered ware is generally among the easier of specific fabrics to identify, it is likely that a certain number of sherds identified as unsourced grog-tempered ware are in fact PKG sherds which may have been burnt or otherwise damaged or discoloured. Similarly some of the unsourced sand-tempered sherds are likely to be Nene Valley grey ware or another specific grey ware, while some unsourced oxidised sherds could in fact be Verulamium region white ware or possibly some other more specific oxidised fabric.

Eleven sherds, or less than 1% of the assemblage, are not Romano-British in origin. All of these are samian ware, one being East Gaulish, probably from Trier, while the other ten are all Central Gaulish (nine probably from Lezoux, while the tenth is probably from Les Martres de Veyre). Other wares which travelled some distance to reach the site are 13 sherds of black-burnished ware 1, from southern Dorset, 21 sherds of Nene Valley colour-coated ware, 14 sherds probably from Alice Holt, near Farnham in Surrey (all probably from the later Alice Holt industry), and 10 sherds of oxidised Much Hadham ware. Pottery types which are likely to have travelled more than 50km to reach the site comprise 5% of the total, whereas 95% of the vessels are likely to have been made within a 50km radius of the site.

The Ceramic Forms

Some 78.3% by sherd-count of the assemblage comprises sherds of unidentifiable form. Most of the rest of the pottery can only be attributed to a general form type such as unidentifiable flagon or jar – by sherd-count specific forms amount to just 3.5% of the assemblage but it represents an entirely Romano-British assemblage with no evidence in the form-types of a pre-Roman culture, despite the rural nature of the site.

Dating

The data has been assessed by Edate (earliest), Ldate (latest) and sherd-count, and indicates that all the stints have date-ranges which end at AD 400, and roughly two-thirds have date-ranges which begin at AD 250 or later.

Table 9: The ceramic fabrics recovered during fieldwalking in 1993

Fabrics	Code	Rows	% Rows	Sherds	% Sherds	Weight (g)	% Weight	Date-range
samian wares								
Central Gaulish samian ware	SAMCG	9	0.5%	9	0.5%	14	0.2%	120-250
Les Martres-de-Veyre samian ware	SAMMV	1	0.1%	1	0.1%	4	0.0%	100-120
Trier samian ware	SAMTR	1	0.1%	1	0.1%	2	0.0%	125-300
Romano-British fine wares								
Much Hadham ware	MHAD	10	0.6%	10	0.5%	31	0.4%	200-400
Nene Valley colour-coated ware	NVCC	21	1.3%	21	1.1%	110	1.3%	150-400
Oxford red/brown colour-coated ware	OXRC	114	6.8%	118	6.4%	529	6.3%	270-400
Oxford white colour-coated ware	OXWC	2	0.1%	2	0.1%	44	0.5%	240-400
black-burnished wares								
black-burnished ware 1	BB1	13	0.8%	13	0.7%	29.5	0.4%	120-400
black-burnished ware 2, fine fabric	BB2F	1	0.1%	1	0.1%	17	0.2%	140-250
black-burnished style ware	BBS	5	0.3%	5	0.3%	50	0.6%	120-400
fine reduced wares								
unsourced fine wares	FINE	34	2.0%	36	2.0%	110	1.3%	50-400
reduced wares								
Alice Holt/Farnham ware	AHFA	14	0.8%	14	0.8%	78	0.9%	250-400
Highgate Wood C ware	HWC	3	0.2%	3	0.2%	5	0.1%	70-160
Nene Valley grey ware	NVG	4	0.2%	4	0.2%	19	0.2%	200-400
unsourced sand-tempered ware	SAND	211	12.6%	221	12.0%	922	11.0%	50-400
tempered wares								
late Roman 'calcite-tempered' ware	CALC	28	1.7%	29	1.6%	188	2.2%	300-400
unsourced coarse ware	COAR	7	0.4%	7	0.4%	75	0.9%	40-400
flint-tempered ware	FLIN	2	0.1%	2	0.1%	11	0.1%	50-200
unsourced grog-tempered ware	GROG	236	14.1%	272	14.7%	1101	13.1%	40-400
unsourced grog- and shell-tempered ware	GROGSH	1	0.1%	1	0.1%	13	0.2%	40-400
pink grog tempered ware	PKG	531	31.7%	613	33.2%	3640.5	43.5%	170-400
unsourced shell-tempered ware	SHEL	72	4.3%	75	4.1%	277	3.3%	40-400
oxidised wares								
North French/southeast English oxidised ware	NFSE	2	0.1%	2	0.1%	5	0.1%	50-160
unsourced oxidised wares	OXID	302	18.0%	334	18.1%	849.5	10.1%	50-400
unsourced fine oxidised fabric	OXIDF	31	1.9%	31	1.7%	67.5	0.8%	50-400
Oxford white ware	OXWW	8	0.5%	8	0.4%	130	1.6%	180-400
Verulamium region white ware	VRW	4	0.2%	4	0.2%	36	0.4%	50-160
miscellaneous fabrics								
unsourced colour-coated wares	CC	8	0.5%	8	0.4%	15.5	0.2%	50-400
Total		1675	100.0%	1845	100.0%	8373.5	100.0%	

TRIAL TRENCHING 1993 AND 1995

Trial trenches in 1995 were opened by machine and no excavation beyond hand cleaning took place. The contexts, therefore, all represent topsoil and or sub-ploughsoil horizons. A total of 1534 sherds, or 326 rows, weighing 19378g, from 27 contexts, were examined in this assemblage. Although the abrasion is generally not enough to hamper identification, many of the sherds are fairly abraded, and small-to-medium sized. All of the contexts are late Roman (AD 200+), or, in the case of five contexts (1022, 1023, 1024, 1026 and 1027), probably residual in post-Roman levels, although a small number of residual sherds are present which may date to the 1st or 2nd centuries.

Only two sherds, one of samian ware from la Graufesenque and one of fine micaceous ware, are definitely residual at AD 200; all the remaining 1532 sherds have date-ranges which end no earlier than AD 250, and some 98.3% of all the sherds recorded have date-ranges which end at *c* AD 400.

The Fabrics

In common with the fieldwalking data both sherd-count (35.8%) and weight (49.1%) indicate that the most common fabric present is pink-grog tempered ware (PKG). By rows the most common fabric is Oxford red/brown colour-coated ware (OXRC; 25.5%): the discrepancy between rows and sherds/weight is caused here by the fact that many more Oxford ware sherds have recognisable forms, each of which requires a separate row, (records, or unique fabric, form and decoration combinations) whereas a much smaller number of PKG sherds have an identifiable form. By sherd-count and weight tempered wares (mainly grog-tempered but also shell-tempered and late Roman calcite-gritted wares) make up at least 50% of the entire assemblage. By sherd-count about 27% of the assemblage is unsourced, probably local sandy reduced or oxidised wares, and about 15% is Romano-British fine wares (mainly Oxford and Nene Valley wares), and the rest accounts for the remaining 8%. Imported pottery amounts to less than about 4% of the assemblage by weight (1.4% by sherd-count).

The Forms

By sherd-count about 60% of the assemblage is composed of either unidentifiable jars or unidentifiable forms. Nearly all of the most clearly identifiable forms are represented by one, two or just a few examples, with the exception of hook-rimmed jars (13 rows, 34 sherds), Dr 38 bowls (11 rows, 18 sherds) and black-burnished-type flanged bowls (16 rows, 32 sherds). Storage jars are also common, but these probably should be classed as an 'unidentifiable form', since they are often simply thicker-walled-than-normal sherds. Not surprisingly, jars and bowls are the largest form categories, whereas flagons are very low in comparison with most urban sites.

Dating

There are no contexts with a *terminus ante quem* earlier than *c* AD 400 (Table 10). To some extent this results from the fact that in the late Roman period (after *c* AD 200) most pottery types have long date-ranges, and most of those date-ranges end in 400 because the types continue to be present in the latest recorded assemblages. The frequent presence of the full variety of Oxford wares along with other obviously late types does, however, suggest that by far the most intensive occupation represented by the pottery belongs to the 4th century. A single sherd of Portchester D ware (PORD) is perhaps not enough to suggest that the bulk of that occupation was in the second half of the century, but at least some may have been that late. All of the Alice Holt Farnham ware (AHFA) from the same production area in Hampshire/Surrey as Portchester D ware was found in a single context in trench 12 (1014). It may be significant that this included no definite examples of large AHFA storage jars, which are usually thought to be *c* AD 330+, but these are generally less common so far north from the production area, and their role would have been very adequately fulfilled by the large pink-grog tempered storage jars.

THE DAMAGE ASSESSMENT 2001

In 2001 English Heritage investigated the line of a watermain dug through the scheduled area at Croughton (Wilmott 2001), a total of 73 sherds, or 38 rows, weighing 722g, from six contexts plus surface finds and un-stratified finds, were examined in this assemblage. There is a maximum of 52 vessels represented. Although the abrasion is generally not enough to hamper identification, many of the sherds are fairly abraded, and small-to-medium sized.

The Fabrics

It should be noted that attempting to assess the quantitative significance of this assemblage is an exercise of somewhat questionable usefulness, since it amounts to less than a kilogram of pottery, and calculating percentages of numbers than less than 100 is always statistically dubious. It is nevertheless clear that in general terms this assemblage is very similar to the pottery from the nearby villa. About one-quarter of the assemblage is pink grog-tempered ware (PKG), for the production of which evidence has been found in the form of pottery and at least one kiln about 6km to the east at Stowe Park (Booth *et al* 2001, 328). Wares imported from outside Britain are represented by just three sherds of Central Gaulish samian ware; Romano-British fine wares, black-burnished ware 1 and a possible sherd of Colchester white ware amount to a total of 13 sherds likely to have been imported from other parts of the province. Almost 80% of the assemblage is thus either likely to have been made locally or of unknown origin (but probably made in the surrounding region). All the wares present are also represented at nearby sites such as Milton Keynes (Marney 1989) and Towcester (Woodfield 1983).

As might be expected the fabric types and fabric origins are similar to those from the trial trenching. This is especially true at the broadest level of comparison: both

Table 10: The dating, by contexts

Context	Trench	Rows	% Rows	Sherds	% Sherds	Weight (g)	% Weight	Edate	Ldate	Comments
1003	1	11	3.4%	33	2.2%	353	1.8%	270	400	
1004	2	14	4.3%	101	6.6%	1382	7.1%	270	400	
1005	3	19	5.8%	69	4.5%	1973	10.2%	270	400	
1007	5	56	17.2%	505	32.9%	6792	35.1%	300	400	Includes 1 sherd of TPW (Transfer Printed ware - post-med)
1008	6	6	1.8%	29	1.9%	307	1.6%	270	400	
1009	7	3	0.9%	17	1.1%	35	0.2%	270	400	
1010	8	2	0.6%	13	0.8%	40	0.2%	170	400	
1011	9i, ii	8	2.5%	12	0.8%	188	1.0%	270	400	
1014	12	19	5.8%	74	4.8%	1230	6.3%	270	400	
1015	13	15	4.6%	29	1.9%	537	2.8%	270	400	
1017	15i	1	0.3%	3	0.2%	30	0.2%	50	400	
1018	15ii	3	0.9%	4	0.3%	9	0.0%	170	400	
1019	15iii	8	2.5%	17	1.1%	109	0.6%	270	400	
1020	16	1	0.3%	2	0.1%	16	0.1%	170	400	
1021	17	2	0.6%	2	0.1%	77	0.4%	170	400	Plus 1 sherd of ENGS INSU (modern)
1032	9 & 11	12	3.7%	31	2.0%	127	0.7%	300	400	All very abraded
Villa Building										
1001	D	15	4.6%	22	1.4%	326	1.7%	300	400	
1002	D	21	6.4%	82	5.3%	845	4.4%	300	400	
1022	B	19	5.8%	117	7.6%	1346	6.9%	300	400	SAND = Northants grey ware; contains 4 sherds TPW (1805-1900)
1023	C	10	3.1%	32	2.1%	326	1.7%	300	400	Contains 22 sherds of 19th-century porcelain (TPW)
1024	A	43	13.2%	282	18.4%	2206	11.4%	350	400	Many sherds very abraded; includes 48 sherds of white porcelain, 20 sherds of TPW and 3 sherds of stoneware (1895+)
1025	D	2	0.6%	3	0.2%	22	0.1%	270	400	
1026	u/s	12	3.7%	15	1.0%	401	2.1%	270	400	Includes 1 sherd of white porcelain and 2 sherds of TPW
1027	E	16	4.9%	29	1.9%	448	2.3%	300	400	Includes 6 sherds of white porcelain and 1 sherd of TPW
1028	E	6	1.8%	9	0.6%	248	1.3%	300	400	
1030	E	1	0.3%	1	0.1%	3	0.0%	270	400	
1031	B	1	0.3%	1	0.1%	2	0.0%	300	400	
Total		326	100.0%	1534	100.0%	19378	100.0%			

assemblages have a total of not less than 94.5% Romano-British wares, and thus a maximum of 5.5% imported wares, or imported wares combined with unsourced miscellaneous wares.

The Forms

Only nine sherds of the 73 come from specifically identifiable forms and apart from a complete lack of amphora sherds, the range of forms represented appears to be entirely normal for the late Roman period.

Dating

The date-ranges indicate that all of the pottery may belong to the late Roman period, and in this respect the

Table 11: Ceramic dating, by contexts from the 2001 damage assessment

Context	Size	Rows	% Rows	Sherds	% Sherds	Weight (g)	% Weight	Edate	Ldate
6204	S	7	18.4%	10	13.7%	36	5.0%	270	400
6206	S	1	2.6%	1	1.4%	5	0.7%	170	400
6218	S	5	13.2%	11	15.1%	113	15.7%	170	400
6222	S	10	26.3%	26	35.6%	303	42.0%	300	400
6239	S	1	2.6%	1	1.4%	5	0.7%	50	400
6246	S	6	15.8%	13	17.8%	72	10.0%	270	400
Surface finds	S	3	7.9%	4	5.5%	51	7.1%	170	400
Unstrat	S	5	13.2%	7	9.6%	137	19.0%	270	400
Total		38	100.0%	73	0.0%	722	100.0%		

assemblage is similar to that from the trial trenching. It is obvious that the greater the number of sherds present in a context, the later the date-range is likely to be.

EXCAVATION 2002

The pottery from 30 contexts was examined, amounting to a total of 220 sherds in 146 rows, an estimated 177 vessels represented weighing 3159g. The quantities in each context are shown in Table 12 below.

Dating

The dating of individual contexts is shown in Table 12, below. Nine of the 30 contexts were found to contain at least some sherds of St Neots ware. This Saxon and early medieval shell-tempered ware can be distinguished from Roman shell-tempered wares made in the Northamptonshire region by the presence of bryzoa microfossils in the tempering. Although the identification of these sherds is not really in doubt, it does seem curious that only one single type of post-Roman pottery was present, even in topsoil (1). Otherwise, however, the Roman pottery present is entirely late, with no context having a *terminus ante quem* earlier than AD 400. The contacts are mainly dated by Oxford ware (OXRC; AD 270-400) and/or by late Roman calcite-gritted ware (CALC; AD 300-400). Demolition material (12) post dates *c* AD 325-400 by the presence of a Young (1978) form 75 bowl. Demolition (28) contains a flanged bowl in late Roman calcite-gritted ware whose form probably dates to the second half of the 4th century (Brown & Woodfield 1983, 100 and fig 30, nos. 256-7; Symonds & Wade 1999, 458 and fig 6.110, nos 11-12). The dating of late Roman fabrics lacks precision in Britain as a whole, and it is difficult with such a fairly small assemblage to say much more than that it probably belongs to the 4th century. There is, nevertheless, no pottery present which unequivocally attests to occupation prior to the second half of the 3rd century. (There is one possible sherd of Verulamium region grey ware (VRG), dated AD 50-200, and one possible sherd of Verulamium region white ware (VRW), but there some doubt about both of these identifications.)

The fabrics

There were no imported (into Britain) fabrics present – no samian ware, no imported fine wares and no amphorae. The assemblage is dominated by late Roman fine wares from the Oxford region (OXRC and OXWC; Young 1977) and the Nene Valley (NVCC; Howe, Perrin and Mackreth 1980; Perrin 1999), as well as fine (FINE) and coarse local grey reduced sandy (SAND) wares, pink grog-tempered ware (PKG; Booth and Green 1989), and late Roman calcite-gritted ware (CALC). The reduced wares are almost certainly all from local or regional productions, as is the late Roman calcite-gritted ware (Symonds 1980, Brown and Woodfield 1983).

One surprising aspect is the presence of just three sherds of Black-burnished ware, probably from only two vessels. Other late Roman sites in the region tend to have much more substantial quantities of the ware, and one might draw the inference that because such sites are likely to have had 3rd century and earlier occupation, their Black-burnished ware probably pre-dates the occupation of this site (Table 12).

Conclusion

The pottery assemblage from fieldwalking, despite the difficulties of identification, is an assemblage which is Romano-British in character not dissimilar to assemblages in urban areas during the late Roman period. Imported pottery occurs in smaller percentages than in urban areas, but by this period imported wares were already very much in decline throughout the province, and rare though they are, some imported wares are still present.

The ceramic assemblage recovered during trial trenching from the periphery of the site area includes among the imported and fine wares a small quantity of amphorae and samian in proportions to be expected at a late Roman rural villa in central Britain. This assemblage is important since the quantities of ceramic types imported into the province had greatly diminished by the time this site was occupied intensively. In this assemblage samian reaches only 3.1% by rows, 1.4% by sherd-count and 3.6% by weight. It compares poorly with about 5% at the Wroxeter Baths Basilica (Symonds 1997, 273, fig 19) where it was residual, in contexts dated between the late 4th century and the 7th century or later, but rather favourably with Milton Keynes, where most of the late Roman sites studied by Marney (1989, Appendix 2, 196-7) were found to contain no samian at all. The rather more substantial amount of Oxford colour-coated ware could be taken to suggest that despite the low quantities of imported wares this site was of high status, since Oxford red/brown colour-coated vessels often occur in samian forms, and could be seen as a Romano-British

Table 12: Context date-ranges

Context	Size	Rows	Sherds	ENVs	Wgt (g)	I/C/R	Edate	Ldate	Comments
Topsoil 1	S	5	5	5	63	C	270	400	
Topsoil 1	M	25	40	37	370	R	300	400	Contains 2 sherds of St Neots ware; all very abraded.
Topsoil 1	S	9	10	10	122	R	270	400	Contains 9 sherds of St Neots ware; mostly very abraded.
Topsoil 1	S	6	8	8	235	C	300	400	All very abraded
Above mosaic 9	S	1	4	3	16	C	300	400	
Above mosaic 9	S	5	7	5	163	R	270	400	Contains 3 sherds of St Neots ware.
Above mosaic 9	S	5	15	5	197	R	270	400	Contains 6 sherds of St Neots ware.
Above mosaic 9	S	10	12	12	305	R	270	400	Contains 2 sherds of St Neots ware; mostly very abraded.
Above mosaic 10	S	4	5	4	23	C	270	400	All very abraded
Above mosaic 10	S	4	6	6	109	C	150	400	
Above mosaic 10	S	12	17	15	259	R	270	400	Contains 2 sherds of St Neots ware.
Demolition 12	S	8	18	10	214	C	325	400	
Demolition 16	S	8	13	9	121	C	300	400	All very abraded.
Demolition 16	S	3	5	3	80	R	300	400	Contains 1 sherd of St Neots ware.
Demolition 17	S	2	2	2	7	C	270	400	
25	S	1	1	1	2	C	50	400	
28	S	4	6	5	98	C	300	400	All very abraded
28 Lower	S	3	5	3	141	C	200	400	
29	S	2	3	3	22	C	270	400	
35	S	4	4	4	75	C	270	400	
38	S	4	4	4	31	C	270	400	All very abraded
39	S	1	1	1	4	C	300	400	?MPOT
41	S	6	10	7	99	C	300	400	
42	S	1	1	1	5	C	270	400	
46	S	4	7	5	118	R	270	400	Contains 2 sherds of St Neots ware.
46	S	5	7	5	105	C	270	400	All very abraded.
53	S	1	1	1	22	C	270	400	
59	S	1	1	1	5	C	50	400	
73	S	1	1	1	133	C	50	400	
76	S	1	1	1	15	C	270	400	
Total		146	220	177	3159				

(S = small, less than 30 sherds; I/C/R = intrusive/contemporary/residual). (See Figs 6 & 8, contexts 35, 39, 53 & 73 not ills)

replacement for the samian which no longer arrived from Gaul.

The low quantity of black-burnished wares, either BB1, BB2, is to be expected with black-burnished wares, including both BB1 and wheel-thrown varieties reaching a maximum of 4% by rows, and only 1.9% by sherd-count or 1.6% by weight. Large quantities of BB1 can be observed on some urban sites in the Midlands region, on average about 23% in the late Roman Baths Basilica at Wroxeter (Symonds 1997, 273, fig 19; White 1997, 313, figs 270-1), reaching a peak above 30% in the late Roman period at Little Chester, Derby (Symonds 2002, 157-8, tables 15-18) (although the figures for black-burnished wares in the Little Chester archive are slightly inflated compared to those quoted for other sites since the totals do not include the samian ware); further south, a peak above 30% has also been recorded at Silchester (Fulford 1984, Group 2.3, 154). By contrast in the

Alcester Road suburb at Towcester the peak of 12.5% is reached in Phase 1 (up to AD 170; Woodfield 1983, 79), while in the town centre the peak of 16% does not arrive until the 3rd century (Phase 6a; Symonds 1980, 82 table 3). At Milton Keynes, however, the percentages of BB1 reach a peak of only 3.97% (Marney 1989, Group 9, 35-6 and 126-8), and the peak at Alcester also reaches only 3.5% (Booth *et al* 2001, 365). The high levels of BB1 in particular at urban sites seems to suggest that the ware benefitted from a distribution system which was certainly as efficient within Britain as the distribution system for samian wares throughout northern Europe. By contrast, however, Allen & Fulford's study of the distribution of BB1 in south-western Britain (1996) seems to miss the fundamental point that quantities of widely-disseminated wares like samian and BB1 were not nearly as affected by the distance from the production site as by the function of the destination site, in particular by whether it was urban or rural in nature. It would seem that the Croughton assemblage provides further support to the conclusion of Booth *et al* (2001, 364-5), along with Evans (2000) and Hancocks *et al* (1998), that ' BB1 was marketed from urban centres and was therefore commoner at those centres'.

The 73 sherds excavated during the damage assessment represent further late Roman occupation of a similar nature and chronology to the assemblage from fieldwalking and trial trenching. Both assemblages are dominated by one regional ware, pink-grog tempered ware (PKG), which accounts for almost half the pottery by weight. *Prima facie* this suggests this site may be unusually isolated, given the low quantities of imported pottery, but the low percentages of well-travelled wares may also be due to the immediate proximity of the nearby pink grog-tempered production centre, whose products have overwhelmed this site, rather than to any decline in trade networks.

CATALOGUE OF PREVIOUSLY UNPUBLISHED CERAMIC FORMS (FIG 15)

44.3	Fieldwalking stint	Flanged bowl, sandy reduced ware SAND 4M
64.4	Fieldwalking stint	Prehistoric or Saxon sherd with ?notched decoration, SHEL
65.9	Fieldwalking stint	Jar, unsourced grog-tempered ware, GROG 2
76.10	Fieldwalking stint	Mortarium, Oxford whiteware (Young 1977 form M22), OXWW 7M22
85.22	Fieldwalking stint	Plain-rimmed dish, Black-burnished ware 2, fine fabric, BB2F 5J
86.2	Fieldwalking stint	2 Bead-rimmed? bowls. Grog-tempered ware, GROG 4? BR
106.1	Fieldwalking stint	Plain-rimmed dish. Nene Valley colour-coated ware. NVCC 5J PR
492	Excavation	Central Gaulish Samian vessel Dr1R dish with rouletting and post-firing holes to accommodate 4-5 lead rivets (CAS492 (1005))

THE CERAMIC BUILDING MATERIAL
P Mills

(The report on the CBM is an abbreviated text of the original specialist report. The full text is available in the archive.)

The Ceramic Building Material (CBM) derived from Croughton is quantified in Table 13 (below) and has been catalogued in the archive (ACBMG 2003, IFA 2001). The majority of the material is small and fragmentary, consistent with an assemblage produced by collapse of the main structures after abandonment, subsequently disturbed by robbing and ploughing. The material is mainly of 3rd-century date, from the comb patterns on the box flue tile and the painting and external decoration on some of the roof tiles recovered. There was a small amount of post-medieval material recovered from the fieldwalking in 1993 (Shaw and Auduoy 1993) (Table 13).

THE FABRICS

Ten fabrics were identified from the assemblage.

CRO01
A hard red fabric with an irregular to fine fracture, and sandy feel. Inclusions of common fine mica, common sub-angular quartz 0.1-0.2mm across, common angular 0.2mm black iron stone and sparse shell, up to 0.2mm across. Used for the production of brick, flue tile, *tegula* and *imbrex*.

CRO02
A hard red fabric with a grey core, a fine fracture and a sandy feel. It has inclusions of common mica less than 0.1mm across, moderate sub-angular 0.2mm quartz,

Table 13: The Ceramic Building Material (CBM) assemblage

Episode	Site Code	Wt (kg)	No	Cnr
Mosaic Excavation 1991	CRV91	8.454	77	4
NA Field Artefact Collection 1993		121.214	4577	20
EH 1993 & 1995 excavation of mosaic and 1995 trial trenches	CAS492	92.345	2210	9
NA excavation 2002	RMF02	121.575	880	128
Total		343.588	7744	161

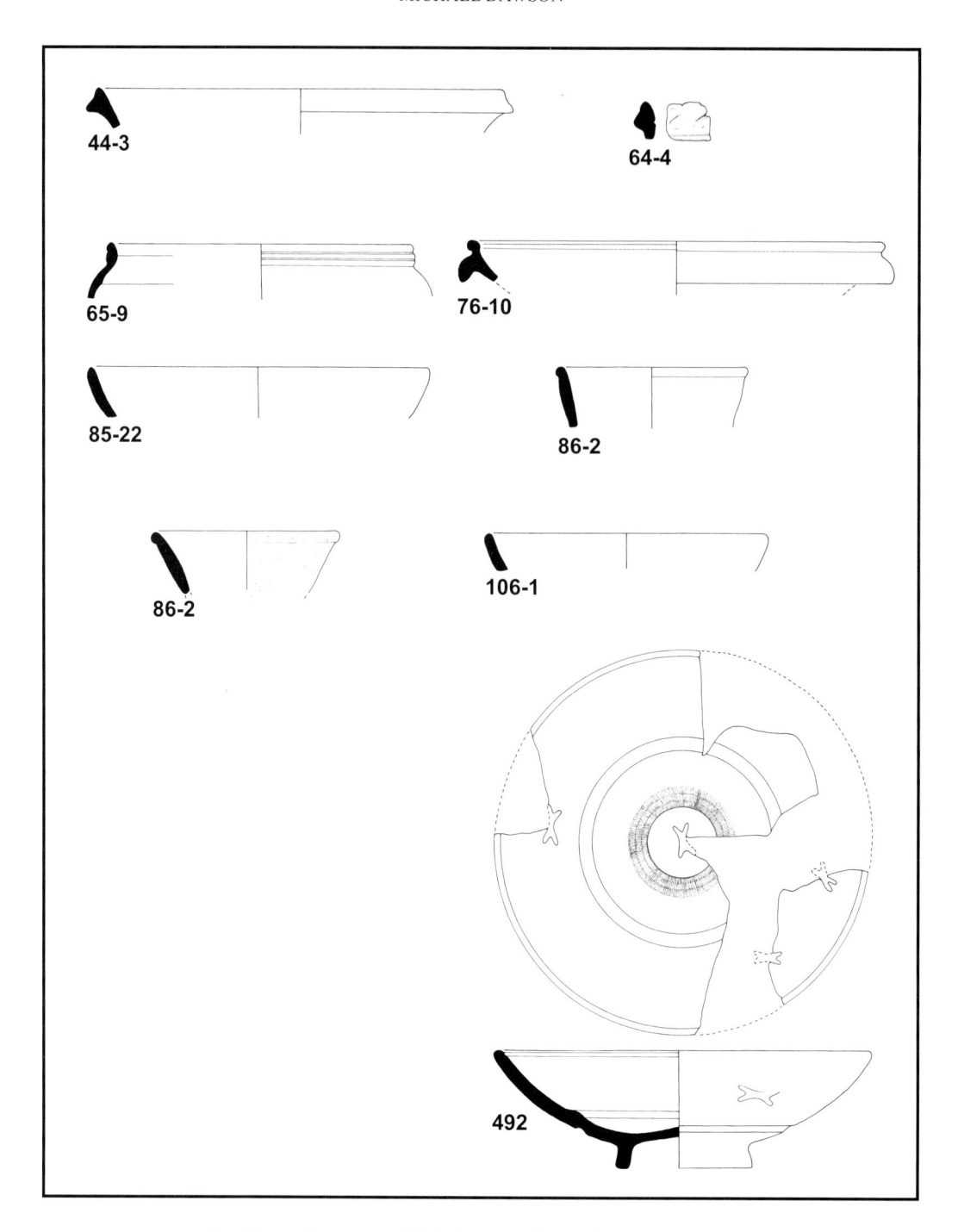

Fig 15 Previously unpublished forms of ceramics from Croughton

occasional sub-angular black ironstone, 0.3mm in size and moderate 0.1mm rounded calcareous material. Used for the production of brick, flue tile, *tegula*, *imbrex* and ridge tile.

CRO03
A red fabric with a grey core. It is hard, having a hackly fracture and harsh feel. It has inclusions of common organic voids, moderate quartz, 0.4mm, common rounded calcareous material 0.3mm, moderate sub rounded grog 0.3mm. This fabric is used for the production of brick, flue tile, tegula, imbrex and ridge tile.

CRO04
A pale variant of CRO02. Used for the production of brick, flue tile, tegula, imbrex and ridge tile.

CRO05
A variant of CRO01 having a slightly more irregular fracture. This fabric is used for the production of brick, flue tile, tegula, imbrex and ridge tile.

CRO06
Pale buff fabric, hard, has a fine fracture and a sandy feel. It has inclusions of common shell, common quartz, moderate mica and occasional flint. This fabric is used

for brick, imbrex and tegula. There is a flint tempered fabric manufactured at Piddington (Fabric 4B, Ward 1999, 12) dated to the 2nd century.

CRO07
This is a red variant of CRO01. There is one example of an imbrex.

CRO08
Pale buff fabric with a dark grey core. Contains abundant angular 3mm across calcite. Used for ridge tile and tegula. Similar to Piddington tile fabric 1A/B (Ward 1999, 12) which is probably manufactured in the 3rd - 4th centuries.

CRO09
This fabric is a pale variant of CRO03. It is used for imbrex and tegula.

CRO10
This fabric is dark red and grey. It is very hard with a fine fracture and sandy feel. It has inclusions of abundant mica and fine quartz and occasional calcareous material. A post-medieval fabric, used for bricks.

The fabric list suggests that there are five Roman groups of fabric utilised on the site: Calcite (CRO08), Lime (CRO02, CRO04) Flint (CRO06), grog (CRO03, CRO09) and shell (CRO01, CRO05, CRO07).

In addition to the possible parallels of flint and calcite-tempered mentioned above there is a wide variety of grog tempered tiles manufactured at Piddington villa from 2nd – 4th centuries (Ward 1999, 14-15). From Croughton there are two main groups, grog and shell-tempered, represented in the material.

FORMS

The forms identified from the settlement are summarised in Table 14. The majority of material was not classifiable and this is coded as 'B/T'. The majority of recognised forms comprised roofing tiles.

Roof tile

No complete examples of roof tiles were recovered. However, the following categories were defined:

Tegula had a thickness between 20mm and 35mm, with a variety of handmade and occasionally knife finished flange types. A number of *tegula* were observed to have nail holes in them. They were typically 7–10mm in diameter and round, having been made pre firing. One *tegula* still had a nail still attached to it. Cutaway types were recorded using the codes in Brodbribb (1987, 16).

Imbrex were identified in two main categories: type 1 which was c 11-15mm thick and type 2 which are 15-20mm thick.

Ridge tiles in Britain are similar to *imbrex*; only they tend to be thicker and less obviously tapered (Brodbribb 1986). In this catalogue, all curved tile with more than 21mm thickness are classified as ridge tile

It would be expected that the normal ratio of *tegula* to *imbrex* by weight would be c 3:1 for a roof. However, as *imbrex* tend to be more recognizable than *tegula* even for small fragments the pattern reflected here is what would be expected from collapsed roofed structures. The small quantity of ridge tiles is expected, as there would only be a few on each structure. There is no specialisation in fabric group by form type (Table 15).

Painted and decorated roof tile

A significant proportion of the roof tiles are decorated, either by paint or by external wavy line decoration, or a combination of these. The wavy line decoration was observed on a small amount of roof tile, usually near the end of a tile. These may have been used for keying in order to help mortar to grip slipped or painted tiles. The painted and decorated tiles were observed in the grog, lime and shell fabric groups. The proportion of painted tiles to the unpainted tiles by number of fragments suggests that the painted tile emanated from one roof. The number of painted tile types by fabric group does suggest that their may have been originally different supplies for the painted *imbrex* and *tegula*.

The painted tiles were treated in several different ways; a deep red slip or paint was coated on the finished tile; a white plaster or slip was coated onto the tile; the tile was covered in white slip or plaster and then red paint in the form of a coat or stripes painted over the white surface. Whilst recreating the original pattern of the roof is beyond the scope of this evidence, a number of suggestions can be made. A couple of examples of nail hole *tegula* had remains of the purple/red paint on them, which suggest that the lowest course of the roof was painted red. The red lines parallel to *tegula* flanges on the whitewashed *tegula* suggest that red painted imbrex were laid down white painted *tegula*. There seem to have been more red painted roof tiles than white painted ones, and a number

Table 14: The CBM forms by project and number of fragments

Form	CAS492	CRV91	CAS 492	RMFO2	Total
B/T	1319	16	2559	32	3926
Brick	5		56	67	128
Flue Tile	25	2	67	167	261
Imbrex	440	16	765	296	1517
Ridge Tile	26	8	32		66
Tegula	395	34	1096	318	1843
Tessera		1	2		3
Total	2210	77	4577	880	7744

Table 15: The amount of roof tile by number of fragments

[Bar chart showing Imbrex, Ridge Tile, and Tegula by Weight (Kg) and Number. Wt(Kg): Imbrex 94.6, Ridge Tile 6.8, Tegula 156. No: Imbrex 1517, Ridge Tile 66, Tegula 1843.]

of tiles had several coats, suggesting that a change in decoration occurred at some point on the roof.

Box flue tile

The box flue tile was mainly fragmentary, and had a thickness of *c* 15- 20mm. It was identified from the assemblage on the strength of the comb decorations. This style of keying is common on flue tiles manufactured in the 3rd-century AD (Ward 1999, 38).

Table 16: Box flue tile by Fabric group

Fabric Group	No	Wt (g)	Cnr
GROG	53	3305	
LIME	197	5248	1
SHELL	11	685	

Bricks

No complete bricks were identified from the assemblage. This is due to the difficulty in determining flat pieces of Roman brick from other forms such as *tegula* and flue tile. The main type of brick identified was a voussoir type – a tapered brick used for making arches. The other Roman bricks are probably from bricks used for flooring and the *pilae* stacks to support the floor.

Markings

Other kinds of marking observed on the material is summarised in Table 17. Signatures are marks made by the tile maker, usually on *tegula*. They are generally seen as a way of recording which tiler has made which batch in a situation where multiple tilers were working in the same location. Tally marks are possible numbers to mark the amount of tile in a pile. Animal prints are often noted on Roman CBM and are formed when animals walk on tiles which are left out to dry prior to firing.

Dating

The main form of dating for this assemblage comes from the box flue tile. The broad combing reflects a mid-3rd-century date (Ward 1999). The use of painted and decorated tile in the vicinity has been observed on mid-3rd-century structures (Ward 1999)

Formation process

The majority of this material was used primarily as roofing or hypocaust for the building. A small quantity of second hand material would also have been used as hardcore in parts of the structure as well as for other deposits close to or within the grounds of the villa. This material was allowed to collapse in its entirety through either abandonment or deliberate destruction. Subsequently material was disturbed by robbing and agricultural activities.

Spatial analysis

The majority of the material from the fieldwalking comprised unidentifiable fragments of CBM scattered around the entirety of the fieldwalked area, with a major concentration over the structures of all types and fabrics. The painted tile and ridge are concentrated in the centre of the scatter. The flue tile is concentrated on the west part of the scatter in terms of weight. The calcite tempered CBM is part of a small scatter in the north-west part of the concentration.

DISCUSSION

The material is consistent with having been produced from the mid-3rd century for a complex of buildings. The similarity of the grog-tempered tile to that manufactured and used at Piddington suggest a similar geological source. The lime and shell-tempered CBM would appear to come from another source. As there is no ready pattern

Table 17: Catalogue of marked tiles

Site	Cxt	Fabric	Wt (g)	No	Cnr	Type	Markings
CAS 492	1024	CRO02	78	1		Tegula	Cat Print?
CAS 492	1024	CRO02	1124	1		Tegula	Sig 2f
CAS 492	1024	CRO02	276	1		Tegula	scored line
CAS 492	1027	CRO03	321	3		Tegula	Sig 1f
CAS 492	1087	CRO02	41	1		Tegula	Sig
CAS 492	1091	CRO03	271	3		Tegula	Sig cl, pp
CAS 492	1092	CRO02	19	1		Tegula	Sig
CAS 492	108	CRO03	157	3		Tegula	Possible tally
RMFO2	1	CRO02	82	1		Tegula	Sig wl
RMFO2	1	CRO02	166	1	1	Tegula	Sig s
RMFO2	9	CRO03	282	1		Tegula	finger prints
RMFO2	16	CRO02	118	1		Tegula	Possible Sig
RMFO2	16	CRO03	1363	4		Brick	Sig cl
RMFO2	16	CRO04	235	1		Tegula	Sig s
RMFO2	17	CRO02	74	1		Tegula	Possible tally
RMFO2	17	CRO03	3463	7	1	Tegula	Sig s
RMFO2	17	CRO03	405	1		Tegula	cat print, pp
RMFO2	28	CRO02	2081	4	2	Tegula	Sig s, pp
RMFO2	28	CRO03	3175	10	3	Tegula	Sig cl, pp
RMFO2	37	CRO03	3591	13	2	Tegula	Sig cl
RMFO2	59	CRO02	66	1	1	Imbrex	tally
RMFO2	76	CRO04	671	1		Tegula	Sig s, pp

Codes: pp = purple paint; sig = signature; cl = curvilinear; S = S shaped; WL = wavy line; 1f = one finger signature; 2f = two finger signature

in the final distribution of these main fabric groups, it would suggest that both these sources were used at the same time for the different structures. The small quantity of flue tile and brick, indicative of a hypocaust structure, may be emanating from a single structure in the west of the complex. The majority of the hypocaust would be underground, so only the top parts are likely to have been disturbed during the post-abandonment activities on the site, hence the relatively small amount.

The painted roof tiles are concentrated at the centre of the complex, and probably relate to a single roof over the mosaic. The main roof was originally painted in red and white, although at some point a number of the white elements of the roof were painted over in red. The pattern was perhaps of a white roof with a red border and possibly with red vertical stripes.

The other structures would have been roofed in well-made orange to red roof tiles. In trying to reconstruct the phenomenology of the late Roman landscape, it is clear that these roofs would have occupied a dominant position. In terms of the surrounding topography they are clearly standing above the land to the south, where the height OD rapidly drops c 30m over 1km and still prominent to the north with the land rising c 5m over 1km. The roof may have been part of a 3rd-century attempt to dominate an existing landscape.

In terms of the wider cultural identity of the material, it has been observed that the painted and combing patterns of some of the roof tiles, as well as probable supply relates it to other sites in Northamptonshire. Unfortunately, given the present lack of retained and properly reported CBM collections from the Roman period comparisons are difficult. The paint and colour of roof tiles in 3rd-century Roman Britain may have been used in some communities as a marker of cultural identity. Whether this reflects resurgence in a confident indigenous community or the arrival of elites from elsewhere in the Roman world remains to be explored.

PLANT MACROFOSSILS
R Scaife

INTRODUCTION

Samples for plant macrofossil analysis were taken from the villa site during the excavations of English Heritage in 1995 and subsequently by Northamptonshire Archaeology in 2002 when total sampling was undertaken of the deposit above the mosaic. Further sampling of the remaining contexts was undertaken under the guidance of Dr J Williams, English Heritage Environmental Science Advisor. Material for analysis comprised processed and previously assessed material (de Rouffignac 1996); processed but unsorted material and, unprocessed bulk samples. The latter have been floated and examined as part of this study. A total of 22 samples from different stages of excavation have now been amalgamated and examined.

During the excavations carried out by English Heritage in 1995, a significant cache of charred grain was recovered which prompted a more comprehensive sampling regime. Samples obtained were taken largely from the excavation of the Bellerophon mosaic floor on which the grain rested and from overlying demolition deposits. The resulting plant remains, predominantly cereal grain, clearly offered potential for study of diet, crop cultivation and the economy of the villa site.

METHOD

Samples of 10 to 40 litres volume were taken from all of the principal contexts (10) and (9) excavated during the two phases of excavation and, especially where these exhibited obvious charred remains lying above the mosaic floor. Of the samples taken by English Heritage, samples of 10 litres were processed using buckets and overflow into sieve sizes of 1mm and 0.5mm. Samples taken from the later excavations by Northamptonshire Archaeology were stored until processing in 2004 using Siraf type flotation tanks by R. Bailey Archaeoservices. The flot was similarly collected in nested sieves down to 0.5u. This resulting flot was air dried. Residues were kept and examined for non-floating botanical and scanned for other archaeological material. Sorting, examination and identification of the plant remains was carried out using a Wild M3c low power binocular microscope (x6 - x40). Material obtained from flotation comprised largely cereal remains with some charcoal and mollusca but with surprisingly few seeds of associated arable weeds. All nomenclature follows that of Stace (1997) and Jacomet (1987). For the purposes of this study, and because of the substantial quantities of grain and its purity, a fraction only of the total quantities was identified and counted for those contexts/samples in which grain was most abundant. The weight of the total flot was measured and of the fractions which were examined. These data are given in Table 19 and allow some broad calculations to be made of total grain numbers.

THE DATA

After assessment of material obtained from the 1995 trenches, the necessity of a detailed sampling strategy in any further excavations was recognised (de Rouffignac 1996, 46). Subsequently, therefore, bulk samples were taken from all of the principal contexts recorded during excavations in 2002. These included the most interesting (10), a fine layer of black silty sediment containing most of the charred plant remains, and the coarser overlying demolition layer (9). Samples were taken from different areas of the mosaic and overlying deposits, as well as the topsoil, sample (9) 1 and a modern layer and fills of a hypocaust (29) 8 and (39) 18. The latter were particularly sparse in plant remains.

Samples from immediately on the mosaic floor, Context 10

Preliminary examination of three samples was carried out by Clare de Rouffignac from (1029) and (1031) excavated from Trench E in 1995. Of these, the former contained perhaps the richest grain samples from the site resting on the mosaic floor on the western side. A single sample (1031) from the fill of a cremation on the western side produced only a very small number of plant remains. The samples of de Rouffignac from (1029) comprised sub-samples of *c* 10 litres which were shown to be exceedingly rich in charred cereal remains and, from restricted sorting of the samples, produced in excess of 6000 cereal grains. De Rouffignac (1996, 45) also noted the presence of pest damage. This aspect has subsequently been re-examined by Dr. M. Robinson who has determined that this phenomenon is in fact a taphonomic/preservation process rather than from insect infestation (Robinson pers comm). For this study, a small proportion of the material previously examined was re-analysed to assess the proportions of grain of different taxa, and to identify the chaff remains (Table 19). This comprised samples 1 and 2 from context (1029), that is, the cache of grain which rested directly on the Bellerophon mosaic floor. In fact, the grain appears to be an almost pure crop of Triticum spelta L. (spelt wheat) with higher proportions of chaff from this grain than recovered from other, subsequently analysed, samples. De Rouffignac does, however, note a single grain of Hordeum sp. (barley) and a rachis fragment, clearly a very small proportion of the overall grain present. Re-examination of this important English Heritage sample 1 (1029) produced solely T. spelta, cf. Triticum spelta and some grain fragments, all of which are likely to be from the same taxon. Identification of grain to spelt and/or emmer wheat is usually only possible from chaff debris alone (the strongly nerved glume bases plus some spikelet forks) since the grain of these glume wheats is morphologically similar (Renfrew 1973). Here, the presence of the former is verified by the chaff remains which were most abundant in this sample. These comprised glumes and spikelet forks of T. spelta L. (Table 19). A single Triticum dicoccum (emmer) glume was also recovered and also confirms de Rouffignac's study who also noted a few similar occurrences. Clearly, however, this was not a major constituent of the crop and was probably from occasional growth as a 'weed' within the crop. More detailed measurements of the grain (spelt) size have been made (Table 18) below.

During excavations in 2002, further samples were taken from above the same mosaic floor on its southern and south-western edge (10). The overlying coarse demolition horizon (9) was also sampled, samples 1a, 1b, 4a, and 4b. Samples of 10 and 20 litres(6a, 6b) from the black silty deposits (10) overlying the mosaic, as expected produced similarly high numbers of almost pure spelt grain (T. spelta L.) being more abundant in samples 5, 6 and 7 (Table 19). Contrasting with the 1995 samples, the quantities of chaff were substantially smaller. Where present, however, these were again glumes and spikelet forks confirming that the grain comprises almost pure spelt. A small number of other grain types were recovered. These included Hordeum vulgare L. (barley) in sample 6 (10) and Avena sp./Bromus secalinus (oat and/ rye brome). In all samples, the number of seeds from non-cultivated crops is remarkably small clearly showing that the grain was at its final stages of processing prior to its grinding for flower.

The demolition layer (9)

Context (9) is a much coarser deposit, described as a demolition layer which seals the plant rich, context (10) overlying the mosaic. The demolition layer (9), (23) and (46): samples 1, 2, 4, 6, 7 and 20 also contained substantial quantities of charred cereal grain which again comprised almost solely spelt wheat. Grain was most abundant in samples 4, 6 and 7 from the south and south-west side of the mosaic and from (23) sample 2 from the north-east corner. Numbers/quantities of chaff remains were small in all samples with occasional glume bases which confirm the presence of spelt. These were most abundant in sample 5. Again, there were notably few weed seeds.

The abundance of these charred grain remains in these demolition deposits and especially in zones above context (10) suggests that mixing and incorporation of grain from the lower layer is likely to have occurred. Certainly, the grain constituents are the same, also suggesting this has occurred.

Other contexts

Although sampling concentrated on the charcoal rich layers overlying the mosaic floor, samples were also taken from the fills of hypocaust (29) and (39) and from pit features (12) and (42). All of these contained few charred remains comprising Triticum indet. and indeterminable grain fragments.

GRAIN MORPHOLOGY

The grain of spelt wheat has typical characteristics with generally flat ventral sides and a broad shape with blunt apices. A relatively small number (100) of cereal grains was examined in greater detail with measurements of length, breadth and thickness made. The following measurements (Table 18) were calculated from the 100 sample grains. Measurements were for maximum dimensions; length of grain; length of ventral surface at right-angles to length and thickness from ventral side to dorsal side.

Table 18: Dimensions of a sample of 100 grains of spelt (Triticum spelta L.)

Minimum length	4.34 mm
Average length	5.69 mm
Maximum length	6.72 mm
Maximum breadth	3.75 mm
Minimum breadth	2.49 mm
Average breadth	3.24 mm
Maximum thickness	3.10 mm
Minimum thickness	1.61 mm
Average thickness	2.55 mm
Ratio of breadth to length	1 to 1.76
Ratio of breadth to thickness	1 to 1.27

DISCUSSION

Overall, the charred plant remains recovered were almost solely of Spelt wheat (*Triticum spelta* L.) with the only special characteristics of this assemblage being the excellent state of preservation of much of the grain, its purity, that is, without much chaff debris or weed seed contaminants. Originally, damage by pest infestation was suggested by de Roufignac. Of 150 spelt grains examined, some 23% showed some degree of damage in the form of holes, pits and gullies. Dr. M. Robinson has, however, carried out a more detailed analysis of this aspect and now supports the idea that these features (damage) were caused during the charring process.

As noted above, the similar morphology of spelt and emmer wheat grain means that identification to species is not generally possible from grain alone and usually relies on the presence of chaff including glume bases and spikelet forks. Fortunately, the richest areas of grain found here, also contained a relatively small proportion of glumes and spikelet forks which verify that the assemblage is indeed of spelt rather than emmer wheat. Chaff debris (and other seeds) was, however, almost non-existent in other samples and overall, it is likely that cleaned grain was processed away from the site and stored for consumption at a later time.

The fact that this is a non-free threshing wheat that requires parching (heating in an oven) to release the grain prior to threshing and winnowing, means that its remains are more likely to be encountered through accidental burning. Here, however, the charring/burning seems to have occurred accidentally through a fire within the villa. Dr. Robinson has suggested the possibility that the grain may have been stored in the roof space and during the fire fell onto the mosaic floor. This may also explain the admixture within the overlying demolition layer (9).

The abundance of spelt here is very characteristic of most Romano-British grain assemblages because of the greater possibilities of accidental burning during parching. It is clear, however, that there was a predilection for spelt wheat during this period and the preceding Iron Age. This phenomenon has been widely discussed since the classic work of Jessen and Helbaek (1944) and Helbaek (1952). Such importance has subsequently been verified from many studies in southern and central England (eg Murphy 1977; Jones 1981; Green 1981; Scaife 1994, 2000a, 2000b). The principal reasons given for this increased importance of spelt which have been made include changes in taste preferences, increased production in response to increased population during the Iron Age (Murphy 1977, 245) and change to Autumn sowing due to the fact that this wheat was more suited to a cooler, wetter climate (Fowler 1984, 163). In addition, Jones (1981) has also suggested it may have been widely used in making porridge. Use in brewing has also been postulated because of sprouted ears which have frequently been recovered. It is also important to note that in the case of spelt, there is some evidence that this crop may have been harvested and transported as whole ears to its place of consumption and possibly stored until its use (Jones 1981). Thus, cropping may not, necessarily, have taken place near the site and, whilst it is more conceivable that this was, in fact, taking place locally, it must also be considered that cultivation was being practised on another farmstead. Thus, as suggested by Jones, there may be a distinction between producer and consumers with final processing for use taking place on the site of the latter. Here, the relative absence of chaff remains suggests that we are dealing with the very final stages of crop production and processing (post-threshing and winnowing) prior to grinding of the grain for flower at the villa. The demise of the crop through burning can, however, only be conjectured.

Table 19: Croughton plant macrofossils (continued below)

Sample No	CAS492 <1>	CAS492 <2>	CAS492	1a	1b	2	3	4a	4b	5
Context	1029	1029	1031	9	9	23	10	9	9	10
Feature Note	On Mosaic	On Mosaic	Cremation	Dem. Layer NW Corner	Dem. Layer NW Corner	Dem. Layer NE Corner	Above mosaic	Dem. Layer S. edge	Dem. Layer s. edge	Below (9) S. edge
Area										
Flot Weight (g)	56	280	10	9	3	5	25	40	38	82
Weight Anal. (litres)	5	20	10	9	3	5	25	10	9.5	10
Grain										
Triticum spelta L.	298	245	1	27	10	82	12	501	418	553
T.cf *spelta*	133	39		19	13	24	23		97	102
Triticum indet				5		6				
T. cf *aestivum* type						6			0 (1)	
Triticum sp.						6				
Avena/Bromus		1							1 (4)	5
Hordeum vulgare								1	0 (1)	
Indet grain	9	113	6	88	15					66
Grain fragments	36		9	34	16	84	31		273	341
Chaff										
gb *Triticum spelta* L.	58	20							3 (3)	2 (7)
gb T. cf *dicoccum*	1									
gb T. indet	9	1							0 (3)	0 (1)
sf T *spelta*	42	17								0 (3)
sf T indet	21									
awn frags.										0 (2)
Seeds										
Vicia/Lath				1	1					1
cf *Arabidopsis*										
Galium sp.			1							

86

Sample No	6a	6b	7a	7b	8	18	19	20a	20b	21	22
Context	10	10	10	10	29	39	25	46	46	12	42
Feature Note	Dem. Layer	Dem. Layer	Dem. Layer	Dem. Layer	Hypocaust Upper fill	Under dem. Subsoil	Mosaic Sand?	Dem Layer	De. Layer	Pit	Pit
Area	SW Corner	SW Corner	SW Corer	SW Corner				W. end	W. end	N. of Mosaic	N. of Mosaic
Flot Weight (g)	38	25	27	13	2	1	6	8	2	8	3
Weight Anal. (litres)	9.5	25	9	13	2	1	6	8	2	8	3
Grain											
Triticum spelta L.	313	143	115	54			43	8	5		4
T.cf *spelta*	208	146	101	22			6	10	2		
Triticum indet											
T. cf *aestivum* type					1			1			
Triticum sp.						1					
Avena/Bromus	4		2								
Hordeum vulgare	2	1									
Indet grain	158	46	30	27		2	16	9	4		4
Grain fragments			74	30		2		9	3		9
Chaff											
gb *Triticum spelta* L.		1		1	1	1					
gb T. cf *dicoccum*											
gb T. indet											
sf T spelta	1			2							
sf T indet				1							
awn frags.	1 (1)										
Seeds											
Vicia/Lath	2 (1)							1			
cf *Arabidopsis*											1
Galium sp.											

Whilst the importance of spelt wheat is evident, there is, nevertheless some evidence for other crop types including *Hordeum vulgare* (barley), *Avena* sp. (oat). The presence of these indicated cultivation and use of these crops but, however, their small numbers may relate to the lesser likelihood of their being preserved due to accidental burning. It is possible that they were inclusions as weeds of the spelt crop and also, the fact that only a small number of different, and obviously rich contexts, were sampled.

DISCUSSION

THE NATURAL ENVIRONMENT

The meagre dating evidence from the early stages of the Roman settlement at Croughton may indicate an origin in the late 2nd century AD, while the single La Tène II spearhead found in the primary fill of a ditch hints at earlier activity in the area. The physical environment at the end of the Iron Age in the Croughton area has not been studied in detail but elsewhere in the region, further north at Wollaston and in the Raunds area, the landscape had been largely cleared of tree cover in the late Bronze Age. Not far from Rowler Manor the ring ditch (NSMR7286) may be sited in a prominent location to take advantage of the cleared landscape. Areas of grazing and cultivation varied in size, but at Crick weed seeds associated with large scale cultivation, rather than garden-type agriculture have been noted (Monckton 2006, 270). Nearby a watching brief on a new grain store at Rowler Manor noted only a very shallow soil above cornbrash on the ridge to the east of the villa, where the absence of data such as tree throws or boundary ditches may hint at the possible location of grazed clearings (Dawson 2001).

EARLY SETTLEMENT

The area of settlement at Croughton in the 2nd century AD may represent a concentration of activity and a shift in the late prehistoric pattern. The latter is evident from a series of cropmark enclosures close to Plomers Firs Farm in the east (NSMR 90) and in the west towards Charlton (NSMR 159, 158), their morphology perhaps an indication of dispersed small scale farming communities. Typically these are occupied from the middle to late Iron Age and are characterised by roundhouses, stock and garden enclosures in a landscape of tree stands and open areas. Whether these farmsteads are occupied over several centuries or a much shorter time, perhaps a matter of few generations, has yet to be confirmed either by ceramic, artefactual or scientific dating.

Coin evidence from the watching brief, not far from the water pipe trench, and ceramics from the trial trenching suggest the earliest settlement at Croughton is in the central and northern part of the area (Fig 2). The dating, ceramics of late 2nd-century date, AD 170 and the small coin hoard deposited between AD 161 and 200, suggests an origin in the late 2nd century. The character of the excavated evidence seems to indicate a combination of post-built and stone-founded structures within or surrounded by ditched enclosures, whilst the geophysical survey and trial trenching has revealed polygonal enclosures which may indicate a settlement form similar to those at Standlake or Appleford in the Upper Thames valley. The dating evidence and the site layout appears to show the settlement grew progressively from the earlier part in the north to include areas to the west and the east by the 4th century, with the villa occupied until the 6th century. The complexity of the geophysics suggests that the settlement layout may have remained stable within a broadly rectangular framework of enclosures on the northern side of the Rowler Brook, with later expansion onto the southern bank.

The character of the settlement at Croughton is firmly agricultural with evidence for iron smithing, crop processing and to a limited extent animal husbandry through the small animal bone assemblage. Together with the enclosures, evident from the geophysics, the settlement may have practised a mixed agriculture of stock rearing and some garden cultivation in the early period and perhaps further afield cereal cropping. There is no evidence to date of the dominance of one form of cultivation and the local soil type today supports both stock rearing and winter cereals.

THE VILLA BUILDING

The villa building in which the Bellerophon and another figured mosaic were located was sited in a prominent position above Rowler Brook to the east. The site, which was previously unoccupied, was clearly chosen to take advantage of the view across the shallow valley to the east and south-west towards what is now Croughton village. Rowler Manor is one of four villa sites along the higher ground above the River Cherwell including Chipping Warden, Thenford and Fringford. An underlying developmental model for this pattern emphasises the origins of villa estates in land controlled by late Iron Age family groups who were able to expand areas of cultivation to exploit the market offered by incorporation into the Roman Empire (Hingley 1990, 122). More emphatically Smith has argued that kin groups were able to combine resources to exploit larger areas and, thereby, gain the economies of scale, which allowed them to achieve the sort of economic growth that permitted the construction of villa type buildings (Smith 1997, 278). The latter model lays emphasis on social change, suggesting architecture became the principal means of status display replacing the retention of a retinue during the first years of the Roman conquest. In addition to economic growth Smith also noted the potential benefits implicit in office holding by one or more members of the kin group, which in turn could have provided the economic basis for the construction of a villa (Smith 1997, 279). Neither model fits comfortably with the evidence from Rowler where the settlement developed without antecedent in the later 2nd century, creating a settlement form which is familiar from several recent excavations, in particular at Water End East, Bedfordshire, and Scotland Farm, Cambridgeshire (Timby *et al* 2007; Abrams 2008). Both these sites and the date of settlement at Rowler hint at the potential for shift in the settlement pattern, perhaps

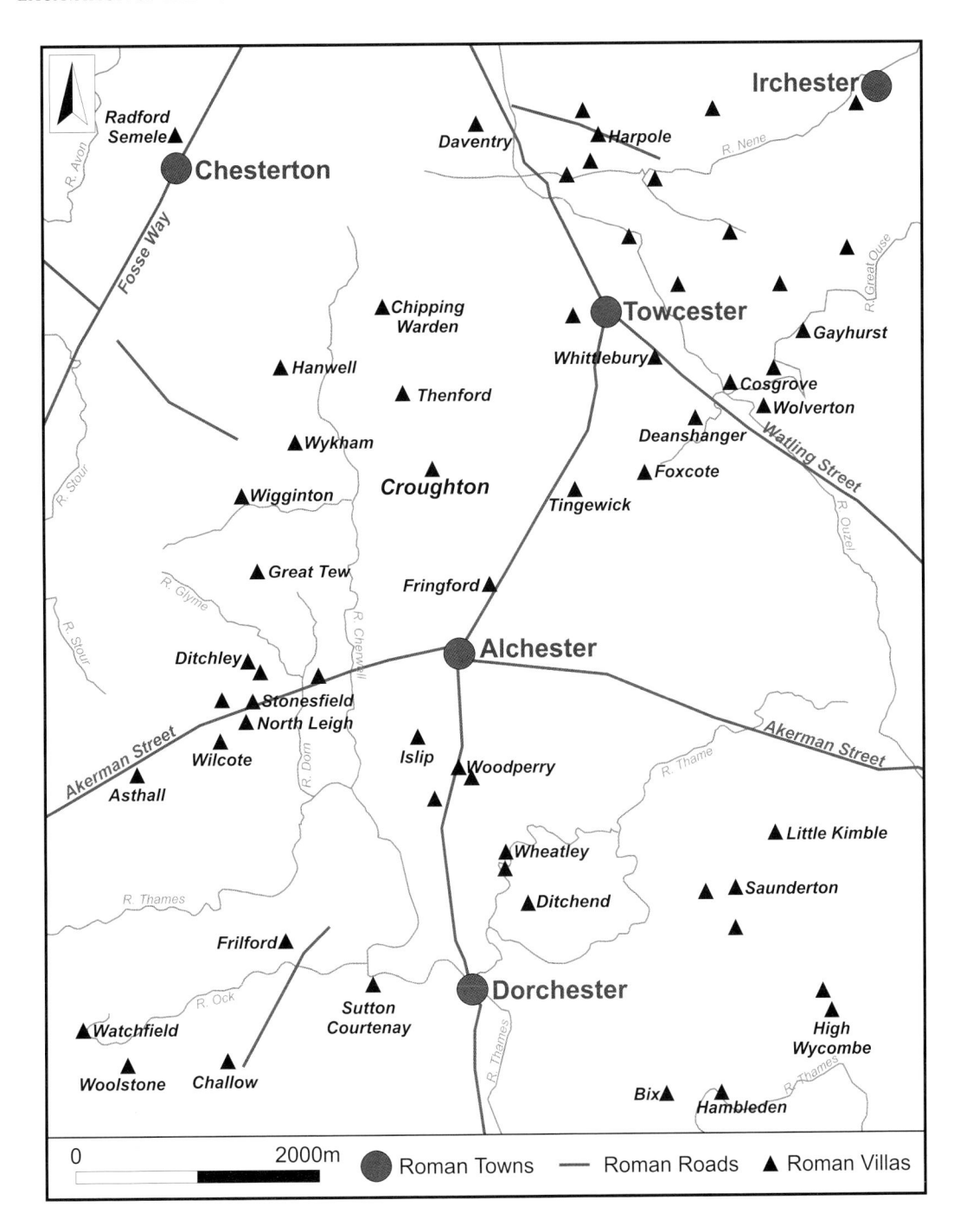

Fig 16 The Roman landscape of Rowler Manor and Croughton

even a period of enclosure and nucleation when the ladder type settlement provided the basis for economic growth. A further factor is the distribution of villas along the River Cherwell. There is no sense of this group, or others in the region, clustering around a potential market at Alchester. Instead the regularity of villas set back but along the higher ground above the River Cherwell seems to imply that there is no specific benefit in proximity to urban centres or even the strategic road system.

The evidence from Rowler is a slim base on which to build a model of settlement practice. Initially perhaps it was a planned complex based on a rectangular land allotment in the late 2nd century, it developed its own internal hierarchy which included other substantial dwellings, but by the 4th century its most significant building, the villa with the mosaics, was located on a pristine site above the local steam and spring. If the distribution of the other villas above the Cherwell is indicative of land holding the villa stood at the apex of a large estate (Fig 16).

The form of the villa may be that of a row type house, with the long axis aligned north to south. The layout of the rooms and the repair to walls [26]/[45] suggest later additions to the original design. The house was stone built probably with some architectural embellishment in the form of worked tufa, but it has been extensively robbed in antiquity.

RITUAL AND STATUS

The status of the villa at Rowler can be gauged in both social and economic terms. The latter is evident from the use of coinage, the mosaic decoration and hypocaust, the stature of the building with tiled roof and satellite farms or dwellings. Located at the core of an estate its wealth may have derived either directly from estate produce and/or indirectly from tribute. Wealth may also have flowed to the estate due to the status of the occupant suggested by the crossbow brooch and late Roman buckle fragment. Both of which are indicators of status and rank.

Models developed around the status of an individual suggest a kin group may be attracted to that individual. This process may lead to the agglomeration of settlement as kin move away from smaller more isolated farms to a more centralised settlement. In some examples symmetrical building plans for the villas themselves have been proposed as the basis for shared occupancy (Smith 1997, 292). At Rowler the pattern of building is more dispersed and alternative factors may have attracted settlement. Perhaps the most potentially significant factor is the combination of high status objects such as the buckle and crossbow brooch terminal together with at least two mosaics. Both the analysis of the mosaic and the coins have suggested the character of the villa in the late 4th century may have been religious, in particular, it may have been Christian. The stone table fragment has also been interpreted in this light (sf 100).

The coinage suggests a similarity between the assemblage at Rowler and the temples at Lamyatt, Nettleton and Uley, and the villas at Gatcombe and Lullingstone (Meates 1979, 73). The latter is particularly associated with Christianity following the discovery of a Chi-Rho monogram painted onto the plaster walls of a room in which there was a Bellerophon mosaic. Similarly the Chi-Rho is associated with the Bellerophon mosaic from Hinton St Mary (Toynbee 1964, 7-14). Although there is no Chi-Rho at Rowler, the presence of high status artefacts, the Bellerophon motif and similarities between the coin assemblage and other religious sites seems to indicate a religious centre which became a house church in the late 4th century. That it may have continued in use, possibly for worship, into the 6th century is suggested by the presence of a late bead from the necklace lost on the mosaic floor.

THE END OF ROWLER

The demise of the villa at Rowler may have occurred as late as the 6th century AD, dated by the appearance of a glass bead in the burnt deposit above the Bellerophon mosaic. The circumstances, however, are far from clear. The deposit above the mosaic (10) which contained a large quantity of charred grain, Scaife has suggested, may have been derived from grain stored in the roof or floor above. It may have been deposited during the fire which destroyed the villa and mixed in with the collapsing remains of the structure. The nails and iron fragments noted by Hylton may relate to timbers burnt in the conflagration, although there is no evidence of significant quantities of charcoal lodged above the pavement. Nor is there evidence of molten glass from broken windows, although there is a small quantity of fused lead. The fire, therefore, may have been limited to the roof but no less final in the life of the building. Neal has suggested the presence of mortar on some parts of the mosaic indicates it was either never completed, postulating that the fire may have occurred during the final construction of the building or during restoration. In either context the bead is problematic and may suggest that the building continued to function into the 6th century before the fire. Subsequently the remains may have stood derelict until the site was finally robbed during the late Saxon period, evident from the appearance of St Neots ware amongst the demolition materials.

BIBLIOGRAPHY

Abbreviations

ACBMG	Archaeological ceramic building materials group
AML	Ancient Monuments Laboratory
B/T	brick or tile
CAS	Central Archaeology Service, English Heritage
CBM	Ceramic Building Material
CK	Carson, R A G, Hill, P V, and Kent, J P C, 1960 *Late Roman Bronze Coinage, AD 324-498*, Part II: AD 346-498, London
EH	English Heritage
HK	Carson, R A G, Hill, P V, and Kent, J P C, 1960 *Late Roman Bronze Coinage, AD 324-498*, Part I: AD 324-346, London
IFA	Institute of Field Archaeologists
NA	Northamptonshire Archaeology
NSMR	Northamptonshire Sites and Monuments Record
RIC	Mattingly, H, and Sydenham, E, (eds) *Roman Imperial Coinage*, Vols **I** (1923) to **X** (1994)

Abrams, J, 2008 *Farming on the edge: Archaeological Evidence from the Clay Uplands West of Cambridge*, East Anglian Archaeol, **123**

ACBMG 2003 *Ceramic building material: minimum standards for recovery, curation, analysis and publication* (http://www tegula freeserve co uk/acbmg/CBMGDE3 htm. Accessed 21/06/03)

Allen, J R L, and Fulford, M G, 1996 The distribution of south-east Dorset Black Burnished category I pottery in south-west Britain, *Britannia*, **27**, 223–281

Andrews, D P, Beckett, M, Clowes, M, and Tovey, S M, 2005 A comparison of rectified photography and orthophotography as applied to Historic Floors – with particular reference to Croughton Roman Villa, *CIPA XX International Symposium Turin, Italy* (http://cipa.icomos.org)

Audouy, M, 1993 Excavations at Berry Hill Close, Culworth, *Northamptonshire Archaeol*, **25**, 47-62

Barker, P, White, R, Pretty, K, Bird, H, and Corbishley, M, 1997 *Excavations at the Baths Basilica, Wroxeter, 1966-90*, English Heritage Report, **8**, 269-318

Beeson, A, 1996 Pegasus the wonder horse and his portrayal on Romano-British mosaics, *Mosaic*, **23**, 18-23

Bird, J, Graham, A H, Sheldon, H, and Townend, P, (eds) 1978 *Southwark Excavations 1972-4*, Southwark and Lambeth Archaeol Excavation Comm, Joint Publication **1**, London and Middlesex Archaeol Soc/Surrey Archaeol Soc, 533-586

Blore, F, 1993 Work Undertaken at Croughton Roman settlement, Northamptonshire, CAS Project **492**, English Heritage

Blore, F, 1996 *Croughton Evaluation report A report on the Archaeological evaluation undertaken at Croughton Roman Settlement, Northamptonshire*, CAS Project, **492**, English Heritage

Booth, P M, Evans, J, and Hiller, J, 2001 *Excavations in the extramural settlement of Roman Alchester, Oxfordshire, 1991*, Oxford Archaeol Monog, **1**, Oxford

Booth, P M, and Green, S, 1989 The nature and distribution of certain pink, grog tempered vessels, *Journal of Roman Pottery Studies*, **2**, 77-84

Brailsford, J W, 1962 *Hod Hill, Volume One, Antiquities from Hod Hill in the Durden Collection*, Trustees of the British Museum, London

Branigan, K, 1977 *Gatcombe: the excavation and study of a Romano-British villa estate, 1967-1976*, British Archaeology Reports, British Series **44**, Oxford

Brodribb, A C C, 1987 *Roman Brick and tile*, Academic Press London

Brodribb, A C C, Hands, A R, and Walker, D R, 1973 *Excavations at Shakenoak Farm, Near Wilcote, Oxfordshire Part IV:Site C*, Oxford

Brown, A E, and Woodfield, C, 1983 Excavations at Towcester, Northamptonshire: The Alchester Road Suburb, *Northamptonshire Archaeol*, **18**, 43-140

Bush-Fox, J P, 1949 *Fourth Report on the Excavations of the Roman Fort at Richborough, Kent*, Oxford: Oxford University Press

Carson, R A G, Hill, P V, and Kent, J P C, 1960 *Late Roman Bronze Coinage, AD 324-498, Part I: AD 324-346*, London: Spink

Carson, R A G, Hill, P V, and Kent, J P C, 1960 *Late Roman Bronze Coinage, AD 324-498, Part II: AD 346-498*, London: Spink

Clarke, G, 1979 *The Roman Cemetery at Lankhills, part II, Winchester Studies 3, Pre-Roman and Roman Winchester*, Oxford: Clarendon Press

Cool, H, 1993 The Copper Alloy and Silver Grave Goods, in D E Farwell and T L Molleson 1993, 89ff

Cooper, N, (ed) 2006 *The archaeology of the East Midlands: an archaeological resources assessment and research agenda*, University Leicester Press Monog, **13**

Cowan, C, 2003 *Urban Development in north-west Roman Southwark, Excavations 1974-90*, MoLAS Monog, **16**, 135-9

Crummy, N, 1983 *The Roman small finds from excavations in Colchester*, Colchester Archaeological Reports, **2**

Cunliffe, B W, 1971 *Excavations at Fishbourne, Volume II: The Finds*, Society of Antiquaries Research Report

Cunliffe, B W, 1984 *Danebury: An Iron Age Hillfort in Hampshire, Volume 2, The excavations 1969-1978: the finds*, Council for British Archaeology, Research Report, **52**

Cunliffe, B W, 1991 *Danebury: An Iron Age Hillfort in Hampshire, Volume 5 The excavations 1979-1988; the finds*, Council for British Archaeology, Research Report, **73**

Cunliffe, B, and Poole, C, 1991 Objects of Iron, in B Cunliffe 1991, fig 7 18, 352

Curteis, M, 2003 Coin List, in M Dawson 2003b

David, A, and Payne, A, 1993 *Croughton near Brackley, Northamptonshire, Site of Roman mosaic find. Interim Report on Geophysical Surveys 1992-3*, Ancient Monuments Lab, Report **15/93**, English Heritage

Dawson, M, 2000a *Iron Age and Roman settlement on the Stagsden Bypass*, Bedfordshire Archaeological Monog, **3**

Dawson, M, 2000b *Prehistoric, Roman and post-Roman landscapes of the Great Ouse Valley*, Council for British Archaeology, Research Report, **119**

Dawson, M, 2001 *Archaeology Desk Based Assessment and Geophysical Survey, New Grain Store Site, Rowler Farm, Northamptonshire*, Unpublished Samuel Rose Report, Dec 2001

Dawson, M, 2003a *Heritage Conservation and Management Plan, Roman Settlement Croughton, Northamptonshire*, Unpublished CgMs Report

Dawson, M, 2003b *Rowler Manor Estate Post Fieldwork Assessment of the Croughton Roman Settlement*, Unpublished CgMs Report

Ekwall, E, 1980 *The Concise Oxford Dictionary of English Place-names*, Oxford: Clarendon Press

Ellis, P, Hughes, G, Leach, P, Mould, C, and Sterenberg, J, 1998 *Excavations alongside Roman Ermine Street, Cambridgeshire, 1996*, British Archaeol Reports British Series, **232**, Oxford

Evans, E, 2000 *Caerleon – canabae: excavation in the civil settlement 1984-90*, Roman Society Monog, **16**, London

Farwell, D E, and Molleson, T L, 1993 *Excavations at Poundbury 1966-80, Volume II: The Cemeteries*, Dorset Natural History and Archaeol Soc Monog, **11**

Fell, C, 1936 The Hunsbury Hillfort, *The Archaeol Journal*, **43**, 57-100

Fowler, P J, 1981 *The Farming of Prehistoric Britain*, Cambridge University Press

French, C A I, 1994 *The archaeology along the A605 Elton-Haddon Bypass, Cambridgeshire*, Fenland Archaeol Trust Monog, **2**

Frere, S, 1972 *Verulamiam Excavations, Vol 1 [Insula XIV]*, Society of Antiquaries Research Report, **28**

Fulford, M G, 1984 *Silchester Defences 1974-80*, Sutton and The Society for the Promotion of Roman Studies, Gloucester

Fulford, M G, 1984 The Roman Pottery, in M G Fulford 1984, 122-195

Galloway, P, 1979 Combs, in G Clarke 1979, 246-248

Galloway, P, 1993 Bone Combs, in D E Farwell and T L Molleson 1993,108-10

Green, F J, 1981 Iron Age, Roman and Saxon crops: the archaeological evidence from Wessex, in M Jones and G W Dimbleby 1981, 129-153

Guido, M, 1999 *The Glass Beads of Anglo-Saxon England c.AD 400-700*, London and Woodbridge

Hancocks, A, Evans, J, and Woodward, A, 1998 The prehistoric and Roman pottery, in P Ellis et al 1998, 232

Hawkes, S C, and Dunning, G C, 1961 Soldiers and Settlers in Britain, Fourth to Fifth Century, *Medieval Archaeol*, **5**, 1-70

Helbaek, H, 1952 Early crops in southern England, *Proceedings of the Prehistoric Soc*, **18**,194-233

Henderson, A M, 1949 Small Objects in Metal, Bone, Glass, etc, in J P Bush-Fox 1949, 106ff

Henig, M, 1997 The Lullingstone mosaic: art, religion and letters in a fourth-century villa, *Mosaic*, **24**, 4-7

Hill, J D, 1995 *Ritual and Rubbish in the Iron Age of Wessex*, British Archaeological Reports, British Series **242**

Hingley, R, 1990 Iron Age 'Currency Bars': The Archaeological and Social Context, *Archaeological Journal*, **147**, 91-117

Howe, M D, Perrin, J R, and MacKreth, D F, 1980 *Roman Pottery from the Nene Valley: a Guide*, Peterborough City Museum Occasional Paper, **2**

Hunter, R, and Mynard, D, 1977 Excavations of a Roman settlement at Thorplands near Northampton, 1970 and 1974, *Northamptonshire Archaeol*, **12**, 97-154

Hutcheson, A R J, 1997 Iron Age or Roman? Ironwork hoards in Roman Britain, in K Meadows et al 1997, 65-72

Hylton, T, and Zeepvat, R J, 1994 Objects of Copper Alloy, Silver and Gold, in R J Williams and R J Zeepvat 1994, 303-321

IFA 2001 *Standards and guidance for the collection, documentation, conservation and research of archaeological materials*, Institute of Field Archaeologists, Reading

Jackson, R P J, and Potter, T W, 1996 *Excavations at Stonea, Cambridgeshire 1980-85*, British Museum Press

Jacomet, S, 1987 *Prahistorische Getreiefunde Eine Anleitung zur Bestimmung prahistorischer Gerstenund Weizen-Fund*, Botanisches Institut der Universitat Abteilung Pflanzensystematik und Geobotanik, Basel

Jessen, K, and Helbaek, H, 1944 Cereals in Great Britain and Ireland in prehistoric and early historic times, *Det Kongelige Danske Videnskabernes Selskab Biologistie Skrifter,* **3** (**2**) Copenhagen

Johns, C, 1996 Bracelets, in R P J Jackson and T W Potter 1996, 334

Johns, C, 1998 *Roman Iconography: A brief Introductory Guide,* British Museum Press, London

Jones M, 1981 The development of crop husbandry, in M Jones and G W Dimbleby, 1981, 95-127

Jones, M, and Dimbleby, G W, 1981 *The environment of man: the Iron Age to the Anglo-Saxon period*, British Archaeological Reports, British Series, **87**, Oxford

Keller, E, 1971 Die Spätrömischen Grabfunde in Südbayern, *Münchener Beiträge zur Vor-und Frühgeschichte,* **14**, Munich

Lambrick, G, 1980 Excavations in Park Street, Towcester, *Northamptonshire Archaeol,* **15**, 35-118

Lloyd-Morgan, G, 2000 Other jewellery and dress accessories in gold, silver and copper alloy, in E Evans 2000, 328-344

Manning, W H, 1985 *Catalogue of the Romano-British Iron tools, fittings and weapons in the British Museum,* British Museum, London

Manning, W H, 1976 *Catalogue of Romano-British Ironwork in the Museum of Antiquities, Newcastle upon Tyne,* Dept of Archaeology, University of Newcastle upon Tyne

Marney, P T, 1989 *Roman and Belgic Pottery from Excavations in Milton Keynes 1972-82*, Buckinghamshire Archaeol Soc Monog, **2**

Marsh, G, and Tyers, P, 1978 The Roman pottery from Southwark, in J Bird *et al* (eds) 1978, 533-586

Meadows, K, Lemke C, and Heron, J, 1997 *Sixth Theoretical Roman Archaeology Conference*, 65-72, Oxbow, Oxford

Meates, G W, 1979 *The Roman Villa at Lullingstone, Kent Vol 1 The site*, Kent Archaeology Society

Monckton, A, 2006 Environmental archaeology in the East Midlands, in N Cooper (ed) 2006, 259-86

Murphy, P L, 1977 *Early Agriculture and environment on the Hampshire chalklands: circa 800 B C - 400 AD,* M Phil thesis of University of Southampton

Neal, D S, and Cosh, S R, 2002 *Roman Mosaics of Britain Vol I Northern Britain incorporating the Midlands and East Anglia*, Illuminata Publishers, London

NA 1995 *Roman settlement at Rowler Farm, Croughton, Northamptonshire Stages 1 and 2 Fieldwork and Desk Based Study*, Northamptonshire Archaeology report

Oakley, G, 1977 The Small Finds, in R Hunter and D Mynard 1977, 133-43

Perrin, J R, 1999 Roman Pottery from Excavations at and near to the Roman Small Town of Durobrivae, Water Newton, Cambridgeshire, 1956-58, *Journal of Roman Pottery Studies,* **8**

Reece, R, 1995 Site-finds in Roman Britain, *Britannia,* **26**, 179-206

Rees, S E, 1979 *Agricultural Implements in prehistoric and Roman Britain*, British Archaeological Reports, British Series, **69** (**ii**), Oxford

Renfrew, J M, 1973 *Palaeoethnobotany, The prehistoric food plants of the Near East and Europe (Studies in prehistory)*, Methuen, London

RN5535/004, 1991 SMR/Archive Report, Cadman G E, Northamptonshire County Council

de Rouffignac, C, 1996 A Summary Assessment of the Environmental Material from the 1995 Evaluation at Croughton Roman Settlement, in F Blore 1996, 41- 48

Scaife, R G, 1994 The plant remains, in C A I French 1994, 154-167

Scaife, R G, 2000a The charred botanical remains, in M Dawson 2000, 107-116

Scaife, R G, 2000b The prehistoric vegetation and environment of the River Ouse Valley, in M Dawson (ed) 2000b, 17-26

Sellwood, L, 1984 Objects of Iron, in B Cunliffe 1984, fig 7 19, 361

Shaw, M, 1979 Romano-British Pottery Kilns on Camp Hill, Northampton, *Northamptonshire Archaeol,* **14**, 17-30

Shaw, M, and Auduoy, M, 1993 *Roman settlement at Rowler Farm, Croughton, Northamptonshire Fieldwalking: Stage 1,* Northamptonshire Archaeology report [Superceded by NA 1995]

Smith, J T, 1997 *Roman Villas: A study in Social Structure,* Routledge, London

Solley, T W J, 1979 Romano-British side tables and chip carving, *Britannia,* **10**, 169-78

Sparey-Green, C, 2002 Excavations on the south-eastern defences and extramural settlement of Little Chester, Derby 1971-2, *Derbyshire Archaeol Journal,* **122**, 154-95

Stace, C, 1997 *New flora of the British Isles,* Cambridge University Press

Symonds, R P, 1980 The coarse ware and other fine wares, in G Lambrick, 1980, 79-98

Symonds, R P, 1997 The Roman pottery, in P Barker *et al* 1997, 269-318

Symonds, R P, 2002 The Roman coarse wares, in C Sparey-Green 2002, 154-95

Symonds, R P, and Wade, S M, 1999 *The Roman Pottery from Excavations at Colchester, 1971-1985*, Colchester Archaeol Report, **10**

Symonds, R P, (ed) 1999 *Recording Roman pottery: a description of the methodology used at Museum of London Specialist Services (MoLSS) and Museum of London Archaeology Service (MoLAS)*, an unpublished guide

Symonds, R P and Rauxloh, P, 2003 A ceramic case-study comparing the data contained in the spot-date files and quantified data from selected contexts at the study area, in C Cowan, 2003, 135-9

Timby, J, Brown, R, Hardy, A, Leech, S, Poole, C, and Webley, L, 2007 *Archaeology along the Great Barford Bypass,* Bedfordshire Archaeol Monog, **8**, Oxfordshire Archaeology

Tomber, R, 1989 Fabric 2: Soft Pink Grogged Ware Thin-Section Analysis, in P T Marney 1989, 67-9

Toynbee, J M C, 1964 *A new Roman mosaic pavement found in Dorset*, Journal of the Roman Society, **54**, 7-14

Tyrrell, R, 1991 *Painted wall plaster from Croughton, nr Brackley,* NSMR

Vouga, P, 1923 *La Tène: Monographie de la Station Publiée au Nom de la Commission des Fouilles de La Tène*, Leipzig: Karl W Hiersemann

Ward, C, 1999 *Iron Age and Roman Piddington: The Roman ceramic and stone building materials 1979 – 1998*, Fascicule **4**, Upper Nene Archaeological Society

Waugh, H, and Goodburn, R, 1972 The Non-ferrous Objects, in S Frere 1972, 114-145

Wheeler, R E M, 1943 *Maiden Castle, Dorset,* Society of Antiquaries Research Report, London

White, R, 1997 Summary of fieldwork carried out by the Wroxeter Hinterland Project, 1994-7, *Shropshire History and Archaeology*, **72**, 1-8

Williams, R J, and Zeepvat, R J, 1994 *Bancroft: A Late Bronze Age/Iron Age Settlement Roman Villa and Temple Mausoleum*, Buckinghamshire Archaeol Soc Monog, **7**

Williams, R J, 1994 Tufa, in R J Williams and R J Zeepvat 1994, 241

Wilmott, T, 2001 *Croughton Roman settlement, Northamptonshire An Evaluation Report on Unauthorised Works*, English Heritage Project **662**, 2001

Windell, D, 1984 Irchester Roman Town: Excavations 1981-1982, *Northamptonshire Archaeol*, **19**, 31-51

Woodfield, C, 1983 The Remainder of the Pottery, in A E Brown and C Woodfield 1983, 74-100 and figs 18-32; 1-272

Young, C J, 1977 *Oxfordshire Roman Pottery*, British Archaeological Reports, British Series, **43**, Oxford

Archaeological recording of a Roman Villa at Brigstock Road, Stanion, Northamptonshire April – May 2002

by

MARTIN TINGLE

with contributions by
Gill Campbell, Greg Campbell, Wendy Carruthers, Andy Chapman, Hillary Cool,
Mark Curteis, Karen Deighton, Tora Hylton, Graeme Lawson, Paul Linford, Donald Mackreth,
Paul Middleton, Margaret Powell and Roy Friendship-Taylor

SUMMARY

In the course of topsoil stripping prior to the construction of a composting facility, part of a Roman villa was unexpectedly revealed, together with ancillary structures. A pond-like feature beneath the excavated part of the villa contained dumped occupation debris, including carbonised plant remains, dating to the later first century AD, and indicating the presence of occupation on the site from at least this time, while pottery from quarry pits to the north, excavated in 1984, may suggest an origin as early as the mid-first century AD.

The main villa building was constructed in the later first century AD. The excavated remains comprised the westernmost room of a villa building aligned west to east, and at least 30-35m long, with a corridor along the northern side, perhaps forming an open veranda. The excavated and aerial photographic evidence would suggest a simple plan form, with the main strip building perhaps comprising some five domestic rooms. There were remnants of tessellated pavements in both the corridor and the excavated room, and displaced smaller tesserae from the room may suggest the presence of a small central mosaic. Fragments of painted wall plaster also came from this room. Amongst the ceramic building material from the demolition rubble there is a small amount of box-flue tile suggesting the presence of at least one room with a hypocaust heating system. A corn drier or malting oven lay to the west of the villa, along with a small oven that incorporated the base of an amphora. In this area there was also a stone-lined well, and its fills contained sherds of amphora, partially articulated cow skeletons and the skeleton of a raven.

In the late second or early third century the building was abandoned. Deposits of burnt debris lying on the scorched surface of the tessellated pavement probably relate to the systematic dismantling of the building, as accumulations of burning debris. Very small quantities of fourth-century pottery indicate that there was some later activity in the vicinity of the villa.

INTRODUCTION

THE DEVELOPMENT

On the 4th April 2002 a site examination was carried out at Brigstock Road, Stanion on a site where topsoil had been stripped from an area of approximately 0.75ha, prior to the site being levelled for the construction of a composting facility (NGR SP 9235 8687, Fig 1). The examination was carried out by the author in order to fulfil the terms of a brief issued by the Northamptonshire County Council Historic Environment Team, which had specified that an inspection was primarily concerned with the potential for the recovery of any evidence of medieval pottery production of Lyveden/Stanion wares.

In fact, at the eastern end of the site, the removal of the topsoil had exposed the remains of part of a Roman villa and further associated structures. Following the discovery of the villa remains, a site meeting was held between the developer and the Northamptonshire County Council Archaeological Planning Officer, to examine whether there was any scope for a 'preservation by-design' solution. Unfortunately, relocation within the immediate vicinity of the proposed site was restricted by the proximity of a sewage treatment plant to the west, problems with access roads to the east, the proximity of a water course to the south and a major road to the north. Relocation to another site in the area was considered impossible because covenants on the surrounding land restricted it to agricultural use. Re-design of the composting facility on the site would have required the importation of substantial quantities of inert material (as the important archaeological remains were located on the highest part of the sloping site).

Consequently, Northamptonshire County Council provided funding for a team from Northamptonshire Archaeology to work with the author to determine the extent of the preserved remains so that an informed decision concerning future action could be made. The ground plan of the building was defined, although at its southern end plough-truncation had reduced the remains to foundation level with no survival of internal horizontal stratigraphy (Fig 2). At the northern end however, it was estimated that floor surfaces were sealed by 300-500mm

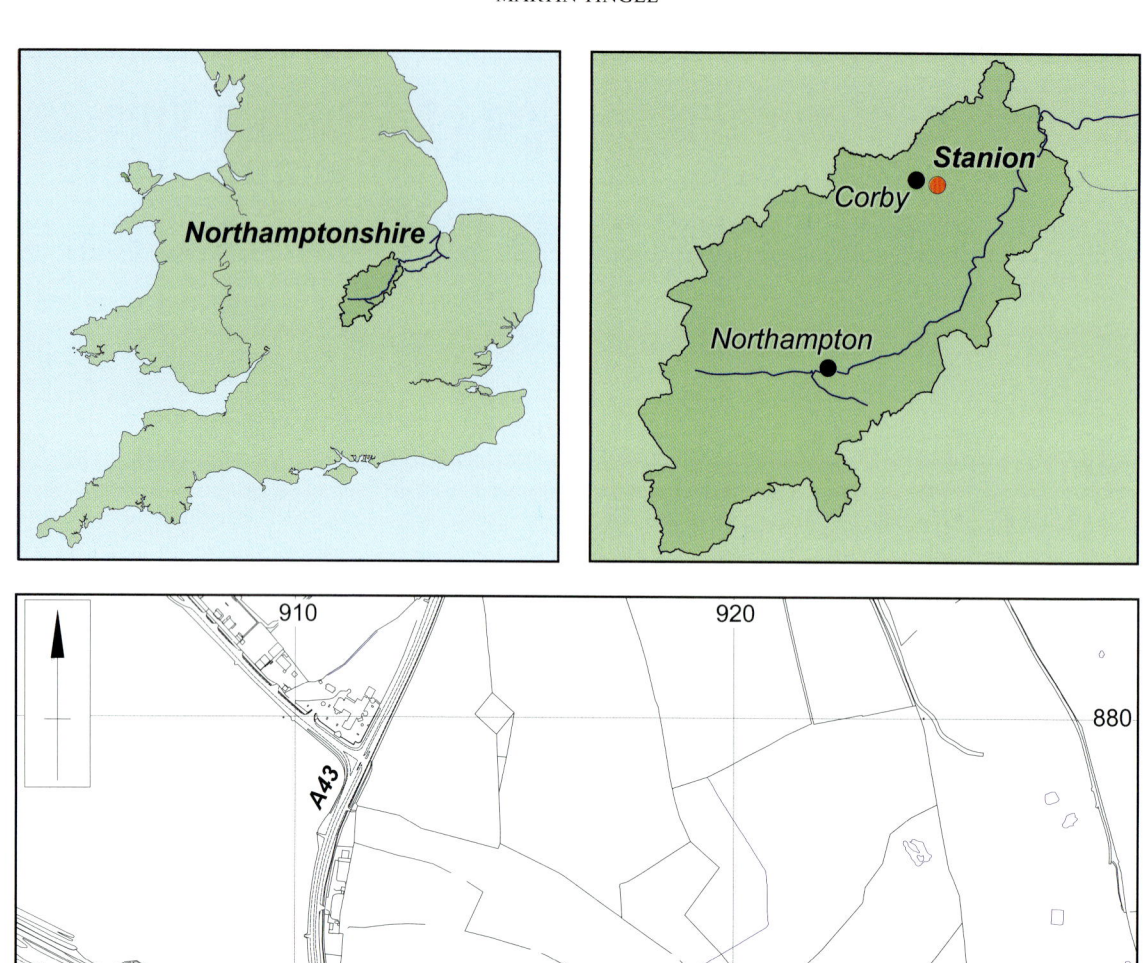

Fig 1 General location plan

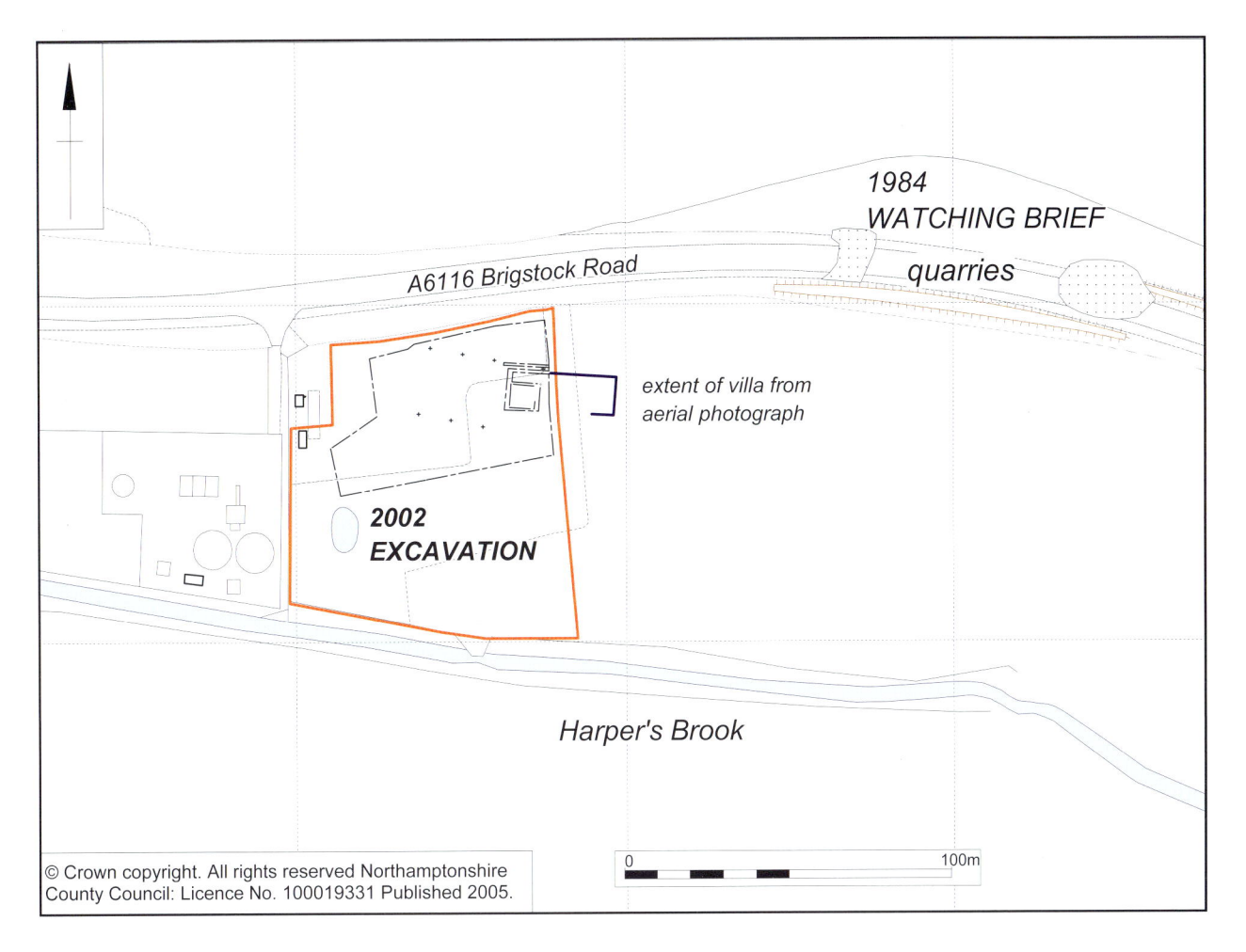

Fig 2 Location of excavated areas and Roman villa

of intact deposits. Two areas of *in situ* tessellated floor were found, as well as fragments of painted wall plaster.

Northamptonshire Archaeology carried out a Geophysical survey within the development and also in an adjoining area, over the presumed location of the undisturbed building. Unfortunately, due to adverse soil conditions, no useful data was revealed. Following on from this work, English Heritage agreed to fund a salvage excavation of the threatened area, concentrating on the known building and the corn drier. The excavation was carried out jointly by Northamptonshire Archaeology, with Rob Atkins carrying out the site recording, and the Northamptonshire Archaeological Society, with the author supervising a group of volunteer society members.

ACKNOWLEDGEMENTS

The author would like to thank the owner of the site, Mr Lawrie Baker, for delaying development and allowing the excavation to take place, although he was under no statutory obligation to do so. He would also like to thank the members of the excavation team from Northamptonshire Archaeology, working under the supervision of Rob Atkins, and the members of the Northamptonshire Archaeological Society and Middle Nene Archaeological Group (MIDNAG) who worked with them, especially Gill Johnston and John Hadman. Thanks are also due to Bob Kings for the initial metal detecting of the site and to Steve Critchley for subsequent detecting, coin identification and geological information.

The author also owes a debt of gratitude to Pat Foster for supplying the plans, slides and the pottery from the 1984 watching brief which added vital information to this report. Thanks are also due to Northamptonshire County Council and English Heritage for funding the work. Finally, the author would like to express thanks to Myk Flitcroft and the other members of the NCC Historic Environment Team (HET), who promptly arranged funding for an initial examination of the site and liaised with English Heritage so that the excavation could proceed.

Since the excavation took place the post of county planning archaeologist has been cut and Myk has moved on to CgMs Consulting Ltd, while the rest of the HET have been dispersed within the County Council. It can only be hoped that when (and it is only a matter of time) the next major archaeological discovery comes to light in similar circumstances there will be someone in the planning department with the responsibility and resources to act as Myk and the HET were able to do.

In post-excavation the project manager for Northamp-

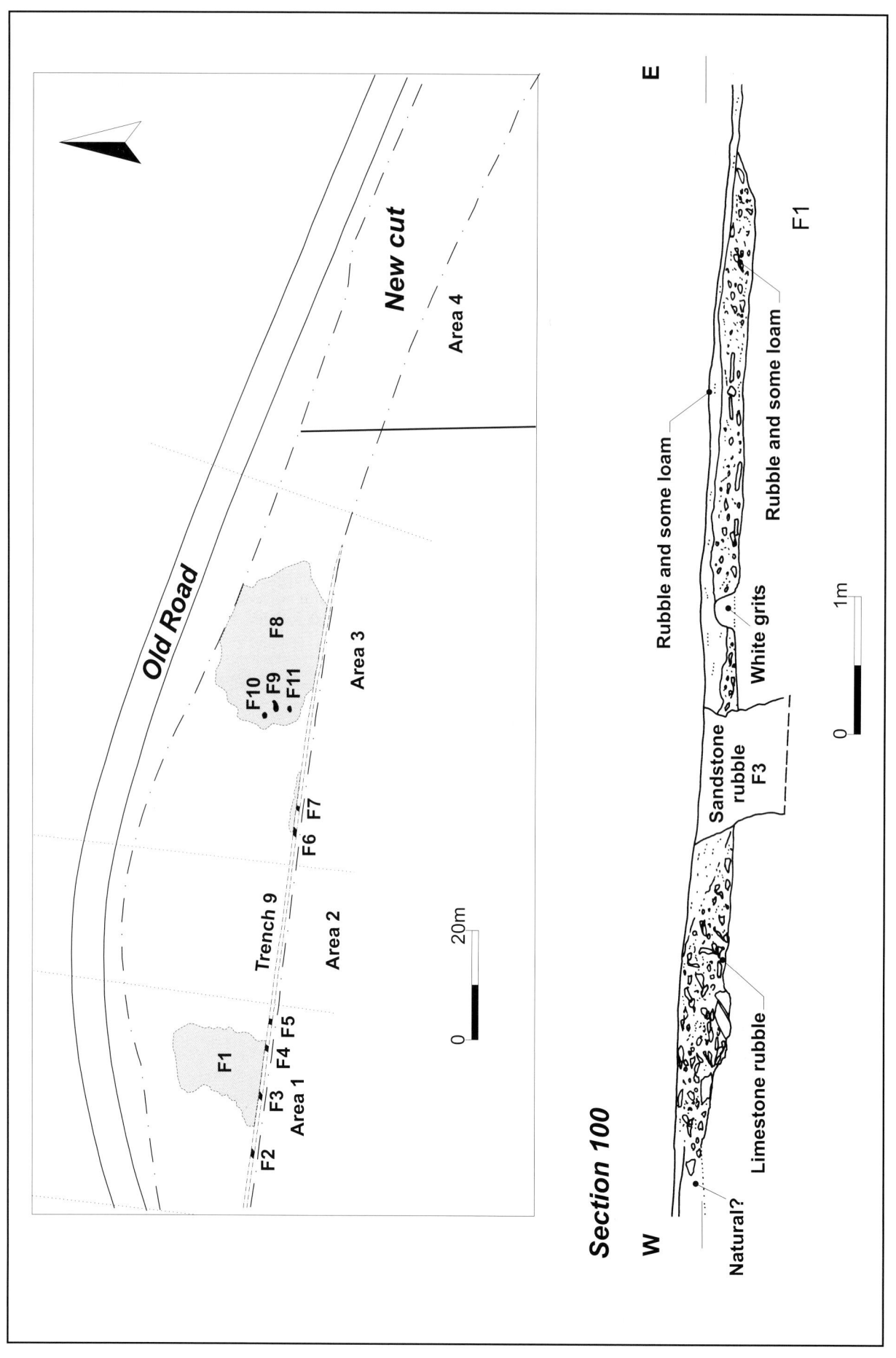

Fig 3 The 1984 salvage excavations

tonshire Archaeology was Tony Walsh. The illustrations were prepared by Pat Walsh, LeeAnne Whitelaw and Jacqueline Harding, and the text has been edited by Tony Walsh and Andy Chapman in line with refereeing comments provided by English Heritage, with Helen Keeley acting as project manager.

TOPOGRAPHY AND GEOLOGY

The site is located adjacent to the A6116 Brigstock Road approximately 1km north-east of the village of Stanion in north-east Northamptonshire. It is on a south facing slope above the Harper's Brook at between 60m to 70m AOD.

The underlying natural geology of the area mainly comprises rocks belonging to the Lias and Inferior Oolite Groups of Middle Jurassic age. Harper's Brook is floored by alluvium covered mudstone of the Whitby Mudstone Formation (formerly known as the Upper Lias), above which and exposed in the banks of the brook are the sandy ironstones of the Northampton Sand Formation (formerly known as the Northampton Sand Ironstone). This in turn is overlain by the Grantham Formation (formerly the Lower Estuarine Series), a succession of laminated clays, silts and sands. Exposures of the Grantham Formation are noted to the west of the villa buildings, which are founded on an apparently unmapped outcrop of course grained, fossiliferous, yellow-brown limestone of the Lincolnshire Limestone Formation. It is likely that there is a faulted junction between the two Formations.

PREVIOUS ROMAN FINDS

PUBLISHED SOURCES

Roman activity at Stanion was first mentioned by John Morton in his *Natural History of Northamptonshire* which described how Roman coins were found in 'Stanion field betwixt the town and the wood' (Morton 1712). The entry for Stanion in Whellan's Directory of 1874 states that 'In Willow Spring Close, near the village, were found some Roman Pavements, some years since' (Whellan 1874, 809). The RCHME (1979, 135) suggests that the find spot may be related to Willow Lane, a street within Stanion.

A survey of historic maps held in the Northamptonshire records Office did not reveal any significant information about the site or indicate the location of 'Willow Spring Close'. The Enclosure Map (NRO 2856) for Stanion dates from 1802 and lists field names surrounding the village which include 'Willow Lane Close' immediately to the south and 'Spring Close' to the north-west. The field in which the site is located is not named, although it appears on an estate map of 1639 (NRO 2991/6) as part of 'Neather Feilde'

Ordnance survey maps from the first edition to the present, show the field in which the villa was found marked with a cross and the appellation 'Roman remains found here 1840'. This is mentioned in the Royal Commission volume, although the precise location of the site is unclear (RCHME 1979, 135). Approximately 200m to the north-east of the site there is another cross recording a coin hoard, also found in 1840. Perhaps because these finds were not precisely located by the Royal Commission, neither appeared on the Northamptonshire SMR in 2002.

During the 1950s there were sporadic reports in the journal of the Northamptonshire Architectural and Archaeological Society describing finds of Roman pottery from an area approximately 300m north of the site which was then part of a modern ironstone quarry (RCHME 1975, 135).

SITES AND MONUMENTS RECORD (SMR)

In the original site assessment carried out prior to the development, an SMR plot revealed indistinct cropmarks approximately 400m south of the site and the known and probable course of a Roman road, which appeared to pass approximately 100m east of the site. The SMR finds record (SMR No 6166/0/1) also noted evidence of Roman iron working, 125m to the north-west of the site (in fact, the finds were located along a stretch of road works and the nearest were approximately 75m from the site and less than 50m from the known extent of the buildings). This had been revealed in 1984 when a watching brief was carried out by Pat Foster, Dennis Jackson and Gill Johnston during road improvements on the A6116 between Stanion and Brigstock. A 400m section of the road works was examined which revealed at least two shallow oval quarry pits, dug into the local Northamptonshire Ironstone (Fig 3, plan, section 100; Fig 4). Both were approximately 30m across and approximately 0.5m deep. As well as the quarry pits,

Fig 4 Watching Brief 1984, quarry pit 3 in section

several other features were noted, including a ditch that was recorded in section, associated with finds of amphora and slag (Fig 3, F3, section 100).

The quarry pits had been backfilled with sandstone *(sic)* rubble as well as slag, ash, mortar and wall plaster and pottery dating from the late first and second centuries. Samian from the pits suggested that while they were open in the second half of the first century they may have been backfilled over a period of a century. The only datable find from the pits was a Hod Hill type brooch that was unlikely to have been manufactured later than AD 60-65.

On completion of the rescue work it was intended that a site report was to be written and placed in the Northamptonshire Archaeological Archive, held at Northampton Museum (Dix 1985, 151). Unfortunately this did not occur, so that much of the above information was derived from unpublished sources and communications with those who worked at the site

Two aerial photographs (NCC Photo Number 9286/033 & 9286/034) (Fig 5) taken in 1996 and held in the SMR archive, show a complex of buildings at the location of the exposed villa. On the reverse of the photographs a possible interpretation of 'WWII Building' is suggested. The photographs indicate buildings that cover approximately 1500 square metres, composed of a rectangular building measuring approximately 10m by 30m which lies wholly outside the excavated area, linked by a substantial wall to the excavated building. It is not clear whether this is the rear wall of another building or the enclosing wall of a courtyard.

Had the Ordnance Survey data, together with details of the unpublished watching brief of the 1984 road scheme been entered on the SMR, this may have led to a different interpretation of the aerial photographs and thus alerted archaeologists within the planning authority to the archaeological potential of the site

THE ARCHAEOLOGICAL EVIDENCE

METHODOLOGY

Due to the limited period that was available, the excavation initially concentrated on defining the ground plan of the villa building, which lay at the eastern end of the stripped area (Fig 6 and Fig 7). Beyond the building, excavation was limited to the small number of prominent cut features, which included a corn drier/malting oven and an amphora-lined oven. In the same area a stone-lined well was uncovered during further machine stripping following the completion of the excavations.

In order to determine the structural sequence of the building, a series of 1.0m wide transects were cut across it and adjacent to one wall, revealing evidence not only

Fig 5 Aerial photograph 1996, looking east

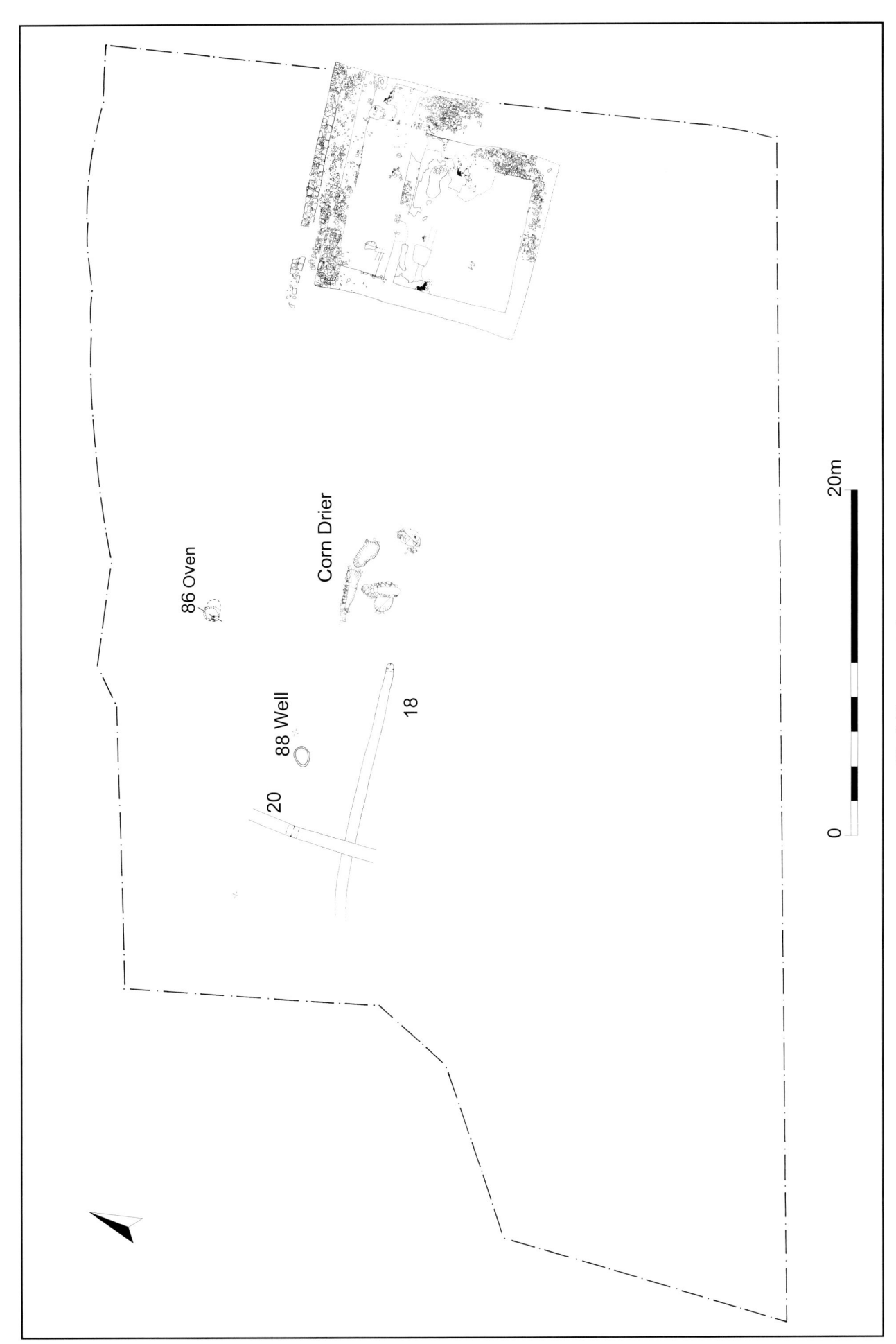

Fig 6 The excavated area

Fig 7 Stanion Villa, after initial cleaning, looking south

for the construction of the building but also the nature of the activity that had preceded it (Fig 8 and Fig 9). However, there was insufficient time to fully explore all the deposits related to the building and the pre-building levels and the significance of some contexts remains uncertain.

Environmental sampling was undertaken following the advice of various specialists, and areas of apparently *in situ* burning on the tessellated floors and within the corn drying oven were sampled for archaeo-magnetic dating.

PHASE 1: PRE-BUILDING DEPOSITS (MID TO LATE 1ST CENTURY AD)

The earliest contexts at the site comprised some lengths of gully and a backfilled hollow, perhaps a former small pond, which predated the construction of the excavated part of the villa building, and may have predated the construction of the entire stone-built villa, although this cannot be demonstrated. The presence of quantities of dumped domestic debris in the pond suggests that there was an episode of clearance, perhaps related to the demolition of a timber precursor to the stone-built villa.

THE GULLIES

In a small area to the east of the excavated room and south of the corridor there were short lengths of shallow gullies running on both roughly north-south and east-west alignments (Fig 8, 65 and 75; Fig 16, Section 8). A further length of gully lay 2.0m to the north, on the margin of the pond and sealed beneath a later cobbled surface, 60. The gullies were 0.70m wide by around 0.30m deep, and on alignments that have no relation to the later building, suggesting that there was a fundamental reorganisation of the building arrangements at the end of the first century AD.

THE POND

Beneath the villa building there was a broad hollow with shallowly sloping sides. As it was only investigated in the series of 1.0m wide transects its plan form was not fully defined, but it may have run on a south-west to north-east alignment, lying beneath the excavated room and extending under the eastern end of the northern corridor (Fig 8). It may have had an irregular plan form and was up to 5.0m wide and 0.9m deep. The primary fill was green brown sand, the colour perhaps suggesting the presence of cess or some other strong organics (Fig 10, Section 9, 66). Above this there were deposits of dark grey brown sandy clay (Fig 10, Section 9, 55, and Section 16, 82). These fills were all rich in charcoal, including charred grain, and dumped occupation debris that included pottery, animal bone and oyster shells. It is uncertain to what extent this represents a slow accumulation of dumped occupation material, or whether it may represent a single episode of backfilling and dumping closely preceding the construction of the villa building. If it was the product of a site clearance, the absence of larger pieces of stone would suggest that it was associated with timber rather than stone buildings.

The soils filling the pond also produced quantities of charred plant remains. Much of this seems to derive from crop processing waste, and spelt appears to have been the principle cereal, along with Bread-type wheat, hulled barley, peas, Celtic beans and probably oats. There were no imported exotic fruits and spices, but the native hedgerows are represented by hazelnut shell fragments and an elderberry seed.

To the east the fills of the pond were overlain by a layer of limestone cobbles (Fig 8, 60). These may represent an attempt to consolidate the area prior to building, with a further soil layer accumulating or being deposited above the cobbles (Fig 10, Section 16, 76).

PHASE 2: THE CONSTRUCTION OF THE BUILDING (LATE 1ST CENTURY AD)

The construction of the building took place during the late first or early second century AD, most probably as part of the provision of the first stone-built house on the site. Aerial photographs (Fig 5) indicate that the excavated part was the westernmost 12.5m of a simple rectangular building some 30-35m long. The excavated part comprised a single square room, with a corridor to the north.

The walls had been heavily robbed so that in places, particularly to the south and west, most of the stonework had been lost and the wall line was only denoted by a shallow deposit of mortar and small stones from 1.0 to 1.4m wide (Fig 8: 5, 7 and 13), which clearly did not indicate the actual width of the standing walls. However,

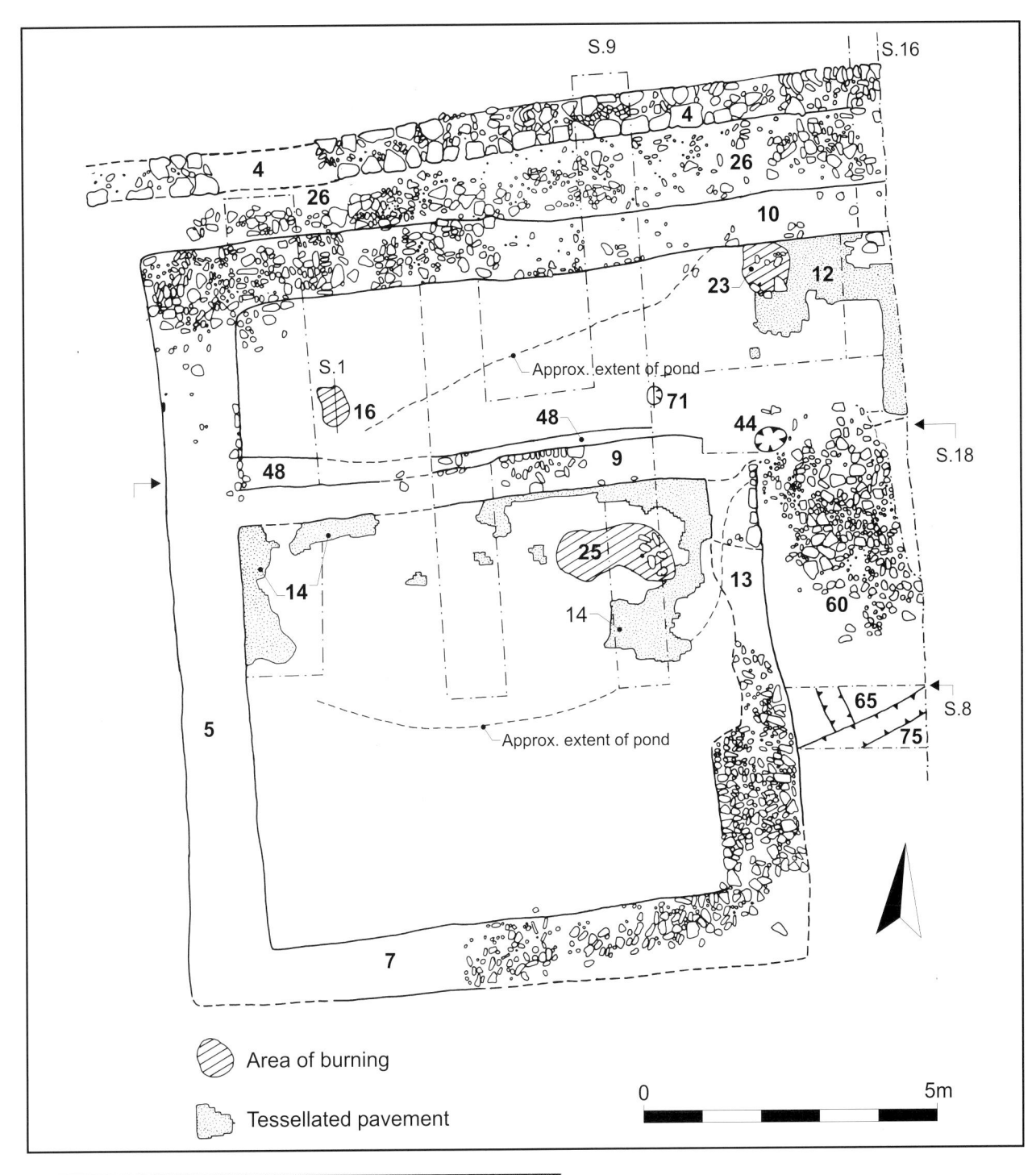

ARCHAEOLOGICAL RECORDING OF A ROMAN VILLA AT BRIGSTOCK ROAD, STANION, NORTHANTS., APRIL–MAY 2002

Fig 8 The excavated west wing of the Roman villa

Fig 9 Stanion Villa, after excavation of section transects, looking south

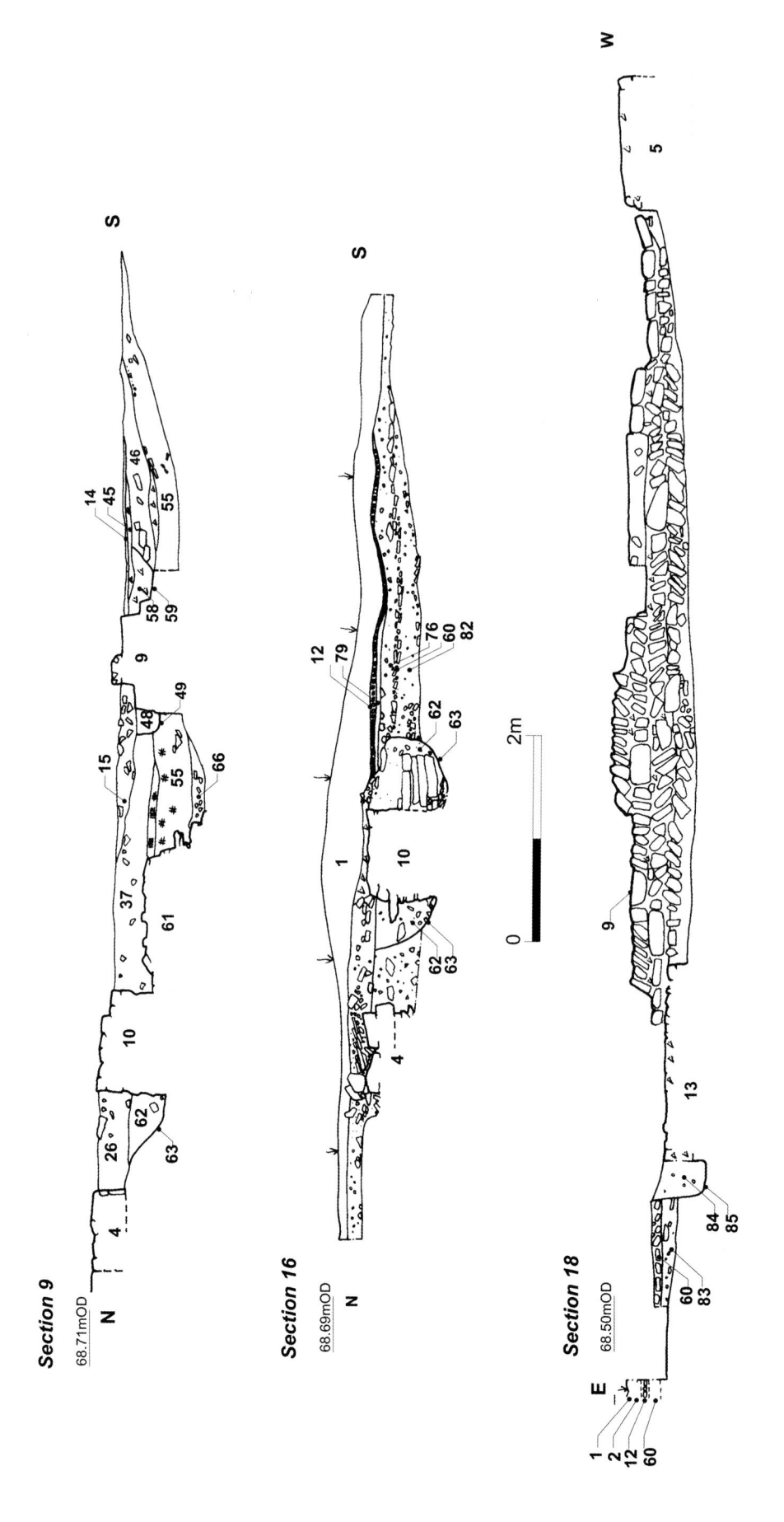

Fig 10 Sections across the villa building

where the walls crossed the soft fills of the pond it had been necessary to provide more substantial foundations. Much of the wall, 9, between the room and the corridor, and the eastern end of the northern wall, 10, had been built within the fills of the pond. For the northern wall a broad construction trench, up to 2.0m wide by up to 0.9m deep, had been cut through the pond silts so that the wall could be founded on the solid bedrock beneath (Fig 10, Sections 9 and 16, 63). The wall, 9, separating the room and the corridor appeared to be set against the northern side of a narrower construction trench, up to 1.6m wide (Fig 10, Section 9, 59).

The wall foundations themselves were 0.9-1.0m wide, 10 and 9, comprising four courses of wall foundations, up to 0.9m deep, formed from large fragments of limestone steeply pitched and bonded with a soft mortar, with the pitching alternating with each course, as seen in the exposed elevation (Fig 10, Section 18, 9). The construction trench had been backfilled, 62 and 58, with a mixture of soil, discarded smaller fragments of limestone and some mortar. Abutting the northern face of wall 9, there was a steep-sided flat bottomed slot (Fig 10, Section 9, 49), up to 0.5m wide by 0.4m deep, that was filled with clean yellow brown mortar containing a few small pieces of limestone. Its function is unknown, unless it was related to the provision of a wall rendering along the southern side of the corridor, which would support the suggestion that this had formed an open veranda.

A further length of wall lay only 0.8-1.2m to the north of the building (Fig 8, 4). This was a ground laid wall, 0.7m wide and standing up to 0.3m high, comprising three courses of flat laid limestone wall facings with a core of smaller limestone. To the east there was a length of pitched stone wall foundation. The relationship of this wall to the building is unclear. To the west remnants of the wall continued beyond the end of the building before all traces were lost to later truncation. Between this wall and the building there was a fill of soil and stones, 26, which was capped with flat-laid limestone that may have been remnants of a stone surface. An intact poppy-headed beaker had been deposited just beneath this surface (Fig 11 and see Fig 17, 1).

Wall 4 may therefore have served as a revetment to a stone surface fronting the veranda, but if this was its primary function it may be questioned why there was a good inner facing, rather than merely a revetment wall with an external face.

PHASE 3: THE OCCUPATION OF THE BUILDING (LATE 1ST TO LATE 2ND /EARLY 3RD CENTURY AD)

The exposed part of the building was 12.5m long by 12.5m wide. The corridor was 3.0m wide and may be presumed to have run the full length of the building. To the east, over the earlier pond fills, an area of plain tessellated pavement had survived (Fig 8, 12). The pavement was laid on a 10mm thick base of clean yellow mortar (Fig 10, Section 16, 79), and comprised large crudely cut sandstone tesserae, 30mm square by 25m deep, pale yellow in colour, which closely resemble pieces used in the Weldon villa (Smith *et al* 1988-9, 39).

At the eastern end of the corridor no evidence for a southern wall survived, which would have been an eastward continuation of wall 9. However, the straight southern edge of the tessellated pavement in the corridor lay adjacent to where the wall face should have lain. This area lay just beyond the pond and would not have required the deep foundations that lay to the west. In addition, there was a substantial post-pit (Fig 8, 44), 0.45m in diameter by 0.65m deep, that may have held the western jamb of a doorway, which may account for the absence of the wall in this area. The fill of this post-pit contained a quantity of painted wall plaster that presumably had accumulated in the hole during the demolition of the building.

It is therefore suggested that the excavated area did include part of a second room to the south of the corridor, but the absence of any evidence for distinctive floor surfaces suggests that it was not elaborately decorated like the room to its west.

The main room was 7.0m wide by 8.0m long. To the north, where it overlay the pond, several areas of plain tessellated pavement survived (Fig 8, 14). These were of the same form as the pavement in the corridor, comprising large yellow tesserae set on a mortar bed. However, a range of displaced smaller tesserae in red, blue and white, and measuring between 10-12mm square, were recovered and these suggest that there was probably a decorative mosaic set within the centre of the room.

In addition, quantities of painted wall plaster were recovered from the demolition rubble within this room. The fragments are too small to say much about the decorative scheme, although it included panels with a white background and framed with striped borders in red and black.

To the south of the building there were patchy remnants of probable former yard surfaces.

PHASE 4: THE ABANDONMENT OF THE VILLA (LATE 2ND /EARLY 3RD CENTURY AD)

The pottery assemblage indicates that the building fell out of use sometime between the late second and the early third century AD. It would appear to have been systematically dismantled. Painted wall plaster and

Fig 11 Near complete poppy beaker in situ

tessera within a door jamb post-pit, 44, suggests that even the doors were dismantled for removal. As the site had been truncated by later activity, only a thin spread of demolition deposits survived, making it even more difficult to quantify what was recovered in contrast to what may have been removed for reuse at abandonment.

Some further evidence for the processes of destruction had survived. At the western end of the corridor and within the main room there were distinct areas of burning (Fig 8, 16 and 25), which appear to be within the demolition deposits and presumably represent the burning of unwanted debris. A further area of burning, 23, described as a hearth on site, lay directly on the tessellated pavement at the eastern end of the corridor, and the surface of the pavement had been blackened and scorched red. This deposit was subject to archaeomagnetic dating, but a date could not be obtained as the magnetic directions were scrambled. This suggests that this was not an *in situ* hearth but an accumulation of burnt and burning debris that had fallen onto the floor whilst still sufficiently hot to scorch the floor surface. This may suggest that accidental or deliberate burning may have either been the catalyst for abandonment or part of the process of destruction.

However, while the bulk of the pottery assemblage indicates that the building was abandoned by the early third century, there is a small amount of third to fourth century pottery and the 14 coins recovered are all dated to between the late third and late fourth centuries, 270s to 370s. This evidence suggests that there was still activity on the site through the later third and fourth centuries, although its nature is unknown. One possibility is that the villa was left as a partial derelict shell, rather than being totally levelled, and the later pottery and coins might be derived from later periodic episodes of wall robbing in which the ruins were being treated as a useful stone quarry.

PHASE 5: ANCILLARY ACTIVITY

In post-excavation the ancillary features beyond the villa building were assigned to a group labelled Phase 5. However, this does not imply a chronological sequence following on from the four phases of defined occupation.

Several cut features lay to the west of the building. These included a corn drier/malting oven, a pit oven constructed utilising the base of an amphora, and a well. Both the pit oven and the well are associated with amphora and appear to relate to the late first century activity that preceded the stone-built villa, while the corn drier and the associated pits are dated to the mid-second to early third century.

THE PIT OVEN

To the north there was a circular oven (Fig 6, 86 and Fig 12). It was formed within a shallow pit, 0.5m in diameter that was lined with part of the body of an amphora, with a complete flat-laid roof tile on one side, probably lining a short flue. A similar oven was located within a fourth century timber barn at the Weldon villa (Smith *et al* 1988-9, 57). The amphora at Stanion was of Dressel 20 type (Peacock & Williams Type 25) of southern Spanish origin, which are dated from late first/early second centuries to the early third century.

Fig 12 Oven base (86) utilising reused amphora

THE WELL

The well was only exposed during levelling of the site following excavation, and had to be excavated rapidly (Fig 6, 88 and Fig 13). It was lined with flat-laid courses of limestone and the shaft was 1.0m in diameter. Finds from the fill include quantities of pottery, including amphora dated to the late first century AD, three partial cattle skeletons and a partial skeleton of a raven. These could be interpreted as rubbish deposits although the possibility that they represent 'closure deposits' should also be considered.

Fig 13 The stone-lined well (89)

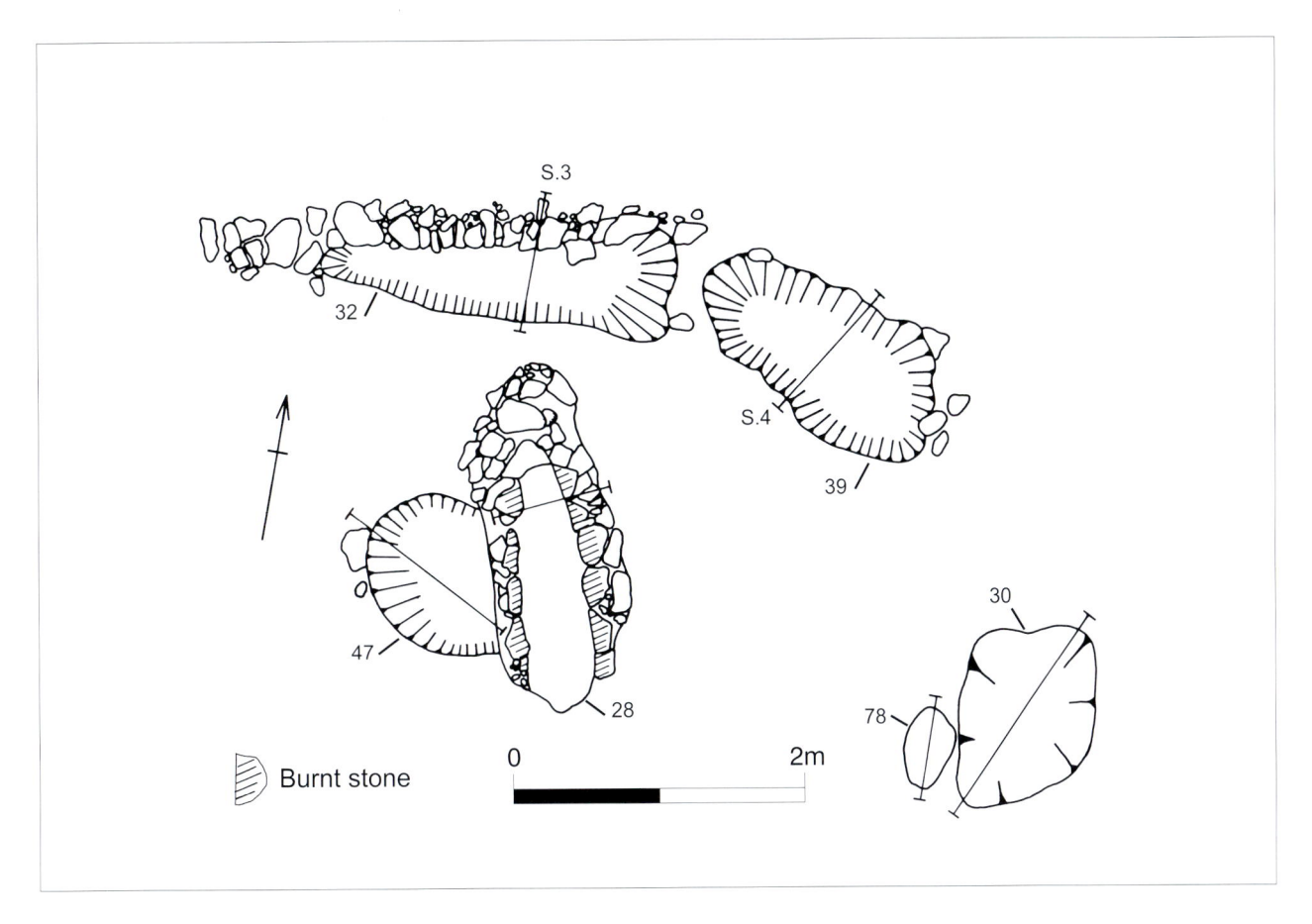

Fig 14 The malting oven and associated pits

THE CORN DRIER/ MALTING OVEN

The most prominent group of features comprised a corn drier/malting oven, 28 and 32, and two associated pits, 30 and 39 (Fig 14 and Fig 15).

As a result of later truncation, the corn drier survived as two separate elements, a linear stone-lined channel to the south, with the limestone lining scorched red, 28, and a channel to the north, aligned east to west, for which a lining only survived along the northern side, 32 (Fig 14 and Fig 16, Section 3). However, it is assumed that these were the remnants of a T-shaped corn drier, with the stokehole at the southern end. The flue was 0.4m wide and would have been 2.7m long connecting with a transverse end channel some 3.0m long.

To the immediate east and south east there were oval to irregular pits (30 and 39) (Fig 14 and Fig 16, Section 4). Both contained dark fills with some charcoal, probably at least partly comprising dumped debris from the oven. Pit 39 also contained a near complete lower stone from a rotary quern 500mm in diameter.

The fills of the oven and the pits were sampled for analysis of the charred seed content. The cereal concentrations from the northern channel and pit 30 were both rich in barley, suggesting that this was the main crop being dried in the oven, although there was no evidence that this was malted barley. The pit, 47, cut by the flue of the oven, contained or had been contaminated with quantities of mixed cereal processing waste, particularly

Fig 15 The corn drier/malting oven, looking north

chaff and also charred spelt. This mixed material may well been remains of the flue used to fire the oven.

Samples for archaeomagnetic dating were also taken but, partly because these are low temperature ovens, a reliable date was not obtained.

DITCHES AND GULLIES

To the west of the corn drier there were two lengths of intersecting ditch or gully (Fig 6, 18 and 20), which ran

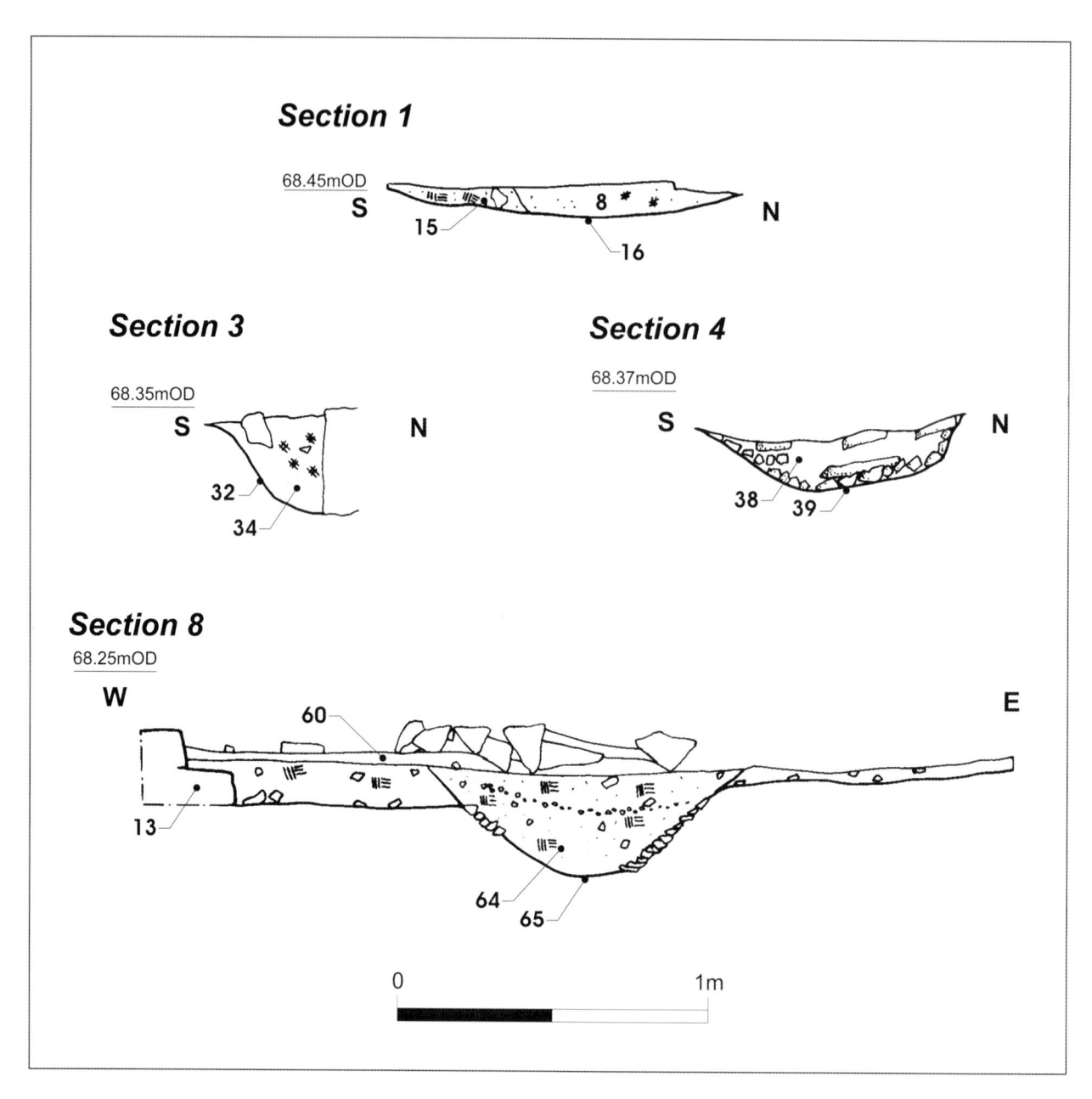

Fig 16 Sections of excavated features

on east-west and north-south alignments that coincided with the alignment of the villa itself. They presumably defined a series of rectilinear plots to the west of the villa, but the full extent of these features had not survived. At best, they were up to 0.65m wide and up to 0.15m deep, but often less.

PHASE 6: POST-ROMAN ACTIVITY

Stanion is principally associated in the archaeological literature with the production of medieval pottery. Small quantities of medieval pottery were recovered from the site, most of which derived from the topsoil or from contexts that could have been disturbed by ploughing and was probably evidence of medieval manuring or post-medieval and modern activity at the site.

THE ROMAN POTTERY
*R M Friendship-Taylor
with M J Darling, B Dickinson and M Powell*

INTRODUCTION

Stanion villa yielded a total of 3150 sherds of pottery, which weighed a total of 58.12 kg.

There were few well-dated groups from the site under investigation, although a general feel for the main periods of occupation was obtained. However, there were few real surprises from the group as a whole (Fig 17).

There were nine medieval sherds (0.29%) from four contexts and seven post-medieval sherds (0.22%) from six contexts. These were presumably from medieval and or post-medieval plough disturbance or other means of contamination.

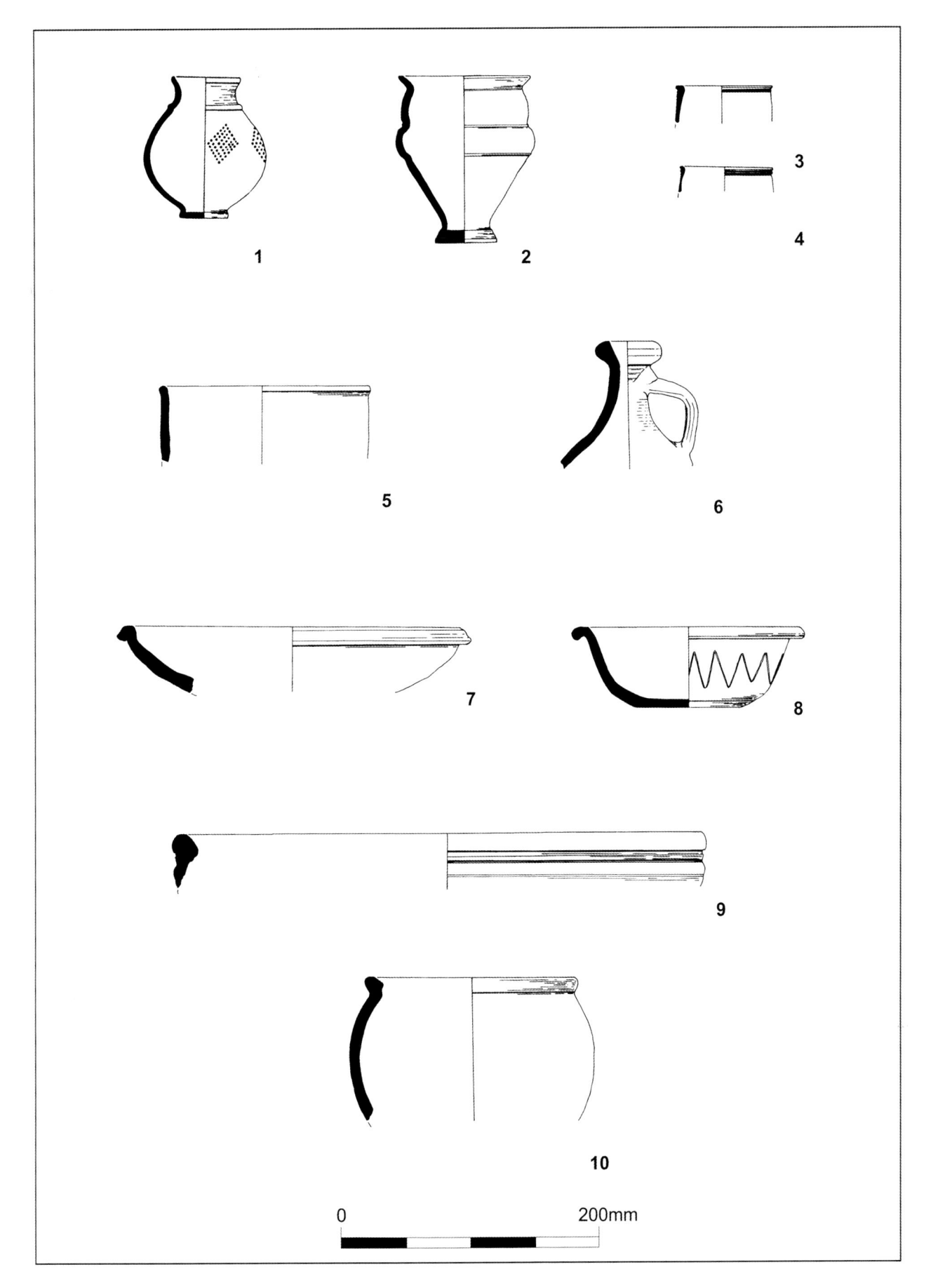

Fig 17 The Roman pottery, 1-10

Table 1: Roman pottery, main fabrics, sherd count by %

Fabric type	Sherd Count	%
Various Grey wares (GRY)	1077	34.19
Lower Nene Valley grey ware (LNVGW)	39	1.24
Grog wares (GR0)	625	19.84
Amphora (DR 20)	251	7.97
Calcite/shell/calcareous (CG)	271	8.60
Lower Nene Valley Col Ct wares (LNVCC)	161	5.11
Samian ware (SAM)	153	4.86
Mica gilt ware (MIC)	15	0.48
London ware (LON)	23	0.73
Post-medieval (P/MED)	7	0.22
Medieval (MED)	9	0.29
Oxford red CC wares (OXRC)	6	0.19
Oxford white mortaria (MOOX)	8	0.25
Other fabrics	505	16.03
Total	3150	100

Generally, the sherd size was small which suggests the site may have been abandoned at a relatively early stage, with a life of only 100 years or so, and had remained open in perhaps a semi derelict state for some time allowing some fourth-century pottery to accumulate. Apart from the main recognisable fabrics as noted below, there was a considerable range of fabrics of which no doubt many had originated from the immediate locality of the Stanion villa.

Samian ware represented 4.86% of the group. Small quantities were present in many contexts. Most of the sherds had fresh breaks, which suggests they had been deposited relatively quickly after breakage. This small group helps greatly to reflect the general date range of the area examined. Perhaps another pointer for an early date is the fact that although the site is not very far from the centre of the lower Nene pottery industry, there was comparatively little lower Nene Valley colour coated fine wares present (5.11%) within the group as a whole. The little that was present possibly reflects the later part of the site's occupation and therefore the end of the main phase of use of the villa, perhaps as early as the late second century or, as late as the early third century AD.

A small but significant quantity of mica gilt ware (mainly beakers) (0.48%) was recovered from various contexts. Most of this appears to have originated in the UK, and may well have come from the lower Nene region during the mid second century; only a single sherd of this ware may have been a continental import.

Also possibly originating from the lower Nene valley were several sherds of the so-called 'London ware' mostly copying samian forms such as Dr. 37 and Dr. 30 types (.33%). (Howe, Perrin and Mackreth *no date*, fig 2, 23 – 25.). This type of pottery was also made at other manufacturing centres such as Packenham (Suffolk) and the north London area (maybe Highgate Wood).

The largest fabric grouping is the ubiquitous grey ware that is represented by 34.19% (1077 sherds). Most of which appears to be of local origin. However, there is a single sherd of rusticated grey ware (which is quite rare in Northamptonshire and may have originated from Lincolnshire to the north-east of Stanion; only two sherds of this ware have been found at Piddington to date and one from Nether Heyford (Stephen Young pers com).

A triangular rim sherd of a bowl, (GRY 27) which could be of Highgate Wood Type, (London) (Brown & Sheldon, 1969a, 1969b & 1971) was also present. Although this ware is not that common in the region, it does occasionally appear in Northamptonshire, for example, several vessels have been recognised at Piddington.

The large Trajanic/Hadrianic kiln complex at Ecton in the Upper Nene Valley (Johnston 1969) is represented at Stanion by only four vessels (GRY 8), comprising three jars and one bowl.

Not surprisingly, the bulk of the grey wares from Stanion possibly originated from the middle Nene area, though no single piece could be recognised from a particular location. The main bulk of the vessels were jars, but bowls and dishes were also present. Grey ware from the lower Nene Valley kilns (LNVGW) seems to be in the minority and is represented by only some 39 sherds (1.24%). Given the location of this site and the low number of LNVGW sherds and together with the colour coated wares, may be a further pointer to an early to mid second century date for the main period of development of this site.

However, the main date range of the pottery conforms largely to the mid to late second and possibly the early third centuries, suggesting that this part of the villa was occupied during this period. There is little pottery of the later third/fourth centuries present within this assemblage, suggesting that activity of some kind may have continued somewhere on the site at least into the fourth century (See above introduction).

Medium sized jars from outside the region have been found at sites such as Stanion, Piddington and elsewhere suggesting that these vessels were likely to have been used as containers to transport commodities such as honey or butter, rather than the local wares which were made for immediate domestic use.

There is a surprisingly large quantity of Amphorae, all of Dressel 20 type (7.97%) comprising one rim and two bases, from at least two, but possibly from three or four vessels. One of these may have been reused as a field oven. The secondary use of this amphora in this way was very similar to an example from the villa at Piddington, where a large storage jar had been laid on its side to create a draught-proof oven. These amphorae had originated from southern Spain and may have contained olive oil.

Apart from the large number of amphorae sherds and the combined grey ware fabrics, the second largest fabric group of vessels present was what is sometimes called 'Roman grogged ware' (termed in this report as GROG) (19.84%). This is a 'lumpy' hard-fired creamy/fawn fabric, which also contains quantities of sand/quartz, grog and sometimes some calcite. It is often used for the larger storage type of vessel, although at Stanion there were many 'developed lid seated jars' (perhaps the most common type of jar) and smaller necked jars also in this fabric.

Surprisingly, there was little shell/calcite tempered pottery (8.60%) within the assemblage as a whole, and again, this may indicate a later start of occupation or a late ending for the site. No late Iron Age forms or fabrics were noted within the assemblage.

The only fourth-century pottery present (Contexts: 1; 15; poss. 27; poss. 37; poss. 43; 48; poss. 60) consisted of a single sherd of Oxford red colour coated ware and an Oxford white mortarium and a little late, lower Nene valley colour coated wares. This fourth-century material could have derived from occupation on another part of the site, which remains unexcavated – or, it may be all that remains of a fourth-century use of the site. Medieval/post-medieval agricultural activity, of which there is ample evidence, may have destroyed and contaminated some of the upper contexts.

SUMMARY AND CONCLUSIONS

Based on the evidence of the pottery, one can suggest a period of occupation from the late first century AD, with the main period of occupation occurring during the early to mid second century. The occupation appears to come to an end in the late second century or more likely by the early third century. However, there must have been some activity during the fourth century, but how intense this was is unclear.

ROMAN POTTERY FROM THE 1984 ROAD SCHEME

During post-excavation a pottery assemblage came to light that had been recovered from rescue excavations undertaken in 1984 during improvements to the road immediately to the north of the villa.

This group of pottery generally conforms to an earlier date range than that from the adjacent villa excavated in 2003. The 1984 group consistently dates from around the mid first century AD through to the early second century AD, but nothing later. Therefore, it would seem that the earliest settlement probably lies somewhere to the north or north-east of the later villa, and that by the second decade of the second century had shifted to the south where the villa later emerged. This earlier settlement may therefore have developed as a simple mid-first-century roadside settlement along the nearby Godmanchester to Leicester road, built probably as a result of early Roman military activity in the area.

The range of forms from this rescue excavation was generally quite limited. The most common form of vessel present was the Developed Channel-rim (lid-seated) jar (JLSD) which should be dated from the late first and into the second century. There were two sherds, both in different fabrics within the group which had attempted to copy the samian form Dr. 30. A grey ware bowl with a burnished lattice decoration and a London Ware copy was represented by a single sherd which was decorated with a burnished fern-leaf design. There may be an element of overlap or continuity, in that both groups have a very limited number of sherds of grey rusticated jars (JRUST) which should both date to the earlier second century. Ecton ware is represented by a single grey ware dish (D) of Trajanic date. There was also a small dish indicating a Gallo-Belgic copy which may also have originated from Ecton. The remainder of the pottery especially the grey wares, probably originated from the locality of the site and the mid Nene valley area.

There seems to be a connection at Stanion with the unusual group of innovative mid-first century pottery found at Rushden by Woods, which he defines as by 'intrusive potters' (Woods and Hastings 1984; Friendship-Taylor 1999). The Stanion vessel is a single narrow-necked jar (JNN) with almost a 'funnel-neck' and a beaded-rim (Fig 18, 18). Around the girth of the vessel are several rows of a notched wheel decoration, above which are double raised cordons and then on the shoulder is a single row of double scratched zig-zags. This matches closely with decorative elements from Rushden. Woods suggested the potters may have arrived with the military from eastern Europe and therefore, its date may be circa Claudio/Neronian (*c* 45-60s AD). The fabric is a burnished grogged ware and its colour is a bright orange/fawn colour (no painted decoration appears to have been applied to this vessel), very similar to many of these fine Rushden vessels, especially the example in Friendship-Taylor 1999 (fig 92, 2). This vessel, when found, seems to have been inverted with its base uppermost and carefully trimmed off, probably at mid point between rim and base. It was found in a pit whose contents suggest may have been part of a 'structured deposit'.

Table 2: Forms present in the 1984 pottery assemblage

Samian	Dr. 18, 27, 30, 37
Channel-rim Jar	JLS
Double Channel-rim Jar (lid-seated)	JLSD
jar with tall upright rim	JNLN
Out-turned rim jar	JO
Small jar	JSML
Medium-sized storage jar	JSS
Large storage jar	JS
Narrow-necked jar	JNN
Reed-rim bowl	BRR
Dish	D
Cover	COV

THE AMPHORAE
R M Friendship-Taylor and M Powell

There are 276 sherds of amphorae, mostly with fresh breaks, weighing 23.20kg. All were from Dressel 20 (Peacock & Williams Type 25) and were mainly from south Spain. These are dated from late first/early second century to the early third century and there are a minimum of 23 vessels present.

There are no stamps, graffiti or *depinti* present on any sherds, but just below a handle springing there is what appears to have been a possible signature incised onto three body sherds in the form of a circle, with its ends overlapping each other and similar to that often seen on the surface of a *tegula* (roof tile).

There is evidence for the reuse of several sherds, such as two handle fragments, which appear to have been used as 'pestles' and two joining body sherds, probably from the base of the neck, just above the shoulder, which had been ground down to a very smooth edge.

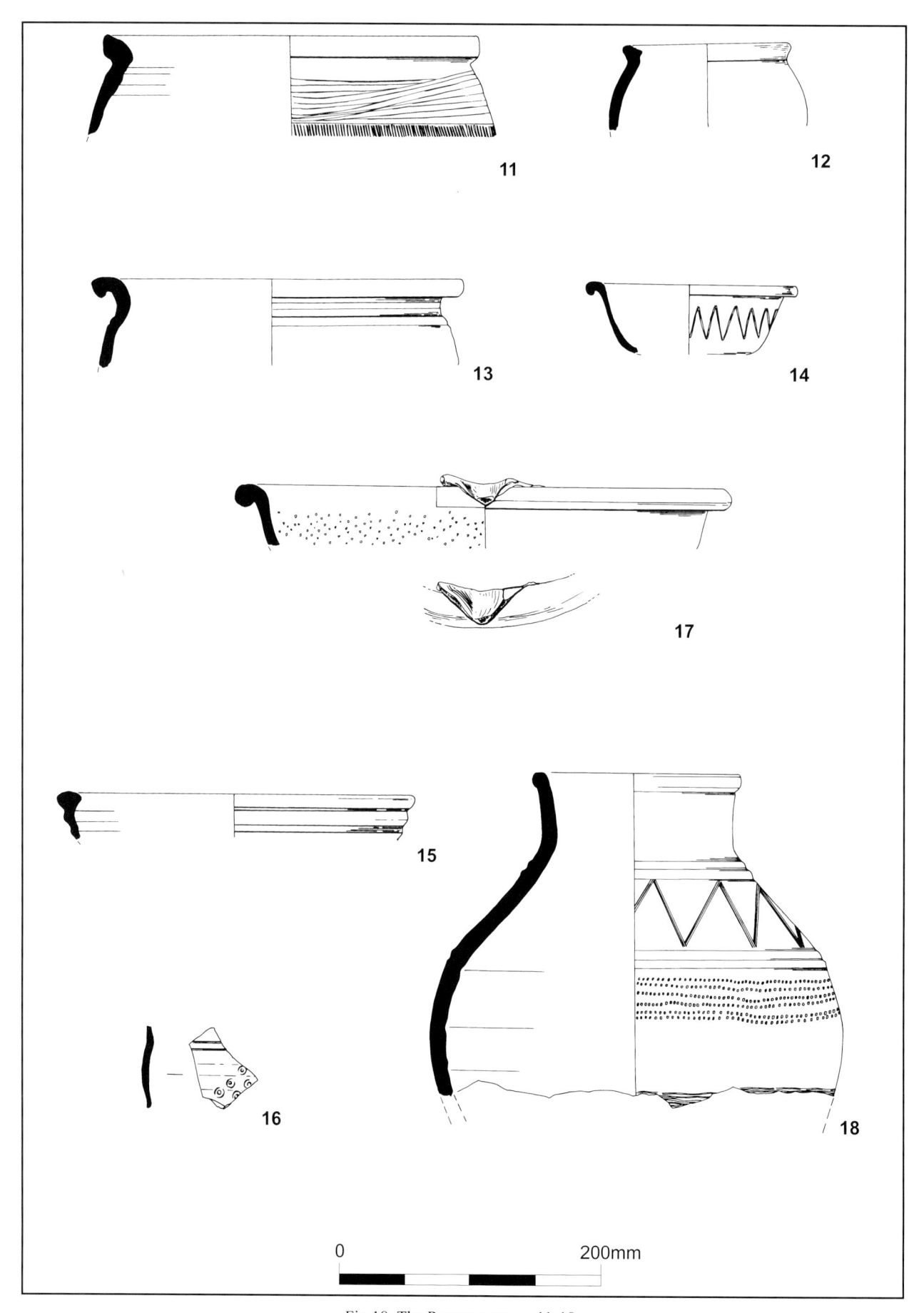

Fig 18 The Roman pottery, 11-18

Table 3: The mortaria

Context no	Fabric	Attribute	Min. Vessels	Sherds	Weight (g)	Date (AD)
1	MOOX-R	BO	1	1	8	3rd-4th century
15	MOOX-W	R	1	1	88	240-400
15	MOOX-W	BO	1	1	19	post 240
15	MONV-L	BO	1	1	13	mid 3rd century
31	MOOX-W	BO	0	1	7	
37	MONV-U	R	1	1	58	late 3rd -3rd century
46	MOMD	R	1	1	75	
53	MONV-L	R	1	1	21	mid 3rd century
64	MONV-L	R	1	2	77	mid-late 3rd century

Two base sherds are also present, one of which shows very clear evidence of the method of manufacture by the insertion of a ball of clay into a pre-cut and scribed hole in the base of the body of the vessel.

Although some discolouration was noted on a small number of body sherds, it was thought that this might not necessarily have occurred as a result of use as a 'field oven'. However, as noted above, the reused sherds with the smoothed edges may have some connection with a 'field oven', although these sherds exhibited no discolouration.

It would appear that most of these vessels were of southern Spanish origin, especially from Cordoba in the valley of the Guadalquivir. Only one fabric (STAN 1) appears to have come from a different source, namely Catalonia in southeastern Spain.

THE AMPHORA FABRICS

Because there was such a diverse range of fabrics present, it was decided to establish a fabric type series (STAN 1 to STAN 8). It was felt that the *National Fabric Reference Collection* (Tomber & Dore 1998) has too few amphorae examples, and therefore only minimal use has been made of it. For all colour references the Munsell soil colour chart was used.

STAN 1   Tomber & Dore, Catalan Amphorae (CAT AM) p.91 Munsell - red-brown (5YR 5/4 – 5/6) to red (10R 5/8 – 4/8 throughout). It is very hard with harsh surfaces and hackly fracture. Common to abundant ill sorted sub angular fine to very coarse sand that consists predominantly of altered alkaline feldspar and quartz with sparse biotite and plutonic rock fragments.

STAN 2   Tomber & Dore, Cadiz Amphorae (CAD AM) p.87. Munsell - pale brown (7.5YR 7/3, 7.5YR 7/4 – 6/4) to pale red or orange (2.5Y 8/2 to 8/3) margins also have slipped surfaces. The fabric is hard with rough surfaces and irregular fracture.

STAN 3   Munsell - pink (7.5YR 7/4). Small ill-sorted white granules less than .5 mm. and larger brown grains up to about 1 mm with fine black grains that may be volcanic ash – no mica is visible.

STAN 4   Munsell - light brownish grey (10YR 6/2). Small white inclusions up to about 1mm. medium sorted. Fine grained matrix containing very small particles of dark material. Sherds tending to delaminate – no visible mica.

STAN 5   Munsell - very pale brown (10YR 7/3). Quartz grains within the fabric up to .2mm. and occasional ?ironstone up to 1.5mm. Hackley surface with sparse surface mica.

STAN 6   Munsell - pink (7.5YR 7/4). Similar to STAN 5 but the white inclusions are long and thin which may be shell; up to 5mm long. Sherds attracted much iron staining.

STAN 7   Munsell - pink (7.5YR 8/4). Sparse mica and quartz grains approximately .5mm. Generally hard fired.

STAN 8   Munsell – pinkish grey (7.5YR 6/2). Similar to STAN 1 but with addition of 'Box Iron' and small flinty fragments up to .5mm.

THE MORTARIA
R M Friendship-Taylor and M Powell
(Notes taken from a discussion with Kay Hartley)

The assemblage of coarse wares includes ten mortaria sherds from eight vessels, weighing 366g. These vessels came from a limited number of sources, such as the lower and upper Nene valleys and Oxfordshire. At least one vessel shows extensive signs of heat discolouration. Recently, pottery specialists are becoming more aware of the numbers of mortaria that show evidence of some form of heat application during use rather than after use.

THE SAMIAN
M J Darling

The samian totals 146 sherds, weighing 825g. The average weight is 5.6g but the group is quite fragmentary, containing many chips or flakes. The pottery has been archived using count and weight as measures according to the guidelines laid down for the minimum archive by *The Study Group for Roman Pottery*.

Table 4: Sources of the samian

Source	Sherds	%	Weight (g)	%
South Gaul	15	10.27	64	7.76
Les Martres de Veyre	7	4.79	21	2.54
Lezoux	124	84.93	740	89.70
Total	146	100	825	100

Three separate groups of sherd links occurred between 31.8 and 37.111; 37.103 and 37.18; 37.46 and 52.44 and 52.52.

Dating of the samian

South Gaulish wares (SAMSG) include two form 37 bowls, both datable to the Flavian to Trajanic period (from 52.32 and 88.24), and a single fragment of a stamp from of Severus I, from 52.77, *c* AD 65-95. The appearance of form 18/31 is consistent with such dating.

Les Martres de Veyre sherds are all tiny fragments and flakes, apart from a form 33 cup stamped by Billicedo from 52.77. All are datable to the Trajanic period, *c* AD 100-120.

The Lezoux ware includes six sherds from form 37, five datable to the Hadrianic to early Antonine period (from 26.7; 37.74; 52.53; 60.10), and one footring of Antonine date (29.4). Three stamps occurred (see below), all datable to the Antonine period, the latest dated *c* AD 155-185.

There are none of the known later second century forms apart from the 31R, first appearing *c* AD 160, and no mortaria, while the stamps indicate *c* AD 185 as the latest date. The overall dating of the samian is therefore from the Flavian period, through to the Antonine period, *c* AD 185.

Table 5: Samian forms by source

Fabric	Form	Sherds	Weight (g)	Comment
SAMSG	18	1	6	Rim
SAMSG	18/31?	1	5	Rim
SAMSG?	18 OR 18/31?	2	3	Rims chip/flake
SAMSG	27	5	14	-
SAMSG	37	2	29	-
SAMSG	-	4	7	-
sub-total		**15**	**64**	
SAMCG	18 OR 18/31	3	8	Rims
SAMCG	18/31 OR 31	18	92	11 rims
SAMCG	27	1	30	Rim/wall
SAMCG	30 OR 37	1	1	-
SAMCG	31	18	246	6 x 31?; 4 rims
SAMCG	31 OR 31R?	1	8	Ftrg only
SAMCG	31R	3	58	1 definite
SAMCG	33	13	67	inc 1 vess MV; 6 rims
SAMCG	35 OR 36	1	1	Chip part rim
SAMCG	36	2	11	Rim
SAMCG	37	5	40	-
SAMCG	38?	1	9	Flange frag only
SAMCG	42	1	4	Rim
SAMCG	BD	26	103	1 vess MV?
SAMCG	-	37	83	4 prob MV
sub-total		**131**	**761**	
Total		**146**	**825**	

SAMSG = Samian southern gaul
SAMCG = Samian Central Gaul
MV = Les Martres de Veyre

POTTERS' STAMPS
B Dickinson

Catalogue of stamped vessels (underlined letters in stamps are ligatured):

[BI]LLICEDOFE on form 33(?): Billicedo of Les Martres-de-Veyre, Die 3b. The potter certainly worked at Les Martres, and the fabric of this piece confirms this. The stamp has also been found at Lezoux, but the pot in question was not demonstrably made there. The fabrics used at Les Martres by Billicedo belong to the Trajanic range. *c* AD 100-120. Context 55.

[ECVLI]AR•F on form 33: Peculiaris of Lezoux, Die 5a (Curle 1911, 238, 72). This stamp is normally found on forms not made at Lezoux after *c* AD 160, such as 18/31, 18/31R and 27. It is known from Carzield and Newstead, and on form 27 from Wallsend. However, it appears occasionally on form 80, and so the die should have still been in use after AD 160. *c* AD 145-170. Context 66.

SABI[NIANI] on form 31: Sabinianus iii of Lezoux, Die 1b. The die from which this stamp comes was used at the Terre-Franche kilns at Vichy, but it was almost certainly also used at Lezoux, to judge by the Stanion pot, and others with the same stamp. The forms associated with it are 31, 31R and 38. *c* AD 155-185. Context 53.

[S]ENII [•M] on form 33: Senea of Lezoux, Die 1a (Dannell 1971, 315, 88, under Senila). Although Antonine, this stamp has not been found on any of the later forms of that period, except on a possible 31R. Another of Senea's stamps occurs on form 27 and in a group of burnt samian from Tác (Hungary) which is taken to have been destroyed in the Marcomannic Wars. *c* AD 140-170. Context 64.

[OFSEVE]RI on form 15/17 or 18: Severus i of La Graufesenque, Die 7aa. This is one of Severus iii's least-common stamps, and there is no internal dating evidence for it. He occasionally stamped pre-Flavian forms, but his output is almost entirely Flavian and his stamps frequently occur on military sites in Britain founded in the 70s, such as Chester and York. *c* AD 65-95, but for this piece, AD 70-95. Context 52

Catalogue of illustrated Roman pottery (Figs 17 and 18)

1. Beaker – poppy head, (BKPH), greyware (GRY9), 2nd century, context 55
2. Out-turned rim jar (JO), greyware (GRY4), 3rd century?, context 27
3. Beaker – bag-shaped (BKBAG), Lower Nene valley colour-coat wares (LNVCC), context 15
4. Beaker – cornice rim (BKCOR), Central Gaulish colour-coat (CGCC), 2nd century, context 37
5. Bowl – imitation form Dr.33 (B33), grog wares (GROG), 2nd century, context 37

6 Flagon – ring-necked (FR), miscellaneous white wares (WT), 2nd-3rd century, context 37
7 Bowl – bead and flange-small (BFBS), silty black with mica inclusions (London ware) (BLKSM), 2nd-3rd century, context 31
8 Bowl – flat-topped rim (BHFT), dense sandy and hard fired (BLK), 2nd century, context 52
9 Grog wares (GROG), (BG225), 2nd century, context 60
10 Jar – neckless (JNL), grog wares (GROG), 2nd century, context 54
11 Double channel-rim (lid seated) jar (JLSD), grog wares (GROG), 2nd century, context 54
12 Double channel-rim (lid seated) jar (JLSD), grog wares (GROG), 2nd century, context 66
13 Jar – large (JL), greyware (GRY21), 2nd century, context 66
14 Dish – rounded out-turned rim (DRR), Black burnished ware – local copy (BB1C), mid 2nd century, context 53
15 Grog wares (GROG), (BHET), mid 2nd century, context 53
16 Greyware (GRY11), (VESS), 2nd century, context 88
17 Oxford white mortaria (MOOX-W), (R), AD 240-400, context 15
18 Narrow-necked jar (JNN), burnished grogged ware, Claudio/Neronian (AD 45-60s), 1984 watching brief

OTHER ROMAN FINDS

T Hylton
with D Mackreth, A Chapman, H E M Cool, M Curteis and P Middleton

INTRODUCTION

In total the excavations produced 148 individual and group recorded small finds, including some of post-medieval date. Finds dating to the Roman period were recovered from all phases; most were located within stratified deposits, while small numbers were recovered from subsoil/topsoil deposits or are unstratified. Although the majority of finds are undiagnostic fragments and nails, there is a small range of artefacts that provide a brief insight into some aspects of life at the settlement. These include items for personal use and a small group of tools, which provide evidence for spinning, sewing, possible leather working and the processing of grain. They are published as individual types within four major functional categories. Miscellaneous and unidentified objects have been considered by material type. The categories are tabulated below along with the quantities recovered (Table 6).

All the copper alloy and iron objects (including nails and small fragments) were submitted for X-ray. This was undertaken by Mehmet Ozgenc and Glynis Edwards of the English Heritage Centre for Archaeology. This not only provided a permanent record, but it enabled identification and revealed details not previously visible. Twelve objects with mineral preserved organic remains adhering to their surfaces were chosen for further investigation. With the exception of one wooden knife handle, most of the organic material was not directly associated with

Table 6: Finds quantified by functional category

Functional category	Ph 1	Ph 2	Ph 3	Ph 4	Ph 5	topsoil
Personal Possessions						
Costume and jewellery	1			3	1	1
Recreational objects	1					
Equipment and furnishings						
General ironwork					1	
Nails (inc. 2 hob nails phase 4)	8	1	10	22	17	
Glass	7		5	15	2	3
Hones/sharpeners	1					
Misc. tools	2		1	1		
Querns				3	1	
Coins				11		3
Miscellaneous and unidentified						
Copper alloy			1	4		
Iron	5	1	1	7		
Lead				4		
Bone	1					
Stone	1			1		1
Total	27	2	18	71	22	8

the objects (Jacqui Watson, English Heritage Centre for Archaeology pers com).

Small numbers of finds, 27, were located within deposits pre-dating building construction. These were mainly associated with a large depression over which the building had been constructed; it is probable that these finds were discarded along with the domestic refuse, which had been used to backfill the feature. There is a dearth of artefacts, two, relating to the construction of the building (Phase 2), while larger numbers, 20, were recovered from deposits associated with its occupation (Phase 3). The majority of finds, 71, were recovered from post-occupation demolition deposits overlying the footprint of the building (Phase 4). Finally small numbers of finds (22) were recovered from an activity area sited to the west of the main structure (Phase 5) and within later deposits together with objects of medieval and post-medieval date.

PERSONAL POSSESSIONS

This category comprises small portable items that would have formed part of a person's general attire, either worn as jewellery, or held by an individual for personal use.

BROOCHES
D Mackreth

(This is a shortened version of the original report, which may be seen in the archive.)

Iron brooch (Fig 19, 1). Only the upper bow and the head survive. In poor condition, the head was formed by beating out the metal and then rolling it to form wings which housed the axis bar of the hinged pin. Although no trace of the slot for the pin can be easily see, this is almost certainly due to the corrosion. The alternative interpretation is that this is not a brooch and no other function comes easily to mind.

Allowing this to be a brooch, it belongs to a type, either in iron or copper alloy, which, by its general distribution, is Durotrigan: well over three quarters of iron ones of this and the chief variant, mentioned below, come from the homeland of that tribe. A secondary distribution favours Hertfordshire and Northamptonshire. The dating is fairly clear: from $c10$ BC – AD 20 (Partridge 1981, 135, fig 87, 11) to the middle of the first century (Fulford and Timby 2000, 325, fig 1349, 10).

Copper alloy brooch (Fig 19, 2). The form of the plate is circular with six insignificant equally-spaced projections. In the middle is a circular hole for some kind of applied central feature. The only other feature of note is a recessed ridge around the periphery on each side of which are marks suggesting that the final form was achieved using a tool. The hinged pin was housed between a pair of lugs. There may be slight traces of a tinned finish..

Exact parallels are not really to be expected. The design recalls a main variant in a large and eclectic family which shares projections, peripheral recessed ridges and holes in the middle. Their distribution is overwhelmingly south-eastern with the Fosse Way military zone forming the north-west boundary. They arrive with the Roman army; at least none has so far been recovered from a pre-Conquest deposit. The dating of the main family is: 20/25-43/5 (Clifford 1961, 184, fig 36, 6) through to middle Flavian times, 71/4-86 (Cool and Philo 1998, 51, fig 13, 99, 100

Copper alloy brooch (Fig 19, 3). The pin is hinged as in the last. The form is that of a shallow dome surrounded by a hollow. On the surface of the dome are two rows of triangular cells having remains of enamel whose colour is too far gone to be sure that it conformed with the normal scheme for this kind of brooch: red alternating with blue. The circular form has four projections. Those at the top and bottom are more prominent and hide parts of the lugs for the pin and the catch-plate. Those on each side are short spikes..

This is a common form and this is a typical example. There may be variations in detail, including a range with cusped borders, but all hang together in as cohesive a manner as could be wished. The distribution is of interest: it favours the east side of England and the area of manufacturing may have been East Anglia. The family was made in large numbers and so there are examples from all over Roman Britain, but the basic pattern is not seriously disturbed. The sites producing the dating belie the true distributions and are a reflection of difficulty in dating isolated second-century finds on ordinary rural sites. The dating of all varieties ranges from 75-120 (Woodward *et al* 1993, 123, fig 62, 46) to the middle of the second century: $c143$-65 (Christison 1901, 405, plate A,2).

ILLUSTRATED FINDS (Fig 19)

1   Iron brooch, only the upper bow and the head survive. Durotrigan, from $c10$ BC – AD 20 to the middle of the first century. SF22, u/s

2   Copper alloy brooch, AD 20/25-43/5 through to middle Flavian times, 71/4-86, SF15, layer 2

3   Copper alloy brooch, AD 75-120 to the middle of the second century $c143$-65. SF106, u/s

FINGER RING

Part of a penannular finger ring (not illustrated) was recovered from a Phase 1 mixed deposit (52) underneath the demolition rubble (15). The finger ring has been manufactured from a single strand of circular-sectioned wire (1mm thick). The terminal folds back on itself and broadens to form a stylised devolved serpent's head (not illus). Although incomplete the small fragment which survives represents a crude example of Johns Type Biv (1997, 36), a style of finger ring comprising snakes head terminals with one or more coils in between which fit round the finger. Such representations on items of jewellery are common during the Roman period and represent health and healing, rebirth and the spirits of the departed (Johns 1998/2000, 7). For a discussion on bracelets and rings in the form of snakes see Johns 1996 (334) and 1997 (34-37).

ARMLETS

Fragments from two copper alloy armlets were recovered from demolition deposits (context 15), they are represented by forms commonly found on Roman

Green

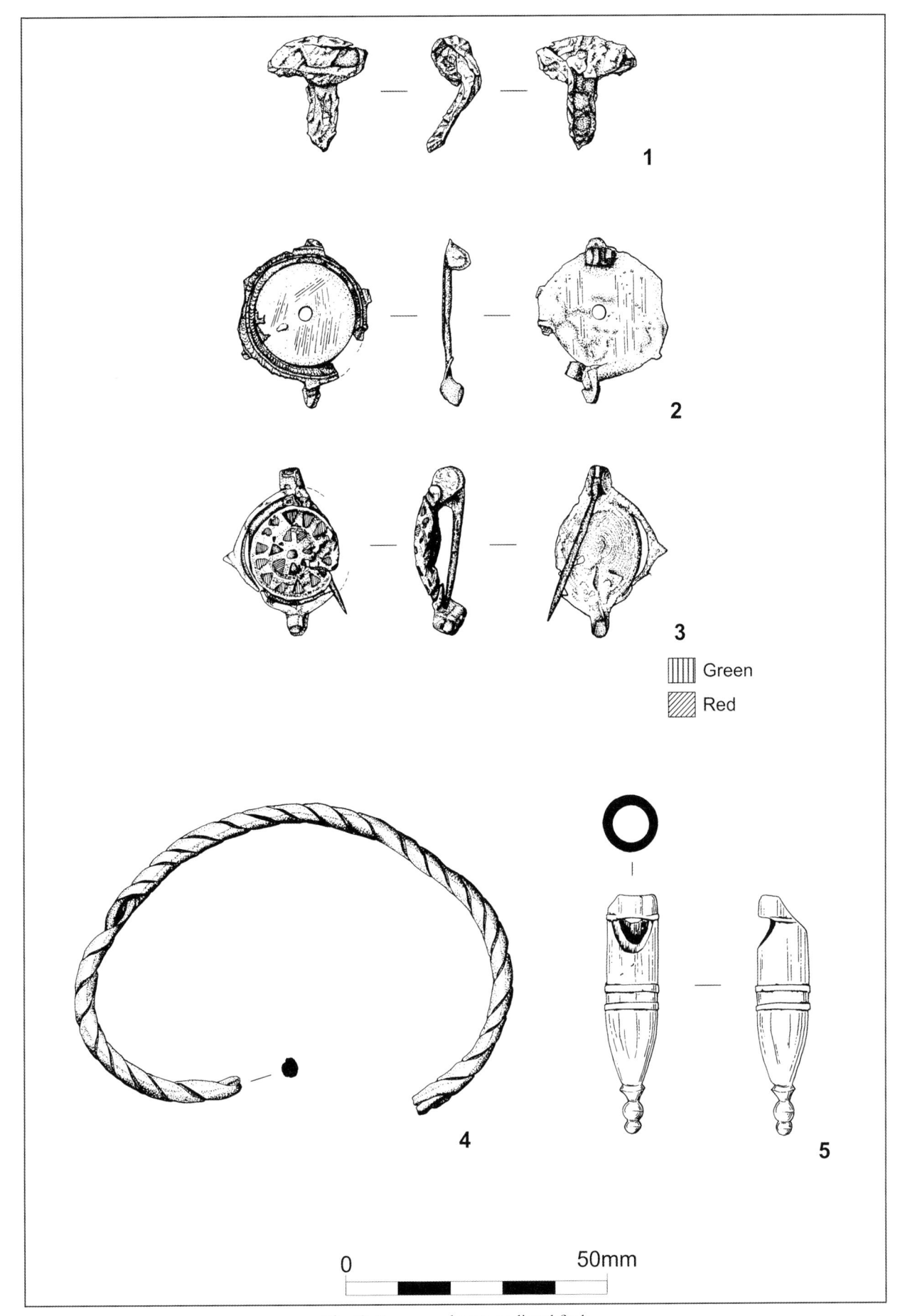

Red

Fig 19 Roman and post-medieval finds

settlement sites in the third and fourth centuries. One is a 'cable' bracelet and comprises three strands of circular-sectioned wire, twisted together in an anti-clockwise direction and then hammered to secure the individual strands (Fig 19. 4). This type may be paralleled by examples from Gadebridge Park Villa, Hemel Hempstead (Neal 1974, fig 61, 164-69) and Bancroft Villa, Milton Keynes (Hylton and Zeepvat 1994, fig 141, 76).

The other is a small fragment (SF 26) from a parallel-sided armlet with a D-shaped cross-section it is decorated with alternating V-shaped notches on the outside edge (not illus) and the X-ray reveals that there are two small centrally placed circular indentations (dots), suggesting that the motif resembles a crudely executed form of 'wave crest' decoration, as seen on fourth-century armlets from Colchester (Crummy 1983, fig 44, 1703 and 1704) and Shakenoak (Brodribb et al 1973, fig 54, 191).

ILLUSTRATED ARMLET (Fig 19)

4   Copper alloy. Incomplete, four fragments (three joining), no terminals. Three D-sectioned strands of wire twisted together in an anti-clockwise direction and them hammered. Thickness 4mm. SF 30, context 15, Phase 4, demolition deposit

PINS

There are two pins, one is manufactured from copper alloy and was recovered from demolition deposits over lying the floor of the Villa (Phase 4) and the other one is made from bone and was located within the fill of the corn drier. Both examples are furnished with simply decorated heads.

The head of the copper alloy pin is ornamented with a single horizontal groove sited at the top of the shaft (not illus); although stylistically plain, the pin appears to correspond with Hilary Cool's Type 5, with simple grooved heads (1990, 157).

The bone pin displays similarities to a group of pins from Fishbourne Villa with lathe turned heads terminating in a conical projection (Cunliffe 1971, 16-24), it also equates to Crummy's Type 2 (1983, fig 18) which are simply ornamented with a tiny reel and cone surmounted on a reel and groove (not illus). Hilary Cool in her typology of metal pins (1990) identifies the similarities between her Type 5 metal pins and Crummy's Type 2 bone pins and suggests that both types were predominantly in use in the first and second centuries (ibid 157).

RECREATION

A single ceramic roundel/counter is formed on a pottery sherd, with the broken edges ground down to form a roundel 26mm in diameter and 8mm high. It is in a hard-fired grog-tempered fabric that dates to the mid to late first century. Similar examples are known from Colchester (Crummy 1983, fig 98, 2449). Ceramic roundels are often recovered from Roman sites and they may have had any number of uses, including reckoning counters or gaming pieces, see Crummy 1983 (93).

BUILDING EQUIPMENT

Considering the nature of the site, there is a distinct lack of objects which may have formed part of or been attached to the original villa structure. With the exception of a single split spike loop, only nails are represented. The split spike loop was recovered from the fill of a pit (context 29, pit 30, Phase 5), it would have been used for attaching rings and fittings. For similar examples see Manning 1985 (plate 61, 39-46).

A total of 57 nails was recovered from Phases 1-5, including two hobnails that presumably derive from footwear. A small number of nails was recovered from deposits pre-dating the construction of the villa (Phase 1), no nails were located within Phase 2 deposits and ten nails were recovered from layers associated with the mortar floor surfaces (Phase 3). The majority of nails were recovered from Phase 4 (22 nails) and Phase 5 (17 nails) deposits. There are two discrete groups of nails, ten were recovered as a group in demolition deposits (Phase 4) and 11 were found in an oven, together with a quantity of metal working debris (Phase 5).

Of the total number, 30% (17 nails) are of indeterminate form, with their heads missing etc, the remainder have been classified according to Manning's Type series (1985, 134ff). The majority of the identifiable nail types are Manning's Type 1B (53%), which range in recorded length from 33-90mm. The majority clustered between 40-55mm and were presumably used for furniture or light structural fixings. Other types include large structural nails, possibly for securing major timbers (Type 1A, 2%), nails with T-shaped heads (Type 3, 7%), nails with 'L' shaped heads (Type 4, 2%), nails lacking a distinct head (Type 5, 2%), nails for upholstery (Types 7, 2%) and hob nails (Type 10, 3.5%).

TOOLS

There are tools associated with textile working, possible leather working and the processing of grain, most probably for domestic consumption. There are two items associated with textile working, a spindle whorl for hand spinning and a needle used for sewing.

The spindle whorl was recovered from a layer of domestic refuse (context 50, Phase 1). It has been manufactured from the base of a pedestal beaker in an oxidised fabric, possibly Oxford ware. The broken edges of the base have been pared down to form a disc and there is a centrally placed perforation, which is waisted, indicating that it had been drilled from both sides. Bases from ceramic vessels are often reused as spindle whorls, for a discussion of these, see Crummy 1983 (67).

The sewing needle was recovered from a mixed deposit (52) under demolition rubble, although complete (c 123mm), it is damaged. The head is squared and there is a small eye set within an elongated groove (not illus), stylistically it conforms to Crummy's Type 3 needles which date to the third and fourth centuries (1983, 67). Similar needles have been recorded at Stonea, Cambridgeshire (Jackson 1996, fig 108, 32-37).

A double-pointed awl measuring 78mm in length was recovered from demolition deposits (context 15, Phase 4). The terminals are separated by an expanded central section and stylistically it resembles Manning Type 4B awl, which has a tapering square-sectioned tang (1985, 40). Awls of this type were generally used for leather working.

Other objects worthy of note include iron wedges and a piece of stone utilised as a sharpener. Two possible wedges measuring from 45-47mm in length were recovered, one from Phase 3 (37) and the other from Phase 4 (15). Wedges had any number of uses, large examples were driven into the timber causing it to split along the grain (cleaving), while smaller wedges may have been used to secure structural fittings and heads of hafted tools. Finally an oval sectioned length of stone displaying patches of wear and longitudinal facets may have been utilised as a sharpening stone for tools (not illus).

QUERNS AND MILLSTONES
A Chapman

There are fragments from four querns and millstones. All have been manufactured from quartz rich sandstones ranging from fine to medium and medium to coarse grained stones, one rich in feldspar. All of these may be categorised as Millstone Grit.

The assemblage includes a near complete, and apparently unused, lower stone from a rotary quern, 500mm in diameter, which came from pit (39), next to the malting oven. The other pieces are all from the demolition rubble over the building (3 and 15). A small fragment from an upper stone retains part of a handle socket, and the grinding surface has almost worn through to the base of the socket, indicating that it had been used to the maximum possible degree.

The other two fragments come from millstones, which indicate the presence either of a watermill on the adjacent Harper's Brook or an animal-powered mill. A small irregular fragment is from a stone up to 68mm thick. A larger fragment is from a well-used upper stone, up to 50mm thick, with a dimpled grinding surface. The back and two edges of the surviving fragment had been reused as a sharpening stone, so it is not possible to accurately estimate the diameter of the original millstone, but it is clearly well in excess of 600mm.

LEAD

Only four pieces of lead were recovered from Roman contexts, all are undiagnostic and were recovered from Phase 4 demolition (context 15) or rubble (context 3) deposits. They include one piece of folded lead sheet and three molten nodules. The paucity of lead fragments on the site is surprising as it was such an important material in building, this together with the dearth of structural fittings may suggest that many of the internal and external fittings may have been removed and recycled after abandonment.

THE ROMAN VESSEL GLASS
H E M Cool

The Roman vessel glass fragments found during the excavations are summarised by Phase and colour in Table 7. The colour of the glass has a chronological significance. Blue/green glass was in use during the first to third centuries whilst bubbly light green glass is typical of the fourth century. As the table makes clear the assemblage is predominantly fourth century and relates to post villa activities.

The material from the pre-villa contexts of Phase 1 consists in the main of undiagnostic body fragments, though one (SF 126 from context 50) is the body fragment of a first to second-century hexagonal bottle (Price and Cottam 1998, 198). The base fragment no. 7 also comes from a Phase 1 context but it is probably intrusive as it is made of the bubbly light green glass typical of the fourth century.

The material that was found stratified in the Phase 3 contexts was also relatively undiagnostic. The light yellow brown colour of two fragments (SF 124, 138; context 37) would suggest a first to mid-second-century date. The same context produced a fragment from either a hexagonal or a square bottle (Price and Cottam 1998, 194) which can only be dated to the broad first to mid-third-century period. The unstratified square bottle base no. 1 could have originally been associated with either the pre-villa or villa occupation. The design on the base is not a particularly common one in Britain, but another square bottle of similar size with this design is known from Southgate Street, Gloucester (unpublished), unfortunately also from a residual context.

It is likely that much of the fourth-century light green bubbly glass from the Phase 4 contexts comes from one or two vessels, but interpretation is made difficult by the fact that they have been heavily burnt. The fragments catalogued as nos. 3 and 6 here are consistent with coming from a large funnel-mouthed jug (for general type see Price and Cottam 1998, 163). These normally have curved handles. Angular reeded handles such as nos. 4 and 5 are more typical of fourth-century cylindrical bottles (see for example Price and Cottam 1998, 204). Such bottles also had funnel mouths like no. 3. Many of the less diagnostic fragments (eg 108, 109) show traces of optic blowing, a typical decoration on the jugs. It is perhaps appropriate to note that though the material is melted, there is no evidence that this was deliberate so that it could be reworked and it seems more likely to be either accidental or the result of rubbish disposal.

Table 7: Roman vessel glass fragments by phase

Colour	Phase 1	Phase 3	Phase 4	Phase 5	Phase 6	Total
Blue/green	3	1	3	1	-	8
Yellow/brown	1	2	-	-	-	3
Bubbly light green	1	-	69	-	1	71
Total	5	3	72	1	1	82

CATALOGUE OF VESSEL GLASS

Blue/green

1 Square bottle; lower body and base fragment. Base design - circular moulding with concave-sided square internally. Moulding diameter 52mm, base width 70mm. SF 131, context 88
2 Body fragment; slightly convex-curved retaining parts of three vertical ribs. Dimensions 27 x 22mm, wall thickness 2.5mm. SF 128, context 52

Light green bubbly

3 Jug rim fragment. Funnel mouth with fire-rounded rim edge; horizontal trail below rim edge. One edge slightly heat affected. Rim diameter 75mm. SF 111, context 15
4 Jug handle fragment; upper part of angular reeded handle retaining part of trail below rim edge. Dimensions 43 x 30mm. SF 110, context 15
5 Jug handle fragment, three joining fragments also 4 chips. Wide straight handle with simple lower attachment, possibly reeded, now heavily burnt and distorted. Present length 115mm, maximum width 80mm. SF 114, context 15
6 Jug base fragment. High pushed-in base ring, probably originally with hollow tube at end; now melted and distorted. Dimensions 54 x 42mm. SF 112, context 15
7 Concave base fragment. Dimensions 27 x 13mm; wall thickness 2mm. SF 123, context 26

THE ROMAN COINS
M Curteis

There is a comparatively small sample of fourteen Roman coins from which few conclusions can be drawn. One coin, a contemporary copy of the falling horseman type of Constantius II (354+) was recovered from context 37, a layer below demolition rubble, possibly dating to phase 3. The majority come from context 15, a mixed layer connected to phase 4. The latest coin from this context is a coin of Valens, providing a *terminus post quem* of 364-78. There are two coins from context 3, which consisted of rubble also pertaining to phase 4. The latest of these coins is also Valentinianic (367-75), giving parity with the dating of phase 4 in context 15. Three coins were recovered from the subsoil (context 2).

CERAMIC TILE

Seventy-two fragments of ceramic tile, weighing 9.74kg, were recovered. Small quantities came from Phase 1, while larger amounts were recovered from the demolition deposits (Phase 4) and ancillary features lying outside the villa (Phase 5). In addition a small number of abraded fragments were recovered from topsoil deposits (Phase 6). Much of the assemblage is fragmentary and displays minimal signs of abrasion.

The bulk of the material comprises identifiable fragments (86%), which can be divided into two broad functional groups: roofing tile and hypocaust tile. The remaining 14% comprises small fragments which are difficult to identify with any certainty. Examination of the fabrics (by eye) indicates that three main fabric types are represented, although there may be slight variations within each type.

1) Sandy fabrics with varying quantities of fine-medium sand, which are generally orange in colour. May be hard fired with a distinct blue/grey core. This type is predominant.
2) Shell-tempered fabrics containing abundant crushed fossil shell and fired to a buff/brown colour. A similar fabric has been recorded at Quinton (Friendship-Taylor 1979, 121ff). Friendship-Taylor suggests that it displays similarities to the material produced at the Harrold Kilns in Bedfordshire (Brown 1974, 9).
3) Sandy fabric with varying amounts of fine-medium sand, tendency for the clays to be 'joggled', sparse white inclusions.

Roof tile makes up 43% of the total by weight. It is represented by fragments of 16 *tegulae* and three *imbrices*, all three fabric types are represented. Twelve fragments of tile join together to form part of a *tegula* measuring 280 by 260mm, they were recovered from a

Table 8: Roman tile types

Context	Tegula No	Wgt (g)	Imbrex No	Wgt (g)	Box flue No	Wgt (g)	Structural No	Wgt (g)	Indeterminate No	Wgt (g)
1	2	448	1	40	1	91	1	293	3	321
8	-	-	-	-	11	888	-	-	4	120
15	2	521	-	-	2	195	-	-	2	50
27	-	-	-	-	2	133	-	-	8	468
31	-	-	-	-	-	-	9	636	-	-
37	-	-	2	100	1	219	-	-	-	-
52	-	-	-	-	-	-	3	970	-	-
53	1	850	-	-	-	-	2	620	1	128
60	-	-	-	-	-	-	-	-	2	306
66	-	-	-	-	-	-	1	124	-	-
86	11	2219	-	-	-	-	-	--	-	-
Totals	16	4038	3	140	17	1526	16	2643	20	1393

hearth (86) together with the base of an amphora. The remainder of the tile was scattered throughout the site.

TEGULA

There is a distinct variation in the shape and thickness of the flanges present, illustrating slight variations in manufacturing technique, knife-trimming, hand soothed etc. Six different shapes were observed, more or less paralleling some of those illustrated by Brodribb (1987). The range includes flanges with flat tops, sloped-tops, rounded and even one that tapers from the base to a rounded point, terminating in line with the outside edge of the *tegula*.

Evidence for the fastening of *tegula* to keep them in place is provided by one perforated fragment (Fabric 2). The hole, positioned 20mm from the top edge and the flange, has been drilled from both sides, after firing. Similar examples have been recorded at Bancroft Villa (Williams and Zeepvat 1994, 120) and Piddington, Northamptonshire (Brodribb 1987, 10).

Four fragments retain worn patches of maroon and dark red paint, on one example the paint only survives close to the flange, where it would have been protected from weathering by the *imbrex*. In general the remains of paint occur on buff-coloured grog-tempered fabrics (Fabric 3) which are pale in colour. Excavations at Verulamium produced a number of pale yellow tiles which had been deliberately painted red. Numerous sites in the Midlands have produced evidence for the use of coloured paints on roof tiles, including Bancroft Villa, Milton Keynes (Williams and Zeepvat 1994, 119) and Croughton Villa (Mills 2008), for further examples see (Brodribb 1987, 137).

Although the assemblage is fragmentary, there are vestiges of grooved indentations on three *tegulae* fragments. One fragment is furnished with two parallel grooves running obliquely across the tile, it is possible that this is part of a makers mark, which are commonly recorded on fragments of *tegula*.

IMBREX

There are a small number of fragments from twenty *imbrices* weighing just over 0.7kg. The survival rate of this type of tile appears to be low, perhaps due to its shape and the thinness of its walls. All three fabric types are represented and one fragment is furnished with a combed wavy line pattern running along the length of the tile.

HYPOCAUST TILE

There are six fragments of box flue, identified by the presence of keying lines on the exterior surface. Two distinct manufacturing techniques have been used to execute the keying lines, combs furnished with seven and eight teeth, had been used to create curved and straight striations, and a roller-stamp, creating parallel, flat bottomed channels (Brodribb 1987, 109ff).

Finally there is a small quantity of structural tile. These fragments are small and generally display signs of having been subjected to heat, it is difficult to determine if they are fragments of pilae or sub-floor tile.

TESSERAE

A total of 657 tesserae were recovered from eight individual deposits, with a few further examples from the topsoil. The majority were recovered from demolition and rubble debris (Phase 4). Within the assemblage three sizes are represented, small (*c* 10 x 10mm) which predominate, medium (*c* 20 x 20mm) and large (30 x 30mm – 35 x 35mm). There are four different colours; red, blue/grey, white and yellow/buff, and as is the norm different materials have been used to represent the colours:

Red tessera: reused ceramic tile and burnt sandstone
Blue tessera: off white/ blue/grey limestone
White: limestone
Yellow/buff: sandstone

THE WALL PLASTER
A Chapman

A total of 2.7kg of wall plaster was recovered, much of it still retaining painted surfaces. The material comprises numerous small fragments usually with a maximum dimension of some 20-20mm. The largest group, 1.7kg, came from context 15, the demolition rubble. The second largest group, a further 0.5kg, was from context 43, the fill of a substantial posthole (Fig 8, 44), which appeared to have held a door post set on the southern wall of the northern corridor.

The material provides only a few indications of the nature of the decorative scheme from which it was derived. Three colours are present: white, red, varying from a pale orange to dark red, and black. The majority of pieces display only a single colour, with white the most common, although some display linear edges between separate colour blocks, typically white and red or white and black. Two pieces show narrow red stripes, 7mm wide, on a white ground. The general indication is therefore that the material comes from panels with a white background, outlined by frameworks of red stripes, and bordered in red and black.

The plaster was submitted for analysis of the pigments used, see below.

RAMAN SPECTROSCOPIC ANALYSIS OF PAINTED WALL PLASTER SAMPLES
P Middleton

METHOD

Twenty-seven samples from five different contexts were examined in this preliminary analysis. The analysis was carried out at Bradford University, under the direction of Prof. H G M Edwards, using FT-Raman spectroscopy and raman spectroscopy with 785nm wavelength.

The samples were heavily contaminated with soot and clay, and this presented certain problems in obtaining clear spectra, as well as resulting in large fluorescence problems (Table 9).

RESULTS

The palette of colours is limited to three: red, grey and white. However, by mixing, a range of 49 colours was

Table 9: Quantification of analysed painted wall plaster samples

Context	Total fragments excavated	Total samples analysed
8	1	1
15	46	10
37	13	4
43	49	11
60	1	1

achieved, with 'red' presented within a colour range from light pink to dark red/purple. Carbon [1310, 1560 cm] is present in almost all samples, in many cases as a result of contamination, but carbon was also certainly used as a darkening agent, whilst calcite [1086, 713, 282 cm] was added to lighten tones. Calcite and carbon were mixed together to produce grey. Some of the white pigment spectra exhibited carbon bands, but these are interpreted as later contamination.

A broad band [centred on 780 cm] appeared with many samples, of all colours, although it was stronger in association with lighter colours. This is assigned to a limewash putty, commonly found on Roman villa sites and is probably best seen as a wall preparation, applied before the coloured pigments.

Four samples are of particular interest in the intensity of the dark red/purple colour achieved. Context (60) and context (15.1) samples both exhibit the characteristic bands [227, 247, 294, 413, 503 and 615 cm] associated with haematite. The strength of the spectra and the presence of band 247 cm suggest that this may be identified as the pigment *caput mortuum* (de Oliveira *et al* 2002). This pigment has also been encountered on recent analysis of samples from Rushton, Northamptonshire (Edwards *et al* 2002). Samples from context (8) and context (43), although superficially similar, present different spectra, assigned to haematite in the case of (8) and to a mixture of iron oxides in the case of (43.1).

DISCUSSION

Although the range of pigments in use appears to have been modest, great ingenuity was employed to produce a range of colour for the decoration of the villa at Stanion. The presence of *caput mortuum* is significant, particularly in the light of its recent discovery at Rushton. Its identification in a context assigned to Phase 1 of the villa building (sample 60) is particularly worthy of note. In contrast, the sample assigned to Phase 2 (sample 43.1), seems to imitate the colour through a complex mixing of a number of iron oxides and without the benefit of the original 'recipe'. This may reflect the availability of a specialist painter in the first instance.

METALWORKING DEBRIS

A Chapman

A total of 4.0kg of metalworking debris was recovered from 14 contexts. However, the majority of the assemblage, 2.9kg, came from a single deposit, context 15, the demolition rubble, while the other contexts produced only the odd fragment or two each.

The material is very mixed. There are some small fragments of tap slag, but the majority comprises irregular lumps of miscellaneous vesicular slag. Some pieces have a single convex surface with fired clay adhering, indicating that they come from broken up furnace or hearth linings. A single small piece, from context 1, the topsoil, has a sausage-shaped projection 18mm in diameter probably resulting from the use of a metal rod to open up holes within a furnace opening to allow the slag to run out. A few pieces of lighter, vesicular fuel ash slag are also present.

The presence of some tap slag would suggest that smelting had been carried out somewhere on the site, while the miscellaneous slag could derive from either smelting or secondary smithing. The small quantity recovered and its fragmentary state suggest that it is secondary within its context and that any metalworking furnaces and heaths, and the large quantities of debris that would be produced by their use, must have lain some distance away within another part of the villa complex.

Although none of the material was available for examination, the quarry pits excavated in 1984 apparently contained quantities of slag, although the nature of the material is not further defined in the surviving notes, as well as some small 'furnace bottoms', and it was assumed by the excavators that the pits had been for the quarrying of ironstone for iron smelting.

The combined evidence does suggest that iron smelting may have been a significant economic activity of this small villa.

MEDIEVAL AND POST-MEDIEVAL FINDS
T Hylton

Medieval and post-medieval artefacts were recovered from topsoil and subsoil deposits. There is one medieval object, a plain, tongue-shaped, two-piece strap-end dated to the thirteenth to fourteenth centuries, for a similar example see Pritchard 1991 (fig 86, 611). Post-medieval finds include a finely crafted bone whistle, two heel irons and a slate pencil.

THE BONE WHISTLE
Dr G Lawson, Cambridge Ancient Music Research Project

This is clearly a pocket whistle with a very loud and shrill pitch. Not a sheepdog-whistle in the modern farming sense, which requires more pitch-control. A personal, more general purpose blast-whistle, like an old police whistle (but higher-pitched). Maybe a gamekeeper's call? The methods of voicing, with the characteristic D-shaped sound-hole and the now-missing block were not well established before about AD 1000, and this looks a lot later even than that. A late date is also suggested by its good condition, unless it is very recent, ie nineteenth century, it would require a very benign topsoil environment to allow such good preservation.

ILLUSTRATED WHISTLE (Fig 19)

5   Whistle, bone. Lathe turned with D-shaped sound hole. Cylindrical with circular cross-section, tapered with a terminal knop. Exterior surface ornamented with a raised linear motif. Length: 44mm diameter: 10mm. SF 82, context 1, topsoil

ARCHAEOMAGNETIC DATING
P Linford

Two features were subject to Archaeomagnetic analysis. These comprised burnt material, interpreted as a hearth on the tessallated floor of the villa, and burnt deposits within the corn drier (28/32). The analysis has shown that, whilst both had been exposed to sufficient heat to acquire thermoremnant magnetisation, the directions of magnetisation measured in individual samples were extremely scattered. In the case of the possible hearth on the tessellated floor the scattering was so marked that it must be concluded that the fired clay was not fired *in situ* but was redeposited after it had been heated.

Some of the samples from the corn drier were magnetised in similar directions, although the majority were highly scattered. Demagnetisation measurements suggest that the firing temperature of the feature was relatively low, but this fact alone would not account for the degree of scattering observed. Disturbance during the time since the feature acquired its TRM is the most likely explanation. It is thus not possible to deduce a reliable date for the last firing of the feature but an approximate estimate can be obtained by subjectively choosing to accept only those seven samples which tend to have similar TRM directions. The date obtained suggests that the corn drier was last heated during the period spanned by the first centuries BC and AD.

THE ANIMAL BONE
K Deighton

METHOD

A small assemblage, two archive boxes, of animal bone was recovered by hand, although bone recovered from wet sieving is also included in the analysis. Sample sizes varied with context but were typically between 20 and 80 litres. Residues of 3.4 mm and 1mm were scanned. The material had been previously assessed (Deighton 2004a) under the guidance of Polydora Baker at the Centre for Archaeology (CfA) English Heritage.

Quantification follows Halstead after Watson (1979) and uses minimum anatomical element (Minau). The following were recorded for each element: context, anatomical element, proximal fusion, distal fusion, side, preservation, fragmentation, butchery evidence and sex (where appropriate). Vertebrae and ribs (with articulating ends) were counted and noted as small or large ungulate but not included in quantification. Partial skeletons are not included in quantification in order to avoid over-representation. Pathology is described after Baker and Brothwell (1980) and fusion follows Silver (1969). Ovicaprid teeth were aged after Payne (1973). Butchery is after Binford (1981). Measurements follow von den Driesch (1976).

RESULTS

PRESERVATION

The occurrence of butchery was low, as was burning, although there was apparently a higher incidence within the material from the ancillary features beyond the building (Phase 5). Skinning was noted on horse bones. Canid gnawing was moderate at 22.4%, but no evidence of bone digested by canids was noted. There was a single instance of rodent gnawing. Fragmentation was fairly high (only 31.5% of bones were whole), although no fresh breaks were recorded and the surface condition was good. Some material from the well (89) exhibited brown staining and exfoliation consistent with waterlogging and rapid drying out. The largest concentration of bone is seen in the dumped occupation debris beneath the building (Phase 1).

TAXONOMIC DISTRIBUTION

Table 10: Species by phase, by number and (percentage)

Phase	horse (*Equus*)	cattle (*Bos*)	Sheep/goat (*Ovis/capra*)	pig (*Sus*)	dog (Canid)	deer (*Cervus sp.*)	chicken (*Gallus*)	Raven (*Corvus corax*)	Total
1	5 (5.6)	22 (24.7)	49 (55)	6 (6.7)	3	1	3	-	89
2	-	-	4	-	-	-	-	-	4
3	-	-	-	-	-	-	-	-	
4	1	3	3	4	-	-	-	-	11
5	1 (2.5)	6 (15.3)	26 (66.6)	5 (12.8)	-	-	-	1*	39
Total	7	31	82	15	3	1	3	1	143

*Partial skeleton

Table 11: Bone from sieved samples by phase

Phase	Sheep/goat (*Ovis/capra*)	pig (*Sus*)	Small bird (Passerine)	Small mammal	amphibians	Total
1	-	-	1	3	-	4
5	4	2	-	13	1	20
Totals	4	2	1	16	1	24

AGEING

The evidence for neonates is an ovicaprid femur from Phase 1 and a *Bos* metacarpal from Phase 5. Only five sheep mandibles were available for ageing from Phase 1, of which four could be assigned to a wear stage (one was 0-2 months, one 1-2 years and two were 8-10 years). One sheep mandible from Phase 4 cannot be assigned to a single age class and of three from Phase 5, one is not assigned, one is 2-6 months and one 2-3 years. A canine mandible has adult dentition present but unworn which could suggest an animal of over 7 months.

MEASUREMENTS

Definition of measurements used in following tables:

M1=breath of proximal articulation (bp)
M2=breath of distal articulation (bd)
M3=greatest length (GL)
M4= Smallest width of shaft (Sc)

Alternative measurements (shown in brackets next to measurements)

Dip= Diagonal of proximal end
Did= Diagonal of distal end
Dd= Depth of distal end
L= Length of Metacarpal
BG=Breadth of glenoid cavity
GLP= greatest length of Glenoid process
SLC=Smallest length of scapula neck
GLi=Greatest length of lateral half
GLm=Greatest length of medial half
DLS= diagonal length of sole

Table 12: Raven bone measurements (mm)

Element	Meas.1 (bp)	Meas.2 (Bd)	Meas.3 (GL)	Meas.4 (SC)
Humerus	23.5	18.2	90	6.7
Ulna	-	10.7 (Did)	-	4
Radius	-	6.7	-	1.2
Carpometacarpus	13	14 (Did)	66	59.6(L)
Tibio-tarsus	-	7.8 (Dd)	-	2.5
Tibio-tarsus	9.5 (Dip)	-	-	-
Tarso-metatarsus	11	7	64	3.5

Table 13: Cattle bone measurements (mm)

Context	element	M1	M2	M3	M4
50 (Phase 1)	Phalanx1	-	29	6.1	-
51	radius	52	54.7	21	190
52	astragalus	-	39	63.5 (GLi)	56.8 (GLm)
52	astragalus	-	46	73	61.1
52	Phalanx1	32.5	28.7	5.6	-
52	metatarsal	-	49	-	21.5
54	Phalanx3	-	-	65(DLS)	-
62 (Phase 2)	Phalanx2	25	21.5	35	-
62	metacarpal	62	62	-	182

Table 14: Sheep bone measurements (mm)

Context	element	M1	M2	M3	M4
52 (Phase 1)	tibia	-	22	-	-
53	Phalanx1	9	7	31.5	-
64	radius	28	-	-	-
83	metacarpal	19.7	-	-	-
29 (Phase 5)	calcaneum	-	-	46	-
29	femur	40.3	-	-	-
88	tibia	-	20.5	-	-

Table 15: Pig bone measurements (mm)

Context	element	M1	M2	M3	M4
21 (Phase 5)	scapula	-	-	35(GLP)	-
27	Phalanx3	-	-	32.5(DLS)	-
31	Phalanx2	15	-	21	-

Table 16: Horse bone measurements (mm)

Context	element	M1	M2	M3	M4
66 (Phase1)	metacarpal	39.5	-	-	17
52	Phalanx1	51	-	-	-

Table 17: Dog bone measurements (mm)

Context	element	M1	M2	M3	M4
53 (Phase1)	Ulna	18	-	-	-
53	Radius	12.1	-	-	-
53	Scapula	-	10.2 (BG)	19 (GLP)	14 (SLC)

SKELETONS

Four partial skeletons were recovered from the fill of a well in Phase five. These were three cattle and a raven. The raven skeleton consisted of a wing, a skull, and lower leg bones.

The cattle skeletons were distinguished from each other by their differing surface conditions. Skeleton 1 with mid brown staining consists of atlas, axis, four cervical vertebra, four thoracic vertebra and four ribs. The vertebral centrums were unfused but present. Two right maxillary tooth rows were also present with the same staining. It seems possible that one was associated with the other remains. Skeleton 2 consists of a light brown partial skull (frontal bone) with left occipital condyle; the sutures of the skull are unfused. Matching right and left maxillary tooth rows or a solitary right maxillary tooth row could be associated, as could a mandibular ramus and a right horn core with a fresh break. The final animal consists of a pair of mandibles with light brown staining; flaking of the deciduous fourth premolar (d4) is present and worn and the third molar (m3) is erupting which suggests an animal of between 18 and 30 months. A right horn core could be associated. Less certain is the association of a left tibia with any of the remains. This has a fusing proximal articulation (damaged) while the distal articulation is unfused.

Table 18: Species by bone element for Phase 1

Element	*Equus* horse	*Bos* cattle	*Ovis/capra* Sheep/goat	*Sus* pig	*Canis* dog	*Cervus* deer	*Gallus* chicken
Scapula	-	1	1	-	1	-	-
P. humerus	-	1	-	-	-	-	-
D. humerus	-	1	1	-	-	-	-
P. radius	1	1	5	3	-	-	-
D. radius	1	1	4	3	-	-	1
Ulna	-	1	1	-	1	-	1
P. metacarpal	1	-	1	-	-	-	1
D. metacarpal	1	-	2	-	-	-	-
Pelvis	-	-	-	-	-	-	-
P. femur	-	1	2	-	-	-	-
D. femur	-	-	2	-	-	-	-
P. tibia	-	-	5	-	-	-	-
D. tibia	-	2	5	-	-	-	-
Calcaneum	-	2	1	-	-	-	-
Astragulus	-	2	-	-	-	-	-
P. metatarsal	-	2	2	-	-	-	-
D. metatarsal	-	2	2	-	-	-	-
Phalanx1	1	4	1	-	-	-	-
Phalanx2	-	-	-	-	-	-	-
Phalanx3	-	1	-	-	-	-	-
Mandible	-	-	7	-	1	-	-
Atlas	-	-	-	-	-	-	-
Axis	-	-	1	-	-	-	-
Horncore	-	-	-	-	-	1(antler)	-
Teeth	-	-	4	-	-	-	-
P. metapodial	-	-	1	-	-	-	-
D. metapodial	-	-	1	-	-	-	-
Total	**5**	**22**	**49**	**6**	**3**	**1**	**3**
Percentage	*5.9*	*26.2*	*58.3*	*7.1*	*3.6*	*1.2*	*3.6*

PATHOLOGY

Two instances of interdental attrition were observed on ovicaprid mandibles. One mandible has an uneven wear pattern on the first molar and interdental attrition, also with possible evidence for an abscess on the mandibular bone. This latter suggests gum disease or infection.

DISCUSSION

The assemblage consists largely of the major domesticates, with ovicaprids as the dominant species. Cattle, sheep/goat, pig, chicken were all utilised as food. The horse was used for traction and transport although the possible evidence of skinning could suggest the use of hides. Dogs were kept for herding, hunting, security and as companion animals and canid gnawing on bones attests to the presence of dogs as well as the actual canid bones.

Little reliance on wild species is suggested. As deer is represented in Phase 1 by a single tine only, this could suggest the collection of shed antler for working rather than hunting or even the import of this material to site. The presence of the raven in the fill of the well (Phase 5) could be the result of pest control or accidental death. The partial cattle skeletons in the well could be butchery waste, the spinal column having been stripped out of a carcass for example. The presence of bone suggests the well had fallen into disuse and was used for rubbish or was deliberately backfilled.

Temporal comparisons are difficult and their value is limited due to the small size of the assemblage and its uneven distribution across the phases. However, this uneven distribution could be an indication of activity. Indeed it appears to confirm the interpretation of structural evidence. The relative concentration of material in Phases 1 and 5 suggests an area of rubbish disposal. For Phase 1 bone could either have been dumped as refuse into the possible pond area or incorporated in the backfill. For Phase 5 the bone could suggest that ancillary activity included the butchery of animal carcasses. In fact, the presence of a corn dryer and charred cereal in this phase could imply that a more diverse range of agrarian produce was processed here. The lack of remains from Phase 3 suggests butchery and rubbish disposal took place elsewhere during villa occupation.

Comparisons between Phases 1 and 5 show sheep are the dominant species, followed by cattle. Cattle appear to decline through time. Phase 1 has the greatest range of species, however, the significance is difficult to interpret without further evidence. Some animals had been present in Phases two and four, however, their numbers are too small for comparison or comment.

Comparisons between sites are only possible in broad terms of the species present and the percentages of domesticates again due to the small size of the assemblage. Comparisons with other small assemblages show varying patterns. For example at Wootton villa (Deighton 2004c) and in Roman levels at Oundle (Deighton 2004b) sheep also dominate. Croughton villa (Deighton 2003a) has equal numbers of cows and sheep whereas *Bos* appear to be the predominant species at Wootton Fields School (Deighton 2003b). Stanwick Redlands farm (Davis 1997) also shows a predominance of cattle, followed by ovicaprids. The larger assemblages at Latimer (Hamilton 1971) and Shakenoak (Cram 1973) villas show lower percentages of sheep and higher of cattle and of pigs. Cattle skeletons in wells are not uncommon for example in the late Roman well from Scole (Baker 1998).

A local example of a raven found on a Roman site was at Park Street, Towcester (Eastman 1980) where two raven ulnas were recorded. The presence of the species at Stanion villa could be the result of pest control or the accidental death of a species, which is not unusual on habitation sites. Eastman (1980) also suggests the birds may have been kept as pets. A ritual explanation should not be ruled out as the bird was associated with the Celtic war goddess. This mythical association possibly has its genesis in the species habit of feeding on carrion, therefore resulting in is presence at battle sites.

THE SHELL
G Campbell

Excavation produced a small assemblage of 69 marine or freshwater shells from 17 contexts, from Phases 1 to 6.

The principal shell recovered was oyster: 35 upper (right) valves and 28 bases (left valves). All were common oysters (*Ostrea edulis*), and almost all were irregular: curved, lengthy, and sharply distended, either anteriorly or posteriorly in about equal numbers. Most shells were thick (the bases putting on growth to keep the shell edge away from the sea-bed) and aged (in some cases very aged). The irregularity and thickness together indicated the great majority of the shells came from beds where oysters were crowded together in the natural manner, without active management to achieve consistent and rapid growth, and with fishing irregular and infrequent. This was confirmed by a base shell from context 29 which had settled and grown on the upper shell of a neighbouring oyster. The exceptions were the examples from context (64), gully [65] predating the villa, which were regular in shape. Fouling organisms were quite common (about half the bases), but all were burrowing worms (probably *Polydora*), a common pest. Oyster shells were distributed through all phases. Most were too broken to measure, or to observe knife-marks caused by opening. Although some were quite large (estimated at over 100mm), most were surprisingly small (about 50mm). Overall, the occupants of the villa consistently imported oysters of low quality (and presumably low in price), aged (and therefore less palatable), smallish, and easily fished (and therefore unpresentable and heavy to transport for the meat contained).

The few mussels were common Atlantic mussels (*Mytilus edulis*), discarded on the site during Phase 1 and intermittently thereafter. As these have a short shelf-life, the site must have had good transport connections with the sea throughout the Roman period.

A single valve of fresh-water mussel (probably *Anodonta complanata*) was found in the Phase 1 deposit 66. This is an edible mussel found in some parts of some slow-moving rivers, and shows this resource was known as a food source to the inhabitants.

Many of the shells recovered were from terrestrial gastropods (common garden snails, mainly *Cepea* and *Helix*), sometimes in quite large numbers. None were the Roman or apple snail *H. pomatia* (the usual snail for escargot). While these snails are edible and might be food remains, it is more likely that these are snails that clustered together to over-winter or survive summer droughts.

Almost half of the deposits that produced shells (eight of the 17) pre-dated the construction of the villa wing (Phase 1), probably because this was the time during the occupation of the site when discard was most likely into the excavated area. Virtually all of the shells came from deposits which would be expected to contain rubbish, such as pit fills and layers. There were only three deposits where it would be unusual to find shells: the primary fill of the pond; the doorpost fill (43) (where the shell was intentionally placed as packing, or the post includes domestic rubbish); and corn-drier fill (27) (which includes post-use domestic rubbish).

The range and nature of the shells recovered are not unusual for the type of site during the period. The indications are of poor quality oysters and close connections with the sea.

THE CHARRED PLANT REMAINS
W J Carruthers

INTRODUCTION

During the excavations an environmental sampling programme was carried out on site under the guidance of Jim Williams (English Heritage, East Midlands Regional Scientific Advisor), resulting in the processing of 40 samples using standard methods of floatation. The samples were assessed by Gill Campbell (E.H. Centre for Archaeology) and, following recommendations in the report, nine samples were selected for full analysis. This report discusses the results of that analysis.

RESULTS

A list of the taxa present in the samples is presented in Table 19. Nomenclature and most of the habitat information was taken from Stace (1997). Cereal identifications follow Jacomet (1987). Ellenberg's indicator values were used to provide information about weed ecology (Hill *et al*, 1999).

Key for Table 19

cf. = uncertain identification; + = occasional; ++ = several; +++ = frequent; +1s = plus one sprouted grain

Habitat Preferences
A = arable; C = cultivated; D = disturbed/waste; E = heath; G = grassland; H = hedgerow; M = marsh/bog; R = rivers/ditches/ponds; S = scrub; W = woods; Y = waysides/hedgerows; a = acidic soils; c = calcareous soils; n = nutrient-rich soils; o = open ground; w = wet/damp soils; * = plant of economic value

Table 19: List of plant Taxa

	Sample	34	26	35	37
	Context	53	54	66	82
CEREAL GRAINS					
T. aestivum/turgidum (free-threshing wheat grain)		cf.1	2	6	-
Triticum dicoccum/spelta (emmer/spelt grain)		16	153+10s	58	-
Triticum sp. (indeterminate wheat grain)		3	73	5	-
Hordeum vulgare L. emend. (hulled barley grain)		3	12	15	-
Hordeum sp. (indeterminate barley grain)		10	13	16	-
cf. *Secale cereale* L. (cf. rye grain)		-	-	-	-
Avena sp. (wild/cultivated oat grain)		3	6	4	-
Avena/Bromus sp. (oat/chess grain)		3	27	11	-
Indeterminate cereal grain		21	202	114	-
CEREAL CHAFF					
Triticum sp. (free-threshing wheat rachis frag.)		1	-	-	-
T. dicoccum (emmer glume base)		-	cf.3	-	cf.1
T. spelta L. (spelt glume base)		114	197	45	-
T. spelta L. (spelt spikelet fork)		3	3	1	-
T. spelta L. (spelt rachis fragment)		8	-	-	1
T. dicoccum/spelta (emmer/spelt glume base)		136	163	53	-
Triticum dicoccum/spelta (emmer/spelt spikelet fork)		39	20	2	7
Triticum dicoccum/spelta (emmer/spelt rachis fragment)		2	-	-	-
Hordeum sp. (barley rachis fragment)		3	-	2	-
Avena sp. (oat awn fragment)		++	+	++	-
Detached cereal sprouts		++	++	++	-
Cereal sized culm node		-	-	+	++++
OTHER ECONOMIC PLANTS & WEEDS					
Ranunculus acris/repens/bulbosus (buttercup achene) CDG		2	3	-	-
Corylus avellana L. (hazelnut shell fragment) HSW*		1	4	1	-
Agrostemma githago L. (corn cockle seed frag.) A		-	1	-	-
Fallopia convolvulus (L.)A.Love (black bindweed achene) AD		-	-	-	-
Polygonum aviculare L. (knotgrass achene) CDo		-	1	-	2
Rumex acetosella agg. (sheep's sorrel achene) GaE		-	-	-	-
Rumex sp (dock achene) CDG		13	84	22	6
Malva sp. (mallow seed) CDGH		-	-	1	-
Viola sp. (violet seed) GDH		-	-	-	-
Thlaspi arvense L. (field pennycress seed) AD		1	-	-	-
Rosa sp. (rose seed) HSW*		-	-	-	-
cf. *Pisum sativum* L. (cf. garden pea) *		-	2	1	-
cf. *Vicia faba* var. *minor* (cf. Celtic bean fragment) *		-	-	1	-
Vicia/Lathyrus sp. (small weed vetch/tare seed) CDG		1	2	-	-
Medicago lupulina L. (black medick fruit) GD		-	-	-	-
Trifolium/Lotus/Medicago sp. (clover/trefoil/medick seed) CDG		11	28	25	8
Linum usitatissimum L. (cultivated flax seed) *		-	-	-	-
Hyoscyamus niger L. (henbane seed) Dn		-	1	-	-
Lithospermum arvense L. (field gromwell nutlet) ADGo		13	43	8	1
Galeopsis tetrahit (common hemp-nettle nutlet) CD		1	-	-	-
Plantago lanceolata L. (ribwort plantain seed) G		-	4	2	-
Odontites verna/Euphrasia sp. (red bartsia/eyebright seed)		-	9	9	-
Rhinanthus sp. (rattle achene) G		-	2	4	-
Galium aparine L. (cleavers nutlet) CGHo		3	25	5	-
G. verum L. (lady's bedstraw nutlet) Gc		-	-	-	1
Sambucus nigra L. (elder seed) CDn		-	1	-	-
Tripleurospermum inodorum (L.)Sch.Bip. (scentless mayweed achene) CD		-	6	3	-
cf. *Centaurea* sp. (cf. knapweed seed frag.) CDG		-	1	-	-
Lapsana communis L. (nipplewort achene) CDGH		-	2	-	-
Eleocharis subg. *Palustres* (spike-rush nut) MPGw		-	6	2	-
Cyperaceae cf. *Schoenoplectus* sp.(cf. bulrush nut)		-	1	2	-
Carex sp. (lenticular sedge nutlet) wGMP		1	1	1	-
Carex sp. (trigonous sedge nutlet) wGMP		1	-	2	1
Lolium-type (grass caryopsis) CG		26	44	9	1
Poaceae (indeterminate grass caryopsis) GCD		24	25	26	2
Bromus sect. *Bromus* (chess caryopsis)ADG		2	203	64	2
Grass-sized stem fragments		-	-	+	-
	Totals	466	1391	530	34
volume of soil processed (litres)		*20*	*70*	*60*	*10*
charred frags per litre		**23.3**	**19.9**	**8.8**	**3.4**
Approximate ratio grain:chaff:weed seeds		*2:10:3*	*1:1:1*	*2:1:2*	*-*

Table 19: List of plant Taxa (continued)

	Sample	12	11	5	10	4
	Context	8	22	31	42	29
CEREAL GRAINS						
T. aestivum/turgidum (free-threshing wheat grain)		-	-	3	3	3
Triticum dicoccum/spelta (emmer/spelt grain)		1	4	27	158+1s	49
Triticum sp. (indeterminate wheat grain)		-	-	4	8	1
Hordeum vulgare L. emend. (hulled barley grain)		7	98	32	18	72
Hordeum sp. (indeterminate barley grain)		4	28	15	4	7
cf. *Secale cereale* L. (cf. rye grain)		-	-	-	2	-
Avena sp. (wild/cultivated oat grain)		-	Cf.1	19	8	12
Avena/Bromus sp. (oat/chess grain)		-	-	12	17	39
Indeterminate cereal grain		-	95	168	257	263
CEREAL CHAFF						
Triticum sp. (free-threshing wheat rachis frag.)		-	-	-	-	-
T. dicoccum (emmer glume base)		-	-	-	2	-
T. spelta L. (spelt glume base)		1	1	7	390	85
T. spelta L. (spelt spikelet fork)		-	-	-	1	5
T. spelta L. (spelt rachis fragment)		-	-	2	1	-
T. dicoccum/spelta (emmer/spelt glume base)		-	-	12	257	7
Triticum dicoccum/spelta (emmer/spelt spikelet fork)		-	-	-	9	2
Triticum dicoccum/spelta (emmer/spelt rachis fragment)		-	-	-	1	1
Hordeum sp. (barley rachis fragment)		-	-	5	2	8
Avena sp. (oat awn fragment)		-	-	++	+	-
Detached cereal sprouts		-	-	-	++	-
Cereal sized culm node		-	-	-	-	-
OTHER ECONOMIC PLANTS & WEEDS						
Ranunculus acris/repens/bulbosus (buttercup achene) CDG		-	-	1	1	-
Corylus avellana L. (hazelnut shell fragment) HSW*		-	-	1	-	1
Agrostemma githago L. (corn cockle seed frag.) A		-	-	-	3	-
Fallopia convolvulus (L.)A.Love (black bindweed achene) AD		-	-	1	1	-
Polygonum aviculare L. (knotgrass achene) CDo		-	-	2	1	2
Rumex acetosella agg. (sheep's sorrel achene) GaE		-	-	-	3	5
Rumex sp (dock achene) CDG		-	-	17	15	59
Malva sp. (mallow seed) CDGH		-	-	-	-	-
Viola sp. (violet seed) GDH		-	-	-	-	2
Thlaspi arvense L. (field pennycress seed) AD		-	-	-	-	-
Rosa sp. (rose seed) HSW*		-	-	-	-	1
cf. *Pisum sativum* L. (cf. garden pea) *		-	-	-	-	1
cf. *Vicia faba* var. *minor* (cf. Celtic bean fragment) *		-	-	-	-	-
Vicia/Lathyrus sp. (small weed vetch/tare seed) CDG		-	-	-	4	30
Medicago lupulina L. (black medick fruit) GD		-	-	-	-	1
Trifolium/Lotus/Medicago sp. (clover/trefoil/medick seed) CDG		-	1	7	1	9
Linum usitatissimum L. (cultivated flax seed) *		-	-	-	2	-
Hyoscyamus niger L. (henbane seed) Dn		-	-	-	-	-
Lithospermum arvense L. (field gromwell nutlet) ADGo		-	-	3	6	10
Galeopsis tetrahit (common hemp-nettle nutlet) CD		-	-	-	-	-
Plantago lanceolata L. (ribwort plantain seed) G		-	-	1	1	3
Odontites verna/Euphrasia sp. (red bartsia/eyebright seed)		-	-	-	-	-
Rhinanthus sp. (rattle achene) G		-	-	-	-	-
Galium aparine L. (cleavers nutlet) CGHo		-	-	6	4	11
G. verum L. (lady's bedstraw nutlet) Gc		-	-	2	-	6
Sambucus nigra L. (elder seed) CDn		-	-	-	1	-
Tripleurospermum inodorum (L.)Sch.Bip. (scentless mayweed achene CD		-	-	-	-	-
cf. *Centaurea* sp. (cf. knapweed seed frag.) CDG		-	-	1	-	-
Lapsana communis L. (nipplewort achene) CDGH		-	-	-	-	2
Eleocharis subg. *Palustres* (spike-rush nut) MPGw		-	-	1	-	1
Cyperaceae cf. *Schoenoplectus* sp.(cf. bulrush nut)		-	-	5	2	-
Carex sp. (lenticular sedge nutlet) wGMP		-	-	2	-	-
Carex sp. (trigonous sedge nutlet) wGMP		-	-	2	-	-
Lolium-type (grass caryopsis) CG		1	-	5	12	9
Poaceae (indeterminate grass caryopsis) GCD		-	-	6	9	4
Bromus sect. *Bromus* (chess caryopsis)ADG		-	3	10	25	7
Grass-sized stem fragments		-	-	++	+	+++
Total:		14	231	392	1232	782
volume of soil processed (litres):		20	30	40	20	?
charred frags per litre:		0.7	7.7	9.8	61.6	?
Approximate ratio grain:chaff:weed seeds		-	10:+:+	11:1:3	5:7:1	10:2:3

DISCUSSION

STATE OF PRESERVATION AND SPROUTING

The state of preservation of most of the charred plant remains was reasonably good. The survival of husks (paleas and lemmas) on many of the hulled barley grains, and the fairly intact state of the spelt glume bases indicated that little surface abrasion or redeposition had occurred. The main reason for cereals being unidentifiable was distortion, vacuolation and fragmentation such as often occurs during charring, particularly in spelt wheat and bread-type wheat. However, some additional distortion was observed in grains that had sprouted. Detached sprouts and grains that had 'caved in' following germination were present in four of the samples, primarily in Phase 1. As evidence of sprouting was not frequent in any of the samples, it was not possible to determine whether this was deliberate sprouting to produce malt, or sprouting due to damp storage conditions. The scant evidence suggests the latter, although examples of the use of spelt to produce malt are known for the Roman period (eg Catsgore, Hillman 1982). Unfortunately very little charred plant material was recovered from the oven fill, flue 29 (context 28), but it may have been used to produce malt at least some of the time. In her review of Roman corn driers in Britain, Van der Veen (1989) found that 28% produced some evidence to suggest that they may have been used to produce malt.

Phase 1

Deposits dated to this phase were associated with activity pre-dating the construction of the villa building. They occurred in a depression that may once have been a pond. The upper fills of this area produced large quantities of pot and an ashy, dark soil, suggesting that it may have been used as a midden prior to the construction of the villa building.

Four samples from this phase of occupation were fully analysed. These consisted of four layers that were rich in charred plant remains from a variety of sources. Although the main crop plants were similar in all of the samples, differences in the type of waste represented can be seen when ratios of grain to chaff fragments to weed seeds are examined (G:Ch:W; see bottom of Table 19).

Sample 34 (context 53, primary fill of pond) was richer in chaff fragments and weed seeds than cereal grains, indicating that burnt cereal processing waste was present (G:Ch:W = 2:10:3). Since burning can change the G:Ch:W ratio, destroying more chaff than cereal grains (Boardman & Jones 1990), this waste material may originally been much richer in chaff fragments before it was burnt. Identification of the grain and chaff fragments indicated that spelt wheat was the principal crop present, with small amounts of hulled barley, bread-type wheat and oats (indeterminate wild or cultivated). These minor cereals probably represented volunteer plants from crops that had previously been grown on the land. Alternatively mixed waste from several crops, perhaps including some hay, may have been present. As many of the weeds can grow in grasslands as well as cultivated fields it is not possible to be certain from where the weed seeds had originated. Where cereal crops follow a grass ley or are sown into a newly ploughed meadow this is even more of a problem.

Sample 26 (context 54, primary fill of pond) also consisted primarily of spelt wheat, but this time the higher proportion of grain to chaff suggested that unthreshed spikelets may have been burnt, since the ratio was roughly 1:1. Alternatively, cereal processing waste and spoilt grain could have been burnt together. Since very small weed seeds such as clover-type (*Trifolium/Lotus/Medicago* sp.) and dock (*Rumex* sp.) were frequent in the assemblage, the latter explanation may be more likely. When ears of hulled wheat are processed up to the spikelet stage (perhaps prior to storage as spikelets; Hillman 1981), it is easy to remove small weed seeds using a relatively large meshed sieve. Only large weed seeds such as chess (*Bromus* sect. *Bromus*) are likely to remain with the spikelets in the sieve.

Chess, an arable weed thought to have been introduced into Britain with spelt (Godwin 1975), was particularly numerous in this sample, outnumbering emmer/spelt grains. Although there is no evidence that chess was cultivated as a crop in its own right during the Iron Age and Roman periods, the fact that it is sometimes abundant in spelt crops (eg a fourth-century enclosure ditch sample from Prickwillow Road, Ely; Carruthers 2003) suggests that it may have been tolerated as a weed and possibly even seen as a useful addition to the crop.

Other crops represented in this assemblage were bread-type wheat, oats (wild or cultivated) barley and possible emmer wheat. Emmer had largely been replaced by spelt on most sites in southern England by the Roman period. Since less than 1% of the glume bases at Stanion were emmer or possible emmer, the remains could represent relict plants persisting within the fields of spelt. One additional food represented was possible pea (cf. *Pisum sativum*), a leguminous plant which would have been useful in helping to restore fertility to the soil. Peas are not commonly found prior to the Saxon period, but this is probably mainly due to problems of preservation by charring.

Sample 35 (context 66, primary fill of pond) produced a similar type of assemblage to sample 26, in that it contained similar quantities of grain, chaff and weed seeds (G:Ch:W = 2:1:2). Once again, spelt wheat was dominant, and weeds such as chess and clover-type legumes were frequent. Both pea and Celtic bean were present, and small amounts of hulled barley, bread-type wheat and oats were recovered. As with sample 26, this deposit may have received burnt material from a variety of sources.

Sample 37 (context 82, fill at margins of pond) produced a very different assemblage, consisting primarily of charred straw fragments and culm nodes ('joints' in the stem). The few identifiable seeds present amongst the straw indicated that it was probably from a spelt crop that had grown on damp soil (providing that the seeds had all come from the same source), since a spelt glume base, spike-rush seeds and a variety of sedge nutlets were present. Arable crops may have been grown along Harper's Brook to the south of the villa, on the fertile alluvial soils. This type of waste would have been removed from the crop in the first stages of processing. It is rarely preserved archaeobotanically, as it usually burns away leaving few traces (Boardman and Jones 1990). It is also a useful resource for fodder, bedding and thatching, so is less likely to be burnt as waste.

As a whole, the Phase 1 samples indicated that spelt was the principal crop in the later first century, prior to the construction of the villa building. Since several types of processing waste were present in the area and the remains were fairly abundant, the crops were likely to have been grown locally. At least some of the crops were being grown on damp soils along the valley bottom. Bread-type wheat, hulled barley, peas, Celtic beans and probably oats were amongst the other crops being grown. There was no evidence that exotic fruits and spices were being imported, although admittedly this type of evidence is less likely to become preserved by charring. However, native hedgerow fruits and nuts were probably being gathered to supplement the diet, as hazelnut shell fragments and an elderberry seed were recovered.

Phase 4

Unfortunately no samples relating to the direct use of the villa were available for study. Two samples from burnt areas probably associated with the demolition of the building were examined; sample 11 (context 22/23, burnt deposit on tessellated floor) and sample 12 (context 8, burnt deposit in shallow hollow, 16). Neither of them was particularly productive, and both consisted of grain with very few contaminants. In contrast to the Phase 1 samples, hulled barley was the principal crop. A few emmer/spelt grains and one possible oat were the only other cereals present. These burnt remains could have been the waste from fodder being fed to the occupants' horses or livestock, or it could have been consumed by the occupants themselves. If so, it represents a change in the diet and a lower status meal than spelt or bread wheat. Since virtually no chaff and very few weeds were present, there was no evidence from this phase that cereal cultivation was taking place locally. The cereals could have been brought onto the site as processed grain.

Phase 5

This phase relates to features outside the villa, including a corn drier/oven, associated pits, a hearth and a well. Unfortunately, although the flue of the corn drier was 100% sampled it produced very few charred plant remains. Only a few poorly preserved emmer/spelt grains and a spelt glume base were preserved in an identifiable state. However, samples from the fill of the northern channel of the oven (sample 5, context 31 in 32) and from the fill of a pit cut by the oven (sample 10, context 42 in pit 47) and a further pit (sample 4, context 29 in pit 30) produced reasonable concentrations of charred cereal remains that probably originated from the oven. Samples 5 and 4 consisted primarily of cereal grains, most of which were hulled barley. When charred, barley produces fewer chaff fragments per grain than spelt wheat, so the larger numbers of grains in these samples in relation to chaff fragments could be due to the dominance of barley.

Sample 10 from pit 47, pre-dating the oven, contained frequent emmer/spelt grains and spelt chaff fragments indicating that either spelt spikelets or mixed cereal processing waste and grain were present. Despite the stratigraphic relationship, the very high concentration of charred plant material in this sample (>61 fragments per litre of soil processed) suggests that they had originated from the oven/kiln, and may have been dumped on top of the pit fills which they have subsequently contaminated.

All three samples probably represent sweepings from the oven, in which case ash from the fuel and any cereals that had become charred accidentally would have become mixed together during redeposition. Fuel residues from ovens are often rich in chaff fragments and weed seeds, since cereal processing waste was a useful source of fuel for ovens and kilns (Van der Veen 1989).

Most of the evidence from Van der Veen's review of Roman ovens indicated that spelt or spelt and barley were the main crops being dried in the ovens. This fits in with the evidence from Stanion, as both hulled barley and spelt were the main cereals present in the samples. Since both cereals require parching to remove the husks, this was likely to have been one use to which the oven was regularly put. Barley that was being used for fodder would not have required parching unless it had been harvested damp. In this case it may have been dried prior to storage to avoid spoilage. Barley may also have been used for human consumption during hard times, or for specific dishes. There was no evidence that it was being used for malting, but this is another possibility

Additional crops represented by smaller numbers of charred remains were bread-type wheat, emmer, oats, possible rye, peas and flax. All of these crops are typical of the period, particularly in central and southern England (Murphy 1997, Greig 1991). Flax is fairly common on Roman sites (Greig 1991). It is likely to have been grown on the damper soils in the valley bottom as it requires a moist root-run. There is some indication that oats were more frequent in the Phase 5 samples than the Phase 1 samples, but too few samples were analysed to be certain. One difference between the two phases that was a little clearer was the increase in indicators of nutrient-poor soils. Sheep's sorrel (*Rumex acetosella*) grows primarily on poor, acidic, sandy soils. It was not present in the Phase 1 samples but occurred in two of the Phase 5 samples. Other poor soil indicators such as vetch/tare (*Vicia/Lathyrus* sp.) and lady's bedstraw (*Galium verum*) seeds were more frequent in the Phase 5 samples. It is possible that the apparent increase in barley cultivation in the Phases 4 and 5 samples was due to some loss in fertility of the local soils, due to intensive cultivation of more demanding crops such as bread-type wheat and spelt wheat during the occupation of the villa. The number of samples examined for this report was too few to draw definite conclusions, but this hypothesis could be investigated if further excavations were undertaken in the area.

There were no other obvious differences in weed taxa through the phases; damp ground taxa were present in small quantities and chess and *Lolium*-type grass seeds were fairly frequent, as in Phase 1. It is likely that both of these arable weed grasses were primarily contaminants of spelt crops, since fewer were present in the barley-dominated samples. Hedgerow fruits and nuts continued to be exploited, as indicated by the recovery of hazelnut shell fragments, an elderberry seed and a rose seed (*Rosa* sp.). There was no evidence for the importation of exotic fruits and nuts, or the cultivation of an ornamental garden, as on the villa estate at Rectory Farm, Godmanchester (Murphy 1997).

COMPARISONS WITH OTHER SITES AND CONCLUSIONS

Very few villa sites have been investigated in detail for archaeobotanical evidence. The small second to fourth-century Roman farmstead at Glapthorne Road, Oundle (Carruthers 2004) produced a very similar range of charred cereal remains, including spelt processing waste and burnt grain or spikelets. The only differences between the charred assemblages at Oundle and those at Stanion were that there was less evidence for the cultivation of barley and slightly more evidence for the persistence of emmer as a minor crop at Oundle. However, at Oundle a well provided useful additional waterlogged environmental evidence, plus seeds of coriander, possible dill, flax, opium poppy and cotton thistle. This suggests that imported spices may have been present at Stanion, but they were not preserved because no waterlogged deposits were available for study.

Larger scale investigations carried out during the A120 road construction scheme in Essex, produced very similar evidence of extensive spelt cultivation on an early Roman farmstead. No exotic foods were present in a waterlogged ditch, although there was evidence for flax processing. Concentrated spelt processing waste was also found on the middle and late Roman sites along the A120. The main differences between the various sites related to the weed taxa, which indicated that some sites were damper than others and some were growing crops on poorer soils. The minor crops were identical to those at Stanion, and hedgerow fruits and nuts were being consumed.

The Roman settlement and later Roman farmstead at Stonea in the Cambridgeshire fens both produced the same range of crop plants as at Stanion, with spelt again being the dominant cereal present (van der Veen 1991). However, lentil was present in both phases of occupation, and fig was found in the earlier, higher status settlement.

The Roman period is remarkable in the uniformity of its arable production across south and central England. There are clearly still unanswered questions, however, concerning the availability of imported foods, and waterlogged deposits such as wells, cess pits and ditches should be given high priority when sites are being sampled. This includes sampling for pollen as well as plant macrofossils, as this could help to detect exotic species. In addition, much more detailed environmental sampling is required on villa sites, in the hope that evidence of garden plants may also be recovered.

DISCUSSION

It cannot be overstated that the excavations at Stanion examined only a small part of the villa complex as it appears on aerial photographs and consequently, what was revealed of the form, function and chronology of the excavated area may not apply to the entire complex.

THE STANION VILLA

The site at Stanion is situated in a valley adjacent to Harper's Brook, a tributary of the River Nene, which it joins near Islip 11kms to the south-west.

Occupation appears to have begun at around the mid-first century AD, perhaps centred on a major timber building. By the end of the first century there had been a major expansion, centred on the creation of a stone-built villa. This comprised a simple strip building some 30-35m long, with a corridor along the northern side, facing uphill, and a suite of rooms to the south. The only room investigated had contained painted wall plaster and a plain tessellated floor, perhaps with a small central decorative mosaic that has been lost. The corridor had been furnished with a similar plain tessellated floor. The adjacent room, which lay at the very edge of the excavated area, appeared to possess no elaborate furnishings. A small quantity of box-flue tile does suggest that at least one room had been provided with a hypocaust, but none of the recovered building material would suggest the presence of a bath house.

This was therefore a fairly small establishment that appears not to have been subject to any major refurbishments in the century or so in which it was occupied, with abandonment occurring at around the end of the second century.

To the west of the building vestiges of associated activities survived, including a pit oven lined with part of an amphora and roof tiles, a corn drier and associated pits, together with a stone-lined well. The economic base of the settlement was further defined by a rich assemblage of charred seed for the fills of a pond sealed beneath the villa, and therefore related to the original first-century settlement. At this time the dominant cereal was spelt, but the assemblage also included a much wider range of crops, including bread-type wheat, hulled barley, peas, Celtic beans and probably oats, and with the native hedgerows represented by hazelnut shell fragments and an elderberry seed. The range of crops found at Stanion Villa further adds to the body of evidence, which indicates the uniformity of arable production across south and central England during the Roman period.

There is less evidence from the second century, but the corn drier was used primarily for drying barley, although there was no evidence that this was malted barley, with chaff and charred spelt present in the mixed charred debris that appeared to be remnants of the flue used to fire the oven.

In addition, large quarry pits to the north of the villa, found in 1984, and smaller amounts of iron slag, including tap slag, from around the villa suggest that iron smelting had played a significant part in the economy of the site.

THE NEIGHBOURING ROMAN-BRITISH SITES

There are at least eight Romano-British sites in the area, most of which were discovered by surface collection on land to the south of the Stanion villa (RCHME 1979, 135). This distribution is almost certainly affected by the widespread ironstone quarrying that has taken place to the north of the site, which would have removed all traces of human activity.

The eight Romano-British sites listed by the RCHME (1979, 135), are characterised by scatters of pottery with building stone and roofing material. One of these (SMR no 2544/0/2) situated 750m south of the Stanion villa is also associated with finds of iron slag. The course of the Gartree Road from Leicester to Godmanchester passes close by, if not actually through this site before crossing the River Nene approximately 10kms to the south-west. From there, river transport would have linked the site with the small towns of Ashton, to the north and Irchester to the south (Fig 20). A second road crosses the Gartree Road close to this location proceeding within 100m of the Stanion villa. This road is observed further north within 75m of the Weldon Villa and possibly links to a known road that passes through Laxton in the direction of Ermine Street, 4kms north of Durobrivae.

COMPARISON WITH NEIGHBOURING VILLAS

Within Northamptonshire, only four villas have been substantially excavated; at Great Weldon (3.5km north of Stanion), Stanwick (17km south of Stanion), Redlands Farm (17km south of Stanion) and Piddington (35km south-west of Stanion). Of these, the villa at Great Weldon is not only the closest, but also shares many characteristics with the Stanion villa, such as its early chronology and its association with iron production.

The villa at Great Weldon has been known of since 1738 and was excavated between 1953–56 (Smith, Hird and Dix 1988-9). No late Iron Age or first century pre-Roman material was found during the excavation suggesting that occupation began in the Flavian period with a rectangular, stone-founded, four roomed building measuring 25.6m by 7.92m. To the north of this structure, a layer of calcined clay from the base of a furnace indicated the preparation of ironstone for smelting and large pieces of iron cinder were incorporated into the foundations of later buildings. The early building was destroyed by fire *c* AD 200 and replaced by one nearly twice as long with a corridor and a small bath suite. Immediately adjacent to this, a separate, circular stone-founded building with a burnt clay floor was constructed during the second century or later. During the fourth century, the main building was extended and embellished with geometric mosaics. The bath suite was enlarged and an enclosed courtyard constructed. On the north side of this was a fourth-century barn that was twice destroyed by fire. The presence of a hoard of 230 coins within a fire damaged room suggests that at least this part of the building was unoccupied at some time after *c* 350 AD. Repairs to the mosaics indicate continuing occupation elsewhere in the building and the coin sequence continues to the end of the fourth century.

The Great Weldon villa was constructed and occupied at approximately the same time as the site at Stanion. Both sites lack evidence of continuous occupation from the late Iron Age, a feature common to other Midland villas, including Apethorpe (RCHME 1979). While the beginning of the third century marks the end of the occupation of the excavated area at Stanion, it is a period of re-building at Great Weldon which leads on to further embellishment in the fourth century. Both villas were constructed in close proximity to roads and are associated with early iron smelting.

The villas at Piddington and Stanwick have yet to be fully published, although interim reports show both similarities and significant differences between these sites and the Stanion villa (Dix 1986-7: Friendship-Taylor 2003). Piddington and Stanwick seem to have developed from late Iron Age occupation, an element absent at Stanion. At Stanwick, the buildings continued to be occupied and embellished into the fourth century, while Piddington followed a similar development as a winged corridor villa until its abrupt abandonment in the late third century, after which occupation on the site seems to continued in small individual family units. This apparently sudden change in site status resembles the sequence from Stanion although in the latter case, they took place in the early third century.

IRONWORKING AND VILLAS IN THE EAST MIDLANDS

The importance of Ironworking in the East Midlands during the Roman period has recently been reviewed, emphasising its importance despite the lack of research comparable with the Weald and the Forest of Dean (Condron 1997; Bellamy *et al* 2000-1; Schrüfer-Kolb 2004). Evidence for early ironworking in the Rockingham Forest around Stanion was noted from the eighteenth century when Morton described extensive scatters of slag at Gretton and Fineshade, although it was not until the nineteenth century that their association with Roman artefacts was recognised (Bellamy *et al* 2000-1,109). Perhaps the most dramatic evidence for the development and the scale of early Roman iron production came from the excavations at Laxton (10kms north of Stanion), where a row of late first century furnaces was found of a type previously unknown in this country, and capable of an unusually large output (Tylecote & Jackson 1988; Crew 1998).

An examination of the Northamptonshire SMR showed there to be 77 sites within a 20km radius of Stanion which had shown evidence of Roman iron working, most of which are found on the ironstone deposits to the north-west of Stanion. Iron smelting is not frequently observed at villa sites, although this may simply reflect the limited areas that are usually excavated. At Sacrewell (20kms north-west of Stanion) a winged corridor villa, occupied from the mid second to the late fourth century, was associated with eight ironworking furnaces (Challands 1974, 13). Unlike Stanion, the ironworking appears to date from the fourth century and to have taken place when at least some of the building was unoccupied. Condron (1997) considered Sacrewell unusual 'in the close association between dirty polluting iron smelting

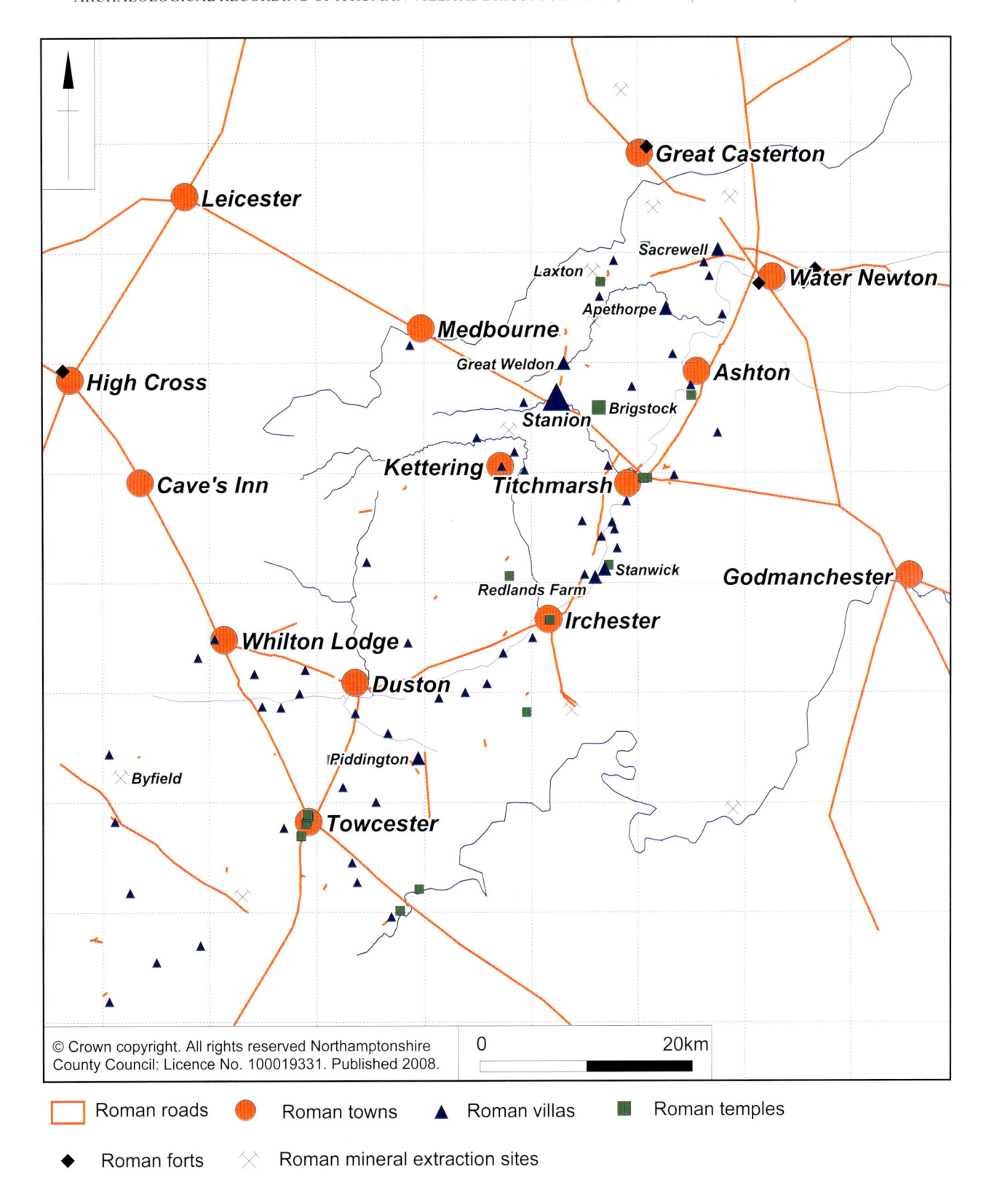

Fig 20 Location of Roman towns and roads

and a high status residence'. However, this perhaps reflects more recent negative associations with industrial processes. At Piddington, iron smelting seems to have occurred within 200m of the villa complex and in a recent gazetteer of Roman iron production sites in the East Midlands, over 30 villas (and possible villas) appear associated with iron smelting (Schrüfer-Kolb 2004, 145-166). The association of villas with iron smelting is seen

Partridge, C, 1981 *Skeleton Green, a Late Iron Age and Romano-British Site*, Britannia Monog, **2**, 1981

Payne, S, 1973 *Kill off patterns in sheep and goats: the mandibles from Asvan Kale*, Anatolian Studies, **23**, 281-303

Peacock, D P S, and Williams, D F, 1986 *Amphorae and the Roman economy: an introductory guide*, London

Price, J, and Cottam, S, 1998 *Romano-British Glass Vessels: a Handbook*, Council for British Archaeology, Practical Handbook in Archaeology, **14**, York

Pritchard, F, 1991 Strap-ends, in G Egan and F Pritchard 1991, 124-161

Renfrew J, 1991 New *Light on Early Farming: recent developments in Palaeoethnobotany*, Edinburgh University Press, Edinburgh

Rollo, B A, 1994 *Iron Age & Roman Piddington, The Mortaria 1979-1993*, Fascicule **2**, Upper Nene Archaeological Society

RCHME 1979 *An Inventory of the Historic Monuments in the County of Northampton: Archaeological Sites in Central Northamptonshire*, **2**, Royal Commission Historical Monuments, England, HMSO

RIC 1923 Mattingley, H, Sydenham E A, Sutherland C H V and Carson, R A G, *Roman Imperial Coinage*, London

Schrüfer-Kolb, I, 2004 *Roman Iron Production in Britain. Technological and socio-economic landscape development along the Jurassic ridge*, British Archaeological Reports, British Series, **380**, Oxford

Silver, I, 1969 The ageing of domestic animals, in D Brothwell and E Higgs (eds) 1969, 283-302

Smith, D J, Hird, L, and Dix, B, 1998-9 The Roman Villa at Great Weldon, Northamptonshire. *Northamptonshire Archaeol*, **22**, 23-68

Stace, C, 1997 *New Flora of the British Isles* (2nd edition), Cambridge: University Press

Taylor, J, 2001 *An Archaeological Resource Assessment of Roman Northamptonshire*, www.le.ac.uk/archaeology/eastmidlands research-framework.htm

Timby, J, Brown, R, Biddlulph, E, Hardy, A, and Powell, A, 2007 *A Slice of Rural Essex, Archaeological discoveries from the A120 between Stanstead Airport and Braintree*, Oxford Wessex Archaeology Monog, **1**, CD-Rom

Tomber, R, and Dore, J, 1998 *The Roman National Fabric Reference Collection*, MoLAS, Monog, **2**/English Heritage/ British Museum

Von den Driesch, A, 1976 *A Guide to the measurement of animal bones from archaeological sites*, Harvard university press

Van der Veen, M, 1989 Charred Grain Assemblages from Roman-Period Corn Driers in Britain, *Archaeol Journal*, **146**, 302-319

Van der Veen, M, 1991 Consumption or production? Agriculture in the Cambridgeshire fens? in J Renfrew 1991

van Zeist, W, Wasylikowa, K, and Behre, K E, 1991 *Progress in Old World Palaeoethnobotany*, A A Balkema, Rotterdam

Watson, J P N, 1979 The estimation of the relative frequencies of mammalian species: Khirokitia, 1972 *Journal of Archaeol Science*, **6**, 127-37

Wedlake, W J, 1958 *Excavations at Camerton, Somerset*, privately printed

Williams, R J, and Zeepvat, R J, 1994 *Bancroft, A Late Bronze Age/Iron Age Settlement, Roman Villa and Temple-Mausoleum*, Buckinghamshire Archaeol Soc Monog, **7**

Wilson, B, Grigson, C, and Payne, S, (eds) 1982 *Ageing and sexing of animal bones from archaeological sites*, British Archaeological Reports, British series, **109**, Oxford

Woodward, P J, Davies, S M, and Graham, A H, 1993 *Excavations at the Old Methodist Chapel and Greyhound Yard, Dorchester, 1981-1984*, Dorset Natural History and Archaeol Soc, Monog, **12**

Woods, P, and Hastings, S, 1984 *Rushden: the early fine wares*, Northamptonshire County Council

Young, C J, 1977 *Oxfordshire Roman Pottery*, British Archaeological Reports, British Series, **43**, Oxford

Zohary, D, and Hopf, M, 1994 *Domestication of Plants in the Old World*, 2nd ed Oxford

Bury Mount: A Norman Motte and Bailey Castle at Towcester, Northamptonshire

by

JIM BROWN and IAIN SODEN

with contributions by
Paul Blinkhorn, Pat Chapman, Karen Deighton, Geoff Egan, Rowena Gale,
Jacqueline Harding, Tora Hylton, Ian Meadows, Jane Timby and Charlotte Walker

SUMMARY

The site of the former motte and bailey castle has recently been the subject of archaeological investigation. The earliest features and deposits preserved beneath Bury Mount were probably of Roman origin. Two substantial pits were excavated, which were sealed by buried soils. The soils accumulated during the post-Roman period and had been continually disturbed. Ditches created during this period were allowed to silt naturally and were redefined and later backfilled in the late 11th century.

A stone building was constructed following the Conquest, and was replaced by the Norman motte in the 12th century. A circular ring of embanked earth formed the base using sandy clay and gravels from the motte ditch and from the surrounding township. Further deposits were tipped onto the ring of earth, raising its height, and spreading down into the centre, where the deposits became thicker to fill the cone-shaped central hollow.

By the later medieval period the motte was probably disused and remained so until the Civil War. During the 19th century Bury Mount was landscaped, planted with trees and the motte ditch was recreated as a watercourse. Two cottages were built into the south side in the mid-19th century and the land was used for garden horticulture. The watercourse was intermittently maintained until the cottages were abandoned and demolished.

INTRODUCTION

Northamptonshire Archaeology was commissioned in July 2007, by South Northamptonshire Council, to conduct an archaeological excavation of the motte and bailey castle at Bury Mount, Towcester (NGR: SP 6856 4915; Fig 1). Plans are being prepared for the consolidation, enhancement and public presentation of Bury Mount as part of the regeneration of the Moat Lane area of Towcester. Bury Mount and its immediate environs comprise a Scheduled Ancient Monument (County No 13623). In accordance with the requirements of the 1979 Scheduled Monuments Act, all progress has been in consultation with English Heritage, advisors to the Department of Culture, Media and Sport. This excavation was designed to provide information on the construction, occupation and demise of Bury Mount, to inform planning advice regarding the scope of design works necessary or desirable to conserve the earthwork and halt the present rate of erosion.

The archaeological works comprised area excavation of two broad trenches, located at the summit and to the south of Bury Mount, with a third slit trench across the north-west side of the motte ditch. The first two trenches investigated the origin and construction of the motte and its subsequent modifications. The third trench investigated the relationship between the motte slope, its ditch and the deposits seen in the evaluation carried out in 2006 at the back of the Wayside Garage, Northampton Road (SP 6928 4888, Foard-Colby forthcoming).

The basis for this publication is the original client report, which has been updated to include the work of Dr Geoff Egan on the lead alnage seals following their conservation (Brown and Soden 2007). The discussion of the long term conservation of the monument has been summarised to provide a more concise overview, empirical data for its condition at the time of fieldwork is contained in the client report.

ACKNOWLEDGEMENTS

The project was managed by Iain Soden and the fieldwork was directed by Jim Brown. Excavation was conducted by Danny McAree, Paul Kajewski, Mark Spalding, David Haynes, Daniel Nagy, Adrian Adams, Peter Burns and Liam Whitby. Environmental processing was by Wallis Lord-Hart. David Parish handled the conservation of finds at Buckinghamshire Museum Service. The illustrations were prepared by Jacqueline Harding and Charlotte Walker. Documentary work was by Iain Soden and the report on the excavations is by Jim Brown.

Northamptonshire Archaeology also wishes to thank Towcester Historical Society for their interest, support and contributions to the project, in particular, Brian Giggins who provided several key documentary sources of interest. The open days held in conjunction with the Society's display at St. Lawrence's Church were a huge success, drawing 650 visitors over the course of two days.

TOPOGRAPHY AND GEOLOGY

Bury Mount is a 1.7ha portion of the regeneration area, the base of which is on level ground at *c* 88.5m

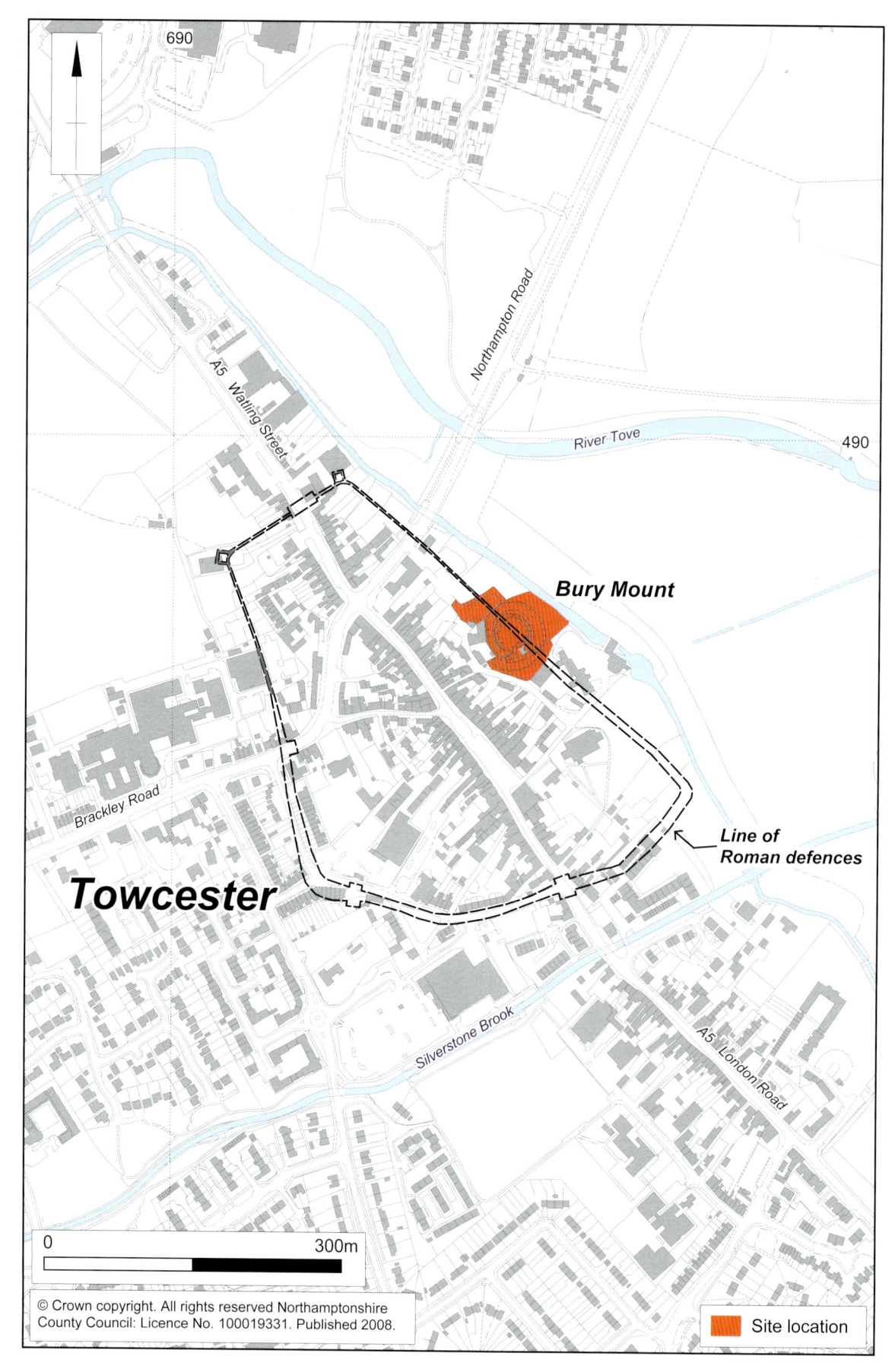

Fig 1 Bury Mount and the Roman town defences

above Ordnance Datum. The site lies in the north-east of the town core (Fig 1). The land is largely open with hardstanding tarmac at the edge of wider, rough areas of grass towards Wayside Garage on Northampton Road. Bury Mount is a flat-topped motte earthwork surmounted by a number of feature trees.

The geology is mapped by the British Geological Survey as Alluvium (BGS 1969). Excavation has demonstrated that it is overlain in part by River Terrace Gravels which form a low plateau on the flood plain.

HISTORICAL AND ARCHAEOLOGICAL BACKGROUND

The motte and bailey castle site lies on the north-east side of the present town centre, close to both the parish church and the medieval market place (Fig 1). The north-east of the site is bounded by the modern line of the mill stream, a later medieval watercourse that may have earlier origins. It served the 19th-century watermill and has been maintained to the present, although the mill is now redundant. To the north-west the site opens onto derelict wasteland, the subject of trial trench evaluation in 1984 and 2006 (Audouy 1984; Foard-Colby forthcoming). This area of ground purportedly contained the disturbed remnants of defences belonging to the Roman town of *Lactodurum*. To the west the site is bounded by modern cottages and a modern workshop housing a light engineering firm, both fronting onto Moat Lane. The south of the site is bounded by Moat Lane itself. To the south-east is a warehouse constructed astride the circuit of an old watercourse. The east of the site backs onto a small car park serving the facilities housed in the buildings opposite the watermill. Bury Mount is also believed to be situated astride the early defensive circuit of the Roman town wall (Woodfield 1992; 1995).

A pre-Roman settlement existed in the sharply-angled bend of the River Tove on the north-east side of the town. Remains of this settlement typified by dark 'Belgic' style pottery were identified during excavations near Bury Mount (Audouy 1984, 25). It is likely that the town may have begun as a *Vicus*, a small civilian settlement, and required defence when it became a focus for Roman political and economic activity. It has been suggested that it was the stage for significant disturbances which were part of widespread conflagrations in the area during the second part of the 2nd century AD (Woodfield 1995, 140-143). The burgeoning Roman town of *Lactodurum* (Towcester) was located on the Watling Street (A5), a major Roman military route built between London and the legionary fortress at Wroxeter, near Shrewsbury. It may have been used as a staging post during periods of military activity and was a likely target for localised insurrection.

There is a significant lack of published work for the archaeology of the town in all post-Roman periods. Although a large number of sites have been investigated in the town and its hinterland over the last 30 years, little evidence has come to light that might elucidate the nature of Saxon, Norman and later medieval settlement. In most extensive excavations in the town, medieval horizons have been largely absent and consequently medieval Towcester is poorly understood. Previous enquiry has only speculated as to the form of the documented Saxon refortification of the town as a Saxon burh (Audouy 1984, 27). Evidence for this has been insubstantial. The motte was previously mentioned as a short-lived structure attributed to the early phase of post-Conquest castle building (Audouy 1984, 29). The presence of a post-Conquest stone building on the site before the motte was raised in the 12th century constitutes a revision to this statement and it now appears likely that the motte belongs to a later period of castle building, perhaps during the tumultuous years 1135-1153, the conflict between Stephen and Matilda.

A wall of possible late medieval date was identified at Meeting Lane during an evaluation, but on the whole evidence has suggested that most medieval activity had been confined to a limited area along the Watling Street frontage (Steadman and Shaw 1991, 7-8, 10; Atkins and Woodfield 1999, 32). This view was supported by the evaluation at 163-165 Watling Street where, despite a reasonable assemblage of residual medieval pottery, only one pit was identified to that period (Prentice 2001, 13). The fragmentary picture of evidence has been mirrored elsewhere with some consistency.

The town history is easier to identify closer to the present as the dearth of artefactual and documentary evidence is replaced with a greater number of post-medieval finds and records. Most prominent amongst these is during the English Civil War (1642-9) when Towcester was garrisoned by the Royalists. Although the vernacular buildings are rather less well represented, several attempts have been made to identify points at which Civil War defences were built. Evidence from the former cinema site, Sponne School and the former filling station, currently Harley Davidson motors, are amongst these (Jackson 1983; Audouy 1984; Woodfield 1992).

Trial excavation was carried out in the open area to the north of Bury Mount in 2006, in the area beyond the Scheduled Ancient Monument. These works remain incomplete due to tenancy issues but included a series of radial core-samples taken by Royal Holloway College, London. The locations of the cores can be seen in Figure 4 and the probable extent of the motte ditch has been compared to map evidence. The excavations were also informed by the conservation management plan for Bury Mount by Shotliffe *et al* (1999), the work by Higham and Barker published in their book, *Timber Castles* (2004), and the place of castle studies within the recent East Midlands archaeological frameworks document (Lewis 2006).

BURY MOUNT

The following maps are retained by Northamptonshire Record Office:

1801	Earl of Pomfret Estate Map (NRO 2923 and 2967)
1811-16	Ordnance Survey, Surveyor's map sheet 53SE
1844	Towcester Tithe Map (NRO T7)
1848-55	Rating map (NRO 4473)
1885	Ordnance Survey 1st edition 25", Sheet LVI.6
1900	Ordnance Survey 2nd edition 25"

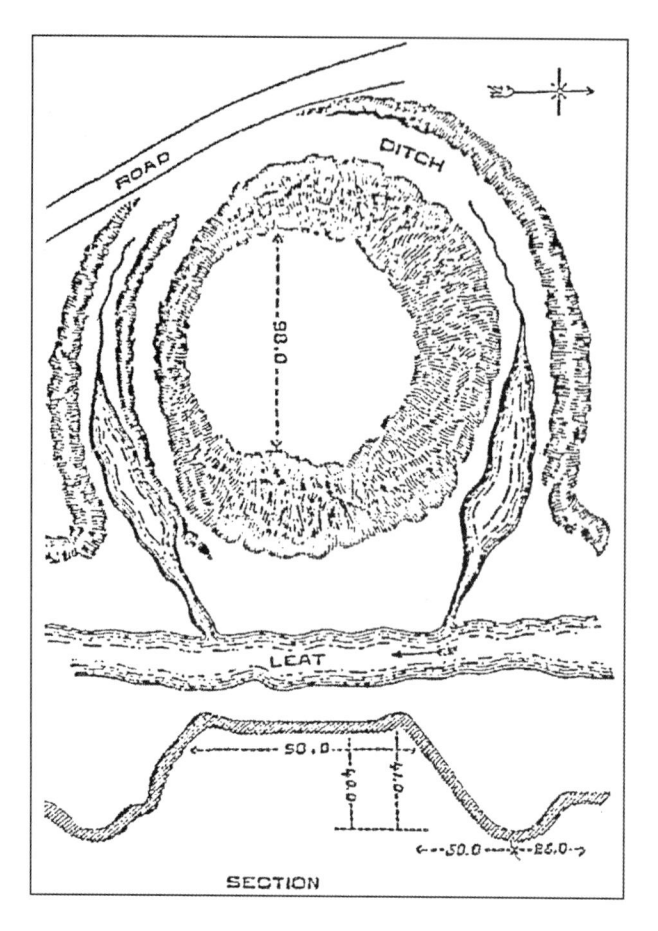

Fig 2 Bury Mount, taken from "The Builder" 13 March 1875

All of these plans show Bury Mount with very little detail, other than to confirm its location. They all show the 19th-century watercourse and the 1848-55 rating map depicts the cottages on the south side of Bury Mount for the first time.

A topographical drawing published in *The Builder* in 1875 shows Bury Mount in a much different light, depicting the channels of the 19th-century watercourse and identifying an earlier ditch (Fig 2). Its accompanying article makes the mistake of identifying the Mount with the Saxon burgh, an earlier development within the town fortified by Edward the Elder against the Danes in 917. Its particular value is in its identification of the medieval ditch much closer to the motte than its 19th-century recreation, mapped in other depictions. In addition a cross-section of the motte appears to show that the flat top was surmounted by a one-foot high earthwork bank around its rim, perhaps for a palisade. No other depiction shows this and there is no trace of this on the ground today. Since the illustrator of 1875 chose to mark its height independently on his cross-section, we must infer that he genuinely believed in what he was looking at. However, the depiction is a reconstruction since it does not show the cottages cut into the south-western quadrant. The mapped and documentary history of the castle, although it comprises precious little, has previously been set out by Courtney (Shotliffe *et al* 1999, 11-17).

There are no records of the castle in the immediate post-Conquest period. The documentary record suggests that the land plot in the late medieval period was waste, later used as a garden and orchard. It was mentioned in a survey in 1391-2, where it was described as 'One moat and within the moat there is one mound tower'; later the *motehyll* was described as being in decay, paying no rent, in the Valor roll of 1467-8 (NRO DL43/14/3; Woodfield 1992, 66-68; Shotliffe *et al* 1999, 12). Records from 1549 and 1551 indicated that much of the site was a garden called Berrymonthyll and a close called Beryorchard (NRO Fermor-Hesketh: MTD/B/28/8, MTD/D/28/13). It was described in 1610 as a garden "planted on every side with cherie trees". Courtney was unable to view a 1606 rental of the fields of Towcester, since it was unavailable due to conservation at the time he wrote (Shotliffe *et al* 1999). This has now been viewed and it can be stated that Bury Mount is not included, the rental being wholly concerned with the open fields around the town (NRO: Fermor-Hesketh: Box A, bundle 1).

Nothing new can be added to Courtney's historical appraisal other than to point out that the association of Bury Mount with a Civil War gun emplacement may be the basis for error (Shotliffe *et al* 1999). The references from the diary of Sir John Luke published by Philip (1947) simply note:

4 August 1643 Skirmish at Towcester began the activity around the town (Philip 1947, 136).

2 Nov 1643 'there are 10 000 horse and foote in about Toster, and seven pieces of ordnance and they intend to fortifie the towne, and to plante their ordnance upon Hunsbury Hill a mile from Northampton' (*ibid* 187-9).

11 Nov 1643 Prince Rupert has 1000 cavalry as a guard at Toster. Stabling was poor and the conditions were very muddy, horses standing in mud up to their fetlocks (*ibid* 191-3).

14 Nov 1643 'as soon as they have finished works at Toster, they resolve to go north leaving a garrison' (*ibid* 195-7).

19 Nov 1643 Two reports arrived 'Toster is entrenched round but not fortified. There are 12 pieces of Ordnance' and 'they have intrenched Toster round but have not yet finished their works' (*ibid* 195-7).

5 Dec 1643 'they have intrenched Toster around, but have not as yet finished there works; there bee many labourers there working daily…. they are making a mount on the farther side of the towne to plant ordnance upon' (*ibid* 206).

6 Dec 1643 'the town is intrenched round about' (*ibid* 207).

18 Dec 1643 'Eight pieces of ordnance in Toster, six in the Markett Place and two planted upon on a hill towards Northampton. That the works are all made up, but are stronger at the end towards London'. Two similar reports (*ibid* 219).

Since these diary entries were made by a Parliamentarian based in Northampton gathering intelligence, he would take great interest in the strengthening of Towcester for the King. We must be clear that very few of the works were observed by him in person, but are the reports of paid scouts as they went out and returned some days later with varied accounts.

Luke seems clear about the use of Hunsbury Hill for a gun emplacement to cover Northampton. It is unfortunate then that the second mention of the construction of a mount gives no specific location, other than to say that it lies on the farther side of the town. The word 'farther' is ambiguous since it assumes the reader knows the movements of the scout relative to the direction from which he approached the town.

If the existing Bury Mount was the place in question it is unclear why its construction was implied, not its modification, since Bury Mount already existed. It is possible that the 'Hill' mentioned as the emplacement on 18 December, is neither Bury Mount nor Hunsbury but another high-point in the landscape with a view of the road from Towcester to Northampton anywhere over a distance of some miles. Such a location outside Towcester would give early warning of an enemy approach, whereas a presence on Bury Mount would add little height and visual advantage. The elevation might add only 250 metres to the range of cannon.

Related documents for the supply of ordnance, powder and ammunition to Towcester during this time suggest that a concerted defence might have been difficult if the Parliamentary forces had been able to attack. While small-arms and horse equipment was constantly transported, the amount of shot made available, split between numerous pieces of ordnance, was strictly limited and it is doubtful whether any more than a brief defensive barrage would ever have been possible before the guns fell silent (Roy 1975). Without firm archaeological evidence, the documentation regarding the Civil War preparations is, at best, ambiguous.

In 1823-4 record was made of a subterranean passage found within the motte, 15 yards in length (Pigot's Directory 1823-4). This has never been substantiated and its nature has formed the basis of much speculation, particularly in respect to the style of construction of the motte, possibly following a retained, South-Mimms type of earthwork construction with an entrance passageway and internal stair to a keep above (Platt 1978, 12-13).

Bury Mount was planted with Scots Pines at the summit by the Earl of Pomfret. Map evidence does not show the planting, although the anonymous author of *The Builder* article of 1875 was aware of them. They were noted once more in the *Northampton Mercury* in 1886-7, when Bury Mount was said to be covered in domestic gardens (NRO: NRS Pamphlet 1592, Answer to Question 96, p31). A dense canopy of trees had matured by the time early photographic postcards were produced *c* 1910 and the gardens were resplendent with serried ranks of vegetables. A few spindly successor pines survive on the motte today, forming less that ten per cent of the original plantation.

It is unusual that such a prominent landmark as Bury Mount has been so widely covered over the years and revealed so few documents. A book on the history of Towcester summarises the documentary understanding of Bury Mount, although archaeological information is absent (Sunderland and Webb 1995, 64-8).

OBJECTIVES

A project design was created by Northamptonshire Archaeology and approved by English Heritage to provide detailed information on the presence or absence, the extent, degree of survival and the depth of burial of archaeological remains across the Scheduled Ancient Monument. Its purpose was to provide sufficient information on the site's surviving archaeology to inform conservation works on the motte and its immediate environs, providing information supporting the field of castle studies and regional research on the medieval period. The project supports the promotion of public interest in the site as a centrepiece of public open space within the wider regeneration plan for Towcester town centre. Particular attention was directed towards establishing the method of construction of the motte and examining the extent and process of its destruction. Work sought to examine the motte ditch and assess its potential to preserve archaeological remains whilst also linking the archaeology of the motte to the known bailey ditch found in the foregoing evaluation (Foard-Colby forthcoming).

METHODOLOGY

Excavation took place in the southern quadrant of Bury Mount, formerly occupied by a pair of thatched cottages, known from photographs of *c*1910 (Fig 3). Investigation

Fig 3 The Bury Mount cottages, c1910

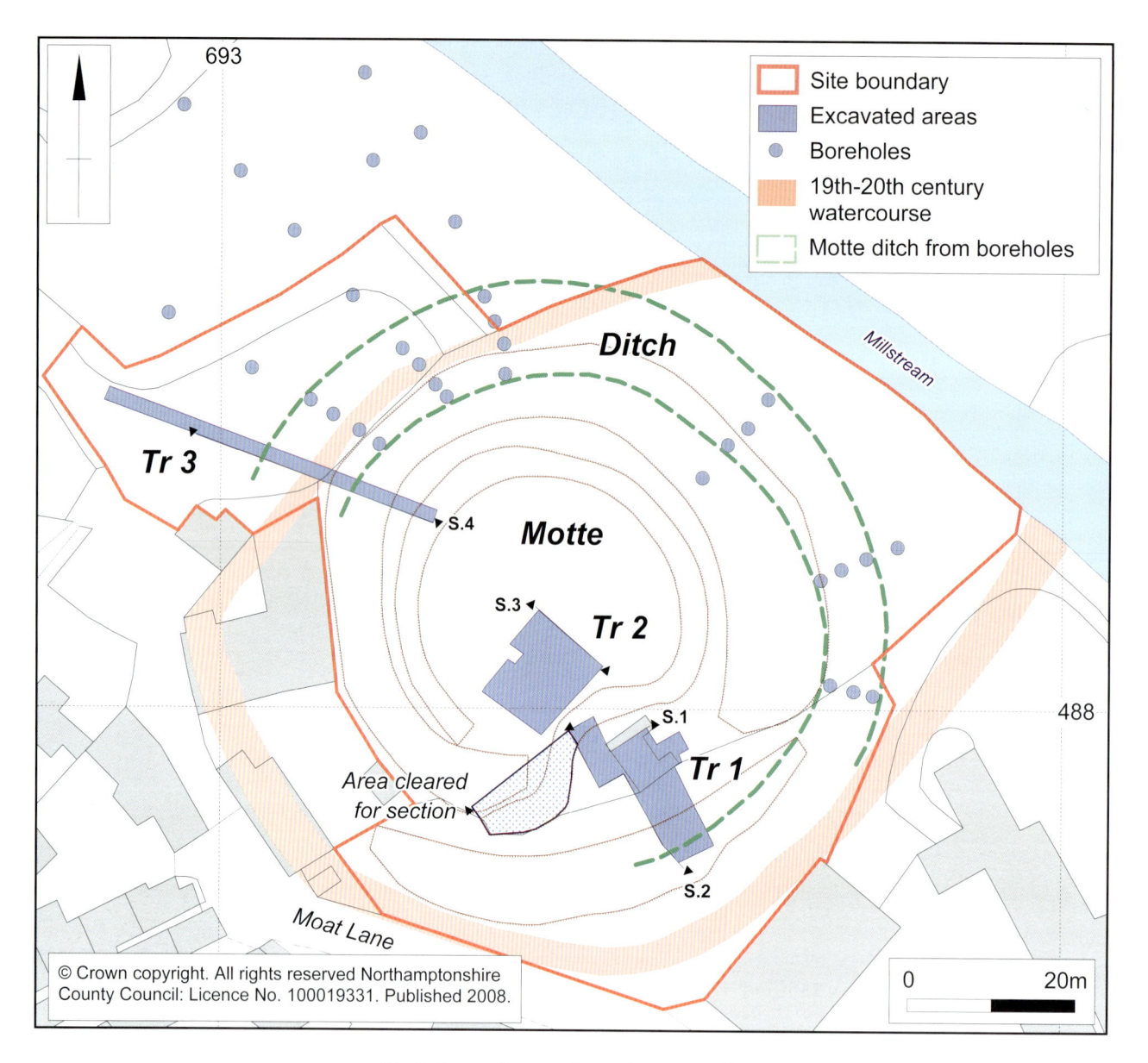

Fig 4 Areas of excavation and core sampling

minimised intervention into undisturbed deposits. It incorporated about one quarter of the surviving motte summit, about one eighth of the slopes and a section to expose the motte ditch on the south-east side (Figs 4-6).

Initial work used a mechanical excavator fitted with a 1.8m wide toothless ditching bucket under continual archaeological supervision. Topsoil, non-structural garden soils and slump deposits were removed to reveal the surface of the significant archaeological remains defined as remains from the English Civil War, or from the medieval, Anglo-Saxon or Roman periods. Excavation of these deposits was continued by hand. At the summit all work was conducted by hand. Spoil was scanned by eye and with a metal detector to assist in the recovery of diagnostic or dateable finds.

The summit was investigated for artillery gabions, emplacements and breastworks or the remains of a stone or timber medieval donjon or tower, all surface evidence having been removed in the landscaping works of the Earl of Pomfret. The slope was exposed to examine motte construction material at the side and base of the earthwork. The encircling ditch was hand-excavated to reveal the last accumulation which was deposited while it was still an earthwork and sampled to assess its environmental potential. Pollen was not retrieved since the reporting timescale was unusually short and infilling of the ditch between the 12th to 20th centuries was a long-term accumulation, making the environment highly changeable. The slit trench was linked to the previous 2006 evaluation trench in the putative north bailey and provided comparison with the sequence noted in the other excavations.

The strategy of fieldwork and post-excavation concentrated specifically on the medieval motte and bailey castle. Roman material was recorded as part of the excavation but was not accorded the same level of attention in post-excavation. Roman finds were not fully analysed and only a commentary was made.

Fig 5 Trench 1, including the Norman defensive ditch in the foreground

EXCAVATED EVIDENCE

SUMMARY OF CHRONOLOGY

Exploration of Bury Mount exhibited a clear sequence of activity (Table 1).

Table 1: The chronological sequence

PERIOD	FEATURES
Roman (1st-4th centuries)	Stone filled pits or postholes, abandonment layers and residual finds
Saxon (5th-9th centuries)	A ditch post-dating Roman abandonment
Saxo-Norman (10th-11th centuries)	A ditch, a pit and buried soils
Norman, pre-fortification (11th-12th centuries)	Stone wall of substantial building
Norman fortification (12th century)	The motte and defensive ditch
Late medieval (13th-14th centuries)	Abandonment and silting of the motte ditch
Early post-medieval (15th-17th centuries)	Cutting of the motte south slope and a large pit at its base
Late post-medieval (18th-20th centuries)	Landscaping, tree planting, a watercourse, two cottages, gardens and an outhouse

Fig 6 Trench 1, view from the base of the motte facing south

ROMAN REMAINS

Cultivable orangey-brown sandy soil had accumulated 300-400mm thick over the natural orange gravels (1078). It contained no finds and appeared to comprise the natural silty infill of undulations in the gravel, disturbed only by worm sorting that had enriched it as a soil (Figs 7-8).

Two pits or postholes, [1111] and [1152], were cut into the natural gravel. Both measured 700-800mm across and had near vertical sides and flat bases, packed with limestone. They were set 2m apart and it is possible that they related to a Roman building of unknown size.

Overlying these features, to a thickness of 250mm at the north end of the trench, was a dark brownish-grey buried soil (1150) containing large amounts of broken roof tile, redolent of a demolition deposit and subsequent accumulation.

A SAXON DITCH

Ditch [1107] measured 750mm wide by 450mm deep, aligned from west to east (Figs 7-8). The south side had subsequently been modified by an off-centre recut on a slightly wider and deeper arrangement [1104]. Fills (1105/8) were similar, being basically firm dark orange-brown clay silt with fragmented limestone and residual Roman pottery trampled into the base. This appears to have been natural silting of the ditch with the pottery probably deposited soon after digging. Fill (1106) comprised loose dark greyish-brown silty loam with white flecks, limestone fragments and root intrusions. It may have been deliberately backfilled and was noted passing eastwards beneath a later wall [1050], although the original, parallel course of [1107] was not visible at this point.

SAXO-NORMAN FEATURES AND BURIED SOILS

Sealing the top of the Saxon ditch was 300-400mm of thick black silty loam (1101; Fig 8). There was no evidence of root intrusion but worm castes were present. This buried soil contained a rim sherd from a Stamford ware jar, manufactured up until the late 11th century and two sherds of Calcareous ironstone coarseware which is a relatively newly recognised pottery type, in production from the late 11th century, shortly after the Norman Conquest.

Ditch [1096] cut the buried soil, aligned from west to east. It measured 1.4m wide by 0.5m deep and was a gentle V-shape in profile, the dark blackish-brown silty loam (1097) fill merging imperceptibly with the layer above.

Pit [1079] also cut the buried soil and was difficult to define in plan, it appeared to have a large rounded irregular

Fig 7 (opposite) Detailed plan of features within Trench 1

Plan of Trench 1

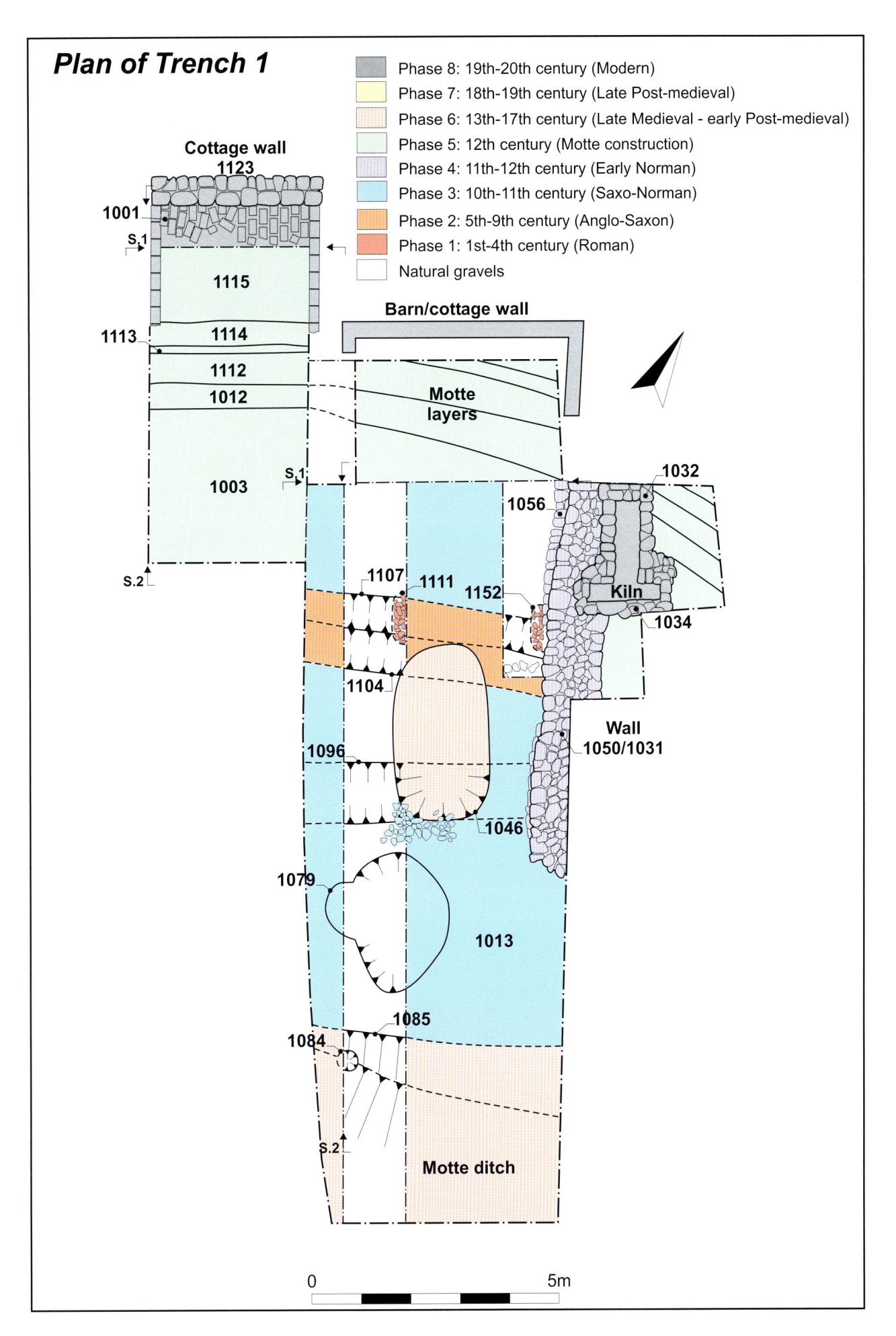

Phase 8: 19th-20th century (Modern)
Phase 7: 18th-19th century (Late Post-medieval)
Phase 6: 13th-17th century (Late Medieval - early Post-medieval)
Phase 5: 12th century (Motte construction)
Phase 4: 11th-12th century (Early Norman)
Phase 3: 10th-11th century (Saxo-Norman)
Phase 2: 5th-9th century (Anglo-Saxon)
Phase 1: 1st-4th century (Roman)
Natural gravels

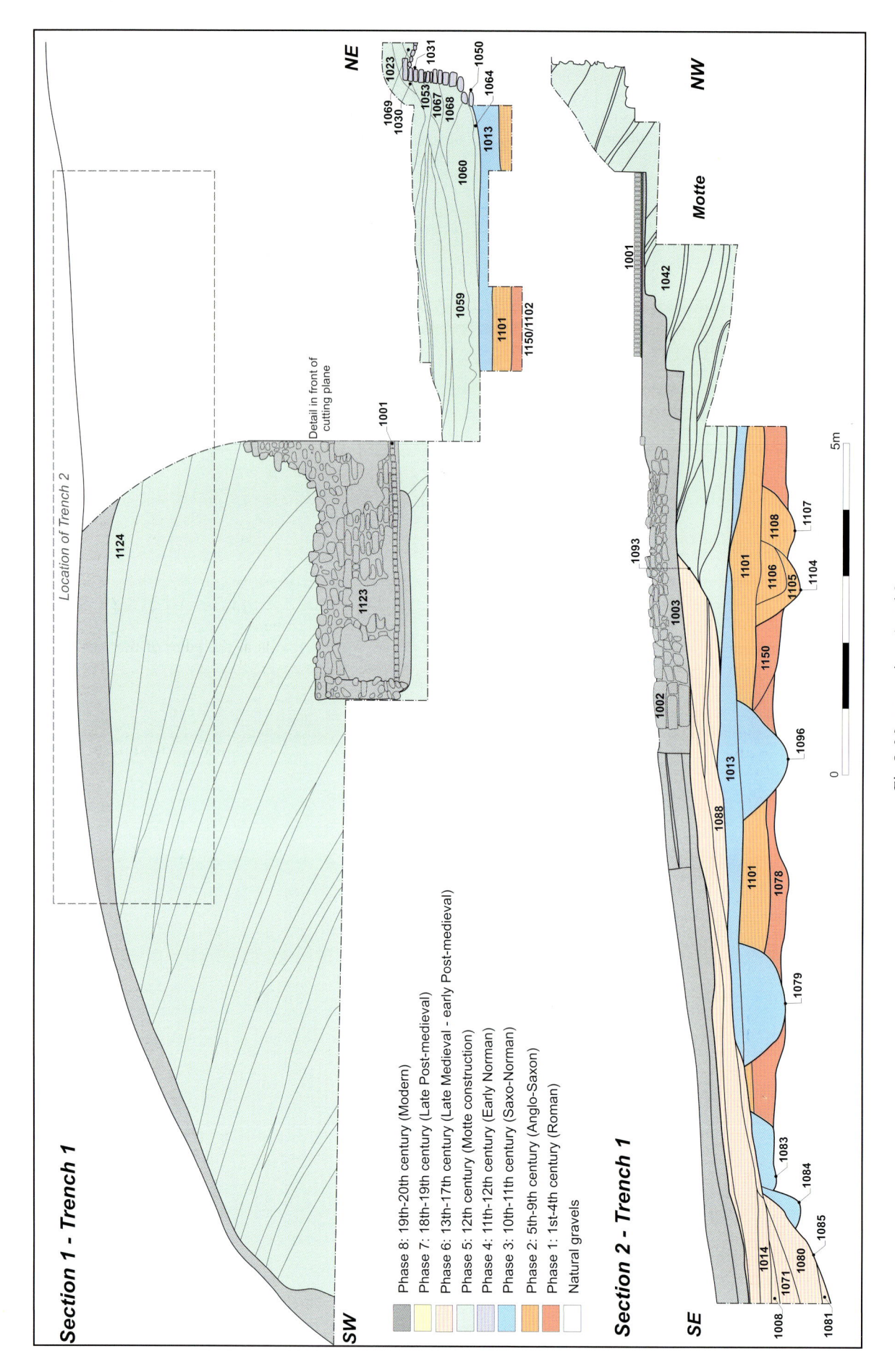

Fig 8 Motte sections 1 and 2

shape *c* 2.7m long by 2.2m wide by 0.56m deep, cutting down into the natural gravel. The fill comprised friable mid-brownish-green sandy clay loam (1075) with very diffuse edges, perhaps suggestive of cess-like material, fluid at the time of deposition. This horizon was overlain by patches of a discontinuous soil up to 290mm thick (1013), which contained large amounts of residual Roman pottery.

A NORMAN WALL

Laid onto the surface of buried soil (1089) was the stone foundation of a wall [1050], aligned north to south, 6.9m long by 1.2m wide by 0.45m high (Figs 7-8). The northern end extended beneath the motte earthwork, whilst the southern terminal had been lost. The masonry comprised blocks of limestone, Northamptonshire Sand with Ironstone and occasional Roman tile fragments used to fill smaller gaps. The block sizes varied considerably, but were generally large faced blocks up to 600mm long by 400mm thick towards the base. Most were crudely shaped and the coursing was irregular. There were six courses at its highest point and four for the larger part. These had been laid dry, but interlocked so that no use of rubble fill was necessary. At the base of the wall was an aperture 260mm wide by 180mm deep which was set beneath the stonework, seemingly where a single stone had been lost in antiquity.

Built into the fabric of wall [1050] was an alteration or repair [1031] (Fig 10). This was distinctly different in character to the preceding stonework. As a distinctive part of the larger wall, it was 3.2m long by 1m wide by 0.8m high, aligned north to south. The stone colour was lighter, the size generally smaller and the wall was offset from the original so that the facing was not flush, incorporating a slight deviation eastwards at the northern end (Fig 7). The larger blocks were 400mm long by 250mm thick, these were crudely-shaped and the coursing was more irregular than the other portion of the wall. There were ten courses at its northern end, thinning to five courses at the southern end where it joined with the stonework of wall [1050]. These were laid dry but, whereas the previous wall had interlocked fairly well, this was crude with stone little more than stacked and the core of the wall comprising merely rubble fill.

It is clear from the pottery from buried soils beneath the wall, and the motte earthwork built above the wall, that its origin lay in the late 11th century. This date is too late for it to have been any element of the Saxon Burgh town defences and it seems probable that the wall is a fragment of an early Norman stone building, possibly a manorial building, buried beneath the motte.

THE NORMAN FORTIFICATION

Sand and gravel deposits sealed the Saxo-Norman buried soil and buried the remains of the Norman wall (Fig 8). The crest of a bank lay closest to the wall, sloping gently down to the west suggesting they were tipped from the top of the wall. One of the layers, (1064), contained one sherd of St. Neots ware (F200) and one sherd of Calcareous ironstone coarseware (F316), placing its deposition in the late 11th century at the earliest.

One peculiarity which was evident from the section of the deposit was that the area 3.1m to 4.4m to the west of the wall was extensively rutted, cutting into layer (1060), perhaps the effect of wheels (Fig 8). Layers were also seen in plan forming the arcs of equally distinctive bands, these mostly lay beyond the cutting planes of the recorded sections and cannot closely be related to them.

Although only a small fragment of the wall was exposed, it was clear that its demolition was swiftly succeeded by its burial beneath the basal layers of the motte (Figs 7-9). Successive dumps of material were built up in layers to raise the overall height of the earthwork by 6m between the surface of the buried soil and the highest point of the 12th-century construction level (1124) in Trench 1 (Fig 8, Section 1) and (2006) in Trench 2 (Fig 9, Section 3). In Trench 3 a similar sequence of deliberate embankment was recorded (Fig 9, Section 4). The surviving summit of the motte appeared not to have been flat. Either due to massive medieval robbing or, just conceivably, because the motte may never have been finished, the central area of the motte contained a hollow which was subsequently filled or re-filled in the 17th century. The height of the motte to the base of this hollow was 4.5m.

Pottery from the lowest motte layer (1064) (Fig 8, Section 2) secured a mid-12th century date for the construction deposits at the base of the motte, a date corroborated at the summit by pottery from layer (2006) (Fig 9, Section 3) and layers (3034, 3035) (Fig 9, Section 4) on the north-west slope.

An embankment of soils at the edge of the earthwork (1093) marked the edge of the motte, within which the next few dumps were laid, forming a soft 'kerb' to what became the motte base (Fig 8). Within this ring, soil was then mounded, each successive layer being shovelled along and sideways over the growing bank towards the centre. The process created a funnelled shape, but the successive embankment of layers constituted a retaining kerb for the next, giving lateral stability as the motte grew higher (Fig 11). The distinct tipping lines sloping downwards towards the centre of the motte would have had the effect of channelling rainwater to the centre of the mound, preventing it from drying out and either spreading or cracking. It would also have the effect of channelling water to a central point where many mottes would have had a well.

The pattern of tip lines between the trenches indicates the approximate centre of the original structure. The suggested radius of the base of the motte from this point is *c*30m which is consistent with a mapped maximum summit diameter of 30m. It also demonstrates the considerable amount of material that was removed from the south side of the site by later activity. According to the excavated evidence in Trench 1, for the west slope of the motte, and in Trench 3, for the north slope of the motte, the median angle of elevation is in the region of 30-35° from the horizontal plane (Figs 8 and 9). The steeper slopes visible elsewhere are accounted for by later modifications and subsequent erosion. Given that both slopes were proportional it is likely that the original motte was a fairly symmetrical mound.

Excavation identified forty-two different blends of material constituting motte construction deposits in Trench

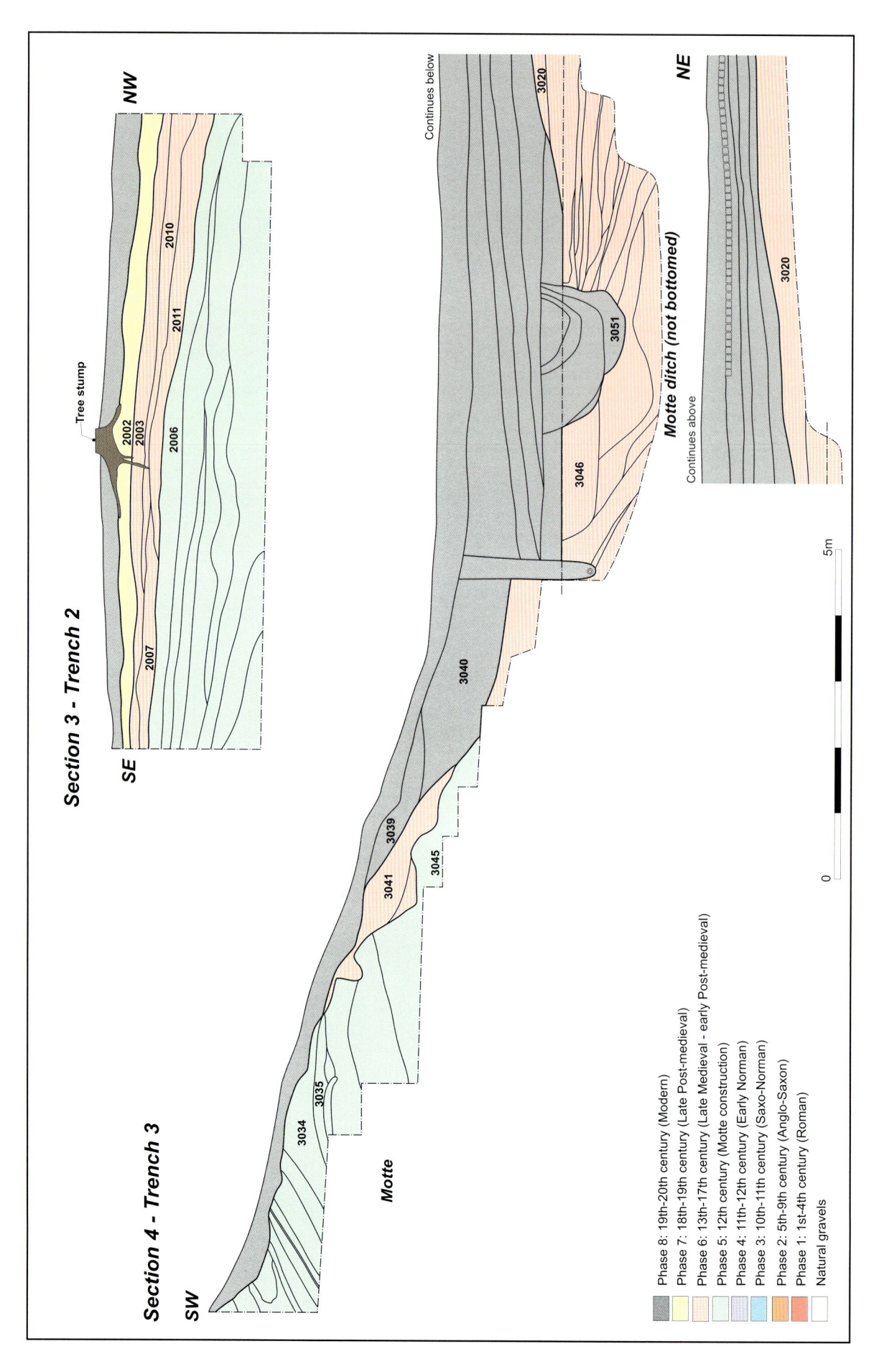

Fig 9 Motte sections 3 and 4

Fig 10 The Norman walls, [1050] and [1031]

Fig 11 Motte construction tipping lines overlying dark buried soil (1089) in the foreground

century pottery, clay tobacco pipes, plastic coated metal bed springs, a flower pot and several lumps of coal. The purpose of the kiln remains unknown. That very little scorching was observed might suggest that it was not fired much before it was abandoned.

LATER PREHISTORIC POTTERY
Jane Timby

A single bodysherd from a handmade vessel decorated with two finger depressions came from layer (1149). The sherd is black in colour and tempered with sparse fragments of coarse limestone. A second bodysherd, in a black grog and limestone-tempered fabric, came from (1086). This piece was decorated with a defined chevron infilled with impressed dots in a style similar to the decorated wares from Chinnor (Richardson 1951, fig. 7). Both pieces could be early Iron Age in date and were residual.

ROMAN POTTERY
Jane Timby

Excavation resulted in the recovery of 1510 sherds of Roman pottery weighing *c* 21kg. With the exception of a small group of 10 sherds from pit [1152] the entire Roman assemblage was redeposited in later contexts. Despite this the sherds are in relatively good condition with good surface preservation and relatively unabraded edges. The assemblage was sorted into fabrics and quantified by sherd weight and count. Named or traded wares were identified using the National Roman fabric reference codes (Tomber and Dore 1998). Other wares were treated more generically and coded according to firing colour and the size and type of inclusions. The data was entered into an MS Excel spreadsheet a copy of which is deposited with the site archive. A summary is provided in Table 2.

The assemblage is chronologically diverse ranging from the 1st to later 4th centuries with a clear bias towards the later Roman period. Continental imports were limited to Samian tableware, Spanish (Baetican) olive oil and Gaulish wine amphorae, and North Gaulish mortaria. Samian accounted for 7.4% of the total assemblage by count, typical of a more urban group. Both plain and decorated wares are present.

Regional imports are well represented with products from Dorset, the Lower Nene Valley, Oxfordshire, Hadham and Verulamium regions. The Oxfordshire wares, mainly colour-coated wares but with some white-ware and white-slipped ware, include examples of Young (2000) forms C45, C48, C51, C77, C81, C84, C99, C100, M22 and WC7 all typical of the later 3rd to 4th centuries. Dorset black burnished ware is mainly confined to examples of jars, plain-rimmed dishes, grooved rim and conical flanged rim bowls. The Lower Nene Valley colour-coated wares form the second largest group at 17.7% by count of the assemblage with beakers, bowls, dishes and jars. Of note amongst these is a dish bearing a post-firing graffiti from layer (2011). The Verulamium wares include a large rim from an amphora imitating a Gallic type and two mortaria, one stamped.

Of the local wares and those with no defined provenance, the grey sandy wares account for 22.5% of the group, pink grogged ware for 7.3% and shelly wares form 14.7%. The latter group includes a number of late Roman forms dating to the last quarter of the 4th century.

Several of the vessels show evidence of use with sooting or the formation of calcareous deposits. Two vessels have holes drilled through the walls after firing and one of the Samian vessels has a rivet repair hole.

Table 2: Summary of fabric weight and sherd count

Fabric	Description	Weight (g)	Sherds
BW	black sandy ware	105	9
BWF	fine black ware	86	6
CC	miscellaneous colour-coated ware	3	1
GREY	grey sandy wares	4074	339
GROG	grog-tempered ware	197	13
GRSA	hard sandy ware with grog	1675	55
GYF	fine grey ware	43	8
GYLIME	grey ware with limestone	54	3
LIME	limestone-tempered	36	4
MORT	miscellaneous mortaria	62	1
OXID	oxidised sandy ware	1193	108
OXIDF	fine oxidised ware	77	8
OXIDGR	grog-tempered oxidised ware	31	2
OXIDLI	limestone-tempered oxidised ware	54	2
PNK GT	pink grog tempered ware	2795	110
SALI	sandy with limestone	21	3
SHELL	shell ware including ROB SH	3115	222
WSOXID	white-slipped oxidised ware	72	29
WSOXLI	white-slipped oxidised limestone ware	11	1
WW	miscellaneous white sandy ware	143	5
WWGR	grog-tempered whiteware	104	3
TOTAL		21165	1510

The small group of 10 sherds from pit/posthole [1152] comprised two mortaria, one from North Gaul, the other from the Verulamium region, two sherds of grey sandy ware and three sherds of grog-tempered whiteware. The Verulamium mortarium had part of a potter's stamp comprising at least two lines but damaged and difficult to interpret. A date in the first half of the 2nd century is likely for this group. The layers post-dating and sealing the Roman features (1149, 1150, 1099 and 1102) contained a mixture of 1st to late 3rd/4th-century sherds but no definite late 4th-century pieces.

The assemblage recovered from Bury Mount, although almost all residual, provides a typical cross section of the range of wares already documented from other sites in and around Towcester. Nearly all the wares can be paralleled in the large published assemblage from the Alchester Road suburb to the southwest of the town, which neatly demonstrates the typical pottery profile throughout the Roman period (Brown *et al* 1983).

ROMAN TILE
Pat Chapman

As the Roman tiles are residual they are only summarised. This assemblage of 298 tile fragments weighs 26.67kg. About a third of the tiles have specific characteristics which can be dated to the Roman or medieval periods, while the remaining two thirds comprise probable body sherds from Roman tile or the occasional medieval brick. As the the same local resources were being used in the Roman and medieval periods the body sherds are difficult to date. The assemblage is very fragmented and abraded.

There are 64 specifically Roman fragments, nearly a quarter of the assemblage. These comprise 36 *tegulae*, 10 *imbrices*, 16 flue tiles and two *bessalis* tiles. Nineteen of the *tegulae* and one *imbrex* have a maroon wash over the upper surface, two *tegulae* have a black wash. One body sherd has black slip on one surface. This is a typical feature of Roman roof tile in this area, such as those from the villas at Wootton, Piddington and Croughton (Chapman *et al* 2005; Ward 1999; Mills 2008). A few of the *tegulae* flange fragments have remnants of the cutaway that links the tiles together. A few tile body sherds are made in a shelly ware fabric, another characteristic of the area, otherwise the tiles are in a range of mainly sandy or softer, finer fabrics, fired to varying degrees.

The thicker fragments are between 25mm and 45mm thick, but usually between 35mm and 40mm. It is most likely that the majority of these are Roman. From layer (1013) there are three fragments made from a pale pink-brown fabric with creamy streaks and grog inclusions, not well mixed, at least 50mm thick. One fragment from layer (1101) was made from an orange red medium sandy fabric 35mm thick. There are two fragments from layer (2003), one 35mm thick in a dark red coarse sandy fabric and the other 40mm thick in a coarse red brown fabric with a grey reduced core. A large brick remnant, minimum measurements 190mm by 105mm and 30-50mm thick from edge to inside, was black and partially vitrified but with white to buff surfaces, partially covered with white mortar/cement.

ROMAN COINS
Ian Meadows

The coins date to the 4th century and were all residual in later contexts.

AD *c*364-75, AE issue of SECURITAS REIPUBLICAE type. Obverse: illegible. Reverse: preserves part of the mint mark of Arles Officina II indicating this coin was issued for either Valens or Valentinian I. layer (1013)

AD *c*367-75, AE3 issue of Valens with a SECURITAS REIPUBLICAE reverse. This coin was minted at Lugdunum by the second officina (mint mark LVGP). layer (1013)

AD *c*3rd/4th century, AE3/4 flan. Obverse: illegible. Reverse: illegible. ditch [1085]

ROMAN GLASS
Tora Hylton

There are 27 fragments of Roman glass, mostly from post-Roman buried soils. The assemblage comprises mainly small body sherds, exhibiting few diagnostic features and measuring no more than 45mm by 20mm. A range of colours is represented and includes two undiagnostic sherds of coloured glass, dark blue and yellow/brown, which date to the 1st and 2nd centuries (Price and Cottam 1998, 15). There are seventeen sherds of blue/green glass and eight sherds of colourless glass, which was in use from the 1st to 4th centuries. Diagnostic forms in blue/green glass include two unguent vessels, one with an uneven sheared rim probably dating to the 1st century and one with an out-turned rim, and part of a tubular rim, representing a bowl or similar type of vessel.

THE SAXON AND MEDIEVAL POTTERY
Paul Blinkhorn

The pottery assemblage comprised 31 sherds with a total weight of 664g. The estimated vessel equivalent (EVE), by summation of surviving rimsherd circumference was 0.61. It comprised a range of ceramic types which suggests that there was activity at the site from the late Saxon period onwards.

The assemblage is most notable for a pottery type which has previously been virtually unknown in the county (F316 Calcareous ironstone coarseware). From the results of this excavation, a watching brief at 147 Watling Street, and work at Sewardsley Priory in Showsley, it appears that it is a medieval coarseware which was manufactured in or close to the town (Brown and Walker 2007).

ANALYTICAL METHODOLOGY

The pottery was bulk-sorted and recorded using DBase IV software. The material was recorded by context, number and weight of sherds per fabric type. Feature sherds such as rims, bases, lugs and decorated sherds were recorded individually. For rimsherds, the form, diameter and percentage remaining of the original circumference were recorded. This figure was totalled for each fabric type to obtain the estimated vessel equivalent (EVE).

The terminology is defined by the Medieval Pottery Research Group (MPRG 1998; MPRG 2001). All the statistical analyses used a Dbase package, which interrogated the original or subsidiary databases, with final calculations made with a calculator. Statistical analyses were carried out to the standards suggested by Orton (1998-9, 135-7).

FABRICS

The medieval pottery was quantified using the chronology and coding system of the Northamptonshire County Ceramic Type-Series (CTS), as follows:

F200:	T1 (2) type St. Neots ware	c1000-1200	3 sherds 14g	EVE = 0.02
F205:	Stamford ware	c850-1150	1 sherd 9g	EVE = 0.06
F330:	Shelly coarseware	c1100-1400	6 sherds 82g	EVE = 0.11
F316:	Calcareous ironstone coarseware	c1100-1400	11 sherds 351g	EVE = 0.25
F329:	Potterspury ware	c1275-1600	2 sherds 85g	EVE = 0.17
F346:	Bourne 'D' ware	c1450-1637	2 sherds 88g	EVE = 0.00
F401:	Late medieval oxidized ware?	1450-?1550	1 sherd 14g	EVE = 0.00
F404:	Cistercian ware	c1470-1700	5 sherds 21g	EVE = 0.00

The pottery occurrence by number and weight of sherds per context by fabric type is shown in Table 4. Each date should be regarded as a *terminus post quem*. The bulk of the assemblage comprises fabric types which are typical of sites of the period in this area of the county, although some of the medieval pottery is a little unusual. The two sherds of late medieval Bourne D ware, a type common in southern Lincolnshire, west Norfolk and north Cambridgeshire, are very rare in the county.

Perhaps the most interesting trait, from a purely ceramic aspect, is the presence of relatively large quantities of fabric F316, the Calcareous ironstone coarseware. Previous excavations in the county have produced extremely small amounts of this material. At Bury Mount it is the dominant medieval ware type, being even more common than Shelly coarseware. There is little doubt that the fabric is broadly contemporary, as it occurs in deposits which produced both pottery types and no later material. From a purely typological point of view, the jar with the thumb-frilled rim is absolutely typical of early medieval pottery (Fig 12, 1). In addition, a single strap handle with stabbed and slashed decoration is very similar to those found on the Shelly coarseware jugs of the 12th century (Fig 12, 3). The technology of manufacture also parallels the production of Shelly coarseware. The rims and upper areas of the body have turning grooves on the inner surface, whilst sherds from the lower body and base do not, showing that the vessels were almost certainly coil-built and then finished on a turntable, or 'slow-wheel'. This is a typical early medieval production technique. The petrology of the ware, containing quartz sand with variable quantities of limestone and ironstone is a reflection of the geology of the region, and a combination seen in a number of different early medieval coarsewares from Brackley (F303, F304), and also in pottery produced nearby in Silverstone.

Recent excavations at Sewardsley Priory (Showsley), a few kilometres to the north of Towcester, have also produced a small assemblage of this material from 12th-century contexts, alongside Shelly coarsewares (Blinkhorn 2007). The fact that it occurs in quantity at this site and at Showsley, with no others represented in the county, suggests strongly that it is of local origin and was produced in or near Towcester. Further finds of the material and evidence of production in the town will enhance the understanding of the ware, but it is potentially an important addition to the picture of ceramic production and use in medieval Northamptonshire.

CHRONOLOGY AND DISCUSSION

The medieval pottery assemblage is somewhat meagre, comprising just 26 sherds, and of these just one dates to the late Saxon period. This is a Stamford ware jar rim from the buried soil (1101) (Fig 12, 4). The rim is fairly typical of the earlier products of the Stamford ware industry, being virtually identical to Kilmurry's vessel form 3, number 2 (Kilmurry 1980, fig 49). It is a long-lived form, being common from the late 9th to the late 11th centuries (*ibid* fig 29). It is possible therefore that the sherd could date to any time between the establishment of the burh at Towcester, c 1014, to the reorganisation of the site in advance of the construction of the motte.

The bulk of the assemblage (20 sherds) dates to the 12th century and represents the main period of medieval activity at the site. It is unremarkable, other than the fabric types present. All the rims were from jars, with the only evidence of any other vessel type being the jug handle (Fig 12, 3). This pattern of vessel occurrence is typical of the 12th century in the region.

Perhaps the most interesting aspect of the entire post-conquest pottery assemblage is the complete lack of

Table 3: RSP phases and major defining wares for the medieval ceramics of Northamptonshire, c850-1550 AD

RSP Phase	Defining Wares	Chronology
LS1	T1(4) St. Neots ware	c850-900
LS2	T1(3) St. Neots ware, Stamford ware, Northampton ware	c900-975
LS3	Cotswolds-type oolitic ware	c975-1000
LS4	T1(2) St. Neots ware	c1000-1100
Ph0	Shelly coarsewares, Sandy coarsewares	c1100-1150
Ph1	Lyveden/Stanion 'A' ware	c1150-1225
Ph2/0	Lyveden/Stanion 'B', Brill/Boarstall ware	c1225-1250
Ph2/2	Potterspury ware	c1250-1300
Ph3/2	Raunds-type reduced ware	c1300-1400
Ph4	Lyveden/Stanion 'D' ware	c1400-1450
Ph5	Late medieval oxidized ware	c1450-1500

Table 4: Pottery occurrence per ceramic phase, all medieval fabrics

Phase	Number of sherds	Weight (g)	EVE
LS1	0	0	0
LS2	1	9	0.06
LS3	0	0	0
LS4	0	0	0
Ph0	20	447	0.38
Ph1	0	0	0
Ph2/0	0	0	0
Ph2/2	2	85	0.17
Ph3/2	0	0	0
Ph4	0	0	0
Ph5	6	94	3
Total	29	635	3.61

glazed jugs, a staple of the high medieval period. Only two sherds of pottery represent the period c1200-1450, both are Potterspury ware bowl rims from (1071), the uppermost layer of the motte ditch.

THE ILLUSTRATED POTTERY (FIG 12)

1   Rimsherd from a large jar with thumb-frilled rim. F316 Greyish buff fabric with a grey core with light sooting on the shoulder. Context (2014), motte construction layer

2   Jar rim. F316 Reddish-orange fabric with a grey core. Patches of sooting on the edge of the rim bead. Context (1073), buried soil layer

3   Jug handle. F316 Reddish-orange fabric with a grey core, slashed edges and stabbing in the centre of the thumb-groove. Context (1073), buried soil layer

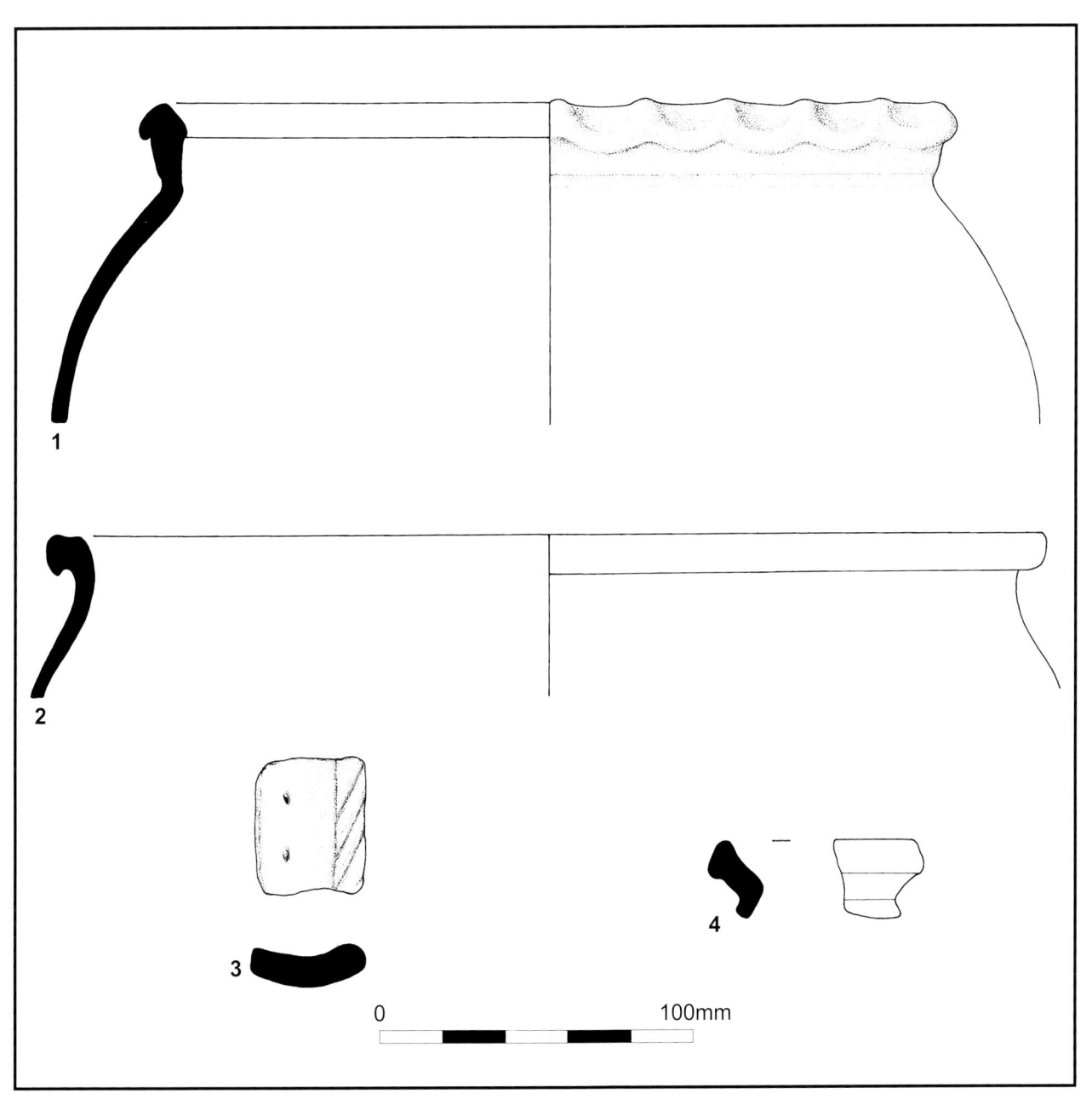

Fig 12 Medieval pottery

4   Jar rim. F205 Brownish-grey fabric with a dark grey core. Extensively sooted. Context (1101), buried soil layer

MEDIEVAL ROOF TILE
Pat Chapman

There are 32 fragments of medieval tile, weighing 1.348kg. The main characteristic is the thickness of the tile, which varies between 10mm to 19mm, but is typically 15mm. There are a variety of fabrics ranging from fine and slightly sandy with fine crushed shell to coarse and sandy with some larger inclusions of grog (recycled fired clay) or gravel and fired to brown, pale red brown, red brown or dark red. Tile from layer (1049) includes one fragment, in an orange-brown coarse sandy fabric, a corner with the remains of a peghole. Two other fragments have green glaze, one very dark green almost black, the other overfired, both in a sandy red fabric.

A MEDIEVAL LACE CHAPE
Tora Hylton

The only find of medieval date is a residual copper alloy lace chape, recovered from the fill (1071) of the motte ditch (1085). The chape is tapered with an edge-to-edge seam and a vestige of the small circular perforation is just visible, which would have attached the chape to the lace. It is similar to Oakleys Type 1 from St Peter's Street, Northampton (Williams 1979, 254, 281).

POST-MEDIEVAL POTTERY
Paul Blinkhorn

This assemblage comprises 51 sherds, weighing 1.28kg. Very little pottery dates to the Civil War and none can be said with certainty to date to the second half of the 17th century due to the broad period of production. Two sherds of pottery may be 17th century, a large fragment of a candlestick in English tin-glazed earthenware from context (1047), and a small piece of a Cologne/Westerwald jug from context (2008). The former is entirely undecorated, suggesting that it is more likely to be of 18th-century date. The latter could have been made at any point in the 17th or 18th centuries.

F406:	Midland yellow wares	c1550-1700	1 sherd, 17g
F407:	Red earthenwares	c1550+	5 sherds, 151g
F410:	English tin-glazed earthenwares	17th-18th centuries	5 sherds, 278g
F411:	Midland blackware	c1550-1700	2 sherds, 80g
F413:	Staffordshire manganese glazed wares	late 17th-18th century	3 sherds, 79g
F420:	Cologne/Westerwald ware	17th-18th centuries	1 sherd, 12g
F429:	White salt-glazed stoneware	c1720-1780	1 sherd, 68g
F1000:	Miscellaneous wares	19th century	33 sherds, 596g

OTHER POST-MEDIEVAL FINDS
Tora Hylton

A small group of post-medieval finds reflect the dress, trade, and Bury Mount's later use as a garden. In addition there is a small group of clay-tobacco-pipes.

COSTUME FITTINGS

Finds associated with dress include a trapezoid buckle chape with internal double spike and pitchfork tongue, exclusively for use with shoes in the mid-18th century (c1720-1770), a Victorian two-piece livery button, marked with the letters G P surmounted by a crown, which probably originated from a Post Office uniform; and a possible cufflink. In addition an annular finger ring with a plain narrow band and D-shaped cross-section was recovered from Trench 2.

BELL-GLASSES

Two handles from glass domes provide evidence for the use of garden glassware during the latter stages of post-medieval occupation. Such glass domes or bell glasses were used to protect fragile plants and seedlings. They are manufactured from green glass, similar to that used for 18th-century wine bottles. The handles are distinctive; they are crudely manufactured, heavy, sub-circular knobs, which have been created by trailing molten glass to form a raised circular knob with centrally placed recess, resembling a doughnut (Noel Hume 1991, 225-226).

CLAY-TOBACCO PIPES

A total of 24 clay tobacco-pipe fragments were recovered, comprising nine pipe-bowls and fifteen stem fragments, which together span the period c1640 to the mid-19th century. Eight bowls are sufficiently complete to enable dating, following the simplified typology using bowl and foot/spur forms (Oswald 1975, 37-41).

The earliest datable bowls are represented by Type G17, which date to c1640-1670; a rouletted example was recovered from the fill (1008) of the motte ditch [1085] and an abraded example was recovered from the summit.

Five bowls are decorated; all are examples of well made Type G24 bowls which date to c1810-1840. All are ornamented with relief-moulded decoration with repeating leaves along the joining seams of the bowl, a motif in use throughout the country and occurring on bowls dated to 1820-60 (Mann 1977, 23). One bowl combines the foliate motif with vertical fluting. Four of the bowls were recovered from the fill of a brick lined kiln pit [1032]. One bowl is in the form of a hand holding a vessel.

Three bowls and one spur fragment preserve makers marks in relief on the spur and, although in some cases the moulding is poor, it is possible to determine that they are all are marked with the initials 'J H'. Although it has not been possible to identify the name of the maker, Robert Moore has recorded that seven other examples marked with the same initials have been recovered from the Towcester area (1980, 30), suggesting local manufacture.

TWO LEAD ALNAGE SEALS
Geoff Egan

These are the first known cloth seals from Towcester. The textile industry of Northamptonshire was not large in the early 18th century but some serges, tammies (thin fabrics used for flags and straining liquids) and shalloons were produced, particularly at Kettering (VCH 1906, 333). It is uncertain whether either of the present seals would have been from a local textile or one woven elsewhere in England.

The seals have been cleaned by David Parish, Conservator for Buckinghamshire County Museum Service. Such seals are generally related to the textile trade and these particular examples would have been attached officially to the merchandise after excise duties had been paid. They are from the last decade of operation of this quality-control and taxation system before it was abolished in 1724. By this time, the alnage had come to be seen as simply a revenue-raising perk enjoyed by the holder of the patent, the Duchess of Lennox, with the industrial aspects being fairly perfunctory if in operation at all. The persistent use of a closing stamp from the previous reign is a reflection of the laxity that had come into the operation of the alnage in its later years. In contrast, the different tax rates for different categories of textile on each seal indicate continuing observance of the fiscal aspect, whether or not any quality control of the textiles to which they were attached was carried out (Egan 1995).

Seal 2 includes the retention of a closing stamp from the preceding reign of Queen Anne that has several parallels on post-Restoration four-disc alnage seals presumably from the early years of the monarch indicated by the portrait stamp in each case. One penny was the tax rate for camlets, chenyes, crapes weighing over eight pounds, single flannels, short lyncies, rugs, single Kidderminsters, petticoats (per dozen) and a range of broad Norwich stuffs (delicate worsteds) according to a list from 1691-2 (HMC 1894, 43).

ILLUSTRATIONS (Fig 13, 1 & 2)

Seal 1 Head of George I (bubble void from casting), lion rampant, 2 ½ to sides, crown over GR, Alnage seal for two and halfpenny tax (a relatively unusual rate), 1714-24. It is not known what fabrics this was the appropriate tax rate for. Dimensions: 13mm by 14 mm, 14mm by 13mm

Seal 2 Head of George I, FIDEI DEFEN around, crown, 1 above left, crude crown over AR ligature, Alnage seal for one penny tax, 1714-24. Dimensions: 14mm by 14mm, 15mm by 14mm

Fig 13 Lead alnage seals (SF6) and (SF7), 1 & 2, from layer (1008) (Conservator's record photograph)

WATERLOGGED AND CHARRED SEEDS
Karen Deighton

Three samples were taken in order to identify macroscopic plant remains. Sample 1 was of 20 litres and seeds within were preserved by water-logging. Samples 2 and 3 were each of 40 litres and seeds were preserved by burning. Sample 1, outwardly showing no signs of water-logging, was at first sieved using standard techniques, only then demonstrating that it was in fact waterlogged. Therefore the collected flot was immediately placed in plastic bags to prevent drying out. A 1 litre sub-sample was analyzed.

Samples 2 and 3 were processed on a 500 micron flot sieve in a modified siraf tank, and then were agitated with water. Any environmental fraction floated off into the mesh. This was then dried and sorted under using a x20 magnification binocular microscope. The seeds were then identified using a variety of published sources.

The seeds recovered in Sample 1 were well preserved by water-logging, with no fragmentation. Samples 2 and 3 carried a large variety of charred seeds of cultivated and wild species within them, amongst which numerous cereal grains were very fragmented, making identification difficult. No chaff was present in any of the samples.

All of the wild plant species were classifiable and a proportion of the cereal grains were identified (Table 5).

DISCUSSION

In Sample 1, the presence of buttercup demonstrates damp/marshy ground. Since other sources indicate a wet motte ditch, this is in full accord. Pottery from the context from which Sample 2 derives includes residual Roman material so may include similarly residual seeds from the Roman landscape mixed with Saxo-Norman material. Environmental data collected from this layer is less informative. Sample 3 was accumulated predominantly in the Saxo-Norman period without much disturbance.

The larger numbers of the wild plants, bramble and stinking mayweed, indicate long periods of abandonment with land left waste. The relatively small numbers involved makes further speculation inadvisable. It was not possible to determine a dominant cereal type due to the poor preservation. Barley and bread-wheat were the most common and there was an absence of chaff indicating that no cereal-processing took place nearby. The wild species are almost all derived from cultivated land.

Sample 1 is most likely material from the local environment blown or washed into the perimeter ditch, which was already water-logged, thus preserving the seeds. Sample 3 is likely to derive from refuse relating to the storage or consumption of cereals. The seeds recovered have been burnt; how they were burnt is not clear. They may be refuse from bread-making and there was also a water-mill nearby so it is likely that the grinding of fully winnowed grain would have been carried out in bulk close to the site. The lack of chaff suggests the wheat is not derived from burning of animal bedding or waste from thatching.

Table 5: Seeds by context and taxa

Sample Number	1	2	3
Context	(1081)	(1013)	(1101)
Feature	Ditch [1085]	Buried soil	Buried soil
Volume (litres)	20	40	40
Barley, *Hordeum vulgare*	--	8	1
Einkorn, *Triticum monococcum*	--	1	3
Emmer, *Triciticum dicoccon* Schrank	--	1	1
Possible *Emmer, cf triticum dicoccon* Schrank	--	--	2
Oat, *Avena sativa*	--	7	--
Oat/Rye, *Avena/Secale*	--	4	--
Rye, *Secale cereale*	--	1	--
Spelt, *Tricticum spelta*	--	1	--
Bread Wheat, *Triticum aestivum*	--	13	3
Wheat/Barley, *Triticum/Hordeum*	--	--	1
Cereal Indet., *Cerealea*	--	187	39
Total Cereal	0	223	50
Common Pea, *Pisum setivum*	--	2	--
Vicia sp., Vetch indet.	--	4	--
Wild Turnip Family, *brassica* sp.	--	1	2
Fat Hen, *Chenopodium album*	--	1	1
Stinking Mayweed, *Anthemis cotula*	--	19	10
Nipplewort, *Lapsana communis*	--	1	--
Possible Rush, cf *Juncus* sp.	--	--	9
Gypsywort, *Lycopus europaeus*	--	--	1
Chess, *Bromus secalinus*	--	3	--
Poa sp., Grass indet	--	--	1
Buttercup, *Ranunculus* sp.	20		1
Sheep Sorrel, *Rumex acetosella*	4	33	2
Bramble, *Rubus fruticosus*	20	--	--
Elder, *Sambucus nigra*	--	2	--
Possible Foxglove, cf *Digitalis Purperea*	--	--	1
Total Number of Seeds	44	289	78
Total Seeds per Litre	2.2	7.2	1.8

WATERLOGGED WOOD
Rowena Gale

A sample containing numerous short fragments of twigs and narrow round-wood from the motte ditch [1085] was received for species identification. The fragments were pieces of desiccated wood. The fragments measured less than 10mm in diameter and had undergone considerable structural collapse. These were prepared using standard methods (Gale and Cutler 2000). Anatomical structures were examined using incident light on a Nikon Labophot-2 compound microscope at up to x400 magnification and matched to prepared reference slides of modern wood. When possible the maturity of the wood was assessed and the stem diameters were recorded.

Sample 1 (1081) contained 32 fragments of cf. willow (Salix sp.) or poplar (Populus sp). Owing to the poor condition of the willow/poplar wood structure it was difficult to examine and it is not possible to provide a positive identification either way. The remaining eight fragments were Prunus sp. In mature wood differences between the ray cells usually enable cherry (P. *avium*) to be distinguished from blackthorn (P. *spinosa*), in this instance the juvenile wood makes differentiation difficult. The structure tends to be more consistent with that of cherry but it is not possible to rule out blackthorn

DISCUSSION

BEFORE THE CASTLE WAS BUILT

The excavations have indicated that the Scheduled Ancient Monument of Bury Mount includes not only the medieval motte from a motte-and-bailey castle but also evidence of activity from the Roman occupation of Towcester to the present day.

The plot is likely to contain further buried Roman features. No buildings of this date were located, although a couple of potential structural features were partly exposed at the base of the excavations. Almost all of the Roman pottery and finds were imported onto the site in later periods and small islands of Roman archaeology are likely to lie undisturbed in the vicinity.

The Saxon and Saxo-Norman periods were marked by the continuous build-up of cultivable soils, into which were dug some substantial ditches. Proximity to wet, low-lying ground, probably pre-dating the mill-stream may suggest these provided drainage. An alternative explanation is that they could have been cultivation trenches. Although the soils were intensely compacted by later construction work on the site, they were of notable thickness with a very long period of accumulation. The small number of features and the scarcity of finds over a period of 600 years indicated sparse, periodic occupation. It may have been marginal land during a period where Roman towns were not a popular focus of settlement activity.

Soon after the Norman Conquest a substantial stone structure was erected on the site. It appears to have been standing long enough to warrant alteration in its alignment and construction. At its northern end it remained beyond excavation, while its southern end was either truncated by the motte ditch or it turned a corner out of the east side of the trench. It is predicted to survive wherever it lies beneath the motte. No floors were identified but the interior of the structure is likely to be on the eastern, unexcavated side. It is possible that it was part of an immediately post-Conquest manor house.

THE FORTIFICATION OF THE SITE

During the 12th century a motte was constructed, formed of successive dumps of soils and gravels brought in from the town, given the large quantity of Roman material amongst its constituents. It was embanked in a distinctive ring, each deposit tipping in towards the centre. The conical central hollow was filled using similar materials that were noticeably richer in clay. The tip lines were clearly distinguished in every section and the full extent of the motte plan can be reconstructed on the ground from the basal layers which survived throughout the excavation. These layers had abutted and covered the earlier Norman structure. The motte had an original base diameter of c60m and the surviving summit diameter is 30m. It is now certain that the motte belongs to the predominant, layered construction-type which is famously depicted on the Bayeux Tapestry. It does not belong to the much rarer revetment type excavated at South Mimms.

Pottery suggests a construction date for the motte in the mid-12th century. The best candidate for this is the period known as The Anarchy, 1135-1153, during which Stephen and Matilda contested over the throne of England. It is less likely that it dates to 1173 during the short civil war led by Hugh Kevelioc, 4th Earl of Chester.

There was no contemporary or later occupation of the summit. Around the base of the motte lay a substantial defensive ditch. Its digging has truncated earlier deposits and features where they extend out from under the motte footprint. No basal silts were identified in the ditch, as excavation was not possible to its full extent, thus its base and its outer edge are unclear.

In the foregoing 2006 excavations an outlying 4m-wide ditch was located north of the motte. It contained an almost complete pottery vessel of St Neot's-type ware, in circulation c 1000-1200. The ditch was relatively shallow and flat bottomed. The series of radial cores also suggest that it is discontinuous since it was not located by a further borehole on its projected eastward line. The 2006 evaluation trench in which this ditch was located was physically linked to Trench 3. The 2006 evaluation is as yet incomplete and the data is not presented here but will be incorporated in a later journal publication.

ABANDONMENT OF THE CASTLE

No late medieval or early post-medieval occupation was present, but during this period there was gradual silting and deliberate infilling of the motte ditch. Restricted sampling has confirmed that for some time at the end of the medieval period and during the early post-medieval period, the motte, called in 1549 Beryorchard, was surrounded by cherry trees, the archaeology confirming the documentation of 1610. The motte ditch is deeply buried and continues to be exceedingly wet, preserving further environmental remains.

The coring work carried out by Archaeoscape from Royal Holloway College in 2006, indicated that the original motte ditch was more extensive than the mapped 19th-century watercourse would suggest. In fact, it was probably a full encircling ditch and was found right around the eastern side of the motte in the boreholes where the organic sediments filling it were as distinctive as where the 2007 works uncovered them to the south and north.

POST-MEDIEVAL REOCCUPATION

During the Civil War (1642-9) Bury Mount may have been occupied for the Royalists, as documents have been purported to suggest. The identification of a mount as a gun emplacement with [Bury] Mount is not beyond doubt. Fieldwork in 2006 has recovered some lead musket-balls and a contemporary Civil War coin but evidence of the motte itself being utilised remains circumstantial. There were no remains present associated with a gun emplacement or contemporary occupation, although Bury Mount was certainly cut back, forming the present scarp of the south face, prior to landscaping works in the 19th century.

In the 19th century the site was occupied by two cottages that stood until recent memory, one of which was later converted into a barn. For a time the cottage was the home of Tommy Roscoe, whose neat and tidy gardens were a notable part of the townscape recorded in a photograph of c1910 (Fig 4). The excavations have shown that although the cottages were benched into the slope of Bury Mount on its south-west quarter, they were built upon the lower levels of motte construction deposits.

During the same century the Earl of Pomfret planted Scots Pines at the summit and may have modified the slopes. There was an absence of archaeological evidence for earlier occupation of the summit that may be the result of preparatory earth-moving. Some of the seeded successors of the trees still stand, but they are very few compared with the many which were depicted in the photograph of c1910, in which perhaps 40 separate trunks can be discerned. A path was cut at this time ascending Bury Mount from the east to the west.

CONSIDERATIONS FOR CONSERVATION

The former footprint of the motte is now known to a considerable extent. Within this sub-circular, 60m-diameter footprint, a considerable thickness of motte construction deposits survive intact. They have been laid down over the pre-existing ground surface which lies above an intact Roman to early Norman sequence of archaeological deposits. The Scheduled Ancient Monument is therefore a multi-period site.

Bury Mount is surmounted by topsoil comprising mainly 19th-century and recent deposits which overlie the buried archaeology on and around the majority of the earthwork. At the summit and on its slopes these are relatively consistent. Around the edges at the foot of the Bury Mount they are thicker where the slope is steepest, the gradient having been instrumental in the amount of hill-wash and other accumulation toward the foot of the earthwork. Where slippage has been greatest on the north and north-east slopes they have masked the inner edge of the motte ditch. In the 19th-century it was partly reused as a minor watercourse which became increasingly choked and nothing is now visible of the ditch as an earthwork. A short length of the 19th-century watercourse can be discerned to the south.

The ditch represents a major, environmentally rich set of Norman, later medieval and early post-medieval castle deposits. Within that ditch are anaerobically-preserved deposits which relate to the land cleared in the 12th century to construct the castle, occupation debris related to the castle, its decline and the greater, longer-term stability of the documented manor to the south which replaced the castle until the later 14th century. Its artefact-content is unknown, but may well include rubbish from the castle occupation and possible remnants of a bridge from the castle baileys, to either south or north. The exact line of the ditch on the western side is unknown. The base of the ditch is buried up to 4.4m below the modern ground surface. Constant water ingress, in volumes a proprietary petrol-driven pump could barely cope with during dry August weather, was encountered at little more than 1m below the modern ground level. Any archaeological excavation within this ditch would therefore be a major engineering exercise.

BIBLIOGRAPHY

Anonymous (ed) 1875 Moated mounds: Cambridge, Towcester, Tempsford, Toternhoe and Caerleon, *The Builder*, 232-233

Atkins, R, and Woodfield, C, 1999 *Archaeological watching brief: Meeting Lane, Towcester, Northamptonshire*, Northamptonshire Archaeology Report, **2420**

Audouy, M, 1984 Bury Mount, in C Woodfield 1992, 25-29

Bailey, B, 1996 Northamptonshire in the early eighteenth century: the drawings of Peter Tillemans and others, *Northamptonshire Record Society*, **39**

Barker, P, and Higham, R, 1982 *Hen Domen, Montgomery: A timber castle on the English-Welsh border*, The Royal Archaeological Institute

Blinkhorn, P, 2007 Medieval and later pottery from Sewardsley, Northamptonshire, Wessex Archaeology (Time Team) report

Blinkhorn, P, forthcoming The pottery, in *Sewardsley Priory, Showsley Grounds, Northamptonshire: An archaeological evaluation and assessment of results*, Wessex Archaeology, unpublished report 65307

BGS 1969 Sheet 202, British Geological Survey

Brown, A E, Woodfield, C, and Mynard, D C, 1983 Excavations at Towcester, Northamptonshire: The Alchester Road suburb, *Northamptonshire Archaeol*, **18**, 43-140

Brown, A E, (ed) *Roman small towns in eastern England and beyond*, Oxbow Monog, **52**

Brown, J, and Soden, I, 2007 *Excavation of a motte and bailey castle at Bury Mount, Towcester, Northamptonshire*, Northamptonshire Archaeology Report, **07/193**

Brown, J, and Walker, C, 2007 *Archaeological watching brief at 147 Watling Street, Towcester, Northamptonshire*, Northamptonshire Archaeology Report, **07/178**

Chapman, A, Thorne, A, and Upson-Smith, T, 2005 A Roman villa and an Anglo-Saxon burial at Wootton Fields, Northampton, *Northampton Archaeol*, **33**, 79-112

Cooper, N, (ed) 2006 *The archaeology of the East Midlands: An archaeological assessment and research agenda*, Leicester Archaeology Monog, **13**, University of Leicester

Creighton, O H, 2002 *Castles and landscapes: Power, community and fortification in medieval England*, Equinox, London

Dawson, M, 2008 Excavation of the Roman villa and Mosaic at Rowler Manor, Croughton, Northamptonshire, *Northamptonshire Archaeol*, **35**

Egan, G, 1995 *Lead cloth seals and related items in the British Museum*, British Museum Occasional Paper, **93**, London

Foard-Colby, A, 2006 *Archaeological evaluation: 147 Watling Street, Towcester, Northamptonshire*, Northamptonshire Archaeology Report, **06/129**

Foard-Colby, forthcoming *Archaeological trial trench evaluation at Wayside Garage, Northampton Road, Towcester, Northamptonshire*, Northamptonshire Archaeology report

Gale, R, and Cutler, D, 2000 *Plants in archaeology*, Otley/ London: Westbury publishing and Royal Botanic Gardens, Kew

Higham, R, and Barker, P, 1992 *Timber Castles*, University of Exeter Press

HMC 1894 *Calendar of Manuscripts of the Most Honourable, the Marquis of Salisbury, Preserved at Hatfield House, Hertfordshire*, part **4**, Historical Manuscripts Commission, London

Hylton, T, 2005 Roman building material from the Centre for Learning, in A Chapman *et al* 2005, 103

Jackson, D, 1983 Defences at the south, The Cinema, in C Woodfield 1992, 29-33

Kilmurry, K, 1980 *The Pottery Industry of Stamford, Lincolnshire. c AD850-1250*, British Archaeology Reports, British Series, **84**

Lambrick, G, 1980 Excavations in Park Street, Towcester, *Northamptonshire Archaeol*, **15**, 35-118

Lewis, C, 2006 The medieval period (850-1500), in N Cooper (ed) 2006, 185-216

Lowerre, A, 2005 *Placing castles in the Conquest: Landscape, lordship and local politics in the South-Eastern Midlands, 1066-1100*, British Archaeological Reports, British Series, **385**

Mann, J E, 1977 *Clay tobacco pipes from excavations in Lincoln 1970-74*

Mills, P, 2008 The Ceramic Building Materials, in M Dawson, 2008

Moore, W R G, 1980 *Northamptonshire Clay tobacco-pipes and pipemakers*, Northampton Museums and Art Gallery

MPRG 1998 *Guide to the Classification of Medieval Ceramic Forms*, Medieval Pottery Research Group, Occasional Paper, **1**

MPRG 2001 *Minimum Standards for the Processing, Recording, Analysis and Publication of post-roman Ceramics*, Medieval Pottery Research Group, Occasional Paper, **2**

Noel Hume, I, 1991(reprinted) *A Guide to Artifacts of Colonial America*

Oakley, G E, 1979, The Copper Alloy Objects, in J H Williams 1979, 248-264

Orton, C, 1998-9 Minimum Standards in Statistics and Sampling, *Medieval Ceramics*, **22-23**, 135-8

Oswald, A, 1975 *Clay pipes for the Archaeologist*, British Archaeological Report, British Series, **14**

Philip, I, (ed) 1947 Journal of Sir Samuel Luke, I: 1643-44, *Oxfordshire Records Society*, **29**, 31, 33

Platt, C, 1978 *Medieval England: A social history and archaeology from the Conquest to 1600 AD*, Routledge, London and New York

Prentice, J, 2001 *An archaeological evaluation at 163-165 Watling Street, Towcester, Northamptonshire*, Northamptonshire Archaeology Report, **2680**

Price, J, and Cottam, S, 1998 *Romano-British Vessel Glass: A Handbook*, Council for British Archaeology

RCHME 1982 *An inventory of the historical monuments in the County of Northampton: Volume IV Archaeological sites in south-west Northamptonshire*, Royal Commission of Historic Monuments, England, HMSO, London

Richardson, K M, 1951, An Iron Age site in the Chilterns, *Antiquities J*, **31**, 132-48

Roy, I, (ed) 1975 The Royalist Ordnance Papers 1642-1646; 2, *Oxfordshire Record Society*, **49**

Schoch, W B, Pawlik, F, and Schweingruber, F, 1988 *Botanical Macro Remains*, Stuttgart, Germany

Scottish Crop Research Seed Identification website, http://www.asis.scri.ac.uk

Shotliffe, D, Steadman, S, and Courtney, P, 1999 *Bury Mount, Towcester, Northamptonshire: Archaeological Management Survey*, Bedfordshire County Archaeology Service

Simms, R S, 1953 Towcester Mote, *The Archaeological Journal*, **110**, 211-212

Steadman, S, and Shaw, M, 1991 *Archaeological evaluation at Meeting Lane, Towcester*, Northamptonshire Archaeology report, **758**

Sunderland, J, and Webb, M, (eds) 1995 *Towcester: the story of an English Country Town*, Towcester and District Local History Society

TDLHS 2006 *Bury Mount Castle, Towcester, Northamptonshire, Discovering Towcester*, Leaflet No **2**, Towcester and District Local History Society

The Ohio University Seed Identification website, http://www.oardc.ohiostate.edu/seedid

Tomber, R, and Dore, J, 1998 *The National Roman fabric reference collection: a handbook*, Museum of London Monog, **2**

VCH 1906 *Victoria County History of Northamptonshire*, **3**, HMSO, London

Ward, C, 1999 *Iron Age and Roman Piddington: The Roman Ceramic and Stone Building Materials 1979-1998*, Upper Nene Archaeological Society, Fascicule, **4**

Williams, J H, 1979 *St Peter's Street, Northampton, Excavations 1973-1976*, Northampton Development Corporation, Archaeol Monog, **2**

Woodfield, C, 1992 The Defences of Towcester, Northamptonshire, *Northamptonshire Archaeol*, **24**, 13-66

Woodfield, C, 1995 New thoughts on town defences in the western territory of the Catuvellauni, in A E Brown (ed) 1995, 129-146

Young, C J, 2000, *Oxfordshire Roman pottery*, British Archaeological Reports, **43**, Oxford (second ed)

A riverside timber revetment at 130 Bridge Street, Peterborough

by

IAN MEADOWS

with contributions by
Tom Higham and Maisie Taylor

ABSTRACT

Archaeological evaluation in advance of development identified a line of upright oak timbers set along the edge of the River Nene and into palaeochannel infilling material containing thirteenth century material, west of the present Town Bridge. The timbers have been radiocarbon dated to the fifteenth century, and may have formed a structure to protect the bridgehead from the effects of tidal scouring or alternatively they could have formed a section of wharf. The occurrence of infilled river channel material to the rear of the revetment indicates a degree of land reclamation and perhaps channel straightening in the medieval period.

INTRODUCTION

Hearthstead Homes commissioned Northamptonshire Archaeology to carry out an archaeological evaluation of 130 Bridge Street (the medieval Hithegate), Peterborough in advance of the construction of a block of apartments (Fig 1; NGR TL 1924 9820). The proposed development lay on the north bank of the River Nene, to the north-west of the present town bridge, on land at about 4.0m above Ordnance Survey datum.

The work was carried out as a series of small archaeological interventions in December 2002, January and February 2003 and May 2006. This report presents the results of this work in a digested form, for the complete report readers are directed to the original client report (Meadows 2004) copies of which are lodged in the Peterborough Historic Environment Record (HER).

ACKNOWLEDGEMENTS

The excavation was directed by Ian Meadows assisted by Ed Taylor, Ailsa Westgarth and Adrian Burrows. Specialist advice was received from Maisie Taylor (wood), Tora Hylton (finds), Paul Blinkhorn (pottery), Ian Tyers (dendrochronology), Tom Higham (radiocarbon dating), Donald Mackreth (documentary history). Work was monitored by Ben Robinson for Peterborough City Council Archaeology Service (PCCAS).

HISTORICAL BACKGROUND

The site was adjacent to the site of previous historical bridges that were probably on the same or very nearly the same location as the first bridge erected in 1307 by Godfrey of Crowland (Mackreth 1994, 35).

Desk-based assessment showed the site's development from the seventeenth century, when Speed (1623) depicted the area as vacant, through a series of building phases, during some of which the river frontage remained clear. In the 1731 prospect of the city (Fig 2), by the Buck brothers, the area is shown edged by a series of closely set upright timbers behind which lay an open area of flood plain on which timbers appear to be present. A map of (1821) showed the simplified outline of the Squire Mansion (erected *c*1760) which occupied the site and was recorded by the artist Fielding in the background to a portrait painting (Fig 3). By the time of the 1884 Ordnance Survey the Squire mansion had gone, additional buildings were present and the site had become a timber yard. In the twentieth century the area continued to be occupied until it was cleared in the 1980s, remaining vacant subsequently.

Although several entries in the Peterborough (HER) record finds of medieval and earlier date for the area immediately around the development, none were known from the site.

EXCAVATED EVIDENCE

STRATEGY AND CONSTRAINTS

The initial strategy was to excavate two trial trenches, one parallel to the riverbank (Trench 1) and the other perpendicular to it (Trench 2) (Fig 4). The one parallel to the riverbank bisected multiple services including a large brick vaulted culvert and two cast iron pipe runs, and was abandoned owing to these constraints. The cast iron pipes may have been associated with the electricity power station that once lay to the north-west. The brick culvert ran north to south across the trench, it was free built in a 2.5m wide trench which was sealed by garden soils and make up layers associated with the later structures on the site. The culvert was built of unfrogged handmade bricks mortared together. The vault was about 1m wide and had an internal diameter of 0.8m high. It is unclear whether it was part of a larger drainage scheme associated with town improvements or simply associated with the Squire Mansion.

The second trench ran north from the river and in its

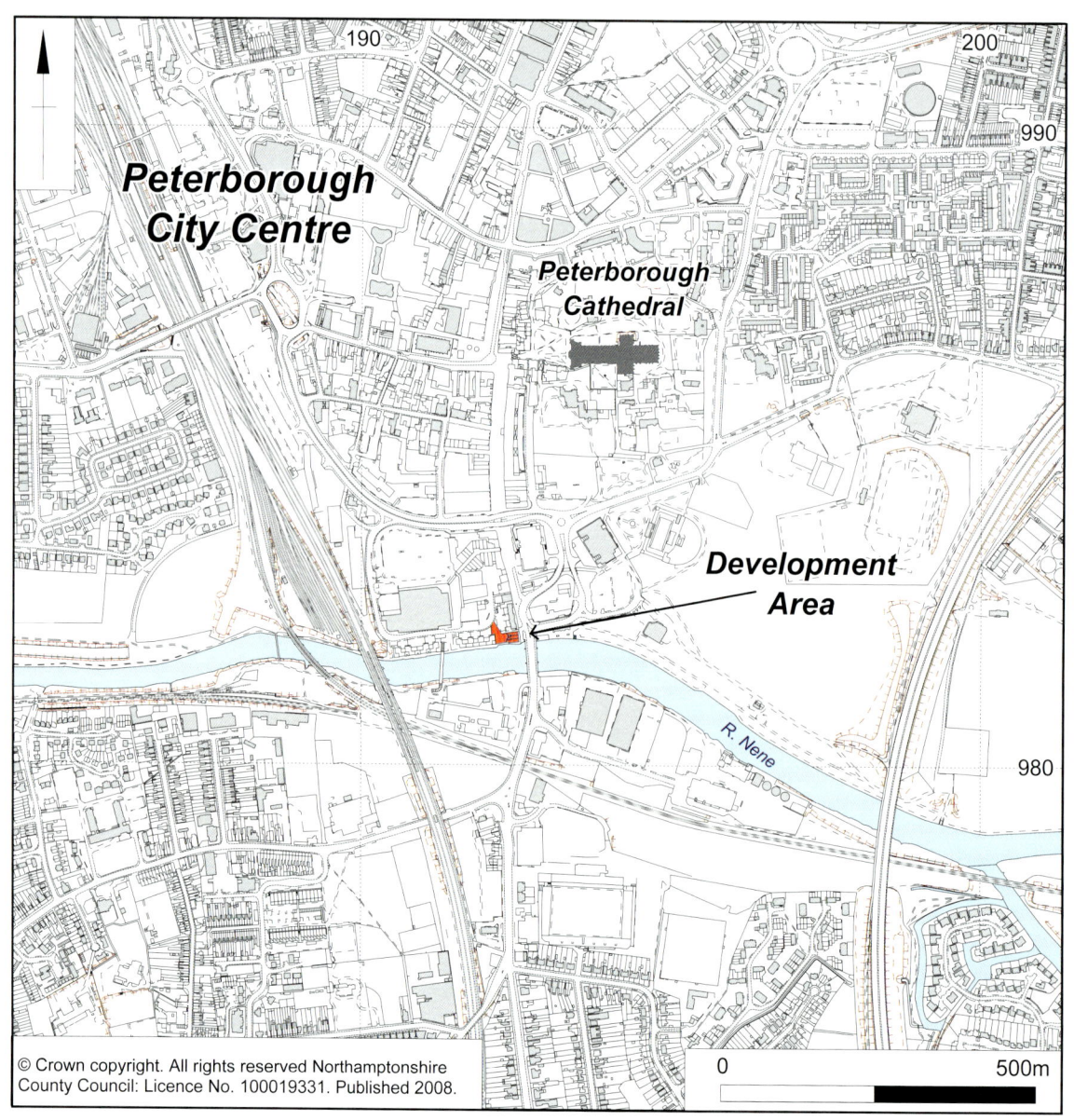

Fig 1 Site location

Fig 2 South West prospect of the city of Peterborough in 1731, by Samuel and Nathaniel Buck

Fig 3 Nathan Fielding (1747-1814), Portrait of Thomas and Charlotte Squire *c*1795, and showing the Squire Mansion in the background (Reproduced courtesy of Peterborough Museum and Art Gallery)

lowest levels there was evidence for possible floodplain and palaeochannel deposits (Fig 5). A 0.4m thick dark organic soil [31], which was very peaty in character and contained only occasional gravel inclusions, sealed a thin mineral soil [32] that was black in colour. This was the limit of the initial exploration but a single deep sounding was mechanically opened through a further 2.5m of organic and clay rich palaeochannel infill deposits [100]. These deposits could not be safely examined but pottery dated to the thirteenth century was recovered from them, although it was unclear from what level. The natural was not reached when the sounding had to be halted.

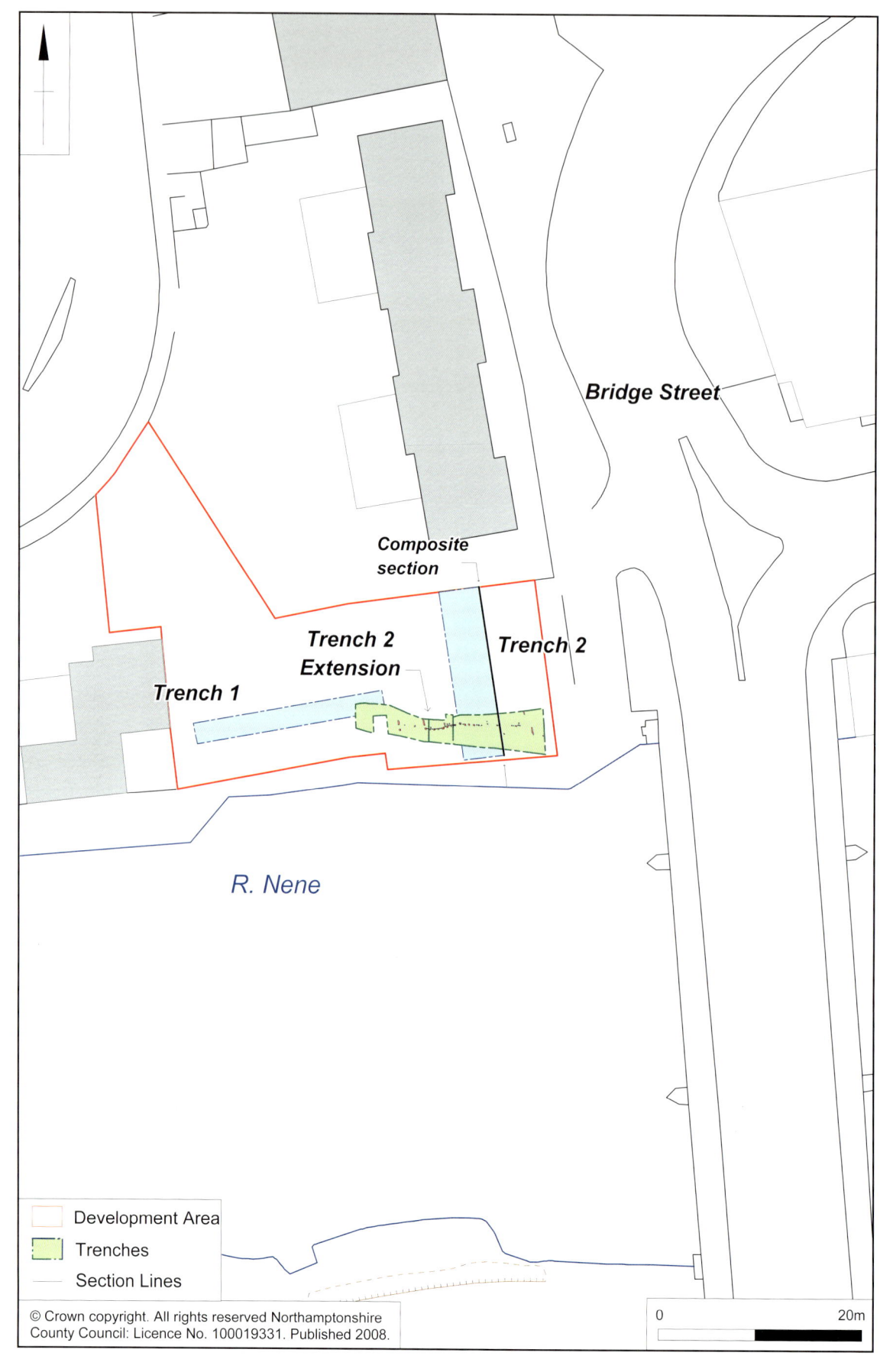

Fig 4 The trench arrangement to the west of the bridge

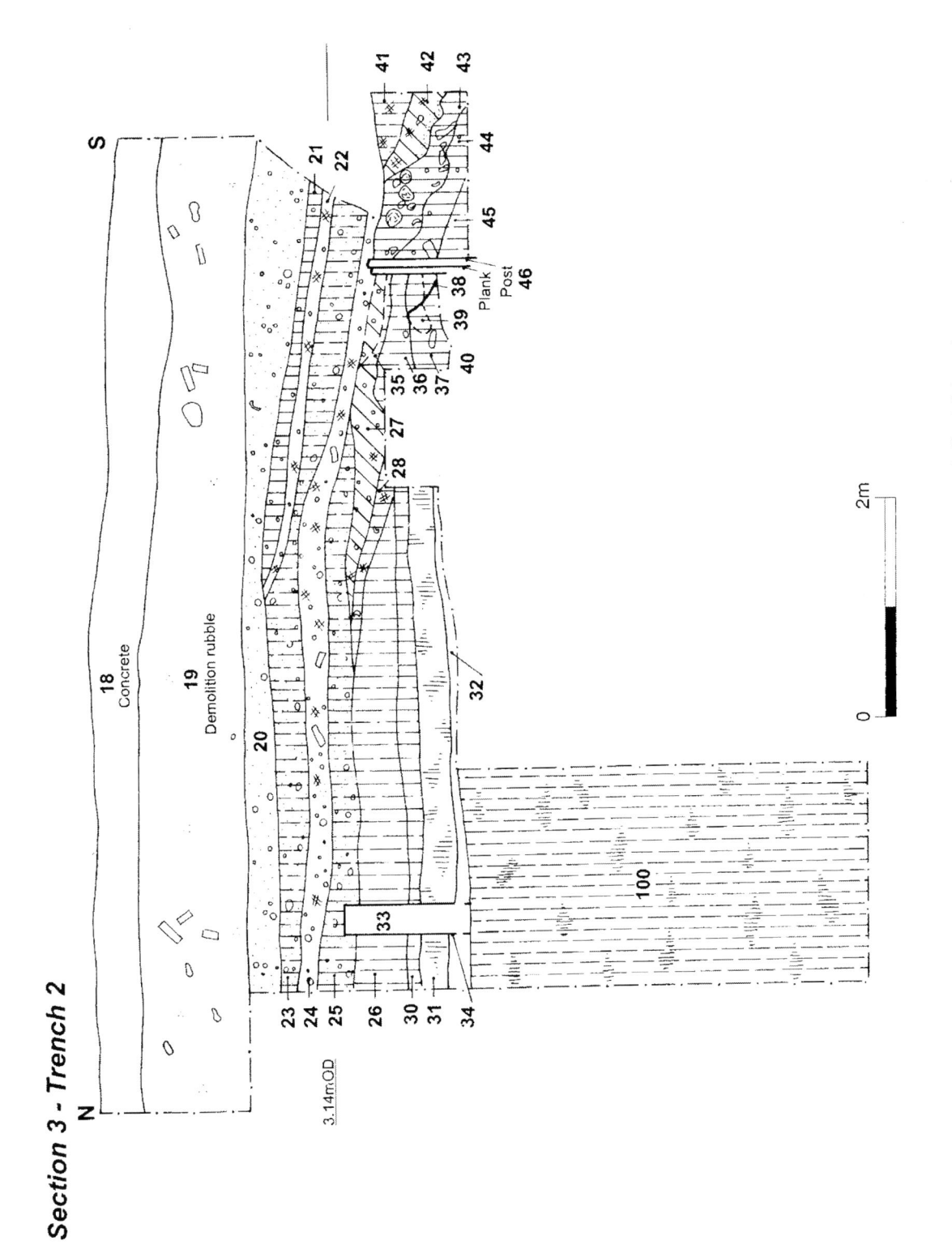

Fig 5 Composite section across the timber revetment and alluvial deposits

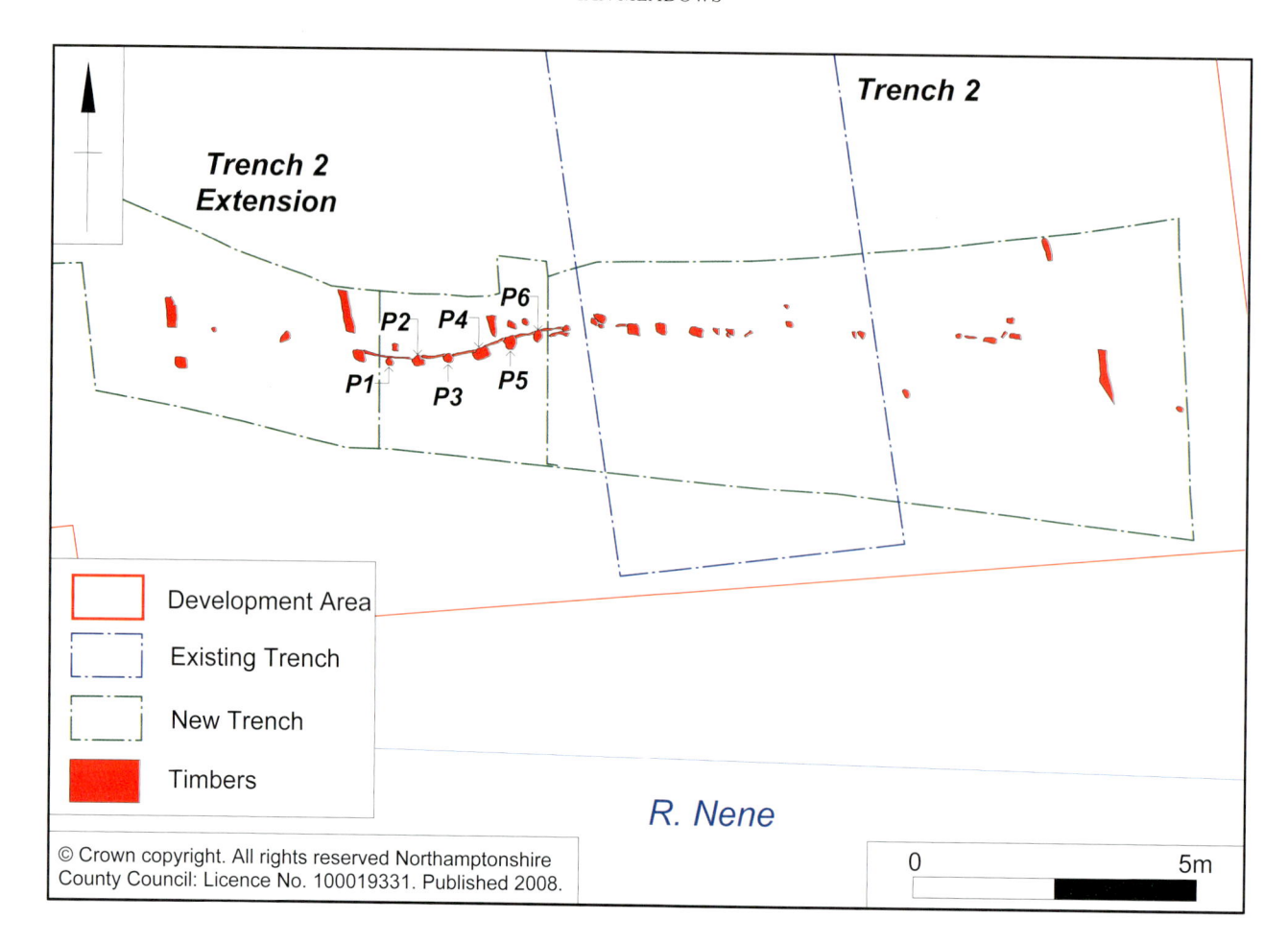

Fig 6 The exposed line of timber posts

While the deep pit was open, discussion took place on site concerning the date and nature of the deep organic fills. Examination of the borehole logs available for the site suggested the presence of a former wide sweeping river meander extending across the site. A relic of this meander may be the inlet portrayed in the 1731 prospect of Peterborough (Fig 2).

At the southern end of the trench the top of a line of timbers was exposed only allowing the partial examination of their northern face. The timbers had to their rear a series of horizontally bedded, often organic deposits, interbedded with clay of distinctly alluvial type [30-32], but at this stage the precise relationship could not be determined.

Due to the limitations of the initial evaluation trench a second stage of work was requested by PCCAS involving the extension of Trench 2 to expose the length of the timberline and allow the examination of both its inner and outer faces. After a number of abortive starts when the water level prohibited safe working, a trench about 20m long and between 7-10m wide was opened. The top of the upright timbers was clearly traced forming a slightly sinuous line from the eastern limit of excavation and stopping after about 12m (Figs 6 & 7). In order to be certain that the end was not just an artefact of shorter timbers a test trench was hand excavated 5m to the west across the line of any potential continuation. This trench was dug to a depth of 0.5m and no upright timbers were observed.

Fig 7 Trench extension, looking east, showing the exposed tops of the posts and the deeper intervention (foreground)

Fig 8 The exposed face of the timber and plank revetment

THE TIMBERS

The timbers comprised roughly squared posts 0.2m x 0.16m, the upper portions of which had been rounded on their riverward face, presumably by erosion and weathering (Fig 8). The rear face of the post was cut with a c 45mm square rebate on each edge in which rested a plank 0.03m thick and 0.27m wide (Fig 9).

A sample length of 2.5m of the timber line was examined to expose both the face and the rear supports of the timber works, they were found to survive in good condition. The face was exposed to a depth of 0.9m.

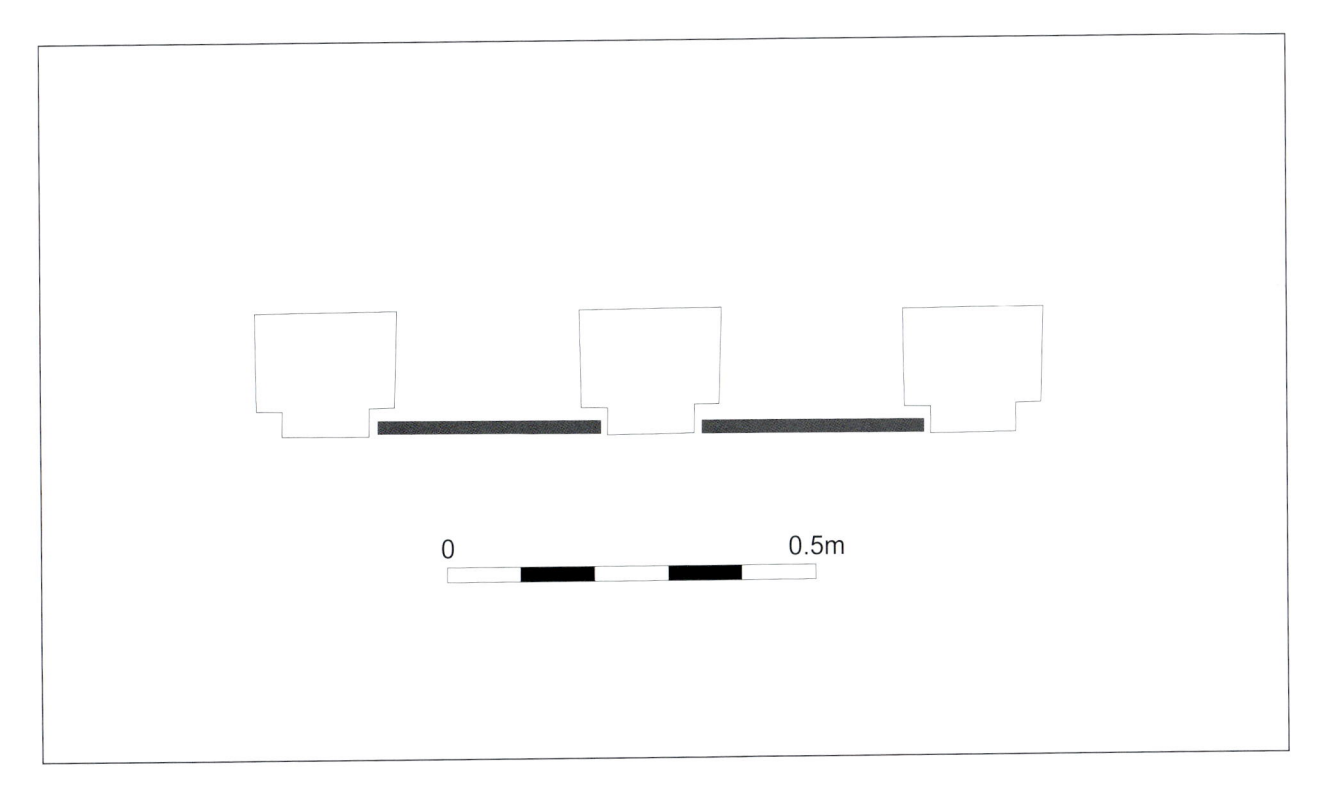

Fig 9 Schematic plan of revetment construction to show rebates with inset planks

ACCUMULATED SILTS

At the limit of excavation to the south of the timbers a firm dark grey silty clay (Fig 5, 45) containing frequent charcoal flecking and isolated small stones was present; its relationship to the timberwork was equivocal, but it dipped south away from the alignment. It was overlain by dark brown silt, a typical riverine deposit, [44] which contained abundant organic material along with occasional small stones and red brick type fragments. This deposit abutted the timbers. Both [44] and [45] contained mid fifteenth-century pottery. These deposits were sealed beneath a deliberate dump of material [43], which contained a substantial amount of waterlogged wood and building material especially limestone roofing slates and pieces of red brick, along with mid-fifteenth-century pottery. At its northern limit this deposit abutted the timber posts [46]. This deposit was perhaps, at least in part, derived from a demolished structure.

A series of further dumps of material were recorded. The earliest was grey clay with frequent charcoal flecks and occasional small stones [42], which was sealed beneath mid brown clay with occasional charcoal flecks and isolated pieces of red brick [41]. These clays both shallowed to the north, they had a maximum combined thickness of 0.7m.

The rear of the timbers was exposed to a depth of about 0.7m. The limit of excavation was into near black silt [37] with an organic content and occasional stones. This was cut by a slot [38], 0.4m wide at the top tapering to 0.1m at the limit of exposure at the base, which contained yellow grey mottled clay with no stone inclusions [39]. It is possible the slot represents a foundation cut for the timberline. These levels were sealed by a firm mid grey silty, possibly alluvial, clay with occasional stone inclusions [36], which also abutted the timbers. This deposit might represent the continuation of the alluvial clays identified to the north [26 & 30]. The uppermost fill that abutted the wood contained mid-fifteenth-century pottery, it was a dark brown clay silt [35] with a high organic content and occasional stone inclusions.

There were two alluvial clays, which possibly represented a continuation of the alluvial deposit identified above [36]. The lowest a homogeneous alluvial clay of mottled blue grey colouration [30], 0.26m thick, containing no inclusions, was overlain by a homogeneous, dark grey clay [26] with no inclusions, 0.47m thick. This deposit was fairly consistent in its thickness except at the southern end where it tapered off or had been scoured off. The colour variation between the two clays may be a reflection of the local soil oxygen conditions rather than actual differences. These deposits were clearly flood derived deposits as a result of overbank flood episodes.

The alluvial level was sealed by a series of more mixed deposits and dumps. The lowest was a silty clay with gravel inclusions [25], which was sealed by a mixed deposit of clay gravel and brick [24], which was overlain by a silty clay [23] containing some gravel. Each of these deposits was horizontally bedded, between 0.2-0.35m thick, except at their southern end where they dipped down as if towards a river channel.

At the southern end of the above levels two deposits [27, 28] were dipping down to the river. The lower, a dark silty deposit, 0.1m thick, which contained moderate amounts of charcoal and both whole and fragmentary pieces of shell, was sealed by a 0.3m thick deposit of mid brown clay [27] with gravel and moderate amounts of charcoal. These deposits may represent encroachment and dumping onto the rivers edge

These mixed deposits were sealed beneath an orange sandy gravel [20] containing frequent small stones. This material was clean and was probably an imported gravel to create a clean flat surface, possibly the court in front of the Squire mansion shown in Fielding's painting. Towards the south this gravel layer sealed two dumps of dirty gravel [21, 22] which contained in the lower layer charcoal and in the upper mortar. These deposits may have been to level the area prior to the deposition of the main gravel horizon [20].

This gravel horizon was sealed by the nineteenth- and twentieth-century deposits comprising a layer [19] of brick and other recent material in turn overlain by a substantial, 0.45m thick, concrete floor raft [18]. This floor was stepped in shallow increments down towards the river suggesting that the ground at the time of development had also possibly sloped towards the river. The stubs of walls were present from the final structure on the site, they incorporated bricks from the Hicks and Gardiner works at Fletton. This was the Temperance Hotel and large timber piles within concreted blocks formed part of its foundations, some of these pile casings were 2m square at the surface and extended 2m down encasing timbers 0.3m across. These timber uprights could be the foundations for the balcony type structure shown in a photograph of the building.

DISCUSSION OF THE TIMBER STRUCTURE
Maisie Taylor

The wooden structure appears to be a stave built revetment. With the exception of a short section, which was exposed to a depth of up to about 1m, only the top of the structure was revealed. The structure has two vertical components: The 'staves' and square framing timbers (Figs 8 & 9). Stave building was a popular method of constructing waterfront revetments in the fifteenth century in London (Period V, in Milne 1982, 29) but there is little comparative material from inland ports.

The staves at Rivergate were sawn planks or boards taken tangentially from the outside of trees. These might have been the by-product from a timber yard that was squaring oak trunks for some other construction work which required large oak timbers. The quality of the timber from which the boards are derived appears to have been first rate. The framing timbers are not such good quality and are of rough squared oak; they may have been reused timbers. There is one framing timber set between every two staves. The square timbers are rebated to receive the boards. This is a profligate use of timber compared with most of the stave-built structures illustrated from London. The oak boards are, however, fairly thin for their width and probably needed the extra support. If the boards were a by-product of oak timber production for some major building project in the city, however, they may have been plentiful and need not have been expensive. As the staves are heavily braced by the square verticals there might not have been a sole plate and the timber could all be earth-fast, alternatively the staves may have been pile driven.

DATING THE TIMBER STRUCTURE
Tom Higham

Lengths of three timbers were removed for dendrochronological analysis. The samples were submitted to Ian Tyers at Sheffield University but were found to have only a maximum of 38 rings, which is below the 50 ring minimum requirement for dendrochronological dating. Instead, samples were submitted for radiocarbon 'wiggle matching', whereby adjoining decadal groups of tree rings are sampled and then dated. A number of lengths of timber from the large squared uprights were taken to the Oxford Radiocarbon Accelerator Unit where two were selected as being potentially suitable by Dr Tom Higham of the Research Laboratory for Archaeology and the History of Art. The results of an initial sample OxA-16871 (617+/-26BP), from what was identified as the exterior of the tree produced a date that was subsequently to prove unlikely.

The other three dates were taken by Dan Miles, the dendrochronologist, they were in the form of a wedge-shaped cut of wood, taken from a single timber, which was mounted and carefully sampled into a section of wood which was polished and which consisted of three blocks of ten tree rings each.

Table 1: Radiocarbon dating results

Laboratory number	Rings	Coventional Age BP
OxA-17656	11-20	543 +/-22
OxA-17657	21-30	535 +/-24
OxA-17658	31-40	593 +/-22

The radiocarbon dated sequence was good but it did present a problem, the sequence did not fit because the date of OxA-16871 (the most recent wood, supposedly) produced an earlier date than other samples. The considered opinion was that OxA-16871 is aberrant. It comes from a different part of the tree wood, was sampled separately, and may date to an older period. For this reason the results were modelled including only the three-date section of the wood, with an additional 15-year gap at the end to account for the gap left by the problematic radiocarbon date, and the estimated sapwood boundary. The felling date for this tree, accounting for these caveats described above, is 1423-1437 Cal AD (68.2% confidence).

DISCUSSION

This excavation identified a previously unsuspected and unique feature in Peterborough, a stave-built timber-faced river frontage. It remains unclear whether the oak timbers formed part of an extra long spillway associated with the bridgehead, if they ever formed part of a wharf arrangement or if they were part of a reclamation scheme. The first suggestion seems more likely since the timberline is only 12m long and that would seem rather short for a wharf. The known wharves all lie downstream of the bridge, which would itself offer an obstruction to most navigation. If the timbers were related to the bridgehead their location would protect it from the effects of tidal scouring which might have weakened the crossing. This would be particularly so as the soils to the north of the bridgehead were soft medieval channel fills which would be easily eroded.

Few medieval or early post-medieval bridgeheads have been examined. Where they have been, the bridgehead was generally replaced in stone before the date of this feature. The bridges recovered from Hemmington across the Trent were of timber from the eleventh to twelfth centuries but from about 1240 onwards the bridgehead was stone rubble with retaining timbers (Johnson pers comm).

The structure cuts channel fills dated to the thirteenth century and the timbers date from the early fifteenth century. It is unclear whether the timbers were erected as a freestanding structure, which then became sealed by dumped material containing fifteenth-century material, or whether the timbers formed a line of driven planks and posts. The former suggestion is perhaps the more likely because of the possible presence of raking timbers however as no timber joints were observed the evidence for the relationship of those pieces to the post and plank line remains equivocal.

It is equally equivocal whether the timbers were new when they were used to create this structure and the squared framing timbers; they could be re-used. The reuse of timber is well attested locally with several references, for example, by William Morton to old timber in the fifteenth century. In one instance a Tom Cooper was paid with old timber (Mellows *et al* 1954, 132).

Examination of other towns where river front structures have been identified does not reveal any that are directly comparable. The examples at Trig Lane, London, were far longer and more extensive in each phase and were undoubtedly a riverfront revetment (Milne 1982). At Hull part of the riverfront was examined at Chapel Lane Staith (Ayers 1979), in a 4m wide trench, and dated to about the second quarter of the fourteenth century. Here it was suggested that for a period of time the revetment was left open to its rear and that some of the sediments present represented settlement from the tidal waters trapped behind the timbers. This is important as it shows that the construction of riverfront structures was not always a rapid sequence of events. At Reading the riverfront revetments were seen to lie in front of deliberate reclamation layers, most of which was probably material derived from dredging of the river as it contained little domestic refuse (Hawkes *et al* 1997). In each of these examples the upright revetments were braced by raking timbers that extended sometimes to the front but always to the rear for up to 3m before being fixed to the ground. The uprights themselves were often also fixed at the base to a horizontal sole plate joined by a top plate at the top.

The structure at Peterborough is perhaps a part of a wider engineering solution to the problems of the tidal flow of the Nene and the need to protect a bridge from erosion on a meander. Monastic alterations to watercourses for drainage, navigation or other reasons can be seen elsewhere and it is possible this may have been a similarly monastically lead exercise. At Ely works included the reclamation of part of a meander of the Ouse and the erection of wharves and warehouses. The excavation evidence coupled with the previous borehole logs both for the Rivergate complex and for developments to the east, indicate that originally the Nene was not as straight as the present course in this area. Slightly beyond the present railway bridge, upstream, the river has a sinuous form that continues westwards. The possible reasons for straightening the channel might be related to the original construction of the bridge over the river in 1307. A meandering course has one edge of active erosion and the other bank is actively depositing. If the meander pattern originally continued through to the present study area then the erosion would have been active on the north bank where the bridgehead lay. By straightening the course the scour effect of the current on the side of the channel would be concentrated into the channel itself.

The stratigraphic position of this structure coupled with the potential for re-use of the timbers still does not rule out the possibility that this structure could be the enigmatic one depicted on the 1731 prospect of Peterborough.

BIBLIOGRAPHY

Ayers, B, 1979 *Excavations at Chapel Lane Staith 1978* (Hull Old Town Report, **3**), East Riding Archaeologist, **5**

Hawkes, J W, and Fasham, P J, 1997 *Excavations on Reading Waterfront sites, 1979-88,* Wessex Archaeology Report, **5**

Mackreth, D F, 1994 *Peterborough: History and guide*

Meadows, I D, 2004 *Archaeological evaluation of 130 Bridge Street, Peterborough, Cambridgeshire 2002- 2003,* Northamptonshire Archaeology report

Mellows and King 1954 *The Book of William Morton, Almoner of Peterborough Monastery,* transcribed and annotated by the late W T Mellows, edited by P I King, Northamptonshire Record Society, **16**, Oxford

Milne, G, and Milne, C, 1982 *Medieval waterfront development at Trig Lane, London,* London Middlesex Archaeological Society, Special Paper, **5**

Excavations at the corner of Kingswell Street and Woolmonger Street, Northampton

by

JIM BROWN

with contributions by
Philip Armitage, Paul Blinkhorn, Pat Chapman, Val Fryer, Tora Hylton, Helen Leaf
Iain Soden, Carol Simmonds, Tim Upson-Smith and Charlotte Walker

SUMMARY

Kingswell Street and Woolmonger Street are integral to our understanding of the layout and development of the medieval town of Northampton. The site is close to the heart of early Northampton and excavation has revealed a sequence of development that relates to the broader pattern of town growth.

In the mid-10th to early 11th centuries there was a large late Saxon cellared structure, similar to others found within the early town, although this area was marginal to the main focus of late Saxon occupation in Northampton. The cellar was succeeded by a Saxo-Norman timber building on the same alignment, although the larger part of the site was open ground, and the roads appear to have been less formally defined.

Intensive occupation of the site did not occur until the 13th-14th centuries when property boundaries were defined by areas of quarrying. Four medieval buildings were constructed within these plots, including a malthouse and a bakehouse. The arrangement of the buildings emphasised the formalisation of both adjacent streets for the first time, although a continuous frontage was not in evidence.

Pottery of the 15th century was sparse, seemingly due to documented civil improvements on Kingswell Street in 1641, but the frontage was developed during this century. Occupation of a medieval building on the Kingswell Street frontage continued in the 16th-17th centuries, with cess pits to the rear. There was no evidence for the Great Fire of Northampton in 1675.

The 17th-18th-century frontage contained at least one surviving medieval building, but this was lost with the erection of new buildings in the 19th century. Clay tobacco-pipemaking debris helped to identify the tenement of Master tobacco-pipemaker, George Henshaw (1767-1774) at 15 Kingswell Street. His tenure formed part of a substantial documented history of the site for the later post-medieval period.

INTRODUCTION

Northamptonshire Archaeology was commissioned in March 2005, by Westleigh Developments Ltd, to conduct an archaeological excavation on 0.3ha of land at the corner of Kingswell Street and Woolmonger Street, Northampton (NGR SP 7532 6033; Fig 1). This was a condition of the planning permission for redevelopment. Northamptonshire Archaeology produced a Written Scheme of Investigation (Soden 2005) that was approved and monitored by the Northamptonshire County Council (NCC) Historic Environment Team Leader. Monitoring visits were conducted on a weekly basis during the course of the subsequent works.

The area excavation comprised a single near square area measuring 25m by 25m area, located within the frontage of the former properties of 14-16 Kingswell Street. This was the area where the evaluation had located the most extensive surviving deposits (Carlyle 2003). As part of an agreed method of reducing the ground level in the remainder of the site, a watching brief was maintained with a contingency for work where additional features survived outside the excavation. This article is a synthesis of results for the combined archaeological programme and is based on the original client report (Brown 2007). It includes details of a silver inlaid iron riding spur following its conservation, which were not available at the time of original reporting.

ACKNOWLEDGEMENTS

The project was managed by Iain Soden and the fieldwork was directed by Jim Brown. Excavation was conducted by Adrian Burrow, Giles McFarland, Nathan Flavell, James Aaronson, Mark Spalding, Sharon Cook, Mark Patenall, Rob Smith and Jennifer Jackson. Environmental processing was by Karen Deighton. The conservation of the finds was carried out through Buckinghamshire Museum Service by David Parish. The illustrations were prepared by Jim Brown, Carol Simmonds and Charlotte Walker. The documentary work and the report on the excavations were produced by Jim Brown. The published report has been condensed from the client report, which is available in archive, in the Historic Environment Record and online through the Archaeological Data Service (ADS) (Brown 2007).

TOPOGRAPHY AND GEOLOGY

The site lies on the northern slopes of the Nene valley. The natural contours of the former hillside slope

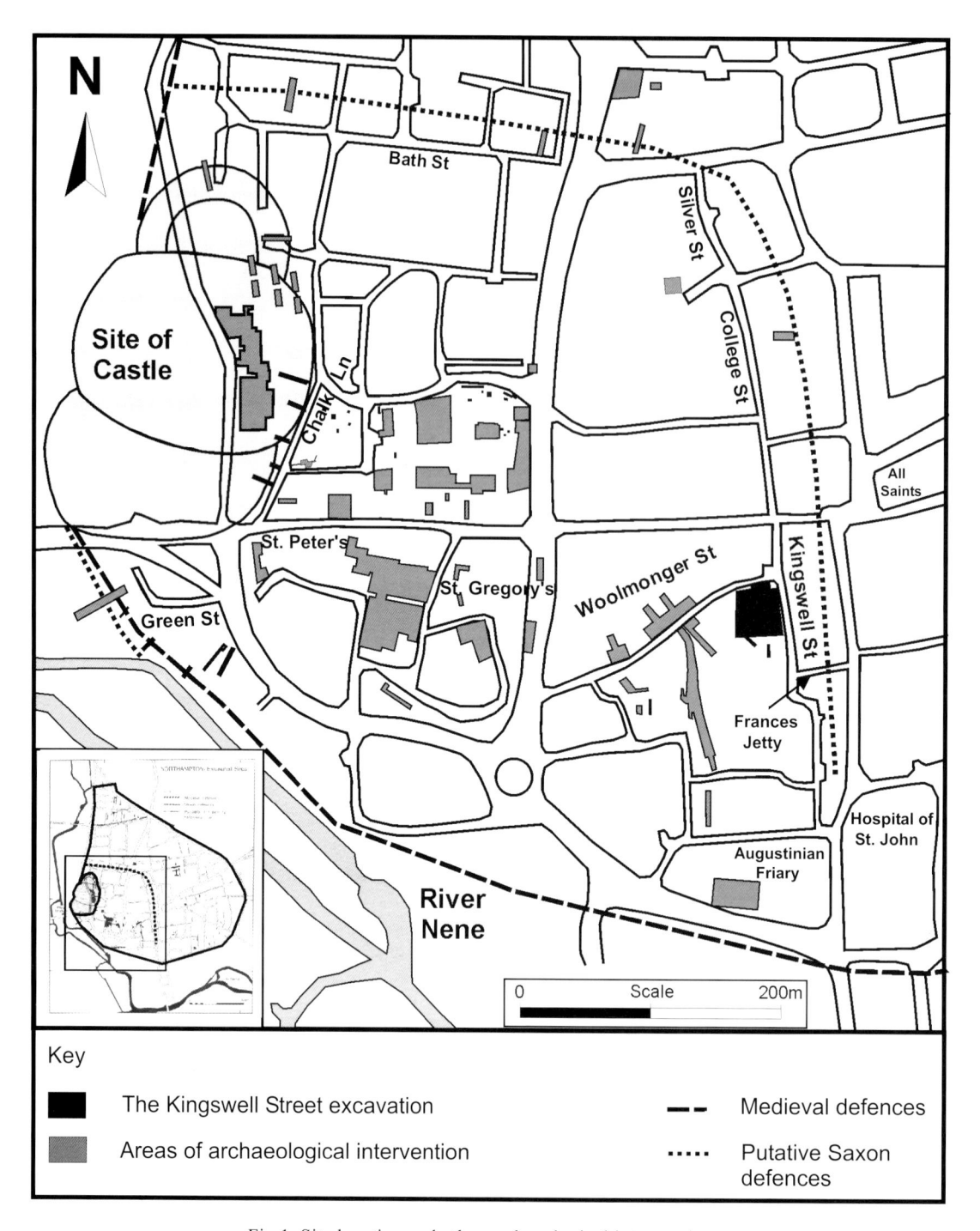

Fig 1 Site location and other archaeological interventions

gradually downwards from 68.2m OD in the north to 67m OD in the south of the excavation area. Modern terracing in the south and dumps of material in the north give the impression of a much sharper gradient. The site is bounded on the eastern side by Kingswell Street, to the north by Woolmonger Street, to the west by the shops around St. Peter's Square and to the south by the delivery access at the former Kingswell Terrace junction. The excavation area, formerly 4-16 Kingswell Street, had Kingswell Street on its eastern side and included an area of watching brief contingency to the north, formerly 1-7 Woolmonger Street.

The geology of the site consists predominantly of sedimentary Jurassic Ironstone and Northampton Sand with ironstone (http://www.bgs.ac.uk/geoindex/index.htm).

HISTORICAL AND ARCHAEOLOGICAL BACKGROUND

The site was situated within the south-eastern quarter of the postulated late Saxon burh, but perhaps outside a middle Saxon precinct around the churches of St Peter and St Gregory (Fig 1; Lee 1954; Williams 1979, 5; Foard 1995, 112). It lay south-west of All Saints Church and the

Norman market place, and north of the Augustinian Friary, in the former parish of St. Gregory, encompassing an area of land on the west side of *Kyngeswell Lane*, south of the junction with *Welmonger Strete* (Williams 1982a, 82).

Archaeological evidence for early to middle Saxon occupation in Northampton comes from the excavations focussed on the land around St. Peter's Church, 300m west of the current site. Around St Peter's settlement was well established by the 8th century and may have formed a provincial or ecclesiastical administrative centre occupying a small precinct (Foard 1995, 111), and this was an early focus for growth throughout the middle and late Saxon periods.

Northampton was ceded to the Danes as part of the treaty between Alfred and Guthrum, *c* 886, fixing the boundary between Saxon England and the Danelaw (Williams 1982b, 21). The town spent 27 years in Danish control before Alfred's son, Edward, recaptured Northampton in 913. How this affected the economy is unclear, but Northampton continued to flourish despite the political upheavals, and evidence of the Danish occupation is scant. By the end of the 10th century the development of the town included a defensive circuit, and Alderman Lee suggested that to the north and east this followed the line of Bath Street, Silver Street, College Street and Kingswell Street (Fig 1; Lee 1954). The line of the defences has only been established archaeologically to the south of the West Bridge, where they have been dated to the 10th century, but with insufficient precision to determine whether they derive from the period of Danish control or were late Saxon in origin, perhaps a response to further Danish aggression (Chapman 1998-9, 42). Kingswell Street is thought to have been an intramural street parallel to these defences, which may have extended south towards the river.

Being enclosed by the defensive circuit did not necessarily mean that the land was intensively occupied or that it contained assets worthy of protection. Excavations conducted at Woolmonger Street, 70m west of the current site, indicate that prior to the 10th century there were few timber buildings in this area to the east of Horseshoe Street (Soden 1998-9, 112-113). This pattern changed from the 10th century onwards as cellared buildings were established in the late Saxon period (*ibid*, 76-78). Clearance and redevelopment took place at Woolmonger Street between the 10th and 11th centuries, when the same cellared buildings were destroyed and replaced by further timber halls, enabling formalisation of the street plan by the Norman authorities (*ibid*, 123).

The town had been a seat of parliament since the reign of Henry I (1100-1135). The New Borough and marketplace was established to the north-east as the town continued to grow and prosper, receiving its first charter in 1189. Such political decisions were catalysts for sustained growth. The construction of a Royal Castle in the mid-12th century under Henry II had a major effect upon the town as a consequence of the Royal investment and even the less important buildings of the town were being rebuilt in stone. Amongst the most influential arrivals were the ecclesiastical houses which were swift to acquire property in Northampton.

In the second half of the 13th century pressure for land in Northampton was intense. The town was a military staging post for campaigns in the north of England and a centre of Royal power. In 1221 the Royal Field Army mustered at Northampton for campaigns in Lincolnshire and again in 1224 in preparation for the siege of Bedford (Norgate 1912). From both strategic and political standpoints Northampton was a key town in central England and a gateway to the north. The needs of Henry III, in his response to unrest, coinciding with the location of the Royal Castle made the town a viable choice for his headquarters. In 1225 Henry III chose to hold his Christmas Court at Northampton, attracting all the magnates in the land and their combined retinues (Turner 1907, 205-62).

The following centuries were less kind. Northampton's documentary record for the 15th century portrays a town in which some areas were in poor repair (Williams 1979, 6). Evidence from excavations at Woolmonger Street demonstrated a distinct lack of evidence for occupation in the 15th-century, combined with signs of property demolition along parts of the street, and no urban regeneration prior to the 17th century (Soden 1998-9). This is a phenomenon that fits a national pattern of urban recession (Schofield 1994, 209). Northampton suffered further at the flames of two large fires, the first in 1516 and a second in 1675. The impact of the Dissolution in the 16th century further curtailed the economic influences of the great ecclesiastical houses, already in decline, and Royal retribution for Northampton's parliamentary stance in the 17th century ended the town's strategic importance.

MAP EVIDENCE

The earliest surviving depiction of Kingswell Street is the 1610 map by John Speed (Fig 2). The street is shown with numerous tenements forming a terraced block on the west side of the street from the junction with Woolmonger Street to the bottom of the hill opposite St. John's Hospital. As with all of Speed's maps the land at the back is not shown, but gives an impression of open space when compared to the walled precincts of the monastic estates.

Noble and Butlin's map of 1746 depicts the site still substantially built up on both frontages and shows a series of property divisions to the rear (Fig 2). The length of the row of buildings on the west side of the street appears shorter, extending beyond Frances Jetty and a large area of lightly-wooded ground occupied the former Augustinian precinct to the south.

Roper and Cole's map of 1807 (not illustrated) provides very little evidence of change from the map of 1746. The rear plots are identical except where two yards and an outhouse at the back of Woolmonger Street had been combined.

Wood and Law's map of 1847 depicts an increasing pressure for space on the site (Fig 2). Several of the rear yards had been developed with buildings and had become increasingly subdivided. Gaps along both streets were far fewer and many more properties had been established over the former Augustinian precinct to the south.

The Ordnance Survey map of 1885 depicts the development of the site with many subdivisions (Fig 2). Small ancillary buildings and outhouses were densely packed. Kingswell Terrace is depicted immediately to the south, with the end tenements, 20-22 Kingswell Terrace,

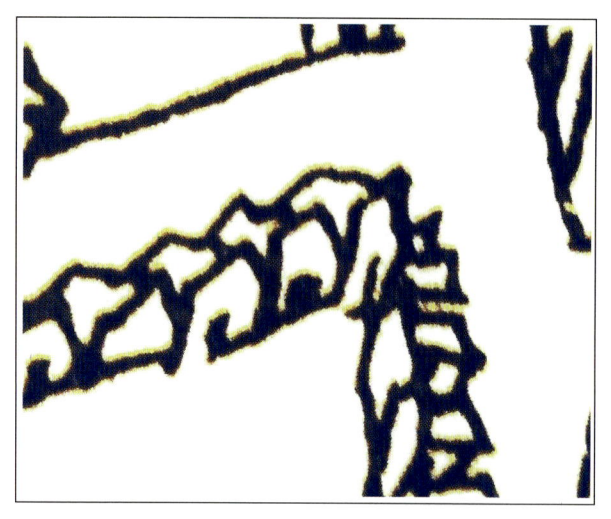

1610 Excerpt from the map by John Speed

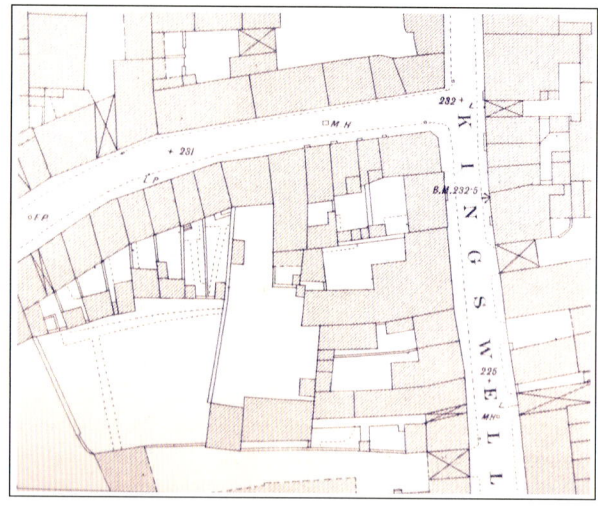

1885 Excerpt from the 1st ed Ordnance Survey

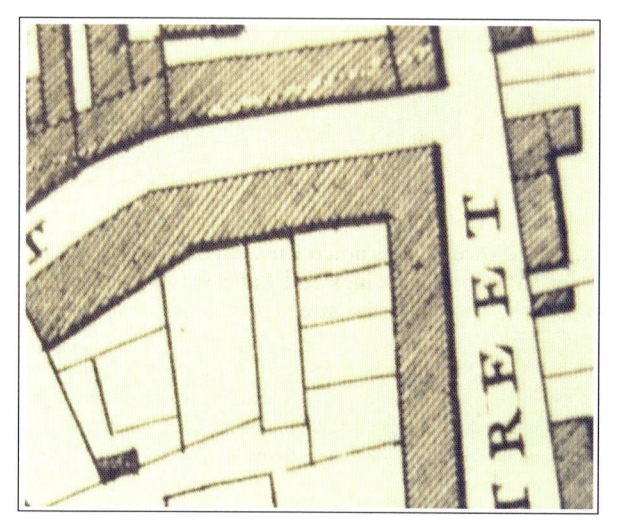

1746 Excerpt from the map by Noble & Butlin

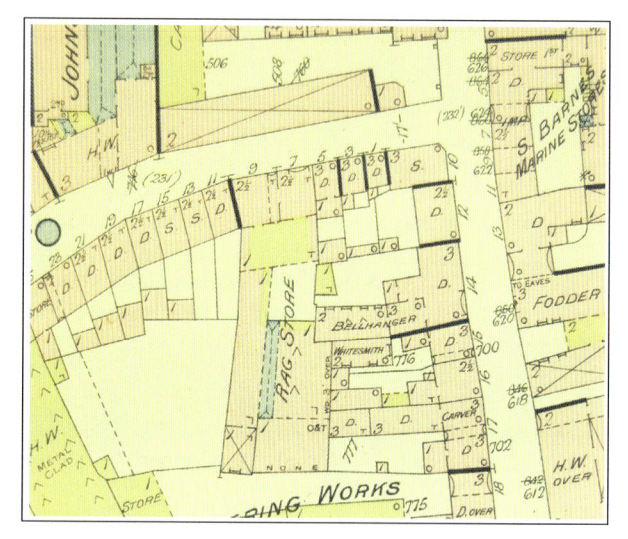

1899 Excerpt from Goad's Insurance plan

1847 Excerpt from the map by Wood & Law

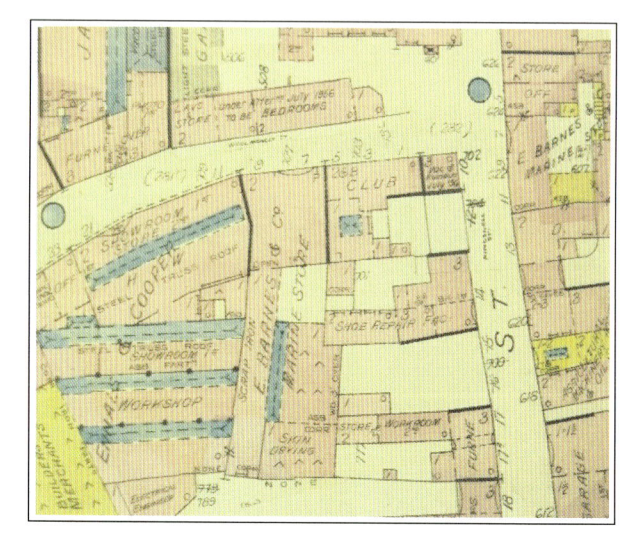

1949 Excerpt from Goad's Insurance plan

Fig 2 Map regression 1949-1610

backing onto the south-west portion of the site. Two alleyways are depicted along Kingswell Street to give access to the rear yards.

The 1899 Insurance Plans of Northampton reveal that the former pattern of street numbers did not run in a predictable sequence (Fig 2; NRO Maps 5970-2). The two alleyways identified on the 1885 Ordnance Survey map lay between 17-17a Kingswell Street and between 17a-18 Kingswell Street, the latter being called J. T. Lowke Engineering Works. A third alley is shown between 15-16 Kingswell Street. The plans also show that a large yard space to the rear of 7-9 Woolmonger Street was succeeded by warehousing for Baines Rag Merchant. Some minor rearrangement of ancillary buildings to the rear of 16-17a Kingswell Street is apparent. A building to the rear of 14 Kingswell Street is labelled 'Bellhanger' and one adjacent, behind 15 Kingswell Street, is labelled 'Whitesmith'. The property at 17 Kingswell Street is labelled 'Carver'.

The Insurance Plans were resurveyed in 1949 and depict a less cluttered arrangement (Fig 2; NRO Maps 5970-2). The property at 10 Kingswell Street is marked as ruinous; 12 Kingswell Street had been demolished; 14 Kingswell Street was a Shoe Repair Factory; 15-16 Kingswell Street had been demolished; 17-17a Kingswell Street housed an Antique Furniture Dealer; and 18-23 Kingswell Street had been rebuilt to accommodate a modernised paintshop and store for Basset-Lowke Engineers. The houses at 24-28 Kingswell Street, immediately south of the excavation site, had been demolished. On Woolmonger Street the tenements between 1-5 and part of 10 Kingswell Street had been replaced by a 'Club'; 7-9 Woolmonger Street and the warehousing was occupied by E. Baines & Co Marine Store, with a skin drying room at the back. Terraced housing between 11-25 Woolmonger Street had been replaced by Ennals & Cooper Agricultural Engineers. Only one alleyway survived, beneath the archway at 18 Kingswell Street, which provided access to the Basset-Lowke yard.

Subsequent Ordnance Survey editions depict minor alterations to ancillary structures between 1927 and 1957. The next major changes were visible on the map of 1972 with the area of a car park replacing the former properties at 14-17a Kingswell Street. The corner plot, 10-12 Kingswell Street and 1-5 Woolmonger Street, had been combined into a public house. A single large building occupied the site of Basset-Lowke Engineers, marked as a 'Scale-model factory'. The south side of Woolmonger Street from east to west showed the club, a warehouse, engineering works and a motor repair works. All of these structures were demolished in 2005.

DOCUMENTS IN NORTHAMPTONSHIRE RECORD OFFICE

The published and archive account of the adjacent Woolmonger Street excavations (Soden 1998-9) contains a detailed account of the documentary information, the relevant parts of which include references to Kingswell Street: Kyngeswellstrete 1431 (Cox 1898); Kyngewell Street 1504 (NBC records 29); Kingswell Lane 1618 (NBC records 86); Kingy Lane 1695 (NRO: NPL 2216); and Lewnys Lane: Venella juxta domum... Lewelini (Rental Edward I); Lewnyslane 1504 (NBC records 29); lane open towards Wolmongerstrete (NBC records 29).

The earliest surviving document that mentions property on Kyngeswell Strete is a Latin Assizes case in 1361 (NRO A97). The case addresses the claim of Henry Vynter against (the Duke of) Buckyngham for illegally appropriating the estates of Criek (Crick) called Vyntersmanere and those fields pertaining to it in Northampton, Coton, Crick and Lilleburne (Lilbourne) in the time of Henry's father, Almeric Vynter, burgager of the town. The land on Kyngeswell Strete is described as a messuage and nothing more, although research during the 1994-7 excavations demonstrated that a tenement belonging to the Vynter family lay at the southern end of Lewnys Lane, probably adjoining Kingswell Street (Soden 1998-9, 66-67).

No further occurrences are traceable until the 15th to 16th centuries. The documents are cited by Cox in his work on the Borough records in relation to Kingswell Lane (Cox 1898). Cox believed two inns were located on Kingswell Lane; 'The Harp' and 'The Lamb and Flag' (Cox 1898, 307). Two documents allude to an inn called 'The Harpe'; the first is dated 1555 and written in Latin; the second is a lease, dated 1568 and endorsed with the seal of the Hospital of St. John, for the 'The Harpe' on Golde Street (NRO YZ3630; FH1118). No reference survives for 'The Lamb and Flag'. In 1580 great overcrowding was noted amongst the poorer houses of Northampton and Kingswell Lane was in need of a refuse policy to clear the street of rubbish (Cox 1898, 264-6). The street is mentioned again in 1586 during the Town Property Survey amongst the 'Lands lying in the south quarter' (Cox 1898, 159-160, 535). Cox catalogues two entries in a list, thus:

(5) A space of grounde lying from his broade gate from his Kingswell Lane to a grounde called Rookes Mucke hyll, tenant William Rainsford, rental 4d.

(21) A hogge stye and a garden in Kingswell Lane; tenant Richard Freeman, rent 2s. 6d.

Rookes Mucke hyll was located in close proximity to St. Peter's Way at its junction with Gas Street (Soden 1998-9, 124). The apparent build up of waste material, its downwind proximity to Rookes Mucke hyll and the apparent late date at which the street was paved, in 1641, leaves the impression that Kingswell Street was low on the list of civic priorities, and probably not a particularly respectable part of the town. Further deeds are recorded for properties on Kingswell Street in 1571, 1608, 1622, 1676, 1696 and 1697; however, all of these documents refer to properties on the east side of Kingswell Street, generally fronting onto Bridge Street or else lying to the north of Woolmonger Street (NRO YZ5156, NPL402, YZ5075, YZ9045-117, NPL2216, NPL1202).

Two covenants are recorded for Benjamin Hill in 1731 for the seizure and lease of a messuage and garden in Kingswell Lane (NRO YZ9092-3). In 1765 Benjamin Hill, a distiller, left three messuages in Kingswell Street to his wife Mary Hill (NRO YZ9094). According to her Will, written in 1782, these were to be transferred to her niece Mary Wye or to her nephews Benjamin and Joseph Hill upon her death (NRO YZ9095-6).

A consultation of the 1768 Election Plan was cross-referenced to the Index of Freemen in the Northampton Record Office, producing a list of residents on the west side of the street and the trades they may have engaged in (NRO Map 1114). The names were recorded in order, but since no street numbers existed, it is not possible to tie these to specific properties:

> From Woolmonger Street walking south
> John Ives, son of William Ives, Cordwainer, 1791
> Thomas Fawcitt, son of James Fawcitt, Tailor, 1766
> Thomas Hewlett, Cordwainer, 1761
> John Johnson, Turner, 1781
> Richard Fox, son of John Fox, Whitesmith, 1757
> James Seeton
> Henry Hewitt
> Charles Seers
> Richard Clayson, apprentice to William Lockett, Hairdresser, 1792
> Joseph Seslove
> George Henshaw, Master Pipemaker c.1768-71; Index of Freemen 1767
> Opening to yard space
> Henry Emmerson
> Names along Kingswell Street resume

Thomas Hewlett was a labourer recorded amongst the tenants in a lease of 1731 but was the only link to the 18th-century deeds consulted (NRO YZ9092). George Henshaw was traced amongst the master clay tobacco-pipemakers of Northampton (Moore 1980, 21). His occupancy of a former tenement, in direct relation to an alleyway and the waste remaining from his trade, make him easier to locate with confidence. The 19th-century maps suggest he lived at 15 Kingswell Street from where clay tobacco-pipe making waste was recovered. Unfortunately in the trade directory and census data for subsequent years, none of the family names continue and it is assumed that these properties did not continue to be occupied for more than one generation or so.

A legal settlement in 1774 provides a period of documentation to 1812 for one particular group of properties in the north of the site (NRO ZB135/32-4). The settlement was between Houghton Wilson and Elizabeth Fisher, and John and Cordelia Manning. Houghton Wilson was presumably a relative of John Wilson living at the eastern end of Woolmonger Street during the Great Election of 1768 (NRO Map 1114). The settlement concerns two adjoining messuages in Kingswell Street that were conveyed to Samuel Fitzhugh, an innkeeper, in 1804. The document records a third conveyance in 1812 from Samuel Fitzhugh to Dennis Slinn, a cordwainer and is inclusive of a messuage in Woolmonger Street with two sheds used as a blacksmith workshop. It seems probable that this relates to 3-5 Woolmonger Street.

A copy lease and release in 1787 between John George, his son Haddon, and John Feyes, records two messuages in Newlands, one in Bridge Street and a garden in Kingswell Street (NRO YZ9055). The same John Feyes is mentioned in a series of conveyance documents, 1800-3, for the messuage on Bridge Street and a garden with Kingswell Street on its east side (NRO YZ9059-61). Later 19th-century documents do not indicate where this might have been, although Roper & Cole's map of 1807 portrays a large area to the rear of the Kingswell Street plots that may have been an allotment belonging to properties not on the Kingswell Street frontage. There is a record of the indenture for lease and release of properties between Thomas Berridge and James Essex, to William Parker the shoe manufacturer and William Boswell in 1819 for a garden, newly erected leather shop and three cottages in Kingswell Street (NRO YZ9064-5). It is not stated which side of the street these lay upon.

TRADE DIRECTORIES

Consultation of Kelly's and Robert's trade directories for the years 1830-1967, combined with the census data from 1841-1901 and knowledge of the map evidence, displays a fairly thorough portrait of changing tenure over the last 200 years (Table 1). The first house numbers do not appear in the documentary record until the census of 1861. Subsequently none of the trades for the years 1791 and 1823 could be identified with specific properties as the family names did not continue.

The corner property at 10 Kingswell Street consistently housed a butcher's shop, 1869-1931, except during the mid-1880s when the tenure was held by H Webb, basket manufacturer. The neighbouring 12 Kingswell Street appeared to be a private tenement throughout the years 1861-1931, first appearing in trade directories under William Jays, turf commission agent. Number 14 was the private residence of Alexander Charles Dickens, 1877-1901. He seems to have been experiencing financial troubles at the turn of the 19th century, for in 1895 he mortgaged his house with George Raunds & Wickham Flower of London (NRO YZ9110-6). In 1899 he was leasing a building to the rear of the property to his neighbour, Henry Perrin, to use as a bellhanger's workshop (NRO Maps 5970-2). In 1911 he sold the property through Bell, Green & Stops Brokers to R T & F J Ashby, the butchers at Kislingbury (NRO YZ9116). They retained an agreement with the General Post Office for use of the yard space to the rear (NRO YZ9117). By 1949 the renovated property had become the site of Modern Shoe Repairs Ltd and was no longer a private residence. Henry Perrin, whitesmith, locksmith & bellhanger was the first 19th-century occupant at 15 Kingswell Street to utilise the buildings and yard space at the back of 14-16 Kingswell Street for trade purposes, around 1884. The house at number 16 appears to have served purely as a residence throughout the 19th century.

The Bosworth family were resident throughout the 19th century and mid-20th century at 17-17a Kingswell Street operating trades that were principally based around handmade wooden household furnishings. Their long tenure suggests that they acquired ownership of Kingswell Court by 1881, when it became known as Bosworth Yard. The differentiation between 17 and 17a, appears to divide the domicile from the shop front. In the 1891 census there is a clear distinction between the Bosworth residence and the workshop, in 1901 the census officer recorded William Bosworth's wife's name at 17. Plot 17a is marked as a 'Furniture Dealer' on the resurveyed Insurance Plan of 1949 (NRO Maps 5970-2). The ancillary building immediately to the rear of number 17, in Bosworth Yard, was marked as a workshop.

EXCAVATIONS AT THE CORNER OF KINGSWELL STREET AND WOOLMONGER STREET, NORTHAMPTON

Table 1: Trades and tenure on the Kingswell Street frontage

Date	No. 10	No. 12	No. 14	No. 15	No. 16	No. 17	Kingswell Court Nos 1 & 2	No. 17a	Nos 18-19 Archway	No. 20	No. 21	No. 22	No. 23
1830											William Cave (Furniture Broker)		
1841						William Bosworth (Cabinetmaker)				James Harley (Plumber)	Ebenezar Cave (Furniture Broker)		
1847						William Bosworth (Cabinetmaker)				William Harley (Painter)			
1851						William Bosworth (Cabinetmaker)	Thomas Humphrey (Plumber)			William Harley (Painter)	Sarah Cave (Widow)		
1854						William Bosworth (Cabinetmaker)				William Harley (Painter)			
1861	William H. Swindell (Shoemaker)	Iain Potter	Daniel Hewitt (Ironmonger)	John Martin (Boot Closer)	William Coleman (Carpenter)	William Bosworth (Pictureframe mfr)	#1 Thomas Humphrey (Plumber) #2 John Leasey (Groom) called Kingswell Court		Absalon Bassett (Boilermaker) called Wilson's Yard William Collins (Boot Closer) Room over the gate	William Harley (Painter)	John Cave (Builder)	Samuel Howard (Builder)	John Perrin (Whitesmith)
1869	John Blunt (Butcher)					William Bosworth (Pictureframe mfr)			Absalon Bassett (Engineer & Boilermaker)		Alexander C. Dickens (Tin Plate Welder)		John Perrin (Whitesmith)
1871	Charles Blunt (Butcher)	Matthew Blake (Chimney Layer)	Thomas Adams (Machine Closer)	Mary Linnell	John Cooper (Carver & Gilder)	William Bosworth (Pictureframe mfr)	#1 Neville Humphrey (Dressmaker) #2 Thomas Flavell (Carpenter) called Kingswell Court		Absalon Bassett (Boilermaker) George Johnson (Railway Labourer) Room over the gate	William Harley (Painter)	William Bell (Carpenter)	Thomas ? (Butcher)	Mary Perrin (Whitesmith)
1877			Alexander C. Dickens (Tin Plate Welder)		Henry Perrin (Whitesmith)	William Bosworth (Pictureframe mfr)			Bassett & Son (Engineers & Boilermakers)				

179

Table 1 (cont.): Trades and tenure on the Kingswell Street frontage

Date	No. 10	No. 12	No. 14	No. 15	No. 16	No. 17	Kingswell Court Nos 1 & 2	No. 17a	Nos 18-19 Archway	No. 20	No. 21	No. 22	No. 23
1881	Richard Higgins (Butcher)	Mrs. Humphrey (Widow)	Alexander C. Dickens (Tin Plate Welder)	John Cross (Ostler)	Samuel Cox (Chairmaker)	William Bosworth (Pictureframe mfr)	#1 James Forskett (Salemonger) #2 William Jacob (Shoe Clicker) called Bosworth Yard		Absalon Bassett (Boilermaker)	William Harley (Painter)	Henry Firkins (Leatherdresser)		
1884	H. Webb (Basket mfr)	Mrs. Humphrey (Widow)	Alexander C. Dickens (Tin Plate Welder)	Henry Perrin (Whitesmith)	Samuel Cox (Chairmaker)	William Bosworth & Son (Carver & Gilder)			Bassett & Son (Engineers & Boilermakers)				
1890	Robert Roddis (Butcher)		Alexander C. Dickens (Tin Plate Welder)	Henry Perrin (Whitesmith, Locksmith & Bellhanger)		William Bosworth & Son (Carver & Gilder)					William Papworth (Milk Seller)	Ralph Smith (Shoemaker)	
1891		George Drage (Engine Fitter)	Alexander C. Dickens (Tin Plate Welder)	Henry Perrin (Whitesmith)	Joseph Ayres (Porter)	William Bosworth (Pictureframe mfr)	#1 Thomas Kirby (Miller's Labourer) #2 Charles ? (Ostler) called Bosworth Yard	Bosworth & Son (Carver & Gilder)	A. Basset (Engineer)		William Papworth (Dairyman)		
1892		George Drage (Engine Fitter)	Alexander C. Dickens (Tin Plate Welder)										
1894	Joseph Ashby (Butcher)		Alexander C. Dickens (Tin Plate Welder)						Basset & Sons (Engineers)	Basset & Sons (Engineers)	William Papworth (Dairyman)	George Smith (Shoemaker)	George J. Russell (Beer Retailer)
1899			Bellhanger	Whitesmith		Carver			Joseph T. Lowke (Engineering Works)				
1901		William Nash (Bricklayer)	Alexander C. Dickens (Electrical Engineer)		Harry Meeks (Driver)	Mary Bosworth (Housewife)			Joseph T. Lowke (Engineering Works)		William Papworth (Dairyman)		

Table 1 (cont.): Trades and tenure on the Kingswell Street frontage

Date	No. 10	No. 12	No. 14	No. 15	No. 16	No. 17	Kingswell Court Nos 1 & 2	No. 17a	Nos 18-19 Archway	No. 20	No. 21	No. 22	No. 23
1910	Ashby & Sons (Butcher)			Henry Perrin (Whitesmith)		William Bosworth (Carver & Gilder)			Joseph T. Lowke & Sons (Engineers)	A. Bell & Co Ltd (Ironmonger)	A. Bell & Co Ltd (Ironmonger)	A. Bell & Co Ltd (Ironmonger)	A. Bell & Co Ltd (Ironmonger)
1924	Roland W. Garner (Butcher)			Ennals & Cooper (Agricultural Engineers)		William Bosworth & Sons (Carver & Gilder)			Joseph T. Lowke & Sons (Engineers)	A. Bell & Co Ltd (Ironmonger)	A. Bell & Co Ltd (Ironmonger)	A. Bell & Co Ltd (Ironmonger)	A. Bell & Co Ltd (Ironmonger)
1931	Roland W. Garner (Butcher)	William Jays (Turf Commission Agent)		Ennals & Cooper (Agricultural Engineers)		William Bosworth & Sons (Antique Dealer)				A. Bell & Co Ltd (Ironmonger)	A. Bell & Co Ltd (Ironmonger)	A. Bell & Co Ltd (Ironmonger)	A. Bell & Co Ltd (Ironmonger)
1940		William Jays (Turf Commission Agent)				William Bosworth & Sons (Antique Dealer)			C. E. Linnet Ltd (Mechanical Engineers) Alfred William Sims (Shopfitter)	A. Bell & Co Ltd (Ironmonger)	A. Bell & Co Ltd (Ironmonger)	A. Bell & Co Ltd (Ironmonger)	A. Bell & Co Ltd (Ironmonger)
1949	Ruinous	Demolished	Shoe Repair Factory	Demolished	Demolished			Furniture Dealer	Paintshop, Store & Fitters	Paintshop, Store & Fitters	Paintshop, Store & Fitters	Paintshop, Store & Fitters	Paintshop, Store & Fitters
1954			Modern Shoe Repairs Ltd			William Bosworth & Sons (Antique Dealer)		William Bosworth & Sons (Antique Dealers)	C. E. Linnet Ltd (Mechanical Engineers) O. Bolton (Joinery mfr) Goodman & Margerets (Leather Goods mfrs)	Basset-Lowke Ltd (Model Engineers)	Basset-Lowke Ltd (Model Engineers)	Basset-Lowke Ltd (Model Engineers)	Basset-Lowke Ltd (Model Engineers)
1967									C. E. Linnet Ltd (Mechanical Engineers) Gordon & Smith (Joinery mfrs) Roberts & Chick (Upholsterers)	Basset-Lowke Ltd (Model Engineers)	Basset-Lowke Ltd (Model Engineers)	Basset-Lowke Ltd (Model Engineers)	Basset-Lowke Ltd (Model Engineers)

JIM BROWN

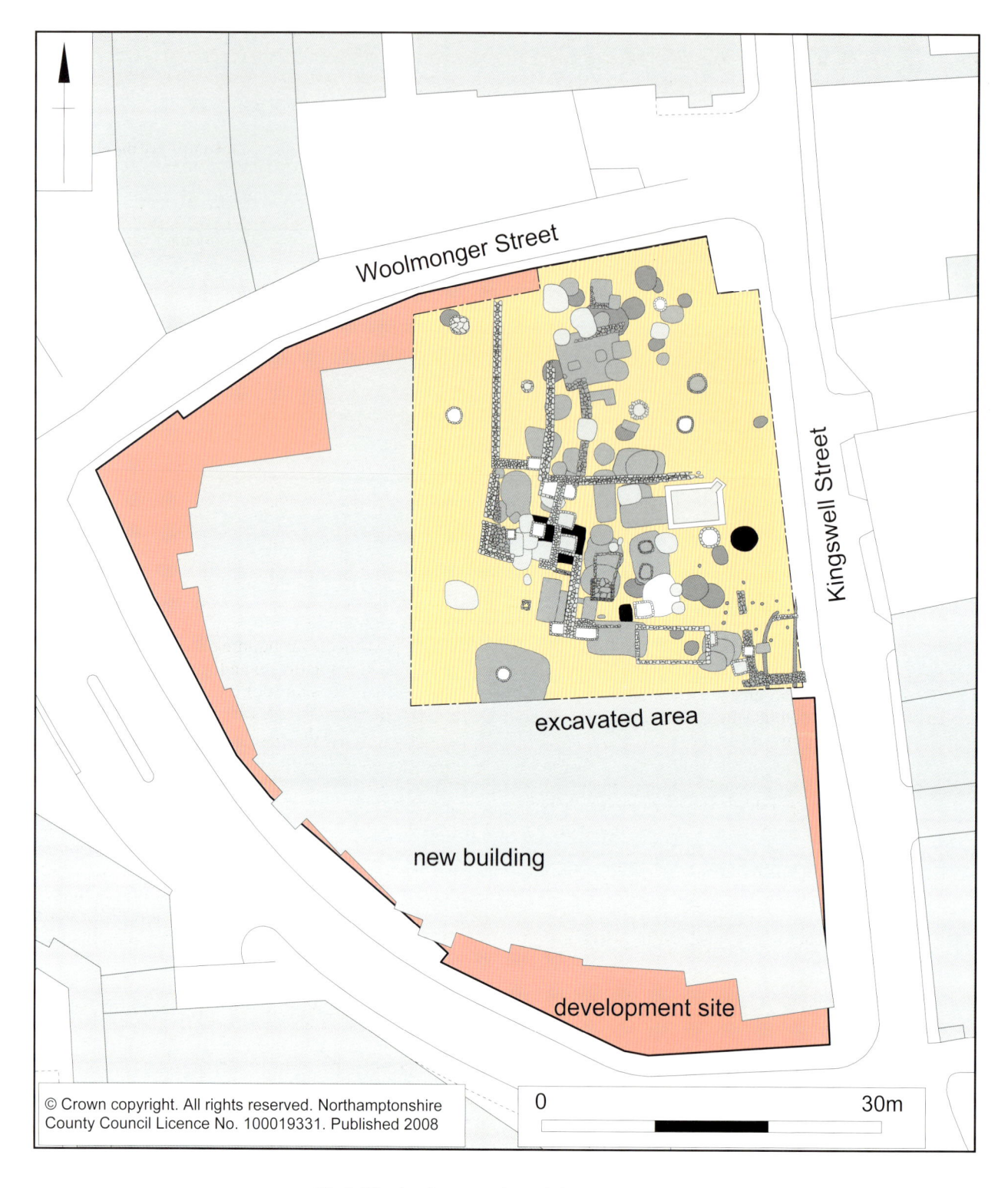

Fig 3 The development site and the excavated area

According to a series of conveyances the properties at 1-5 Woolmonger Street were sold by John Trasler to Kathleen Finnegan in 1898 (NRO ZB1348/3). These were subsequently sold to Northampton Tradesman's Club Co Ltd in 1930, which then expanded the premises in 1946 by purchasing 10 Kingswell Street from Joseph Basset-Lowke Ltd (NRO ZB1348/4).

BASSET-LOWKE LTD, MODEL ENGINEERS

The boilermaker Absalon Basset, occupied 18-19 Kingswell Street and enjoyed possession of the large works yard to the rear, 1861-1910. By 1894 Basset & Sons engineering works had expanded to occupy neighbouring number 20 and was no longer renting out the room above the gateway. The yard moved into new ownership in 1899 under Joseph Thomas Lowke, then experimenting with an offshoot business based in the shop front of number 19 called Miniature Railways of Great Britain Ltd. Lowke kept the engineering works running at least until 1924. Over the following 40 years parts of the yard were sold for development and the buildings were leased to a series of smaller manufacturing firms. It seems likely that ownership of the property remained with the Lowke family until they had enough capital to establish a new factory facility on the site. In 1954 the trade directory records Basset-Lowke Ltd, railway model engineers, operating at 20-25 Kingswell Street and is recorded on the Northampton Insurance Plan of 1949 as a paint shop, store and fitters, presumably serving the new Basset-Lowke enterprise (NRO Maps 5970-2). The retail outlet was located at 78 Derngate Road and a considerable collection survives for the premises including photographs, greetings cards and the model railway catalogues 1914-1929 (NRO ZB498 1-67). The firm was still successfully manufacturing miniature railway models on the site in 1972. Corgi purchased the Bassett-Lowke brand name in 1996 and re-launched the railway locomotive products in 1999 (www.bassettlowke.co.uk).

OBJECTIVES

The objectives were to determine the sequence of occupation on the site, giving attention to the former Kingswell Street frontage and the back-plots that supported it. This would establish the nature of the site during the early to middle Saxon, late Saxon, medieval and post-medieval periods. Remains of these were present in the nearby Woolmonger Street excavations of 1993-7 (Soden 1998-9). It was also desirable to realise the artefactual and ecofactual potential of the site and use this to identify changing industries and the domestic economy of the site. The cut-off date for this was established as the Great Fire of Northampton in 1675 after which the town centre was substantially redeveloped. The project aimed to place the site within the wider historic street-plan and examine the possibility of features fronting the former Lewnys Lane, as identified by the 1993-7 work.

METHODOLOGY

The area of the main excavation and a portion of the watching brief area were excavated concurrently. The combined excavation area measured 25m by 36m, including the entire north-east corner of the development site, covering plots 10-17a Kingswell Street, 1-7 Woolmonger Street and the known location of surviving deposits (Carlyle 2003, 16) (Fig 3). Subsequent to excavation, the whole area was monitored under a continuous watching brief.

Ground clearance was conducted using a 360° excavator fitted with a toothless ditching bucket. Modern surfaces and underlying non-structural post-medieval and modern layers were removed under archaeological supervision. Deep homogeneous garden soils were also removed after examination and were monitored to identify archaeological deposits or undisturbed natural horizons as they were exposed. Mechanical excavation stopped at the surface of the archaeological horizon and a process of hand excavation was employed for the remainder of the works. Excavation extended to the back of the Kingswell Street frontage, over half of its length in one continuous trench and took in a large portion of the former Woolmonger Street frontage.

The late post-medieval building plots were identified and investigated in relation to underlying deposits before removal. Pits and structures of the 16th to 17th centuries were fully excavated and their distribution used to predict the layout of the back-plots. Late medieval soils were initially cleaned to identify cutting features, and these were excavated prior to the removal of soil layers. All features that were exposed were hand-cleaned and sampled sufficiently to determine their character and date, and to reveal the underlying stratum (Fig 4). A cross-section of deep features such as wells and quarry pits were sampled to a depth of 1.2-1.5m. Individual buildings or structures were fully excavated and their distribution used to interpret early plot divisions and alignments. Pits

Fig 4 General view of the site during excavation, looking south-west

and postholes that produced pottery of Saxon or Saxo-Norman date were fully excavated where undisturbed by later activity. A site record was maintained to include plans, section drawings, levels, photographs, context descriptions and details of environmental samples. Artefacts pre-dating the fire of 1675 were recovered from secure contexts and retained with the exception of large assemblages of non-diagnostic building materials.

The palaeo-environmental potential was reviewed and samples were retrieved from significant deposits at depth and processed for environmental and industrial residues.

Arrangements for the preservation *in situ* of significant unexcavated deposits such as the fill of wells and cess pits were made by Westleigh Developments Ltd who organised a concrete raft for the northern area of the site.

THE EXCAVATED EVIDENCE

SUMMARY OF CHRONOLOGY

The excavation identified a clear sequence of development (Fig 5):

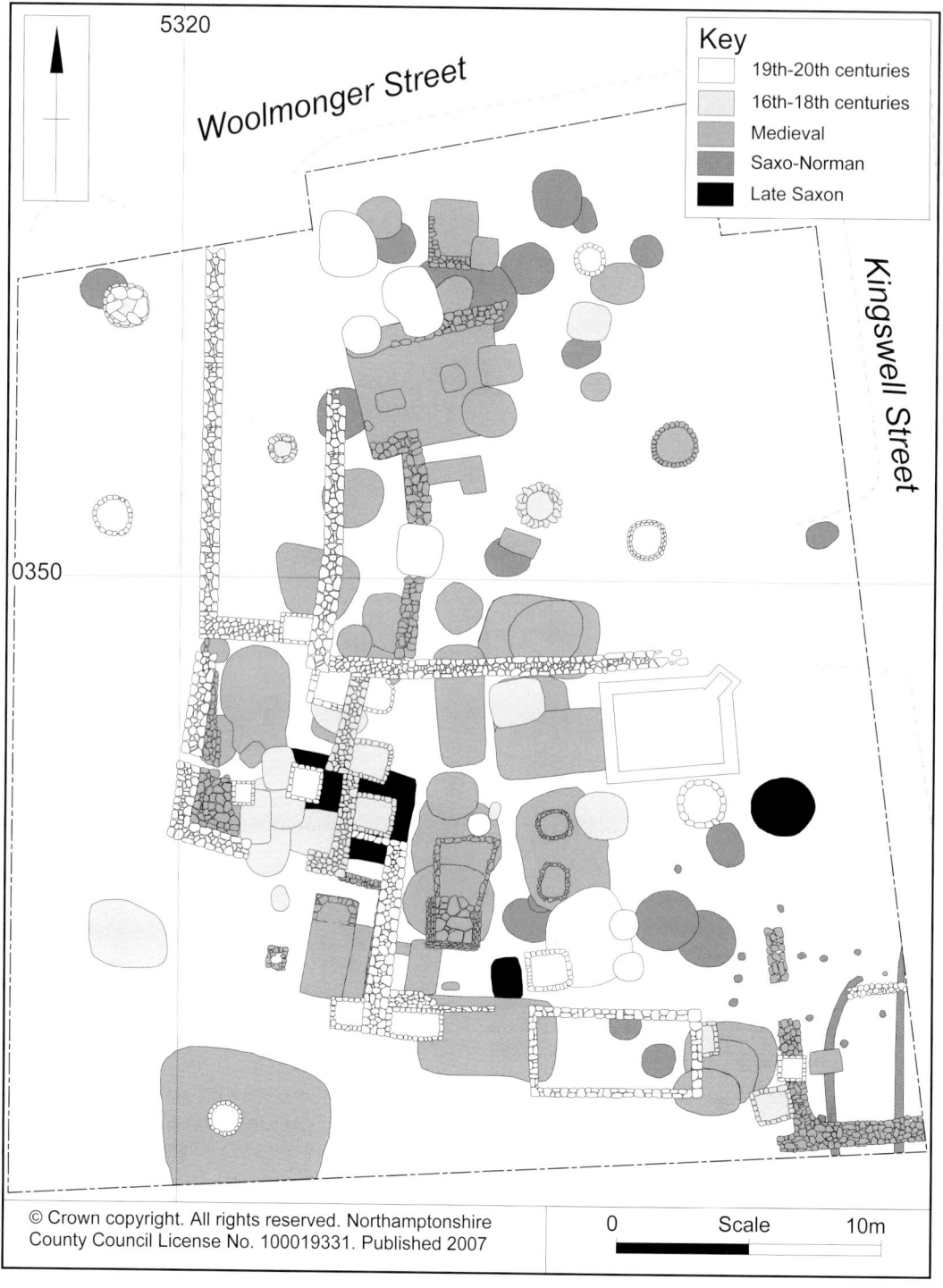

Fig 5 General plan showing all periods of activity

PERIOD	FEATURES
Late Saxon (mid-10th to early 11th centuries)	A cellared building and three large pits
Saxo-Norman (mid-11th to 12th centuries)	Two gullies and a timber building next to Kingswell Street
Medieval (13th to 15th centuries)	Four stone buildings, two malting ovens, a bread oven, two wells and numerous other pits
Post-medieval (16th to 18th centuries)	Late occupation of a tenement on Kingswell Street; four cess pits, three wells and robbing of medieval features
Late post-medieval & modern (19th to 20th centuries)	Below ground disturbance included five wells, two cellars, six boundary walls and nine cess pits

A LATE SAXON CELLAR AND PITS

THE CELLAR (BUILDING A)

A rectangular cellar with near vertical sides and a flat base measured 5m long by 3.5m wide by 1.16m deep and was aligned west-north-west to east-south-east (Fig 6; Building A). The fill comprised a sequence of seven layered deposits forming tipping lines from the backfill process. The lowest of these comprised an accumulation of firm mid-greyish brown silty clay with frequent charcoal inclusions and fragments of ironstone that contained coarse St. Neots ware pottery. The top four layers were disturbed by 16th to 17th-century pits, particularly at the southern side of the cellar. The cellar was of the type observed during the 1993-7 Woolmonger Street excavations (Soden 1998-9, 76-78). It was somewhat larger and deeper than the 10th-century Grubenhäuser described amongst the St. Peter's Street excavations (Williams 1979, 92-94). The best preserved Northampton example was post-pit building B79 excavated at Chalk Lane with which these dimensions compare favourably (Williams and Shaw 1981, 98). The distribution of sunken buildings at Chalk Lane and St. Peter's Street each reflected an arrangement based on social and economic paradigms with no clear alignment (Williams and Shaw 1981, 100). In all three instances this unplanned settlement growth was succeeded by timber buildings arranged upon a street frontage and attributed to the Norman reorganisation of the town.

The pits

Three large pits lay in close proximity to the cellar and produced exclusively late Saxon pottery (Fig 6; 54, 82, 316). Each pit was unique in shape and size. Pit 54 was circular, 1.98m in diameter and 1.66m deep with steep sloping sides and a broad rounded base. It was filled with domestic waste and garden soils, and sealed with a crushed ironstone cap. The pottery was highly fragmented and may have been stored in a midden before burial. Animal bone amongst the waste included evidence for butchery at all stages of meat preparation. It also produced a small, heavily corroded oval buckle. Pit 82 was sub-circular and so heavily truncated by later medieval pits that its true dimensions could not be defined. Pit 316 was sub-rectangular, 1.78m long by 1.1m wide and 1.6m deep, with steps cut into the southern side.

A SAXO-NORMAN TIMBER BUILDING AND PITS

THE TIMBER BUILDING (BUILDING B)

In the south-east corner of the excavation, extending beyond the modern frontage of 17-17a Kingswell Street, lay a timber-framed structure comprising twelve postholes (Figs 6 and 7). The dimensions of the building were estimated to be over 8m long by 6m wide. The main postholes defining the corner of the building were roughly circular, with the largest 0.4m in diameter by 0.27m deep and the smallest 0.22m in diameter by 0.1m deep. The interior postholes had no clear alignment. Only the rear of Building B was exposed within the excavated area and the southernmost extent of the structure was destroyed by later medieval activity. The front of the building is likely to survive beneath the modern road. Its alignment matched the earlier Saxon Building A, it either did not front Kingswell Street or the angle of the street has moved.

Within Building B was a small pit, 28, that was roughly circular with shallow sloping sides and a bowl-shaped base, 0.75m wide by 0.15m deep. The pit contained dark reddish-brown heat-scorched silty loam, 27, with charcoal flecks, noted in the evaluation as a possible hearth (Carlyle 2003, 16). A high proportion of charcoal, together with herbaceous seeds indicative of burning dried grasses, grassland herbs and hedge brush was found (sample 3). A crude musical flute or whistle was recovered from the floor of the building. The floor was similar to the Saxo-Norman buried soil, although more compacted. The building is thought to have been a dwelling.

Cutting the floor of Building B, were two gullies, 24 and 193. Both were aligned roughly north to south and were of similar size, up to 0.45m wide and 0.18m deep. They were probably drainage gullies cut after the building was demolished, and suggest a period where the ground remained open.

THE BURIED SOIL

A patchy deposit of light mid-orangey-brown silty clay, 137, less than 80mm thick, overlay the natural ironstone. It was the first definable occupation or cultivation soil layer and was only found in proximity to the features in this part of the site since it was mixed into later medieval soils elsewhere.

Fig 6 Late Saxon and Saxo-Norman features

Fig 7 Saxo-Norman timber building, Building B, looking east

RUBBISH PITS

Immediately west of the building were two large circular pits (Fig 6). Pit 199 was 2.25m wide and 1.34m deep, and cut by a similarly sized pit 116. Both had steep sides, broad flat bases and were filled with ash layers, garden soils and substantial quantities of pottery. The primary fill of pit 116 contained loose pulverised ironstone. Much of the Saxo-Norman pottery was recovered from this pit and comprised 67.4% jar forms. Soil samples indicated a high density of bread wheat grains. The pit also produced a small axe and a knife. It is probable the pits were dug to clear midden waste from outside the dwelling and the finds suggested domestic activity nearby.

CESS PITS

In the north of the site was a substantial scatter of pits that were filled by firm greenish-brown and mid- to dark brown silty clay, often containing charcoal and dated by pottery. The pits varied in size, the largest measured 3.7m long by 2.8m wide, but most were considerably smaller and more circular around 1.7m wide. As these lay in an area of watching brief contingency, excavation was limited to a level of sampling sufficient to characterise and date the nature of the features and precluded full excavation (Fig 8). The pits were for the disposal of sewage, as demonstrated by the high level of faecal concentrations amongst the samples.

Fig 8 Saxo-Norman and medieval cess pits sampled by watching brief

MEDIEVAL LAND PLOTS AND BUILDINGS

THE MEDIEVAL BURIED SOIL

A spread of homogeneous soil lay up to 0.28m thick comprising firm dark greyish-brown silty clay, 22, with frequent charcoal flecks mixed with domestic waste. The soil was found throughout the site. It predated construction of later medieval buildings, possibly the result of garden horticulture, subsuming evidence of earlier soil layers, and producing a relatively late deposit containing residual material.

THE MEDIEVAL LAND PLOTS

The 13th to 14th centuries were an intense period of activity (Fig 9). Four possible medieval land plots were indicated with little concordance to later mapped layouts. It seems appropriate to discuss the medieval features within the context of these divisions. Initial activity within each comprised the quarrying of ironstone, perhaps for the buildings that occupied them.

THE STREET CORNER (PLOT 1)

This area lay within the watching brief and was sampled within the scope of the contingency but precluded full excavation. The area was heavily truncated by 20th-century cellars and the possibility of surviving features had been considered relatively low.

Cess pits and refuse pits

A total of eleven pits were recorded and investigated. They varied between 1m and 2.2m in diameter, six of them were rectangular and the rest were sub-circular. Most of the pits were filled with light to mid-greenish brown silty clay indicative of faecal content. Pits 385 and 387 were filled with firm dark blackish-brown silty loam soils mainly comprising ash and domestic waste.

The largest pit was partly stone-built, 373 (Fig 10). The stonework was shaped but un-coursed ironstone forming a sturdy retaining wall against earlier disturbed ground. Where the pit cut natural ironstone no retaining wall was constructed. It was rectangular, 2.2m by 1.6m, and was sampled to 0.7m deep showing alternating bands of dark greenish-brown silty clay and decayed organic brush. Within a couple of weeks of excavation this pit was heavily colonised with moss, germinating amongst the high levels of mineralised faecal concretions found in the soil. The moss growth was not only an indicator of rich organic matter, but perhaps also of the toiletry habits of those who deposited its original contents.

An ancillary building (building C)

A rectangular area, 6.5m long by 4.75m wide, was filled by a 0.21m thick deposit comprising firm mid-greyish brown clay loam. It defined a probable building of which the walls only partially survived, c 0.96m wide, unbonded, with only one course. The masonry comprised ironstone blocks up to 340mm by 280mm by 150mm in size, roughly-shaped and faced on both sides with a rubble core. On the east and south sides they had been obliterated by robbing. Wall 367 extended south from the structure probably linking with wall 296, but broken by 20th-century disturbance. It was suggestive of a back wall for a plot on Kingswell Street.

Three square pits lay within the interior (369, 385 and 389) and were most likely linked to the building itself. The pits varied between 0.2-0.6m deep and were largely filled with a mixture of domestic waste, ash and green tinged soils, perhaps belonging to a yard building rather than a tenement or workshop.

A medieval well

Well 330 was 1.55m in diameter and its fill was excavated to 0.63m deep. The stonework was roughly hewn, un-mortared, arranged in an interlocking pattern and faced

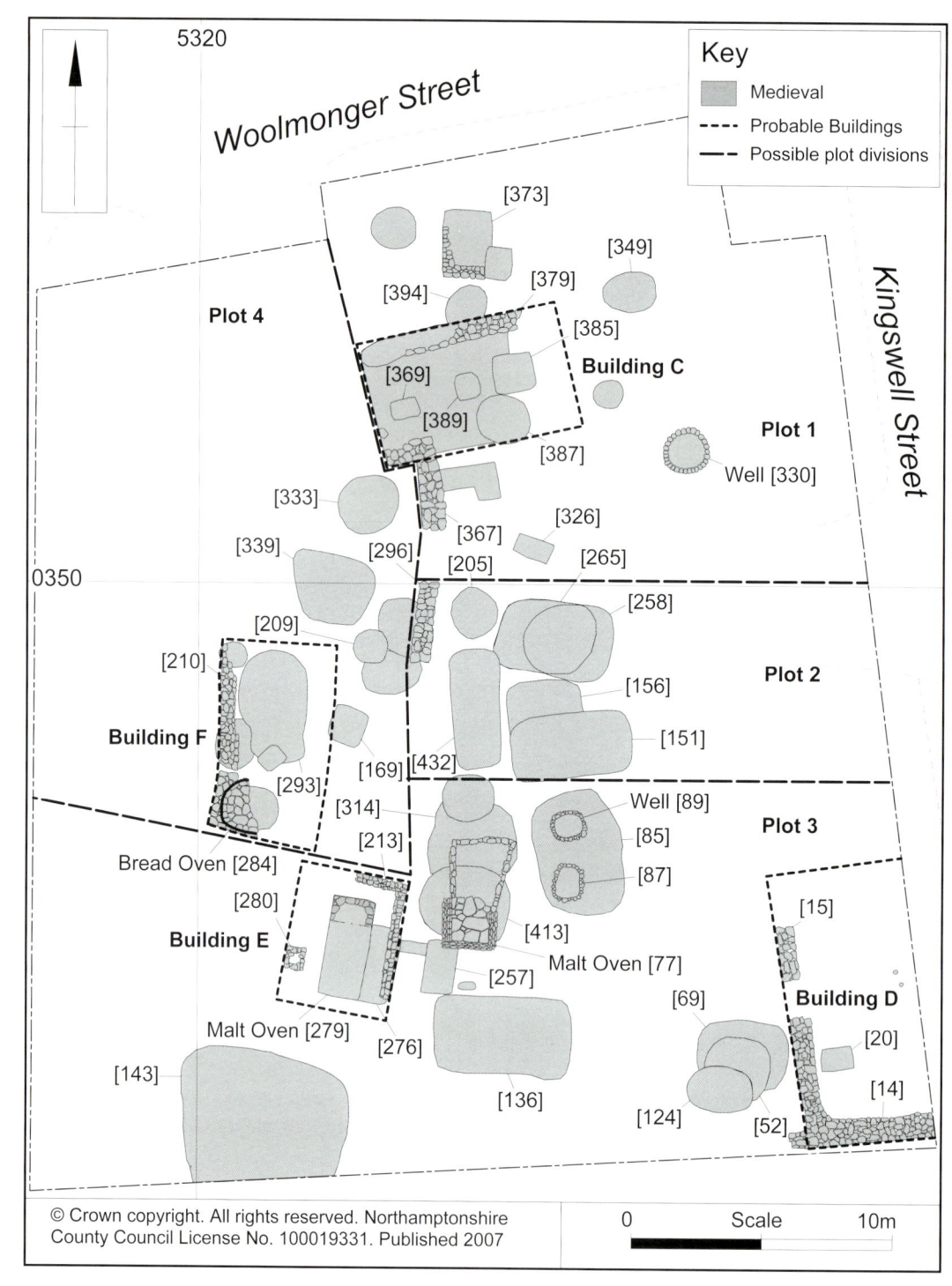

Fig 9 Medieval features

Fig 10 Medieval stone-lined cess pits, [373] & [394]

internally. No construction pit was present. The fill comprised firm dark brown silty clay, 329, with frequent chunks of ironstone and exclusively 13th to 14th-century finds. An augur was used in an attempt to determine the full depth, which was still not reached at 2m below the archaeological level (65.96m above OD). The solid ironstone natural provided stable sides for construction provided it was wide enough for a man to dig by hand.

BENEATH THE SHOE REPAIR FACTORY (PLOT 2)

The 20th-century brick cellar of 14 Kingswell Street had heavily truncated deposits in this plot and there was much disturbance in the upper horizons (Fig 9).

Quarry pits
Pit 258 was sub-rectangular, 1.8m wide by 3.9m long by 1.89m deep. Within the pit there was a stack of quarried ironstone blocks, which were generally 260mm by 150mm by 120mm in size. These were irregularly-shaped, laid flat, eight courses high and stacked edge to edge. The pit had been backfilled with dumps of domestic waste, garden soils and shattered ironstone. It was later used as a sump, 265, containing material similar to the nearby cess pits.

Three other sub-rectangular quarry pits were also identified. All of these pits contained dumps of fragmented ironstone, domestic waste and mixed soils (151, 156, 265 & 432). Pit 151 was 2.5m by 4m and 1.45m deep. The south side was cut by pit 156, which was 2.5m by 1.23m and 1.72m deep. A soil sample contained faecal waste.

A cess pit
Pit 205 was circular with vertical sides, 1.6m wide by 1.6m deep. The fill comprised firm mid-brown silty clay with the characteristic greenish tinge suggestive of cess. As with cess pit 373, this became heavily colonised with moss within a short time of exposure.

The rear boundary wall
Wall 296 had been built at the rear of the plot within a foundation trench aligned from north to south. It was probably the southern extension of wall 367. Further sections of the wall had been destroyed by post-medieval activity.

BENEATH 15-17 KINGSWELL STREET (PLOT 3)

The 19th-century maps show these properties as three distinct tenements, which is not visible amongst the later medieval features (Fig 9). Quarrying on the site was succeeded by construction of two stone buildings (Buildings D and E). There was a building on the frontage, and a malthouse at the back. The longevity of the malthouse was shorter than that of the frontage building, the latter surviving well into the post-medieval period.

Quarry pits
Six large quarry pits lay to the rear of the plot. Pit 136 was rectangular, aligned east to west, with vertical sides 4m long by 3m wide by 2.2m deep, truncated at the eastern end by a 19th-century cellar. Pit 143 was sub-circular, with irregular overhanging sides 6.4m long by 3.6m wide; the base was not reached within 1.6m. Pit 257 was rectangular, aligned north to south, with sharp 80° sloping sides that were excavated down to 1.78m without encountering the substrate. A 2.5m length of walkway of weathered ironstone separated this from pit 276. Its surviving extent suggested proportions in excess of 2.5m wide and 1.47m deep. Pits 413 and 314 were also heavily disturbed and their proportions would not have been dissimilar. These pits had been cut with vertical sides to a sufficient depth that the unweathered natural Jurassic ironstone bedrock could be quarried in substantial blocks. The fill comprised dumps of firm greyish-black silty clay containing ash, charcoal, animal bone, pottery and shattered ironstone.

The frontage building (building D)
The east wall of the building lay beyond the excavated area and the north wall did not survive. It is estimated to have been 10m long by 5m wide (Figs 9 and 11). Remnants of the western wall, 15 and 14, were 0.63m wide, with two courses. The southern wall was 0.8m wide, with three courses. The walls were faced on both sides and built from ironstone blocks up to 330mm by 220mm by 140mm in size. The stones interlocked such that minimal rubble packing was necessary to maintain its integrity.

Fig 11 Medieval tenement, Building D

Within the south-west corner was a rectangular pit, 20, that was 1.4m by 1.3m and 1m deep. The pit had steep sides and a slightly rounded base, filled with brownish-grey silty clay and shattered ironstone.

A series of refuse pits
Several large pits lay behind Building D. The earliest and largest of these pits, 69, measured over 2.8m wide and 0.5m deep, and had been disturbed by later pits (52 and 124). They were filled with household waste that included predominantly shelly ware pottery and some medieval glazed wares of ceramic phases Ph2/0 and Ph2/2.

The malthouse and ovens (building E)
Wall 213 formed the north-east corner of Building E which was 5m long by 4.5m wide (Fig 12). It was built from shaped ironstone blocks, 190mm by 180mm by 90mm in size. The stone was arranged in a non-uniform

Fig 12 Medieval malthouse, Building E

dry-stone fashion with a crude inner face. The walls were 0.22m thick and 0.4m high comprising four courses. Additional supporting foundations had been established where the wall crossed quarry pit 276 (Fig 13). Here the wall foundation was 0.94m deep comprising eleven courses supported by a buttress. The position of the west wall was estimated by the sudden change in ground level (Fig 9). A stone pillar support 280 was located 3m from both the north and east sides of the building and marked the socket of a timber upright.

Malt oven, 279, was inside the building (Fig 14). Between the malt oven and the wall was a 20mm thick deposit of compact pale yellowish-grey clay all around the outside of the pit. The malt oven was 2.1m wide at the top with sharply angled sides sloping to 0.5m depth before becoming vertical and joining a flat base, 1.38m wide by 1.04m deep. An ironstone hearth lay at the base of the pit formed by two courses of unshaped stone set at the sides and filled with charcoal rich scorched red silty clay, 80mm thick. Samples produced puffed cereal grains from combustion at high temperatures and amphibian remains following disuse. The pit was filled with firm mid-brown silty clay, fragments of ironstone, broken roof tiles and pottery. Above this the whole of the interior of Building E was covered by loose pale greyish-brown silty loam, fragmented ironstone and large quantities of green glazed roof tile. The layer formed a levelling deposit, 200mm thick, in the footprint of the building. Pottery suggests that the building was demolished prior to the 15th century.

Outside, malt oven 77 was roughly rectangular, aligned north to south and opened out slightly at the northern end (Fig 15). It measured 1.45m across at its narrowest point and was 1.9m across at its widest point. The oven chamber was 1.8m long by 0.58m deep with a broad flat base. It was constructed using shaped ironstone blocks to form the sides

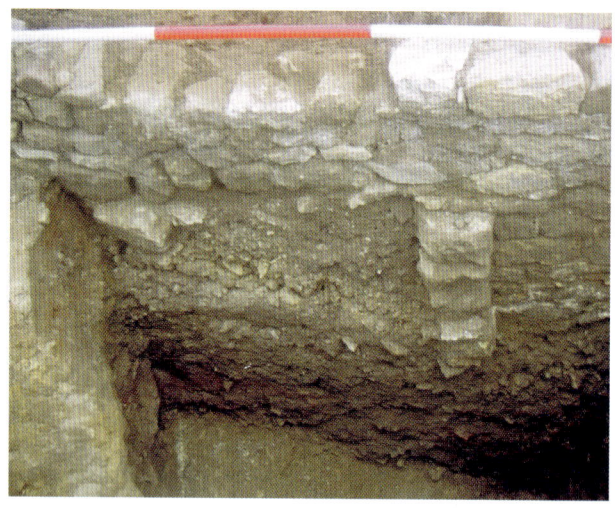

Fig 13 A medieval wall built over a quarry pit [276], Building E

Fig 14 Medieval malt oven [279], Building E

Fig 15 Medieval malt oven [77]

and flagstones lining the base. The stoke hole had been robbed on the northern side during the 17th century. The ironstone blocks averaged 250mm by 170mm by 100mm in size, arranged to interlock in a non-uniform dry-stone fashion. The flagstones were irregular, arranged to provide the best coverage of the base and measured up to 550mm by 390mm by 60mm. The sides were built at a 45° angle to the base. There were four courses surviving at the southern end and only one course surviving where robbing had taken place. The flagstones showed evidence of scorching concentrated in a circle at the centre, within the lost flue opening. The majority of the feature was filled with compact mottled creamy-white clay containing flecks of orange, red and grey, overlain by 0.22m of compact brownish-grey clayey silt.

A medieval well

A large sub-rectangular construction pit, 85, measured 4.5m long by 3m wide and was 1.25m deep. Within the pit was well 89 comprising shaped ironstone slabs varying in size, 240-380mm across, forming a circular shaft that was excavated to 0.9m deep. The well was 1.4m wide at the top with an internal shaft, 0.74m wide. The well had been filled with loose dark brown sandy silt containing frequent charcoal and small ironstone fragments. The top of the well had been robbed away by a pit of similar proportions, removing stone to 0.5m deep. Cut into the well pit, was a stone lined pit 87. The pit was rectangular, 1.2m long by 0.75m wide by 0.9m deep. It was lined with seven courses of rough unfaced ironstone no larger than 180mm across.

BENEATH BAINES & CO MARINE STORE (PLOT 4)

Quarry Pits

The area at the back of 7 Woolmonger Street contained many pits. Pits 293, 333 and 339 were associated with quarrying, as elsewhere. Pit 293 was excavated showing an irregular oval shape, aligned north to south along the plot. It was 4.7m long by 2.7m wide and was excavated to a depth of 1.4m showing different tip lines of shattered ironstone and silty clay. Frequent charcoal flecks were evident throughout together with dumps of charcoal, ash, sand and blue-white powdered lime, perhaps waste from building work nearby.

A cess pit

Pit 169 was rectangular, 1.6m long by 1.2m wide, excavated down to 1.72m. The sides were vertical, cutting into the natural, and the fill was firm dark greenish silty clay.

The bakehouse (Building F)

The dimensions of the building were estimated to be 7.5m long by 4.5m wide. The west wall 210 was constructed from ironstone blocks up to 380mm by 320mm by 120mm. The stone was mostly unfinished although a clear face survived on the exterior. The wall survived in two parts, 6.3m long and 0.58m wide, having partially collapsed in antiquity. Accumulated against the wall was compact mottled silty clay 285, 0.25m thick, containing ironstone chips scorched by heat radiated from a bread oven, 284, above (Fig 16).

Fig 16 Medieval bread oven [284], Building F

The circular bread oven, 284, was 1.65m in diameter. Only the hearthstones survived, large flat slabs of scorched ironstone, up to 400mm by 300mm by 100mm thick. The stone had been interlocked directly on top of a silty clay and ironstone gravel bed. It had been incorporated into wall 210 indicating that it was an integral part of Building F (Fig 9). Much of the building been destroyed by 19th-century disturbance.

POST-MEDIEVAL PITS AND WELLS

The 16th to 18th-century activity was largely confined to scattered pits and wells (Fig 17). The frontage houses that they served had been lost to later redevelopment. Property boundaries had moved implying a continuous process of redevelopment in which new arrangements were regularly re-defined. Stone lost from medieval walls and structures was robbed during this period creating a 190mm thick spread, 166, of mixed silty clay and charcoal above the remains of the demolished bakehouse. It extended north and east creating a horizon mixed with later garden soils and burning. It is probable that if there had originally been a horizon for the Great Fire of Northampton in 1675 it had been blended and mixed with these later deposits.

REFUSE PITS

Five pits were cut into spread 166, three of which were excavated (161, 163 and 254) (Fig 17). The largest of these, pit 161, was 0.97m deep. Most of the pits contained tip lines generally comprising greyish-brown silty clays flecked with charcoal and ironstone. The rear of post-medieval was littered with refuse on what was probably open ground. Pottery dates bridged the 15th to 17th centuries.

THE WELLS

Three wells predated the 1885 buildings and were situated where other structures would eventually have been built over them (295, 297 and 365). The construction of the shaft was similar in each case, comprising roughly-shaped blocks of ironstone arranged in an interlocking dry-stone fashion, including pieces of reused masonry (Fig 18). These produced pottery of 15th to 17th-century manufacture.

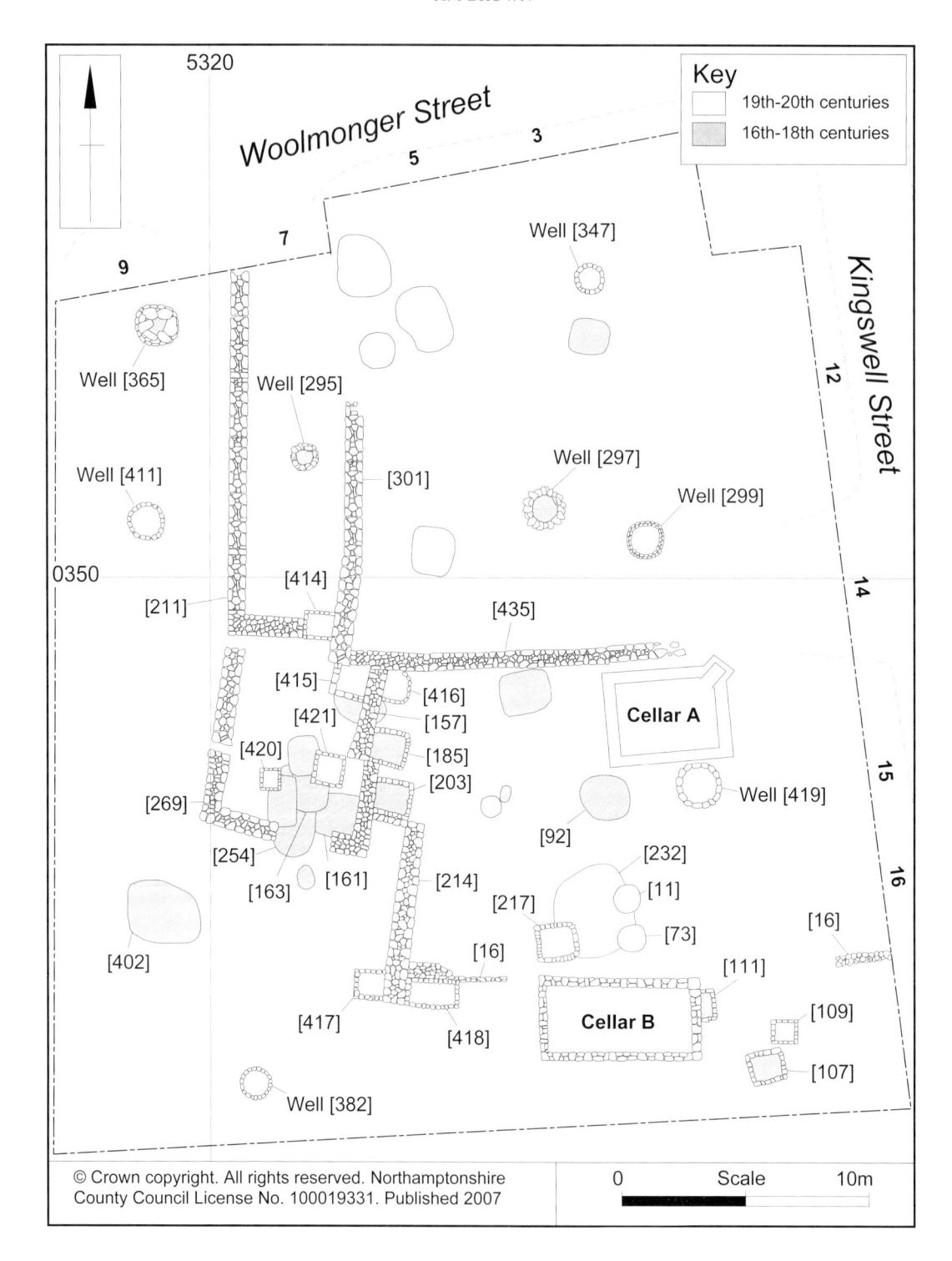

Fig 17 Post-medieval and modern features

THE REAR BOUNDARY WALL OF 14-16 KINGSWELL STREET

Above the pits two sections of wall established the rear of the plot comprising ironstone blocks, shaped and faced on both sides with rubble fill 157. The wall was 7.8m long by 0.6m wide with one course of stone, 200mm high. The boundary survived as a partition into the 19th century according to the historic map evidence (Fig 2).

STONE-LINED CESS PITS

Pits 107 and 111 were each 1m by 1.4m long, rectangular and no deeper than 0.3m. The stonework lining the pits was crude, comprising roughly-shaped ironstone with a rough interior face. The fills were dark greyish-brown clay loam containing animal bone and pottery. Their shallow depth suggests a degree of truncation by later buildings. Sampling produced no evidence for faecal mineralization normally associated with cess pits, although items of

Fig 18 Post-medieval stone-lined well [365]

food debris recovered from pit 107 included bones of eel, pike and herring. The pit also contained part of a broken candlestick. It abutted the outside of the medieval Building D and produced 16th to 17th-century pottery, suggesting that the building was still in existence when the pit was constructed. This supports the view that the building was still occupied up until the late 17th century (Carlyle 2003).

Two other cess pits, 185 and 203, were roughly square, being 1.0-1.3m wide by 0.4-0.6m deep. Both pits were lined with rough hewn, unshaped, ironstone up to 250mm by 260mm by 100mm in size, with a crude inward face and an irregular interlocking pattern. Various dumps of dark greyish-brown and black soils filling them contained late 17th to 18th-century pottery, clay tobacco-pipe and animal bone. Other finds included window and vessel glass, a knife, a bow-saw and a decorated riding spur. Pit 185 also produced the remains of a whole perch, a fish adding diversity to food remains evident on the site. The cess pits were to the rear of a tenement yard space and marked the western extent of the property occupied by George Henshaw, master clay tobacco-pipemaker, c 1768-71 (Moore 1980, 21).

CLAY TOBACCO-PIPE WASTE

Pit 232 at 16 Kingswell Street (Fig 17) was filled with various dumps of garden soil, ironstone shale and domestic waste including clay tobacco-pipes debris (Fig 22, 16). Documentary sources suggest that this was a shared yard during the Great Election of 1768 and was divided between the properties before 1885. It is likely that the clay tobacco-pipe muffle and wasters are from the occupation of 15 Kingswell Street by George Henshaw.

LATE POST-MEDIEVAL AND MODERN ACTIVITY

There were five wells, two cellars, five boundary walls and nine cess pits of the 19th to 20th centuries. Many of the later features are identifiable on the 1885 Ordnance Survey map or can be associated with a mapped structure (Fig 17).

WELLS

All of the wells were filled during the 19th to 20th centuries and cannot have had long periods of use. They were constructed using a level of engineering unavailable in previous centuries. Two of the wells had been capped and exposure of the archaeological horizons by machine had disturbed the brick cap, allowing demolition material to fill the void below (382 and 419). Where this was not the case, wells were examined to confirm the period of backfill (299, 347 and 411). Each well had its own peculiar characteristic patterns of stonework and had been finished in a different style. Most reused building masonry or roughly shaped and unfinished ironstone. Four of the wells lay within buildings, suggesting that they were situated within well houses depicted upon the maps of 1885 (347, 382, 411 and 419). One well was situated in the yard space of 14 Kingswell Street, 299.

CELLARS

Cellar A was 5m long by 4m wide and 1.4m deep. The walls were of red brick, and it had been filled with demolition rubble. The rubble contained an assortment of materials including a champagne magnum, several jars in Nottingham stoneware and an assortment of poorly preserved shoes and leather offcuts. Cellar A served the Shoe Repair Factory which was present from around 1949 (NRO Maps 5970-2). None of these items were retained.

Cellar B was situated at the back of 17 Kingswell Street and beneath the former 'Carver's workshop' (NRO Maps 5970-2). The cellar, 6.5m long by 2.2m wide and 1.6m deep, was constructed from ironstone blocks, shaped and finished on both faces. There were no finds of interest from within the cellar fill.

BOUNDARY WALLS

Many of the property boundaries survived that are visible on the 1899 and 1949 Insurance plans (NRO Maps 5970-2). Most of these were aligned on 18th-century precursors. The walls which formed the boundaries of 7 Woolmonger Street were present (211, 269 and 301). The north boundary wall of the 1899 Bellhanger's workshop was present to the rear of 14 Kingswell Street, 435. This was later incorporated into the 1949 shoe repair factory. The rear wall, 214, of 16 Kingswell Street was visible along with the partition with 17 Kingswell Street. The latter having abutted Cellar B below the 1899 Carver's workshop.

CESS PITS

Most of the cess pits lay within small ancillary buildings, likely to have been outhouses (414, 415, 416, 417 and 418). Two cess pits were situated in the open yard at 7 Woolmonger Street, 420 and 421. One cess pit was situated in the yard space of 16 Kingswell Street, 217, and one lay behind 17 Kingswell Street, 109.

MODERN DISTURBANCES

Four other pits were dug within the bounds of 5 Woolmonger Street. They post-date the demolition of the tenement, but predate the construction of *The Cobblers* public house, which was demolished in 2005. There were three minor surface disturbances located within the yard of 15-16 Kingswell Street that probably originated around the time when Henry Perrin was in residence at 15 Kingswell Street, but had no relationship with his trade as a whitesmith.

THE POTTERY
Paul Blinkhorn

The pottery assemblage comprised 3,975 sherds with a total weight of 76.517kg. The estimated vessel equivalent (EVE), by summation of surviving rimsherd circumference was 44.66. The range of pottery indicates continuous occupation at the site from the 11th century onwards. The assemblage is typical of the period for Northampton, comprising local wares and a small number of regional and continental imports. It is well-preserved, with many large sherds and reconstructable vessels (Figs 19-20).

METHODOLOGY

The pottery was bulk-sorted and recorded using DBase IV software. The material was recorded by context, number and weight of sherds per fabric type. Feature sherds such as rims, bases, lugs and decorated sherds were recorded individually. For rimsherds, the form, diameter and the percentage remaining of the original circumference were recorded. This figure was totalled for each fabric type to obtain the estimated vessel equivalent (EVE).

The terminology is defined by the Medieval Pottery Research Group (MPRG 1998; MPRG 2001). All the statistical analyses used a Dbase package, which interrogated the original or subsidiary databases, with final calculations made with a calculator. Statistical analyses were carried out to the standards suggested by Orton (1998-9, 135-7).

FABRICS

The pottery was quantified using the Northamptonshire County Ceramic Type-Series (CTS) (table below):

F100:	St Neots ware	*c* 850-1100	6 sherds, 74g	EVE = 0.3
F110:	Rhenish greyware	12th-13th centuries	2 sherds, 29g	EVE = 0
F111:	Pingsdorf ware	11th-13th centuries	1 sherd, 4g	EVE = 0
F130:	Northampton ware	10th-11th centuries	29 sherds, 404g	EVE = 0.66
F200:	T1 (2) type St Neots ware	*c*1000-1200	1777 sherds, 18170g	EVE = 18.19
F205:	Stamford ware	*c*850-1250	50 sherds, 466g	EVE = 0.03
F319:	Lyveden/Stanion A ware	*c*1150-1400	27 sherds, 876g	EVE = 0.16
F320:	Lyveden/Stanion B ware	*c*1225-1400	57 sherds, 2650g	EVE = 0.31
F324:	Brill/Boarstall ware	*c*1200-1600	85 sherds, 2299g	EVE = 0.84
F329:	Potterspury ware	*c*1250-1600	293 sherds, 5391g	EVE = 3.84
F330:	Shelly coarseware	*c*1100-1400	1471 sherds, 38150g	EVE = 19.38
F331:	Developed Stamford ware	late 12th to early 13th centuries	10 sherds 146g	EVE = 0
F343:	London ware	12th-14th centuries	3 sherds, 29g	EVE = 0
F345:	Oxford ware	late 11th-14th centuries	6 sherds, 92g	EVE = 0.20
F347:	Nuneaton ware	13th-15th centuries	3 sherds, 22g	EVE = 0
F360:	Miscellaneous sandy coarsewares	*c*1100-1400	22 sherds, 233g	EVE = 0.17
F365:	Late medieval reduced ware	*c*1400-1500	1 sherd, 9g	EVE = 0.
F403:	Midland purple ware	*c*1450-1600	10 sherds, 843g	EVE = 0.22
F404:	Cistercian ware	*c*1470-1550	15 sherds, 250g	EVE = 0.2
F405:	Tudor green ware	*c*1450-1600	10 sherds, 48g	EVE = 0.16
F406:	Midland yellow wares	*c*1550-1700	1 sherd, 19g	EVE = 0
F407:	Red earthenwares	*c*1400 onwards	1 sherd, 212g	
F408:	Rhenish stonewares	*c*1450 onwards	1 sherd, 4g	EVE = 0
F409:	Staffordshire slipwares	*c*1680-1750	18 sherds, 1077g	
F410:	Tin-Glazed earthenwares	17th-18th centuries	16 sherds, 350g	
F413:	Staffordshire manganese ware	late 17th-18th centuries	20 sherds, 801g	
F426:	Iron-glazed earthenwares	late 17th-18th centuries	6 sherds, 2435g	
F1000:	Miscellaneous wares	19th-20th centuries	22 sherds, 926g	

The following, not included in the CTS, were noted:

F1   Early-middle Saxon organic-tempered ware 1 sherd, 12g
       Moderate to dense organic voids up to 5mm.

F377   Ely ware, 12th-15th centuries. 8 sherds, 297g. (Spoerry 2002)

       Generic name for a quartz sand and calcareous tempered group of pottery fabrics mainly manufactured in Ely, with a second possible source in Huntingdonshire. Jars, bowls and jugs dominate. Earlier vessels hand-built and turntable finished, later vessels finer and usually wheel-thrown. Formerly Grimstone software, Kings Lynn.

CHRONOLOGY

The late Saxon and medieval pottery is dated using the Relative Seriated Phase (RSP) chronology (Blinkhorn 2006, 114-115). In addition to the previously published RSP, phase LS4, for the period *c* 1000-1100, is defined by F200, T1 (2) type St. Neots ware (Table 2).

The data shows that there was intense activity at the site from the 11th century until the 15th century. The sherd size is large due to the number of near-complete vessels. All the deposits are of a primary nature, comprising waste from the dwellings on or close to the site (Table 3).

The occurrence of the major wares demonstrates a pattern typical of the Saxo-Norman and medieval periods in Northampton. The Saxo-Norman assemblage is dominated by St. Neots ware, with Shelly coarsewares dominant in the 12th century. From the 13th century onwards, Shelly coarsewares remain important, but first Lyveden/Stanion wares, then Brill and Potterspury wares make up the bulk of the glazed fabrics. Residuality is fairly low, apart from during the first half of the 13th century, when considerable disturbance of Saxo-Norman deposits is caused by quarrying.

THE ASSEMBLAGE

LATE SAXON TO SAXO-NORMAN (LS4, *c* 1000-1100)

The period is dominated by T1(2) St Neots ware, forming over 98% of the phase assemblage with small quantities of Stamford and Northampton wares. The presence of Northampton ware in 11th-century contexts, despite it being a primarily 10th-century type, is probably not evidence of earlier occupation at the site. Denham (1985) has noted this phenomenon at other sites, and it may represent a late floruit of the industry.

Rimsherds largely comprised jars and bowls. Other vessels included a St Neots ware pedestal lamp and a Stamford ware crucible. Decorated sherds were largely absent, other than a St Neots ware storage jar with thumbed applied strips.

Over two-thirds of this pottery came from pit [54], weighing 8.1kg, but produced few refitting sherds and no vessels were reconstructable. The pottery was very fragmented and despite some large sherds, the average sherd weight was only 9.8g, which is very low. The lack of refitting sherds indicates probable secondary deposition cleared from a midden for burial.

Table 2: Pottery occurrence per ceramic phase by number, weight (g) and EVE

RSP	Period	Quantity	Weight (g)	EVE	Mean sherd weight (g)
LS4	*c* 1000 - 1100	1240	12107	12.95	9.8
Ph0	*c* 1100 - 1150	483	14105	8.69	29.2
Ph1	*c* 1150 - early 1200s	129	7719	2.50	59.8
Ph2/0	*c* early 1200s - late 1200s	1069	18657	10.46	17.5
Ph2/2	*c* late 1200s - 1400	834	15228	8.33	18.6
Ph4	*c* 1400 - 1450	34	348	0.31	10.2
Ph5	*c* 1450 - 1500	69	1001	0.83	14.5
	c 1500 - early 1600s	5	274	0	54.8
	c 1600s	3	211	0.20	70.3
	c late 1600s - 1700s	72	3178	0.39	44.1
	c 1700s - 1800s	5	2002	0	400.4
	c 1800s	28	1134	0	226.8

Table 3: Pottery occurrence per ceramic phase by weight (g) expressed as a percentage of the total phase assemblage

Phase/Fabric	LS4	Ph0	Ph1	Ph2/0	Ph2/2	Ph4	Ph5
F130	1.1%	0.1%	1.0%	0.3%	0.7%	0	0
F205	0.7%	0.4%	0.3%	1.5%	0.2%	0	0
F200	98.1%	13.5%	6.0%	17.9%	2.5%	56.0%	0
F330	-	85.8%	89.5%	60.8%	47.1%	0	57.9%
F319	-	-	3.0%	2.1%	1.7%	0	0
F331	-	-	0.1%	0.4%	0.4%	0	0
F320	-	-	-	12.9%	1.5%	4.9%	0.4%
F324	-	-	-	1.7%	11.6%	0	21.4%
F329	-	-	-	-	33.4%	13.2%	13.3%
F365	-	-	-	-	-	2.6%	0
F403	-	-	-	-	-	9.8%	1.9%
F405	-	-	-	-	-	12.4%	0
F408	-	-	-	-	-	1.1%	0
F401	-	-	-	-	-	-	0
F404	-	-	-	-	-	-	2.9%
Total	12107	14105	7719	18657	15228	348	1001

T1(1) St. Neots ware occurred in this phase, such pottery had a period of use into the mid-11th century. There was a lack of Anglo-Saxon pottery dating to before the 11th century, unlike the nearby St. Peters Walk excavations (Soden 1998-9). A single residual sherd of early to middle Saxon pottery was noted in a high medieval context and it would appear that this area of Northampton was marginal until the 11th century.

SAXO-NORMAN (PH0, c 1100-1150)

Shelly coarsewares, the major ware at medieval sites in the northern and eastern areas of Northamptonshire, were introduced. The material forms over 85% of the phase assemblage, along with smaller quantities of St. Neots ware, Stamford ware, Lyveden/Stanion unglazed wares, Northampton ware, and Developed Stamford ware. A single bodysherd from a glazed Oxford ware tripod pitcher was present. The Stamford and Oxford wares were the only glazed pottery available at that time, with the latter less common on sites at St. Peters Walk (Soden 1998-9, 88) and Derngate (Blinkhorn 2002, 46).

Vessel forms were limited to jars, bowls and jugs, with jars forming a 67.4% of the phase assemblage. There were four rims from cylindrical jars, a speciality of the shelly ware industry. Finds from West Cotton suggest that they were specialist cooking vessels, and all the vessels from this phase showed heat scorching. Vessels were represented by large fragments, including the complete profiles of two shelly ware jugs (Fig 19, 1). One of these vessels shows sooting on half of the base and part of the lower body from having been placed on the edge of a fire to heat the contents. The location of the sooting indicates that the handle was positioned over the heat source and would have been extremely hot when removing it from the fire.

Also of note are two bodysherds from a shelly ware storage jar with stamped applied strip decoration, and another in the same fabric from a pitcher, with rouletted decoration. Decoration of any kind is extremely rare on shelly wares.

The phase assemblage was fairly fragmented, although a number of vessels were represented by more than one sherd. As in the preceding phase, the majority of the refuse was removed from a midden for burial, with a few vessels thrown in at the time of burial.

SAXO-NORMAN (PH1, c 1150-1200)

Shelly wares continued to dominate making up nearly 90% of the phase assemblage, along with Lyveden/Stanion A ware, another type of unglazed shelly limestone-tempered ware. St. Neots ware represented only 6%, which saw the end of the industry. Residual Northampton ware was also noted, along with Stamford and Developed Stamford ware and a bodysherd from a Rhenish greyware vessel. German imports have been noted before on sites in Northampton, they are always rarities, none were noted at St. Peter's walk or Derngate.

The range of vessel types is typical of the early medieval period, dominated by an 82.4% proportion of jars with smaller quantities of bowls and jugs. One decorated sherd from a St. Neots ware bowl with rouletting on the rim was present. The pottery was well preserved with two near-complete shelly ware jars apparent (Fig 19, 2). These vessels showed a similar sooting pattern to those noted earlier. The first of the jars has sooting on half the base and side, and extensive internal limescale from heating water beside a fire. The second has two areas of sooting on the base and sides, showing heating a similar manner on more than one occasion.

MEDIEVAL (PH2/0, c 1200-1250)

Medieval glazed wares from Lyveden and Stanion in the north-east of the county, and Brill on the Oxfordshire and Buckinghamshire border were introduced. The former comprises nearly 13% of the phase assemblage, with jugs, often with slip stripe decoration, being the sole glazed product of the industry. Brill jugs, which were also often highly decorated, make up 1.7% of the assemblage (Fig 19, 3). One of the Lyveden/Stanion B ware jugs has crude incised facemasks. Two very similar vessels were noted at the Derngate excavations (Blinkhorn 2002, fig 9, 1 & 2). Other glazed wares were also noted; three sherds of London ware jugs, rare in Northampton; and two sherds of Oxford ware baluster jugs, a typical product of the tradition in the 13th century.

The unglazed assemblage consisted mainly of shelly wares, nearly 61% of the phase assemblage with 16 sherds of F360 Sandy coarseware also present. Shelly ware jugs were well represented, some of them showed scorching consistent with heating. One, rather unusually, had a strap handle covered in stamping (Fig 19, 4). Another had rows of triangular rouletting. A large shelly ware jar with applied strip decoration was also present (Fig 19, 5).

Pingsdorf ware was present, an import from the Rhineland. One sherd was also found at the Moat House Hotel on King Street (Blinkhorn 2001, 99).

Eight non-joining bodysherds of a curfew (*couvre feu*) or fire-cover were present in Ely ware. They were partially scorched on the inside, with applied strips and incised wavy lines on the outside. Curfews are occasionally found on medieval sites, particularly in the towns, used to cover the fire at night and allow the embers enough oxygen to keep them glowing. At a time when many buildings were made of thatch and timber, fire was a constant danger.

The assemblage was dominated by 75.4% jar forms, with bowls and jugs making up roughly equal proportions of the remainder. Residual fragments of two St. Neots ware pedestal lamps and a Stamford ware crucible were present.

LATE MEDIEVAL (PH2/2, c 1250-1400)

Potterspury ware was introduced, common in Northampton in the later 13th-14th centuries. The material comprises 33.4% of the phase assemblage, although shelly wares are still the major pottery type. Brill wares are also common, comprising over 11%, whereas Lyveden/Stanion glazed wares are much less common, representing only 1.5%. Six sherds of early medieval Sandy ware were present, with two sherds of glazed Oxford ware and Nuneaton ware. These are likely to be contemporary, although the Oxford ware was reaching the end of its manufacturing period. A fragment of a Rhenish Paffrath ladle was

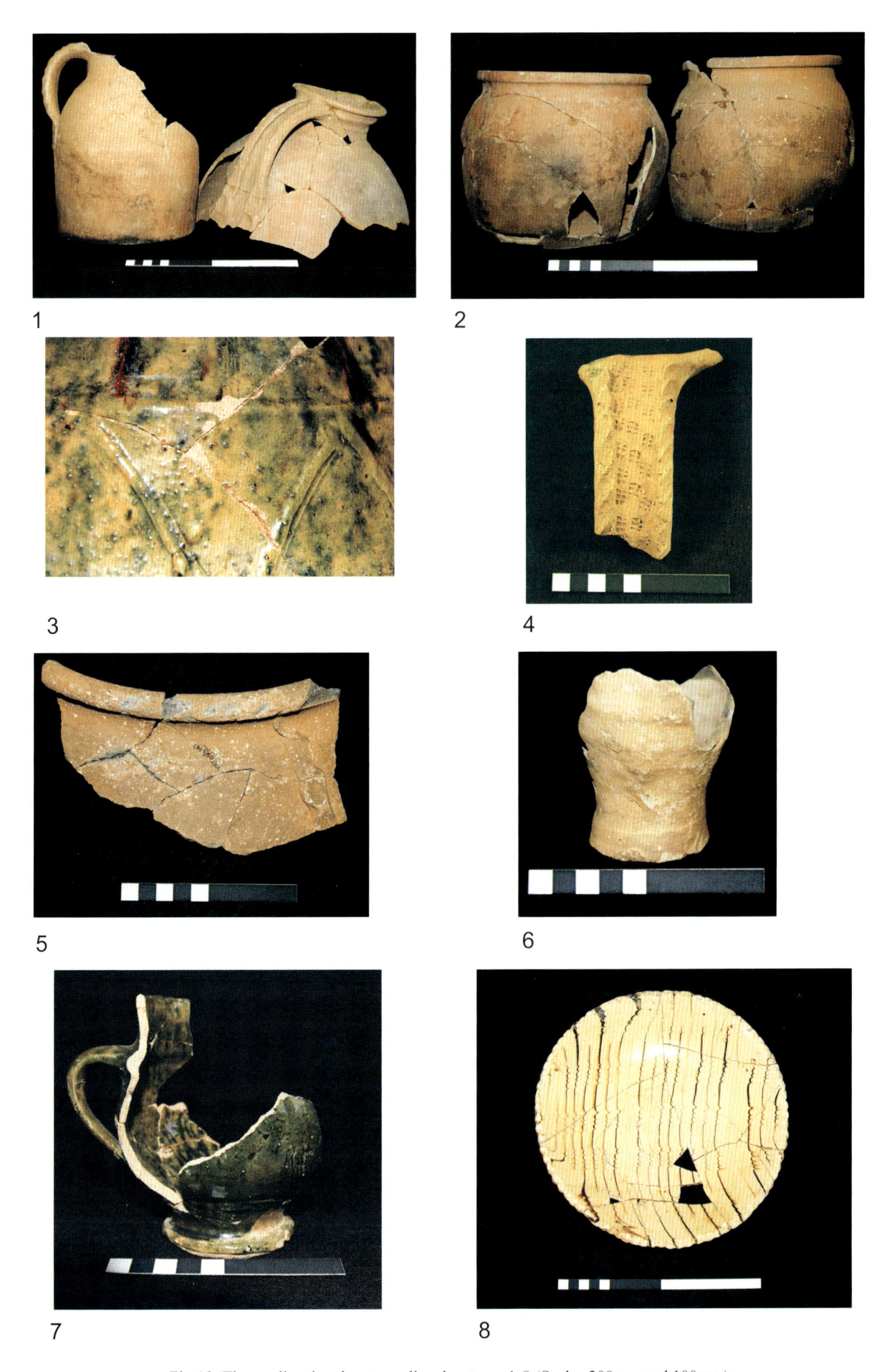

Fig 19 The medieval and post-medieval pottery, 1-8 (Scales 200mm and 100mm)

present, more common in later 11th and 12th-century contexts.

The Potterspury assemblage is fairly fragmented, with no vessels reconstructable to a full profile. Residuality is low, comprising only 3.4% of the group. One residual sherd of note was an early-middle Saxon hand-built pot. Over 100 such sherds were noted at St. Peters Walk (Soden 1998-9, 84), confirming that the area of the town was marginal until the 11th century.

Jars are the most common vessel type forming 49.1% of the phase assemblage. Jugs are also well represented, making up 35.1% of the assemblage. The rest of the group comprises bowls and a single fragment of a Brill skillet. A residual St. Neots ware lamp rim was present. Non-rim sherds included the base of a Potterspury drinking jug, which is a miniature version of the larger vessels and is quite a rare find (Fig 19, 6).

The pattern of vessel consumption at this site is typical. Jars dominate in the early part of the period, with jugs becoming more and more common. By the end of the 14th century, specialist pottery like the skillet and the drinking jug came into use.

LATE MEDIEVAL (PH4, c 1400-1450)

The low occurrence of pottery reflects the depressed nature of the economy of the later 14th century. Contemporary pottery comprised jars, bowls and jugs in Potterspury, Lyveden/Stanion B ware, a single sherd of Reduced ware, and Midland purple ware. Drinking pottery such as cups and mugs in 'Tudor Green' types and German Stonewares were also present, all highly fragmented.

LATE MEDIEVAL TO EARLY POST-MEDIEVAL (PH5, c 1450-1550)

Pottery of this date is lacking, residuality is high, with nearly 58% of the pottery being shelly wares. Brill wares comprise over 21% of the phase assemblage as 'Tudor Green' wares, particularly mugs and cups (Fig 19, 7). A large group of late 15th-century kiln waste of this type was recently discovered at Ludgershall near Brill (Blinkhorn and Saunders 2004, 131-144). Cistercian ware was present, along with Potterspury ware, Midland purple ware and Nuneaton ware, no other contemporary pottery was noted.

LATER POST-MEDIEVAL POTTERY

Post-medieval pottery was generally sparse, although a number of near-complete vessels from the late 17th-18th centuries were noted. The pottery is typical, comprising utilitarian, plain tin-glazed earthenware plates, dishes and mugs in Staffordshire earthenware (Fig 19, 8). A pictorial Staffordshire slipware plate has a suspension hole and initials, possibly of the maker, at the top (Fig 20, 9). The overall scheme is uncertain, although the hind quarters of an animal are visible.

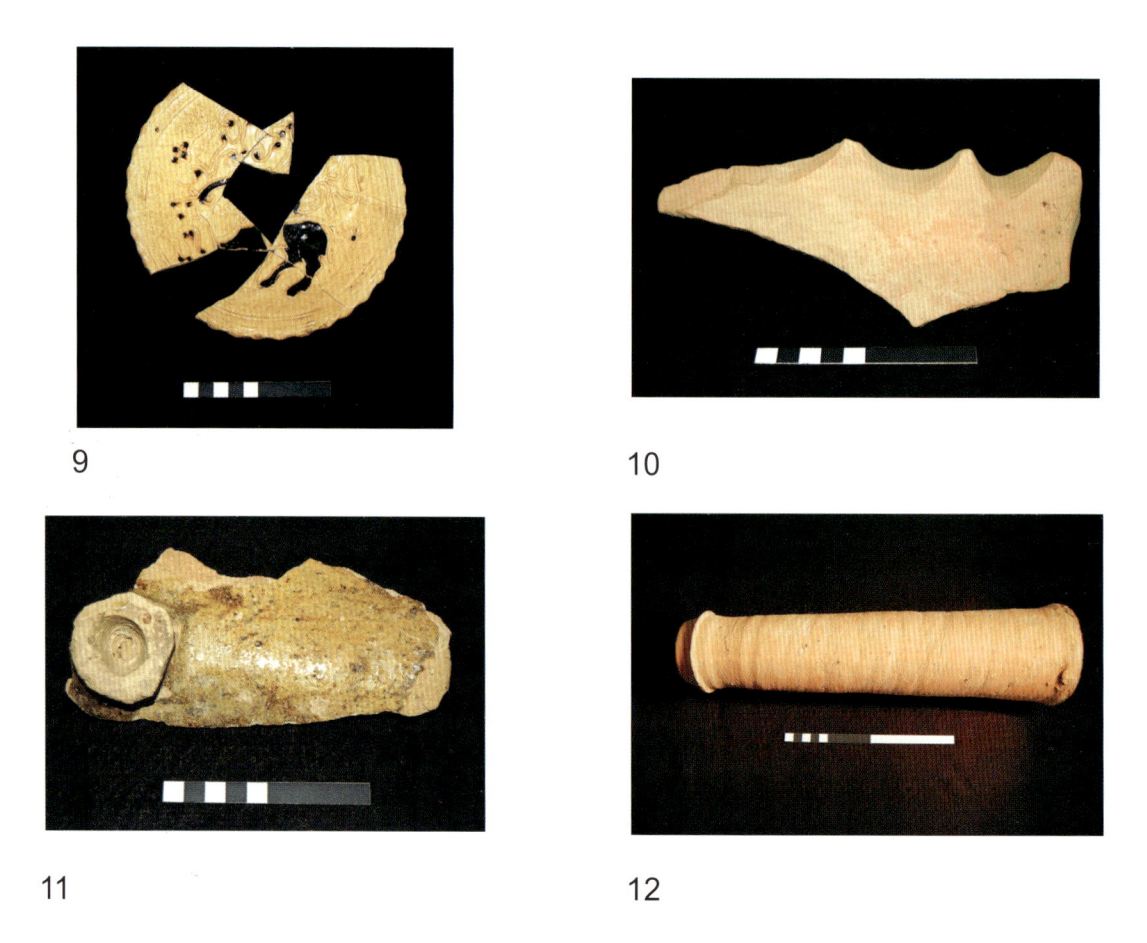

9

10

11

12

Fig 20 The post-medieval pottery, 9, ceramic ridge tiles, 10-11 (Scales 100mm) and a ceramic water pipe, 12 (Scale 200mm)

CATALOGUE OF ILLUSTRATED POTTERY (Figs 19 and 20)

1 Two 12th-century shelly ware jugs (scale 200mm)
2 Two shelly ware jars (scale 200mm)
3 Brill jug showing detail of slip stripe decoration
4 A stamped jug handle (scale 100mm)
5 Applied strip decoration on a shelly ware jar (scale 100mm)
6 Base of a Potterspury drinking jug (scale 100mm)
7 A 'Tudor green'-style cup (scale 100mm)
8 A Staffordshire slipware bowl (scale 200mm)
9 Fragments of a Staffordshire slipware pictorial plate (scale 100mm)

THE BUILDING MATERIALS
Pat Chapman

CERAMIC ROOF TILES

This assemblage of 156 fragments of roof tiles weighs 13.8kg and comprises 113 fragments of unglazed flat peg tiles and 43 fragments of green-glazed ridge tiles with four crests. The majority are from two contexts; a 14th to 15th-century demolition layer (212) of the malthouse (Building E) and a 15th to 16th-century garden soil (64) above it.

The ridges are gently curved with straight sides. Calculations based upon the most complete ridge tile from Corby Road, Stanion in Northamptonshire, show that the height of the ridge tile from the base to the apex of the ridge would be 135mm, with an estimated base width of 260mm (Chapman 2008).

The main fabric is smooth and sandy, varying from red to buff, with occasional small calcareous inclusions and a dark grey to black core. This is similar to CTS Fabric F322, Lyveden/Stanion 'D' ware. It dates to c 1350-1500 according to the revised date of the waster kilns at Stanion (Blinkhorn 2008) and is similar to the Greyfriars tile fabric 1 (Eames 1978, 125). A few tiles are in a sandy fabric with frequent fine crushed shell and occasional small ironstone inclusions, fired to brown, orange-brown or red and usually with a medium grey reduced core. They vary in thickness from a thin streak to the whole fabric excepting its surfaces. This is identical to the ridge tile from Corby Road, Stanion.

The ridge tiles are 8-10mm thick, the only measurable dimension. They are almost all copper glazed varying in shade from a light to a very dark green. One end of the single unglazed tile is decorated with three upstanding knife cut triangles with curving rather than straight edges, probably as part of a series (Fig 20, 10). Similar ridge tiles have been found at the Fishergate House site in York (Spall 2005, plate 9) and in Southampton, dated to the 13th-14th century (Garside-Neville 1996, 295; Dunning 1975, 189). A similar fragment has been found at a tile kiln site at Bread and Meat Close, Warwick (Chapman 2007). Tiles from the Laverstock kilns in Salisbury are dated to the 13th century (Saunders 2001, 174, fig 62, Cat 293).

A green-glazed ridge tile has a stubby cylindrical crest rising 20mm above the tile (Fig 20, 11). It has an external diameter of c 50mm and a slightly oval internal diameter of 30mm by 22mm which narrows to a point, but does not penetrate the body of the tile. It has been made from added clay. The crest does not appear to be part of a broken dome style crest as the rim has some remnant glaze and it is smooth where it is undamaged. A finial may have been separately made to socket into it.

The peg tiles are 10-12mm thick, the only measurable dimension. The pegholes are 12mm in diameter and the three pieces with two holes for fixing to laths have gaps between them of 65-72mm, thus one tile was probably about 155mm wide. The fabric is fine orange to orange-pink to brown, with fine grog and ironstone and occasional bigger ironstone inclusions. The core is sometimes a medium grey of varying thicknesses. A few tile fragments are in shelly ware.

CATALOGUE OF ILLUSTRATED ROOF TILE (Fig 20)

10 An unglazed decorated ridge tile (scale 100mm)
11 A green glazed decorated ridge tile (scale 100mm)

STONE ROOF TILES

There are eight perforated limestone roof tiles of varying sizes. They are generally rectangular and the pegholes are all neatly drilled to an average 8-10mm in diameter, narrowing from the top surface down. Two other pieces are possible fragments, while the remaining four pieces are small surface fragments split from other stones.

The largest rectangular tilestones are almost complete. They are 613mm long and up to 270mm wide, and 500mm long up to 250mm wide, with both up to 40mm thick. Each tapers in at the top, to reduce the overall weight of the tiles on the parts that were concealed by the overlapping row of tiles above. Neither has extant pegholes.

One medium sized example measures 240mm long and up to 190mm wide, with a remnant peghole close to the left hand edge and a possible remnant on the right hand side. An iron fragment adhering to the back of this tile may be the head of the nail fixing the tile that was overlapped, indicating a vertical overlap of at least 50%.

Two smaller tiles are 180mm by 110mm wide and up to 25mm thick, with the pegholes more central. The complete surviving edge of one has been chamfered out from the top along one side and the base.

One example is slightly trapezoidal, measuring 50mm at the apex to 145mm at the base and is 13mm thick. It may have been used as a ridge or valley tile.

The tile sizes are similar to those from a medieval moated manor at Tempsford, Bedfordshire (Chapman 2005, 97, Fig 37.12). Stone tiles were graded, with the biggest laid at the eaves with courses of diminishing size to the ridge. Stone tiles were laid at quite a steep pitch, 50 degrees or more, being pegged or nailed to laths that were attached to the rafters (Brunskill 1978).

FLOOR TILES

There are seven fragments of floor tile, four of which are green glazed, one is lead glazed, another is plain and the last is too worn to determine. Six of them come from 13th-14th-century contexts and one was residual in a 17th-18th-century pit.

DRAINPIPE

An unglazed coil made, wheel-finished red brown ceramic waterpipe came from an 18th-19th-century layer (140). It measures 402mm (16½ inches) long with an external diameter of 110mm (4¼ inches) at one end, c 15mm thick, tapering to 65mm (2½ inches) in diameter and 5mm thick at the other end. The internal diameter of the pipe is 60mm. The narrow end has a collar 25mm below the top and 20mm wide to fit inside another pipe, while the wide end has an internal collar 20mm deep to fit over another pipe (Fig 20, 12).

ILLUSTRATED WATER PIPE (Fig 20)

12 An unglazed coil-made ceramic water pipe (scale 200mm)

A green glazed water pipe of similar dimensions, tapering rather than being flanged, was found at Ely in 1964, together with 13th-century pottery (Briscoe and Dunning 1967, 86). Pottery water pipes were used for secular and monastic houses and can be of either the tapering or the flanged type. Similar looking pipes were also found at Basing House, Hampshire, dating to c 1540 (Moorhouse 1991, 110-112, fig 8.12).

OTHER FINDS
Tora Hylton

There are 91 finds from the Saxo-Norman to the post-medieval period. A single heavily corroded oval buckle was recovered from pre-Conquest deposits. Small numbers of finds were recovered from 11th to 12th-century features relating to Saxo-Norman Building B. The greatest numbers of finds were recovered from the 13th to 14th-century pits which covered the site. A few residual medieval finds occurred in later deposits.

The range of finds provides a brief insight into some aspects of life at the site and forms a small assemblage that may be compared to the excavations at St Peter's Street and Woolmonger Street (Oakley *et al* 1979; Hylton 1998-9). There is evidence for domestic settlement that includes items for personal use and recreation. A small group of tools attests to textile manufacture and woodworking. With the exception of nails there is a distinct lack of structural fittings. Most finds were recovered from quarry backfill deposits.

A total of 26 iron objects, excluding nails and small fragments, were submitted for X-ray by David Parish of the Buckinghamshire County Museum Service. This provided a permanent record of identification and revealed technical details not previously visible. One iron object, a spur, coated in a silver inlay, was chosen for further investigation (Fig 21, 1). This entailed selective cleaning, using air abrasive to reveal decorative features (Fig 21, 2) (Table 4).

HOUSEHOLD ITEMS

Items for household use include a limestone mortar recovered from medieval pit 349, and part of a candlestick from a post-medieval pit 107. Mortars for the preparation of food are common finds on medieval sites. About a quarter of the original object survives

Table 4: Finds quantified by functional category

Functional category	Late Saxon	Saxo-Norman	Medieval	Post-medieval	Late post-medieval
Personal possessions					
Costume and jewellery	1	2	6	3	-
Recreation	-	1	1	-	-
Miscellaneous objects	-	-	1	-	-
Equipment and furnishings	-	-	1	-	-
Building materials					
Nails	-	8	14	6	-
Glass - window	-	-	1	5	-
Household items					
General	-	-	2	1	-
Glass - vessel	-	-	2	4	2
Knives	-	1	-	1	-
Hones/sharpeners	-	1	2	-	1
Tools					
Textile working	-	-	4	-	-
Woodworking	-	1	-	1	-
Miscellaneous tools	-	-	1	-	-
Transport					
Sledge runners	-	-	1	-	-
Horse fittings	-	-	1	1	-
Miscellaneous and unidentified					
Copper alloy	-	1	10	1	1
Iron	-	5	4	1	-
Stone	-	-	-	2	-

1

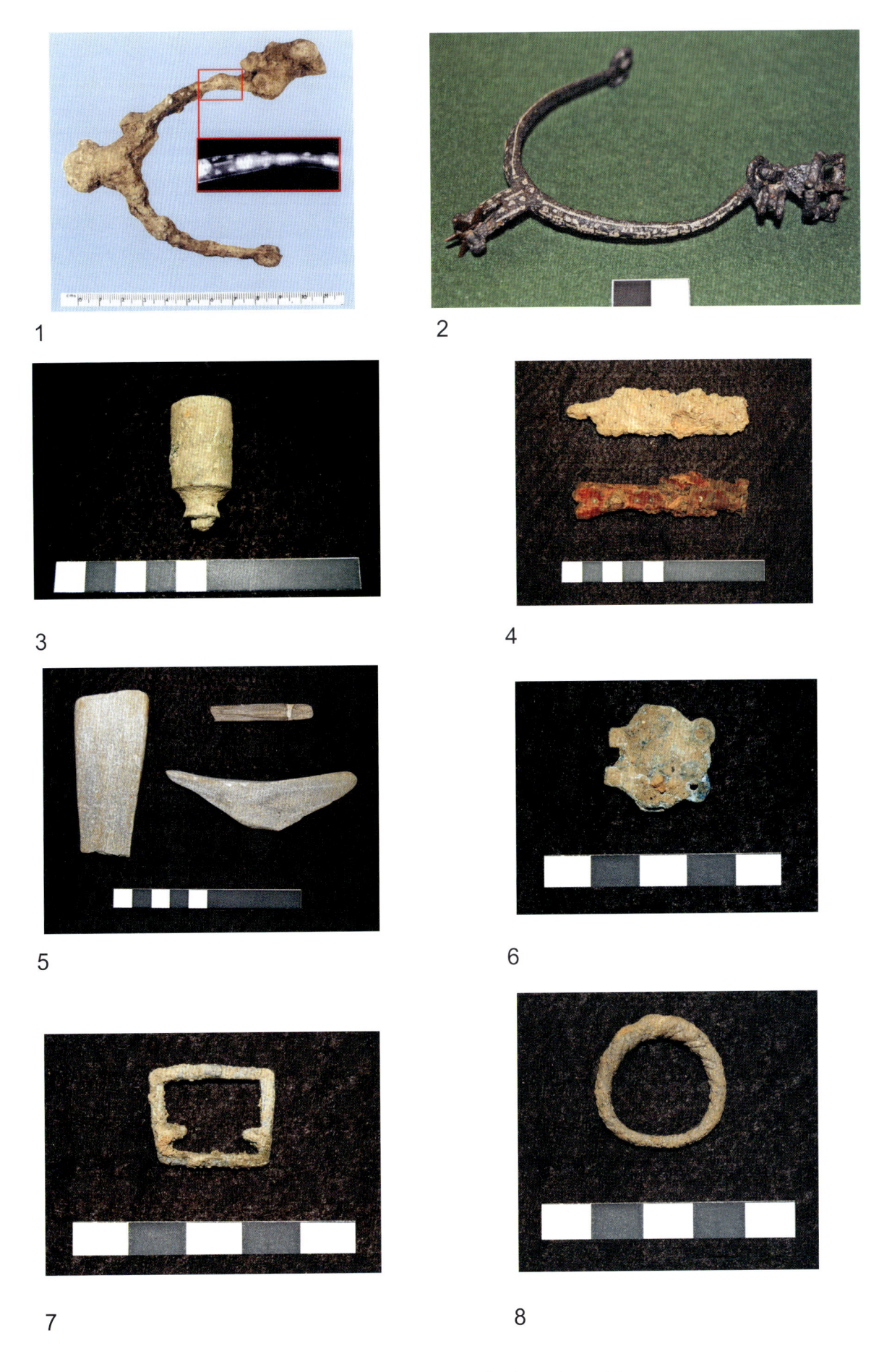

2

3

4

5

6

7

8

Fig 21 Other finds, 1-8 (scales 10mm intervals)

201

and would have measured c 220mm in diameter. The internal diameter of the mortar is c 100mm. The exterior surface is smooth, the wall and base are c 65mm and c 60mm thick respectively. The rim is flat topped with external moulding and a vertical rib protrudes from one side. Originally there would have been two or four ribs furnished with a runnel. The vertical edge of the rib is decorated with a simple motif.

The candlestick is incomplete and comprises a cup with circumferential grooves, a short stem and an angled collar above a socket (Fig 21, 3). This would have been fixed to a branched double socket candleholder (Brownsword 1985, fig 3, 4). Candleholders of this type have a base with supporting stem, surmounted by a spike which is flanked by two curved branches with sockets or cups at theirs ends, they generally date to the late 15th and early 16th centuries.

PERSONAL EQUIPMENT

There are two knives, a whittle-tang knife from Saxo-Norman pit 116 and a scale-tang knife from post-medieval cess pit 185 (Fig 21, 4). The former terminates in a tapered prong, onto which an organic handle of wood, horn or bone would have been hafted. In contrast, scale-tang knives terminate in a parallel-sided strip, to which scales of wood or bone would have been fixed. This particular example has a tang with biconvex terminal and displays similarities to an example from London which dates to the 16th century (Egan 2005, fig 63, 354).

The excavation produced three whetstones for sharpening ferrous metal knives and tools (Fig 21, 5). Two types are represented, small hones, perforated at one end for suspension from a leather thong and larger unperforated hones. The former is represented by a small slate hone recovered from the floor of Saxo-Norman Building B and the latter by two unperforated hones of micaceous schist (Norwegian Ragstone) from later deposits.

PERSONAL POSSESSIONS

This category comprises small portable items which would have formed part of a persons clothing such as costume fittings, items worn as jewellery or items held by an individual for personal use such as recreational items like musical instruments and toys.

COSTUME FITTINGS

One buckle and two buckle plates were recovered. An iron buckle with a plate attached was recovered from late Saxon pit 54. Although heavily encrusted in corrosion deposits, the X-ray reveals a buckle with simple oval frame with part of a rectangular plate furnished with a recess for the pin and two perforations (Egan 1991a, fig 41, 265). A copper alloy buckle plate was recovered from a layer of post-medieval soil dumping (Fig 21, 6); the plate is small with concave sides and pierced terminal lobes, patches of gilding are evident on the surface and the presence of a slot for the pin is the only thing that confirms its identity. This piece is medieval in date.

Pins

There are ten pins, one from the Saxo-Norman gully, 24, which is intrusive, four from medieval pits and soil dumping, and five from a post-medieval well, 295. With the exception of one that has lost its head, the remainder are all drawn copper alloy wire pins with wound wire heads, that measure up to 39mm long. Oakley's classification of pins from St Peter's Street, Northampton shows that there are two main types; five Type H1 pins with simple wire wound heads and four Type H2 pins with wire wound heads moulded into a spherical shape (Oakley 1979, 260).

Other objects associated with dress include a complete strap loop from a medieval pit, 52 and a copper alloy lace chape from a medieval quarry pit, 339. The strap loop comprises a rectangular frame with two internal projections (Fig 21, 7). A similar example from London was recovered from c 1200-1400 deposits (Egan 1991b, fig 139). The lace chape is made from a rolled copper alloy sheet and would have been used to secure the lace terminals, which would in turn have fastened items of clothing. It is comparable with examples from St Peter's Street (Oakley 1979, fig 103, 254, 278).

Jewellery

One item of jewellery was recovered, an incomplete finger ring from a medieval pit, 339 (Fig 21, 8). It is made from four circular-sectioned wires comprising two large tapered wires of 3mm diameter and two fine wires of 1mm diameter. The wires have been twisted together in a clockwise direction to produce a ribbed coil. Chunky finger rings were common in the Viking period and occur as late as the 1170s (Pritchard 1991, 331). A similar example was recovered from a late 10th to early 11th-century context at Winchester (Hinton 1990, fig 165, 2064).

A goose ulna whistle
Helen Leaf

This object is a crudely made whistle from the floor of the Saxo-Norman Building B (Fig 22, 9). It has been made from a goose ulna, a bone used for just under a third of all currently known flutes (Leaf 2006, 13). A typical goose ulna flute has a D-shaped window or sound hole at the proximal end, three finger holes at the distal end, and uses the entire length of the ulna once the epiphyses have been removed. Though this example differs from this, its features have parallels elsewhere.

The whistle is short; it measures 67mm long and 11mm in diameter, and uses only about a half of the possible length of bone. The blowhole is sited 7mm from the distal end. The visible cut marks indicate that this is its intended length. Comparable whistles without finger holes have been found at Rayleigh Castle and Winchester (Francis 1912, 171; Megaw 1990, 718-723). It may have originally been longer and subsequently shortened, as appears to have occurred with the example from Folkestone (Pitt-Rivers 1883, 464).

The window of this whistle measures c 6mm across and is roughly oval, an uncommon shape evident on the whistle from Westbury-by-Shenley (Riddler 1995, 392). In the process of manufacturing a whistle, a block of wood or other substance is fitted into the proximal end

9

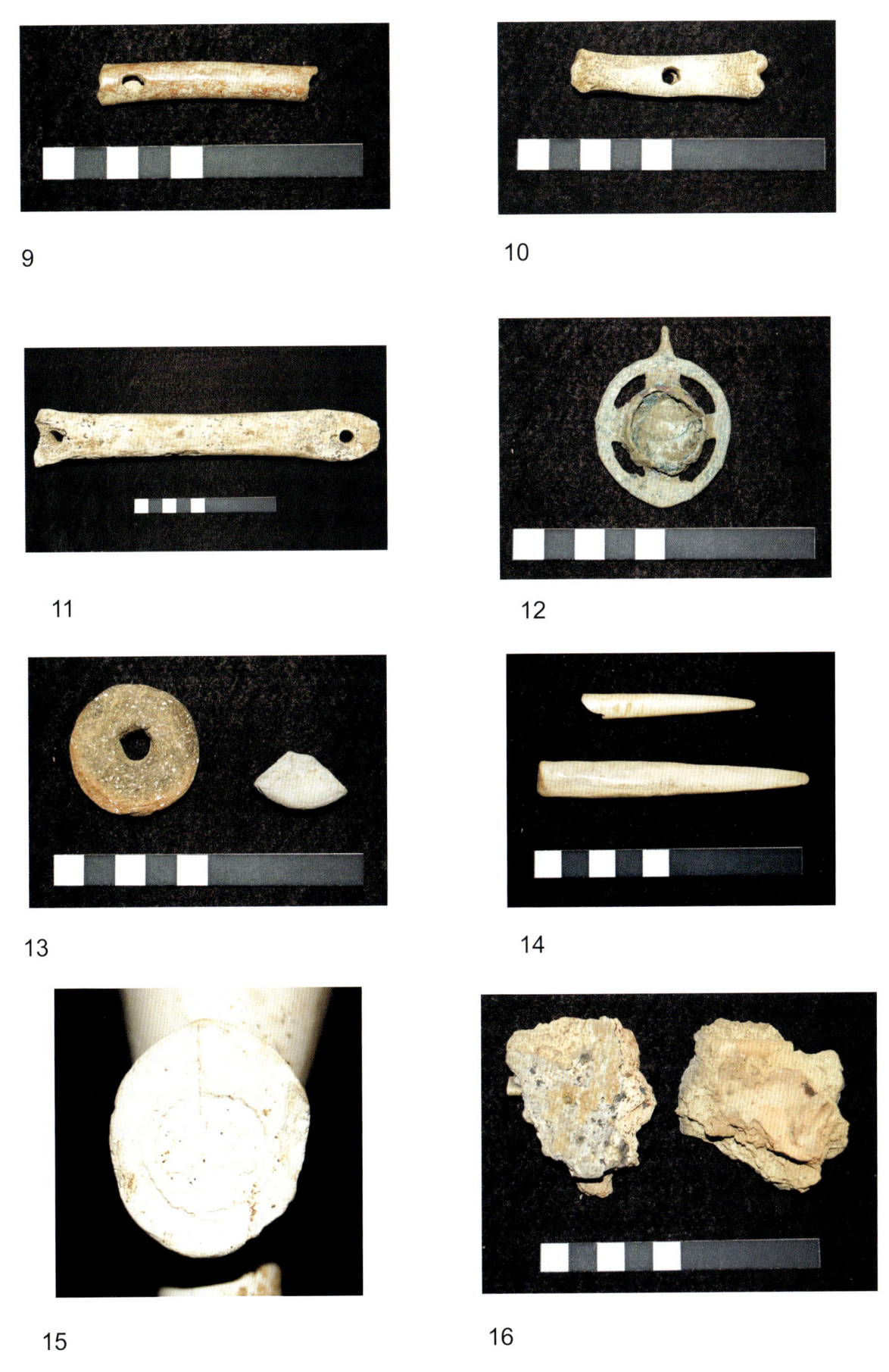

10

11

12

13

14

15

16

Fig 22 Other finds, 9-16 (scales 100mm)

to direct the stream of air to the window when blown. If fitted well this gives a strong and clear sound. The oval window of the Kingswell Street example, along with the presence of spongy cancellous bone on the internal surface of the bone, may have made it more difficult to fit a good block and the resulting sound would have been of low quality.

A feature seen on the external surface of this example, and common to many, is the presence of 'chatter marks' made during manufacture when the bone was scraped with the blade of a knife.

The 'buzz-bone'

The 'buzz-bone' is manufactured from a pig metapodial, perforated laterally through the anterior and posterior surfaces and the terminals have been knife-trimmed to remove unwanted protrusions (Fig 22, 10). Seven similar examples were recovered from St Peter's Street where they were identified as bobbins or toggles (Oakley 1979, 313). They may also be spinning, buzzing musical toys (MacGregor 1985, 102-3; Lawson & Margeson 1993, 213-4). In recent years this latter interpretation has gained support, with an example from Beverley recovered with a knotted leather thong (Foreman 1992, fig 74, 505; Lawson 1995).

EQUIPMENT AND FURNISHINGS

There is a dearth of structural related ironwork with little to characterise the nature of the buildings on the site. Many fittings which may have been in use were notable by their absence and appear to have been removed, possibly reused or recycled. Twenty-eight nails were recovered, eight from Saxo-Norman deposits, four from later medieval deposits and six from post-medieval deposits. The majority are undiagnostic, but those identifiable are mainly flat sub-circular heads and square-sectioned shanks. There is one wedge-shaped nail with a tapering profile and no distinct head.

TRANSPORT

THE SLEDGE-RUNNER

Of particular interest is the presence of a sledge-runner found within later medieval soil dumping deposits (Fig 22, 11). The sledge runner has been made from a horse metapodial and measures 234mm long and, although fairly well preserved, the posterior surface shows signs of decay. The distal (toe) and proximal (heel) ends have been modified, the articular surfaces have been partially removed and both ends have been perforated by a 9mm hole drilled through the shaft. The toe is slightly upswept, formed by oblique cuts from either side. The underside of the runner (anterior surface) appears to display little sign of wear, suggesting that it may not have been used. Very few sledge-runners have been identified from England and their dating is largely dependant on continental examples (MacGregor 1985, 145). Similar 14th-century examples manufactured from horse radii have been recorded at West Fen Road, Ely and in post-medieval deposits at Stonea, Cambridgeshire (Riddler 2005, fig 4.16, 277; Smithson 1996, fig 237, 1 and 2).

Sledge-runners resemble bone skates, the main difference is that runners have vertical holes to fasten the runners to the sledge, while bone skates have horizontal toe holes or transverse heel holes for attaching straps. Sledge runners manufactured from the metapodials or radii of horses were introduced during the middle to late Saxon period and were in use until the early 19th century.

RIDING EQUIPMENT

A harness pendant was recovered from late medieval pit, 124 (Fig 22, 12). It comprises a gilded, circular, openworked frame with integral suspension loop. The frame has a reversed 'Z' motif and at its centre there is a circular collet, the interior of which retains the remains of a paste that would have secured a cabochon. Horse harness pendants were common in the 13th-14th centuries (Griffiths 1986).

An iron spur was recovered from a pit 185. The X-ray image revealed a spur decorated with an inlaid silver motif (Fig 21, 1). This has since been cleaned and conserved by David Parish at Buckinghamshire Museum Service (Fig 21, 2). It is 85mm long with a span 80mm wide, the neck is 10mm long and the length of the rowle box is 13mm.

The spur is complete with slightly tapered sides and a D-shaped cross-section. The terminals broaden to accommodate two circular holes for attaching fittings which would secure the spur to leather straps. The neck is divided for most of its length by the rowle box but the rowle is missing.

A buckle and a hooked fitting are still attached to one of the terminals. The buckle is asymmetrical and there is a sheet roller on the outside edge of the frame, in addition, a pin and an attachment plate for connecting the buckle to the terminal of the spur is attached to the central bar. The motif which occurs on the sides of the spur is also repeated on the buckle. A hooked fitting is attached to the other hole in the terminal, it has an integral plate with a button or knop for connecting to a leather strap, and is not dissimilar to that seen attached to a buckle from London (Egan 2005, fig 18, 121).

Initially the type of terminal, which is a Ward-Perkins Type Bii, and the style of the spur suggested a relatively early date around the 13th century, but its fragile proportions, the fittings and the type of decoration suggest that the piece probably dates to the 17th century, when the spur became an object of fashion, with a variety of decorative finishes (Ellis 1990, 1038). Of the two main types in vogue, one had tapered straight sides and a small neck rather like the Kingswell example. Stylistically and functionally spurs of this type would be more suitable as an item of fashion rather than for use on long journeys (Ellis 1990, fig 321, 3872-3).

CRAFT MATERIALS AND TOOLS

TEXTILE WORKING MATERIALS

Two spindle-whorls relate to hand spinning and were recovered from later medieval pits, 151 and 326 (Fig 22, 13). One is manufactured from the base of a shell-tempered pot (F330). The edges have been knife trimmed to form a disc measuring 40mm in diameter, at the centre there is a waisted, circular perforation, cut with a knife. The other is a lath turned biconical, limestone whorl measuring 35mm in diameter. Examples of both types have been found in Northampton. Ceramic whorls pre-date 1450 and limestone whorls may be of late Saxon or early medieval date (Oakley 1979, 286).

Two pin beaters manufactured from animal bone were recovered from a later medieval quarry pit, 257 (Fig 22, 14). The earliest is a double-pointed pinbeater for use with a warp-weighted loom. This example is incomplete and is 65mm long, it has an oval cross-section and it tapers to a rounded point. The exterior surface is highly polished and a series of short oblique grooves are present on the anterior and posterior surfaces, set just above the point. Such tools are commonly found on settlement sites of early to middle Saxon date. The later example has a pointed terminal at one end and a squared, 'chisel-like', end at the other. It has a D-shaped cross-section, tapers to a rounded point and measures 101mm in length. There is a worn groove or notch on the right hand side, on both anterior and posterior surfaces, suggesting contact with the threads on the loom. This example would have been for use with the vertical two-beam loom, which was introduced in the 9th century and was in use until the 13th-14th centuries (Brown 1990, 227-31).

WOOD WORKING TOOLS

Wood has always been an important material used in the manufacture of items, building materials and as a fuel. No wooden objects survive from this site, but there are two items that provide evidence for the preparation of wood. An axe head was recovered from Saxo-Norman pit, 116, adjacent to Building B. Much of the blade is missing and what remains suggests that the axe was quite small for light tasks such as chopping kindling or honing timber. The socket is complete with an oval-shaped eye and flat top.

A bow-saw was recovered from a post-medieval cess pit, 185. The saw comprises a parallel single-sided blade, with six teeth per 20mm, set at 90° and 35° to the back of the blade. The example is probably a rip saw as the teeth are alternately angled out. A vestige of the tang onto which a handle would have been hafted protrudes from one end of the blade and the other end is perforated for securing to the handle.

Miscellaneous tools

A bone implement of unknown use was recovered from a medieval quarry pit, 257. It has been manufactured from a small splinter of hollow bone that is the radius of a sheep or goat. The terminal has been knife-trimmed to form a short faceted point, rather like a pencil. The exterior surfaces are extremely worn, suggesting that it was hand-held. A shallow depression, close to the point, shows signs of extreme wear from the fingers and thumb when the tool was in use.

GLASS

The glass is a poor representation of the types which are known to have been in use. Much of it is abraded, with the decayed surfaces display lamination, flaking and crumbling, characteristics of dehydration. There are six fragments of window glass from post-medieval deposits and soil dumping layers. Only one fragment has blackened manganese surfaces and grozed edges, indicating that it is medieval in date.

Eight fragments of vessel glass were recovered; two fragments from 13th-14th-century deposits, four from 17th-century deposits and two from a 19th-century pit. The clearly identifiable pieces were a rim from a clear glass flask decorated with heavy spiral mould-blown ribbing, the lower portion of a wine glass and a complete phial in opaque bluish-green glass. These three were recovered from a cess pit, 185.

CLAY TOBACCO-PIPES AND MUFFLE
Tim Upson-Smith

A group of 117 clay tobacco-pipe fragments were recovered, 79 examples were from a pit, 232, and 23 were from a cess pit, 185. The majority of bowls provided a closely dated range *c* 1660-1710. A small quantity of pipe kiln muffle was also recovered from a pit, 232. The assemblage was dominated by 39 examples of Oswald's Type G9, *c* 1680-1710, and 20 examples of Type G18, *c* 1660-1680 (Oswald 1975). Two examples of Oswald's Type G8, *c* 1680-1710, were recovered from a cess pit, 185. One of these was marked in relief with the initials 'JA' within a circle on the foot and could possibly be attributed to John Anderson of Wellingborough who died in 1723 (Moore 1980, 19; Fig 22, 15). Two bowls both 18th-century, Type G23, *c* 1760-1800, were also recovered from cess pit, 185.

The majority of bowls and stems were burnished and all the bowls were ornamented with a partial or complete milled band or groove below the lip of the bowl, a common motif until *c* 1710 (Moore 1980, 6). The majority of the pipe bowls show no signs of use and are wasters from the manufacturing process. The stem fragments measured up to 147mm long and 11 examples retained their mouthpieces.

Four fragments of muffle-kiln debris were recovered from the pit, 232, in light buff coloured clay reinforced with pipe stems. The clay matrix contained small voids, a result of burnt-out organic matter. The exterior surfaces were fired-damaged, resulting in a pale grey surface (Fig 22, 16). A further single fragment was recovered from cess pit, 185, that consisted of an Oswald G9 pipe bowl with stem of 112mm length and a fired clay lump adhered to it.

One clay tobacco-pipe manufacturer is documented living at 15 Kingswell Street, *c* 1767-1774, called George Henshaw (Moore 1980, 21). The two features which produced the assemblage were located within the yard of this property. The pipes and the kiln waste date to *c* 1680-1710, although the pottery and two of the clay tobacco-pipe bowls date the pits to *c* 1680-1800. It is unlikely that there was an earlier manufacturer on the site since there was a complete lack of earlier clay tobacco-pipe manufacturing waste elsewhere. It seems probable that George Henshaw was using an older mould producing pipes with a short stem length. These pipes would have been up to 10 inches (255mm) long, the fashionable length for clay pipes in the second half of the 18th century was up to 15 inches (378mm) long, but were not practical for labourers or craftsmen.

CATALOGUE OF ILLUSTRATED FINDS (Figs 21 and 22)

1   An iron riding spur as recovered, with X-ray inset (scale 120mm)
2   The iron riding spur showing the silver inlay, after cleaning (scale 20mm)
3   A 15th to 16th-century candle holder (scale 100mm)
4   A Saxo-Norman whittle tang knife (top) and a 16th-century scale tang knife handle (bottom) (scale 100mm)
5   Whetstones (scale 100mm)
6   A copper alloy buckle plate (scale 50mm)
7   A medieval copper alloy strap loop (scale 50mm)
8   A 12th-century copper alloy finger ring (scale 50mm)
9   A whistle made from a goose ulna (scale 100mm)
10 A 'buzz-bone' made from a pig metapodial (scale 100mm)
11 A sledge runner made from a horse metapodial (scale 100mm)
12 A gilded horse harness pendant (scale 100mm)
13 Two spindle whorls (scale 100mm)
14 Two bone pin beaters (scale 100mm)
15 A manufacturer's stamp on the base of a clay tobacco-pipe bowl
16 Examples of muffle from a clay tobacco-pipe oven (scale 100mm)

MAMMAL, BIRD AND FISH BONES
Philip Armitage

A total of 2,994 hand-collected and sieved animal bone specimens were analysed (Armitage 1998-9, 102-103). A total of 2,112 specimens are identified to species and the part of the skeleton, forming 70.5% of the assemblage, the remaining 29.5% were unidentified owing to fragmentation or the absence of surviving diagnostic features.

SPECIES

Of the 2,112 identified specimens, 81.9% are from mammals, 13.4% from birds, 4.1% from fish and 0.6% from amphibians. The species represented are listed below:

BIRDS

Grey-lag/domestic goose, *Anser anser*/domestic
Domestic fowl, *Gallus gallus* (domestic)
cf Partridge, *Perdix perdix*
Teal/domestic duck, *Anas platyrhynchos* (domestic)
Carrion crow, *Corvus corone*
Turdidae cf Songthrush, *Turdus ericetorum*

FISH

Cod, *Gadus morhua*
Haddock, *Melanogrammus aeglefinus*
Herring, *Clupea harengus*
cf Turbot, *Scophthalamus maximus*
Thornback ray (or roker), *Raja clavatus*
Freshwater eel, *Anguilla anguilla*
Pike, *Esox lucius*
Perch, *Perca fluviatilis*
Amphibians
Common frog, *Rana temporaria*

MAMMALS

Horse, *Equus caballus* (domestic)
Cattle, *Bos* (domestic)
Sheep, *Ovis* (domestic)
Goat, *Capra* (domestic)
Pig, *Sus* (domestic)
Dog, *Canis* (domestic)
Cat, *Felis* (domestic)
Fallow deer, *Dama dama*
Brown hare, *Lepus* cf. *capensis*
Rabbit, *Oryctolagus cuniculus*
Black rat, *Rattus rattus*
House mouse, *Mus musculus*

Fragmented mammal bones form 96.4% of the specimens not identified to species, with only 2.5% from indeterminate fish species, and 1.1% from indeterminate bird species. This area small mammal bone fragments from sieved samples.

The animal bones from Kingswell Street were divided into three main periods based on the dating from finds and the structural and stratigraphic relationships. The periods are defined as follows:

Table 5: Period groups of analysed bone

Site phase	Period	Chronology
Phases 1 & 2	Late Saxon to Saxo-Norman	Pre-Conquest to 12th century
Phase 3	Medieval	13th to 15th centuries
Phase 4	Post-medieval	16th to 18th centuries

CONDITION

The preservation is good with relatively few specimens exhibiting weathering, erosion or leaching. Even in the bones from pit 54, which on the ceramic evidence included midden material, there is little sign of these effects. Of note is the apparent 'brittleness' of bones from the later medieval quarry pit 293, the result of lime present in the fill. The incidence of dog gnawing is relatively low, only 2% of the total NISP, and the frequency of burnt bones makes up 1.8% of the assemblage. There is no direct association between the burnt bones and hearth pits or malting ovens. There are eleven specimens of burnt sieved mammalian bone fragments from soil layer 294, probable food detritus.

RECORDED DATA

The data is a useful resource for larger scale studies. Determinations of the ages at death of the major domestic species based on dental eruption and wear were examined and recorded. This data and the epiphyseal fusion in these same species are held in the site archival records. A summary of the identified females, males, and castrates in the domestic livestock, and sex profiles for the adult domestic fowl are also retained. There are also GL measurements on mammal and bird bone elements together with estimates of the withers heights for cattle, sheep, pigs and horses.

THE ASSEMBLAGE

LATE SAXON AND SAXO-NORMAN (MID-10TH TO 12TH CENTURIES)

A total of 670 bones were examined, of which 73.6% are identified to species and anatomy. Pit 54 yielded 62.9% of the total identified bone specimens from this period. On the basis of anatomical distributions this is debris from primary and secondary butchering, intermingled with kitchen waste. The overall diet was dependant on the meat of domestic livestock, predominantly cattle and sheep, some pig, and supplemented with domestic fowl. There are no wild game species such as deer or hare, and fish are limited to the occasional cod and freshwater eel. The thrush, cf Songthrush, humerus may also represent food debris as discussed by Sergeantson (2006, 142), the bones of thrushes are found quite often 'confirming that these birds were eaten from an early period'. The carrion crow bones from pit 54 do not represent food debris, this bird was as common an urban scavenger as it is today (O'Connor 1993, 159).

There is an absence of dog bones, a feature also noted in general amongst later deposits which presumably indicates their burial elsewhere. The lack of dog bones is in marked contrast to the quantities of dog bones, including partially articulated skeletons, recovered from Woolmonger Street, 1994-7 (Armitage 1998-9, 103-4). Cat bones are also absent but do feature in later deposits.

MEDIEVAL (13TH TO 15TH CENTURIES)

A total of 2,149 bones were examined of which 69.9% are identified to species and anatomy. The diet of the inhabitants during the later medieval period comprised beef and mutton, augmented by pork, domestic fowl, lamb and veal. Warren-bred rabbits also featured in the diet and along with domesticated duck. Unlike the earlier deposits there is evidence for the consumption of venison and hare. Wildfowl were also represented by the part-skeleton of a young partridge recovered from the malt oven fire pit, 279. There was increased consumption of geese and an expanded variety of both marine and freshwater fish. The fish include at least one pike comparable to a modern specimen of 457mm length. Pike in the later middle ages was generally associated with a high status diet (Woolgar 2000, 39; Dyer 2000, 106-8). Dyer discusses the cost of fish quoting a price of 2-3 shillings in the 15th century for a mature pike, the equivalent to a week's wages for a skilled craftsman.

On the basis of the meat quality the food debris indicates that the dietary profiles of the inhabitants were beyond subsistence needs, and even beyond 'solid sufficiency', reflecting a certain degree of affluence (Ervynck et al 2003). The food remains do not reveal evidence of the luxurious or extravagant dietary levels enjoyed by the privileged classes, which often featured exotic and prestigious foods like swan. Local inhabitants merely enjoyed a prosperous standard of living.

Much of the meat, fowl and fish consumed locally would have been procured from butchers, poulterers, and fishmongers in the town. The keeping of small livestock such as chickens, pigs and goats supplemented domestic provisioning. Evidence of this is strongly indicated by the domestic fowl bone elements. The age and sex profiles established for the 32 domestic fowl represented suggested they had been kept primarily as egg producers with a higher ratio of hens to cock birds (Albarella et al 1997, 48). Meat production was of secondary importance. The newly hatched chick was probably a natural casualty indicative of fowls raised on the site. Such urban backyard chicken rearing was a common subsistence enterprise in the medieval period, with the birds being fed on household scraps (Serjeantson 2006, 137-47). The medieval birds would have been somewhat scrawny to the modern eye, of a size similar or smaller than modern Bantams.

Anatomical distributions of the cattle and sheep indicate that some of the animals may have been slaughtered on site. This accounts for the presence in the refuse of all body parts, including those of the head and extremities of the feet. Whole untrimmed carcasses of these animals may also have been purchased from the local meat market (Armitage 1998-9, 105). The market place was a short walk to the north-east of the site and ideal for transporting goods. The close proximity of the Augustinian precinct to the south and both the Hospitals of St. Thomas and St. John would have also been large affluent consumers.

An alternative interpretation is that butchers', tanners' and horn-workers' waste had been dumped in the area, becoming intermixed with the household refuse of the local district. The presence of two detached and chopped sheep horn cores, a cranium with the horn cores removed and a single goat horn core add support to this suggestion. They may represent the waste products of leather and horn working in the area. The soils in which they were found predated the establishment of the later medieval street frontage and were not confined to a single part of the site.

It will be of interest to scholars researching the early history of sheep breed-types in Britain that the later medieval deposits also yielded a cranium of a polled, naturally hornless, sheep. This was recovered from the demolition layer of the malthouse which was deposited before the 15th century. A cranium with a scur, a small bony 'knob', in place of a horn was recovered from a well, 330. No examples of such polled or scurred sheep are represented in the Saxo-Norman and medieval deposits, where all the sheep appear to have been horned. Polled and scurred sheep crania were also recorded in the 1994-7 excavations along Woolmonger Street which produced identical results (Armitage 1998-9, 105).

Two rodent species are present in the later medieval deposits. Black rat is represented by one innominate bone and one metapodial bone from a well, 89. A house mouse skull, one lower jawbone and one femur were amongst sieved samples from a cess pit, 373. Rodent activity is evident from three rat-gnawed sheep bones post-dating the later medieval street frontage, and in one case, the demolition of the malthouse. Given the presence of vermin, it is not surprising that a population of domestic or feral cats were present, attested by the recovery of 39 bone elements from at least 14 cats, 8 of which were adults and 6 of which were kittens. These cats also scavenged kitchen scraps as indicated by a cat-chewed chicken ulna.

Frog bones were recovered from sieved samples taken from the malt oven fire pit, 279. Two individuals were represented. Other frog bones included one vertebra from the outdoor malt oven, 77, and a femur from a cess pit, 373. An aquatic habitat is not essential outside of the breeding season for the common frog but their presence indicates that at least part of the site was overgrown and close to wetland countryside. Frogs were often attracted to urban sites in large numbers due to an abundance of household refuse and middens providing the ideal environment for the proliferation of flies and a bountiful food source for frogs (O'Connor 2000, 17). Deposits from which amphibian evidence was recovered comprise mainly demolition debris predating the 15th century with some silting towards the base of the pits. The pits themselves were left open after disuse, at least long enough for the frogs to inhabit them. They appear to have been backfilled when the malthouse was demolished.

POST-MEDIEVAL (16TH TO 18TH CENTURIES)

A total of 175 bones were examined, of which 66.9% are identified by species and anatomy. Analyses of the food debris from a pit, 107, and a cess pit, 185, indicate a surprisingly varied diet, which included both freshwater as well as marine fish. The sieved contents of the pit, 107, yielded freshwater eel, pike and herring. Cess pit, 185, yielded four fin spines and 28 scales from a perch. From the same deposit came the skull of a domestic duck. In addition to the consumption of beef, veal, mutton, pork, and chicken, at least one suckling piglet had been eaten as evidenced by a tibia from a pit, 402. A foetal or neonatal calf is represented by 14 bone elements from a pit, 73, perhaps an aborted or still born calf of a milk cow, kept locally. Overall the diet of the inhabitants from the 17th century onwards appears to have been substantial, indicating a rejuvenation of prosperity.

DISCUSSION

The results are compared against the faunal assemblages from the 1994-97 excavations along Woolmonger Street (Armitage 1998-9; Locker 1998-9). Food bones from the different sites highlight the paucity of fish in the diet of the Saxo-Norman and medieval inhabitants in the district. This is in marked contrast to the rich spectrum of both marine and freshwater fish consumed further to the west (Locker 1998-9). Meat consumption patterns in the later medieval period exhibit a much greater diversity compared with the adjacent site. Evidence suggests that local inhabitants supplemented their staple fare of beef, mutton and pork with wild game species that included deer, hare, partridge, rabbit and duck. They also enjoyed a variety of fish species, predominantly marine, but also including freshwater eels and pike. In stark contrast, the meat, fowl and fish eaten by the inhabitants further westwards along Woolmonger Street appears to have been somewhat restricted.

Caution should be exercised in considering the differences outlined above. The quantity of bones from Saxo-Norman and medieval deposits in the 1994-97 excavations is much greater than that from the Kingswell Street excavation, whilst the reverse holds true for the respective later medieval assemblages.

Settlement at Kingswell Street was still fairly peripheral to the core of the parish of St Gregory in the 11th to 12th centuries, as emphasised by the low density of features and smaller quantity of period material from the site. Woolmonger Street was, however, already well established in this period and the full extent of urbanisation was not to reach Kingswell Street until the 13th century. Evidence for the food consumption of Saxo-Norman inhabitants is therefore likely to be a reflection of occupation density.

Later medieval patterns are more complex. Fishing rights on the Nene may have been restricted by the Augustinian Friary in the 13th century. It was not uncommon for monasteries to have fishing rights on the local river, whilst the opportunities to fish for the common man were restricted. There is evidence that the various monasteries and richer individuals over-fished the Dee at Chester in the late 12th century (Barraclough 1988, 264, doc 263). According to the Coventry Benedictine Priory Cartulary the monks were at pains to claim their fishing rights at nearby Styvechale, despite their ownership of fishponds (National Archives E164/21, 62-5). In turn this opened the way to poaching. The same Benedictine Priory which had been so ready to assert its fishing rights was now complaining that its stocks in its own fishponds were regularly filched during the night. Restrictive practises had to be relaxed as the economic constraints suffered by the monasteries began to bite towards the turn of the 15th century, forcing them to let out previous monopolies to tenants.

Another possibility is the presence of mills on rivers which severely effect fish stocks. Milling practises regularly empty the ponds and kill the fish. The construction of fish-weirs keeps them away to such an extent that large stretches upstream of a mill can be devoid of fish. The Nene close by certainly contained numerous mills and at various times the banks of the Nene may have been unsuitable for fishing.

The local economy may also have been responsible. Wealthy local consumers within the Kingswell Street area were the Augustinian Friary and the Hospitals of St. Thomas and of St. John. The site was situated in easy walking distance to the market, ideal for anyone whose livelihood was based on food preparation. It is possible that produce was not necessarily being consumed by the people of Kingswell Street, but slaughtered and prepared for the tables of these more affluent consumers.

PLANT REMAINS
Val Fryer

Soil samples were taken from undisturbed single phase features and bulk floated by Northamptonshire Archaeology with flots collected in a 500 micron mesh sieve. The dried flots were scanned under a binocular microscope at magnifications up to x16, and the data of the plant macrofossils and other remains noted were recorded according to recognised nomenclature (Stace 1997). A small number of mineral replaced macrofossils were recorded, the majority of the plant remains were charred. Modern contaminants, including fibrous and woody roots, seeds, arthropods and fungal sclerotia, were present throughout.

Table 6: Sampled features

Features	Interpretation	Samples
54	Late Saxon pit	4
28, 82, 116	Saxo-Norman pits	3, 7, 6
77, 279	Medieval malting ovens	2, 10
89	Medieval well	17
294	Burnt spread within later medieval garden soil, Plot 4	12
373, 394	Medieval cess pits	14, 15, 16
432	Medieval quarry pit	18
107	Post-medieval	9

PLANT MACROFOSSILS

Cereal grains, chaff, seeds of common weeds and wetland plants, together with tree and shrub macrofossils were present within all thirteen samples. Preservation was variable, although a high density of the cereal grains and seeds were heavily puffed and distorted through combustion at very high temperatures.

CEREALS AND OTHER FOOD PLANTS

Oat (*Avena* sp.), barley (*Hordeum* sp.), rye (*Secale cereale*) and wheat (*Triticum* sp.) grains were recorded, with wheat occurring most frequently. Cereal chaff was generally rare, bread wheat (*T. aestivum/compactum*) type rachis nodes with diagnostic crescentic glume inserts were present within Saxo-Norman pit, 116, and medieval cess pit, 394. A single poorly preserved rivet wheat (*T. turgidum*) type node with persistent glume bases was in medieval cess pit, 373. Detached cereal sprouts and grains with concave profiles were present within malt oven 77. This is indicative of the presence of germinated grains, the quantity recovered was very low and it was not possible to state whether deliberate or accidental germination was represented. Possible charred pea (*Pisum sativum*) seeds were noted within post-medieval pit, 107, and malt oven 279, although neither retained an intact testa or hilum. Indeterminate fragments of large charred pulses (*Fabaceae*) were also recorded with mineral replaced bullace or damson (*Prunus domestica* ssp. *insititia*) type fruit and apple (*Malus* sp.) seeds.

WILD FLORA

Common segetal weeds were present within most of the assemblages studied. Taxa noted included corn cockle (*Agrostemma githago*), fat hen (*Chenopodium album*), small legumes (*Fabaceae*), corn gromwell (*Lithospermum arvense*), knotgrass (*Polygonum aviculare*), dock (*Rumex* sp.), corn spurrey (*Spergula arvensis*) and scentless mayweed (*Tripleurospermum inodorum*). The presence of seeds of stinking mayweed (*Anthemis cotula*) within all but three of the assemblages indicates that most crops were being grown on the local heavy clay soils. Grasses (*Poaceae*) and grassland herbs including medick, clover, trefoil (*Medicago, Trifolium, Lotus* sp.) and ribwort plantain (*Plantago lanceolata*) were all present.

Seeds of wetland plants occurred relatively infrequently. Taxa recorded from the burnt spread (294) included sedge (*Carex* sp.), spike-rush (*Eleocharis* sp.), rush (*Juncus* sp.) and reed mace (*Typha* sp.). Tree and shrub macrofossils, namely hazel (*Corylus avellana*) nutshell fragments and elderberry (*Sambucus nigra*) 'pips' were also rare, occurring in only four assemblages.

OTHER PLANT MACROFOSSILS

Charcoal fragments and charred root or stem were abundant. Mineral replaced root and stem fragments were recorded from a cess pit, 394, and a quarry pit, 432. Other plant macrofossils included indeterminate buds, culm nodes, inflorescence fragments and thorns.

OTHER REMAINS

Black porous, tarry material and the siliceous globules, which occurred at varying densities in all samples, are probable residues of the combustion of organic remains at very high temperatures, including cereal grains and straw/grass. Mineralised faecal concretions were common or abundant in samples 14-18. Other remains included pellets of fired clay within the Saxo-Norman pit, 116.

DISCUSSION

LATE SAXON AND SAXO-NORMAN (MID-10TH TO 12TH CENTURIES)

The assemblages are broadly similar in composition and all would appear to be derived from small deposits of burnt domestic detritus. Wheat and barley grains, some of which may have been accidentally spilled during culinary preparation, are recorded throughout and include a large number of oats. The latter may be present as contaminants of the main cereal crops as, in the absence of oat floret bases, it is not possible to ascertain whether grains from wild or cultivated species are present. Cereals used on site may have been imported as batches of semi-cleaned grain as weed seeds are also common, in particular larger specimens of a similar size to the grain such as corn cockle, brome (*Bromus* sp.), smaller legumes and large grasses. Some contaminants like oats and larger grasses may have been tolerated, others, like the corn cockle seeds, were toxic if consumed and would have been removed by hand during the final stage of processing.

The assemblage from pit 116 contains a high density of wheat grains along with a number of bread wheat type rachis nodes and some weed seeds. As eggshell and fish bone are also present, this assemblage is likely to be derived from domestic hearth waste.

Wood and charcoal appear to have been the principal fuels used during this period, although other materials including dried grasses, grassland herbs and hedge brush may have been used as kindling and to add aroma to the fire (sample 3).

MEDIEVAL (13TH TO 15TH CENTURIES)

Samples from the malt ovens represent the residues from the last firing of the ovens mixed with silting at the base of the abandoned pits. The assemblages are less than 0.1 litres in volume, but both contain a moderate to high density of cereal grains and weed seeds, many of which are severely puffed as a result of combustion at very high temperatures. Germinated grains and detached cereal sprouts are present in sample 2. The density of material recovered is insufficient to be indicative of primary malting waste. Similarly composed assemblages have recently been recorded from other contemporary ovens in Norwich (Fryer, forthcoming). In Norwich they have been interpreted as either batches of semi-cleaned grain accidentally destroyed during drying, or residues of the fuel used within the ovens.

Samples 9, 14, 15 and 16 are all from cess pits (107, 373, 394). The assemblages differ greatly in composition. Pit 107 contained only a very small quantity of charred material, with no evidence of the phosphatic mineralisation commonly seen within sewage deposits. Sample 14 is largely composed of charred remains constituting backfill material. Sample 15 consists almost entirely of mineralised faecal concretions. Sample 16 represents the entire contents from the bottom half of a shelly coarseware jug, used latterly as a poe and dumped in pit, 394. This variety of composition clearly indicates that the cesspits were non-specific features and were commonly used for the deposition of a range of waste materials. Faecal concretions are abundant within Sample 18, illustrating that sewage and dung became mixed into features across the excavated area. Sample 18 was retrieved from the lower fill of a quarry pit, 432, and it was clear from the stratigraphic sequence that fluid cess deposited in pits percolated down into the fills below.

Sample 12 is the only sample studied which contains a moderately high density of wetland plant macrofossils, namely sedge and spike-rush fruits. The assemblage may include burnt flooring materials and domestic hearth waste, burnt and raked into the soil, 294.

SUMMARY

Assemblages from both the Saxo-Norman and medieval deposits are composed of domestic waste. Similar assemblages were also noted at Woolmonger Street (Carruthers 1998-9). The two samples from the medieval period indicate that they were also used for corn drying rather than for malting alone, since medieval ovens were multi-functional structures. Pits across the site were used for the deposition of both charred refuse and sewage.

Cereals appear to have been of considerable importance to the occupants of the site, and much of the grain present was probably produced on the local clay soils. Wheat appears to have been of particular importance, probably due to its suitability to clay land production. Oats are also common in some assemblages, probably as contaminants of the main wheat crop. The same may also be true of the barley, rye, peas and other large pulses, none of which appear in any significant quantity, but all of which can survive as weeds. The presence of small legume seeds may indicate that some attempts at soil improvement by rotational cropping were being undertaken.

The assemblages give little indication of the environment of the site during either the Saxo-Norman or medieval periods, although the few wetland plant remains indicate the proximity to the river margins. Dried grasses and grassland herbs were being used as kindling for both the ovens and the domestic hearths and were within easy reach of the site.

DISCUSSION

The earliest features show an alignment orientated west-north-west to east-south-east (Fig 6). Residuality of the late Saxon pottery was limited and suggests that the extensive disturbance by later features was not responsible for the low level of late Saxon activity present. A late Saxon cellar, Building A, was present in an area of the town that was perhaps largely marginal until the 11th century. The pit was probably a cellar of the type observed at Woolmonger Street (Soden 1998-9, 76-78), Chalk Lane (Williams and Shaw 1981, 98) and Sol Central, Marefair (Miller et al 2006). The pit alignment was repeated in the later Saxo-Norman timber building, Building B, and was also evident in the 13th-14th-century malthouse, Building E. Although the land was initially marginal to occupation further north and west, the early foundation laid a pattern which was apparently incorporated into the subsequent growth of the area.

When Building B was established in the 12th century, the majority of the area was still sparsely occupied. The building extended to the east of the site and evidence for the frontage was lacking. Enquiries into Kingswell Street as an internal route along Lee's postulated defensive perimeter remain inconclusive (Lee 1954). The Saxon defences have been clearly identified on the western side of the burh at Green Street, they have not been positively identified on the eastern side of the burh (Foard 1995; Chapman 1998-9; Soden 1998-9). It is possible the street existed by the 12th century, but given the sparse occupation of the site at the time, the building could have occupied an open area of ground, not necessarily adjacent to a road and set some distance back from Woolmonger Street or aligned upon its earlier course. Woolmonger Street was not fully metalled upon its present alignment until after c 1250 (Soden 1998-9, 113). Several Saxo-Norman pits produced household waste, presumably relating to the occupation of the Building B since animal bone represented primary deposition that was unexposed to the effects of weathering, erosion or leaching. The pottery showed that a good deal of other rubbish was being stored in middens as evidenced by the level of fragmentation and lack of cross-fits and supports a more peripheral location casting doubt on the extent of urbanisation at this time.

There remained a lack of growth into the second half of the 12th century. Few features were positively identified to the period, limited entirely to a sparse scatter of pits. Pottery supported domestic occupation close by in the form of soot-stained cooking vessels (Fig 19, 2).

In the early part of the 13th century the ground was still open and undeveloped. Garden soils sealed the features associated with Building B showing that it had been demolished and the ground left vacant. Topsoil continued to be mixed, possibly by garden horticulture, eradicating earlier soil layers, and producing a loamy deposit.

In the second quarter of the 13th century quarrying was taking place on the site to extract blocks of the natural ironstone for building. It was apparent from the distribution of the extraction activities that some degree of demarcation had been introduced on the site. Quarries were reinstated soon after their excavation with whatever materials were easily available to hand, largely comprising midden waste. Quarrying had been demarcated on loose principles with some comparison to property divisions in later centuries (Fig 9). The general pattern was recognisable as a series of yard spaces, but the exact positions of boundaries were subject to variation. Certain quarries were contained within the partitions of the later plots, fossilising these divisions upon the 19th-century maps.

In the second half of the 13th century pressure for land in Northampton was intense and the site had become fully developed. The town became a military staging post for campaigns in the north of England and a Royal Castle was built (Norgate 1912; Turner 1907, 205-62). From both strategic and political standpoints Northampton was a major town in England and a gateway to the north, a major factor in sustained growth.

Four stone buildings lay within the medieval land plots. One of the buildings is thought to have been a tenement, Building D, possibly attached to a neighbouring building, fronting onto Kingswell Street. The frontage was established around the time that we know Woolmonger Street to have been replanned and diverted north of its previous course (Soden 1998-9, 112-3). This tenement was located on top of the former Saxo-Norman timber building, Building B, with a clear soil horizon between the two demonstrating a break in the occupation. It would seem that the building was not replaced in stone as swiftly as had happened along Woolmonger Street (Soden 1998-9, 112-3, 123). Substantial walls survived beneath 17a Kingswell Street, partially extending into 17 Kingswell Street. The remainder of the original frontage had not survived redevelopment in subsequent centuries or had not extended the full length of the street.

The three other buildings would appear to have been workshops or ancillary structures comprising; a malthouse (Building E), a bakehouse (Building F) and a yard house (Building C). The malthouse was in the south of the site and may have fronted a narrow street or alleyway, its alignment slightly eccentric to Building D and yet consistent with a timber building that had already been demolished over half a century before. This is potential evidence of the alignment of Lewnys Lane, a narrow street that is documented as connecting Woolmonger Street to Kingswell Street from the late 13th century until the turn of the 16th century (Soden 1998-9, 66, 112-3). Combined with the building remains in Trench 3 of Woolmonger Street 1994-7, it lends further weight to this short-lived thoroughfare.

The medieval pattern was subject to alterations in later centuries. The shortening of the rear of 15-16 Kingswell Street indicated that after the medieval period the formalisation and restructure of the properties only partially incorporated existing boundaries so that it is the boundaries between neighbouring properties that continued in use rather than the position of the rear wall, which appeared staggered and irregular in all periods.

On the basis of the stratigraphy and the amphibian remains, the malt ovens were disused some time before they were backfilled. Pottery dates the demolition debris of the malthouse to before the 15th century, probably at some point in the mid-14th century. A broad distribution of feral activity associated with a district in poor sanitary condition was apparent from the presence of rat, frog and cat bones. This is in stark comparison to the century immediately thereafter. There was a distinct lack of evidence for 15th-century activity, limited to small dumps of waste material in the vicinity of the demolished malthouse, and the construction of the pit, 107, abutting the rear of Building D. The tenement property was still inhabited, although the ground to the rear of the property appears to have been left undeveloped. Extensive spread deposits of post-medieval garden soils suggest that the ground remained undeveloped through to the documentation of 'gardens' to the west of Kingswell Street, 1787-1803, which were associated with detached properties on Bridge Street (NRO YZ9055; 9059-61). Pottery for the period *c* 1400-1550 was limited to small groups indicative of low density habitation with virtually no dumping of perishable waste. There was no evidence for the fire of 1516. In 1580 the area was documented as overcrowded and in need of a refuse policy (Cox 1898, 264-6). A good deal of material may have been removed outside of the town for disposal before 1641 when civic improvements were made to the area and Kingswell Street was paved.

Occupation of the street frontage continued in the 17th-18th centuries with the establishment of distinct pit groups along the rear wall of 15 Kingswell Street and within a yard space shared with 16 Kingswell Street. These cess pits, together with a pit behind 16 Kingswell Street, produced clay tobacco-pipe manufacturing evidence. The pits were securely dated *c* 1680-1750 by Staffordshire manganese ware and Staffordshire slipware pottery. Food debris recovered from the pits suggest that the diet of the inhabitants in the 17th century was varied and of relatively high status including such foodstuffs as perch, suckling pig and venison indicative of a return of prosperity in the area following the civic investment.

It is not clear at what date the later medieval tenement building was replaced. Documentary evidence suggests it had been lost before the 18th century, and although it survived the Great Fire of Northampton in 1675, the refurbishment of the district in 1641 indicates that many medieval tenements could have been demolished before the fire.

BIBLIOGRAPHY

Albarella, U, Beech, M, and Mulville, J, 1997 *The Saxon, Medieval and Post-medieval Mammal and Bird Bones Excavated 1989-91 from Castle Mall, Norwich, Norfolk*, English Heritage Ancient Monuments Laboratory Report, **72/97**

Armitage, P L, 1977 *The Mammalian Remains from the Tudor Site of Baynard's Castle, London: A Biometrical and Historical Analysis,* PhD Thesis, Royal Holloway College & British Museum of Natural History

Armitage, P L, 1998-9 Faunal remains, in I Soden 1998-9, 102-106

Bailey, G, Charles, R, and Windsor, N, (eds) 2000 *Human Ecodynamics*, Oxford: Oxbow Books

Barraclough, G, 1988 The Charters of the Anglo-Norman Earls of Chester, 1071-1237, *Record Society Lancashire & Cheshire*, **126**, doc 263, 264

Biddle, M, (ed) 1990 *Object and Economy in Medieval Winchester; Artefacts from Medieval Winchester,* Winchester Studies, **7.2**, Oxford

Blinkhorn, P, and Saunders, J M, 2004 A late 15th-century manufactory of the Brill/Boarstall pottery industry at Ludgershall Buckinghamshire, *Medieval Ceramics*, **23/24**, 131-144

Blinkhorn, P, 2001 The Saxon and medieval pottery, in A Chapman 2001, 99

Blinkhorn, P, 2002 Excavations at Derngate, Northampton, 1997-2000, *Northamptonshire Archaeol*, **30**, 31-61

Blinkhorn, P, 2003 The pottery, in A Thorne 2003, 116-119

Blinkhorn, P, 2006 Saxon, medieval and early post-medieval pottery, in J Brown 2006, 114-117

Blinkhorn, P, forthcoming The medieval pottery from St. James' Abbey, Northampton, report submitted to Northamptonshire Archaeology

Blinkhorn, P, 2008 The medieval pottery, in P Chapman *et al* 2008

Bond, J M, and O'Connor, T P, 1999 *Bones from Medieval Deposits at 16-22 Coppergate and Other Sites in York,* The Archaeology of York, **15/5**, York Archaeological Trust

Briscoe, G, and Dunning, G C, 1967 Medieval pottery roof-fittings and a water-pipe found at Ely, *Proceedings Cambridge Antiquarian Society*, **60**, 81-89

Brown, A E, (ed) 1991 *Garden Archaeology Papers presented to a conference at Knuston Hall, Northamptonshire, April 1988*, Council British Archaeology Research Report, **78**,

Brown, D, 1990 Weaving Tools, in M Biddle 1990, 225-232

Brown, J, 2006 The archaeology at 46-50 Sheep Street, Northampton, *Northamptonshire Archaeol*, **34**, 103-123

Brown, J, 2007 Archaeological excavations at the corner of Kingswell Street and Woolmonger Street, Northampton: March-May 2005, Northamptonshire Archaeology, **07/60**

Brownsword, R, 1985 *English Latten Domestic Candlesticks 1400-1700*, Finds Research Group 700-1700, Datasheet **1**

Brunskill, R W, 1978 *Illustrated Handbook of Vernacular Architecture*, Faber

Carlyle, S, 2003 *Desk-based assessment and archaeological trial excavation of land off Kingswell Street and Woolmonger Street, Northampton, September 2003*, Northamptonshire Archaeology report

Carruthers, W, 1998-9 Charred Plant Remains and the Arable Environment, in I Soden 1998-9, 108-112

Chapman, A, 1998-9 Excavation of the Town Defences at Green Street, Northampton, 1995-6, *Northamptonshire Archaeol*, **28**, 25-60

Chapman, A, 2001, Excavation at the Moat House Hotel, Northampton, 1998, *Northamptonshire Archaeol,* **29**, 93-101

Chapman, P, Chapman, A, and Blinkhorn, P, 2008 A medieval potters' tenement at Corby Road, Stanion, Northamptonshire, 2002, *Northamptonshire Archaeol*, **35**

Chapman, P, 2005 Stone roof tile, in A Maull and A Chapman 2005, 97

Chapman, P, 2007 Ceramic and stone building materials, in D McAree 2007

Chapman, P, 2008 Ceramic roof tiles, in P Chapman *et al* 2008

Cox, J C, 1898 *The Records of the Borough of Northampton*, Volume 2

Denham 1985 The pottery, in M Shaw 1985, 213-133

Dunning, G C, 1975 Roofing Materials, in C P S Platt and R Coleman-Smith (eds) 1975, 186-93

Dyer, C, 1994 (reprinted 2000) *Everyday Life in Medieval England*, London and New York, Hambledon and London

Eames, E, 1978 The Ceramic Tiles, in J H Williams 1978, 121-128

Egan, G, & Pritchard, F, 1991 *Dress Accessories c.1150-c.1450*; Medieval Finds from Excavations in London, **3**

Egan, G, 1991a Buckles, in G Egan and F Pritchard 1991, 50-123

Egan, G, 1991b Mounts, in G Egan and F Pritchard 1991, 162-246

Egan, G, 2005 *Material Culture in London in an age of transition: Tudor and Stuart period finds c1450-c1700 from excavations at riverside sites in Southwark*, MoLAS Monog, **19**

Ellis, B, 1990 Spurs, in M Biddle 1990, 1037-41

Ervynck, A, van Neer, W, Hüster-Plogman, H, & Schibler, J, 2003 Beyond affluence: The zooarchaeology of luxury, *World Archaeology*, **34 (3)**, 428-441

Evans, D H, and Tomlinson, D G, 1992 *Excavations at 33-35 Eastgate, Beverley 1983-86*, Sheffield Excavation Report, **3**

Foard, G, 1995 The early topography of Northampton and its suburbs, *Northamptonshire Archaeol*, **26**, 109-122

Fock 1966 in A von den Driesch and J Boessneck 1974

Foreman, M, 1992 Objects of bone, antler, and shell, in D H Evans and D G Tomlinson 1992, 163-74

Francis, E B, 1912 Rayleigh Castle: New Facts in its History and Recent Explorations on its Site, *Transactions of the Essex Archaeological Society*, **12**, 171

Fryer, V, forthcoming Plant macrofossils from the Millennium Library Site, Norwich, *East Anglian Archaeol*

Garside-Neville, S, 1996 Ceramic Building Materials, in R L Kemp and C P Graves 1996, 294-299

Griffiths, N, 1986 *Horse Harness Pendants*, Finds Research Group 700-1700, Datasheet, **5**

Grigson, C, 1982 Sex and age determination of some bones and teeth of domestic cattle: a review of the literature, in B Wilson *et al* (eds) 1982, 7-23

Gryspeerdt, M, 1978 The Pottery, in J H Williams 1978, 133-47

Hinton, D A, 1990 Metal Finger-Rings, in M Biddle 1990, 646-652

Hylton, T, 1998-9 Small finds, in I Soden 1998-9, 97-101

Ivens, R, Bushby, P, Shepherd, N, 1995 *Tattenhoe and Westbury. Two Deserted Medieval Settlements in Milton Keynes*, Buckinghamshire Archaeol Society Monog, **8**

Jackson, R P J, and Potter, T W, 1996 *Excavations at Stonea, Cambridgeshire, 1980-85*, British Museum Press

Jones, E T, Laughton, J, and Clark, P, 2000 *Northampton in the Late Middle Ages*, Centre for Urban History, University of Leicester

Kemp, R L, and Graves, C P, 1996 *The Church and Gilbertine Priory of St Andrew, Fishergate*, The Archaeology Of York, **11-2**, York

Kiesewalter 1888 in A von den Driesch and J Boessneck 1974

Lawson, G, and Margeson, S, 1993 Musical Instruments, in S Margeson 1993, 211-15

Lawson, G, 1995 Pig *Metapodial 'Toggles' and Buzz-discs: Traditional Musical instruments*, Finds Research Group 700-1700, Data Sheet, **18**

Leaf, H, 2006 English Medieval Bone Flutes: A Brief Introduction, *The Galpin Society Journal*, **59**, 13-19

Lee, F, 1954 A new theory on the origins and early growth of Northampton, *Archaeol Journal*, **110**, 164-74

Locker, A, 1998-9 Fish bone, in I Soden 1998-9, 106-108

MacGregor, A, 1985 *Bone, Antler, Ivory & Horn: The Technology of Skeletal Materials since the Roman Period*, London & Sydney: Croom Helm

Margeson, S, 1993 *Norwich households: The Medieval and Post-Medieval Finds from Norwich Survey Excavations 1971-1978*, East Anglian Archaeol, **58**

Maull, A, and Chapman, A, 2005 *A medieval moated enclosure in Tempsford Park*, Bedfordshire Archaeol Society Monog, **5**

Mayer, J J, and Brisbin, I L, 1988 Sex identification of Sus scrofa based on canine morphology, *Journal of Mammalogy*, **69 (2)**, 408-412

McAree, D, 2007 *Archaeological excavation at Bread and Meat Close, Warwick, Warwickshire, 2003*, Northamptonshire Archaeology, **07/108**

McCarthy, M, 1979 The Pottery, in J H Williams 1979, 151-242

Megaw, J V S, 1990 Bone Whistles and Related Objects, in M Biddle 1990, 718-723

Miller, P, Wilson, T, and Harward, C, 2006 *Saxon, medieval and post-medieval settlement at Sol Central, Marefair, Northampton: Archaeological excavations 1998-2002*, Museum of London Archaeological Service Monog, **27**

Moore, W R G, 1980 *Northamptonshire Clay tobacco-pipes and pipemakers*, Northampton Museums and Art Gallery

Moorhouse, S, 1991 Ceramics in the medieval garden, in A E Brown (ed) 1991, 100-117

MPRG 1998 *Guide to the Classification of Medieval Ceramic Forms*, Medieval Pottery Research Group Occasional Paper, **1**

MPRG 2001 *Minimum Standards for the Processing, Recording, Analysis and Publication of post-Roman Ceramics*, Medieval Pottery Research Group Occasional Paper, **2**

Mudd, A, and Hallam, T, 2000 *Former Burgess Site, St. Peter's way, Northampton: Archaeological Evaluation, May 2000*, Northamptonshire Archaeology report

Norgate, K, 1912 *The minority of Henry III*, London

O'Connor, T P, 1993 Birds and the scavenger niche, *Archaeofauna*, **2**, 155-162

O'Connor, T P, 2000 Human refuse as a major ecological factor in medieval urban vertebrate communities, in G Bailey *et al* (eds) 2000, 15-20

Oakley, G E, 1979 The Copper Alloy Objects, in J H Williams 1979, 248-64

Orton, C, 1998-9 Minimum Standards in Statistics and Sampling, *Medieval Ceramics*, **22-23**, 135-8

Oswald, A, 1975 *Clay pipes for the Archaeologist*, British Archaeological Report, **14**

Payne, S, 1973 Kill-off patterns in sheep and goats: the mandibles from Asvan Kale, *Anatolian Studies*, **23**, 281-303

Peacey, A, 1996 *The Development of the Tobacco Pipe Kiln in the British Isles* (www. intarch.ac.uk/journal/issue1/peacey/toc.html)

Pearce, J, 1992 *Border Wares*, Her Majesties Stationary Office

Pitt-Rivers, A H L F, 1883 Excavations at Caesar's Camp near Folkestone, *Archaeologia*, **47**, 439, 456, 464, and Pl. XX, No. 35

Platt, C P S, and Coleman-Smith, R, (eds) 1996 *Excavations in Medieval Southampton 1953-69*, **2**, Leicester

Pritchard, F, 1991 Finger rings, in G Egan and F Pritchard 1991, 325-35

RCHME 1985 *An Inventory of Archaeological Sites and Churches in Northampton*, Royal Commission on Historical Monuments of England

Riddler, I, 1995 in R Ivens *et al* 1995, 392

Saunders, P, (ed) 2001 *Salisbury Museum Medieval Catalogue, Part 3*, Salisbury and South Wiltshire Museum

Schofield, J, 1994 Medieval and Later Towns, in B Vyner (ed) 1994, 195-214

Serjeantson, D, 2006 Birds: Food and a mark of status, in C M Woolgar *et al* (eds) 2006, 131-147

Shaw, M, 1985 Excavations on a Saxon and medieval site at Black Lion Hill, *Northamptonshire Archaeol*, **20**, 113-138

Shaw, M, and Steadman, S, 1993 *Archaeological Evaluation at St. John's Street, Northampton, 1990*, Northamptonshire Archaeology report

Shaw, M, and Steadman, S, 1994 Life on the Medieval Backstreet: Archaeological Excavations at Swan Street, Northampton, 1989, *Northamptonshire Archaeol*, **25**, 127-159

Smithson, V, 1996 Post-medieval Bone Objects, in R P J Jackson and T W Potter 1996, 668-670

Soden, I, 1998 *St. Peters Walk, Northampton: Archaeological excavations on Woolmonger Street, 1994-7*, Northamptonshire Archaeology report

Soden, I, 1998-9 A story of urban regeneration: Excavations off St. Peter's Walk, Northampton 1994-7, *Northamptonshire Archaeol*, **28**, 61-127

Soden, I, 2002 *Pettifer Estates Ltd, Former Burgess Site, St. Peter's Way, Northampton: Archaeological Mitigation Strategy*, Northamptonshire Archaeology report

Soden, I, 2005 *A written scheme of investigation for pre-emptive archaeological excavation of land at Kingswell Street and Woolmonger Street, Northampton*, Northamptonshire Archaeology

Spall, C A, and Toop, N J, (eds) 2005 *Blue Bridge Lane & Fishergate House, York. Report on Excavations*, Archaeological Planning Consultants (APC), Monog, **1**

Spall, C, 2005 Medieval building material, in C Spall and N J Toop (eds) 2005

Spoerry, P, 2002 Medieval pottery production, marketing and the growth of urban forms and functions: evidence from Ely, *Proceedings Cambridgeshire Antiq Soc*, **91**, 152

Stace, C, 1997 *New Flora of the British Isles*, 2nd edition, Cambridge University Press

Starkey, D, Ramston, J, and Reid, C, (eds) 2000, *England's Sea Fisheries: The Commercial Sea Fisheries of England and Wales since 1300*, Chatham Publishing, London

Thorne, A, 2003 Excavation of a medieval tenement at Deene End, Weldon, Northamptonshire, *Northamptonshire Archaeol*, **31**, 105-124

Turner, G J, 1907 The minority of Henry III: Part II, *Trans Royal Historical Soc*, 3rd series, Vol **1**, 205-62

von Becker, C, 1980 *Untersuchungen an Skelettresten von Haus- und Wildschweinen aus Haithabu, Neumunster*, Karl Wachholtz Verlag

von den Driesch, A, and Boessneck, J, 1974 Kritische Anmerkungen zue Widerristhöhenberechnung aus Langenmassen vor-und frühgeschichlicher Tierknochen, Saugetierkundliche, *Mitteilungen*, **22**, 325-348

Vyner, B, (ed) 1994, *Building on the Past*, The Royal Archaeological Institute

Ward-Perkins, J B, 1993 *London Museum Medieval Catalogue 1940*, reprinted 1993

West, B A, 1982 Spur development: recognising caponised fowl in archaeological material, in B Wilson *et al* (eds) 1982, 255-261

Williams, J H, 1978 Excavations at Greyfriars Northampton 1972, *Northamptonshire Archaeol*, **13**, 96-160

Williams, J H, 1979 *St. Peter's Street, Northampton: Excavations 1973-1976*, Northampton Development Corporation, Archaeol Monog, **2**

Williams, J H, 1982a Northampton's Medieval Parishes, *Northamptonshire Archaeol*, **17**, 74-84

Williams, J H, 1982b *Saxon & Medieval Northampton*, Northampton Development Corporation

Williams, J H, and Shaw, M, 1981 Excavations in Chalk Lane, Northampton, 1975-1978, *Northamptonshire Archaeol*, **16**, 87-135

Wilson, B, Grigson, C, and Payne, S, (eds) 1982 *Ageing and Sexing Animal Bones from Archaeological Sites*, British Archaeological Reports, British Series, **109**

Woolgar, C M, Sergeantson, D, and Waldron, T, (eds) 2006 *Food in Medieval England: Diet and Nutrition*, Oxford University Press

Woolgar, C M, 2000 'Take this penance now, and afterwards the fare will improve': seafood and late medieval diet, in D Starkey *et al* (eds) 2000, 36-44

A medieval potters' tenement at Corby Road, Stanion Northamptonshire

by

PAT CHAPMAN, PAUL BLINKHORN and ANDY CHAPMAN

with contributions by
Karen Deighton and David Leigh

SUMMARY

Excavation by Northamptonshire Archaeology of a house plot at Corby Road, Stanion uncovered a cluster of pits within a potters' tenement containing waster dumps. A total of 600kg of pottery comes from over 200 vessels. Glazed jugs were the major product but jars and bowls are also present. This assemblage adds significantly to the understanding of the Lyveden/Stanion pottery industry, which supplied much of medieval Northamptonshire and parts of the surrounding counties with its more utilitarian table ware. There are also smaller quantities of glazed roof ridge tiles, a few with crests, and ceramic kiln furniture.

There were two distinct phases of pottery production, dating to the second half of the 14th century, and the second half of the 15th century. The evidence comes from a combination of the dating of associated pottery of other types and typology. It is now certain that the production of Stanion B ware was considerably longer-lived than first anticipated. It has been regarded as ending in the 14th century, but the evidence from this site shows that production was still taking place in the later years of the 15th century. It would therefore seem appropriate now to give the tradition a chronology of AD 1200-1500.

The evidence also indicates a revision of the Lyveden/Stanion D ware, generally regarded as starting around AD 1400 to replace the B ware, based on the evidence from Lyveden. However, wasters of both fabrics have been found at Stanion in all the pit groups. It is suggested that it should now be dated AD 1350-1500, and may even have started earlier.

It is notable that none of the kiln waste from this site is wheel-thrown, it has all been coil-built and finished on a turntable. The Stanion potters were very late in taking up the wheel, and the evidence from this site indicates that it was in the early 16th century at the earliest.

A review and a gazetteer of other archaeological work in Stanion, including details of a kiln excavated in 1990, is also provided.

INTRODUCTION
Pat Chapman

Northamptonshire Archaeology carried out a developer-funded excavation of a new house plot at 2 Corby Road, Stanion, Northamptonshire, within a plot running between Little Lane, to the east, and Corby Road, to the west (Figs 1 and 2: NGR SP 9145 8701).

An evaluation trench had been excavated in 1993 (Soden 1993). The northern end of this trench had located the well-preserved remains of a late medieval stone building, and to the south there was a cluster of pits that evidently contained large quantities of wasters from a nearby kiln, although the pits were not excavated at the time.

This area was shown as an empty plot on a map of 1730 (Soden 1993, 6, NRO map 4090), indicating that it probably had not been disturbed since the pottery industry came to an end at the end of the 15th century.

When a planning application was submitted for the building of a house (Planning Application Reference: 00/00444/OUT), the plot was assessed by the then Northamptonshire County Council Historic Environment Team (NCCHET) as containing archaeology of national importance. The mitigation strategy called for the pre-emptive excavation of the house plot, which lay over the identified cluster of waster pits, and the *in situ* preservation of all other archaeological deposits (*Brief for Archaeological Recording Action* issued by NCCHET on 15th February 2002). The excavation of the house plot was carried out in December 2002, often in very poor weather conditions. Given the time constraints, work focussed on the recovery of waster assemblages from the central group of pits (Fig 3). Subsequently, a watching brief was carried out along the northern margin of the site during groundworks for the provision of an access road, to ensure that the underlying archaeological deposits were subject to minimal disturbance.

TOPOGRAPHY AND GEOLOGY

The site is level, but the ground slopes gently away to the south and east. The underlying drift geology has been mapped as Till overlying a solid geology of Inferior Oolite rock (BGS 2003).

ACKNOWLEDGEMENTS

The excavations were carried out on behalf of Mr A Taylor during December 2002 and were managed by Andrew Mudd. The fieldwork team, directed by Simon Carlyle, was Adrian Burrow, Nathan Flavell, Mick Garside, Giles MacFarland, Rebecca Pullen, David Stacey and Jo Young,

Fig 1 Location plan

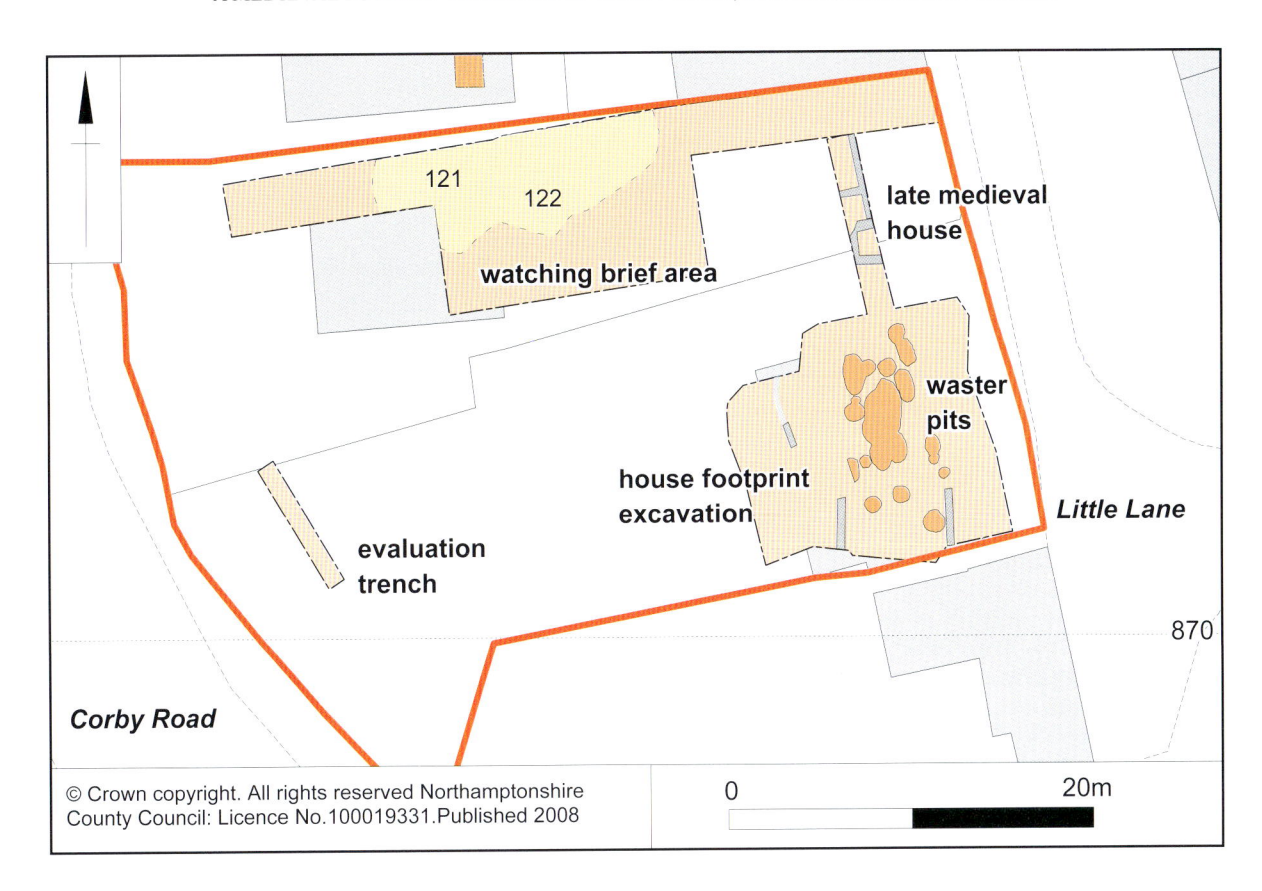

Fig 2 General plan of excavated area

who all achieved a great deal through the poor weather conditions at the time which hampered the excavation. The watching brief was carried out by David Leigh.

Given the exceptional quantity of pottery recovered, we would like to thank those individuals who freely volunteered their time to assist in the washing and

Fig 3 A display of jugs and a bowl from the waster dumps at 2 Corby Road, Stanion

reconstruction of the pottery. These included members of the Young Archaeologists Club organised through the Upper Nene Archaeological Society; Paul Thompson and Alex Thompson (née Thorne) who organised volunteers through the Herbert Art Gallery and Museum, Coventry, and volunteers organised by Ian Meadows. The logistics of keeping the material in order and under control was organised by Pat Chapman.

The post-excavation programme was managed by Andy Chapman. The fieldwork analysis and the report were prepared by Pat Chapman, who has also analysed the roof tile and kiln furniture. Paul Blinkhorn analysed and reported on the extremely large and important pottery assemblage. Andy Chapman has reviewed the available archaeological evidence for the Stanion pottery industry. The illustrations are by Andy Chapman and Carol Simmonds, and the pottery photographs are by Andy Chapman. The costs of post-excavation analysis have been met by Northamptonshire Archaeology.

Given the lack of a sufficient developed-funded budget to cover the costs of post-excavation analysis for this exceptionally large quantity of pottery, it has not been possible to have the vessels drawn. Instead a photographic archive has been compiled providing side views of the largely reconstructed vessels. Each image includes a scale bar and the pottery reference number. These images form an appendix and a full set is also included on the CD attached to this volume.

THE STANION POTTERY INDUSTRY
Andy Chapman

This review of the Stanion pottery industry draws on an overview of the pottery industry of the Rockingham Forest by Glenn Foard (1991) and the single previously published kiln (Bellamy 1983). In addition, it uses unpublished notes and records compiled by Burl Bellamy (and loaned to Graham Cadman) and the site records compiled by Graham Cadman during his excavation of another kiln in 1990. More recent evaluations carried out by Northamptonshire Archaeology as developer-funded projects, in addition to the site being reported, are also summarised. A new gazetteer listing the archaeological interventions on and around the known production centre, largely lying at the northern end of the historic village between Little Lane and Corby Road, is also provided.

THE POTTERS' TENEMENTS AT STANION

In 1086 two holdings are recorded in Stanion. One was part of the manor of Brigstock, an important royal estate, and this probably corresponds to the post-medieval Nether Hall manor (Foard 1991, 17). The second was held by Edwin from the Bishop of Coutances, and this must be the same as Upper Hall manor, which was independent of the Brigstock manor. The evidence for pottery production in Stanion has all come from the northern half of the medieval village, and all from tenements of Upper Hall manor, which mainly lay at the northern end of the village (see Foard 1991, fig 4).

It is also significant that the Upper Hall manor held a large area of woodland that no doubt supplied the fuel for the potters' kilns, while the woodland belonging to the Brigstock manor supplied the charcoal burners who provided the fuel for the iron industry (Foard 1991, 17).

It has been argued by Foard (1991, 17 & fig 4) that post-medieval tenements shown on the map of 1730 correspond closely to the layout of the medieval village (Fig 1). What the 1730 map depicts is a series of tenement plots fronting onto High Street, with further tenements at the northern end of the village, between Little Lane and Corby Road. Here there were cottages fronting onto Little Lane to the east and open plots to the west.

The Ordnance Survey map of 1900 shows much the same pattern but with the appearance of some new houses extending back from the frontages. It is only more recently that there has been further infilling within the historic core, as well as new estates that have covered the former fields to the west of both High Street and Corby Road, with more limited expansion onto the fields to the east of High Street and a minor expansion to the south (Fig 1). At the northern end of the village it has been the building of new houses and the sub-division of the plots between Little Lane and Corby Road that has led to the disturbance of the long abandoned kilns and waster dumps that had lain undisturbed in the former gardens and orchards (Fig 4).

DISCOVERY AND INVESTIGATION

From the beginning of the expansion of new housing in Stanion in the 1930s evidence began to slowly emerge that Stanion had been an important pottery producing centre from the 13th to 15th centuries, like Lyveden, four miles to the east.

A series of rescue excavations on deserted crofts at Lyveden in the late 1960s to early 1970s provided much information about the kilns, workshops, homes and the products of the Lyveden potters (Steane 1967, Bryant and Steane 1969, Steane 1971, Steane and Bryant 1975). As a result, Lyveden came to be viewed as the centre of the local medieval pottery industry, when the number of kilns that appear to have been functioning in Stanion would suggest that it was in fact Stanion that was the dominant production centre (Foard 1991). However, the comparable crofts at Stanion lay within the living village, so it has not been possible to investigate the industry in a systematic manner. Instead, the evidence from Stanion has accrued on an *ad hoc* basis, largely comprising salvage and rescue digs on active building sites as new houses were constructed on the plots between Little Lane and Corby Road, and on other nearby sites. In some cases, see below, this has meant that only an hour or two was available to grab a collection of vessels, often already disturbed from waster dumps, with perhaps the partial investigation of evident kilns visible in the sides of house construction trenches. There has been no opportunity to look at the arrangement of even a single tenement. To compound the problems of the lack of proper opportunities for fieldwork investigation, even a quick 'smash and grab' raid could produce substantial quantities of pottery, and there has been a lack of resources to enable much of this material to be even partially analysed and published.

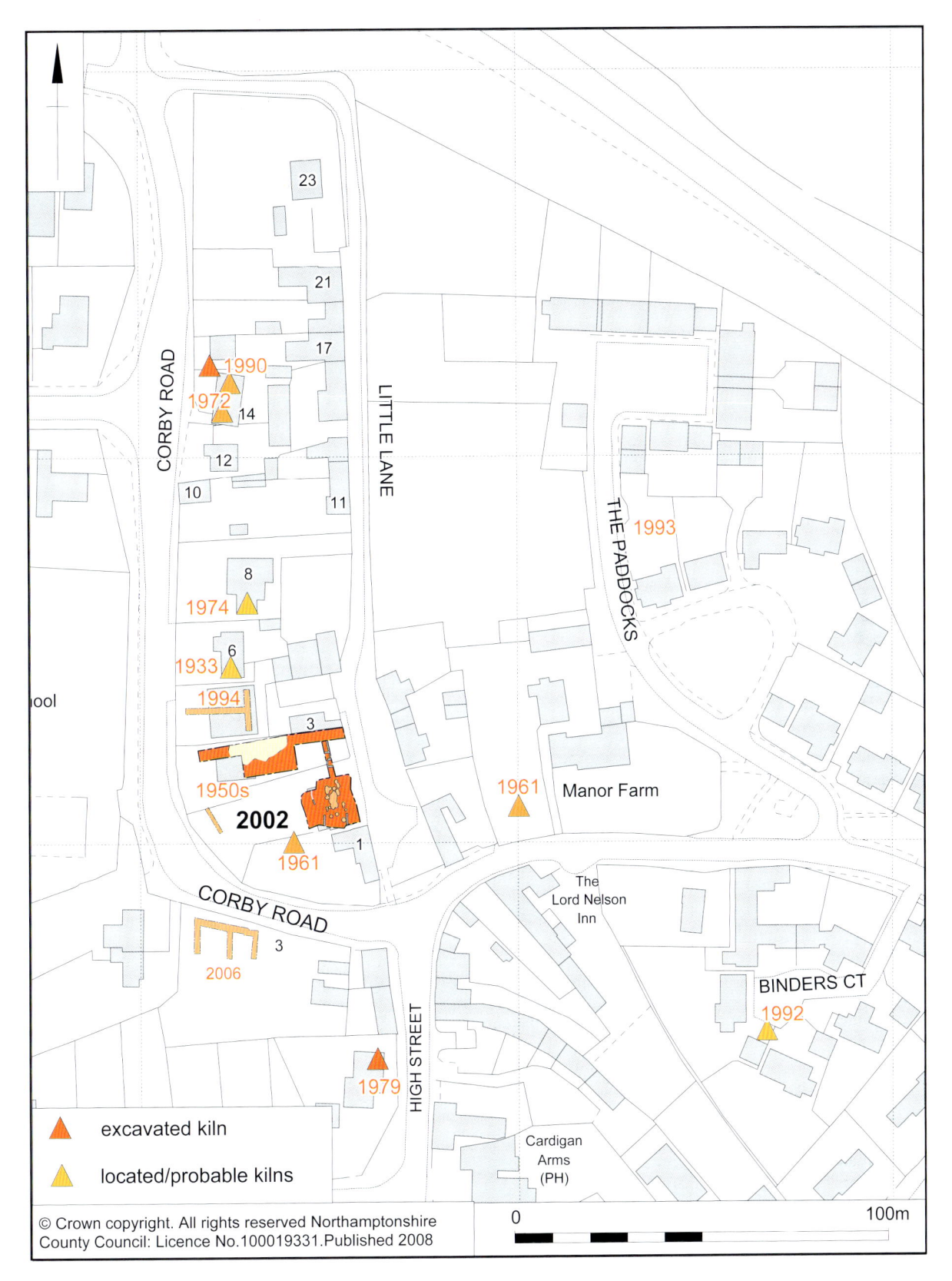

Fig 4 The potters' tenements at Stanion, showing all archaeological interventions

The information concerning the Stanion pottery industry is therefore a collection of incomplete, and sometimes uncertainly located, fragments of ground evidence accompanied by large quantities of largely unanalysed pottery, and all spread over some 70 years of sporadic work, as listed below and summarised in the gazetteer (Fig 4).

6 CORBY ROAD, 1933

The story begins in 1933 when the *Kettering Leader* carried an article entitled 'Roman Kiln and Ancient Pottery Unearthed'. 'Remains of ancient pottery and a kiln...have been discovered at Stanion by workmen building a bungalow. The men... for a week have been excavating in an orchard near the Corby Road at Stanion in order to lay the foundations of the bungalow... when only a few inches below the surface huge quantities of broken pottery... were found. Later in a corner of the foundations huge stones burnt red by fire were found in the ground.' The Roman remains were, of course actually medieval, and Burl Bellamy identifies this site as 6 Corby Road, a bungalow built by Joseph Streather of Corby.

2 LITTLE STREET (SP 91428702), 1950s

Pottery was recovered in the mid-1950s, and it was suspected that there were kilns in the garden (Foard 1991, Appendix 1, information from Mr Thompson, 2 Little Street). This reference is to the same property as the subject of this present article, where the excavated waster pits further indicate the presence of kilns, presumably on the western part of the site.

MANOR HOUSE GARDEN (SP 91508701), 1961
1 CORBY ROAD (SP 91448700), 1961

The Ordnance Survey record cards record a kiln in the garden at 1 Corby Road and a kiln seen in a sewer trench in the Manor House garden (Foard 1991).

14 CORBY ROAD, 1972, J R FOX

In November 1972 about 4cwt (c200 kg) of medieval pottery, mostly wasters, were rescued from two houses built on an orchard plot (Fox 1975). Part of a kiln stoke hole and flue, filled with wasters, was excavated. Four courses of dry stone wall remained, but much of the structure had already been destroyed by the house foundations.

The material recovered covered at least six distinctive pottery styles as summarised below by Fox (1975). The earlier material was the course hand-made 'Stanion wares', but without the applied white strips typically of Lyveden/Stanion pottery. The later medieval wares were wheel made and fired to a high temperature. They included three sizes of jugs, typically pear-shaped with sagging bases. The smallest had rod handles with stab holes; the medium had plain strap handles, and the largest wide multiple grooved handles. Large slashed bibs of cream slip were applied to the body and covered with green glaze speckled a bright green. The lowest level of ash produced a white iron-free ware, resembling Stamford ware. The material also included some later material, including cisterns with several patterns of bung hole, fish dishes, and flat roof tiles and crested ridge tiles. A report on the later aspects of the pottery was published by Bellamy (1983, 159-61).

8 CORBY ROAD?, 1974, J HADMAN

John Hadman and Steve Upex were given half an hour to retrieve what they could from the site during the building of a house extension. It was not an excavation, more of a smash and grab (Hadman pers comm). They recovered numerous wasters, some pretty complete, and remains of a kiln or kilns were evident (Hadman 1974). Burl Bellamy records the location as 8 Corby Road, a house that had been built in 1938. No account of this material has been published.

HIGH STREET (SP 91468695), 1979, B BELLAMY

Burl Bellamy carried out a rescue operation over a weekend when a building site on the west side of High Street had been stripped down to the limestone bedrock, with building due to commence the following week (B Bellamy pers comm). A kiln was fully excavated (Bellamy 1983). It had been constructed within a vertical-sided hole cut 0.6m into the limestone bedrock, which formed the walls of the kiln. The kiln chamber was 3.4m long by 2.3m wide, with an oval pedestal, 1.6m long by 1.16m wide, built of limestone blocks with a rubble and earth core (Fig 5). In front of the pedestal there was a central flue arch support, and the flues were 0.50m and 0.55m wide defining this as a parallel flue kiln. On the northern side the flue had been narrowed before its first firing by the insertion of dry stone walling. After a period of firings the kiln was lined with limestone slabs pitched against the walls, and after a period of ash accumulation a new lining was added at a higher level. The extant flue arch support had also replaced an earlier support. The kiln as found was completely filled with ash at the rear of the chamber, with this deposit sloping down towards the stoke hole, and at least 27 separate layers of black, red, grey and white ash were observed.

The pottery was recovered from the kiln and the stoke pit and it is all likely to be wasters from vessels fired in this kiln. The main fabric was buff/pink or grey with oolitic inclusions and sometimes ironstone (within the Northampton T2 range). Other fabrics included a hard, white iron free fabric often carrying a bright green glaze, and a shelly fabric similar to Lyveden ware. The vessels included both coil built and wheel-made jugs, decorated with white painted slip bands or white applied strips and pads with grid stamps, and an olive green glaze (Bellamy 1983, fig 3). There were also skillets with plain pulled handles, and a range of bowls and jars. In addition there were green-glazed crested ridge tiles, and four floor tile fragments (Bellamy 1983, figs 3 & 4).

THE EXCAVATION OF A KILN AT 17 LITTLE LANE, 1990

THE EXCAVATION

In 1990 a rescue excavation was carried out by Graham Cadman of the Curatorial Section of the Northamptonshire Archaeological Unit during redevelopment of the property at 17 Little Lane (NGR: 9143 8713. Site Code: 17LL). The following description is drawn from the site records, which the excavator has made freely available to the author. Graham Cadman was assisted in the excavation by the late John Hartigan, Christine Addison and Gill Johnston. An initial assessment of the pottery was provided by Paul Blinkhorn, see below, who also described and published the pottery bird whistles (Blinkhorn 1991).

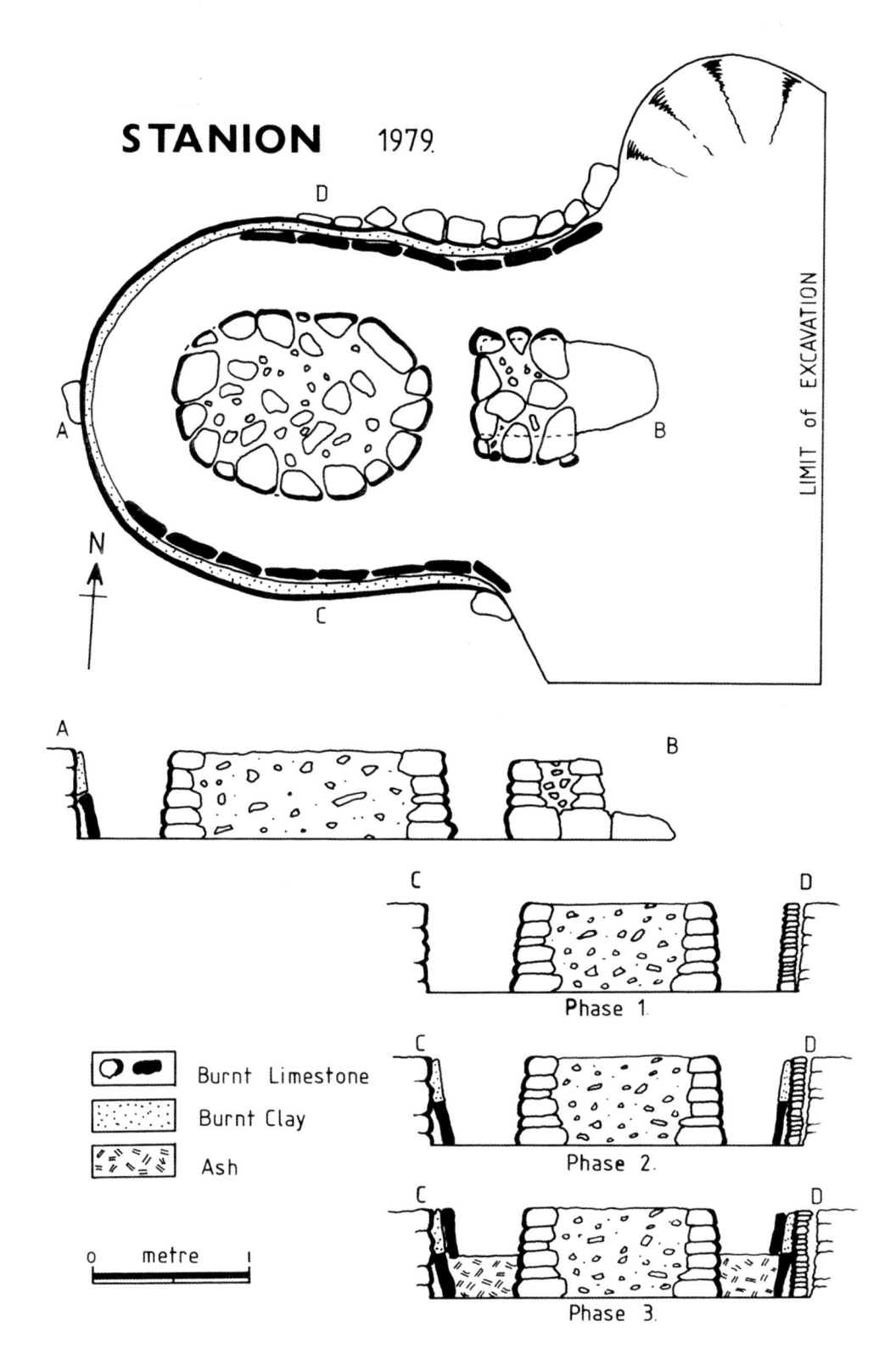

Fig 5 Plan and sections of kiln excavated by Bellamy in 1979 (from Bellamy 1983, fig 2)

On the first site visit the topsoil had been removed over the greater part of the property, to expose a natural of buff-coloured clay. Features were seen cutting into the natural and were excavated in difficult conditions over a period of some 11 days in late January and early February.

THE KILN

The kiln lay at the western end of the site against the southern property boundary, so that only the northern half of the kiln could be excavated (Figs 6-9). This was evidently a parallel-flue kiln built within a construction

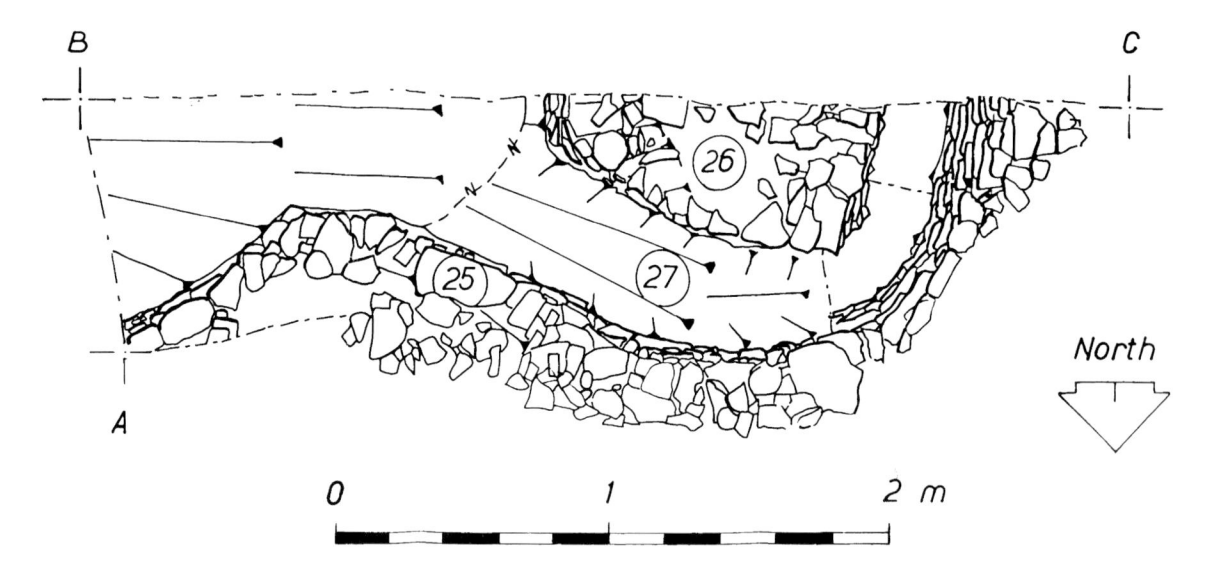

Fig 6 Plan of kiln excavated at 17 Little Lane by Cadman in 1990

Fig 7 The kiln at 17 Little Lane during excavation in 1990, looking west

pit, broadly similar to the kiln excavated by Bellamy (Fig 5). The kiln chamber was 2.5m long, lined with rough courses of dry stone walling in limestone (25), which at the west end of the kiln stood 0.95m high (Figs 6, 8 and 9). The lining continued eastward for at least 1.0m into the stoke pit. The pedestal (26) was 1.2m long, with a rubble and clay core faced with coursed limestone the same as the chamber lining. The flue was from 0.4-0.5m wide. To the north it contained lenses of red-orange-black clay-sand-ash accumulated through a succession of firings, while to the west the fill clean clay had been a deliberate infilling of this end prior to the first firing.

The kiln chamber and stoke pit was filled with tumbled limestone in a clay matix, from the kiln superstructure, and above this there was a thick layer of clay (Fig 9).

THE DITCHES

A length of ditch (F5), 1.0m wide by 0.50m deep, had been infilled with kiln debris, probably from the excavated kiln, although there was no stratigraphic relationship. The upper fill was of grey-black silty clay, containing much ash, presumably largely debris from kiln firings.

Cut into the top of the clay infill above the collapsed kiln superstructure, there was a gully (F2), which contained quantities of dumped pottery, evidently from another nearby kiln in use at a later date. Towards the southern side of the area at the eastern end of the property

Fig 8 The excavated kiln, showing the coursed limestone lining of the chamber and pedestal

Fig 9 The kiln, looking south, showing rubble fill in section

an 8.0m length of gully (F1), also aligned west to east, was probably a continuation of the same feature. It had a U-shaped profile and was 0.60m wide by 0.35m deep. The fill of the gully contained large amounts of closely-packed dumped pottery, although whether this was a backfill or a hardcore to assist drainage was unclear.

The western end of the site had not been fully stripped, and the ground surface sloped gently up and was higher than the adjacent properties. This may have been the remnant of a low bank adjacent to the west end of the plot, made up of topsoil and much pottery.

The excavations produced a total of 21 archive boxes of pottery (including roof and floor tile fragments), estimated to weigh 4cwt (c 200kg).

THE POTTERY ASSEMBLAGE FROM 17 LITTLE LANE
Paul Blinkhorn

In 1990 Paul Blinkhorn prepared an assessment of the pottery assemblage and recommended that full analysis and publication should be carried out. Unfortunately, no funding was available and the only outcome was the publication of a note describing the exceptional bird whistle pots (Blinkhorn 1991). Below we provide a summary of the assemblage extracted from that unpublished assessment report.

FEATURE (F5)

A very large group (c 5 boxes). The initial impression is that it was from a different kiln to the material found in Features 1 and 2. The fabric is quite dissimilar, being the coil-built oolitic B-type ware, having a heavier tempering of white ooliths, with moderate amounts of rounded and angular ironstone, up to 10mm. This material is usually dated to the 13th century (eg Steane and Bryant 1975, 75). The range of colours is usual, ie mainly orange or dark grey.

Some 75-80% of the assemblage comprises jugs, bowls, tiles and jars. There are no bifid rims. A few sherds of the white sandy fabric and the buff-orange oolitic wheel-thrown ware are present, but the vast majority of the vessels are coil built, and, in the case of jugs, show obvious differences in form to the jugs in the other fabrics. They are generally much larger, and although there are a few of the grooved strap handles (one slashed), the vast majority are thicker and heavier with an ovoid cross-section, decorated with single shallow thumb groove and a single line of stab marks running longitudinally down the centre. There is also a single pipkin/skillet handle in a similar fabric with the same stabbed decoration.

It is also worthy of note that there are only two sherds with geometric slip decoration (overall scheme uncertain), as this usually appears to be the commonest form of decoration on coil-built jugs, with all the other vessels having a patchy green glaze, and apart from a single vessel with a perfunctory applied slip on the shoulder, no applied plastic decoration or stamping occurs.

The jars and bowls have the usual forms of body and rim profile for Lyveden/Stanion ware, but are made in the jug fabric, and many are glazed. This is most unusual, as these vessels only usually occur in the shelly limestone A fabric and are unglazed. There were two glazed jars in this B fabric at West Cotton, one of which had the quite soft, ironstone-rich fabric found here (Blinkhorn in press).

Perhaps 20-25% of the material consists of coarse, conical pipe-like vessels with flat bases, which were probably kiln spacers.

A single large base sherd from a Brill/Boarstall-type jug was amongst this material.

FEATURE (F1)

The fill of this feature contained many fragments of wasters, apparently with a high degree of reconstructablility. The fabric appears to be the Lyveden D type, ie wheel-thrown vessels with oolith tempering, although with a fair degree of variation in colour, hardness and inclusions. The majority of the sherds are of an orange-buff fabric, with a grey or orange core, and a sparse tempering of fine white ooliths, < 1mm, with an occasional piece of crushed limestone, up to 5mm.

A few vessels occur in a soft, pure white fabric, a soft grey, and a hard purplish brown, with the latter having no ooliths in the temper, merely a very few pieces of angular limestone.

Many of the vessels are glazed green, but only on the top part, with most having only a few patches or splashes on the shoulders, with 'runs' down to the lower body. A few vessels have patches of white slip under the glaze, although none have any sort of geometric pattern which is typical of vessels from the earlier period of the industry. The majority of the vessels appear to be jugs, with the rim/handle count suggesting around 10 to 15 vessels present, with the predominant form appearing to be globular, with simple strap handles, which are either plain, stabbed or longitudinally grooved, with some having the latter two techniques employed.

The rim forms suggest that a fairly large number of jars are present, as were fragments of kiln spacers, a bung-hole from a cistern and a few fragments of glazed roof tiles.

FEATURE (F2)

A broadly similar assemblage to that from ditch (F1), but more fragmentary. There appears to be a lower proportion of jars and a far larger proportion of roof tiles. There are a few fragments from the neck, handle and rim of a jug in a white sandy fabric very similar to Stamford ware, with patches of thick yellowish-green glaze, and a few sherds of a similar pinkish fabric with no visible inclusions. There are also about a dozen quite thick sherds from the base of a vessel in a very soft, sandy, orange-pink fabric, also with no visible inclusions except for a large piece of angular red ironstone, 10mm. Three bird whistles in a similar, although slightly harder fabric were also found in this feature.

SUMMARY AND DISCUSSION

It would seem apparent that the excavated pottery came from two distinct phases of production.

The earlier material is probably derived from the excavated kiln. Within this group the glazed jars and bowls are quite rare, although a few are known from Lyveden (Steane 1967, figs 3a-3e, Bryant and Steane 1969, fig 5c). The jugs are of the normal coil construction and form, but there is none of the usual form of slip and/or stamp decoration which appear to be virtually standard for jugs of this type, as at the kiln excavated by Bellamy (1983) and as in the assemblage from West Cotton, Raunds (Blinkhorn in press).

The published material recovered from the adjacent property, 14 Corby Road (Fox 1974 and Bellamy 1983), would suggest that the kilns on this property may have been the source for the wheel-thrown vessels, Lyveden D type, recovered from ditches (F1) and (F2), with the assemblages sharing such common features as bifid rims, and a lack of slip decoration on the glazed jugs. It is difficult to be certain of a date for this material, but one of post-1400 can be suggested by association. Wheel-thrown Lyveden/Stanion wares are generally dated to the 15th century at the kiln sites (eg Steane and Bryant 1975, 91), and West Cotton, Raunds has very little of the material with the latest coin date coming from the end of the 14th century (Chapman in press).

The bird whistles are of considerable interest, as only one other example of this type is known from an English source (Pearce and Vince 1988, 128, no.210), although similar vessels are more well know on the continent, but usually with an anthropomorphic form rather than as miniature jugs (*c*50mm high) as in the case with these (J Hurst pers comm) (Figs 10 and 11). The whistle pots are in a hard, pink-buff slightly sandy fabric with rare white-grey ooliths and reddish-brown rounded ironstone (Blinkhorn 1991). Throwing marks and glaze splashes are visible on the inner surface, which has a patchy mottled green and yellow copper glaze. A tubular clay whistle, with a rectangular cut-out on the upper side, projects into the vessel through the side and ends just above the base. When the vessel is filled with water and air is blown down the stem, a warbling sound akin to bird song is produced. They are thought to have been used as both toys and hunting lures (Blinkhorn 1991).

It is striking that there is such a high proportion of conical vessels, which were probably kiln spacers, in the earlier pot deposits. These objects appear to be quite rare. There are two examples illustrated from kiln D1 at Lyveden (Adams in Bryant and Steane, 1969, 25 and figs 8c & d) and they were found associated with kiln D2 (Steane 1971, 35), but not with kilns G and J. No mention is made of kiln props by Bellamy (1983). The large number in this deposit at 17 Little Lane could be due to a high failure rate during firing, or even the failure of a kiln load consisting of these objects alone. It would seem probable that each potter made his own kiln furniture, but proof of this through fabric analysis is still needed.

RECENT EVALUATIONS

Apart from the excavation at 2 Corby Road reported in this article, Northamptonshire Archaeology has also carried out other evaluations in the area since 1990, although these have provided largely negative evidence.

In March 1992 a field south of Brigstock Road (SP 916869) was subject to fieldwalking and resistivity survey prior to development. A small mound in the western half of the area had a recent disturbance that had exposed sherds of medieval pottery, although no evident wasters. The above average resistance readings suggested the possible presence of a kiln, but this could not be confirmed by magnetometer survey due to the proximity of a modern sewer. This land, Binders Court, has since been developed for housing.

In March 1993 three trial trenches were excavated in a field to the north of Manor Farm (SP 915871), now occupied by The Paddocks housing development (Fig 3, 1993: Steadman 1993). It had not been possible to carry out geophysical survey because of the presence of concrete foundations and rubble from former farm buildings. No features or artefacts were recovered which might indicate the presence of nearby kilns.

In 1994 at 3 Little Lane (SP 91428703) a T-shaped evaluation trench failed to find any surviving archaeology (Blinkhorn 1994). It was concluded that the site had been levelled by terracing and that any former remains had been lost. This conclusion was supported by a comparison of the ground levels, which stood around 1.0m higher to the south within the property of 2 Corby Road.

More recently, in 2006 there was an evaluation to the immediate south of Corby Road (Fig 1, 2006: Foard-Colby 2006). This E-shaped pattern of trenches located a sparse scatter of cut features some of medieval date. However, only relatively small quantities of pottery were recovered. It would therefore appear that this particular property was never involved in pottery production despite the presence of kiln sites to both the north and south-east.

Fig 10 A pottery bird whistle from the kiln excavated in 1990 (scale 50mm)

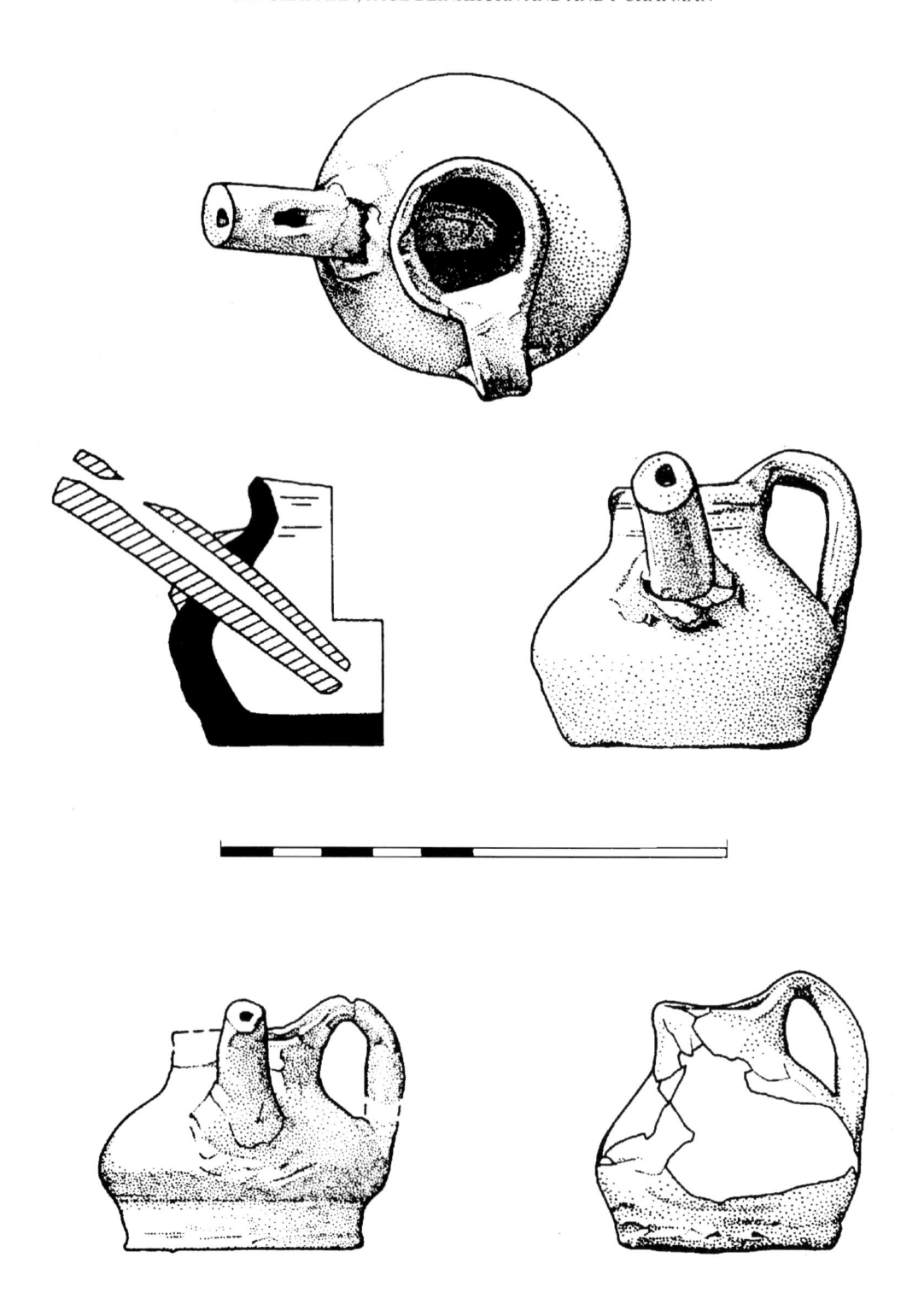

Fig 11 The pottery bird whistles from the kiln excavated in 1990 (scale 100mm)

A GAZETTEER OF ARCHAEOLOGICAL INTERVENTIONS

Date	Location	Summary	Publication
1933	6 Corby Road ?	Workmen report finding of numerous wasters and part of a kiln	*Kettering Leader*, 9 May 1933
1950s	2 Little Street (SP 91428702)	Pottery recovered and kiln(s) suspected in garden (see 2 Corby Road, 2002 and waster pits on same property).	Foard 1991 (house owner pers comm)
1961	1 Corby Road (SP 91448700)	Kiln in garden recorded by Seabourne.	Foard 1991 (OS record card SP98 NW23)
1961	Manor House garden (SP 91508701)	Kiln recognised by Seabourne in sewer laying, and sherds reported from gardens in vicinity.	Foard 1991 (OS record card SP98 NW20)
1972	14 Corby Road (SP 914871)	Salvage/Rescue by J R Fox when building work uncovered deposits. Limited excavation of stoke hole and flue of one kiln and another kiln suspected. Numerous wasters. Records and finds deposited with Northampton Museum.	Fox 1975 and Bellamy 1980, 159-61
1974	8 Corby Road ? (SP 914872 ?)	Salvage work by J Hadman and S Upex Numerous wasters and remains of kiln. Location identified by B Bellamy.	Hadman 1974
1979	High Street SP 91468695	Rescue excavation on west side of High Street following stripping of site for building. Kiln and numerous wasters.	Bellamy 1980
1990	17 Little Lane (SP 91438713)	Rescue excavation by G Cadman in advance of building work. Kiln and numerous wasters, including bird whistle pots.	Blinkhorn 1991 Chapman, Blinkhorn and Chapman 2008
1992	S. of Brigstock Road (SP916869)	Earthwork survey and resistivity survey. Possible kiln at SP91568695. Now built over	Masters *et al* 1992
1993	N. of Manor Farm (SP 915871)	Trial trenching before housing development. No evidence of former kilns or waster dumps	Steadman 1993
1994	3 Little Lane (SP 91428703)	Evaluation by P Blinkhorn for NA in advance of new house. No evidence of former kilns or waster dumps, but site had been truncated.	Blinkhorn 1994
2002	2 Corby Road	Excavation by S Carlyle for NA in advance of new house. Group of waster pits.	Chapman, Blinkhorn and Chapman 2008
2006	3 Corby Road	Evaluation by A Foard-Colby for NA in advance of new house. Archaeology survived, but no evidence of former kilns or waster dumps	Foard-Colby 2006

THE EXCAVATED EVIDENCE
Pat Chapman

The excavated area was almost square, measuring 13.0m north-south by 13.9m east-west, 0.14ha, taking in the proposed house plot (Figs 12 and 13). The stone building within the northern end of the previous trial trench is also considered.

The area of the house plot was stripped by mechanical excavator to expose the intact archaeological deposits (Fig 13). The western side of the area, which was almost devoid of features, was stripped down to natural, while an adjacent area, which included two boundary walls, was left at a slightly higher level, and was not fully excavated. The area containing the waster pits was stripped to natural and the pits were excavated by hand. A small area of stratified deposits to the south-east was only partially investigated (Fig 13).

The natural substrate comprises bright orange yellow silty clay with occasional lenses of blue grey clay. The clay becomes more orange with depth and contains pieces of ironstone. The pit fills comprised grey brown

Fig 12 General view of site during excavation, looking south-east towards Little Lane

clay silts with occasional flecks of charcoal and small cobbles, with variations mentioned below.

CHRONOLOGY

A ditch running along the southern edge of the excavation probably marked the southern boundary to the tenement from the 13th century. In the 14th century this boundary was perhaps relocated slightly further to the south, perhaps to the present line, when a stone building was constructed, fronting onto Little Lane.

According to the dating of the pottery, the excavated group of waster pits fall into two periods, between 1350-1400 and 1450-1500, with the earlier group lying slightly to the east (Fig 14).

The stone building to the north, partially investigated in the 1993 evaluation, was probably broadly contemporary with the waster dumps, and had certainly been levelled by the late 16th century. A small clay dump in this area was of clean clay, perhaps prepared for potting.

To the west, two walls running north to south were probably boundary walls. They were certainly still in use in the 16th century, following the demise of the pottery industry, and may have been built to sub-divide the plot following the abandonment of the potters' tenement (Table 1).

Table 1: Site chronology

FEATURES	DATE
Southern plot boundary ditch	13th-14th centuries
Waster dump; early phase	1350-1400
Northern building	14th-16th centuries
Southern building	14th-16th centuries
Waster dump; later phase	1450-1500
Abandonment of potters' tenement Western boundary walls	16th century
Overlying soil horizons	16th to 18th centuries

The whole area was covered by soil layers containing a sparse scatter of post-medieval pottery dating from the 16th to 18th centuries. Part of the plot became an orchard, indicating it was left under grass rather than being a garden. In the 1990s the plot was divided into two, longitudinally, to permit the building of the new house on the southern half of the plot.

Fig 13 (opposite) Plan of excavated area

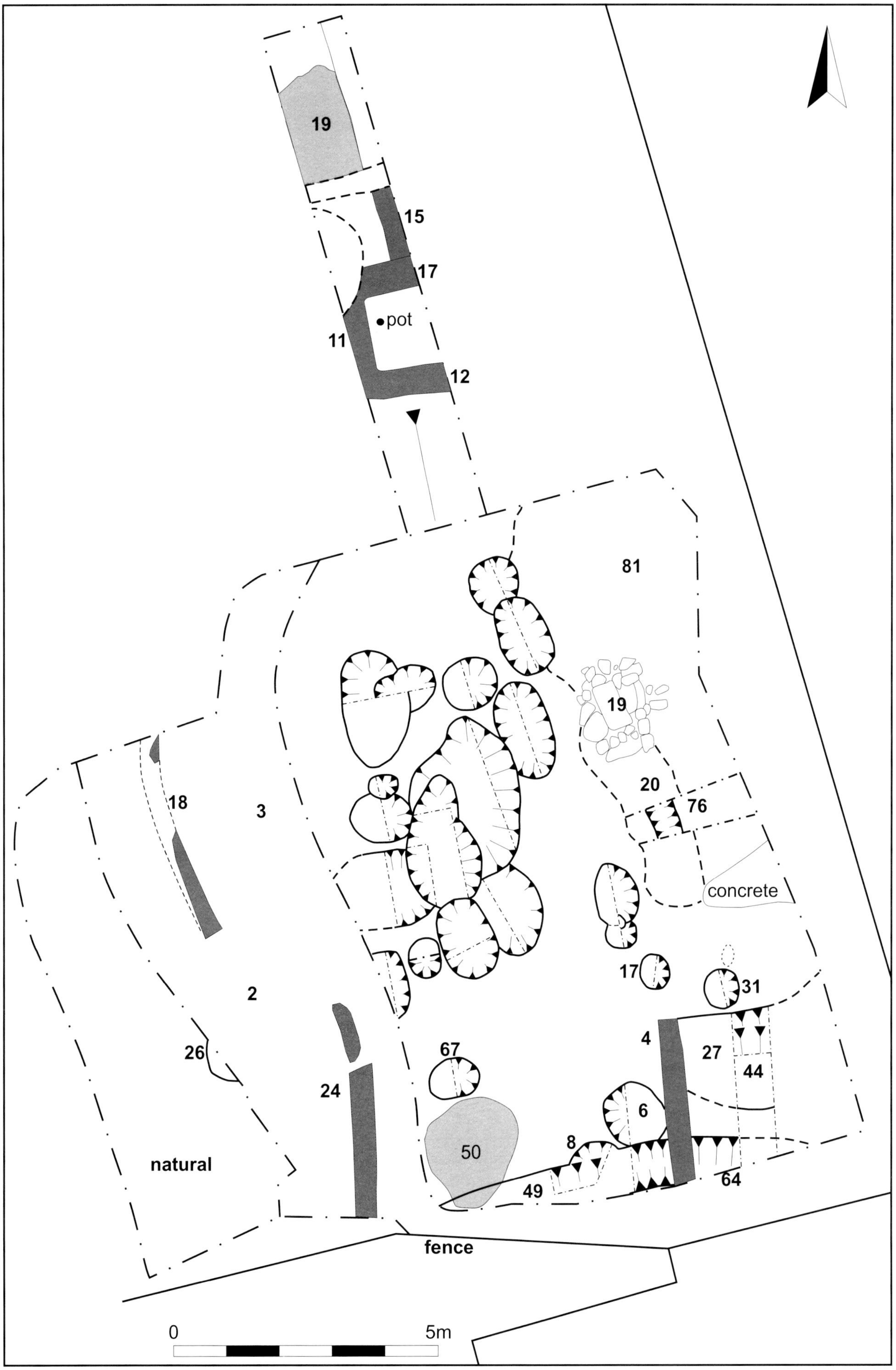
19
15
17
pot
11
12
81
19
20
76
18
3
concrete
17
31
2
4
27
26
67
44
24
6
8
50
natural
49
64
fence
0
5m

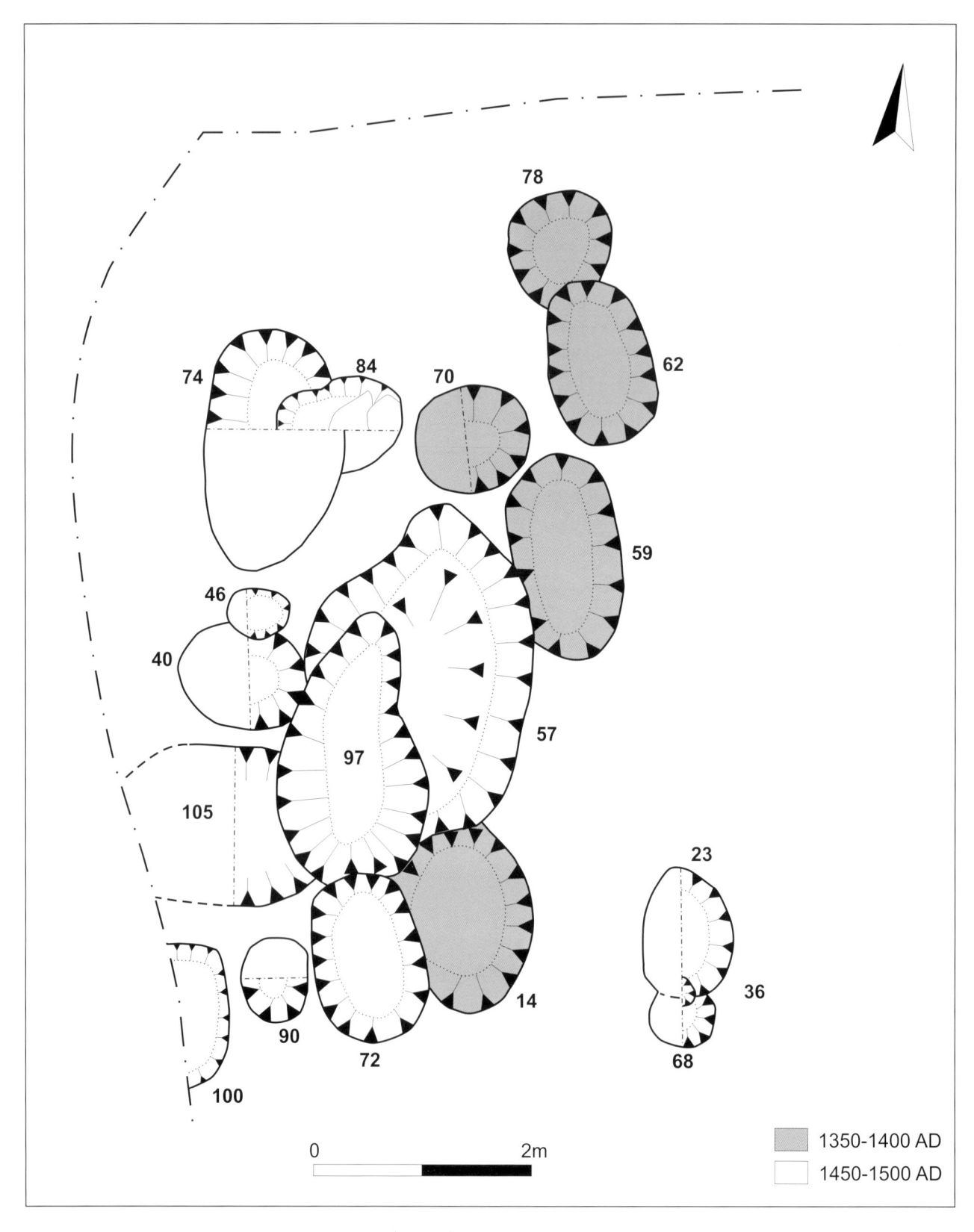

Fig 14 The central pit group

PLOT BOUNDARY

A ditch ran along the southern margin of the excavated area (Fig 13, 49/64). It was 0.55m deep, with a steep northern side and a flat bottom, and was perhaps slightly in excess of 1.80m wide, although the southern edge lay beyond the excavated area. To the west, the primary fill comprised grey blue clay containing frequent small limestone slabs and flecks of charcoal, along with a few sherds of Lyveden/Stanion B ware. To the east larger limestone slabs, up to 40mm by 30mm, within the primary fill were set upright on the base of the ditch, perhaps to consolidate the backfill before the construction of the overlying building. An upper ditch fill of brown clay silt (29) contained a fragment of a curfew. The presence of Lyveden/Stanion B ware indicates that the ditch was open in the 13th and into the 14th century, with the building perhaps dating to the 14th century. The close coincidence with the modern plot boundary might suggest that the early ditched boundary was perhaps relocated just a few metres to the south when the building was constructed.

THE EARLY PHASE OF WASTER PITS
(c 1350-1400)

A combination of stratigraphy and pottery dating indicate that there were two phases of waster pits, with the earlier group lying slightly to the east (Fig 14). The pits were steep-sided and flat-bottomed. Three were oval, between 1.50 and 1.75m long, and the other two were 1.0m in diameter. Pit 14, at 0.58m deep, was the deepest and contained over two thirds of the pottery assemblage from the earlier pits. These pits also contained small quantities of roof ridge tile and kiln furniture.

To the east of these pits, a layer of brown clay silt, (81), about 0.05m deep and containing charcoal flecks and occasional small fragments of limestone, covered an area c 7.0m long and 3.80m wide (Fig 13). It appeared to be an area of trampled natural contemporary with the pit complex.

PIT 14

This pit was 1.70m long by 1.00m wide and 0.58m deep, with very steep sides and a flat base (Fig 14). It was filled with a tumbled mass of waster pots, most of which had gone in as complete or near complete vessels, and the density would indicate that this material probably comprised the waste from the failure of no more than one or two kiln firings. They were perhaps particularly disastrous failures in which a larger than normal number of vessels were lost. The total weight of pottery was 200kg, and 15 vessels have been reconstructed from this group.

The initial dump of pottery lay against the south-western side of the pit, and included nine jugs within a grey and ashy charcoal-flecked fill (65) (Figs 16-18). A further dump of pottery included a number of almost complete vessels within a grey brown silty clay (13), including a small jug (Fig 34, SJ1) and a small internally glazed bowl with six pulled lips, which appears to be unique (Fig 34, SB1).

The range of vessels comprises jars, bowls and jugs of Lyveden/Stanion B ware giving a date of AD 1350-1400.

PIT 59

This shallow oval pit was 1.60m long, 0.97m wide and only 0.28m deep. There was relatively little pottery, only c21kg, within the fill of greyish brown clayey silt, but

Fig 15 Central pit group looking south, pit 59, bottom left, and pit 14, centre back

Fig 16 Pit F14 during excavation of primary pot deposit

Fig 17 Pit 14, with a deposit of largely complete jug wasters

Fig 18 Pit 14 with the primary deposit of pots *in situ*

some material had been removed from the surface when the pit had first been uncovered during the evaluation in 1993.

The vessels comprise largely jugs with some bowls, and the lack of jars would indicate a date of about AD 1350.

PIT 70

This circular pit, was 0.95m in diameter and 0.40m deep (Fig 14). Within the soft grey brown silty clay there was a cluster of medium sized limestone slabs on the north side. The small amount of pottery, 7.5kg, included a complete jug (Fig 29, ST12) and one with an unusual rouletted decoration (Fig 33, ST22). The Lyveden/Stanion A ware sherds, date the group to before AD 1400.

PITS 78 AND 62

To the north-east there were two intercutting pits (Fig 14). Pit 78 was 1.0m in diameter by only 0.10m deep, and contained 6.9kg of pottery, all predating AD 1400.

Pit 62 was 1.41m long by 0.85m wide and 0.17m deep. Despite being so shallow, it contained 50kg of pottery in brown silty clay. The bulk of the pottery comprises Lyveden/Stanion B ware jars and jugs and four dripping dish rimsherds, with a small amount of Lyveden/Stanion D ware and two large Lyveden/Stanion A ware rimsherds, which date the assemblage to before AD 1400. In particular, there are three jug rims with face masks, different to previously known examples from 13th-century contexts, which have very little parallel in the Lyveden/Stanion industry. If they are copies of, or inspired by other industries such as those in Norfolk, they would be dated to the 13th to 14th centuries (Blinkhorn this report) (Fig 22, ST28, 29, 30).

PIT 17

To the south-east of the main group of pits, this steep-sided, flat-bottomed pit was only 0.55m in diameter and 0.44m deep (Fig 13). There was very little pottery, only 106g, but this included three Lyveden/Stanion A ware sherds, which would date the pit to AD 1330-1400. In the upper fill there were frequent blocks of limestone, measuring 15-30mm long and up to 10mm thick.

THE LATER PHASE OF WASTER PITS
(c 1450-1500)

The second phase of waster deposition saw a concentration of larger, intercutting pits in the centre of the site (Fig 14). These contained just over half of the total pottery assemblage, and a majority of the roof tile and kiln furniture. There was also a scatter of smaller pits in the southern area (Fig 13).

PIT 57

This, the largest pit on the site, was 3.10m long by 1.30m wide and up to 0.65m deep, with steep sides and a relatively flat bottom (Fig 14).

The primary fill was a thin layer of grey blue clay, 0.08m thick, in the deepest part of the pit, suggesting that it had been left open for sometime, with water accumulating in the bottom. The secondary fill was c 0.25m thick, and contained only some pottery sherds.

The main dump of pottery, nearly 80kg, was in the upper fill (55) of dark grey clay silt, which also contained over 19kg of the ridge tile, nearly one third of all the assemblage.

Most of the assemblage comprises Lyveden/Stanion B ware jars, bowls and jugs in broadly similar proportions to those in pit 14. There are also some sherds of Lyveden/Stanion D ware. One sherd has part of an inscription '. . *naria*', extremely rare on medieval jugs, and there is a wider range of decorative techniques. This, in addition to a single sherd of Midland Purple ware, date this pit group to about the middle of the 15th century.

PIT 105

This was a shallow pit with indistinct edges, and the only pit with its long axis aligned east to west (Fig 14). It measured 1.41m long by 1.30m wide and 0.25m deep.

The primary brown clay fill was overlain by a thin band of dark grey brown clay silt, 0.03m thick, with dense comminuted charcoal. Only the upper fill (104), the usual grey brown clay, contained a very small amount of pottery, 2.4kg. It was cut on its eastern side by pit 97.

PIT 97

This pit, 2.20m long by 1.30m wide and 0.50m deep, had been cut into the fills of pits 57 and 105 (Fig 14). The primary fill (96) was soft loose ashy grey silt containing some pottery sherds. This was overlain by a thin layer of yellow brown silty sand, followed by soft dark grey clay silt (94), which contained most of one jug and was overlain by anther thin layer of yellow brown silty sand. The main fill (92) was a brown clay silt, which contained 61kg of pottery as well as some ridge tile and a near complete kiln prop.

The stratigraphic sequence suggests that this pit was not filled with wasters and sherds from only one or two kiln firing, as with pit 14, but with some initials odds and ends deposited at intervals wide enough apart for some silting to occur. The main act of deposition then followed.

The entire assemblage comprises jars, bowls and jugs in Lyveden/Stanion B wares, which would probably be dated to the second half of the 15th century, especially as this pit post-dates pit 57.

PIT 72

The final pit in the central sequence, cutting the end of pit 97, was 1.65m long by 1.25m wide and only 0.25m deep, with steep sides and a roughly flat bottom (Fig 14). Unlike the other pits, in which complete or at least large parts of single vessels had been deposited, the grey brown clay silt of this pit was packed with a dense mass of individual pottery sherds (Fig 19). It seems most likely that these were sherds from several previous kiln firings, which had probably lain for some time in surface waster dumps before being redeposited in this pit. It was not possible to reconstruct any of these vessels because of the mixed and fragmented state of the assemblage (Figs 14 and 19).

This is the largest assemblage of pottery of this later phase, at over 120kg, again mainly Lyveden/Stanion B ware jars, bowls and jugs, with a small amount of Lyveden/Stanion D ware sherds. There are also three fragments of face-masks, similar to those from pit 62. These are usually dated to the 14th century, in contrast to the rest of the pottery which is mid to late 15th century, but as the group contains redeposited material the face

Fig 19 Section of pit 72, showing the fill of re-deposited pottery sherds

masks may have been residual sherds from the earlier phase of activity. There was also 2.7kg of ridge tile, the second largest amount after pit 57, and the remains of a few kiln props.

PITS 84 AND 74

Pit 84 was 1.30m long by 0.86m wide and 0.98m deep, with near vertical sides. There were two large limestone blocks *c* 500mm by 300mm by 160mm, within the yellowish grey clay silt (Fig 14). It contained only 2.8kg of pottery and roof tile.

Pit 74 was also steep-sided, 2.10m long by 1.40m wide and 0.55m deep, cutting pit 84. The primary fill was dark grey silt containing comminuted charcoal. It was overlain by yellowish clay and a grey brown silty clay, which contained 9.5kg pottery and a little roof ridge tile.

As well as Lyveden/Stanion B and D ware jars, bowls and jugs, the presence of a sherd of Midland Purple and the only two bifid type jar rims from the excavation, date the assemblage to post AD 1450.

PITS 40 AND 46

Pit 40 was 1.12m long by 0.86m wide by 0.55m deep, with near vertical sides (Fig 14). It contained a small assemblage of pottery and roof ridge tile, including seven crests (Fig 25) and the largest amount of kiln furniture from any context.

Pit 46, which cut the northern edge of pit 40, was a small circular feature, 0.51m in diameter and only 0.36m deep. The fill contained lumps of blue grey clay near the base.

PIT 90

This shallow pit was *c* 0.70m in diameter by 0.14m deep, with a stony clay fill and very few pottery sherds.

PIT 100

Pit 100 was 1.30m wide and 0.55m deep with vertical sides. The western half was concealed by a later soil horizon. Both the primary and upper fills contained very little pottery, which is surprising as it was so close to the central pottery pit group.

PITS 36, 68 AND 23

The earliest feature in this group, pit 36, was 0.40m wide and 0.62m deep with steep sides (Fig 14). It had been cut by a circular pit, 68, 0.51m in diameter and 0.55m deep, with vertical sides. The final cut, pit 23, was 1.22m long by 0.81m wide and 0.44m deep, with steep sides into a concave base. There were occasional fragments of limestone and about 5kg of pottery in the fills, comprising mainly bowls.

PIT 67

Lying to the south of the main group, this was a circular pit, 0.86m in diameter but only 0.11m deep (Fig 13). There were lumps of blue grey clay within the brown silty clay and one large slab of limestone, and a few sherds of pottery.

PIT 6

Also lying to the south, this bowl-shaped pit was 1.21m

long by 0.99m wide and 0.36m deep (Fig 13). There were frequent pieces of limestone, 7mm to 20mm long, in the primary fill, which was overlain by a thin ashy band, containing comminuted charcoal, covered by a soft silty grey clay. There was very little pottery, mainly Lyveden/Stanion B ware and a single sherd of Cistercian ware, giving an end date in the late 15th century.

PIT 31

A very shallow pit, 0.64m diameter and only 0.008m deep (Fig 13).

Pit 26

This was a partially exposed waster pit west of the boundary walls (Fig 13). Pottery collected from the surface included the full profile of a pancheon.

Pit 8

A sub-circular hollow, [8], had been cut into the upper ditch fill. It was 2.30m long by 1.80m wide, but only 0.14m deep. The fill was blue grey clay with fragments of burnt stone and burnt clay and containing some Lyveden/ Stanion B ware pottery.

Burnt surface, (50)

To the south, and extending over the western edge of infilled boundary ditch, 49, there was an irregular burnt patch, c 2.00m by 1.80m (Fig 13, 50). The clay natural was burnt to a dark pinkish red, with the burning penetrating to a depth of 0.12m.

SOUTHERN BUILDING

The south-eastern corner of the excavated area was not fully excavated. The earliest feature was a large oval pit, 44 (Fig 13). It was up to 1.80m wide and perhaps up to 6.0m long, but the eastern end was not defined in plan, and 0.6m deep, with steep sides and a flat base. The primary fill was greenish brown clay silt, perhaps suggesting that it had been used as a cess pit. The secondary fill was soft brown clay silt, which was overlain by thin layer of yellow brown clay with blue grey lumps and small limestone cobbles. On the surface of this layer there was an area of burning, perhaps associated with use of an overlying building.

A rough limestone wall was built across the backfilled boundary ditch, 64, and also across the end of pit 44 (Fig 13, 4). The wall was 0.50m wide, built of roughly coursed angular limestone and survived up to five courses high at the northern end. A length of 3m length was uncovered, and it continued beyond the southern limit of excavation. The northern end was disturbed, and it is uncertain whether it was the original northern end or marked the survival of the wall only where it had subsided into the underlying pit fill. The absence of any return wall may suggest the latter. Part of the eastern wall face was scorched, and this face was abutted by a brown clayey layer containing fragments of limestone, (27), which may have been a remnant of a floor level, also preserved by subsidence of the underlying ditch fills.

It is therefore suggested that a small stone building, of unknown overall dimensions, had stood here during the 14th and 15th centuries, broadly contemporary with the usage of the nearby pits.

NORTHERN BUILDING

This building was partially exposed during the trial trench evaluation in 1993 (Fig 13) (Soden 1993). The plan is too incomplete to define the plan form and size, but it is likely that they formed the rear of a building fronting onto Little Lane. The walls were all 0.50-0.60m thick, built of roughly coursed oolitic limestone around a rubble core.

A wall aligned north-south, 15, which to the north had been robbed, may have formed the rear of the building. To the south it was abutted by a wall at right angles, 17, with a parallel wall, 12, only 1.4m to the south. These may have formed a small chamber with an end wall, 11, to the west, although only the inner face of this wall survived undisturbed. Within this chamber a complete Lyveden/Stanion B ware jar had been inverted and buried in the earth floor.

The western face of wall 15 was abutted by a layer of light grey clay, (19), heavily contaminated with charcoal and small stone fragments, and containing quantities of late medieval pottery and roof tile wasters (not excavated), which may have accumulated as a waster dump against the rear wall of the building.

In the junction of walls 15 and 17, there was a small deposit of pure, clean light grey clay, which appears to have had its natural contaminants removed, possible in preparation for potting.

The pottery associated with these features was no later than 15th century in date, suggesting that the building was contemporary with the waster pits and was part of the potter's workshop.

THE WESTERN BOUNDARY WALLS

There were two sinuous lengths of boundary wall, aligned north to south, in the western part of the area (Fig 13, 18 and 24). Wall 18 was 0.41m wide with two courses of unmortared limestone surviving, and wall 24 was 0.45m wide, also with two unmortared limestone courses surviving. There was a scatter of limestone running diagonally between the two wall ends, perhaps suggesting that they were part of a single boundary system despite the marked offset between their alignments.

The homogeneous soil horizons abutting these walls, (2) and (3), which were up to 0.35m thick, contained both medieval and post-medieval pottery. Above this, there was a dark grey brown clay silt layer (10), removed by machine excavation, which contained 19th-century glass and pottery as well as scatters of gravel.

OTHER POST-MEDIEVAL FEATURES

A line of limestone, interpreted in excavation as the possible remnant of a wall, ran east to west across the top of the fills of pits 57 and 97 (not illustrated). There is however, too little surviving to determine what this derived from and whether it may have been the remnant of a wall that survived only where it had subsided into the underlying pit fills.

To the east of the pit group, the area of trampled natural, (81), was cut by a broad U-shaped gully, 76, about 3.50m long, 0.46m wide and 0.33m deep (Fig 13). The fill of grey brown silty clay, contained limestone blocks up to 150mm long, and some post-medieval pottery. Overlying the gully there was a layer of fine to coarse limestone fragments up to 0.11m thick 20).

At the northern end of these features there was a limestone slab, 500mm by 970mm and 100mm thick, surrounded by smaller slabs over a bed of small limestone fragments in dark grey brown clay silt, which also included 19th and 20th-century white china (Fig 13, 19). The hollow sound given out when the fill was tapped suggested that there was a void below, implying that the limestone was the modern capping for a well.

WATCHING BRIEF
David Leigh

A watching brief took place in early January 2003 along the northern end of the plot during the removal of topsoil ahead of laying an access road (Fig 2). In the central part of this area slightly deeper excavation exposed the top of a compact layer containing pottery and roof tiles, in an area *c* 15m long. Within this area, another deeper cut exposed a small area containing stone fragments and wasters within sandy clay burnt red. This suggests that further intact deposits lie in this area, at least comprising further waster dumps while the quantities of stone and burnt clay may suggest the presence of a kiln.

WESTERN EVALUATION TRENCH

An evaluation trench was excavated at the western end of the plot at the request of the landowner who was proposing to build a garage here (Fig 2). Archaeological features in this area were covered by a greater depth of overburden, nearly 1.0 m, than those at the eastern end of the plot.

At the southern end of the trench there was a roughly circular pit, 0.8m diameter, filled with mid grey clayey silt. There were several sherds of medieval pottery on the surface of the fill, but their provenance was uncertain and they were not retained. No other archaeological features were noted in the trench.

The subsoil, which was up to 0.6m thick, comprised mid brown slightly clayey silt with very occasional pebble inclusions and moderate roots. The topsoil was 0.35m thick. Several abraded sherds of medieval pottery were recovered from these layers, but not retained.

The trench was inspected by the NCCHET Planning Archaeologist and no further work on the trench was considered necessary. There would be appear to be no activity related to pottery production in this part of the plot.

THE POTTERY
Paul Blinkhorn

The pottery assemblage comprises 620,690g (Table 2). The estimated vessel equivalent (EVE), by summation of surviving rimsherd circumference is 200.9. The pottery was quantified using the chronology and coding system of the Northamptonshire County Ceramic Type-Series (CTS). The majority of the material comprises groups of Stanion ware kiln waste from isolated pits, although small quantities of other pottery types are present, as follows:

F209:	?South Lincs Oolitic ware	AD 1100-1300	215g,	EVE = 0.33
F319:	Lyveden/Stanion A ware	AD 1150-1400	1244g,	EVE = 0.53
F403:	Midland Purple ware	AD 1450-1600	30g,	EVE = 0
F404:	Cistercian ware	AD 1470-1550	3g,	EVE = 0

FABRIC

The majority of the kiln waste comprises the standard Lyveden/Stanion fabric (CTS F320. 583,178g, EVE = 192.56), but some of the material is in a different fabric, classified in the CTS as Lyveden/Stanion D ware (CTS F322) which is smoother and sandier than F320, and contains considerably fewer ooliths (16,674g, EVE = 7.48).

PREVIOUS WORK

Since the first recorded evidence of medieval pottery production in Stanion in 1933 (A Chapman above), Stanion has produced plentiful evidence for medieval pottery manufacture in the form of kilns and/or potting waste, but very little of this material has been analysed and published. Bellamy's summary of 1983 is, up until now, the best-published group of material from the village. It dealt with two different groups of kiln waste from different locations, one of which also had a kiln in association. One group was dated to the late 13th to 14th centuries, the other to the mid-15th to 16th centuries.

Other than this, and notes of reports of finds, very little else has been published. The material from the evaluation at 2 Corby Road was examined by Stewardson (unpublished MA dissertation), although that report is superseded by the present analysis. The material from 2 Corby Road therefore offers the first real opportunity to examine in detail a large group of stratified kiln waste from this important industry.

Most of the kiln waste occurred within a cluster of pits, with some intercutting. The earlier phase comprised the pits lying at the eastern margin of the group, including pit 14 which contained the single largest quantity of pottery.

THE EARLY PHASE OF WASTER PITS
(*c* 1350-1400)

PIT 14

This was, stratigraphically, the earliest of the central

Table 2: Quantification of the ceramic assemblage

FEATURE/ (FILLS)	NATURE OF DEPOSIT	TOTAL POT (kg)	WHOLE/PARTIAL VESSELS	RIDGE TILE (kg)	KILN FURNITURE (kg)
		EARLY PHASE PITS 1350-1400			
78 / (77)	--	6.86	--	0.26	--
62/ (61)	B ware with A and D sherds	50.35	3 face sherds	0.86	0.21
70 / (69)	B and A ware	7.50	1 jug (ST12)	1.18 (Fig 25, 1)	0.09
59 / 58	B ware	22.84		0.27	
14 / (13, 65)	B ware in both deposits	201.61	12 jugs (ST1, 2, 3, 4, 5, 6, 7, 8, 9, 10, 16, SJ1) 2 pots (SC1, SC2) 1 bowl (SB1)	1.58	0.96
17 / (16)	A ware	0.10	--		
Total		**289.26**		**4.15**	**1.26**
		LATER PHASE PITS 1450-1500			
84 / (82, 83)	--	2.81	--	1.01	0.25
74 / (73, 79, 80)	B and D ware, Midland Purple bifid rims	9.51		2.33	4.34 (Fig 26, 4)
57 / (55, 56, 88)	B and D ware, Midland Purple Inscription	82.44	--	19.34	1.09
105/ (104)		2.36			
97 / (92, 93, 94, 96)	B ware, 2 deposits	61.39	8 jugs, (ST13, 14, 15, 17, 18, 20, 21)	8.19	1.21 brick, kiln furniture (SP1)
72 / (71)	B and D ware redeposited	121.78	--	2.69	0.28
40 / (39)		12.94	--	3.2	11.63 (Fig 26, 1 & 2) part brick
46 / (45)		1.73	--	--	
90 / (89)		1.96	--	--	
23 / (22)		5.63	--	--	0.16
6 / (5, 38)	B ware, Cistercian	1.75	--	--	--
67 / (66)		0.12	--	--	--
Total		**304.42**		**36.76**	**18.96**
		OTHER FEATURES			
44 / (27, 41, 42, 43)	Building, cess pit south-east corner	4.31		0.27	--
8 / (7)	Hollow, B ware	0.96			--
49:64/(47, 48, 63)	Boundary ditch B ware	0.21			--
layer 3		15.68		0.86	0.28
layer 2		5.85		1.10	0.81
Total		**27.01**		**2.23**	**1.09**
TOTAL		**620.03**		**43.14**	**21.31**

pit group along with pit 59 (Fig 14). The fills, 13 and 65, produced 200.734kg of pottery with a total EVE of 74.53. It is all Stanion B ware (CTS fabric 320) with the exception of 543g (EVE = 0.14, from one jar rim) of Lyveden/Stanion A ware (CTS F319). Stanion D ware did not occur. The Stanion B ware assemblage therefore comprises 200.191g with a total EVE of 74.39. The assemblage comprises mainly glazed jugs (EVE = 53.53, 72.0%), along with jars (EVE = 8.28, 11.0%) and bowls (EVE = 12.68, 17.0%).

The range of vessels and the fabric is fairly typical of the Lyveden/Stanion B ware tradition. One vessel of note, however, is a small bowl with an internal glaze and a total of six pulled lips evenly spaced around the rim (Fig

34, SB1). The vessel, which is nearly complete, appears to be unique amongst all the known products of the industry, and its function is far from clear. It is possible that the vessel was intended as a multi-wick lamp. Medieval lamps often have a single pulled lip in which the wick is located, and so the vessel would certainly work in such a manner, but this vessel does not have any obvious parallels, and must remain something of an enigma.

Chronology

The dating for this group is almost entirely dependant upon typology and the presence of other pottery types. The only pottery present in pit 14 other than Stanion B ware, are a few sherds of Lyveden/Stanion A ware, which is generally dated AD 1150–1400. The A ware sherds were, however, quite large and fresh, and do not appear to be residual. It is likely therefore that this particular pit group dates to before AD 1400. The range of vessel forms also suggests such a date. The assemblage comprises entirely jars, bowls and jugs; all of the more sophisticated pottery forms of the 15th century, such as dripping dishes and cisterns are entirely absent, although a case can be made, on size grounds, that some pipkins were also present. Such vessels are known from the 14th century, however. The presence of a relatively large number of B ware jars is a highly significant trait. Such vessels are extremely rare at medieval sites in the county. A number of glazed jars were noted at the kiln site at nearby Lyveden, where they were given a date of the early-mid 14th to early 15th century (Webster 1975, fig 27 and 91).

Lyveden/Stanion B ware jar rims were noted at a medieval tenement at Deene End, Weldon, where the evidence from other pottery types suggested that they dated to the first half of the 13th century. However, nearly all the medieval assemblage at that site comprised Lyveden and Stanion wares (1,429 sherds), with only four sherds in other fabrics datable to the period AD 1250–1450 (Blinkhorn 2003). It is highly likely, therefore, that they are later than the given date. A single B ware jar rim was also noted at Warmington in Northamptonshire, in a context datable to AD 1200-1400 (Blinkhorn forthcoming). Again, Lyveden wares comprised nearly all the medieval assemblage.

The most persuasive evidence perhaps comes from the medieval hamlet of West Cotton, Raunds, despite B ware being plentiful, only two B ware jars were noted (Blinkhorn in press). It appears that West Cotton went into decline after the middle of the 14th century, so the fact that B ware jars were so rare suggests that they were only just being introduced at the time, and a date of AD 1350–1400 for the pottery from pit 14 appears therefore to be the most likely.

Jars

The jars show a fairly restricted range of rimforms, with just six different types (Table 3). Rim type 105 was by far the commonest (32.7%), with types 101, 102 and 104 well-represented, but types 103 and 108 were very rare. Many of the vessels are glazed (total EVE = 1.85, 22.3%), with, of the commoner forms, type 104 having by far the highest proportion of glazed pottery.

The data in Table 3 also shows the mean rim diameters of the vessels. The main rim forms show some variation, with type 102 having the largest mean at 190.9mm, and 104 the smallest, at 171.4mm. For such relatively small populations, this difference is unlikely to be significant. Overall, the mean jar rim for the entire population was 166.9mm. Unglazed vessels had a mean diameter of 177.7mm, glazed examples 165.0mm.

The data in Table 4 shows the occurrence of the different

Table 3: Jar rimform occurrence, pit 14, by EVE

Form	101	102	103	104	105	108
EVE	1.79	1.97	0.19	1.54	2.71	0.08
%	21.6%	23.8%	2.3%	18.6%	32.7%	1.0%
Glazed	0.20	0.07	0.14	0.87	0.57	0
% glazed	11.2%	3.6%	73.7%	56.5%	21.0%	0
Mean rim diameter (mm)	183.6	190.9	180.0	171.4	182.7	160

Table 4: Rim diameter occurence (20mm intervals), in EVE, pit 14, jars

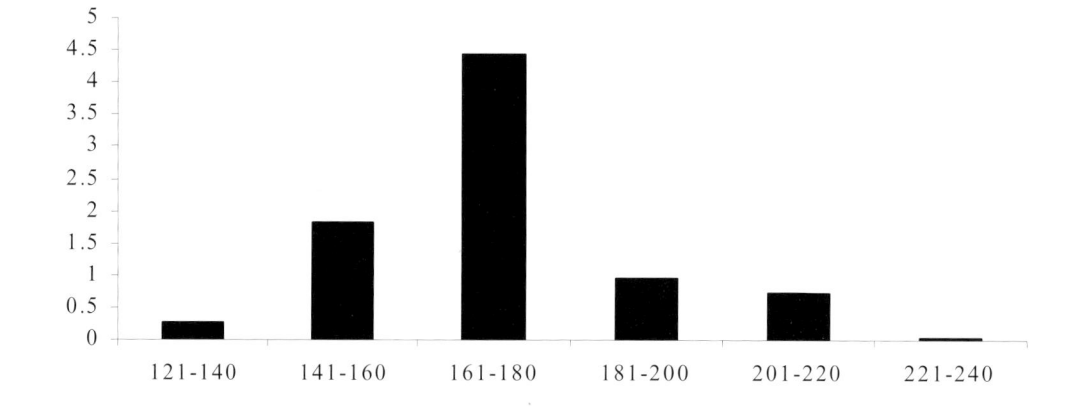

rim diameter sizes for all the jars from this pit. The data shows a classic unimodal distribution, indicating that jars in the 161-180mm diameter range were the preferred size, with smaller numbers of larger and smaller vessels also made.

None of the jars have slip decoration, despite such vessels occasionally being noted at other sites in the region, such as West Cotton, Raunds (Blinkhorn in print). Incised, applied and stamped decoration was also absent, other than stabbing on the handle of an extremely unusual handled jar. The three vessels which survived to full profile all had sagging bases.

ILLUSTRATIONS (Fig 34)

SC1 Near-complete jar. Grey fabric with orange surfaces. Glaze splashes on the outside base pad. Context 13, pit 14
SC4 Full profile of jar. Dark grey fabric with pale orange surfaces. Context 65, pit 14

Not illustrated

SC2 Full profile of jar. Grey fabric with pale orange-brown surfaces. Numerous glaze spots on outer surface. Context 13, pit 14
SC3 Full profile of jar. Grey fabric with brick-red surfaces. Sooting on lower outer body. Context 65, pit 14
SC5 Upper part of jar. Dark grey fabric with pale orange-brown surfaces. Context 13, pit 14

Bowls

The bowls showed slightly more variation in form, with ten different rim types noted (Table 6). The most common forms are 201, 203, 206, 207 and 208, with the rest all represented by less than 6%. The vessels which survived to a full profile or near-full profile suggest that most vessels had glaze on the inside, covering the base-pad and the most of the inner surface of the vessel. Other than this, none of the bowls were decorated in any way. Unusually, 11 of the bowl rims (total EVE = 2.18, 17.2%, Table 5) have pouring mechanisms in the form of a pulled lip, including one vessel with a number of them (Fig 34, SB1). Lipped bowls had a mean rim diameter of 220mm.

Table 6: Bowl rimform occurrence, pit 14, by EVE

Form	EVE	%	Mean Rim Diameter (mm)
201	1.73	13.6%	281.3
202	0.32	2.5%	312.0
203	2.11	16.6%	247.1
204	0.66	5.2%	280.0
205	0.74	5.8%	275.5
206	3.42	27.0%	316.0
207	1.41	11.1%	298.2
208	1.84	14.5%	304.1
209	0.26	2.1%	300.0
210	0.19	1.5%	300.0

Most of the rim forms have a mean diameter which fall in the range of 275–316mm, although type 203 rims are by far the smallest, with a mean size of 247mm. The mean diameter for the whole assemblage is 308.2mm. The data in Table 5 shows that there are broadly two peaks in the rim diameter occurrence of bowls, one in the 161-180mm range, the other in the 261-280mm bracket. This again suggests very strongly that the smaller lipped vessels had a different function to the larger ones, and that the former were indeed skillets or pipkins. Unfortunately, no horizontal handles of the type usually found on skillets or pipkins were noted amongst this group of pottery, although they did occur in others from this site.

The data in Table 7 shows the rim diameter occurrence for bowls from this feature. The bulk of the assemblage is over 280mm in diameter, and the distribution appears broadly unimodal. However, the occurrence of the vessels with a diameter of 280mm or less has a somewhat erratic occurrence. Previous work, on the pottery from West Cotton (Blinkhorn 1999) has shown that bowls made at other manufactories in the region, particularly shelly coarseware (CTS fabric 330) and Lyveden/Stanion A ware (CTS fabric 319) have a trimodal size distribution at some consumption sites, with the choice of size related to function. It is possible that something similar is occurring here, at the point of manufacture, although the data is not clear enough for this to be certain.

Table 5: Lipped bowl rimform occurence (20mm intervals), pit 14, by EVE

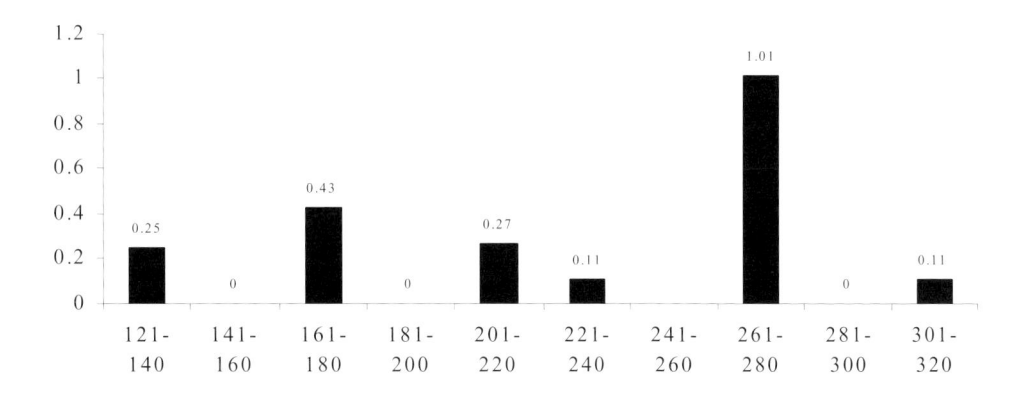

Table 7: Rim diameter occurrence (20mm intervals), in EVE, pit 14, bowls

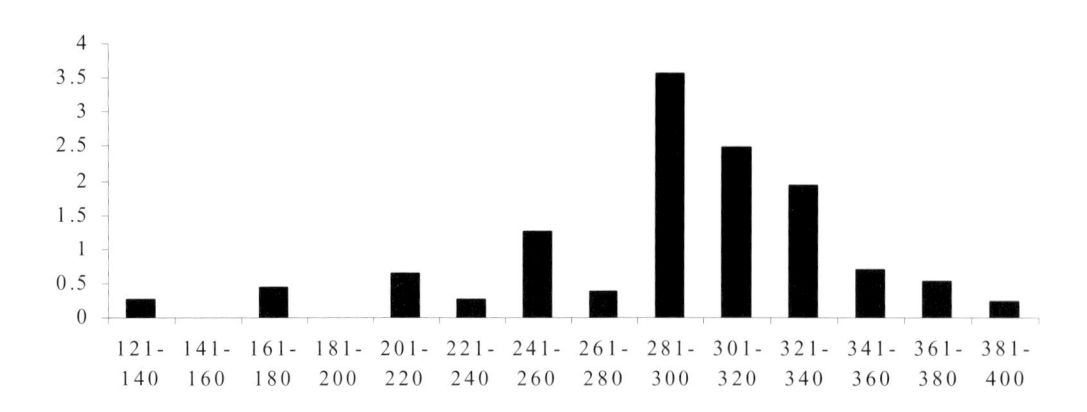

ILLUSTRATION (Fig 34)

SB1 Near complete, multi-lipped bowl. Grey fabric with orange-brown surfaces. Inner surface covered with a glossy green, copper-spotted glaze, numerous glaze spots and runs on the outer surface. Context 13, pit 14

Not illustrated

SB3 Full profile of pancheon. Grey fabric with browner surfaces. Glossy green glaze on lower inner surface. Context 13, pit 14

SB6 Full profile of bowl. Grey fabric with dark reddish-brown surfaces. Glossy dark green glaze on inner surface. Context 13, pit 14

SB9 Full profile of pancheon. Grey fabric with brick-red surfaces. Patchy, glossy green glaze on the inner surface. Context 13, pit 14

Jugs

Jugs are, as noted above, the commonest vessel type from this group, as is usually the case with Stanion B glazed wares (eg Fig 20, ST1 and Fig 21, ST3 and ST6). They had a limited range of rim forms, as shown in Table 8, types 301, 303 and 304 are by far the commonest types, with all types having a similar rim diameter.

Table 8: Jug rimform occurrence, pit F14, by EVE

Form	301	302	303	304	305
EVE	10.35	0.66	18.83	18.95	4.64
%	19.3%	1.2%	35.2%	35.4%	8.7%
Mean rim diameter (mm)	103.6	112.0	108.2	107.1	106.2

The data in Table 9 shows the rim diameter occurrence for the jugs and shows that, like the jars, they have a unimodal distribution. The mean rim diameter for the jugs was 106.8mm.

All the complete or near-complete jugs suggest that all the vessels have a similar overall form. They are all high-necked and shoulderless, with the widest point at the waist, and the area below the waist tapering slightly towards the base, although the bases were generally only slightly narrower than the waists. The exceptions to this

Table 9: Rim diameter occurrence (20mm intervals), in EVE, pit 14, jugs

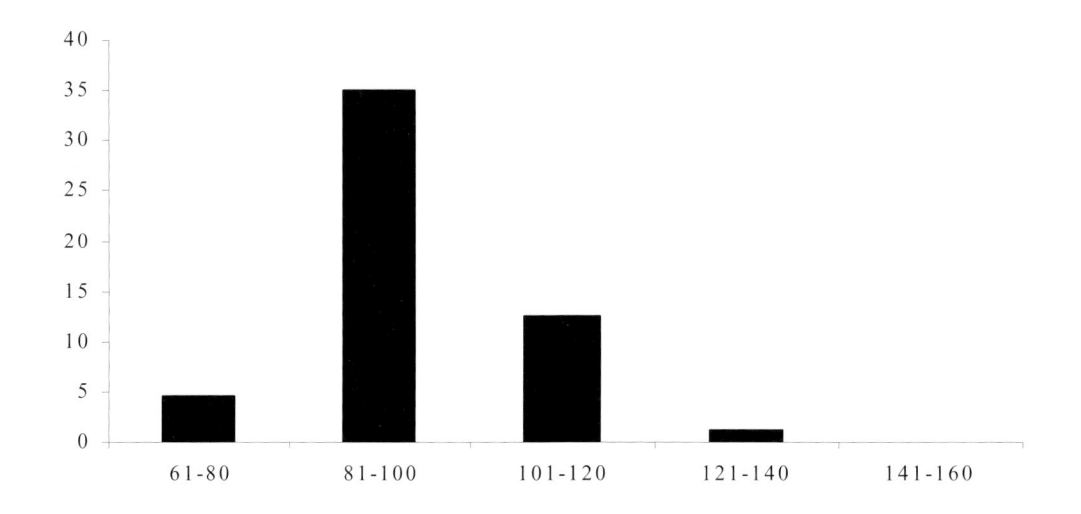

Fig 20 Jugs ST1, pit 14 (left) and ST15, pit 97 (right)

Fig 21 Jugs ST3 and ST6, pit 14 (centre and right) and ST17, pit 97 (left)

were ST6, which had rounded shoulders and a cylindrical lower body, and SJ1, which was very squat (see Figs 27-28, ST1 –10; Fig 30, ST16; Fig 34, SJ1). The commoner form is typical of the Lyveden/Stanion B ware tradition. All the jugs have pulled lips as the pouring mechanism, and handles are generally round-sectioned rods. A total of 59 complete or fragments of jug handles were noted, all bar one of which had stabbing.

A total of 126 bases sherds were noted, all of which were flat apart from two examples with thumb-frilling. Such treatment is very rare on B ware jugs, despite being quite common on the products of other industries. No parallels are known from settlement sites in the region.

Decoration was predominantly glazing, which was a little patchy, but universally covered the area of the vessel from just below the waist to the rim top. A number of vessels also had geometric slip decoration in a white-firing clay which generally appeared yellow under the glaze. Five different geometric schemes were used with the commonest, noted on 12 vessels, being simple, evenly-spaced longitudinal stripes which ran slightly diagonally across the upper body of the pot. Much less common was a scheme which comprised standing arches divided by vertical stripes, but in all cases, where a vessel had slip decoration, the scheme always included a single horizontal stripe which ran around the waist of the pot, with the rest of the decoration always above it. Stamped pellets, which are often noted on glazed B ware jugs were entirely absent, and the slip decoration was always thinly applied, probably with a brush. Stylistically, these are quite different from the 'classic' slip-decorated B ware jugs, where the slip lines are usually narrower and thicker, and given the appearance of being trailed onto the vessel rather than painted. It may be that such vessels are earlier than the group from this site; certainly, such vessels were only present in contexts dating to before 1350 at Black Lion Hill in Northampton (Denham 1985, 126). Excavations of one of the Lyveden kilns also suggested that the stamped jugs with trailed decoration were much earlier than the types with painted stripes and no stamping (Webster 1975, fig 21).

ILLUSTRATIONS (Figs 27, 28, 30, 34)

ST1 Near-complete jug. Grey fabric with brown surfaces, green glaze on upper body and neck, kiln scars on upper body. Context 13, pit 14

ST2 Near-complete jug. Grey fabric with brown surfaces, green glaze on upper body and neck, stripes in a cream slip appearing pale green under the glaze. Context 13, pit 14

ST3 Near-complete jug. Uniform orange fabric. Orange glaze with dark-green copper-spotting on upper half of body and neck and rim. Context 65, pit 14

ST4 Near-complete jug. Grey fabric with purplish-brown surfaces. Glossy green glaze, white slip decoration appearing pale green under the glaze. Context 65, pit 14

ST5 Near-complete jug. Dark grey fabric with lighter surfaces, glossy green glaze with unfused blobs of copper oxide. White slip stripes, appearing pale green under the glaze. Context 65, pit 14

ST6 Full profile of jug. Grey fabric with browner patches on the outer surface. Large streak of glossy green glaze on and below the handle. Context 65, pit 14

ST7 Near-complete jug. Grey fabric with orange-brown surfaces. Glossy green glaze on upper part of body and rim. Sherd with slip-stripe decoration fused to outer surface. Context 65, pit 14

ST8 Full profile of badly distorted jug. Grey fabric with browner surfaces, spots and runs of glossy green glaze on the outer surface. Context 65, pit 14

ST9 Near-complete jug. Dark grey fabric with orange surfaces, glossy green glaze on upper part of body and neck. Context 65, pit 14

ST10 Body and base of jug. Grey fabric with orange inner surface. Glossy green glaze, white slip decoration appearing pale green under the glaze. Context 65, pit

ST16 Near-complete jug. Grey fabric with brick-red surfaces. Variegated green and blue-green glaze over most of body and neck. Context 65, pit 14

SJ1 Near-complete squat jug. Grey fabric with orange brown surfaces, dull green glaze on the upper body, unglazed around the handle. Context 13, pit 14

Not illustrated

ST11 Near-complete jug. Uniform brick-red fabric. Green glaze, largely unvitrified, over white slip stripes appearing light green under the vitrified areas. Context 65, pit 14

PIT 59

This feature is, like pit 14, the earliest stratigraphically in the central pit group (Fig 14). It does not have a direct relationship with pit 14. The fill, 58, produced 21.42kg of pottery, with a total EVE of 8.79. It is mainly Stanion B ware, although unlike F14, some D ware vessels are also present (384g, EVE = 0.59, 1.8% of the assemblage by weight). Of the B ware, the main vessel type is jugs (EVE = 8.08, 91.9%), with bowls making up most of the rest of the group (EVE = 0.59, 6.7%). A single jar rim is also present (EVE = 0.12, 1.4%). A single fragment from the rim of a dripping dish (SD1) was also noted, but as these are asymmetrical, it is not possible to calculate the EVE.

Chronology

This assemblage shows a number of differences to that from pit 14. The most striking trait is the range of vessel forms. Jugs are far more common, with only one jar rim present. If, as discussed above, such vessels were not common until after the middle of the 14th century, this would suggest that this group is earlier than that from pit 14, and dates to around AD 1350.

A single bodysherd was noted in the pit 59 group with both slip decoration and rows of comb-stabbing. Again, such sherds were absent from pit 14, but were noted at Bellamy's 1983 kiln again suggesting a similar date (Bellamy 1983, fig 4. 4, 46).

The pottery

The relatively small assemblage size coupled with the

preponderance of jugs means that detailed statistical analysis of this group would serve little purpose.

Only one jug was reconstructable to a full profile (Fig 33, ST24). It is of a similar form to the majority of the jugs from pit 14, and has glaze limited to the upper part of the outer surface. It is not slip-decorated. Slip decoration on jugs was not common amongst this group; just four vessels (EVE = 1.2) were noted, and all had simple vertical stripe schemes, again painted rather than trailed. As with pit 14, all the jug handles were round-section rods, all with a single line of stabbing running down the centre. All the spouts were simple pulled lips.

A total of 21 sherds from jug bases are noted, of which five are thumb-frilled bases. This is a much higher proportion than was noted amongst the pottery from pit 14, and again suggests that this group is of a different date.

No lipped bowls were noted, but it is worthy of note that even though the assemblage was small, the bowls again appear to favour two different sizes. Three rims were noted in the range 140–180mm, the rest in the 300-320mm category.

ILLUSTRATION (Fig 33)

ST24 Near complete jug. Grey fabric with dark reddish-brown surfaces. Glossy dark green glaze with copper-spotting on upper part of body. Context 58, pit 59

Not illustrated

SD1 Dripping dish fragment. Uniform brick-red fabric. Unvitrified glaze on inner surface. Context 58, pit 59

PIT 78

One of the two most northerly pits, this feature only produced 6.86kg of pottery. It was cut by pit 62, and therefore is likely to pre-date AD 1400. Seven rimsherds were noted, all from jugs. One of the jugs had slip stripe decoration. Two rod handles, both with stabbed decoration, were also present.

PIT 62

Pit 62 yielded 48.14kg (EVE = 20.07) of pottery. The assemblage includes two large A ware rimsherds (280g, EVE = 0.32) in good condition, indicating that the assemblage dates to before AD 1400. The bulk of the assemblage comprises B ware, with 800g (EVE = 0.10, 1.7%) made up of D ware. The B ware assemblage comprises jars (EVE = 0.4), bowls (EVE = 0.34) and jugs (EVE = 19.01). In addition, four rimsherds from dripping dishes were noted, as was the handle from the same or a skillet. None of the bowl rims produced any evidence of spouts. They all have a rim diameter of 300mm or greater, apart from a single example with a diameter of 200mm, again suggesting a bimodal size distribution.

The dripping dishes all have simple upright rims and were glazed internally. The group is also notable from the presence of three jug rims with face-mask decoration.

Jugs

The jug assemblage had a fairly wide range of rimforms, with types 303 and 304 by far the most common (Table 10). The mean rim diameter was 107.9mm, with the unimodal size distribution show in Table 11.

Table 10: Jug rimform occurrence, pit 62, by EVE

Form	301	302	303	304	305	306	307
EVE	0.99	0.92	7.13	6.28	2.84	0.12	0.85
%	5.2	4.8	37.5	33.0	14.9	0.6	4.5

All the jug handles are round section rods with a single line of stabbing. A total of 118 jug rims was noted, of which 15 have slip stripes. No other forms of decoration were noted, other than five sherds with fragments of facemasks.

Table 11: Rim diameter occurrence (20mm intervals), in EVE, pit 62, jugs

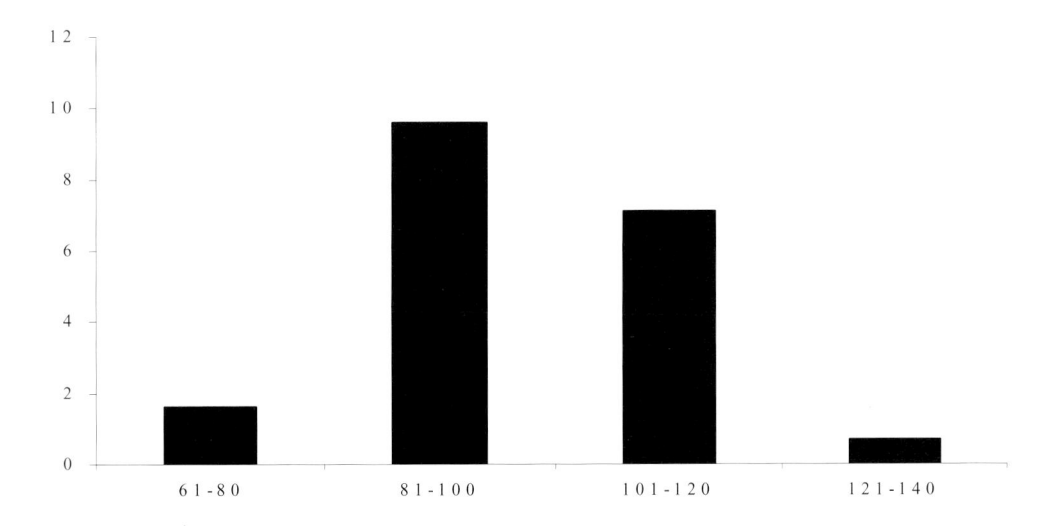

Fig 22 Face mask sherds, ST30 (top), ST 28 (left) and ST 29, pit 62

The facemask sherds (Fig 22, ST 28, 29 and 30) are somewhat unusual, and different to previous known examples, which have been noted in 13th-century contexts at other sites. The early examples comprised dots of white slip into which crude faces had been cut (eg Blinkhorn 2002, fig 10, 1 & 2), whereas these examples consist of an incised mouth and slashed applied strip around the lip of the jug, to form a mouth and beard, with one of them (ST29) having a simple slashed eye or eyebrow just below the rim. The other (ST28) is damaged and insufficiently complete to know if eyes were present. The third sherd is much smaller, and only a fragment of the beard is present, although this one has slip stripe decoration as well (ST30). Such vessels appear to have very little parallel in the Lyveden/Stanion industry. A sherd from Lyveden kiln D1 had a slashed pad below the lip which may be an attempt at a similar enhancement, but the illustrated vessel is said by the authors to be '*derived from two similar jug bits*', and its date is unknown (Bryant and Steane 1969, 21 and fig. 9). There are no other published parallels.

It is possible that the facemask vessels are copies of, or at least inspired by, the products of other industries. Anthropomorphic and face-jugs are well-known products of the Grimston industry in Norfolk (eg McCarthy and Brooks 1988, fig 157), and at least one anthropomorphic Grimston jug is known from Lyveden (Webster 1975, fig 34, 8.01). Such vessels tend to be 13th to 14th century, which is in keeping with the mid-late 14th-century date given to this group.

ILLUSTRATIONS (Fig 22)

ST28 Fragment of face-jug. Dark grey fabric. Dull green glaze on outer surface. Context 61, pit 62
ST29 Fragment of face-jug. Orange fabric with unvitrified glaze on outer surface. Context 61, pit 62
ST30 Fragment of face-jug. Orange fabric, slip stripe decoration. Context 61, pit 62

PIT 70

Adjacent to pits 59 and 62, this pit produced a small assemblage of jug sherds including a single near-complete example (Fig 29, ST12) and a single bowl rim. One of the jugs, unusually, has rouletted decoration (Fig 33, ST22). There were also four small sherds of 'A' ware present, suggesting that the group may date to before AD 1400.

ILLUSTRATIONS (Figs 29 and 33)

ST12 Near-complete jug. Light grey fabric with orange surfaces. Green, partially unvitrified green glaze on upper part of the vessel, white slip stripes appearing yellow under the vitrified areas. Context 69, pit 70
ST22 Fragment of jug. Grey fabric with brick-red surfaces, concentric rows of rouletting above the waist. Glossy dark green glaze with copper spotting. Context 69, pit 70

PIT 17

This small feature to the south-west produced only 98g of pottery, including three small A ware sherds.

THE LATER PHASE OF WASTER PITS
(c 1450-1500)

PIT F57

This feature was later than pit 14 and pit 59, and cut both (Fig 14). It comprised three contexts, 55, 56 and 88. The bulk of the pottery came from context 55, comprising 75.325kg (EVE = 20.24), with 56 producing 5.07kg (EVE = 1.95) and 88 yielding 2,02kg (EVE = 0). The total EVE for the feature was 22.19.

Most of the assemblage comprises the standard B ware, but 1.944kg of D ware is also present (2.3% of the assemblage by weight), along with a single sherd (10g) of Midland Purple ware (CTS fabric F403). The B ware comprises jars, (EVE = 2.76, 12.4%), bowls (EVE = 3.58, 16.1%) and jugs (EVE = 15.85, 71.4%), which is broadly similar to the proportions in the stratigraphically earlier pit F14.

Chronology

The presence of the single sherd of Midland Purple ware in this feature offers an excellent *terminus post quem* for the pottery. Such wares are well dated in the region, and were in widespread use by the mid-15th century. They are often found conjunction with Late Medieval Oxidized Wares (CTS fabric 401) which date to the second half of the 15th century. It would appear therefore that this pit group dates to around the middle of the 15th century.

Further possible support of this chronology comes from a sherd with a fragment of a single line inscription (Fig ST26). The inscription appears to read '...*naria*', although it is somewhat difficult to decipher, and other interpretations are possible.

Any sort of lettering on medieval jugs is extremely rare. A small sherd with a fragment of a roller-stamped inscription is known from fieldwalking at Flore near Northampton (Blinkhorn and Dix 1992). It appears to have been part of a vessel which is the same as a 15th-century example from Coventry. The latter appears to have the same inscription, and, almost certainly, was made by the same potter. Dunning's (1967) overview of medieval jugs with lettering illustrates how rare such vessels are. He noted an inscribed jug handle from Abthorpe near Towcester in Northamptonshire (*ibid*, fig 67), dated to the late 14th to 15th centuries, and the Coventry vessel noted above. A vessel from Spilsby in Lincolnshire, with a free-hand inscription was also dated to the 15th century (*ibid*, fig 70). The sherd from this pit, with its mid-late 15th century date is, chronologically, entirely in keeping with all the other known examples.

The assemblage

This group does show some typological differences to the material from the earlier pits, 14 and 59. The range of vessel forms is basically the same, comprising jars, jugs and bowls, and a single skillet or dripping dish handle was also noted. The main difference appears to be a somewhat wider range of decorative techniques. The most notable of these is a sherd with an inscription,

In addition to the inscribed sherd, a further five bodysherds were noted with decoration, four of which were in D ware. The one sherd which was not had fingertip impressions and an incised wavy line, as did one of the sherds in D ware fabric. The rest comprises one sherd with fingertipping, one with a wavy line, and one with horizontal cordons.

Jars

A total of 20 jar rimsherds were noted, with a mean rim diameter of 185.0mm, which is a little larger than that for pit 14. The rim diameter occurrence is collated in Table 12, and shows a unimodal distribution, as once again was the case for pit 14. Just two of the rims showed traces of glaze.

Bowls

A total of 52 bowl rimsherds were present, 20 of which showed evidence of internal glazing. A wide range of rimforms were noted, as shown in Table 13. It was similar

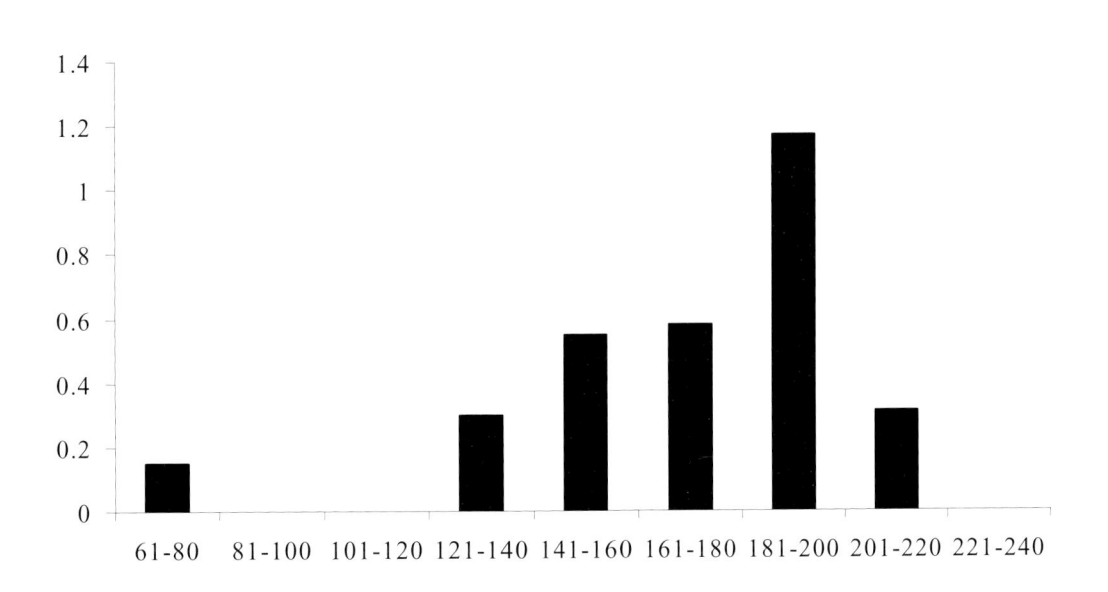

Table 12: Rim diameter occurrence (20mm intervals), in EVE, pit 57, jars

to that from pit 14, and there were some variations in occurrence. For example, type 203 rims, which were one of the most common types in pit 14, were one of the rarest here.

Table 13: Bowl rimform occurrence, pit 57, by EVE

Form	EVE	%	Mean Rim Diameter (mm)
201	0.25	7.0%	313.3
202	0.35	9.8%	288.0
203	0.10	2.8%	290.0
204	0.09	2.5%	320.0
206	0.87	24.3%	300.0
207	0.16	4.5%	300.0
208	0.48	13.4%	317.1
210	0.48	13.4%	336.7
211	0.59	16.5%	320.0
212	0.04	1.1%	300.0
213	0.17	4.7%	370.0

The rim diameter occurrence is shown in Table 14. It shows a trimodal distribution, suggesting that there were three main favoured sizes and, in diameter terms, they were more or less the same as those in pit 14. Just two bowls with pulled lips were noted, and these were again at the smaller end of the size range, one with a diameter of 240mm, and the other 260mm. This suggests that they are also likely to be from skillets.

Not illustrated
SB5 Full profile of bowl. Grey fabric with dark reddish-brown surfaces. Glossy dark green glaze on inner surface. context 55, pit 57
SB10 Rim of decorated bowl. Grey fabric with brick-red surfaces, unvitrified glaze on the inner surface. Rim top decorated with fingertipping. context 55, pit 57
SD2 Dripping dish/skillet handle. Uniform brick red fabric. context 55, pit 57

Jugs
The range of rimforms from this pit group is broader than that from pit 14, and different forms are favoured (Table 15). The most common form is type 305, comprising over 55.8% of the assemblage, as opposed to just 8.7% of the pit 14 jugs. Type 301 rims, which comprise over 19% of the pit 14 group, represent less than 1% of this assemblage, and the other forms have noticeably different representation. This is perhaps what one would expect for two groups of pottery with a chronology which indicates that they were made by different potters. Certainly, it has been observed in the past that potters tend to favour a particular rimform, even when working within the constraints of a tradition (J Hudson pers comm).

The assemblage mean rim diameter was 112.4mm, which is a little larger than the jugs from pit 14, but probably not significantly so.

The distribution of the jug rim diameters (Table 16) shows a similar distribution to that for F14.

In terms of decoration, many of the jugs were glazed, but only two had slip decoration, in the form of painted vertical stripes similar to those in the earlier features. Just 11.2% of bodysherds were noted with slip decoration, but as this includes all vessel types, it would suggest that the proportion of slip decoration on jugs is somewhat higher, and the apparently low occurrence of slip decorated jugs as suggested by the rimsherds is just a statistical anomaly.

Table 14: Rim diameter occurence (20mm intervals), pit 57, bowls, by EVE

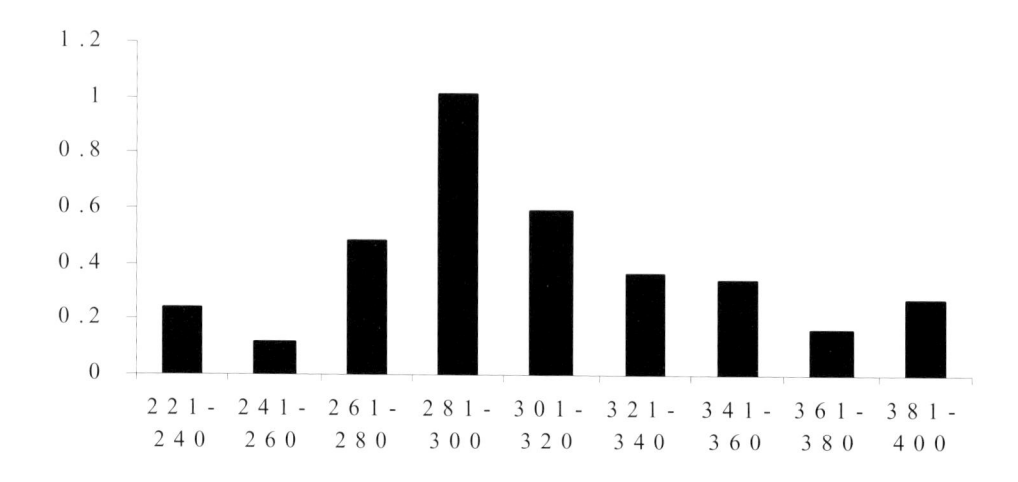

Table 15: Jug rimform occurrence, pit 57, by EVE

Form	301	302	303	304	305	306	307	308
EVE	0.15	0.22	2.93	2.12	8.84	0.10	0.28	1.06
%	0.9%	1.4%	18.5%	13.4%	55.8%	0.6%	1.8%	6.7%
Mean rim diameter (mm)	80.0	126.7	116.0	110.0	111.7	140.0	100.0	112.5

Table 16: Rim diameter occurrence (20mm intervals), in EVE, pit 57, jugs

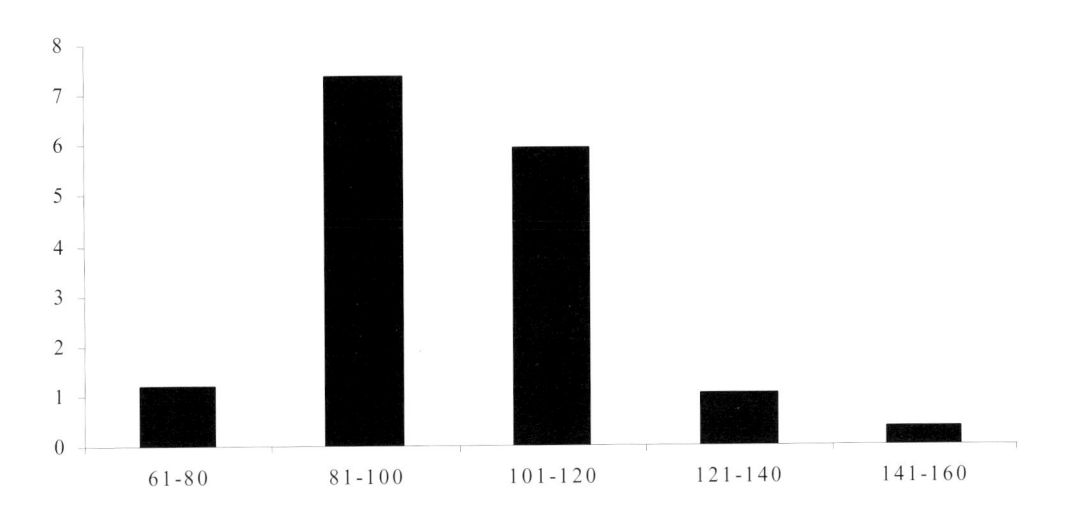

A total of 28 handles were noted. Of these 26 were round-sectioned rods, all of which had a single line of stabbed dots running down them. The other two handles were a single horizontal example from a skillet or dripping dish, and a strap handle with slashed decoration. The latter is more typical of the Brill and Potterspury industries, and is most unusual on B ware vessels, although a small number were noted at West Cotton.

Not illustrated

ST25 Full profile of jug. Grey fabric with dark reddish-brown surfaces. Glossy dark green glaze with copper-spotting on upper part of body. Context 55, pit 57

ST26 Sherd with incised lettering. Grey fabric with browner surfaces, glossy variegated green and purple glaze on outer surface. Context 55, pit 57

PIT 97

This feature cut both pits 57 and 105, although the latter only produced a small assemblage (1,692g). Pit 97 produced 63.261kg of pottery with a total EVE of 14.65, of which 5.773kg (EVE = 2.01) was D ware. It comprised mainly jars (EVE = 1.46, 10.0%), bowls (EVE = 1.71, 11.7%) and jugs (EVE = 10.52, 71.8%), along with a single skillet (EVE = 0.11, 0.8%).

Chronology

The entire assemblage comprised B wares, meaning that any dating could only be given on stratigraphic and typological grounds. The group obviously post-dates pit 57, which was reasonably closely dateable to around the middle of the 15th century, but that is all that can be said. It is therefore given a tentative date of sometime in the second half of the 15th century.

Jars

Jars were slightly less common than in pit 57. Just six rimsherds were noted, with rimforms 101, 103, 104 and 107. All the vessels were in the 140–180mm size range, with a mean diameter of 165.0mm. Four had traces of glazing, one of which also had slip stripes.

Bowls

A total of 18 bowl rims were present. They almost all had type 211 rimforms, apart from single examples of types 201, 206, 207, 213 and 216. They had a mean rim diameter of 313.3mm, with the size occurrence again suggesting a trimodal distribution (Table 17). The only skillet from the assemblage had a rim diameter of 160mm, which is considerably smaller than any of the bowl assemblage, although the only two bowls with pulled lips were again at the smaller end of the distribution range, being 220mm and 260mm diameter respectively. Six sherds produced traces of internal glazing.

Table 17: Rim diameter occurence (20mm intervals), pit 97, bowls, by EVE

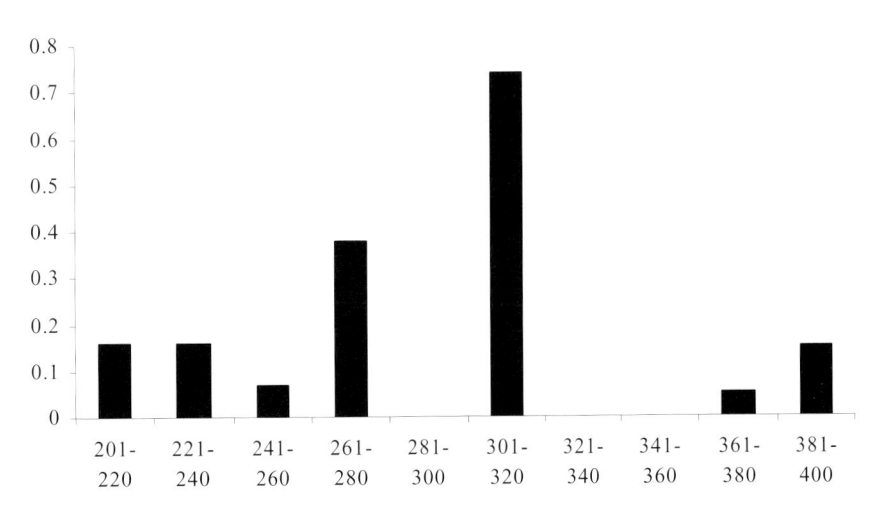

Fig 23 Jugs ST13 (right) and ST14, pit 97

Jugs
The range of rimforms was this time somewhat restricted, as shown in Table 18. The data show a broadly similar pattern to those for pit 57, with type 305 by far the most common. The rim diameter occurrence is shown in Table 19. It once again shows a unimodal distribution, with the mean rim diameter being 114.7mm. The vessels which survived to a full profile (Figs 20-23, 29-32, ST13

Table 18: Jug rimform occurrence, pit 97, by EVE

Form	303	305	307	308
EVE	2.30	5.92	0.46	2.30
%	21.9%	56.3%	4.4%	21.9%
Mean rim diameter (mm)	125.0	118.5	113.3	100.0

Table 19: Rim diameter occurrence (20mm intervals), in EVE, pit 97, jugs

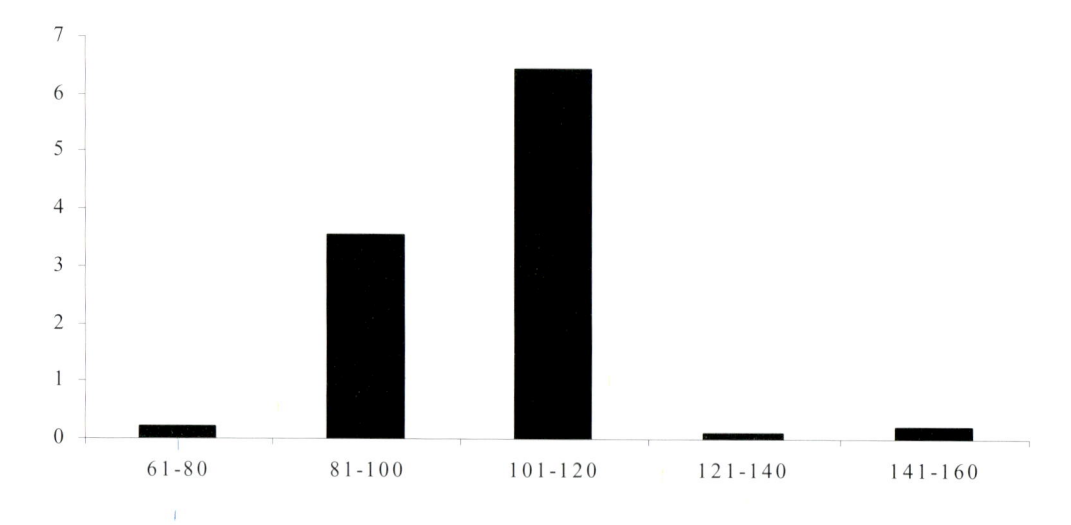

Fig 24 Jugs ST20 (right) and ST21, pit 97

– ST15, ST17 – ST21) showed a little more variation in form. The globular balusters noted in the earlier groups were still represented, but some were a little taller and more slender than previously (eg Fig 21, ST17), and a single small squat example was also present. This deposit also contained two jugs in a distinctive white fabric with pale buff surfaces and a bright apple green glaze (Fig 23, ST13 and ST14).

A total of 18 handles were noted, all of which had a single line of stabbing running down the centre. Six vessels had slip decoration, again brushed on and entirely limited to vertical stripes with the exception of two vessels (ST20 and ST21, Fig 24 and Figs 31 and 32, ST20 and ST21) which had what appear to be an inverted horseshoes painted between widely-spaced stripes. These two large globular jugs were also both evidently decorated by the same individual, as the patterns are near identical, although the horseshoe pattern is more clearly executed on the smaller jug, ST20.

Two bodysherds, probably from jugs, had incised cordons, but no other decoration was noted.

ILLUSTRATIONS (Figs 29 to 32)

ST13 Near-complete jug (Fig 23). White fabric with pale buff surfaces. Pale, apple green glaze with sparse darker copper-spotting. Context 92, pit 97
ST14 Near-complete jug (Fig 23). White fabric with pale buff surfaces, bright apple green glaze with sparse copper-spotting. Upper part of body glazed and lightly incised. Context 92, pit 97
ST15 Near-complete jug (Fig 20). Grey fabric with orange surfaces, patchy green glaze on most of body and neck. Incised wavy line around girth. Context 92, pit 97
ST17 Near-complete jug (Fig 21). Grey fabric with orange patches on outer surface. Sparse drips of glossy green glaze on outer surface and handle. Context 92, pit 97
ST18 Grossly distorted waster. Orange fabric with patchy, glossy green glaze, white slip decoration appearing yellow under the glaze. Context 92, pit 97
ST19 Near-complete jug. Grey fabric with brown surfaces, glossy green glaze with white slip decoration, appearing yellow under the glaze. Context 92, pit 97
ST20 Near-complete jug (Fig 24). Grey fabric with orange brown surfaces. Glossy green glaze, white slip decoration appearing yellow under the glaze. Context 92, pit 97
ST21 Near-complete jug (Fig 24). Grey fabric with orange brown surfaces. Glossy green glaze, white slip decoration appearing yellow under the glaze. Context 92, pit 97

Not illustrated

ST27 Highly decorated sherd. Uniform pink fabric, incised decoration on outer surfaces, glossy variegated yellow and brown glaze. Context 92, pit 97

SC7 Jar rim. Dark grey fabric with brick-red surfaces. Variegated dull orange and green glaze on both surfaces, white slip decoration on outer surface, appearing yellow through the glaze. Context 92, pit 97

SB8 Full profile of bowl. Grey fabric with red surfaces. Context 92, pit 97

PIT 72

This was, stratigraphically, the latest of the central pit group. It was also the second largest, comprising 117.505kg of pottery with a total EVE of 40.1. The D ware totalled 1.511kg (EVE = 0.5). The B ware assemblage comprised entirely jars (EVE = 2.96, 7.4%), bowls (EVE = 3.58, 8.9%) and jugs (EVE = 33.56, 83.7%).

It was most notable for three vessels which had three fragments of face-masks. They are basically the same as those from context 61, pit 62, with an applied beard and incised mouth below the pouring lip. The fact that the examples from this context are obviously later indicates that they were either still being made in the mid-late 15th century, or are redeposited.

Chronology

This group is also lacking any other pottery apart from B ware, and so the dating is arrived at purely on stratigraphic grounds. Once again, given the range of fabrics and forms, a mid-late 15th-century date seems the most appropriate.

Jars

Most of the rimforms comprised type 102 and 105, as shown in Table 20. A total of 27 rimsherds were noted,

Table 20: Jar rimform occurrence, pit 72, by EVE

Form	101	102	105	108
EVE	0.12	1.49	1.05	0.30
%	4.1%	50.3%	35.5%	10.1%
Mean rim diameter (mm)	180.0	190.9	203.3	193.3

of which just three had traces of glaze (eg SC6). None had slip decoration.

The assemblage had a mean rim diameter of 196.3mm. The diameter occurrence is shown in Table 21. The data again shows a unimodal distribution. The two classes at the extremes of the distribution appear a little over-represented, but there was just one sherd in each class, and both were relatively large, and have thus skewed the data.

Bowls

A total of 56 bowl rim sherds occurred. They had a wide variety of rimforms, but by far the most common was type 206 (see Table 22). There was a wide variation in the mean rim diameter of the various types, but this is likely to be due to some classes only having one or two examples. The assemblage mean was 298.6mm.

Table 22: Bowl rimform occurrence, pit 72, by EVE

Form	EVE	%	Mean Rim Diameter (mm)
201	0.21	5.9%	260.0
202	0.12	3.4%	280.0
203	0.12	3.4%	200.0
204	0.07	2.0%	360.0
206	1.52	42.5%	300.0
207	0.59	16.5%	294.0
208	0.71	19.8%	315.4
209	0.11	3.1%	300.0
210	0.16	4.5%	266.7

The rim diameter occurrence is shown in Table 23. It once again suggests that there were two different size-classes of vessel, one clustering around the 201-220mm class, the other around 281 – 300mm. Three rims were noted with pulled lips, one from a vessel with a rim diameter of 200mm, the other two being 220mm. This again suggests that the smallest vessels in the bowl class were skillets or pipkins. Only 20 of the rims did not show traces of internal glazing.

Table 21: Rim diameter occurence (20mm intervals), in EVE, pit 72, jars

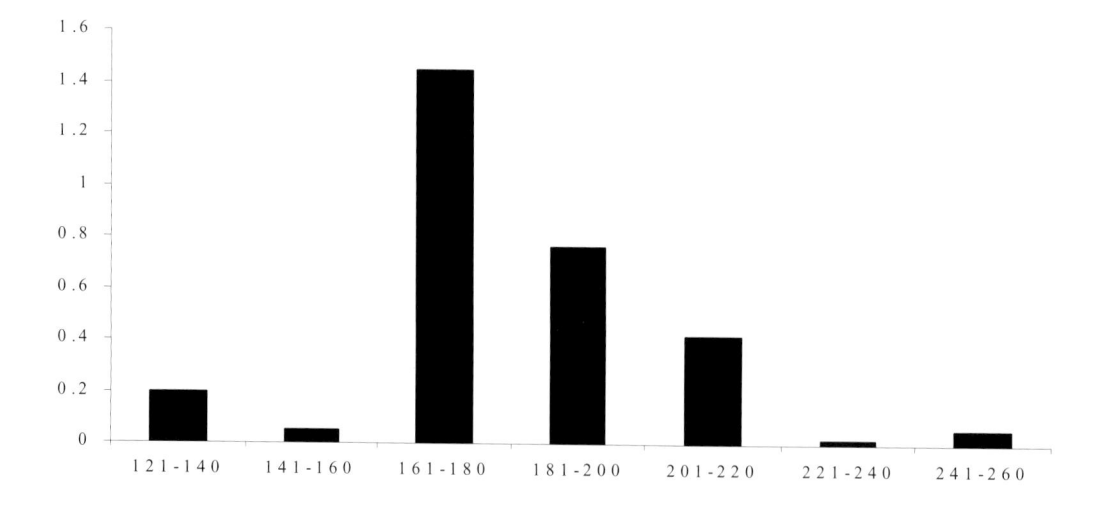

Table 23: Rim diameter occurence (20mm intervals), pit 72, by EVE, bowls

Jugs

A total of 198 rims were noted from jugs. The range of forms is shown in Table 24.

Table 24: Jug rimform occurrence, pit 72, by EVE

Form	301	303	304	305	306	307	308
EVE	2.55	12.53	13.40	1.82	0.08	2.19	0.96
%	7.6	37.3	39.9	5.4	0.2	6.5	2.9
Mean rim diameter (mm)	103.1	109.4	107.0	116.7	120.0	107.7	116.0

The assemblage had a mean rim diameter of 108.6mm. The rim diameter occurrence is shown in Table 25. Once again, they have a purely unimodal distribution.

A total of 62 handles were noted. They are all round-section rods with a single line of stabbed impressions running down them. There are fifteen vessels with slip decoration, one with arches, the rest with vertical stripes. None of the jugs had survived to a full profile, so it is difficult to make any meaningful assessment of the vessel forms.

Not illustrated

SC6   Rim of jar. Uniform dark grey fabric, large splash of dark green glaze on inner shoulder. Context 71, pit 72

SB4   Full profile of pancheon. Grey fabric with pale brown surfaces. Context 71, pit 72

PITS 84 AND 74

These two features were in the northern area of the site, just north of the two larger pits 57 and 97 (Fig 14). Pit 84 was cut by pit 74 giving it a *terminus post quem* of the mid-15th century. Pit 84 produced just 2.81 kg of pottery,

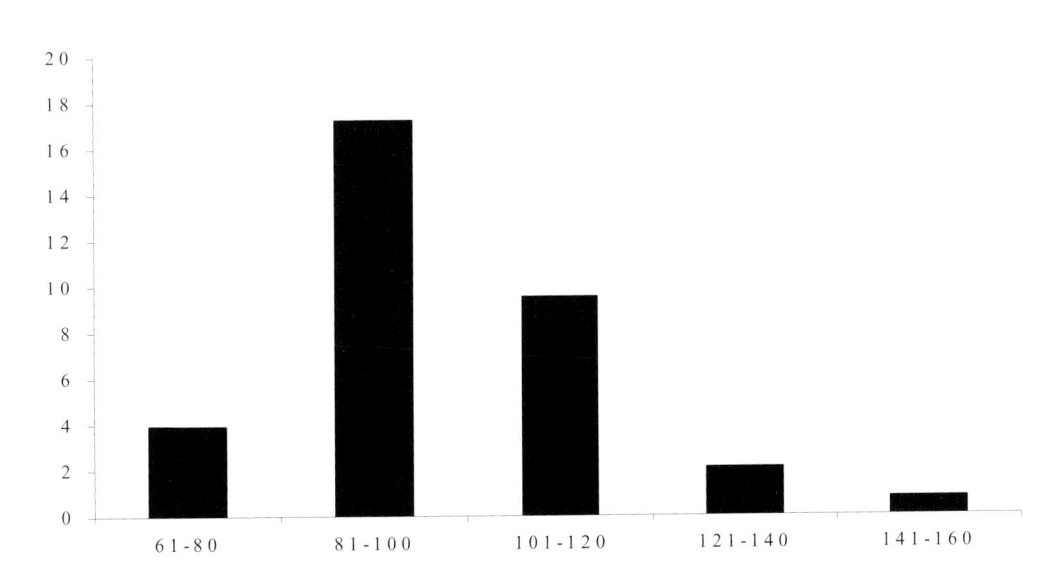

Table 25: Rim diameter occurence (20mm intervals), in EVE, pit 72, jugs

all of which is B ware, except for 2.98kg of D ware. Only six rims were noted, two each from jars, bowls and jugs. Four handles are present, one being a rod of the usual type, one from a skillet handle and the other two are slashed straps, both in D ware. One bodysherd was noted with slip stripes.

Pit 74 produced 9.51kg of pottery. As well as B ware, it also produced a fairly large sherd of Midland Purple ware, which dates the assemblage securely to post-AD 1450. The rest of the assemblage comprises B ware, but only 2.38kg is in the standard fabric, with the bulk of the assemblage (5.41kg) made up of the D ware. Only 11 rimsherds are present; four from jars, three from bowls and four from jugs. It is certainly significant that two of the four jar rims are the bifid type 109. Bifid rims are universally a late medieval form, and the fact that they occurred in this feature along with a sherd of Midland Purple, offers considerable support to the late medieval date given to this group. These are the only two rimforms of this type from the entire excavation.

None of the jars or jugs have slip decoration, although two bodysherds were noted with such treatment. Five handles are present, which were all stabbed in the usual manner.

PIT 6

This pit yielded just 1.33kg of pottery, most of which was B ware, but a single sherd of Cistercian ware is also present, given the group a *terminus post quem* of the late 15th century. It produced four rims: two from jars, one from a bowl and one from a jug. The feature was cut by a ditch, 49/64, which contained a small assemblage of B ware and a fragment of a possible curfew in the gully overlying the ditch east of wall 4.

PIT 67

This small pit to the south of the main group yielded just 182g of B ware.

PIT 23

A group of three small pits lay east of the main group. The largest group of pottery from these pits came from pit 23, with 5.093kg (EVE = 1.89). It comprised mainly bowls, all with a rim diameter of 320mm or greater, along with a single jar rim and three jug rims. One of the jugs was reconstructable to a full profile, and also showed that the handle was luted to the body by the pottery pushing a finger through the body of the pot from the inside.

ILLUSTRATION (Fig 33)

ST23 Full profile of jug. Grey fabric with pale orange surfaces. Extensive patches of partially unvitrifed green glaze on upper part of body. Context 22, pit 23

OVERVIEW AND DISCUSSION

This group of pottery is significant on many levels, and offers a useful insight into the later part of the Stanion B ware pottery industry. Perhaps the most important finding is the chronology of the industry. The past, rather scanty evidence has suggested that the B ware industry had finished by the end of the 14th century; the evidence from this excavation shows that there is no doubt that it in fact continued more or less to the end of the 15th century.

The presence of other pottery types suggests that this site contains wasters from an earlier phase of manufacture, and that there were two distinct phases of potting. The groups in association with A wares almost certainly date to before AD 1400, with the presence of B ware jars, a post-mid 14th century vessel type, indicating a date of AD 1350-1400.

Also, the presence of two sherds of Midland Purple ware and a sherd of Cistercian ware in direct association with wasters shows that B ware pottery was still being made in the last quarter of the 15th century. This chronology is supported by the presence of two bifid rimforms in a late pit group, pit 74, which produced one of the sherds of Midland Purple ware. Bifid rims were not noted as being present at the Lyveden potteries (Bryant and Steane 1969; Webster 1975), but several were noted by Bellamy at the kiln at 14 Corby Road in Stanion (*ibid* 1983, fig. 5 nos 12–15). That group was given a date of AD 1450–1550 (*ibid* 161), which is broadly the same as the chronology for the examples from this site.

Thus it offers an opportunity to examine two large and reasonably well-dated groups of B ware which were made around a century apart. In the following analyses, these will be referred to as the 'early group' in the case of the former, and the 'late group' in the case of the latter.

EARLY GROUP: PITS 14, 59, 62, 78

Vessels
The proportions of the main vessel types, in EVE is shown in Table 26. There is very little difference between the two. Jars are slightly more common in the later groups, but the difference does not appear significant. It would seem therefore that there was little change in the output of the Stanion potters between the mid-14th and the late 15th centuries.

Table 26: Comparison of vessel types, early and late groups

	Jars	Bowls	Jugs	Total EVE
Early Group	8.4%	13.0%	78.4%	104.8
Late Group	10.9%	11.6%	77.6%	80.41
Total	17.55	22.9	144.49	185.21

The minor wares, skillets and dripping dishes, were mainly represented by handles or, in the case of the latter, asymmetrical vessels, meaning that the EVE could not be calculated. It is certainly worthy of note that the five dripping dish fragments from this excavation all appeared in early groups.

The date of introduction of dripping dishes within the Stanion pottery industry is uncertain, but such vessels were being made at other kilns in the region in perhaps the 13th century and definitely the 14th century, at, for example, Olney Hyde and Brill (Mynard 1984; Mellor 1994). They were not present at West Cotton, Raunds, but status considerations are a likely factor. Dripping dishes are rare finds and are usually only found on sites of somewhat above average status; they were used to catch the fat dripping from roasting meat for use in sauces etc, and they are usually found in an urban context or at a manorial site or similar. Stanion dripping dishes are very rare finds, with few obvious parallels. A couple of fragments, interpreted as skillets, were noted at a kiln in Stanion, along with a probable handle (Bellamy 1983, fig 3; 29, 30 and 32). The group was dated to the late 13th–early 14th century, on stylistic grounds, although the presence of three glazed B ware jar rims, one with slip decoration, suggests perhaps a slightly later date, around the mid-14th century.

A large fragment of a dripping dish was noted at the manufactory at Lyveden (Webster 1975, fig 32, 4.26), although that example was in a different fabric, probably Lyveden E ware (CTS fabric 325), and was dated to the late 15th century, which is the time when that fabric type was current.

The evidence from here and elsewhere therefore suggests that dripping dishes were probably being made at Stanion around the mid-14th century. The lack of such vessels from the later group at this site also suggests that they had ceased to be made by the mid-15th century, although they are such rare vessels, and the fact that other industries in the region were still making them at that time, means that this end date cannot be advanced with confidence.

Vessel Size

This section will concentrate solely on jars and bowls. The rim diameter of jugs does not seem to be related to vessel size, whereas evidence from elsewhere, particularly West Cotton, has indicated that the rim diameters of, particularly, bowls and, to a lesser extent, jars, is related to the capacity of the vessel (Blinkhorn 1999).

Jars

The mean rim diameter for the early group was 183.5mm, while for the late group it was 191.0mm. This difference does not appear greatly significant, but the data (Table 27) shows that the late group had a wider range of sizes, and that there is a small secondary peak at the larger end of the size range. This would suggest that, in the later period, small quantities of large jars with a specialized function were being produced. These are likely to have been storage vessels, perhaps even bunghole cisterns, but no bungholes were noted amongst the entire assemblage. It is uncertain whether such vessels were produced in the B ware. Bellamy (1983, fig 6, 21 and 22) noted two bungholes amongst a group of kiln waste at 14 Corby Road, Stanion, but these were the wheel-thrown E ware (CTS fabric 325) which date to post-1450. A few were also noted at Lyveden (Webster 1975, 3.09, 4.09, 4.10; Bryant and Steane 1969, fig 12n), but these were again all in the E fabric.

Bowls

The mean rim diameter for the early group was 305.7mm, for the late group, 306.5mm. The data is shown in Table 28. It shows that both early and late groups have a broadly unimodal distribution, but that the early group has a much wider range of sizes. There are also some of the smaller categories of early vessels (less than 220mm) which are not represented at all. It is most likely due to there being two categories of bowl, one having a pouring mechanism in the form of a pulled lip. Most of the lipped bowls had a rim diameter of 280mm or less, with the majority 220mm or less. The mean size was 220mm, which is considerably lower than the assemblage mean.

Conversely, of the unlipped bowls, only three examples had a diameter of 220mm or less, and the sherds were so small that they could easily be lipped examples with the pouring mechanism unrepresented. The small mean size of the lipped bowls suggests very strongly that at least some of these may have been pipkins or skillets, which often have a pouring mechanism such as a lip. Pipkins/skillets tend to be smaller than the large pancheons which make up the bulk of this assemblage, but usually have a horizontal handle at 90 degrees to the position of the lip. Thus, it would be difficult to say that a rimsherd came from such a vessel unless it was complete enough to include the area where the handle would have been located.

A similar picture was noted with the late group. Only seven lipped bowls were noted, but they were all at the smaller end of the distribution, being 260mm or less, with a mean diameter of 231.4mm. This is again considerably smaller than the assemblage mean.

It would appear therefore that the bowls broadly fell into two functional categories; small vessels, often with lips, which cluster around the 220-240mm diameter range, and large ones, without lips, in the 300-320mm range (Table 28).

Jugs

As noted above, the rim diameter of the jugs does not appear to be related to the vessel capacity, and there seems to be considerable variation in the latter parameter, at least partially related to vessel form.

Rimforms

Jars

The jar rim form occurrence, in EVE, as a proportion of the assemblage, is shown in Table 29. It provides confirmation that the type 109 bifid rims only occur amongst waste in the 'late group', as noted above.

Bowls and Jugs

There appears to be considerable variation in the proportion of the bowl and jug rim forms in the different groups, but

Table 27: Jar rim diameter occurrence, in EVE

Diameter (mm)	121-140	141-160	161-180	181-200	201-220	221-240	241-260	261-280
Early Group	0.26	1.99	4.57	0.97	0.97	0.04	0	0
Late Group	0.81	0.97	3.09	1.93	1.40	0.13	0.21	0.06

Table 28: Rim diameter (mm) by EVE

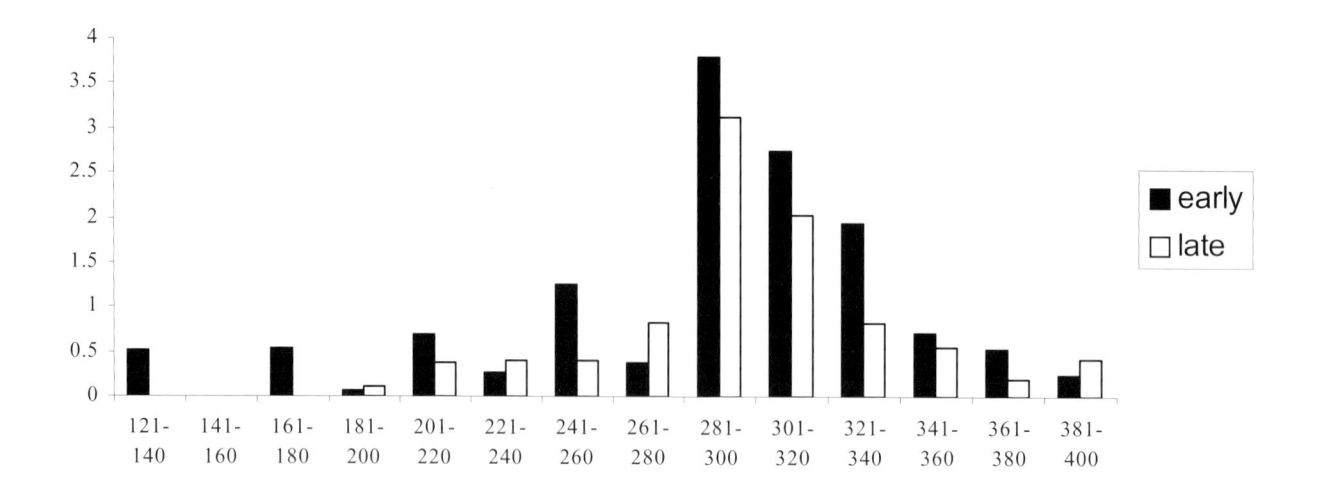

Table 29: Jar rim occurrence by type, in EVE, expressed as a percentage of the period assemblage

Form	101	102	103	104	105	107	108	109	Total
Early	20.3%	26.3%	2.1%	17.5%	32.8%	0	0.9%	0	8.80
Late	3.7%	30.4%	6.7%	8.0%	15.8%	27.9%	3.4%	4.1%	8.75

none appear to have typological significance. As noted above, it is entirely possible that each rimform represents the work of a different potter, with the implication that the wasters were from a number of different kilns, or, conversely, if this represents the output of a single kiln, then a number of different potters were using the same kiln. At this time, we have very little knowledge of how medieval pottery industries were organized. Villages such as Stanion, where pottery production was a staple of many of the inhabitants in the medieval period, are well known, but how the various potters interacted with each other is not.

Decoration
The Stanion B ware pottery from this site is typical of the industry in that decoration is extremely limited. Glazing was noted on all the vessel forms, although not all vessels were glazed. The same applies to slip decoration, mainly in the form of painted stripes, although a small number of vessel with other schemes, such as standing arches, were also noted.

Glazing on jars usually occurred on the upper body and rim, although a number of examples simply had splashes and drips of glaze, indicating that they were essentially unglazed, but had been fired at the same time as glazed vessels. Slip decoration did also occur on jars, but only in the form of vertical stripes.

Some bowls were glazed, but always on the inside. Again, some vessels were essentially unglazed, with splashes and drips from other vessels.

Jugs were most often decorated, but the range of techniques was somewhat restricted when compared to some other contemporary industries. Glazing was usually limited to the upper part of the vessel, and where slip stripes occurred, they were limited to the glazed area, usually with a single horizontal cordon defining the lower limited of the decorated area. Stamped pads, which are common on Lyveden/Stanion wares, were not noted.

One vessel had a fragment of an incised inscription, which is extremely unusual in medieval pottery generally, and a small group of vessels with faces modelled below the pouring lip were also noted. Incised decoration was generally very rare, other than a few vessels with comb-stabbing or incised cordons or wavy lines.

CHRONOLOGICAL SUMMARY

The evidence indicates that the pottery from the pits at this site represents two distinct phases of production, one in the second half of the 14th century (the 'early group'), and the other in the second half of the 15th century (the 'late group'). The dating comes from a combination of the dating of associated pottery of other types and typology. In the case of the early group, associations with A ware, which had fallen from use by AD 1400, and in the case of the latter, Midland Purple and Cistercian wares, which were introduced in the mid-late 15th century. The fact that the whole site was sealed by a layer which produced pottery of the mid-16th century onwards offers some general support to the end date of production.

One of the most striking aspects of the two groups of pottery is how little difference there is in terms of the style of most of the pottery, and the range of vessel and decoration types. Despite this, the assemblage has provided some very useful insights into the Stanion pottery industry, and has allowed some refinement of the chronology of this regionally important industry.

It is now certain that the production of Stanion B ware

was considerably longer-lived than first anticipated. It has always generally been regarded as ending in the 14th century, but the evidence from this site shows that production was still taking place in the later years of the 15th century. It would therefore seem appropriate to now give the tradition a chronology of AD1200-1500.

The site has also offered evidence to make a case for the revision of Lyveden/Stanion D ware. This was generally regard as starting around AD 1400 based on the evidence from Lyveden, and was thought to replace the B ware, but wasters of both fabrics have been found here, in all the pit groups. It is therefore suggested that it should now be dated AD 1350-1500, and it is entirely possible that it may even have started earlier.

The excavation has also confirmed that bifid-rim B ware jars, although rare, are a reliable chronological tool. They appear solely in the late group, and thus can be dated AD 1450-1500.

Similar comments apply to dripping dishes. They mainly occur in the early group, so it can be confidently stated that such pots were first made in Stanion around AD 1350.

The slip decoration used on the vessels found at this site is somewhat different, in terms of the technique of application used, to other vessels. All the slip-decorated vessels from this site were had the designs painted on in a generally rather thin slip. The thick, possible piped slip decoration known from other kilns and excavations is entirely absent, as are stamped pads, another common technique elsewhere. It would appear therefore that thickly applied slip and/or stamped pads are an early product of the industry, dating from perhaps AD 1200 – 1350, whereas painted, thin slip decoration is later, and datable to AD 1350-1500.

It is also possible that techniques of incised decoration, such as comb-stabbing, are also early, and again dates to AD 1200-1350.

Finally, it is notable that none of the kiln waste from this site is wheel-thrown, it all being coil-built and finished on a turntable. It has long been known that Stanion potters were very late in taking up the wheel, and in the past it has been suggested that a true fast wheel was not used until the late 13th or early 14th century. The evidence from this site indicates that it was later still, and likely to be the early 16th century at the earliest.

CERAMIC ROOF TILE
Pat Chapman

This assemblage comprises 474 sherds, weighing 42.8kg, of exclusively ceramic roof ridge tile (Table 30). They come from both phases of waster pits, together with the pottery and kiln furniture. About half of the assemblage, 202 sherds, came from fill 55 of pit 57, and a further 64 sherds are from fill 92 of pit 97, part of the central pit group of the later phase. The tile assemblage includes 31 ridge crests, all but three being of a single basic standard type, rather like a blacksmith's anvil, with small variations. There are single examples of three other types.

The tile is generally about 13mm thick with variants from 9mm to 15mm thick. The largest 11 sherds from fill 55, pit 57 are a maximum of 194mm by 65mm, while most of the rest average 110mm by 70mm, with some smaller sherds. In fill 92 pit 97 there are six sherds, c 140mm by 110mm, while the majority of the rest are about 130mm by 70mm, with a few smaller sherds.

Most of the sherds are in a hard, smooth to rough fabric, which has a generally rough fracture, with mainly frequent to dense fine crushed shell, sometimes with occasional small ironstone inclusions. The tile is brown, orange brown or red, usually with a medium grey core varying in thickness from a thin streak to the whole width except for the surface. This has a similarity to the Lyveden/Stanion D ware fabric (CTS F322) which is dated 1350-1500, according to the revised dating (Blinkhorn this report). It is also similar to the tile fabric 1 from the Greyfriars site, Northampton (Eames 1972, 125). Some of the sherds had been overfired to grey or black. A few sherds and one crest are in a silty pink fabric, the crest with some large ironstone inclusions. Laminated flaking was noted particularly on sherds from pit 57 and pit 97.

The majority of the ridge tile are green glazed, while one is lead glazed, and a few were left plain.

Table 30: Quantification of ceramic ridge tile

Context/feature	Number	Weight (g)	Crests	Comment
13 / pit 14	23	1581	1	Early phase
58 / pit 59	11	273	1	Early phase
61 / pit 62	8	868	3	Early phase
69 / pit 70	13	1187	1	Early phase
77 / pit 78	3	262		Early phase
39 / pit 40	37	3196	7	Later phase
43 / pit 44	1	273	1	Later phase
55 / pit 57	202	19347	10	Later phase
71 / pit 72	42	2692	1	Later phase
73 / pit 74	9	590		Later phase
79 / pit 74	18	1744		Later phase
82 / pit 84	16	992	1	Later phase
83 / pit 84	1	25		Later phase
92 / pit 97	64	8194	4	Later phase
2 layer	13	1101	1	Later phase
3 layer	13	869		Later phase
Totals	**474**	**43094**	**31**	

All the sherds had been stabbed from the underside of the tile for firing purposes, sometimes through to the upper surface. An implement, typically c3mm square in section, was used and a more or less regular pattern of holes was creating, spaced very approximately 30mm apart. Sometimes this had been done around the crests from the outside. Some crests had vertical or near vertical slashes along each side, similar to those on vessel handles.

Only part of one ridge tile could be reconstructed to give measurable dimensions, the tile from pit 70 (Fig 25, 1 and 2). The height of the ridge tile from the 'base' to the apex of the ridge, not including the crest, is 135mm; from the base midpoint to the edge of the tile is 130mm, giving an estimated base width of 260mm. The surviving length is 245mm. The measurement of 137mm from edge to the crest, gives a projected complete length of c334mm, assuming the crest was central.

CRESTS

The crests were added separately to the tile by pushing the clay upwards from inside whilst pressing the crest down, and then smoothing the clay into the tile both underneath and on top. This can be seen clearly on those crests with only a remnant base. The top and the curves at each end were knife-trimmed and the edges smoothed.

The basic crest shape is that of an anvil or hammerhead (Fig 25, 3). Each end is usually a matching concave shape or flared out in a straight line or occasionally as a convex curve. However, occasionally the ends are slightly different. The crest base length varies between 40mm and 95mm, although 50mm to 70mm is the most common, while the top length measures between 40mm and 80mm. The height is typically 33mm, although that can range from 20mm to 42mm (Table 31).

Three single examples of other crest styles were found. One is triangular, 40mm long at the base, narrowing to 22mm at the, broken, top (Fig 25, 4a). It is possible that it may have been similar to the horned crest (see below), but with the second horn missing. One crest is an asymmetrical triangle (Fig 25, 4b). A few examples have been found elsewhere, including at least three partial examples at Greyfriars, Northampton (Eames 1972, fig 18). The horned crest is 95mm long at the base, rising to blunt points at each end, 45mm apart (Fig 25, 4c). One point is 28mm high, 15mm long at the base narrowing to 10mm on top and 12–7mm thick. The other point is 34mm high, 22mm long at the base narrowing to 14mm on top and is 17mm thick. Both sides are slashed. The green glaze has been overfired.

The tiles and crests were found in both phases of waster pits, indicating the general conservatism of the roof furniture.

ILLUSTRATIONS (Fig 25)

1 & 2 Ridge roof tile with crest
3 Crests, anvil type, one with slashes
4 a: pointed, triangular crest, b: asymmetrical triangular crest, c: horned crest

Table 31: Crest descriptions and dimensions

Context/ feature	Base length (mm)	Top length (mm)	Height (mm)	Thickness base to top (mm)	Description
13 / pit 14	73	85	40	20-10	Vertical slashes, convex curve upwards, green glaze
58 / pit 59	58		30	25 - 10	Stabbed, ends broken, green glaze
61 / pit 62	40	22	23	25 - 10	Triangular, possibly formed from tile, top broken, slashed, green glaze
61 / pit 62	70	80	30	25 - 8	Slashed, ends more upright, white slip
61 / pit 62	65	--	0 - 20	25 - 10	Diagonal longwise, slashed, possibly formed from tile, white slip
69 / pit 70					Partial, green glaze, slashed
39 / pit 40	50	60	25	25 - 10	Pink fabric, ironstone inclusions, white slip
39 / pit 40	55	60	30	25 - 10	Straight and convex ends, some stabs, green glaze
39 / pit 40	50	63	25	22 - 10	Flared sides, white slip, glaze?
39 / pit 40	50	60+	30	25 - 10	One tip broken, green glaze
39 / pit 40	68	75	30	25 - 10	Tips broken, green glaze
39 / pit 40	60	70+	33	25 - 10	Winged end, other broken, green glaze
39 / pit 40	50+	50+	33	25 - 10	End missing, green glaze
55 / pit 57	55	50+	35	25 - 10	Flared end, one broken, green glaze
55 / pit 57	58	85	32	20 - 9	Flared, green glaze
55 / pit 57	58	78	35	23 - 9	One end pointed, other convex, pink fabric, ironstone, inclusions, white slip
55 / pit 57	65	73	30	25 - 9	Slashed, tip missing, green glaze
55 / pit 57	51	65	32	25 - 10	Winged, tip missing, green glaze
55 / pit 57	70	50+	42	28 - 10	Occasional stabs, both ends broken,
55 / pit 57	68	--	--	25	Base only, stabbed, green glaze
55 / pit 57	--	--	--	32	Half base, green glaze
55 / pit 57	--	--	--	30	Base end, green glaze
55 / pit 57	--	--	30	25 - 10	One end only, white slip
71 / pit 72	--	--	--	--	Partial, one winged end, green glaze
82 / pit 84	95	45	28&34	12-7, 17-14	Slashed, horned, green glaze
92 / pit 97	70	85	33	30 - 10	One tip missing, stabbed one side, slip
92 / pit 97	65	80	34	25 - 10	Green glaze
92 / pit 97	55	78+	35	23 - 10	Tip missing, green glaze
92 / pit 97	--	--	35	25 - 10	One end only, green glaze
43 / pit 44	90		35	25 - 8	One end broken, green glaze
layer 2	64	60+	37	20 - 10	Winged, one end broken, green glaze

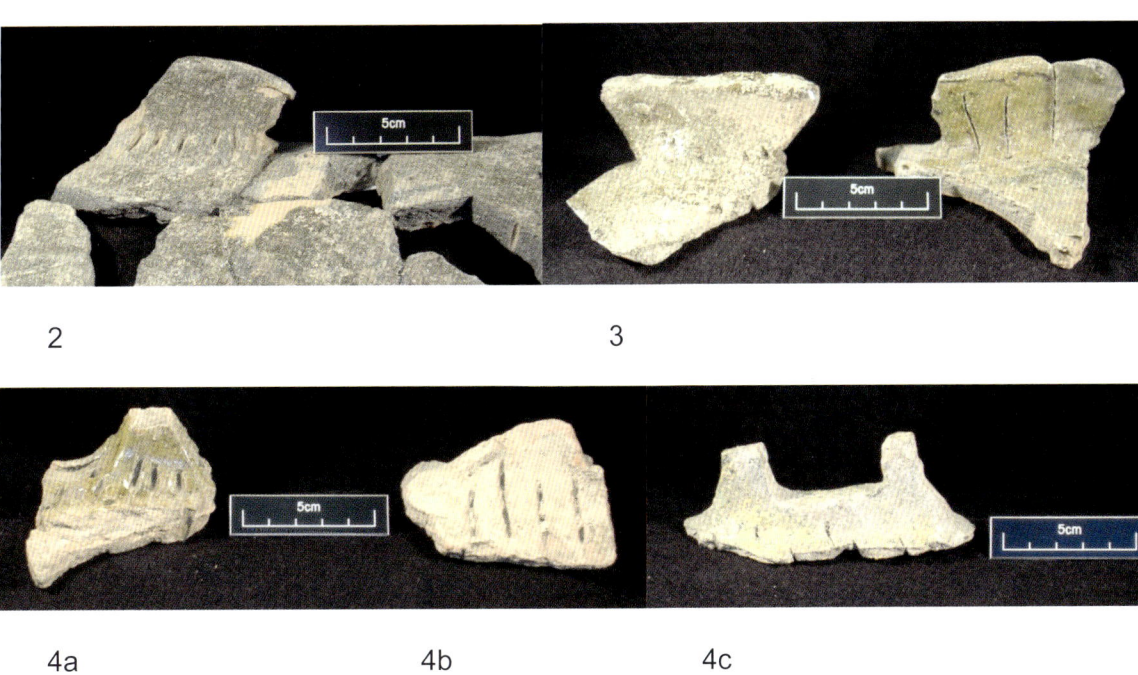

Fig 25 1: roof ridge tile partially reconstructed; 2: detail of crest; 3: anvil style crest with and without slashes; 4: a, triangular crest; b, asymmetrical crest; c, horned crest

KILN FURNITURE
Pat Chapman

KILN PROPS

A quantity of more crudely-made items has been identified as cylindrical kiln props or spacers. The assemblage comprises 198 sherds, weighing 20.9kg (Table 32). Half the assemblage by number and weight comes from the fill (39) of pit 40, of the later phase, 1450-1500. There are eleven separate kiln props by rim count.

The fabric is hard with a generally rough fracture and medium to frequent fine crushed shell and occasional to some small ironstone fragments up to 9mm in length. The colour is red brown with a medium grey core of varying thickness. The surface is often buff to grey, sometimes hard fired to dark grey or black. There are a few sherds that are fine and silty, pink in colour with occasional ironstone inclusions, similar to a few of the tile sherds. The remains of the prop from fill 65, pit 14, is red-brown with very frequent shell, of up to 1mm in length, standing proud of the surface. Unusually it has been stabbed, in places only 15mm apart.

These kiln props are all coil made. The coils are usually quite broad, typically 30mm thick, and the breakages have almost invariably occurred at the coil joins, leaving a steep diagonal sheer, which indicates how poorly the coil joins were smoothed over in manufacturing. The narrower upper ends of the props are occasionally very simply finished, and in one case the section is an irregular oval rather than circular (Fig 26, 2). However, the tops have more usually been given a reasonable finish internally for a finger's length down from the rim, which has itself been simply shaped in a fashion similar to the contemporary jugs (Fig 26, 1). In many cases this finishing is more than would have been required, and it may be that these props were made by trainee potters who were practising their skills in turning a rim.

The body is generally smoothed on the outside, and they are furnished with flat bases. There are occasional splashes of glaze on the bodies, and two large sherds have glaze down the edges, perhaps suggesting use as spacers after having already been broken. The body of the props are typically 10-12mm thick, with the more crudely made props about 14mm thick. The rims vary in diameter between 60 and 70mm.

The most complete example, SP1, from the fill (92) of pit 97, stands 290mm high, with a rim diameter of 110mm and a base 180mm in diameter (Fig 26, SP1). It broadly resembles a medieval jug in form, but it is complete enough to be certain that it never had a handle attached. It may have been a partially made jug that was rejected and utilised as a kiln prop.

It is possible that the few larger, wider props could have been used as saggars; containers to hold and protect small items in the kiln, such as the pottery whistles from 17 Little Lane (see A Chapman above). The best preserved example has an oblique, oxidised 'rim', suggesting that it was a kiln prop that lost its upper part during initial firing, and may subsequently have been used as a saggar (Fig 26, 4).

Kiln props were noted at Lyveden kilns D1 and D2 (Bryant and Steane 1969, figs 8c and 8d, and Steane 1971, 35). They are of broadly similar form to the examples from this site. Bellamy (1983) does not mention kiln props as being found at either of the groups of material he published. About a quarter of the vessels within the pottery recovered from the kiln at 17 Little Lane are described as coarse, conical pipe-like vessels with flat bases used as kiln spacers (Blinkhorn in A Chapman above).

Table 32: Quantification of kiln props

Context/feature	number	weight (g)	comments
13 / pit 14	8	754	Early phase
61 / pit 62	2	218	Early phase
65 / pit 14	2	208	Early phase
69 / pit 70	2	91	Early phase
39 / pit 40	101	11634	Later phase
55 / pit 57	11	1090	Later phase
22 / pit 23	1	167	Later phase
71 / pit 72	9	280	Later phase
73 / pit 74	29	3889	Later phase
79 / pit 74	5	459	Later phase
82 / pit 84	3	255	Later phase
92 / pit 97	10	1217	Later phase
2 layer	11	815	Later phase
3 layer	4	287	Later phase
Total	198	20993	

ILLUSTRATIONS (Fig 26)

1. Kiln prop, jug-type rim, diameter 50mm widening to 110mm near base, surviving length 285mm. Context 39, pit 40
2. Kiln prop, oval, upright rim, diameter c65mm widening to 85-95mm near base, surviving length 195mm. Context 39, pit 40
3. Kiln prop, jug type, diameter 110mm, base diameter 180mm, length 290mm. Context 92, pit 97
4. Kiln prop, top missing, base diameter 160mm, surviving height 170mm. Context 73, pit 74

STRUCTURAL TILE

There are two structural tiles associated with the kiln waste. One from fill 92 of pit 97, is large, rectangular and weighs 3.6kg, but is broken in half. The fabric comprises poorly mixed clay, with frequent fine shell inclusions and the occasional small fragment of ironstone, reduced to a dark grey, except for the surface which is a pale pinkish brown.

The tile would have measured 256mm long by 145mm wide and 70mm thick, (10 inches long by 5¾ inches wide and 2¾ inches thick). One face is smoothed if slightly uneven, has squared corners and sharp edges, with a fine cracked surface, the other face has rounded edges and corners. The tile had been stabbed from both sides although the entrances were obscured.

The tile fragment, weighing 0.5kg from fill 39 of pit 40, was formed from a batch of clay that had been mixed

1   Pit 40

2   Pit 40

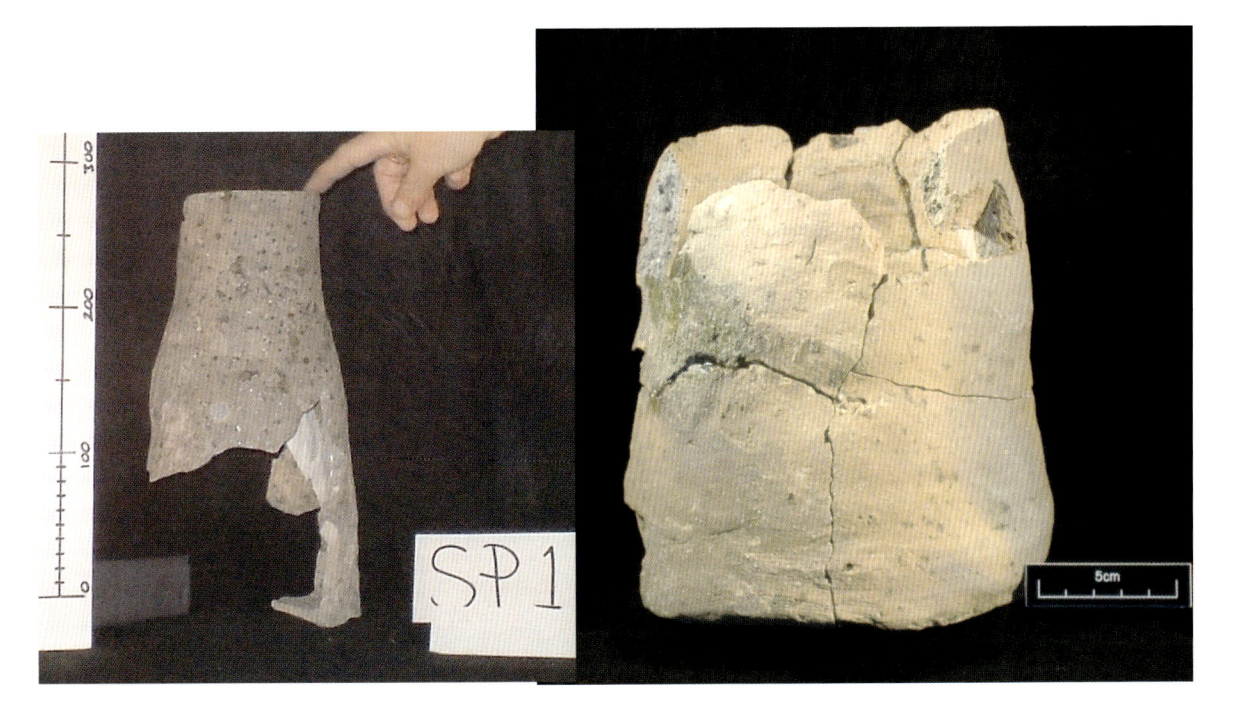

3   SP1, pit 97

4   Pit 74

Fig 26 Kiln furniture 1 – 4

in a circular fashion, leaving a 'hole' in the centre. The fabric is very similar to the above example if slightly darker. The surviving surface is smooth, but with fine cracks and has been stabbed with an implement with a 3mm squared section at 20mm intervals in rows 20mm apart. The surviving dimensions are 135mm by 133mm and 53mm thick (5¼ by 4 by 2inches thick. Two further fragments also came from this context.

These are similar to structural tiles found at a tile kiln in Warwick (Chapman 2007) and the contemporary 13th to 14th century-tile factory at Danbury, Essex (Drury and Pratt 1975, 123 and fig 54). A similar style of tile was also recovered from the 17th to 18th-centuries pottery kiln at Donyatt in Somerset, indicating the ubiquitous nature and longevity of this element of kiln structure (Coleman-Smith 2002, 158, fig 24).

KILN BAR

There is one small fragment of a possible kiln bar from fill 69 of pit 70. It is 60mm long and a minimum of 38mm thick, broken at both ends. It is made from a very hard reduced fabric with a partial red surface.

FIRED CLAY

This small assemblage comprises 40 fragments weighing 1.4kg. There are eight fragments of irregular, grey, overfired, powdery, vesicular, fired clay with fine shell and ironstone inclusions. One piece has small fragments of red shelly pot fabric embedded in it. The largest piece is 75mm by 70mm by 38mm, the remainder being smaller. Eleven pieces are orange to brown to black with a flat combed or smoothed surface, averaging 40mm by 50mm by 15mm thick. The thickness is the same with smaller fragments. These fragments are presumably debris from the nearby kilns.

FLOOR TILE

From pit 62 there is a fragment of plain unglazed floor tile. It is 30mm thick made from a coarse dark red fabric with occasional large inclusions. A thinner, larger fragment comes from pit 72, with surviving dimensions of 90mm by 70mm and 20mm thick. The fabric is similar to the other tile but one surface is light orange.

ANIMAL BONE
Karen Deighton

Animal bone weighing 1.11kg was recovered. Identifiable bones were noted. Ageable and measurable bones (after Von Den Driesch) were also noted. Ageable elements included cheek tooth rows and bones with fusion and neonatal bones. Animal bone from wet sieving (3.4mm and 1mm residues) was also included.

Fragmentation was heavy with few whole bones recovered. Surface condition was reasonable A single instance of butchery was noted, a chopped *Bos* femur. No evidence of burning or canid gnawing was observed. The material appears to be domestic refuse.

Table 33: Identifiable bones by species

Bos cattle	*Ovicaprid* sheep/goat	*Sus* pig	*Avis* bird	*Cervid* deer	Amphibian	Total
7	6	4	1	2	4	24

ENVIRONMENTAL EVIDENCE
Karen Deighton

Two 20 litre samples were hand collected. These were processed using a siraf tank fitted with a 500-micron mesh and flot sieve. The resulting flots were dried and analysed using a microscope (10xmagnification). Analysis was undertaken to establish the nature, preservation and presence of ecofacts and their potential contribution to the understanding of the function and economy of the site.

Preservation was moderate with some cereal grains exhibiting fragmentation and abrasion.

Table 34: Finds by sample and context

Sample	1	2
Context/feature	43 / 'cess' pit 44	98 / pit100
Charcoal	Very frequent	Very frequent
Cereal	3	10
Pulse	1	
Weed/wild	2	
Other	Mollusc	

Note: Numbers for plant marcofossils refer to number of finds.

Cereal in sample 1 could not be identified beyond Wheat/barley (Triticum/Hordeum). The pulse in sample 1 appeared to be common vetch (*Vicia sativa*). The wild / weed species in sample 1 were possible raspberry (*Rubus* cf *idaeus*). Cereal types present in sample 2 were Spelt/bread wheat (*Triticum spelta/aestivum*), possible rye (Cereale cf *Secale cereale*) and possible naked barley (*Hordeum vulgare* cf var.nudum).

BIBLIOGRAPHY

Bellamy, B, 1983 Medieval Pottery kilns at Stanion, *Northamptonshire Archaeol*, **18**, 153 - 63

Blinkhorn, P, 1991 Three pottery bird whistles from Stanion, Northamptonshire, *Medieval Ceramics*, **15**, 21-24

Blinkhorn, P W, 1999 The Trials of Being A Utensil: Pottery Function at the Medieval Hamlet of West Cotton, Northamptonshire, *Medieval Ceramics*, **22-23**

Blinkhorn, P W, 2002b The Pottery, in J Hillier *et al*, 46-51

Blinkhorn, P W, 2003 The Pottery, in A Thorne, 116-9

Blinkhorn, P W, in press, The Saxon and medieval pottery, in A Chapman in press

Blinkhorn, P W, forthcoming b Saxon and Medieval Pottery from Warmington, Northants, in I Meadows forthcoming

Blinkhorn, P W, and Dix, B, 1992 A sherd of medieval pottery with a roller-stamped inscription from Flore, Northamptonshire, *Northamptonshire Archaeol*, **24**, 107-8

BGS 2003 http://www.bgs.ac.uk/geoindex/index.htm

Bryant, G F, and Steane, J M, 1969 Excavations at the Deserted Medieval Settlement at Lyveden. A Second Interim Report, *J Northampton Mus*, **5**

Chapman, A, in press *Raunds, West Cotton: A study of medieval settlement dynamics*, Oxbow books

Chapman, P, 2007 Ceramic and stone building materials, in D McAree 2007

Coleman-Smith, R, 2002 Excavations in the Donyatt potteries: site 13, *Post-medieval Archaeol*, **36**, 118-172

Denham, V, 1985 The Pottery, in M Shaw 1985, 123 – 33

Drury, P J, and Pratt, G D, 1975 A late 13th and early 14th century tile factory at Danbury, Essex, *Journal Soc Med Archaeol*, **19**, 92-164

Dunning, G C, 1967 Late medieval jugs with lettering, *Medieval Archaeology* **11**, 233-42

Eames, E, 1972 The Ceramic Tiles, in J Williams 1972, 121-128

Foard, G, The medieval pottery industry of the Rockingham Forest, Northamptonshire, *Medieval Ceramics*, **15**, 13-20

Foard-Colby, A, 2006 *Archaeological evaluation on land at 3 Corby Road, Stanion*, Northamptonshire Archaeology Report, **06/149**

Fox, J R, 1975 Stanion (SP914871), in Archaeology in Northamptonshire, *Northamptonshire Archaeol*, **10**, 1975, 170-1

Hadman, J, 1974 Stanion (SP914872), in Archaeology in Northamptonshire, *Northamptonshire Archaeology*, **9**, 1974, 110

Hillier, J, Hardy, A, and Blinkhorn, P W, 2002 Excavations at Derngate, Northampton, 1997 – 2000, *Northamptonshire Archaeol*, **30**, 31-61

Masters, P, Parker, M, and Webster, M, 1992 *Archaeological survey at Stanion, Northants*, Northamptonshire Archaeology Unit (Contracts Section)

McAree, D, 2007 *Archaeological excavation at Bread and Meat Close, Warwick, Warwickshire, November 2003*, Northamptonshire Archaeology Report, **05/78**

McCarthy, M R, and Brooks, C M, 1988 *Medieval Pottery in Britain AD900-1600*, Leicester University Press

Meadows, I, forthcoming *Excavations at Warmington*, Northamptonshire Archaeology

Mynard, D, 1984 A Medieval Pottery Industry at Olney Hyde, *Records of Buckinghamshire*, **26**, 56 - 85

NA 2002 *Project design: archaeological recording action, construction of a new dwelling at 2 Corby Road, Stanion*, Northamptonshire Archaeology

NCCHET 2002 *Brief for Archaeological Recording Action*, Northamptonshire County Council Historic Environment Team

Pearce, J, and Vince, A, 1988 *A Dated Type-Series of London Medieval Pottery. Part 4: Surrey Whitewares*, Trans London and Middlesex Archaeol Soc, Special Pap, **10**

Shaw, M, 1985 Excavations on a Saxon and Medieval Site at Black Lion hill, Northampton, *Northamptonshire Archaeol*, **20**

Soden, I, 1993 *An archaeological evaluation at 2 Corby Road, (Land at Little Lane), Stanion, Northants, 1993*, Northamptonshire Archaeology Report

Steadman, S, 1993 *Archaeological evaluation at land north of Manor Farm, Stanion, Northamptonshire: March 1993*, Northamptonshire Archaeology Unit (Contracts Section)

Steane, J M, 1967 *Excavations at Lyveden 1965-67*, J Northampton Museums and Art Gallery, **2**

Steane, J M, 1971 *Excavations at the Deserted Medieval Settlement at Lyveden 1965-67: a third interim report*, J Northampton Museums and Art Gallery, **9**

Steane, J M, and Bryant, G F, 9875 Excavations at the Deserted Medieval Settlement at Lyveden, Northants, *J Northampton Mus* **12**

Stewardson, A, unpublished *Report on the Ceramics from 2 Corby Road, Stanion, Northants*, Leicester University MA Dissertation

Thorne, A, 2003 A Medieval Tenement at Deene End, Weldon, Northamptonshire, *Northamptonshire Archaeol*, **31**, 116-9

Von den Driesch, A, 1976 *Guide to the identification of animal bone from Archaeological sites*, Harvard University

Webster, P A, 1975 Pottery Report, in J M Steane and G F Bryant, 60 - 95

Williams, J, 1978, Excavations at Greyfriars, Northampton 1972, *Northamptonshire Archaeol*, **13**, 96 – 160

APPENDIX 1: PHOTOGRAPHIC ARCHIVE (Figs 27-34)

Given the lack of a developed-funded budget to cover the costs of post-excavation analysis for this exceptionally large quantity of pottery, it has not been possible to have the vessels drawn. Instead a photographic archive has been complied providing side views of all the largely reconstructed vessels. Each image includes a scale bar and the pottery reference number. On the following pages (Figs 27-34) the vessels are reproduced at consistent scales. A full set of these images is also included on the CD attached to this volume.

ST1, pit 14

ST2, pit 14

ST3, pit 14

ST3, pit 14

ST4, pit 14

ST5, pit 14

Fig 27 Pottery catalogue, jugs ST1-ST5, pit 14

ST6, pit 14

ST6, pit 14

ST7, pit 14

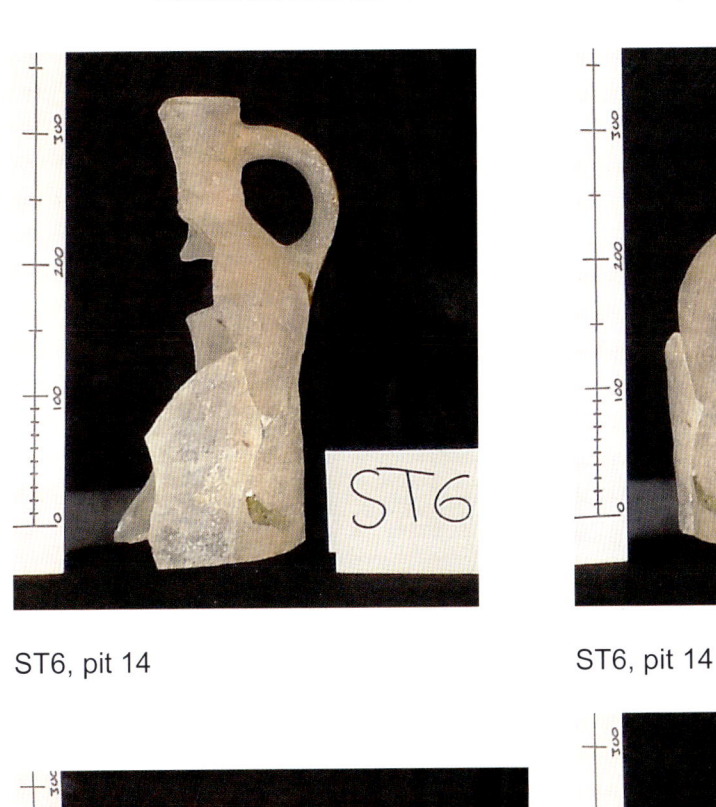

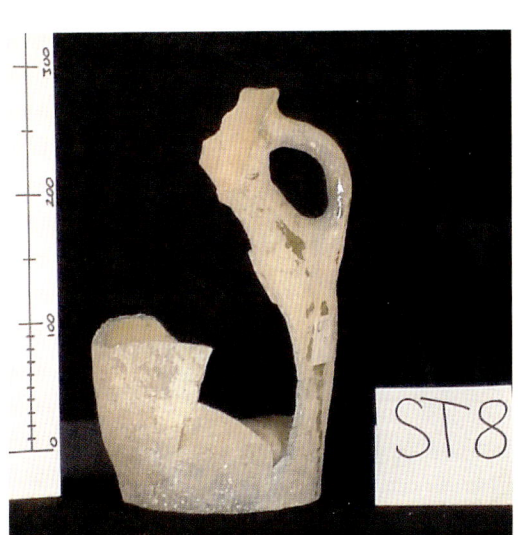

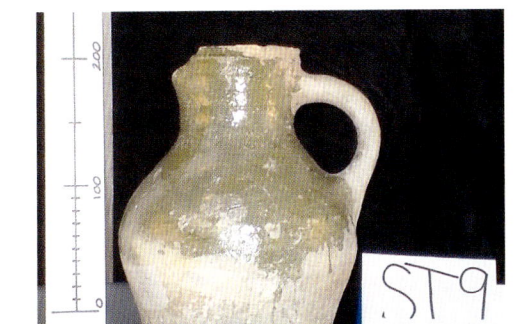

ST8, pit 14

ST9, pit 14

ST10, pit 14

Fig 28 Pottery catalogue, jugs ST6-ST10, pit 14

ST12, pit 70

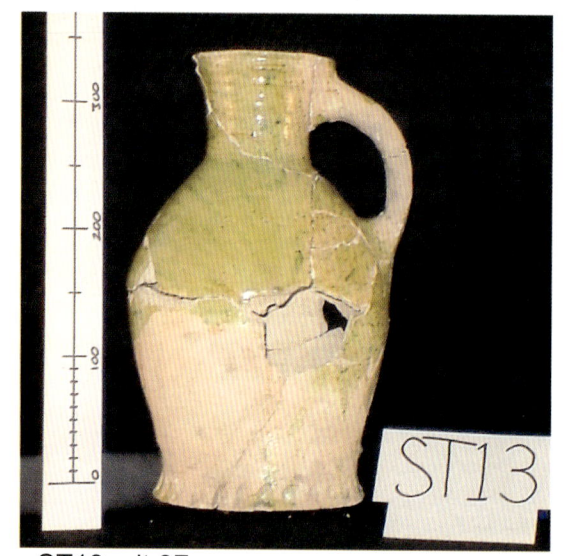

ST13, pit 97

ST14, pit 97

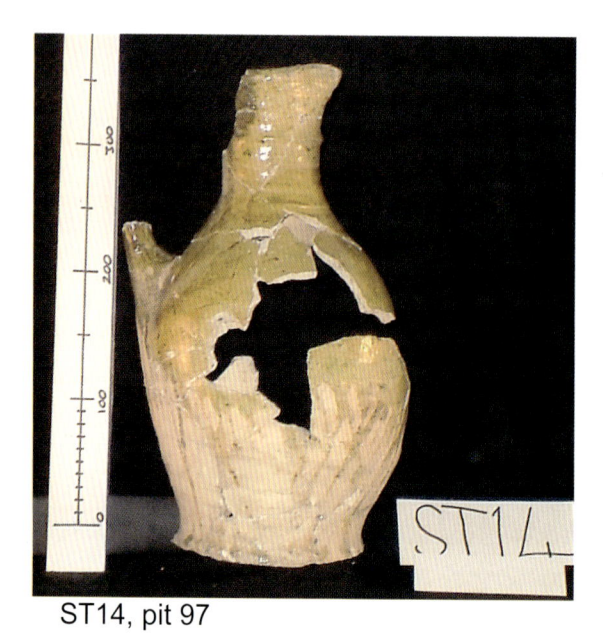

Fig 29 Pottery catalogue, jugs ST12, pit 70; ST13 and ST14, pit 97

ST15, pit 97

ST16, pit 14

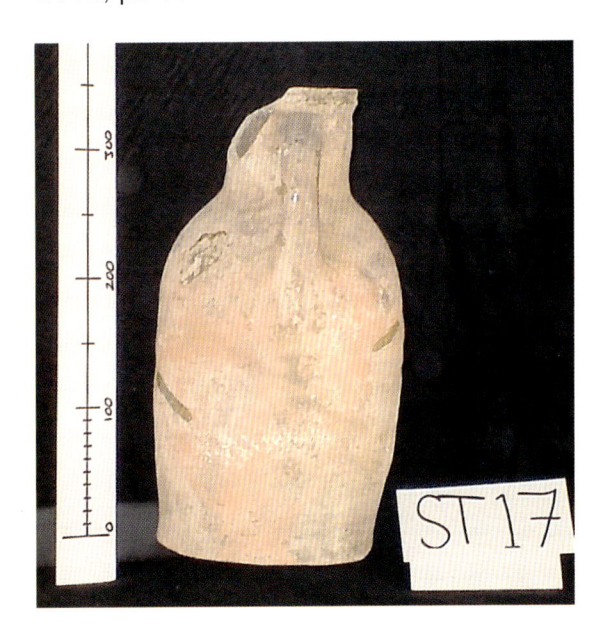

ST17, pit 97

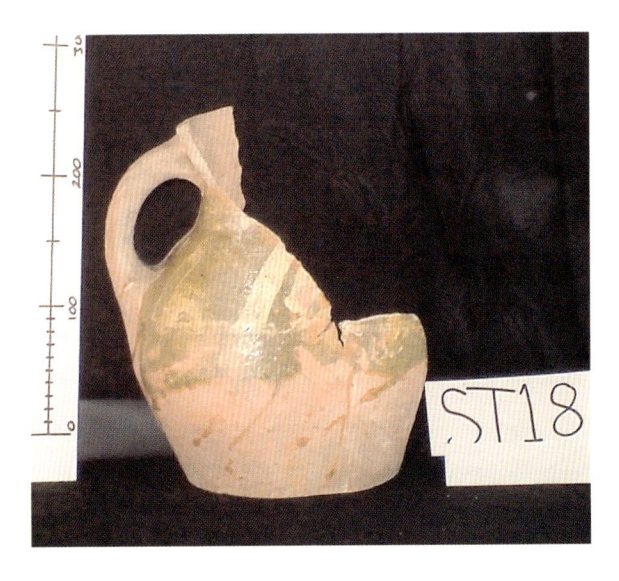

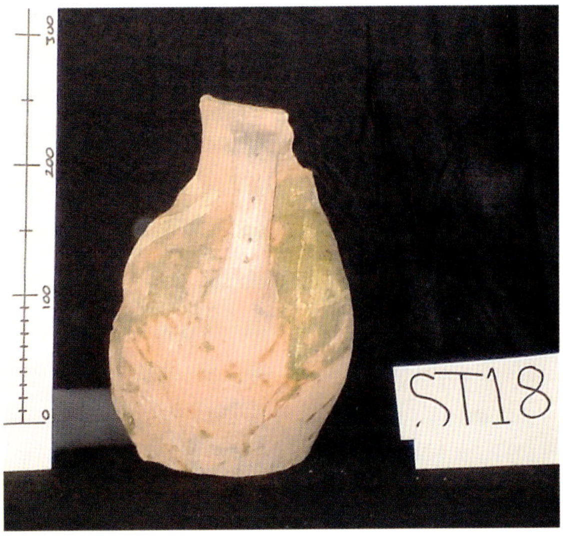

ST18, pit 97

Fig 30 Pottery catalogue, jugs ST16, pit 14; ST15, ST17 and ST18, pit 97

ST19, pit 97

ST20, pit 97

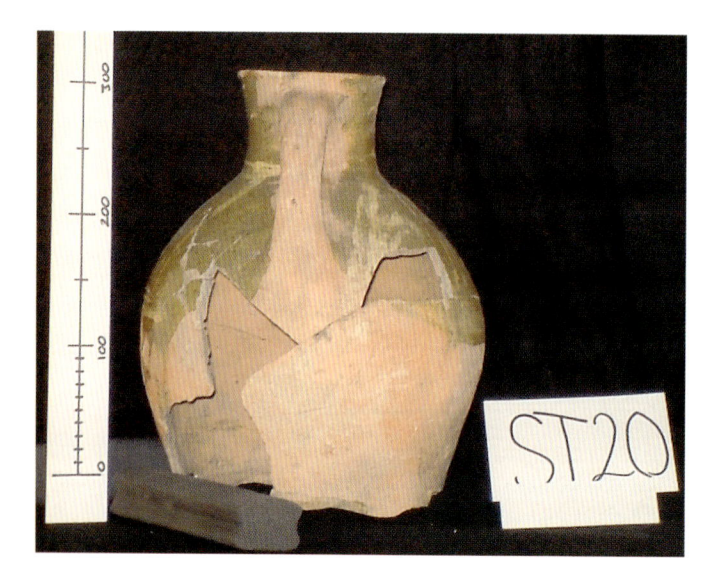

ST20, pit 97

Fig 31 Pottery catalogue, jugs ST19 and ST20, pit 97

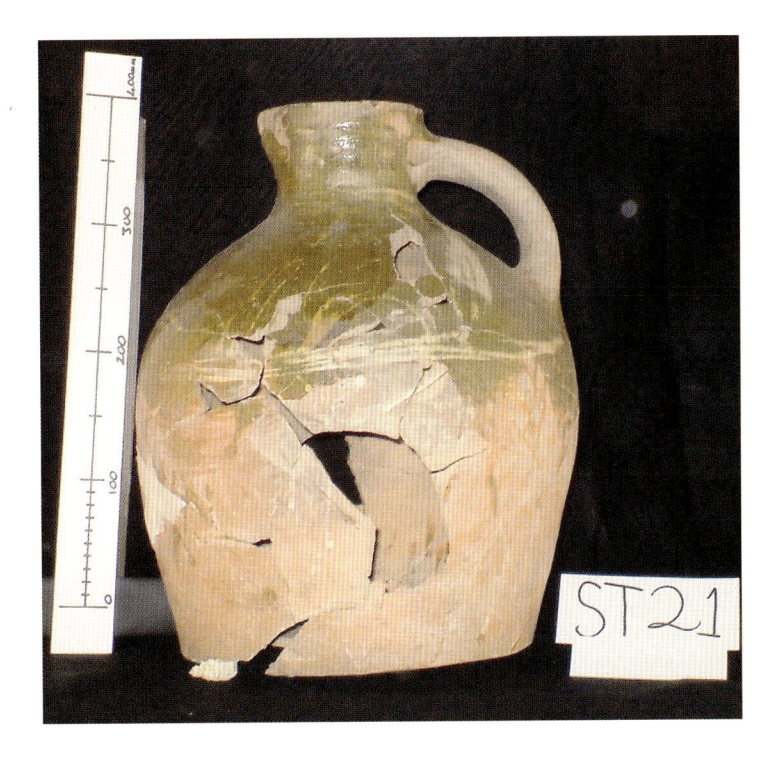

ST21, pit 97

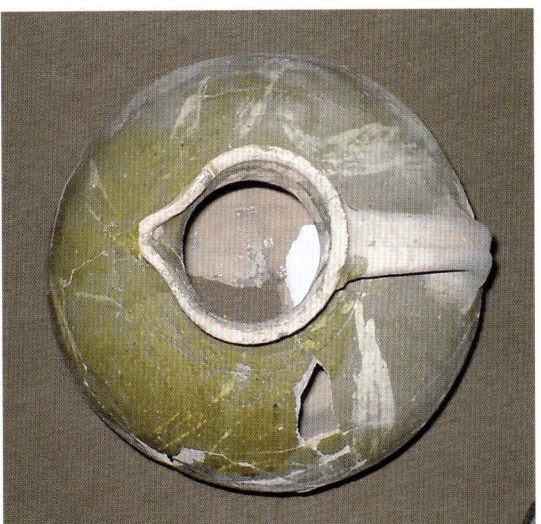

Fig 32 Pottery catalogue, jug ST21, pit 97

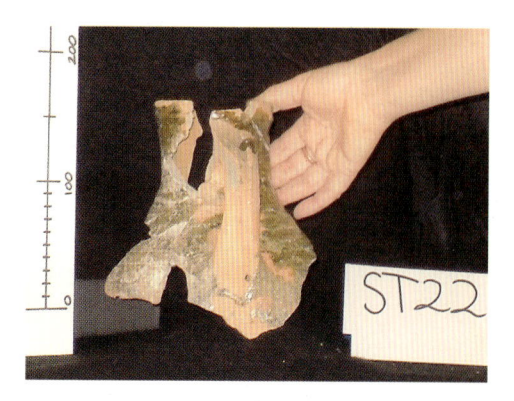

ST22, pit 70

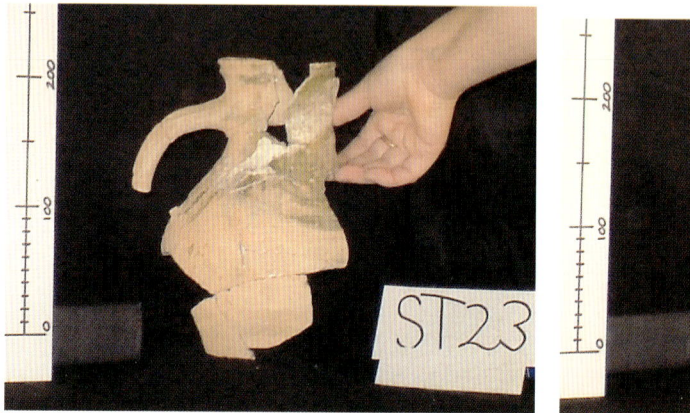

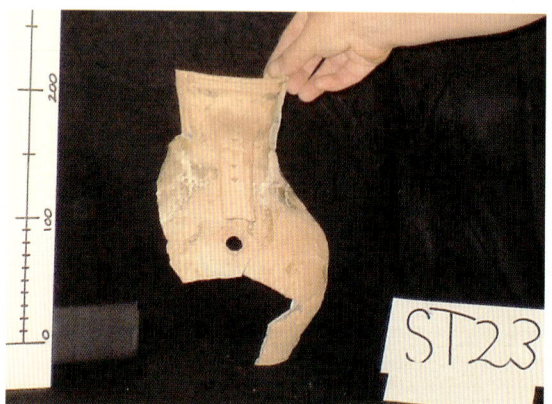

ST23, pit 23

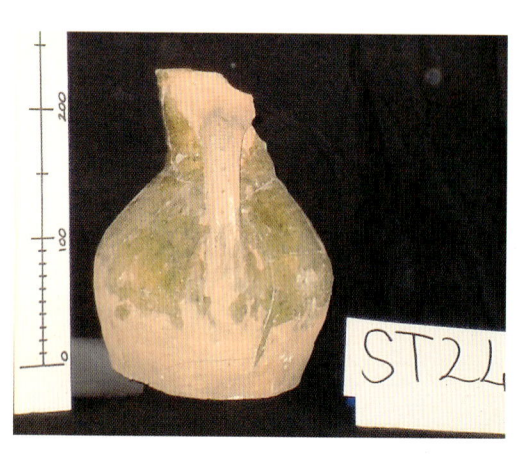

ST24, pit 24

Fig 33 Pottery catalogue, jugs ST22, pit 70; ST23, pit 23 and 24, pit 59

SJ1, pit14

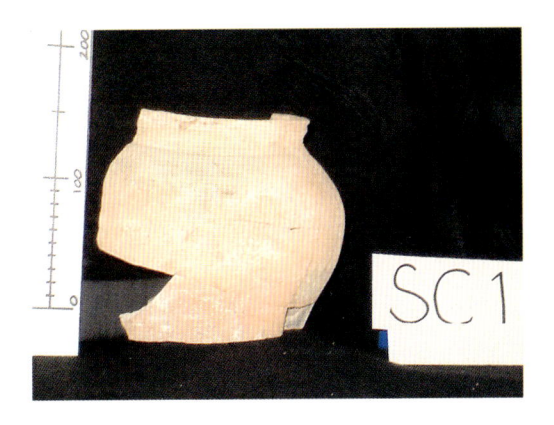

SC1, pit 14    SC4, pit 14

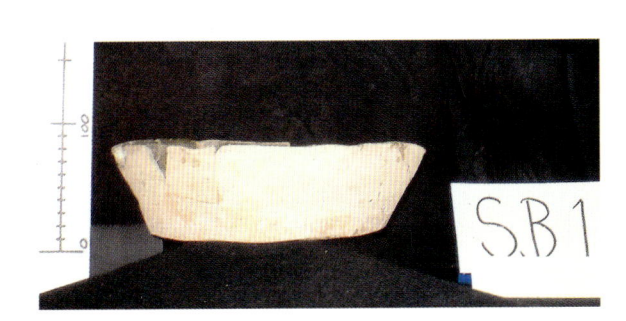

SB1, pit 14

Fig 34 Pottery catalogue, jug SJ1, jars SC1 and SC4, six-lipped bowl SB1; pit 14

The Tin Tabernacle, Havelock Street, Desborough

by

JOE PRENTICE

SUMMARY

The Tin Tabernacle on Havelock Street, Desborough dates from the late nineteenth century. It is a prefabricated, timber-frame building clad with corrugated iron and lined with tongue and groove match board pine. These buildings were used primarily by non-conformist churches which were springing up all over the country in huge numbers and, as congregations grew, funds were raised to provide affordable dedicated buildings of worship. The Desborough Tin Tabenacle has survived through different usages with the basic structure largely intact, and the building has provided an uncommon and distinctive element of the local architectural landscape.

INTRODUCTION

The Tin Tabernacle stands on Havelock Street, Desborough, Northamptonshire, near its junction with Station Road, an area due for redevelopment (Fig 1). Northamptonshire Archaeology was commissioned by Kettering Borough Council to carry out a basic desk-based assessment and photographic building survey of several properties under council ownership in the small town of Desborough prior to decisions being taken concerning their future. The general objective was to set the buildings into a local historical context using basic map regression to trace their development, and to provide a written and photographic appraisal of the buildings to form an archive record before any change.

Site visits were made in December 2007 to make a written and photographic record of the buildings and their settings. Desk-based assessment was undertaken in the Northamptonshire Record Office to identify maps and other documents relevant to the properties. A drawn record was not required, and the principal record was by digital photography with additional detail recorded in written notes.

The project was managed by Steve Parry and the fieldwork was conducted by Joe Prentice and Yvonne Wolframm-Murray. The full report on all the properties was prepared by Joe Prentice (2007), and is available in the county *Historic Environment Record* and will be available online through the *Archaeology Data Service* (ADS), Unpublished Fieldwork Reports (Grey Literature). The account of the Tin Tabernacle has been extracted from the larger report and edited for publication by Andy Chapman.

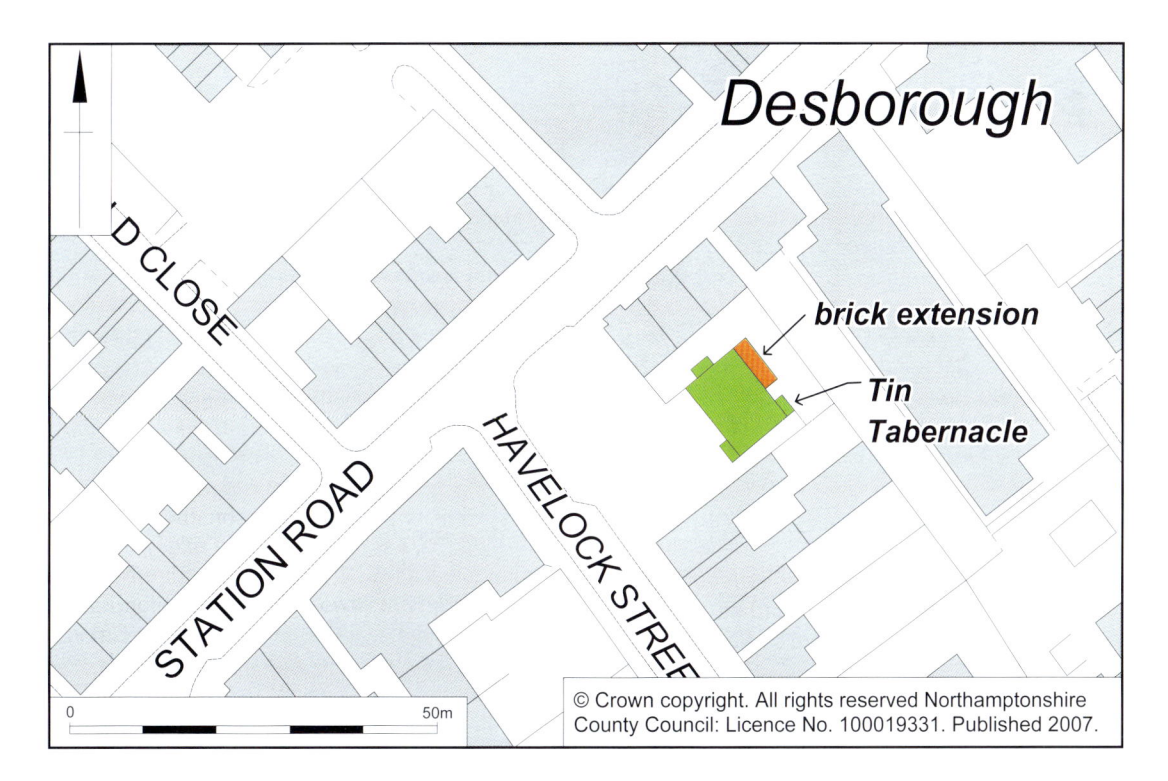

Fig 1 The location of the Tin Tabernacle, Desborough

DESK-BASED ASSESSMENT

DESBOROUGH

Historic maps show Desborough to be a small town until well into the nineteenth century. In 1857 the London, Midland and Scottish Railway was opened through the town, and shortly following it came ironstone quarrying, which quickly spread across the parish. There was a small boot and shoe industry in the mid-nineteenth century which developed widely during the 1880s and 1890s. In 1854 there was just one boot and shoe maker, by 1894 there were eight manufacturers and two shoemakers. By 1880, when the 1st edition Ordnance Survey map was published, some new building of housing and factories had taken place. By the time of the 1900 edition there had been much further development, and both Havelock Street and the Tin Tabernacle were in existence. At that time the Tin Tabernacle had a porch at the northern end and two small rooms at either side of the southern end. It appeared to sit within an open-fronted plot.

TIN TABERNACLES

Corrugated iron was being mass produced in Britain as early as the 1830s and with the invention of galvanisation in France in 1837, it rapidly became a widely used building material. The first of the prefabricated churches, or "Tin Tabernacles" as they became known, was built in London in 1855 (Smith 2004). Various companies produced buildings in kit form which could be chosen from catalogues to suit every need, though mostly the deciding factor on the size and complexity of the building is likely to have been cost.

A number of engineering companies showed corrugated iron buildings at the Great Exhibition in 1851. They were used primarily by non-conformist churches which were springing up all over the country in huge numbers and, as the congregations grew, funds were raised to provide dedicated buildings of worship. Prices began at under £100.00 (approximately £8,000.00 now, using the Retail Price Index) and the erection of the building would often be undertaken by the congregation. The buildings arrived, often by train, in their constituent parts and the wooden frames were erected on simple brick or stone rubble bases. The land on which the building was erected was often donated by a local landowner at a peppercorn rent which explains why so many churches have such a small plot.

The inside walls were lined with tongue and groove match board pine and the corrugated iron sheeting provided the external weatherproofing, a rudimentary form of insulation was provided by felt sandwiched between the inner and outer skins of the building. The floor ranged from beaten earth, wooden boards, brick, tile or stone depending on funds. Similarly the windows could be simple standard squares or rectangles, but also included ecclesiastical styles and occasionally stained or painted glass, and the most elaborate churches had steeples and bell towers. Heating was sometimes provided by a wood or coal stove, and lighting either by candles or paraffin lamps, later superseded by gas and electricity. Sometimes the tin tabernacles were intended to have only a short lifespan, until sufficient funds could be raised for a permanent building in brick or stone. If this was achieved the tin buildings were either sold on to have other uses, or were kept to be used as Sunday School rooms, reading rooms or any number of other uses. Their simple construction meant that they could be moved easily or adapted by locals without any specialist skills or great expense.

THE DESBOROUGH TABERNACLE

Though the history of the building type is well known and documented, the history of this particular example is not clear. It was not present in 1880, but its depiction on the 1900 Ordnance Survey map shows that it stands in its original position, having been erected at some point in the previous decade.

It is not known which denomination built the hall, and it is possible that it may not have been built for a directly religious purpose, as many such buildings were erected for use as halls, meeting rooms and Temperance Clubs, and a brick-built Temperance Room and Café still stands just across the road at Desborough. Temperance Halls were often started in temporary buildings, so it could have been linked with that movement, though at present no evidence has been found to prove this.

It is understood to have served as the town Fire Station until *circa* 1980 when a new, purpose-built, station was erected a few streets away, on Station Road, though it is not clear when it became the Fire Station. It has been used as a commercial garage since the mid 1980s.

BUILDING ASSESSMENT

The Desborough Tin Tabernacle is constructed from a timber frame covered externally in corrugated iron sheeting, some of this is original and some later replacements (Fig 2). The building is simple in plan, a main rectangular room in which the meetings were held, with a small entrance porch at the north-west end (Fig 1). At the south end on the east side there is a small room which may have served as a simple vestry, and there is a similar room on the west side, which is now the lobby to the garage workshop. Both side rooms are clearly shown on the 1900 Ordnance Survey map.

The porch at the north end has double doors on the exterior (Figs 3 & 4) and a second set of doors which open into the body of the church (Fig 5). The two sets of doors have the same configuration and are typical of factory made pine doors with recessed panels bordered with a simple moulding. Above the doors the gable end of the porch is decorated with a shaped barge-board, which is also used on the main building (Figs 3 & 4). The porch has no windows but there are two in the north end of the main building (Fig 3). These are simple lancet style timber frames, the lower part fixed, the upper portion opening inwards and held in place by curved iron stays Figs 6 & 7). The glass is slightly ribbed and is thought to be original. Other windows on the east and west sides suggest there were originally four sets of two lancets on each side. It is not known if there were any on the south end as this façade is not accessible from the exterior and the interior has been covered by modern decoration.

Fig 2 The western frontage of the Tin Tabernacle, showing the inserted Fire Station doors and one of the southern side rooms (right)

Fig 3 The northern end of the building, showing the porch and the later brick extension (left)

The roof is supported on simple timber trusses with a collar strengthened by iron tie rods between the collar and the apex of the frame and from the underside of the collar to eaves level (Fig 8). The interior of the building is finished with vertical tongue and groove match board pine originally varnished a dark brown but now with numerous later coats of paint added at various times (Figs 5 & 8). It is not certain if any of the window frames or doors retain original colouring, but this is probably unlikely.

There are no fixtures or fittings which relate to its original usage, or indeed any period apart from its current use as a garage. The floor is partly concrete, inserted most likely when the building became a fire station, and partly timber, the latter being replaced by the current tenant. On the west side of the building opening onto Havelock Street glazed double doors had been inserted to make the access for a fire engine (Fig 9). Traces of the fire station red paint can be seen on the double doors beneath a later green paint. The exterior of the west side has been fitted with modern square-section corrugated metal sheeting; it is not known if this has been fitted over the original corrugated iron or replaces it. On the east side an additional room has been added in brick (Figs 1 & 3).

DISCUSSION

The Havelock Street garage is a good example of a pre-fabricated building type generally known as a "Tin Tabernacle". Produced in huge numbers in the latter part of the nineteenth, and early part of the twentieth centuries, these buildings are increasingly being recognised as

Fig 4 The porch, showing the decorated bargeboards on the porch and main gable

Fig 5 The interior showing the windows and the internal doors from the north porch, and the tongue-and-groove match boarding

Fig 6 Exterior view of a typical lancet-style window

Fig 7 Interior view of a typical lancet-style window, with curved stays to support the opening top light

Fig 8 The interior showing the wooden roof trusses and strengthening iron rods, and the matchboard lining

Fig 9 Inserted Fire Station doors on the west side of building

an important part of the development of both non-conformist religion and architectural innovation. Their constructional method, however, means that unless maintained regularly and carefully, they have a relatively short lifespan, though this of course was part of the original design as they were cheaply manufactured and were never intended to be permanent. The Desborough building, whilst preserving some elements remarkably intact, such as the decorated barge boards on the north gable ends, has undergone significant changes. The insertion of the double doors when the building became a fire station has compromised the western side of the building, but such an alteration could be relatively simply un-done. This western side has also been clad with modern corrugated sheeting, although the original corrugated iron may survive beneath.

It does not appear that the use of the building as a garage has had much effect at all since it uses the internal space and does not seem to have resulted in any substantial changes to the structure. The building's continued occupation has almost certainly ensured its survival to the present, since once unused these building's become derelict very quickly. There do not appear to be any fixtures or fittings which relate to the buildings original use, which is still unknown. Future uses for the building are limited; the main room space is versatile but the construction of the building means that there is practically no insulation and it contains limited facilities. The structure itself appears to be in reasonable condition, but some repair is needed. The constricted nature of the plot on which the building stands limits the use of outside space, and long term prospects for the structure depend on a regular repair and maintenance regime. Alternatively the building could find a new use elsewhere, its pre-fabricated construction meaning that it could be dismantled and re-erected for a new lease of life.

The Tin Tabernacle, along with the houses and factory recorded at the same time, represents an aspect of life in Desborough now gone, but nevertheless integral and essential to its history and development. Whilst individually not of great local, regional or national significance, recognised by the fact that they are not individually Listed, such buildings are all important to the locality as they each have distinct visual and social impacts.

The Tin Tabernacle would be a difficult building to find an alternative use for and, though it has been on the site since at least 1900, it does not have an obvious visual impact on its surroundings due to its location and small size. It is hard to perceive how it could continue to find a use in its present location or condition, and offering it for re-use elsewhere might be the best solution, though even if offered for nothing it might not be easy to find a group or individual eager to take on the challenge. However, at least this scenario would give the building a chance for survival, and before its removal or dismantling an opportunity could be made to try to find out more of its history by contacting locals, perhaps by an advertisement in a local paper asking for information.

BIBLIOGRAPHY

Ballinger, J, 2000 *Extensive Urban Survey of Northamptonshire: Desborough*, Northamptonshire County Council

Prentice, J, 2007 *Archaeological Building Assessment at The Lawrence Boot and Shoe Factory, Cottages on 15-21 Harborough Road and The Tin Tabernacle on Havelock Street, Desborough, Northamptonshire: December 2007*, Northamptonshire Archaeology, 07/198

Smith, I, 2004 *Tin Tabernacles. Corrugated Iron Mission Halls, Churches and Chapels of Britain*

A prefabricated temporary building at Cranford Primary School, Kettering, Northamptonshire

by

ANTONY WALSH

SUMMARY

The implementation of the 1944 Education Act raised the school leaving age from 14 to 15 in 1947. As a result a rapid expansion of space was required to accommodate the additional pupils. One response was the provision of temporary accommodation in prefabricated buildings, utilising the designs for standard huts issued by the Ministry of Works during World War II. A prefabricated building was erected in the grounds of Cranford school in 1946 but, far from being temporary, this was still in use some six decades later. Once common, these buildings are becoming increasingly scarce, and this example was recorded before demolition. The basic structure remained largely as built although the windows had been replaced and few original internal fixtures or fittings survived. The construction method was as described in the Ministry of Works construction manual, although the dimensions of the building and some use of materials suggest that it was a modified form of a standard type 24 hut.

INTRODUCTION

An application was made by Northamptonshire County Council (Buildings and Capital Development Section) for Conservation Area Consent to demolish a 1940s prefabricated 'HORSA' building (Hutting Operation for the Raising of the School-leaving Age) at Cranford Church of England Primary School, Church Lane, Cranford, Kettering, Northamptonshire (Fig 1, NGR SP92589, 76976). A condition to provide a photographic, drawn and written record of the building prior to demolition was provided by Myk Flitcroft, as Senior Environmental Planner, Northamptonshire County Council (NCC).

Northamptonshire Archaeology was commissioned to carry out this work. A site visit was made on 27th July 2006, and scale drawings provided by NCC were checked and annotated. A photographic record was made using 35mm film, both black and white negative and colour transparency and by digital SLR. Written descriptions were made using Northamptonshire Archaeology pro forma record sheets.

ACKNOWLEDGEMENTS

The project manager was William Boismier and the fieldwork and photography was by Antony Walsh. The client report was prepared by Antony Walsh with assistance from Joe Prentice, and this report has been edited for publication by Andy Chapman. The illustrations are by Jacqueline Harding.

BACKGROUND

The 1944 Education Act formed an important part of the programme of post-war social reconstruction. Amongst its many provisions was the intention to establish a nationwide system of free, compulsory schooling from age 5 to 15, with a further rise to 16 as soon as was practicable. As a consequence, the school leaving age was raised from 14 to 15 in 1947. In this post-war period this placed a considerable burden on school facilities, with an evident need for more space to accommodate the additional pupils at a time of austerity and shortages.

As with housing, a quick, cheap and 'temporary' solution was found in the use of prefabricated buildings. These were allocated by the Hutting Section of the Ministry of Works during the 1940s to provide temporary accommodation until such a time as permanent buildings could be constructed. The name 'HORSA' that has been attached to these buildings stands for 'Hutting Operation for the Raising of the School-leaving Age'.

The Standard 24 Hut was a sectional structure which allowed buildings of different sizes to be built by the addition of extra 6-foot sections (or bays) as required. The 24 denotes the span of the building at 24feet (7.32m). The construction manual, issued by the Ministry of Works, Hutting Section, Cleland House, Page Street, London SW1 in August 1943 issue, describes the form of these huts in some detail (MoW 1943). Copies of two pages showing the plan form and a method for erection of the framework are illustrated (Figs 2 & 3). These huts were to be erected on a prepared base of the most minimal specification-'strip turf and remove vegetable soil, excavate additional depth if directed for hardcore (to be kept to a minimum). Excavate for post foundations. Establish carefully the post positions'. The posts were to be set in sockets 'which must not exceed 10″ by 9″ and be 9″ deep exactly', with the posts grouted in using a mortar comprising a ratio of 1:2 of cement and sand. A framework of reinforced concrete ribs was bolted to the bracketed posts and held at the ridge by a continuous tie. The description of the framework erection allowed for a minimum of four workmen to manhandle the posts and beams using A-frames and a light portable gantry (Fig 3).

The posts forming the ends were flat-topped, without ribs, and concrete floor sills and lintels spanned the walls between the posts to form standard sized panels

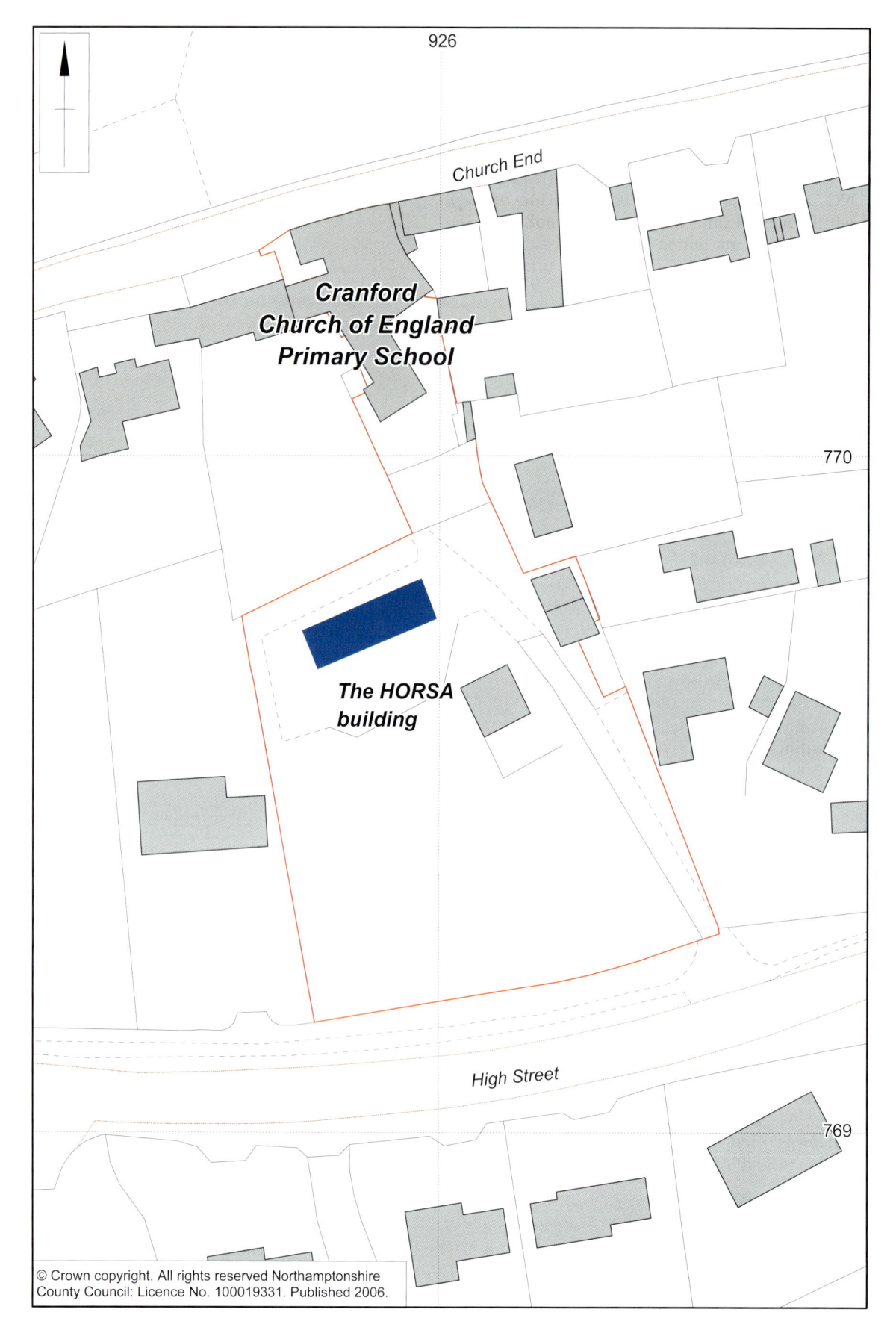

Fig 1 The location of the HORSA building at Cranford School

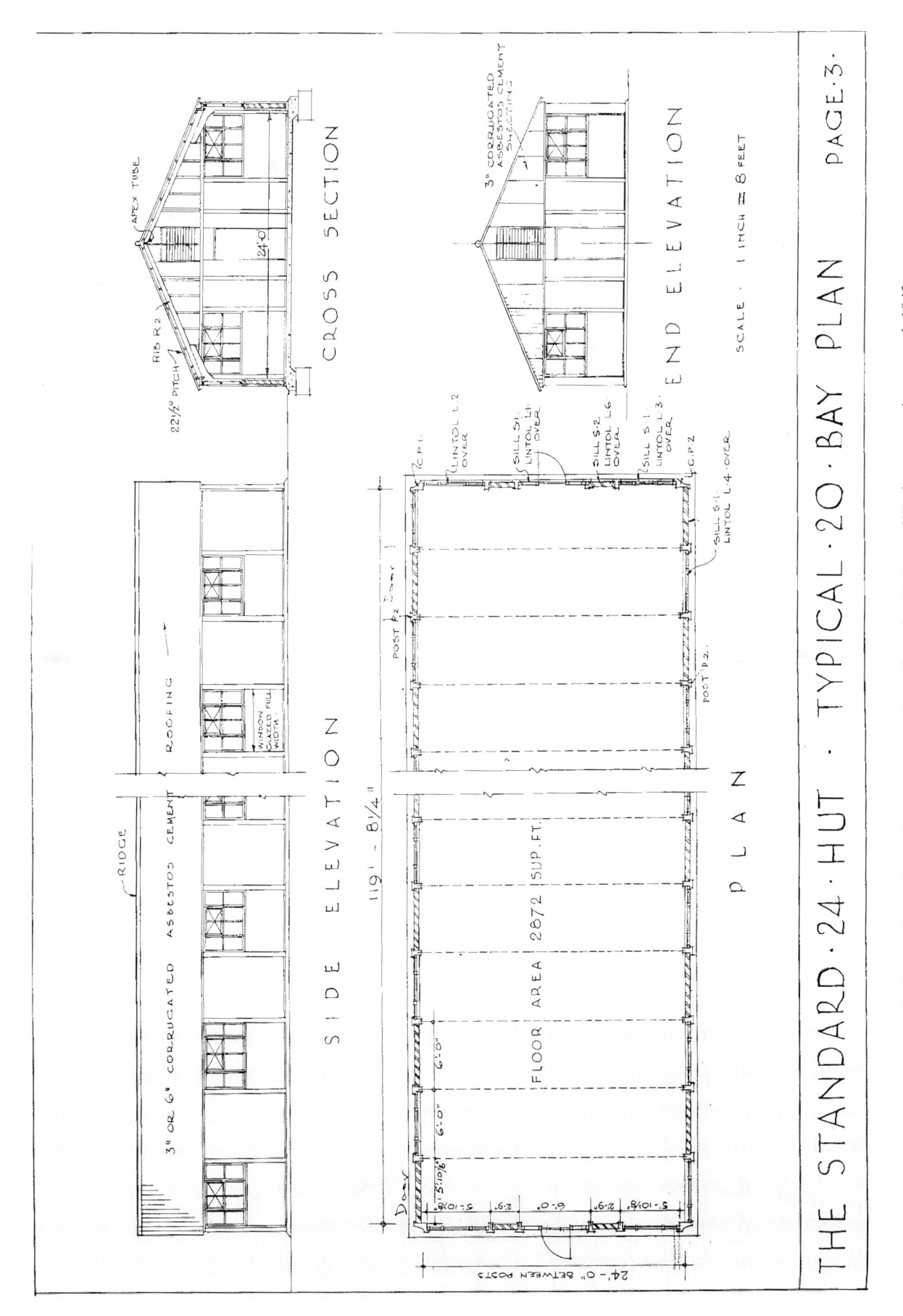

Fig 2 Plan and elevations of a typical type-24 hut, from the *Ministry of Works* construction manual, 1943

● A COMPLETE BASE WITH CORRECTLY SET OUT & LEVELLED POST HOLES IS ASSUMED.
   SEE PAGES 6 & 7

1. SET UP, ALIGN, PLUMB, & SECURE WITH WEDGES AS SHOWN. THE WHOLE OF THE POSTS GROUT THE POSTS IN, EACH ONE BEING SUPPORTED BY AN 'A' FRAME — AND NO FURTHER OPERATIONS BEING PERFORMED · UNTIL THE CONCRETE HAS HARDENED

2. SET UP A LIGHT PORTABLE GANTRY ABOUT 10'0" HIGH, BY 13'0" BY 4'0" IN LINE BETWEEN A PAIR OF OPPOSITE POSTS. HOIST ONTO IT A PAIR OF RIBS
   A PORTABLE CRANE OR SHEAR LEGS, WITH NON-OVERHAULING BLOCK & TACKLE MAY BE USED. THE LOAD BEING SUSTAINED BY THE TACKLE WHILE THE RIBS ARE BEING OFFERED TO THE POSTS BOTH RIBS MAY BE ERECTED SIMULTANEOUSLY BY THE USE OF TWO HOISTING APPLIANCES
   ● IF LIFTING TACKLE IS USED THE RIBS MUST BE PROTECTED FROM DAMAGE BY THE SLING

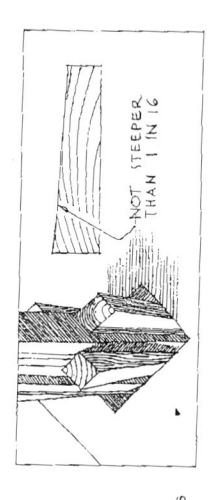

3. TWO MEN ON THE GANTRY NOW OFFER A RIB TO ITS POST, WHILE TWO MEN MAKE THE BOLTED CONNECTION. REPEAT WITH THE OPPOSITE POST, THE CONNECTIONS BEING HANDTIGHT ONLY. MAKE NECESSARY ADJUSTMENTS & THEN FIX APEX PIN

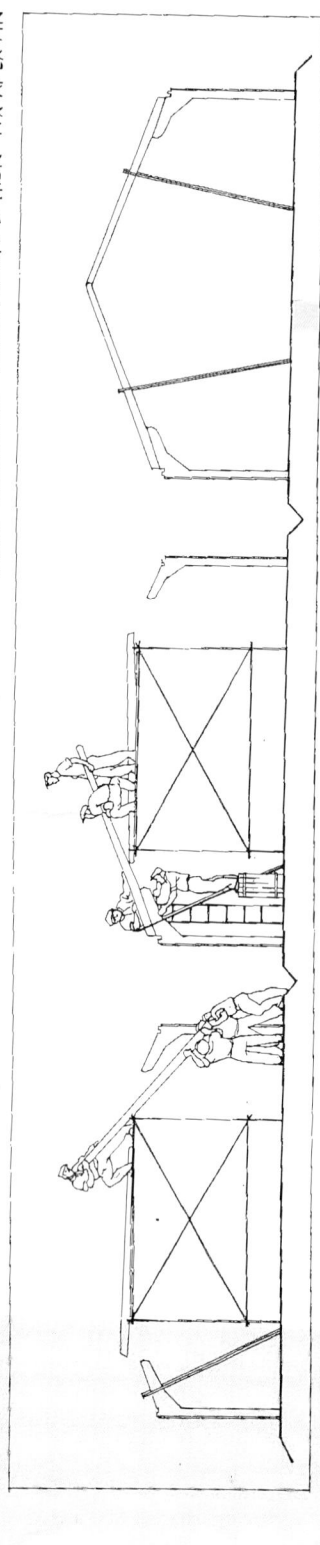

4. ON REMOVAL OF THE GANTRY TO THE NEXT BAY AN 'A' FRAME SHOULD BE PLACED BENEATH EACH RIB OF THE COMPLETED FRAME, AND THESE 'A' FRAMES MUST REMAIN IN POSITION UNTIL CONNECTIONS ARE FINALLY TIGHTENED
   CONTINUE SIMILARLY WITH THE ERECTION OF THE SUCCEEDING RIBS
   ● RIDGE TIES BEING FIXED AND LINTOLS GROUTED IN AS THE WORK PROCEEDS
   ● ON EXPOSED SITES AN 'A' FRAME SHOULD BE LEFT UNDER EVERY FOURTH FRAME UNTIL THE PURLINS HAVE BEEN FIXED
   ● POST · TO · RIB BOLTS ARE TO BE PLACED WITH NUTS UPPERMOST

This method matches the erection & grouting-in of all posts preceding the erection of the ribs.

HE STANDARD · 24 · HUT · ERECTION of FRAMEWORK · METHOD 2 · PAGE · 9 ·

Fig 3 Instructions for hut erection, from the *Ministry of Works* construction manual, 1943

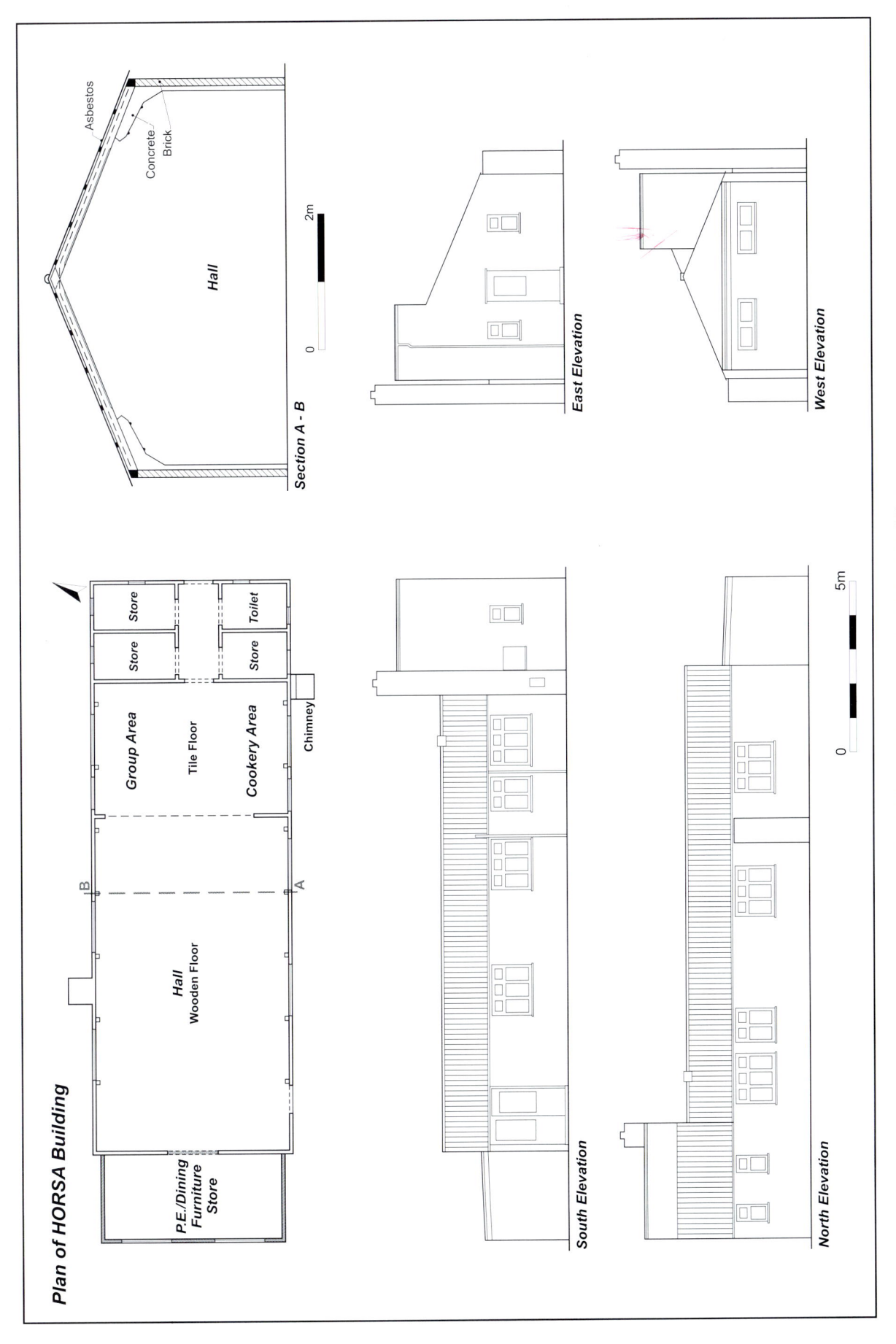

Fig 4 Plan and elevations of the HORSA Building

throughout for the wall cladding. The cladding between the posts could be of any material but the following were standardized; bricks, clay blocks, mineralised siding board, plasterboard or wood cement. Windows were also prefabricated and it was suggested that they should be top hung sashes opening outwards as these could be incorporated in mineralised siding boards, if this method of infill was chosen. Roofs appear to have always been standard three or six-inch corrugated asbestos sheeting screwed to timber purlins fixed to the ribs, and building-board lining.

The buildings were clearly relatively quick and cheap to erect and required minimal foundations. The manual provides full and clear instructions from the arrival of the separate parts at the site and the recommended method of storage to the finishing and decorating, and even the fitting of blackout screens.

THE SCHOOL PLOT

The HORSA building at Cranford primary school stood centrally within the school plot (Fig 1). To the south was the school field; which is contained by a fence and accessed by a gated footpath onto the High Street. Two buildings to the south, an office and a temporary classroom, had recently been replaced by an extension to the main school and a 'new' temporary classroom. A new playground had been constructed south of the HORSA building, which involved levelling the natural slope, which rises towards the High Street. It is likely that the site of the HORSA building also required levelling. The main school buildings lie to the north, facing onto Church End. The surrounding properties are residential, with gardens.

Following the demolition of the prefabricated building, the school now has a new hall on this site.

THE CRANFORD PREFABRICATED BUILDING

The building was aligned east to west and the original structure was 17m long (55' 9"), with a 2.5m long modern extension on the western end (Figs 4 & 5). The internal width of the building was 5.7m (c19 feet), 5-feet less than the 24-feet specified for the Type 24 Hut. The maximum internal height was 3.4m.

The construction method was clearly visible within the open room that comprised most of the interior. Seven concrete posts and brackets formed seven and a half bays bounded by end walls of brick (Figs 4 & 6). The ceiling ribs were simply bolted to the brackets (Fig 7). The ribs were halved at the apex and had a chamfer on their underside, which was repeated on the brackets (Fig 8). Between the posts there was brick infill to the wall plate and the apex of the gables. The external finish was of pebble-dashed render (Figs 5 & 9). Originally the windows would have contained metal frames, but these had been replaced with UPVC units. The roof was of corrugated asbestos sheeting. The northern elevation of the building was fenced off and very overgrown, and could not be photographed due to the close proximity of trees and bushes. The northern wall of the building was clearly the least stable, and had recently been reinforced with timber shoring. A possible disused chimney was noted between the western and central windows.

Fig 5 The southern elevation, with the service rooms (right) and the modern extension (left)

Fig 6 Interior of hall looking east, showing the partial partition between the main room and the cookery and group area (background)

Fig 7 Detail of single bracket, showing bolts retaining rib

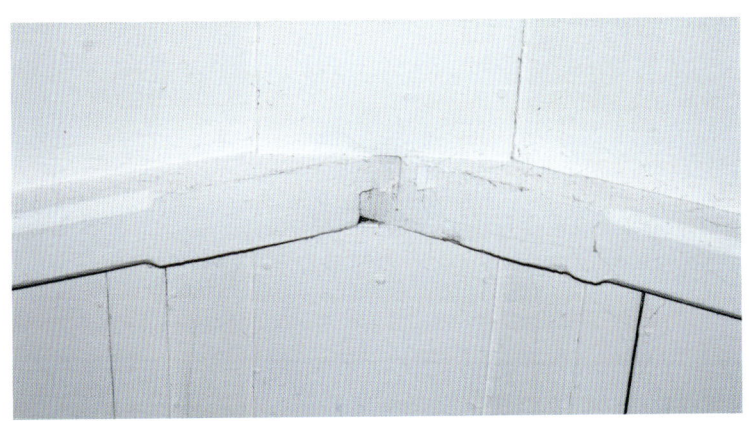

Fig 8 Detail of apex of ribs, showing halved joint and chamfering

The main part of the building was an open hall (Fig 6). At the east end, two and a half 'bays' were a cookery area, containing a sink and kitchen units, and on the north side was a 'Group Area' for teaching. These bays were partially separated from the hall space to the west by a brick wall extending *c* 2m from the southern wall and a projecting brick post on the northern wall. The division was also reflected in the flooring, with the cookery area having a red tile floor while the hall had wooden parquet flooring.

Originally the space was probably more formally divided, by a full wall or partition, with a stove or fireplace serving each. The chimney serving the eastern area still stood against the southern elevation (Figs 4, 5 & 10). The capped remnant of a chimney serving the larger western room stood against the northern elevation at the centre of the five-bay hall (Fig 4). The position of a former fireplace or stove base was indicated by a rectangular area of different flooring. Recently, the wooden-floored end of the building had been used for PE, as well as a dining area, with swing-out climbing bars on the south wall and brass fixing points in the floor.

The internal decoration and finishing was very simple, with painted brickwork and a hardboard ceiling. Lighting consisted of suspended striplights hung on chains. The electric wiring was surface mounted in pipes or pinned to the wall with plastic clips, and passing through spaces in the concrete brackets. The headteacher remarked that there was minimal insulation in the building, and that it was very cold in winter.

Although now occupied by new UPVC units, the arrangement of window openings on the southern elevation was probably original, and was mirrored on the northern side. Four windows were present in each elevation, in an asymmetrical arrangement; with two widely-spaced three-light windows in either elevation of the larger western room and closely spaced three- and two-light windows serving the cookery and group area.

A door at the western end of the southern wall contained a UPVC door and window, but the former presence of a simpler door here was suggested by a surviving outside step.

At the western end of the building there was a more recent flat-roofed extension, built of breeze blocks. This was used to store PE and dining furniture, and was accessed by double doors. The extension had a clear straight joint with the original west wall of the building and the pebble dash render on the original external wall still survived within the extension. It may be conjectured that the double doors had replaced an earlier main entrance at the western end of the hall.

The eastern end of the building was occupied by four small service rooms flanking a short lobby/corridor that led to a door in the east elevation, slightly south of the central axis. All the rooms had similar design panel doors and concrete floors.

Over the southern storeroom and toilet, the building was of double height with a flat roof, with a separate sloped roof to the north (Figs 9 and 10). On the southern elevation, at the junction of the single and double storeys there was a slender chimney, with a metal flue access panel. The chimney was held together by a series of

Fig 9 The eastern elevation, showing the raised water tank storage over the service rooms

Fig 10 The service rooms, showing the chimney, with supporting metal bands, and hatch opening into the possible coal store

Fig 11 Store room, with stone slab shelf on brick piers, and wooden-slatted shelving

metal brackets. Immediately east of the chimney was a square hatch, presumably allowing access to the adjacent storeroom (Fig 10). This and the absence of a window, suggest that it once served as a coal store. The only fittings in this room were more recent, comprising the remains of veneered (MDF/chipboard) shelves. This room also contained a high-level access door into the double height roof space, through which a water tank could be seen.

The toilet/washroom to the east was lit by two small windows.

On the northern side of the corridor, the western storeroom had stone-slab shelves upon brick bases (Fig 11), suggesting that it was used as a pantry, while the eastern storeroom contained the service controls, electricity meter etc, and also remnants of wooden slatted shelving. They were each lit by a single small window.

CONCLUSION

It is understood that the expected life of such prefabricated buildings was approximately ten years. That at Cranford had stood for sixty years, although it was showing signs of subsidence, presumably a result of the shallow foundations. Following increasing cracking of the walls and floors, timber raking supports had been erected against the northern elevation in an attempt to restrict further movement.

The Cranford building appears to have been a slightly later model than that described in the Ministry of Works manual for 1943, as it had certain improvements to the specification, such as brick walls to the apex of the gables rather than corrugated asbestos sheets above eaves level, and a pebble-dashed external finish and metal window frames (recently replaced with UPVC units).

The original asbestos roof had become brittle and the chimney was held together by a series of metal brackets. At the opposite end of the building a small flat-roofed extension, built of breeze blocks, was also suffering from the movement of the HORSA building and was showing cracks to its walls.

In consequence of its condition, a decision was made to demolish the old 'prefab' and it has now been replaced by a new hall.

REFERENCES

MoW 1943 *Standard 24 Hut (24' 0" span): Description and Method of Erection*, Ministry of Works, August 1943

Notes

AN ELEVENTH-CENTURY COPPER ALLOY STIRRUP-STRAP MOUNT FROM OVERSTONE, NORTHAMPTONSHIRE

Some time ago, whilst metal detecting in the Overstone area of Northamptonshire, Mr Brian Hemmington discovered an interesting stirrup-strap mount. In August 2007, Mr Ian Wagstaff brought the object to the present author, in his capacity as the local Finds Liaison Officer for the *Portable Antiquities Scheme* (PAS), and the find was subsequently identified and recorded on the PAS database.

GENERAL BACKGROUND

The distinctive group of finds we now know as stirrup-strap mounts are items of early medieval horse furniture, and are so-called as they seem to have been fixed between the stirrup and its associated strap, in order to prevent wear on the leathers. They were originally identified as book clasps, but this has been reassessed in the light of metal detected finds. Indeed, the most comprehensive study of the form (Williams 1997) is a survey of artefacts very largely collected by this means. Examples from excavated contexts are few, and chronology is thus insecure, but on art historical grounds (particularly the use of debased Ringerike and Urnes style ornament), most are believed to date to the eleventh century (though see Lewis 2007). One of the few Northamptonshire examples from an excavation is from the deserted medieval hamlet of West Cotton, Raunds (Chapman in press, fig 11.38, 1), although even that is an unstratified metal detector find.

THE OVERSTONE MOUNT

This object (Fig 1) is made of cast copper alloy, and is in good condition, with an even green-brown patina. It measures 56mm long by 34mm wide, and weighs 29g. It is most notable for its anthropomorphic design; it features a central, facing, male figure surrounded by zoomorphic motifs. The central figure's head is in high relief, and bears traces of what may have been a beard or moustache, as well as a hairline or stylised helmet. The figure is naked, and some effort has been made to suggest muscle tone in the torso. The figure's arms and legs are apart, and some form of girdle lies around his upper legs, with an M-shaped profile. Below this hangs a straight rod (probably a phallus), terminating between the figure's feet, which are rather crudely rendered, being three-toed, and grasping the horizontal base in a manner comparable to bird claws. This base is pierced by two circular perforations, and the upper suspension loop (now broken away), emerges from behind the figure's head.

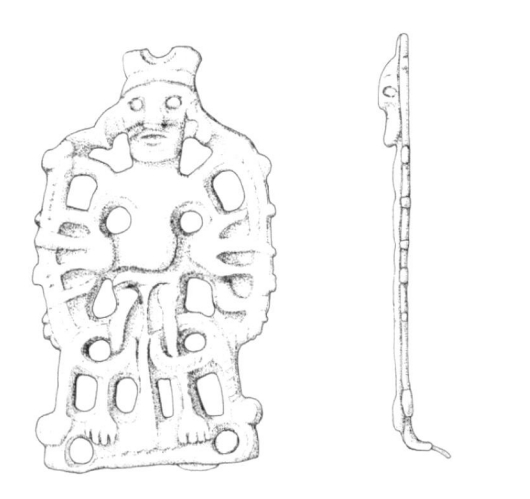

The figure is flanked by a pair of rudimentary serpents, whose tails entwine the figure's legs, with their heads (characterised by gaping mouths and bulging eyes) either side of that of the central figure. The serpents' bodies are grasped by the central figure's hands, and an unclear zoomorphic motif lies horizontally behind the arms of the man. Comparison with Williams' (1997) drawings suggests that this animal lies with its tail and hind legs to the left, and its head and forelimbs to the right, where it bites the body of the serpent. A number of grooves and facets on the lower sections of the serpents' bodies may have been intended for niello and silver wire ornament, as seen on similar examples from elsewhere in the country (Williams 1997, fig 25).

DISCUSSION

Artefacts dating to the late Viking Age/Anglo-Norman period are unusual. Indeed, PAS examples known from Northamptonshire number only 42 at the time of writing (see Ashby *in prep.*). These finds include strapends, buckles, brooches, and horse harness fittings. There are eleven stirrup-strap mounts from the county, including good examples from Abthorpe, Weedon, and Potterspury, but finds from excavated contexts are less common. The Overstone stirrup-strap mount thus holds particular importance as one of very few indicators of Anglo-Scandinavian/Late Saxon activity in the county.

The Overstone example is particularly unusual, being large in size, and of Class A type 3 (Williams 1997, 36-39). This type is poorly represented across the country (ten examples are recorded in the 1997 corpus, with only four others on the PAS database at the time of writing), but Williams (1997, 14) suggests that the type may have its origin at Winchester. Notably, most examples found thus far are rather debased in ornament, with all the PAS examples being degenerate. The present find, though not demonstrating the same level of craftsmanship as that apparent in the manufacture of the stirrup-strap mount from Sherborne St. John, Hampshire (Williams 1997, no.70) - which the author cites as one of the finest

Fig 1 The Overstone stirrup-strap mount

stirrup-strap mounts in his corpus - nonetheless sits with the more accomplished examples of the type. The Overstone find is thus an exciting addition to the corpus, and its preservation by record with the PAS is important. The find is recorded at www.finds.org.uk, with reference number NARC-6C5583.

ACKNOWLEDGEMENTS

I am grateful to Mr Brian Hemmington and Mr Ian Wagstaff for bringing the find to the PAS, and thanks to all those who gave opinions on the artefact, including David Williams and Michael Lewis. Thanks are also due to Michael Lewis for information regarding his recent work, and to Pat Walsh of *Northamptonshire Archaeology* for the drawing.

BIBLIOGRAPHY

Ashby, S P, (in prep) *Viking Age Northamptonshire: an archaeological survey based on data from the Portable Antiquities Scheme*

Chapman, A, in press *West Cotton, Raunds: a study of medieval settlement dynamics, AD 450-1450*, Oxbow Books

Lewis, M J, 2007 A new date for 'Class A, type 11A', stirrup-strap mounts, and some observations on their distribution, *Medieval Archaeology*, **51**, 178-184.

Williams, D, 1997 *Late Saxon stirrup-strap mounts: a classification and catalogue*, Council for British Archaeology, Research Report, **111**, York

STEVEN ASHBY
FINDS LIAISON OFFICER, PORTABLE ANTIQUITIES SCHEME,
NORTHAMPTONSHIRE COUNTY COUNCIL

THE NORTHAMPTONSHIRE PORTABLE ANTIQUITIES SCHEME, 2007

2007 has been an interesting year for the Portable Antiquities Scheme in Northamptonshire. Some uncertainty surrounds the security of the national scheme's long-term funding, but the local scheme - now well established in Northamptonshire County Council's *Archives and Heritage Service* - has continued to thrive. Increased numbers of finders (detectorists, field walkers, and casual finders alike) bring their finds for identification and recording to the Northamptonshire Finds Liaison Officer (FLO). In 2007, 118 people reported finds, and the total number of objects recorded in the year was 1387, surpassing the figures for 2006 by some margin. More importantly, these data are beginning to show signs of what they can tell us about the economic, settlement and landscape history of the county, and in some respects (for the Roman period in particular) the region stands out nationally, showing an unusually high concentration of finds.

The Scheme has attempted to maintain a high level of contact with existing finders, as well as encouraging others to come forward and volunteer their finds for recording. As well as meetings with members of the public, the FLO has maintained contact with finders by attending meetings at metal detecting clubs, and running finds surgeries held at regular intervals across the county. These currently take place at Corby, Daventry, Kettering, Northampton, Oundle, Towcester, and Wellingborough, with key support from the district councils, as well as at Piddington Roman Villa Museum, in collaboration with the *Upper Nene Archaeological Society*. There have also been a number of 'one-off' surgeries, in order to assess demand, and an event at Stanwick Lakes proved to be a particular success. The FLO has also attended and lectured at a number of archaeological conferences, and has spoken at the meetings of a number of local history and archaeological societies. We would like to extend opportunities for community engagement with the scheme, by encouraging more finders to come forward and introduce themselves, and by creating the chance for those already participating to become even more involved. It is hoped that finders might be interested in keeping their own detailed records, helping to record on the database, or producing short notes and reports for publication in local journals and magazines (such as *Northamptonshire Archaeology*).

Publicity for the scheme has been stepped up, both within and outside the county. In particular, attention has been paid to the promotion of the scheme in academic fora, and to liaison with local museums, partner authorities, and community interest groups. The latter have included metal detecting and local history societies, townswomen's guilds, and even Brownie groups. The FLO has also developed particularly close links with members of the CLASP community archaeology 'umbrella' group, and spoke to them at their AGM.

In August 2007, the FLO, together with colleagues from the PAS, participated in *English Heritage's Festival of History* at Kelmarsh Hall. This event, at which the PAS's presence is now well established, once again proved to be a superb promotional event, and their small team of five staff spoke to over 1400 people, including large numbers of children. Such outreach will no doubt pay dividends in terms of public awareness of the Scheme, for both finders and interested researchers. The FLO has also worked with a number of undergraduate and postgraduate archaeology students who were interested in researching the PAS data for their own projects.

The Northamptonshire FLO continues to act as Treasure advisor for the county, and is often the first point of contact for finders of potential Treasure. Rates of reporting of treasure finds continue to increase; this is testament to the increasing publicity and good will that the Scheme enjoys, and thanks are due to the county's finders and landowners for their continued cooperation. Such collaboration is now beginning to bear fruit in the form of tangible results; readers may recall a Bronze Age founder's hoard reported in a previous note (Brindle 2004). This hoard has been placed on display in Northampton Museum, and stands as an example of what can be achieved when finder, landowner, Finds Liaison Officer (Tom Brindle, Northamptonshire FLO 2003-2006), and authority work together.

In addition to seeing finders in his office, at club meetings and at surgeries, the present FLO has, together with other FLOs and PAS colleagues, attended a number of

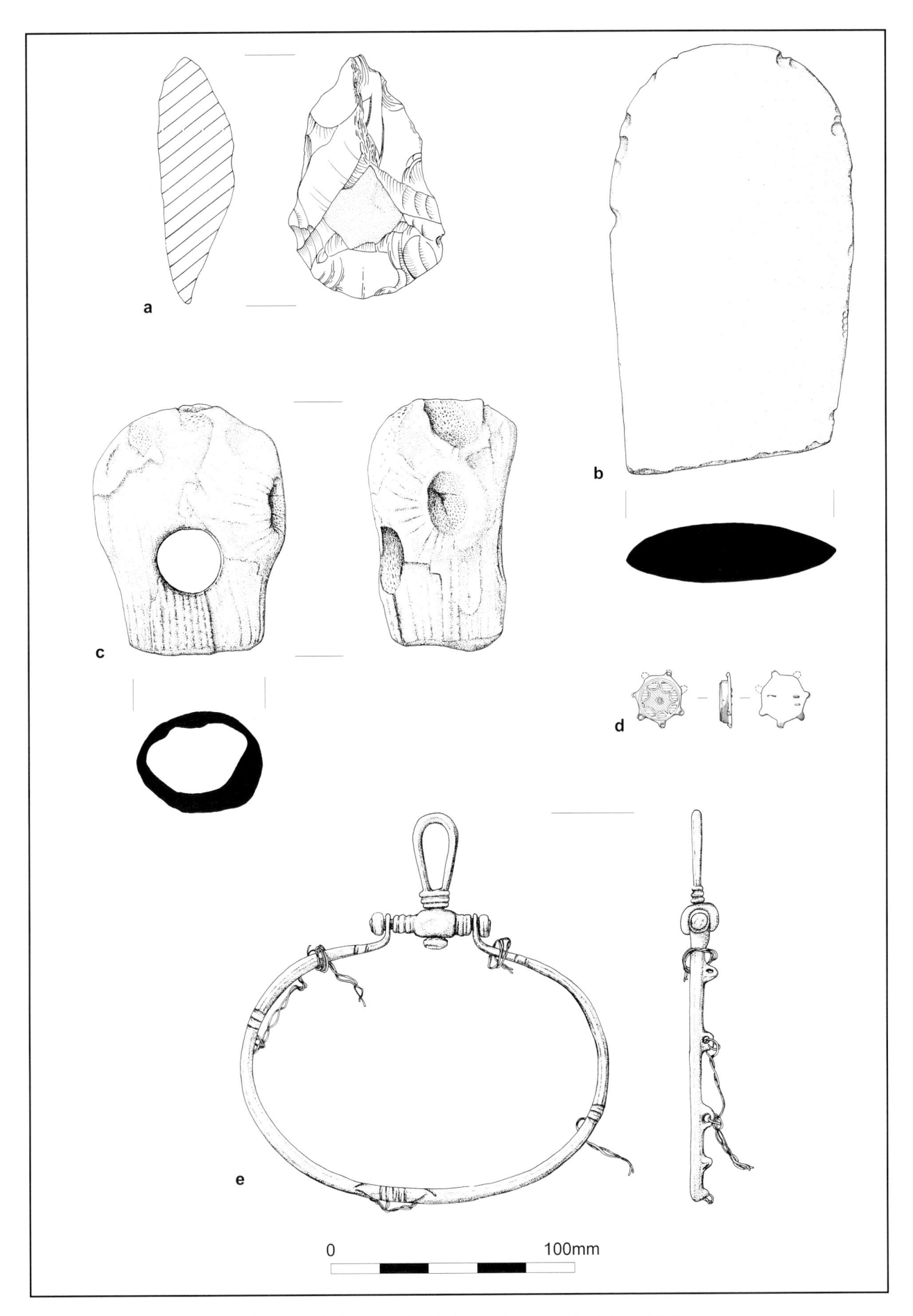

Fig 1 Key finds recorded with the Northamptonshire PAS in 2007

metal detecting rallies over the year, both within and without Northamptonshire. PAS intervention at these events was invaluable, as large numbers of finds were found, some of which may not otherwise have been recorded by the Scheme.

In 2007, a total of 1387 finds from Northamptonshire have been recorded onto the national database (www.finds.org.uk). These finds are arranged within 705 records, as they include large collections of pottery sherds and bulk material. Notwithstanding, since 1999, over 7000 records have been made for Northamptonshire. This year, many of the more interesting artefacts (detailed below) seem to have been found in the districts of Northampton and South Northamptonshire, but with other finds continuing to be recorded from Daventry, Kettering, Wellingborough, Corby, Kettering, and East Northamptonshire in roughly equal quantities. A brief account of some typical finds from each period follows, as a means of demonstrating the range of material encountered in the region.

The following are amongst those finds recorded by the Northamptonshire FLO in 2007 (reference numbers relate to the PAS database, publicly available for searching at www.finds.org.uk, illustrated in Figure 1. The oldest Northamptonshire artefact recorded by the PAS to date is a Lower Palaeolithic flint axe (NARC-FD1537, Fig 1a), found by a detectorist in the Gayton area. From the Neolithic we have an incomplete greenstone adze (NARC-180DE7, Fig 1b), and a macehead carved from red deer antler (NARC-181793, Fig 1c), comparable to finds from Liff's Low, Derbyshire (see Edmonds 1995, fig 82). Little has been reported from the Bronze Age in 2007, though the completion of treasure proceedings for the much-publicised Northampton founder's hoard (NARC-77BD13; see above) is of note. From the Iron Age, a number of coins have been recorded, including gold staters (eg NARC-5F5173) and silver units (eg NARC-FEA435); these are usually of types minted by the kings of local tribes, such as Cunobelin and Tasciovanus.

From the Romano-British period, one might note a folding 'hare and hound' knife (NARC-03BF62) and numerous brooches, but the real value lies in the large numbers of coins that have been recorded; to date, a total of 1003 coin records have been made. The archaeological utility of this data will no doubt become clearer with the completion and publication of doctoral research projects being undertaken at the University of London by former Finds Liaison Officers Tom Brindle (previously FLO for Northamptonshire) and Phillippa Walton (previously FLO for Cambridgeshire and the North-East). Both projects are likely to incorporate PAS data from Northamptonshire.

From the early medieval period, Anglo-Saxon cruciform and small-long brooches have been reported, and are arguably suggestive of hitherto unrecorded cemeteries (see NARC-EFCE90 and NARC-7A8DC6 for examples). Of particular interest is a radiate-headed brooch (NARC-9BD914) from South Northamptonshire, which may be of continental (eg Frankish) origin. The Middle Saxon period (c AD 600-800) is relatively under-represented, though we have a number of coins, including sceattas (eg NARC-419B22; NARC-A61021), and silver pennies of Offa (NARC-DC37D2) and Coenwulf (NARC-C472D2),

kings of Mercia, and the later Saxon king Edward the Elder (NARC-D203C1). Interestingly, the Late Saxon period / Viking Age (cAD800-1050) fares a little better than the preceding period in terms of artefactual finds. In addition to the Northampton stirrup-strap mount (NARC-6C5583, see Ashby this volume), we may also note a Late Saxon cloisonné brooch (NARC-C34DE6, Fig 1d), an Anglo-Scandinavian lead alloy disc brooch (NARC-56D604) and a Norse bell (NARC-D9C172) all from South Northamptonshire. In general, the finds from the early medieval period are beginning to build into a useful dataset, and one which the present author plans to exploit in forthcoming research on identity and regionality in Viking Age England (Ashby *in prep.*)

From the medieval period, the most notable find is a scatter of coins and artefacts in an area of South Northamptonshire that may relate to a previously unknown 15th-16th century market or meeting place (investigations ongoing). There is also a complete purse frame (a particularly unusual find) from South Northamptonshire (NARC-182644, Fig 1e). All of these finds are testament to the wealth and level of activity in rural Northamptonshire around the end of the Middle Ages, and provide a useful dataset for future research on Northamptonshire's later medieval and post-medieval economy and society.

In closing, it should be pointed out that the successes of the scheme would not be possible without the cooperation, support, and assistance of Northamptonshire County Council, the various partner authorities, and of course the finders themselves. With their help, it should be possible to build upon recent achievements, and encourage ever greater numbers of people to record their finds with the scheme, for the benefit of local communities and the academic establishment alike. Particular thanks are due to Norton Northamptonshire Portable Antiquities Search Team (*NNPAST*), Northampton Detecting Association (*NDA*), Steve Young and *CLASP*, and the Nene Valley Detecting Group (*NVDG*), but all finders, whether detectorists, gardeners, fieldwalkers or dogwalkers have played an enormous role in the scheme's successes. With particular regard to the present note, the author is indebted to the following finders: Iain Barrie, Tim Binns, Dave Derby, Steve Gibson, Ian Giggins, Robert Hemmington, John Marchant, Steve Pulley, and Paul Warren. Finds illustrations for Figure 1 were prepared by Pat Walsh and Jacqueline Harding of Northamptonshire Archaeology.

The Northamptonshire Finds Liaison Officer is based at County Hall in Northampton, and can be contacted care of the *Archives and Heritage Service*. To search for finds from Northamptonshire and elsewhere in the country, and to find out more about the PAS, please visit our website: www.finds.org.uk.

Catalogue of illustrated finds (Fig 1)

a   Palaeolithic flint axehead (NARC-FD1537)
b   Neolithic greenstone adze (NARC-180DE7)
c   Neolithic antler macehead (NARC-181793)
d   Early medieval cloisonné brooch (NARC-C34DE6)
e   Medieval/post-medieval purse frame (NARC-182644)

REFERENCES

Ashby, S P, in prep *Viking Age Northamptonshire: an archaeological survey based on data from the Portable Antiquities Scheme*

Brindle, T W, 2004 The Northamptonshire Portable Antiquities Scheme, 2004-2005, *Northamptonshire Archaeology*, **32**, 132-135

Edmonds, M, 1995 *Stone Tools and Society*, London: Routledge

DR STEVEN P ASHBY
FINDS LIAISON OFFICER FOR NORTHAMPTONSHIRE
C/O ARCHIVES SERVICE
NORTHAMPTONSHIRE COUNTY COUNCIL
PO BOX 163, COUNTY HALL
NORTHAMPTON, NN1 1AX
Tel: 01604 237249
sashby@northamptonshire.gov.uk

SOME RECENT ARCHAEOLOGICAL PUBLICATIONS

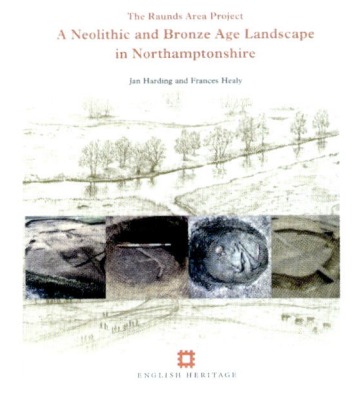

A Neolithic and Bronze Age Landscape in Northamptonshire by Jan Harding and Frances Healy
English Heritage 2007; 324 pages
ISBN: 9781873592991 Product Code 51176

Like all aspects of the Raunds Area Project, this report has been long awaited, and is now finally available. English Heritage, Northamptonshire Archaeology and Oxford Archaeology investigated more than 20 Neolithic and Bronze Age monuments in the Nene Valley between Raunds and Stanwick. From c4000 BC to the early 1st millennium BC a succession of ritual mounds and burial mounds were built as settlement along the valley sides increased and woodland was cleared. The Long Mound, the Long Barrow, part of the Turf Mound and the Avenue were built in the 5th millennium BC. With the addition of the Long Enclosure, the Causewayed Ring Ditch, and the Southern Enclosure, by c3000 BC there was a chain of five or six diverse monuments stretched along the river bank for well over a kilometre. From c2200 BC monument building accelerated again and included at least 20 round barrows, almost all containing burials, at first inhumations and then cremations, continuing down to c1000 cal BC, by which time two overlapping systems of paddocks and droveways had been laid out, indicating a change to domestic occupation of the valley.

In terms of getting hold of a copy of this report there is good news and bad news. The good news is that a digital copy can be obtained free of charge on the English Heritage web site (www.english-heritage.org.uk). Just follow the path: Home/Learning and Resources/Publications/Research Monographs. You can then choose this report from the list of research monographs now available online as pdf files. The full report is provided as chapter by chapter downloads; eight altogether.

The bad news is that if you want a printed copy it is available as Print On Demand (POD) but at a cost of £45 plus £5.00 postage and packing (payable to English Heritage). To obtain a copy email or write to English Heritage Postal Sales, c/o Gillards Worldwide Warehousing & Distribution, Trident Works, Temple Cloud, Bristol BS39 5AZ (email: ehsales@gillards.com or phone: 01761 452966).

What is available at present is the synthesis of the results, and this does not include conventional finds and environmental reports, although interesting aspects are highlighted in a series of "Panels" that appear at intervals. There is, therefore, a second volume still to come that will include the specialist reports. I assume that this too will be published free of charge as a download and as a POD hardcopy at a similar price to volume 1.

Iron Age and Roman Piddington: 6th Interim Report and phase descriptions of the late Iron Age settlement, military phase, Roman villas and Saxon phases at Piddington, Northants
by R M & D E Friendship-Taylor
The Upper Nene Archaeological Society 2008,
£5.00 to members, £5.50 to non-members, available from the museum or by post (+£1.40 p & p) from Roy & Liz Friendship-Taylor, 'Toad Hall', 86 Main Road, Hackleton, Northampton NN7 2AD.

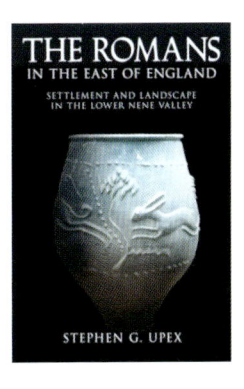

The Romans in the East of England: Settlement and Landscape in the Lower Nene Valley
by Stephen G. Upex
Tempus 2008 224 pages, 79 figures and 23 colour plates
ISBN: 9780752441184
Paperback price £19.99 (+p&p) (In July it was available for £13.19 from Amazon)

Professor Upex shows how the Nene Valley and East

Midlands area provides an ideal case study of the Roman occupation of Britain. The book deals with the region's Iron Age origins, its significant sites and roads, and its association with the Boudican revolt, and accounts for the reasons why it became one of the wealthiest areas of Roman Britain by the end of the third century. Villa occupation was lavish, and different villa systems have been detected and mapped. The importance of the area is seen in spectacular fashion with the late Christian hoard of church silverware and other buried treasure.

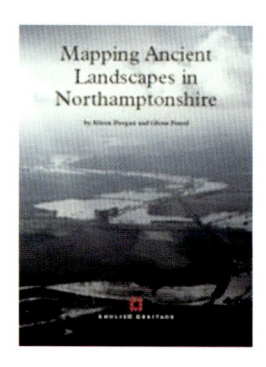

Mapping Ancient Landscapes in Northamptonshire
by Alison Deegan and Glenn Foard
English Heritage 2008

The Northamptonshire NMP project team are pleased to announce the simultaneous release of the Northamptonshire NMP Project data via the Archaeology Data Service (ADS) and the publication of Mapping Ancient Landscapes in Northamptonshire. This marks the conclusion of the Northamptonshire NMP Research, Dissemination and Archiving Project. This project was started in 1994 as part of the National Mapping Programme (NMP) and was one of the first to embrace a totally digital methodology. Mapping and recording was completed in 2001 and was following by a scheme of research and analysis and dissemination of the project's data, funded by English Heritage (EH) and supported by Northamptonshire County Council (NCC).
Mapping Ancient Landscapes in Northamptonshire is published by English Heritage and is authored by Alison Deegan and Glenn Foard with contributions from Alex Gibson and Graham Cadman. It will shortly be available to purchase from the EH online shop. It will also be available to download by chapter from the publication downloads page.

The mapping and recording stage of this project data generated a considerable range and quantity of digital data and much of this is now available via the pages dedicated to the *Northamptonshire NMP Project* on the *ADS* website. On the *ADS Interactive Map* users can view all the Northamptonshire NMP mapping and key information from the associated databases. The Interactive Map can also display the original transcription files, which indicate the photographic source of an individual feature and a distribution plot of the air photographs covering the county. At present the Interactive Map is displayed against 1km and 5km grid lines but there are plans to include base mapping from a service such as Google Maps or Multimap in the future.

These data, including over 450 NCC air photographs, are also available for download. This will enable the user to manipulate and display the spatial data in their own GIS and to interrogate the wealth of morphological and interpretative information that lies behind this mapping. The ADS will also maintain the archive of this data.

And yet more news from the Raunds Area Project:

Raunds: The origin and growth of a midland village, AD 450-1500 Excavations in north Raunds, Northamptonshire 1997-1987
by Michel Audouy and Andy Chapman (editor)
Oxbow Books 2008; 168pages and 130 illus, plus CD containing specialist reports
ISBN: 9781842173374

This volume, also long awaited, presents the results of open area excavation in north Raunds between the late 1970s to the end of the 1980s, work of great significance in developing our understanding of the origins of the English village. The excavation focused in particular on the evolution of Furnells Manor, and examined the processes of village development from the early Saxon period through to the desertion of the outlying manorial centres at the end of the medieval period. Most significantly, it defined the formation of the village in a system of regular plots created by the mid tenth century, probably following the English reconquest and the creation of the Danelaw, as part of a widespread reorganisation and nucleation of settlement. The work began a transformation of medieval settlement studies.

In order to keep the cover cost down, and to be consistent with both the companion volume describing the work at nearby West Cotton and the presentation of the prehistoric aspects of the project, as outlined above, the decision was taken to present the overview and the excavated evidence in the volume with the specialist reports on an attached CD. In the case of north Raunds, which is relatively short for a monograph, the cost impact is not significant, but for the forthcoming West Cotton report, which is over twice the length of the Raunds report, there will be a significant difference, as in this case it would have been necessary to publish two volumes, or one extremely thick volume, to encompass all of the material.

However, the benefit from publishing in this form is

not considered to be the saving on publication costs but the hope that the cheaper cover price will encourage more people to buy the volume to access and make use of the evidence.

The intention with both the Raunds and West Cotton volumes will be to make them available online as pdf files once the hard-copy sales have run their course.

ANDY CHAPMAN

NORTHAMPTONSHIRE ARCHAEOLOGY REPORTS ONLINE

In commercial archaeology a report is produced detailing the results of every developer-funded project from, say, extensive open area excavation on a quarry site running for several years to a single visit to check the footings for a new garage in one of our historic villages. The size of these reports is therefore anything from hundreds of pages down to a handful of pages and a single location plan.

These grey literature reports are only produced in small numbers and are available within the county Historic Environment Record (HER) and from the archaeological contractor who carried out the work. Only the most significant of these projects will go on to formal publication in the journal or elsewhere, and then sometimes only in summary form, while many of them will be covered by a paragraph or two in the annual summaries in this journal and the annual regional round-up, *South Midlands Archaeology*, and in other national and period journals.

As reported in the notes section in the last journal (volume 34, 2006, 142) *Northamptonshire Archaeology*, the archaeological contractor within *Northamptonshire County Council*, are now making their client reports available online through the national *Archaeology Data Service* (http://ads.ahds.ac.uk), who have established a library for *Unpublished Fieldwork Reports (Grey Literature)*. You just need to go to the home page of *ADS* and click on the *ArchSearch* option and choose *Library* and then *Unpublished Fieldwork Reports (Grey Literature)*. From here you can search by county, by archaeological contractor or a host of other options. For any single report you are given basic details of title and have the option to open a pdf copy of the full report, which you can either view online or download to your computer for later viewing or printing.

Below we provide a full bibliography for the 60 reports on projects in Northamptonshire carried out by *Northamptonshire Archaeology* that were available online at the end of June 2008. By the time this journal appears there may be even more available. The list does include a number of sites for which reports have been published in *Northamptonshire Archaeology* in recent years. In some instances the two will be nearly identical; in other cases the client report may contain additional material such as full finds reports, perhaps with additional illustrations.

BIBLIOGRAPHY

Brown, J, 2006 *The Roman villa at Deanshanger, Northamptonshire: Excavations 2004-2005*, Northamptonshire Archaeology, **05/085**

Brown, J, 2005 *Archaeological Excavations at the Former Swan Garage, 46-50 Sheep Street, Northampton, 2003-2004*, Northamptonshire Archaeology, **05/134**

Burrow, A, 2005 *Archaeological Evaluation at Oundle School, Oundle, Northamptonshire*, Northamptonshire Archaeology, **05/094**

Butler, A, and Fisher, I, 2005 *A Geophysical survey on land at Weston Favell Upper School, Northampton*, Northamptonshire Archaeology, **05/116**

Butler, A, and Fisher, I, 2005 *A geophysical survey on land at Buckton Fields, Whitehills, Northampton, Northamptonshire, July 2004 -January 2005*, Northamptonshire Archaeology, **05/036**

Butler, A, and Foard-Colby, A, 2006 *Geophysical survey and archaeological evaluation at Quinton House School, Upton, Northamptonshire*, Northamptonshire Archaeology, **06/039**

Carlyle, S, 2002 *Archaeological evaluation at Milton Ham, Northampton, 2002*, Northamptonshire Archaeology

Carlyle, S, 2006 *Archaeological Evaluation in College Place and Market House Courtyard, Brackley, Northamptonshire*, Northamptonshire Archaeology, **06/080**

Carlyle, S, 2006 *Watching brief at County Hall, George Row, Northampton*, Northamptonshire Archaeology, **06/097**

Carlyle, S, 2006 *Archaeological excavation at Pineham North, Upton, Northampton, December 2006, settlement 2, assessment report*, Northamptonshire Archaeology, **06/177**

Chapman, A, 1999 *Archaeological recording of a Roman villa at Wootton Fields, Northampton January-February 1999; asseessment report and updated project design*, Northamptonshire Archaeology

Chapman, A, 2000 *Archaeological evaluation of the former Express Lift Company, Abbey Works, Weedon Road, Northampton, 1999-2000*, Northamptonshire Archaeology

Chapman, A, 2002 *Earthwork and metal-detecting surveys at land adjacent to Spring Croft, Church Street, Sibbertoft, Northamptonshire, December 2001*, Northamptonshire Archaeology

Chapman, A, and Atkins, R, 2004 *Iron Age and Roman settlement at Mallard Close, Earls Barton, Northampton*, Northamptonshire Archaeology

Chapman, A, and Stevens, C, 2002 *Archaeological recording action and watching brief, Brackmills Link Road, Northampton*, Northamptonshire Archaeology

Chapman, P, 2005 *Watching brief for canopy walkway tower foundations at Salcey Forest, Northamptonshire*, Northamptonshire Archaeology, **05/119**

Chapman, P, 2006 *Edgcote House, Northamptonshire, new lift pit*, Northamptonshire Archaeology, **06/089**

Chapman, P, and Holmes, M, 2006 *Iron Age Settlement at Swan Valley Business Park, near Rothersthorpe, Northampton*, Northamptonshire Archaeology, **06/005**

Field, L, and Chapman, A, 2006, *Archaeological excavation at Harlestone Quarry, near Northampton, October 2006*, Northamptonshire Archaeology, **06/173**

Foard-Colby, A, 2006 *Archaeological evaluation Jubilee Street, Rothwell, Northamptonshire*, Northamptonshire Archaeology, **06/006**

Foard-Colby, A, 2006 *Archaeological evaluation at South-West Sixfields, Northampton, Northamptonshire, February 2006*, Northamptonshire Archaeology, **06/032**

Foard-Colby, A, 2006 *Archaeological watching brief at Thorpe Castle House, Thorpe Waterville, Northamptonshire*, Northamptonshire Archaeology, **06/066**

Foard-Colby, A, 2006 *Archaeological Mitigation Strategy and Watching Brief at Barnes Meadow, Northampton*, Northamptonshire Archaeology, **06/102**

Foard-Colby, A, and Fisher, I, 2006 *Geophysical survey, archaeological evaluation and a watching brief for Upton Way Flood Attenuation Scheme, Upton, Northamptonshire*, Northamptonshire Archaeology, **06/121**

Foard-Colby, A, 2006 *Archaeological evaluation at 147 Watling Street, Towcester, Northamptonshire Archaeology*, Northamptonshire Archaeology, **06/129**

Foard-Colby, A, 2006 *Archaeological Trial Excavation at 3 Corby Road, Stanion, Northamptonshire*, Northamptonshire Archaeology, **06/149**

Foard-Colby, A, 2006 *Archaeological Trial Trench Evaluation on land at Upton, Northampton (CVLR Phase)*, Northamptonshire Archaeology, **06/166**

Holmes, M, and Walford, J, 2007 *Geophysical Survey of Land to the North of Rothwell, Northamptonshire*, Northamptonshire Archaeology, **07/184**

Jones, C, 2005 *An archaeological excavation, Watling Street Byway, Northamptonshire*, Northamptonshire Archaeology, **05/050**

Jones, C, 2006 *Archaeological excavation at St Bartholomew's Church, Greens Norton, Northamptonshire*, Northamptonshire Archaeology, **06/065**

Jones, C, 2006 *Archaeological evaluation, Buckton Fields, Northamptonshire*, Northamptonshire Archaeology, **06/131**

Jones, C, and Chapman, A, 2005 *Archaeological watching brief at Earls Barton Quarry (southern extension), Northamptonshire*, Northamptonshire Archaeology, **05/157**

Leigh, D, 2002 *Middlemore Farm, Daventry, Northamptonshire, archaeological watching brief, May to September 2002*, Northamptonshire Archaeology

Leigh, D, 2003 *Excavation of Roman features at Plot 1, Middlemore Farm, Daventry, Northamptonshire, February to March 2003*, Northamptonshire Archaeology

Leigh, D, 2005 *An archaeological watching brief at the Church of St. Bartholomew, Furtho, Northamptonshire*, Northamptonshire Archaeology, **05/102**

Leigh, D, 2005 *An archaeological watching brief on land at DIRFT Central, Northamptonshire*, Northamptonshire Archaeology, **05/086**

Leigh, D, 2005 *An archaeological watching brief on land to the rear of Parson Latham's Hospital, Oundle, Northamptonshire*, Northamptonshire Archaeology, **05/075**

Leigh, D, 2006 *An Archaeological Watching Brief during Phase II of Infrastructure Works on land at Middlemore Farm, Daventry, Northamptonshire*, Northamptonshire Archaeology, **06/123**

Lewis, B, 2004 *Archaeological Watching Brief at Tove Valley Business Park, Towcester*, Northamptonshire Archaeology

McAree, D, 2006 *An archaeological warching brief at Harper's Brook, Islip, Northamptonshire*, Northamptonshire Archaeology, **06/183**

Mason, P, 2005 *Archaeological Geophysical Survey and Trial Trench Evaluation: Hardingstone allotments, Hardingstone, Northampton*, Northamptonshire Archaeology, **05/131**

Mason, P, 2006 *A Romano-British settlement at West Haddon, Northamptonshire*, Northamptonshire Archaeology, **06/059**

Mason, P, 2006 *Archaeological Test Pits North-West of Irchester Roman Town*, Northamptonshire Archaeology, **06/040**

Mason, P, 2006 *An Archaeological Watching brief and Excavation north-west of Irchester Roman Town, Northamptonshire*, Northamptonshire Archaeology, **06/158**

Mason, P, Butler, A, Fisher, I, Burrow, A and Mudd, A, 2005 *Archaeological Fieldwalking, Geophysical Survey and Trial Trenching on land west of Kettering, Northamptonshire, October-November 2005*, Northamptonshire Archaeology, **05/143**

Maull, A, and Masters, P, 2004 *Excavations of a Roman farmstead on land west of Glapthorn Road, Oundle, Northamptonshire, 1999-2001*, Northamptonshire Archaeology

Morris, S, 2005 *Archaeological Evaluation (Geophysical survey and Trial Trenching phase), Ellands Farm, Hemington, Northamptonshire*, Northamptonshire Archaeology, **05/107**

Morris, S, 2006 *Archaeological evaluation (trial trenching), Saffron Road, Higham Ferrers, Northamptonshire*, Northamptonshire Archaeology, **06/017**

Pears, B, 2005 *Archaeological Evaluation at Pineham North, Upton, Northamptonshire*, Northamptonshire Archaeology, **05/081**

Prentice, J, 2005 *An assessment of three dormer windows at Barton Seagrave Hall, Northamptonshire*, Northamptonshire Archaeology

Prentice, J, 2005 *Building recording at Glebe House, Easton-on-the-Hill, Northamptonshire*, Northamptonshire Archaeology

Prentice, J, 2005 *Desk-based assessment and building recording survey at St. George's School, Northampton*, Northamptonshire Archaeology

Simmonds, C, 2005 *Archaeological earthwork survey at Salcey Forest, Northamptonshire*, Northamptonshire Archaeology, **05/ 084**

Simmonds, C, 2005 *Archaeological watching brief at Harvey Reeves Road/Sixfields, Northampton*, Northamptonshire Archaeology, **05/093**

Soden, I, and Leigh, D, 2006 *An Archaeological Watching Brief at St John's Hospital Chapel, Northampton*, Northamptonshire Archaeology, **06/104**

Thorne, A, and Chapman, A, 2004 *Further excavation at Wootton Fields Roman villa, Northampton, 2002*, Northamptonshire Archaeology

Thorne, A, 2005 *Archaeological watching brief on the compound for the Anglian Water Sewage Scheme, Tansor and Cotterstock S101A*, Northamptonshire Archaeology, **05/038**

Upson-Smith, T, 2005 *A43 Corby Link Road, Northamptonshire: Archaeological Geophysical Survey and Trial Excavation*, Northamptonshire Archaeology, **05/151**

Upson-Smith, T, 2005 *Archaeological evaluation of main access at Chester House Farm (Module 6), Irchester, Northamptonshire*, Northamptonshire Archaeology, **05/058**

Walford, J, 2006 *A509 Isham to Wellingborough Improvement: Archaeological Geophysical Survey*, Northamptonshire Archaeology, **06/180**

ANDY CHAPMAN
SENIOR ARCHAEOLOGIST
NORTHAMPTONSHIRE ARCHAEOLOGY

Archaeology in Northamptonshire 2007

Compiled by Pat Chapman (Northamptonshire Archaeology)
with additional contributions from Richard Ivens

PREHISTORIC

EARLS BARTON, QUARRY EXTENSION
NGR SP 847 613
Evaluation
Northamptonshire Archaeology
A trial excavation was conducted by Paul Mason on *c* 29 ha of arable land to the west of Earls Barton Quarry, on behalf of Phoenix Consulting Archaeology Ltd and their client Hanson Aggregates. The site lies in the floodplain of the River Nene within a landscape known to contain important Bronze Age remains. As a result of the fieldwork a small number of archaeological features and a system of river palaeochannels were discovered. A middle Bronze Age cremation deposit comprised the partial remains of an infant, who was burned on a pyre of hazel, blackthorn and oak sometime between 1440–1280 cal BC (95% confidence). This burial is probably slightly later in date than the nearby upstanding round barrow mound (SAM17135) which occupies a position in the centre of the application area on a gravel 'island', and would be presumed to be of early Bronze Age date.

HANNINGTON, NORTHAMPTONSHIRE TO EMPINGHAM, RUTLAND PIPELINE
Geophysical survey and evaluation
Northamptonshire Archaeology
Geophysical prospection followed by test pit excavation carried out by Ian Fisher and Jason Clarke, was commissioned by Mott MacDonald, on behalf of Anglian Water Services, as part of the archaeological evaluation of a proposed pipeline route from Hannington in Northamptonshire to Empingham in Rutland. The test pits were excavated to the underlying natural geology in areas of archaeological potential to establish the depths of overburden over archaeological deposits. Individual areas within Northamptonshire are summarised separately below by period, here comprising the parishes of Broughton, Great Cransley and Rushton.

Broughton
NGR SP 827 752
A ditched sub-rectangular enclosure was detected by geophysical survey, with additional ditches and several small features. The complex is probably a small prehistoric or Roman farmstead. Two other ditches formed opposite sides of a small rectangular enclosure of unknown date.

Great Cransley
NGR SP 838 782 to SP 7630 8305
Extensive archaeological remains were detected by geophysical survey along the pipeline corridor. Several are ditched enclosures of later prehistoric or Romano-British date as well as a trackway.

Rushton
NGR SP 8530 8480 to SP 8408 8075
Parts of ditched enclosures were located by geophysical survey. Three semicircular ditches appear to be prehistoric or Roman settlement enclosures.

MOULTON, PITSFORD ROAD
NGR SP 7730 6712
Strip, map and record
Northamptonshire Archaeology
Archaeological strip, map and record was carried out by Anne Foard-Colby during the removal of topsoil and subsoil for construction of sports pitches for Moulton College at Pitsford Road. Archaeological remains consisting of two ditches, one containing five sherds of probable Iron Age pottery, one possible furrow, one old land drain and a small pit were found.

NORTHAMPTON, SHELFLEYS
NGR SP 733 578
Evaluation
Northamptonshire Archaeology
Archaeological evaluation was undertaken by John Walford and Nathan Flavell on land in Shelfleys, Northampton for Hepher Dixon Ltd, acting on behalf of the developer Genesis Housing Group. Geophysical survey covering about half the site revealed part of an enclosure ditch. Trial trenches examined part of the ditch as well as areas each side. Archaeological features and finds were very sparse but the limited evidence indicates that the enclosure is of later prehistoric or Roman date. It is suggested that the enclosure was not a focus of habitation, but may have been a corral for stock.

SALCEY FOREST
NGR 79449 51996
Evaluation
Northamptonshire Archaeology
An auger survey and trial trenching was carried out by Stephen Morris, on behalf of the Forestry Commission, within Salcey Forest to determine the character and original date of a series of earthworks forming a ditched and banked enclosure. The auger survey was initially carried out in transects in three locations to identify which of the landscape features had the best potential for further examination. The excavation clarified the presence of an early bank, with a later ditch and further bank make-up, although the dates of the features were not determined. A small amount charcoal recovered from a deposit at the base of the bank was radiocarbon dated to the early Iron Age, 770-400 cal BC (95% confidence), but may have been residual material pre-dating the bank by a considerable time.

THORPE MANDEVILLE TO GREATWORTH PIPELINE
NGR SP 521 443 to SP 568 422
Geophysical survey
Northamptonshire Archaeology

A magnetometer survey by Paul Clements, for Anglian Water Services, was undertaken along the easement of a new pipeline between Thorpe Mandeville and Greatworth. The survey identified several areas of archaeological interest, including two enclosure complexes of probable later prehistoric or Roman date, two isolated enclosures, and several linear ditches representing boundaries or trackways. Traces of medieval ridge and furrow were ubiquitous.

THRAPSTON, HUNTINGDON ROAD
NGR TL 003 782
Evaluation
Northamptonshire Archaeology

Evaluation was conducted by John Walford and Paul Mason on c 16.5ha of pasture land at Thrapston, on behalf of Henry H Bletsoe and Son. Geophysical survey confirmed evidence for an important Bronze Age ringwork lying within the proposed development site, which had been previously located by aerial photography and partially excavated in 1997. Trial excavation on land surrounding the ringwork revealed widely dispersed archaeological features including parts of three possible roundhouses, a human cremation and gravel quarry pits.

TOWCESTER VALE
NGR SP 689 479 to SP 692 465
Geophysical survey
Northamptonshire Archaeology

Geophysical survey by Carol Simmonds comprising 145ha of magnetic susceptibility reconnaissance and 22ha of targeted detailed magnetometry were carried out at Towcester Vale, encompassing the southern hinterland of Towcester town, on behalf of University of Leicester Archaeological Services (ULAS). Five areas of interest were identified. Follow-up survey revealed a 5ha palimpsest of late prehistoric curvilinear enclosures, roundhouses, pits and linear ditches west of Watling Street. A probable occupation site including an ovoid enclosure and roundhouses was also identified, along with other small enclosures and ditches, including a probable part of the medieval Wood Burcote.

ROMAN

HANNINGTON, NORTHAMPTONSHIRE TO EMPINGHAM, RUTLAND PIPELINE
Geophysical survey and evaluation
Northamptonshire Archaeology

Geophysical prospection followed by test pit excavation by Ian Fisher and Jason Clarke, was commissioned by Mott MacDonald, on behalf of Anglian Water Services as part of the archaeological evaluation of a proposed pipeline route from Hannington in Northamptonshire to Empingham in Rutland. The test pits were excavated to the underlying natural geology in areas of archaeological potential to establish the depths of overburden over archaeological deposits. Individual areas within Northamptonshire are summarised separately by period, comprising the parish of Rushton.

Rushton
NGR SP 8530 8480 to SP 8408 8075
Parts of ditched enclosures were located by geophysical survey. Three semicircular ditches appear to be prehistoric or Roman settlement enclosures. Linear anomalies appear likely to be Roman, but they do not seem to be associated with buildings or dense archaeology despite the presence of a Roman villa complex nearby, whose extent remains undefined.

HIGHAM FERRERS, FERRERS COLLEGE
NGR SP 9655 6814
Evaluation
Northamptonshire Archaeology

An archaeological evaluation, comprising geophysical survey and trial trench excavation, was carried out by Nathan Flavell and Carol Simmonds on c 10.7ha land comprising a field adjacent to the A6 Higham Ferrers/Rushden Bypass and a playing field of Ferrers College. The work was commissioned by the Duchy of Lancaster, via GSS Architecture, in advance of planning proposals for the residential and commercial development. Evaluation revealed a pattern of ditches and gullies associated with settlement activity in the late Iron Age/early Roman period.

SYWELL, SYWELL AERODROME
NGR SP 8240 6875
Watching brief
Northamptonshire Archaeology

An archaeological watching brief was carried out by Anne Foard-Colby during the removal of topsoil prior to the infilling of land to the west of runway 5/31 at Sywell Aerodrome. Any archaeological remains would have been sealed beneath subsoil and therefore not visible during the present work. However, in small areas where the subsoil was shallow a number of features were partially exposed, including a Roman oven with an associated pitched-stone surface, a ditch and two pits. A small assemblage of 1st to 2nd-century Roman pottery was recovered from the oven and the ditch.

WHILTON LODGE, BANNAVENTA
NGR SP646 611
Geophysical survey
Northamptonshire Archaeology

A geophysical survey was conducted by Adrian Butler, on behalf of CLASP (Community Landscape and Archaeology Survey Project), on an area of land of approximately 5.2ha covering the site of a known Roman Small Town, *Bannaventa*, at Whilton Lodge. Magnetometer survey revealed a large area dominated by the double and triple-ditched defences enclosing probable building remains of uncertain form. These were arranged as a ribbon development along the line of a road, likely to be the Roman Watling Street, passing through the centre of Bannaventa.

MEDIEVAL

FOTHERINGHAY, CASTLE FARM
NGR TL 0615 9305
Watching brief
Richard Ivens

A watching brief was carried out during extensive groundworks at Castle Farm, Fotheringhay. Several minor features were observed amongst much modern disturbance. Some evidence was recovered regarding the form of the Outer Moat, and the line of its now infilled northern route. Remains of a massive and probably medieval stone structure were revealed between the farmyard and the inner edge of the Outer Moat. The remains of another stone building were also identified in the same area.

FURTHO, ST BARTHOLOMEW'S CHURCH
NGR SP 7734 4309
Watching brief
Northamptonshire Archaeology

An archaeological watching brief by Iain Soden was undertaken during a final phase of groundworks connected with the replacement of floors in the tower and nave of the interior of The Church of St Bartholomew. The present church dates to around 1620 with remodelling in the later 17th and 18th centuries, although windows and other details date to the 14th century. The church has been largely disused since c 1920. Excavation beneath the present tower revealed a single large limestone wall, the foundations of the former west end of the nave. A 190mm-long stone weight was recovered from beneath the floor. The object, made from Oolitic Limestone, comprises a sub-circular/rectangular shaft with a T-shaped head at one end. Stylistically it is of a type of medieval basket-trap weight used for catching fish in rivers and ponds.

HANNINGTON, NORTHAMPTONSHIRE TO EMPINGHAM, RUTLAND PIPELINE
Geophysical survey and evaluation
Northamptonshire Archaeology

Geophysical prospection, followed by test pit excavation, conducted by Ian Fisher and Jason Clarke, was commissioned by Mott MacDonald, on behalf of Anglian Water Services, as part of the archaeological evaluation of a proposed pipeline route from Hannington in Northamptonshire to Empingham in Rutland. The test pits were excavated to the underlying natural geology in areas of archaeological potential to establish the depths of overburden over archaeological deposits. Individual areas within Northamptonshire are summarised separately below, comprising the parishes of Gretton, Rockingham, Cottingham, Middleton, Rushton, Rothwell, Thorpe Malsor, Great Cransley, Broughton, Walgrave and Hannington.

Broughton
NGR SP 827 752
Medieval ridge and furrow was detected in the fields.

Cottingham
NGR SP 8635 8965
A single, short length of ditch and ridge and furrow cultivation were located.

Great Cransley
NGR SP 838 782 to SP 7630 8305
Extensive ridge and furrow is present along the length of the corridor.

Gretton
NGR SP 878 930
Palaeochannels of the River Welland were recorded by geophysical survey. A cluster of archaeological features comprising part of a small ditched enclosure and other associated ditches are likely to relate to the deserted medieval hamlet of Cotes, whose earthwork remains lie in the neighbouring field. A recently ploughed-out north-south field boundary was also detected. Ridge and furrow with various orientations were recorded throughout the area. A medieval ditch directly under topsoil was recorded in a test pit.

Hannington
NGR SP 8255 7225
Geophysical survey revealed remnants of medieval ridge and furrow.

Middleton
NGR SP 8605 8890
A broad, linear, highly magnetic anomaly detected by geophysical survey may reflect a former road or trackway.

Rockingham
NGR SP 872 921
Boundary ditches, a small pit and ridge and furrow cultivation were located by geophysical survey.

Rothwell
NGR SP 8412 7980
South-westerly aligned ridge and furrow cultivation was observed.

Rushton
NGR SP 8530 8480 to SP 8408 8075
Medieval ridge and furrow was identified along the length of the corridor.

Thorpe Malsor
NGR SP 840 794
Three linear ditches and one curvilinear ditch were found by geophysical survey. A negative anomaly was also detected, possibly a wall or gravel filled ditch.

Walgrave
NGR SP 8225 7375 to SP 8225 7300
Geophysical survey revealed ridge and furrow cultivation.

IRTHLINGBOROUGH
NGR SP 708 936
Geophysical survey
Northamptonshire Archaeology

A magnetometer survey, commissioned by CgMs Consulting, was conducted by Mark Holmes across a proposed development area to the west of Irthlingborough. A number of highly magnetic features suggestive of lime kilns were identified. Magnetically disturbed areas were detected, likely to be a by-product of the industrial past of the site. Several former quarry pits of various sizes were also located. The site retained the patchwork pattern of medieval field systems.

POST-MEDIEVAL

BARNWELL, OLD RECTORY
NGR SP 0488 8497
Building recording
Northamptonshire Archaeology
Building recording and a desk-based assessment by Iain Soden, ahead of renovation, have indicated that the Old Rectory was probably purpose-built in local limestone, with a limestone tile roof, in the very early 19th century, perhaps around 1810. It comprises a number of simple phases but all were probably completed in quick succession, the house reaching its current size by 1822. It is split into distinct areas, comprising private, devotional, reception and service areas. Other alterations continued through the 19th and much of the 20th centuries to suit individual rectors. Map evidence suggests that an earlier rectory building may lie to the north or east of the current building while human remains discovered during previous archaeological fieldwork indicate that graves lie widespread under the lawns between the rectory and the church tower.

BLISWORTH, CHURCH OF ST JOHN THE BAPTIST,
NGR SP 72529 53413
Watching brief
Richard Ivens
A watching brief was carried out during the excavation of a service trench connecting the north-west corner of the north aisle with Church Lane. Three brick-built burial vaults were observed, but not disturbed. Evidence of numerous burials (undated) was noted along the north side of the church. Minor details of the north aisle foundations were also recorded.

CRANFORD ST ANDREW, THE OLD RECTORY
NGR SP 9205 7753
Evaluation
Northamptonshire Archaeology
The kitchen garden at The Old Rectory, a Grade 2 Listed Building, occupies a 0.19ha site to the east of the property, the wall being evaluated by Joe Prentice. Although it is now in separate ownership from the Old Rectory, the site forms part of the property's curtilage, most recently acting as a kitchen garden supplying the Rectory with vegetables, fruit and flowers. Though a high brick and stone wall runs along the eastern boundary, there is no evidence from historic maps or from the structure and layout of the area to imply that it was historically a walled garden. The wall is likely to have been built to screen the property from the adjacent road.

COTTAGES AT 15-21 HARBOROUGH ROAD, LAWRENCE BOOT AND SHOE FACTORY, DESBOROUGH
NGR SP 8020 8346
Buildings recording
Northamptonshire Archaeology
The former Lawrence Boot and Shoe factory and the cottages at 15-21 Harborough Road are properties owned by Kettering Borough Council, who commissioned a basic desk-based assessment and photographic building survey carried out by Joe Prentice prior to decisions being taken concerning their future.

Cottages at 15-21 Harborough Road
These were originally a row of three separate houses, built in the late 19th century, which have been knocked through and now comprise a single residence. They are built of red brick bonded in a lime mortar beneath a concrete tile roof with a single chimney stack at the south gable end and a second, double stack between the original central and north cottage. House 21/21a was built as a separate property. The building is L-shaped in plan, constructed of red brick with gauged brick window heads symmetrically placed either side of a central front door; the roof is of modern concrete tiles but was probably originally of Welsh slate.

Lawrence Boot and Shoe factory
The former Lawrence Boot and Shoe factory, now empty and derelict, comprises three distinct parts; a long range of three storeys lying north-south (the original building pre 1880), a hipped-roof block and an adjacent single-storey range immediately to the east added 1900-1916. The walls are constructed of red Fletton-type bricks and the corners are dressed with limestone quoins, and a flat limestone string course divides the upper and lower storeys. The roofs are of concrete tiles or Welsh slate.

FOTHERINGHAY, PERIO MILL
NGR TL 0438 9253
Buildings recording
Northamptonshire Archaeology
A buildings recording was carried out by Joe Prentice on the redundant mill prior to conversion to residential accommodation. The mill buildings date from the 18th and 19th centuries and are predominantly constructed of coursed limestone bonded in lime mortar. The quoins, doors and window openings are finished with dressed limestone blocks. At the southern end on the first floor, two bays on the east side and four bays on the west side have been infilled with red brick between the oak uprights to eaves level. The southern gable end of the group is of limestone and the whole range is roofed with corrugated asbestos. A single-storey outbuilding has been added to the west side of the range to the south of the mill race and is also built of limestone, but is roofed in Collyweston slates.

Little remains internally of the machinery which it would have contained during its working life apart from a dressing machine used to grade the flour and occasional brackets, sockets and chutes. Nothing remains of the fixtures and fittings which were associated with paper making on the site between 1718 and 1851, before it reverted to being a corn mill.

GREENS NORTON, ST BARTHOLOMEW'S CHURCH
NGR SP 669 499
Watching brief
Northamptonshire Archaeology
The hand excavated footprint of a new extension adjacent

to St. Bartholomew's Church was monitored by Iain Soden on behalf of the Diocesan Advisory Committee's archaeological adviser. Previous work in 2001 and 2006 (Volume 34, 148), had established that articulated, but undated burials lay at between 1.20m and 1.70m below the modern ground surface.

A northerly extension to the tower and the west end of the north aisle, dated 1923, were uncovered. This was constructed of stone, brick and concrete over a slate damp-proof course; the whole resting on a foundation of concrete laced with crushed brick. A buttress for the north aisle of the church was offset on unmortared stone foundations. A brick drainage gully lay at foundation level at the foot of an escarpment in the churchyard, designed to prevent water from collecting in the foundations.

Disarticulated human bone and post-medieval coffin handles were found and reburied. Three articulated burials were also partially exposed and reburied.

HIGHAM FERRERS, CHICHELE COLLEGE
NGR SP 9569 6865
Watching brief
Northamptonshire Archaeology
An archaeological watching brief was carried out by Mark Patenall during the renovation of part of the western boundary wall and gateway of Chichele College. Modern cement mortar and a fragment of probable 19th-century brick were observed in the wall core on either side of the gateway. It was noted that the gateway to the wall was of similar design to the doorway of the north wall of the college building.

HIGHAM FERRERS, DOVECOTE
NGR SP 687 961
Evaluation
Northamptonshire Archaeology
Three hand dug test pits within the structure of the dovecote were excavated by Mark Patenall on behalf of Higham Ferrers Tourism Board to evaluate the site of the Dovecote, part of the castle (Scheduled Ancient Monument, County No 13607). The work was carried out under Scheduled Monument Consent preliminary to proposals for the conservation and presentation of the dovecote remains, which lie under a garden to the rear of the Green Dragon Public House. The standing fabric comprises three sides, one of which is rebuilt, of a rectangular building, roofless and with a largely grassed centre. An accumulation of 19th to 20th-century waste material covered the entire dovecote interior to a depth of c 0.65m deep.

KELMARSH, CHURCH OF ST DENYS
NGR SP 7351 7920
Recording action
Richard Ivens
A recording action was carried out on archaeological remains exposed during remedial works to the foundations of the east wall of the chancel. The remains included parts of brick burial vaults and a brick-built and blocked archway through the foundations of the east wall of the chancel. This burial complex lies within a railed enclosure immediately east of the chancel, which today contains only the chest tomb of the 1st Lord Bateman (dated 1845). Lord Bateman was a member of the Hanbury family and presumably the railed enclosure is a family burial plot. Many Hanburys are buried in the church and the archway through the east wall of the chancel possibly linked burial vaults below the chancel and within the railed enclosure, or may have been a burial niche. The foundation of what appears to be an angled buttress of an earlier church was exposed at the northeast corner of the chancel. A second, rather fragmentary stone structure was revealed at the south-east corner of the chancel, however, there are indications that this postdates the present chancel foundations.

KISLINGBURY BRIDGE
NGR SP 6996 5982
Evaluation
Northamptonshire Archaeology
An assessment, required by WS Atkins on behalf of Northamptonshire County Council, was carried out by Joe Prentice for Kislingbury bridge. The bridge is a single-width five arch structure, built primarily of local ironstone across the River Nene to the north of Kislingbury village. It is thought in part to date from the 17th century, although the majority dates to the late 18th or 19th centuries. The two northernmost arches contain the earliest stonework but are both suffering decay, cracking and partial collapse.

NORTHAMPTON, NUNN MILLS
NGR SP 763 597
Survey
Northamptonshire Archaeology
A photographic survey was undertaken by Tony Walsh for Rolton Group, of derelict and partially demolished buildings at Nunn Mills ahead of redevelopment. The larger buildings comprise the remains of Nunn Mills Power Station; operational from the 1930s to the mid 1960s. Following decommissioning of the station buildings, part of the site was occupied by light industrial buildings concerned with motor services.

POLEBROOK, POLEBROOK HALL
NGR TL 06 87
Buildings recording
Northamptonshire Archaeology
A buildings recording was undertaken by Joe Prentice at Polebrook Hall, listed Grade II. It was built in the 17th century with alterations and additions during the 18th and 19th centuries. It is constructed of Northamptonshire limestone, apart from the west side of the servants' range which is of yellow brick. A portion of the 19th-century additions to the hall were demolished in the mid twentieth century, and most of the remaining elements of the building have undergone various alterations.

STANWICK, STANWICK HALL
NGR SP 9751 7113
Buildings recording
Northamptonshire Archaeology
Stanwick Hall is a fine country house, Grade II* listed,

dating to the 18th century. Building recording was undertaken by Joe Prentice ahead of renovation and refurbishment to be a family home. It is built of coursed dressed limestone with ashlar rusticated quoins and a Collyweston stone roof. The 19th-century extension is built of brick and roofed in Welsh slate. Like most houses of this period it has undergone various alterations and additions, but it also suffered a fire in the early 20th century which resulted in the replacement of a significant part of the interior features, most significantly the main staircase.

SULGRAVE, CASTLE GREEN
NGR SP 5566 4524
Watching brief
Richard Ivens

Archaeological watching briefs were maintained during the construction of a new path and the repair/rebuilding of a boundary wall. The remains of two stone walls were found at the north-east corner of the site; possibly demolished in the 17th century these walls may represent two distinct structures. The works on the boundary wall revealed nothing of significance and the existing wall appears to have been constructed in the 19th century.

SULGRAVE, DIAL HOUSE FARM
NGR SP 5544 4539
Buildings recording
Northamptonshire Archaeology

A group of limestone buildings roofed with Welsh slate forming the farmyard complex associated with Dial House Farm was recorded by Joe Prentice prior to their conversion to domestic dwellings. They comprise simple buildings suitable for a variety of functions throughout the farming year, and only two, the stable and carriage house appear to have been built with a single purpose. They all date to the late 18th or 19th centuries.

THRAPSTON, MULBERRY HOUSE, 15 CHANCERY LANE
NGR SP 9960 7877
Buildings recording
Northamptonshire Archaeology

Buildings recording was carried out by Iain Soden on Mulberry House, an 18th-century cottage, listed Grade II. The corner property was originally separate, and later joined to the adjacent house, both beginning as small cottages, then being greatly enlarged by the addition of a second floor throughout, probably in the later 19th century. Few original features survive inside although many small alterations have left clear evidence in the fabric.

TOWCESTER, 147 WATLING STREET
NGR SP 6938 4854
Watching brief
Northamptonshire Archaeology

A watching brief by Jim Brown and Charlotte Walker monitored groundworks for a concrete raft designed to enable preservation *in situ* for known Roman remains beneath the new building (Volume 34, 147). The remains of two rubble stone walls and a stone drain were encountered outside the evaluated area and were dated by the pottery to the late medieval and post-medieval periods.

UPTON, QUINTON HOUSE SCHOOL
NGR SP 7168 6020
Buildings recording
Northamptonshire Archaeology

Quinton House School occupies a Grade I listed Building, Quinton House. Building recording and a watching brief were carried out by Joe Prentice ahead of construction of a new dining room which will occupy a courtyard to the north side of the current buildings. A porch, added to the building before 1886, is to be demolished and the surface of the courtyard is to be lifted and drains diverted. A cellar found beneath the courtyard probably dates to the early 19th century.

PERIOD UNKNOWN

CANONS ASHBY, CANONS ASHBY HOUSE
NGR SP 577 505
Watching brief
Northamptonshire Archaeology

An archaeological watching brief was undertaken by David Leigh on behalf of the National Trust, during groundworks connected with the installation of two security bollards on land at Canons Ashby House. The bollards were installed as part of the anti-theft measures taken for the security of *The Shepherd Boy* statue that stands within the gardens of the house. The excavated holes revealed a truncated natural substratum sealed by post-medieval roadway material. No archaeological deposits were revealed and no artefacts were recovered.

DESBOROUGH, GRANGE PARK
NGR SP 7990 8400
Watching brief
Northamptonshire Archaeology

A watching brief during the initial stages of development was undertaken by Chris Jones on behalf of Magnetic Park Partnerships. Extensive areas of the site had been quarried for ironstone in the 19th and 20th centuries, so only undisturbed areas were investigated. Observation concentrated on the west side of the development close to the general location of a Saxon cemetery discovered before 1757. However, no archaeological features or artefacts were found during the present work.

FINESHADE WOOD
NGR SP 978 987
Evaluation
Northamptonshire Archaeology

An archaeological evaluation was carried out by Carol Simmonds, on behalf of the Forestry Commission, on a 9.4ha parcel of land at Fineshade Wood. Five trenches were opened exposing natural Jurassic limestone directly beneath the topsoil, although in one trench two layers of colluvium overlay the natural. Four features were investigated, including two linear gullies, a possible gully terminal and a probable pit/tree throw hole, but no dating evidence was found. Slag was retrieved from the topsoil in one area.

GREAT OAKLEY, OAKLEY BROOK
NGR SP 869 852
Geophysical survey
Northamptonshire Archaeology
A magnetometer survey, carried out by Adrian Butler, was commissioned by Wardell Armstrong across a proposed development area of 19ha to the south of Great Oakley. Other than a large amount of ferrous debris in the topsoil, only three ferrous pipelines and a possible square brick-built feature were located.

HANNINGTON, NORTHAMPTONSHIRE TO EMPINGHAM, RUTLAND PIPELINE
Geophysical survey and evaluation
Northamptonshire Archaeology
Geophysical prospection followed by test pit excavation, carried out by Ian Fisher and Jason Clarke, was commissioned by Mott MacDonald, on behalf of Anglian Water Services, as part of the archaeological evaluation of a proposed pipeline route from Hannington in Northamptonshire to Empingham in Rutland. The test pits were excavated to the underlying natural geology in areas of archaeological potential to establish the depths of overburden over archaeological deposits. Individual areas within Northamptonshire are summarised separately below, comprising the parishes of Rockingham, Cottingham, Middleton, Wilbarston, Thorpe Malsor and Great Cransley.

Cottingham
NGR SP 8635 8965
A single, short length of ditch and ridge and furrow cultivation were located by geophysical survey.

Great Cransley
NGR SP 838 782 to SP 7630 8305
Two areas of rounded magnetic anomalies may represent furnaces or other industrial features, although they may be modern intrusions. Several disturbances are likely to relate to the former quarry and mineral railway.

Middleton
NGR SP 8605 8890
A broad, linear, highly magnetic anomaly detected by geophysical survey may reflect a former road or trackway.

Rockingham
NGR SP 872 921
Boundary ditches and a small pit were located by geophysical survey.

Thorpe Malsor
NGR SP 840 794
Three linear ditches and one curvilinear ditch were found by geophysical survey. A negative anomaly was also detected, possibly a wall or gravel filled ditch.

Wilbarston
NGR SP 85565 8620
Two long curving ditches were detected by geophysical survey. Another ditch was also located, with a ferrous object central to it.

KETTERING, LOWER STREET
NGR SP 8624 7885
Watching brief
Northamptonshire Archaeology
An archaeological watching brief, behalf of Stepnell Ltd, Rugby acting for their clients Brackley Investments Ltd, was undertaken by David Leigh during groundworks connected with the construction of a new medical centre on land at Lower Street. A truncated natural substratum was present across all the development area. No archaeological deposits or artefacts were present.

NORTHAMPTON, BILLING LANE
NGR SP 811 647
Evaluation
Northamptonshire Archaeology
An archaeological evaluation was carried out by John Walford and Leon Field on land for proposed development at Billing Lane for Hepher Dixon Ltd, acting on behalf of the developer Genesis Housing Group. Detailed geophysical survey was undertaken, but no archaeological features were revealed. Subsequently, fifteen evaluation trenches, totalling 450m in length were excavated. There was one modern gully and evidence for ploughing, but no archaeological features or finds were found.

NORTHAMPTON, GOLDINGS, WOODVALE PRIMARY SCHOOL
NGR SP 801641
Evaluation
Northamptonshire Archaeology
An archaeological trial trench evaluation was carried out by Anne Foard-Colby on land proposed for a new school on the site of the former Woodvale Primary School, Goldings. A small ditch and a shallow gully were recorded, but no archaeological artefacts were present.

RUSHTON, TRIANGULAR LODGE
NGR SP 83040 83035
Evaluation
Northamptonshire Archaeology
An archaeological investigation was undertaken by Jim Burke to determine the nature of a circular stone feature at land next to The Triangular Lodge, Rushton. The feature proved to be a probable flower bed. No artefacts were present.

SULBY, FORMER SULBY HALL
NGR SP 6597 8167
Northamptonshire Archaeology
In the last volume (2006, **34**, 149), the recovery of human bone disturbed by a badger set on the site of the former Sulby Hall was reported. Bones collected by the police forensic team were examined by and deposited with Northamptonshire Archaeology, and further bones collected by local residents were deposited with local residents the late Chris Lowe and his wife (Alison Lowe

pers comm). Given a local interest in the possibility that these bones could relate to the Battle of Naseby, a bone sample was sent for radiocarbon analysis, and Mrs Lowe has kindly provided details of the results. The radiocarbon date places these bones firmly in the medieval period, mid-11th to mid-13th centuries (1040-1230 Cal AD, 95% confidence, 874+/-27BP, OxA-16456), and most probably in the later 12th to early 13th centuries (1150-1220 Cal AD, 64% confidence). This indicates that the bones derive from disturbed burials within a cemetery attached to an early church, perhaps the parish church of St Botolph, where the nave is recorded to have fallen down long before 1451. It would therefore appear that the later hall was built partly over the site of the former parish church and its cemetery.

SULGRAVE, SULGRAVE CASTLE GREEN
NGR SP 5565 4525
Geophysical survey
Northamptonshire Archaeology
A geophysical survey was conducted by Adrian Butler, on behalf of the Sulgrave Castle Green Management Committee, on two areas of the Castle Green in the village of Sulgrave. Putative building platforms have been identified together with possible demolition deposits and foundations in the south-west of the green. A potential former hollow-way was detected crossing the green from the south-east to north-west. Further possible building remains were identified to the south of the castle earthworks.

THURNING, LONGBROOK FARM
NGR SP 967 826
Watching brief
Northamptonshire Archaeology
An archaeological watching brief was undertaken by Paul Kajewski during groundwork associated with the creation of a lake at Longbrook Farm, Winwick Road. Examination revealed a number of modern land drains, and one undated gully.

UPTON
NGR SP 724602
Watching brief
Northamptonshire Archaeology
Archaeological watching brief was carried out by Jim Burke, Anne Foard-Colby and David Leigh from August 2006 to January 2007 during the groundworks for the construction of roads and housing at the Barratt site (D2), Upton, on behalf of English Partnerships followed by Barratt Developments plc. The development was situated at the eastern margin of an extensive Iron Age and Roman settlement, previously subject to open area excavation. There were no archaeological features or finds present.